Programming with
Turbo Pascal®

David W. Carroll

Micro Text Productions, Inc.
McGraw-Hill, Inc.
New York, NY

Library of Congress Catalog Card Number: 85-60357

Micro Text Productions, Inc.
McGraw-Hill Book Company
1221 Avenue of the Americas
New York, NY 10020

10 9 8 7 6 5 4 3 2 1

ISBN 0-07-852909-3

Table of Contents

Preface
1. Introduction to Turbo Pascal 1
2. The Turbo Environment 17
3. Introduction to Computer Programming 33
4. The Turbo Pascal Language 41
5. Pascal Program Structure 46
6. Data Types 60
7. Expressions and Simple Statements 74
8. Procedures and Functions 87
9. Terminal Input and Output 110
10. Simple Programs 124
11. Decision Statements 130
12. Data Structures: Part I. Arrays and Strings 153
13. Data Structures: Part II. Records and Sets 180
14. Pointers and Dynamic Data Structures 192
15. Device and File I/O 209
16. Advanced Programs 226
17. Machine Level Interface 252
18. Advanced Compiler Topics 273

Appendices
A. Turbo Compiler Directives 282
B. Turbo Editor Commands 283
C. Turbo Pascal Reference Guide 285
D. Turbo Pascal Syntax 289
E. Compiler Error Messages 296
F. Run-Time Errors 298
G. I/O Errors 298
H. Binary and Hexadecimal Numbers 299
I. Keyboard Return Codes 300
J. IBM PC Character Set 303
K. Turbo Pascal Public Domain Library 305
L. Bibliography 306
   Index 308

Dedication

To Carol—her support, patience, and love have made this book a reality.

Acknowledgments

I would like to acknowledge the Turbo Pascal products from Borland International, which this book is about. Turbo Pascal has proven that high quality software can be sold successfully at an affordable price. Thanks also to Borland for providing the demonstration Turbo Pascal compiler for inclusion with this text.

A special note of gratitude to Stephen R. Davis and J. Glen Wood for granting permission to use their public domain memory resident programs "LASTCOM.PAS" and "THELP.PAS" as a basis for the TURBOHLP program included on the program diskette.

Thanks also to Peter Grogono for permission to use the Turbo Pascal cross-reference utility included on disk which is based on a program he originally wrote in 1978.

Finally, I would like to thank Carol, my wife, for editing and proofreading the entire manuscript and offering many helpful suggestions, and Georgia Cantando, my step-daughter, for keyboarding many of the tables and reference sections included in the text.

NOTICE TO READERS

The author welcomes your EMAIL through the Borland SIG on CompuServe Information Service. Please address your comments or questions to David W. Carroll.

The author also operates an IBM PC based Remote Bulletin Board System which is normally on-line 24 hours a day, 7 days a week at (209) 296-3534. This system has hundreds of public domain Turbo Pascal, BASIC, and other utility programs available for the IBM PC and compatible computers.

The MS-DOS TURBOHLP program and source files from the example Pascal programs in the text are available from the author in machine readable form in several popular CP/M diskette formats. Specify system type and send check or money order for $15.00 to:

David W. Carroll
P.O. Box 699
Pine Grove, CA 95665

Preface

This book is an introduction to programming in Pascal using the Turbo Pascal compiler from Borland International. It may serve to familiarize an experienced programmer with the Pascal language and the Turbo Pascal compiler, or it may be used in a classroom/lab environment as a hands-on introductory programming course.

This text includes a diskette containing a special limited Turbo Pascal compiler/editor for MS/PC-DOS computers as well as source code for the programming examples in the book. The compiler is a limited version of the original Turbo Pascal version 1.0 compiler especially designed for this book. It supports virtually all of the features of ISO Standard Pascal.

The limited Turbo Pascal compiler/editor can be used to input, edit, and compile programs to memory—no stand-alone ".COM" files can be produced—and the length of program source code is limited to 3490 bytes (characters) when error messages are loaded into memory or 4803 bytes if the error message file is not loaded. Although "Include" files and the IBM PC's special screen and graphics features are not supported in this version, most of the example programs presented in the text can be compiled and run within these limits. A special memory resident help facility for Turbo Pascal, a listing program, and a cross reference program are included on the diskette. These utility programs may be used with any version of the Turbo Pascal compiler/editor.

The focus of this book is primarily on learning the basic concepts of programming in Standard Pascal, as opposed to the many advanced features and extensions provided by the various versions of Turbo Pascal. It provides a good basis for moving on to use the full capabilities of the commercial version of Turbo Pascal. Thus, the use of a limited compiler with the text actually aids in learning Standard Pascal without the distraction of the large number of extensions available in the commercial version of Turbo Pascal. The example programs in the Pascal tutorial are used to illustrate the concepts being presented, and are therefore short and to the point. Also, most programs developed in this text are reasonably portable and most will run on other Pascal implementations without major changes.

The programming examples in this book can be compiled on any version (1.0—3.0) of Turbo Pascal, except where noted otherwise. Any version or operating system dependent features are clearly noted.

The text is designed for hands-on use with the Turbo Pascal compiler and an IBM PC or compatible computer.

David W. Carroll
September, 1985

## CHAPTER ONE

Introduction to Turbo Pascal

Microcomputers are becoming commonplace in our society. Today they can be found almost everywhere—at work, at school, in a briefcase, on airplanes, and at home. Although these machines can solve many types of problems very quickly, they are not "smart." Before a computer can perform a useful task, someone must provide complete instructions to it in the form of a *computer program*.

Computer programs may be written in any of dozens (or even hundreds) of ways, using a variety of methods from hand-encoded binary commands to high-level computer programming languages like FORTRAN, BASIC, and Pascal. Such high-level languages allow programs to be written in a form similar to English and are designed to speed the development of programs and insure their portability, maintainability, and overall reliability.

Programs written in high-level languages must be changed to the *machine language* commands understood by a particular computer before they can be used. This interfacing task can be performed either by an *interpreter* program like BASIC or by a *compiler* program like Turbo Pascal. An interpreter evaluates each *source program* instruction as the program is run and activates the appropriate machine language routines in its library as required. A compiler, on the other hand, actually translates the high-level code to a new machine language program, which may then be run independently. Compiled programs are usually much more efficient than interpreted programs in in terms of execution speed and memory requirements.

Many high-level programming languages for expressing computer programs have been developed in the thirty years since FORTRAN, the first popular high-level language, was introduced. These languages each have had their strengths and weaknesses. FORTRAN (for FORmula TRANslation) allows easy algebraic manipulations while having limited text handling features. BASIC (for Beginners All-purpose Symbolic Instruction Code) offers powerful text and math capabilities and is easy to learn. However, it is unstructured, it features so many extensions as to be nonportable, and it requires a slow interpreter or generates very large compiled files. Other languages, like C and PL/I, are extremely powerful and fast, but are not easy to learn and can result in programs that are difficult to understand and maintain.

The Pascal programming language was designed by Professor Niklaus Wirth of the Technical University (ETH) in Zurich, Switzerland. The language definition was first published in 1974 in the *Pascal User Manual and Report* by K. Jensen and N. Wirth.

Pascal was originally intended as an easy-to-learn yet powerful programming language for use as a learning tool by computer science and programming students. Pascal tends to encourage the use of many of the structured programming techniques which have evolved since 1960 as methods for designing and developing high-quality, error-free programs.

Much to the surprise of its inventor, Pascal has become a popular commercial programming language as well as a useful instructional tool. The inherently structured nature of the language and its powerful error detection capabilities have increased the overall productivity of programmers (as well as the reliability and portability of their programs). Although the definition of the Pascal language was published in 1971, Pascal did not achieve anything like the widespread popularity of interpreted BASIC among microcomputer users until recently. Pascal is both powerful and easy to learn, but early implementations required many steps to create and develop programs due to the inherent complexity of using editors, compilers, linkers, and assemblers. The development time required to repeat all of these steps when writing and debugging programs was unacceptable to many users when compared to the ease of using interpreted BASIC.

The UCSD Pascal p-code compiler for the Apple II computer was popular for software developers, but did not reach a really broad market. Later microcomputer Pascal compilers (DRI's Pascal MT + and Microsoft/IBM Pascal) suffered from bulky, slow code and a frustrating development environment, again involving the use of several separate programs for editing, compiling, and linking program files to create working programs.

In October 1983, Borland International released its revolutionary Turbo Pascal compiler for Z-80 and 8086/8088-based microcomputers. This product features a complete one-step programming environment that in many ways brings the convenience of BASIC to Pascal. Turbo Pascal includes a sophisticated full screen editor similar to WordStar, an advanced source code linked error detection system, and a one-pass native machine code compiler which is more than 10 times faster than any other microcomputer Pascal compiler available. The Turbo compiler produces stand-alone executable program files and offers a large number of extensions to Standard Pascal including access to low-level machine features. Best of all, this package was originally priced at $49.95. Since then, the price has increased to $69.95—but it is still a great deal.

Since its release, over 400,000 copies of Turbo Pascal have been sold, and the Turbo Pascal product has been significantly enhanced, increasing both its power and speed. Some market analysts credit Borland's product with revitalizing interest in Pascal, even suggesting that (Turbo) Pascal may become the language of choice for educators, software developers, and "hackers" alike, and that it may even replace the venerable BASIC as *the* microcomputer programming language through the 1980s and 1990s.

1.1 Getting Started

Since this book is a hands-on tutorial, we will start with a discussion of setting up your Turbo Pascal work disks and the operation of the compiler and editor. This section will assume you are using an IBM PC or compatible computer with the PC-DOS or MS-DOS operating system and either the limited Turbo Pascal compiler/editor included with this text or commercial Turbo Pascal, version 2.0 or 3.0. Since the limited compiler is a subset of the commercial version, the set up instructions will be similar.

If you are using CP/M-86 on a 16-bit computer or CP/M-80 on an 8-bit Z-80 computer, you will need to purchase a commercial version of Turbo Pascal compatible with your operating system and computer format. The installation and set up instructions for these systems will differ from the material presented here. Refer to your computer, operating system, and Turbo Pascal reference manuals. A disk containing the example Pascal programs from the text is available separately from the author in most popular disk formats.

1.2 System Requirements

The minimum equipment recommended to use the Turbo Pascal compiler, Turbo help program, and examples in this book is an IBM Personal Computer equipped with a color or monochrome monitor, one or two double- sided disk drives, 128K bytes of memory, a printer, and the PC-DOS 2.0 or later operating system.

An alternative minimum configuration is an Enhanced IBM PCjr with a color monitor, one disk drive, 128K bytes of memory, a printer, and the PC-DOS 2.10 operating system.

IBM PC compatible computers may be used with the included diskette provided that they use PC-DOS or MS-DOS in an IBM compatible format and that they have IBM compatible screen display capabilities and disk formats.

1.3 IBM PC and PC-DOS Basics

For those readers who are not familiar with the IBM Personal Computer and its disk operating system, PC-DOS, we will provide a brief introduction here to help get you started with Turbo Pascal.

IBM PERSONAL COMPUTER

The IBM Personal Computer is a 16-bit microcomputer system based on the Intel 8088 microprocessor chip. The IBM PC can support between 64K bytes and 640K bytes of Random Access Memory (RAM) and up to 48K bytes of Read-Only Memory (ROM). It includes an 83-key keyboard and one or two floppy disk drives. The IBM PC-XT includes one floppy disk drive and one 10-megabyte hard disk drive. The IBM PC can be equipped with either a special high-resolution monochrome monitor and a monochrome display card or a color graphics adapter (CGA) card and a composite monochrome monitor, a composite color monitor, or a special RGB color monitor.

IBM PC KEYBOARD

The IBM PC keyboard is perhaps the most important interface point between the user and the computer system. In applications like programming, where heavy user interaction is required, the keyboard (and monitor) become the focal point of the user interface. In this section we will discuss the keyboard layout and important keys referred to in this book.

Keyboard Layout

The IBM PC keyboard has 10-dedicated function keys and a 15 key combined numeric entry/cursor control pad. The 10 function keys may be used to generate up to 40 different special function commands (when combined with the three "shift" keys discussed below) whose meaning is defined by software. The numeric pad may be used either for entry of numbers or for cursor control commands, depending on the state of the "Num Lock" mode key.

In addition to the two normal case shift keys (both marked ↑), the IBM-PC keyboard has two special shift keys—"Ctrl" (Control) and "Alt" (Alternate). These three types of shift keys can be used to change the meaning of almost every key, enabling the keyboard to generate over 200 different codes. To input a shifted code, the appropriate shift key is depressed and held while a second key is pressed, then both keys are released.

The IBM PC, like most computers, has a *Control shift* key (marked Ctrl) which enables the keyboard to produce special, non printing ASCII characters which have special meanings in text files. These ASCII control characters are produced when the "Ctrl" key is used as shift key with normal ASCII characters (like Ctrl-A). The control key can also be used to create unique codes for program control when it is used to shift "special function keys" (like Ctrl-F3).

The IBM PC keyboard has another special key called the *Alternate shift* key (marked "Alt"). This shift key allows all of the keys on the keyboard to take on a special meaning when depressed with the ALT key. ALT shifted characters are often used to control the operation of a program that handles text input. Pressing the ALT key with another key does not output an ASCII character to the program—rather it generates a special code which the program can detect and interpret easily.

Keystroke Notation

Because of the multiple key combinations sometimes required to generate a specific code on the IBM PC keyboard, a simple form of keystroke notation will be adopted in this book. Any time a special, "shifted," or multiple key input is needed, it will be shown enclosed in right and left angle brackets—"⟨" and "⟩". For example, to reset the IBM PC and reload DOS, you must type:

⟨Ctrl-Alt-Del⟩

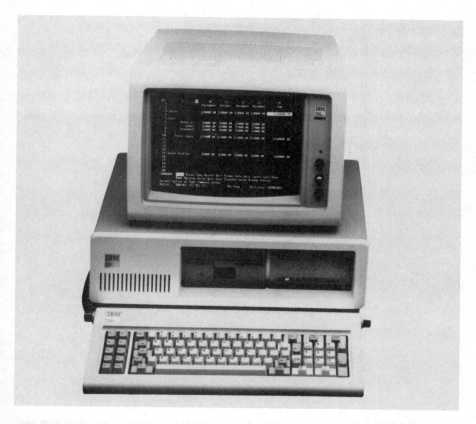

The IBM PC XT system with the system unit, keyboard, and monitor.
Photo courtesy of IBM.

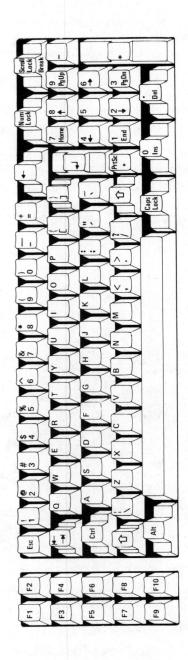

Figure 1-1 IBM PC Keyboard Layout. Reprinted from the *IBM PC Technical Reference Manual* by permission of IBM.

This means depress the Ctrl, Alt, and Del keys at the same time.

If you are using a shifted key combination, depress and hold the special shift key first, then press the key to be shifted, just as you would to type upper case letters with the normal case shift keys. For example, type

⟨Alt-C⟩

means depress the Alt key and hold it, then press the letter C key, then release both keys. Similarly, type

⟨Ctrl-C⟩

means depress the Ctrl key and hold it, then press the letter C key, then release both keys. Other keys with special functions will also be written in this way. Thus, type

⟨Enter⟩

means press the Enter key (marked ↵ on the IBM PC). The Enter key is also called input, return, or carriage return on some keyboards. Most keyboard entries must be terminated by pressing the ⟨Enter⟩ key—this tells the computer to enter or accept the data you have just typed.

The other special function keys are also noted this way. For example:

⟨F2⟩ means the Function 2 (F2) key

⟨TAB⟩ means the tab key (marked →| on the IBM PC)

⟨Esc⟩ means the Escape key (Esc)

One other convention will be used throughout the text—all user keyboard input to programs will be shown in bold type for clarity. This should clear up any questions on the keyboard input instructions, but some reminders will be included in the examples in the next few sections of the text.

DISKETTES

The IBM Personal Computer with PC-DOS 2.0 and later uses 5¼" double-sided, double-density, soft-sectored floppy diskettes. The format used provides a total of 360K bytes of storage on each floppy diskette and a maximum of 112 files (without the use of subdirectories).

The diskette included in this edition requires PC-DOS version 2.0 or later and an IBM PC or Enhanced PCjr with at least one double-sided disk drive. All of the programs will operate on systems with PC-DOS version 1.1 or later, but the work disks must be created on a system using PC-DOS 2.0 or later.

STARTING UP THE SYSTEM

At the beginning of each session with your IBM PC, you will probably need to *boot up* the system. Booting up (also called the *initial program load* or IPL) loads the DOS program into your computer's memory. To boot up your system, first turn on the power to the computer and any peripheral equipment (monitors, printers, etc.). Next, insert a diskette containing the PC-DOS system—either the PC-DOS 2.0 (or later) master disk or a working copy—into disk drive A (the left-hand or top drive, depending on your system's configuration) and close the door of the drive.

Each time DOS is loaded or the computer is reset, you will be asked to enter the current date and time to enable the computer to date-time stamp your disk files (unless your system has an automatic clock/calendar card installed). After a few seconds, you will hear a beep and the monitor will display:

```
Current date is Tue 1-01-1980
Enter new date:
```

Enter the correct date in the format MM-DD-YY (i.e., 5-1-85 for May 1, 1985) and press the Enter key (↵) to enter the data. Next, you will see:

```
Current time is 0:00:40.92
Enter new time:
```

Enter the correct 24-hour (military) time in the format HH:MM:SS (i.e.,10:40:45 for 10:40:45 AM and 14:20:10 for 2:20:10 PM, or in other words add 12 hours to all times beginning at 1:00 PM) and press the Enter key (↵) to enter the data. Finally, DOS will sign on with:

```
The IBM Personal Computer DOS
Version 2.10 (C)Copyright IBM Corp 1981, 1982, 1983
A⟩
```

PC-DOS

PC-DOS is the *disk operating system* (DOS) for the IBM PC. It enables the computer to access program and data files on diskettes (and the hard disk) in an organized way. It also provides a number of utility functions and programs for working with disk files. MS-DOS is a similar operating system sold by Microsoft for IBM compatible computers. Most MS-DOS commands are identical to the equivalent PC-DOS command.

The "A)" is called the DOS prompt. It indicates that DOS is ready to accept your command and that the current or *default* disk drive for DOS commands is the A drive. The A drive is the left-hand, top, or only floppy drive on most systems. The other floppy drive, if available, is the B drive. On hard disk systems, drive C is the hard disk, and is usually the default drive after booting up the system.

DOS DEVICE NAMES

DOS uses *device names* to refer to various input and output (I/O) devices connected to the computer. For example, disk drives are normally named A: and B: on a two-drive system. Other reserved device names include:

CON =   Console keyboard/screen
AUX or
COM1 =   First serial port
LPT1 =   First parallel printer port

DOS FILE IDENTIFIERS

File identifiers in DOS are made up of two parts— the *filename* and the optional filename extension or *filetype*. The filename can be from one to eight alphanumeric characters in length. The filetype can be from zero to three characters in length. The filename is followed by a period (.) and the filetype. Upper and lower case characters are the same.

The following characters can be used in file identifiers:

A-Z 0-9 $ & # ! % ' ' ( ) - { } _ / \

Here are some typical file identifiers:

TEST.PAS   (Pascal program file)
TEST.BAK   (Turbo backup file of edited TEST.PAS file)
PART2.CHN   (Turbo Chain file)
MATH.000   (Turbo overlay file—version 2.0 and later)
VAR.INC   (optional type for Turbo Include files)
TURBO.DOC   (Document file)
IBM.TXT   (Text file)
MUSIC.BAS   (Tokenized BASIC program file)
STARS.ASC   (BASIC source file in ASCII text format)
FORMAT.COM   (Program command file)
BASICA.EXE   (Program execute command file)
DEVICE.SYS   (DOS system file)

Other file types may be assigned to meet the user's needs, as long as they do not conflict with reserved DOS file types.

PROGRAM COMMAND FILES

Executable program command files have COM or EXE filetypes. To load and run (execute) a program command file, type the program command filename (without the file type extension—".COM" or ".EXE") followed by the ⟨Enter⟩ key at the DOS prompt. For example, to run the program ALPHA.COM, type:

A⟩ **ALPHA**⟨Enter⟩

and the program ALPHA.COM will be loaded into memory from the default disk drive and execution will begin. Of course, the named program must be on the diskette in the default drive.

To reference a drive other than the default drive, simply prefix the file identifier with the drive letter and a colon, as:

A⟩ **B:ALPHA**⟨Enter⟩

DOS Commands

For the purposes of this book, you will need to be familiar with only a few of the many PC-DOS commands. Some of the most often used are: DIR, FORMAT, COPY, ERASE/DEL, RENAME, MODE, SYS, and TYPE. You will find descriptions of these commands in the IBM PC-DOS user manual.

1.4 Making Working Copies

Before using the Turbo Pascal compiler or the other programs provided on the diskette included with this edition, you must make working copies of the master distribution diskette. This will insure that you have a backup copy in case anything happens to your work diskette(s) and will also allow you to place a copy of your DOS system on your work diskettes so you can boot up your computer from them. Using work copies also increases the workspace available on your diskettes for the demonstration and example programs in the text.

PC-DOS 1.1 USERS

If you require work disks compatible with PC-DOS 1.1, they must be created on a system running PC-DOS 2.0 or later because the distribution diskette uses the DOS 2.0 double-sided format. In that case, follow the instructions in the DOS 2.0 manual for using the FORMAT command with the /B option instead of the /S option specified in the "Formatting" section below, then copy the distribution files and programs as described in the "Copying the Turbo Programs" section below. Finally, place the PC-DOS 1.1 system on the work disks by rebooting with PC-DOS 1.1 and using the SYS command, followed by copying the COMMAND.COM file to the work disks. PC-DOS 1.1 disks have somewhat less space available than DOS 2.0 or later disks due to the different format used and two diskettes will be required to hold all the files.

HARD-DISK USERS

If you are using a system with a hard disk drive, you can either use the floppy work diskettes as described below, or you can place the programs and files on your hard disk drive.

To copy the files to a hard disk drive, first create a subdirectory named TPAS (or anything else you like):

C)**MD \TPAS**

and change to the new directory with the command:

C)**CD \TPAS**

Now, place the distribution disk in drive A and copy all the files to the hard disk with the command:

C)**COPY a:*.***

The demonstration Turbo compiler, utilities, and all the example programs are now on the hard disk. Whenever you wish to use the Turbo Demo system, just change to the Turbo subdirectory with the command:

C)**CD \TPAS**

Hard-disk users should translate references in the text to floppy drives A and B to drive C (the hard disk), and otherwise proceed as described in the book for floppy diskette users. Skip the next two sections on creating floppy work diskettes.

FORMATTING

To create your floppy work diskette, the first step is to format a new diskette. Place your working DOS diskette in drive A and boot up your computer. Either turn on the power and close the A drive door or press the special system reset key combination ⟨Ctrl-Alt-Del⟩ on the keyboard. Next, type:

A⟩ **FORMAT B:/S**

and follow the instructions on the screen. First, place a new diskette in drive B and close the door. Then press ⟨Enter⟩ to start the format process. At the end of the format, remove the diskette from drive B and press "Y" to format another. You can use the DIR command when you are done to check the diskette. The complete process for one diskette will look something like this:

A⟩**format b:/s**
Insert new diskette for drive B:
and strike any key when ready

Formatting. . .Format complete
System transferred

　　362496 bytes total disk space
　　40960 bytes used by system
　　321536 bytes available on disk

Format another (Y/N)?**n**

A⟩**dir b:**

　　Volume in drive B has no label
　　Directory of B:\

COMMAND COM 17792 10-20-83 12:00p
　　1 File(s) 321536 bytes free

A⟩

COPYING THE TURBO PROGRAMS

To make working copies of your Turbo compiler and program diskette(s), place the Turbo Pascal compiler master diskette in drive A and a newly formatted diskette in drive B. Now type:

A⟩ **COPY A:*.* B:**

This procedure will copy all of the Turbo Pascal program, help, install, utility, and message files to the new diskette. You now have a usable programming work diskette. Remove the diskette from drive B and label it:

"Programming with Turbo Pascal WORK"

You can now boot your system from this work disk and use it to compile and run all the examples in the book. You will still have some room on the disk to experiment with the sample programs.

1.5 Installing Turbo Pascal

Turbo Pascal for the IBM PC comes pre-installed for the computer system's default display mode. The default will be MONO mode if a monochrome display adapter is installed in the computer and CO80 (COlor 80 column) mode if the Color Graphics Adapter (CGA) card is installed. CO80 mode will only operate properly with a color monitor— a composite monochrome monitor connected to the CGA card will display a distorted image. The system display mode may be changed by using Option 2 of the DOS MODE command or by installing your Turbo compiler program to match your computer's display. Refer to the DOS user manual for a detailed explanation of the meaning and use of the MODE command Option 2 display parameters.

To use the MODE command, either copy MODE.COM from the system diskette to your Turbo work diskettes (or hard disk subdirectory) or insert the PC-DOS system diskette in drive A. Now, for example, to allow a composite monochrome monitor to work properly on the CGA card, you must type:

A⟩ **MODE BW80**

each time before you start a new session with your Turbo system. The MODE command may be included in an AUTOEXEC.BAT file on your Turbo work diskette for automatic execution each time you start your system.

To permanently install your Turbo Pascal compiler and utility programs for the type of display used on your system, follow these instructions for each of your work diskettes: Place your work diskette in drive A and press ⟨Ctrl-Alt-Del⟩ to reboot. (Hard-disk users change to your Turbo subdirectory.) Now type:

A⟩ **TURBOINS**

or if you are using a commercial version of Turbo Pascal, type:

A⟩ **TINST**

(Note: If you cannot read the screen at this point, you must press Q to exit the install program and then use the PC-DOS MODE command as described above to reset the system default display mode to match your monitor. Now run the install program again and proceed.) If you are using the TURBOINS program with demonstration compiler, you will see a selection of programs which may be installed for your type of display.

Programming with Turbo Pascal
by David W. Carroll
Published by Micro Text/McGraw-Hill
Copyright 1985 Micro Text Productions

Display Installation for Demonstration Programs
Version 4.1 of October 24, 1985

Install display mode for:
1.   TURBODE.COM—Demo Compiler Program
2.   TURBOINS.COM—Turbo Install Program
3.   TURBOHLP.COM—Turbo Help Program
4.   TURBOLST.COM—Turbo List Program
5.   TURBOXRF.COM—Turbo Cross-reference Program

Which program? (Enter no. or Q to quit):

Figure 1-2 TURBOINS Main Install Menu.

TURBO Pascal installation menu.
Choose installation item from the following:

[S]creen installation | [C]ommand installation | [Q]uit
Enter S, C, or Q:

Note: the *[C]ommand installation* option is not available with the demo Turbo system install program.

Figure 1-3 Turbo 2.0 TINST and TURBOINS Installation Menu.

Choose one of the following displays

    0)   Default display mode
    1)   Monochrome display
    2)   Color display 80x25
    3)   Color display 40x25
    4)   b/w display 80x25
    5)   b/w display 40x25

Which display? (Enter no. or Q to exit):

Figure 1-4 Turbo Display Install Menu for IBM PC.

Simply select the correct display configuration, and your Turbo Pascal compiler will be updated to automatically use that display mode each time you start the program.

1.6 Starting Turbo Pascal

To start up your Turbo Pascal system, place your WORK diskette in drive A and press ⟨Ctrl-Alt-Del⟩ to reboot. (Hard-disk users change to your Turbo subdirectory.) Now type:

A)**TURBOHLP**

to load the Turbo Pascal memory resident help program provided with this edition. Next, type:

A)**TURBODE**

to load and run the limited demonstration version of the Turbo Pascal compiler/editor included with this text. (NOTE: If you are using a commercial version of Turbo Pascal, use the command:

A)**TURBO**

to load and run the compiler/editor.)

    You will now see the Turbo Pascal sign-on followed by the Main Menu on your screen, something like this:

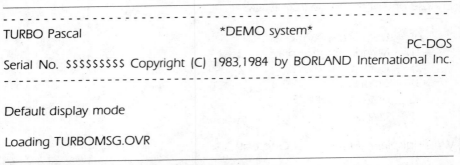

- -

TURBO Pascal   *DEMO system*

PC-DOS

Serial No. $$$$$$$$$ Copyright (C) 1983,1984 by BORLAND International Inc.

- -

Default display mode

Loading TURBOMSG.OVR

Figure 1-5 Demo Compiler Sign-on Screen.

If you are using a commercial version of Turbo Pascal, you will be asked whether to load the compiler error messages file. Answer "Y" for yes or "N" for no. This file provides a text explanation of each compiler error code. Once the error message file has been loaded, you will see the main Turbo menu screen:

Logged drive: A

Work file:

Edit   **C**ompile   **R**un   **S**ave

Dir   **Q**uit

Text: 0 bytes
Free: 3490 bytes
>

Figure 1-6 Demo Compiler Menu.

Now you have completed the preliminary "housekeeping" steps and you are ready to start working with Turbo Pascal. Let's move on to the next chapter, which will introduce you to the Turbo Pascal Programming Environment.

## CHAPTER TWO

The Turbo Environment

The Turbo Pascal compiler differs from most other compilers for high-level programming languages in a number of ways, including:

1) The speed of program compilation and execution;
2) The small compiled size of programs;
3) The ease of generating stand-alone, runnable programs;
4) The ability to "run" programs in memory for testing;
5) The powerful, easy-to-use, built-in editor;
6) The advanced error detection and location system;
7) The many extensions to the Pascal language (in the form of built-in procedures and functions).

These factors make Turbo Pascal one of the most productive microcomputer programming languages available today. Together they form the Turbo "programming environment."

The Turbo Pascal programming environment consists of a fast, one-pass native code compiler for either Z-80 or 8088 microprocessors; a full screen editor; and an advanced compile- and run-time source code linked error detection and display capability. These functions are tied together into a single system by a simple menu-driven user interface.

To see how the Turbo Pascal system works, start up your computer and insert your WORK disk. Load the TURBOHLP program and start the Turbo Pascal demonstration system or start your commercial Turbo Pascal system. Refer to Chapter 1 if you have problems. You should now see the Turbo Pascal menu on your screen.

2.1 The Turbo Pascal Menu

The Turbo Pascal menu system links all of the separate features of the Turbo environment together into one easy-to-use package. The examples in this section are for Turbo Pascal 3.0. However they are also appropriate for earlier versions (including the demo compiler). Just ignore any functions not supported by your version.

The master menu allows the user to select the main and work files, view the disk directory, select the default disk drive (and active subdirectory in Turbo 3.0), activate the compiler and editor, run the current program in memory mode, select compiler options, save workfiles, and exit to DOS. It also shows the workfile size, remaining free space, the logged drive, and the active directory. Menu selections are made by pressing a single key corresponding to the highlighted letter in the desired menu item.

```
Logged drive: B
Active directory: \

Work file:
Main file:

Edit     Compile   Run   Save

Dir       Quit compiler Options

Text:    0 bytes
Free: 62024 bytes

>
```

Figure 2-1 Turbo 3.0 Master Menu.

From the main menu, the user may load an existing workfile or create a new workfile by typing **W** for Work file. The system will prompt for the file identifier. If no filetype is entered, the default type of .PAS will be assumed. Try typing **W** followed by the filename TEST . You will see something like this:

```
>W Work file name: TEST
Loading B:\TEST.PAS
New File
>
```

The edit function is activated by typing **E** for Edit. Try the editor by pressing **E**. The screen will clear and a status line will be displayed at the top. Try it out by typing a few lines—in many ways the editor works just like a typewriter. Press ⟨Enter⟩ to start a new line. The editor commands will be covered later in this chapter. When editing is completed, type ⟨Ctrl- K⟩⟨D⟩ to return to the main menu. This command DOES NOT save the workfile to disk; the workfile remains in memory. If the Quit menu option is selected after an edit, the system will ask if the workfile should be saved. You do not need to save the TEST file you just created.

```
Logged drive: B Active directory: \

Work file:TEST.PAS
Main file:

Edit      Compile   Run    Save

Dir       Quit compiler Options

Text:       0 bytes
Free: 62024 bytes

)Q
Workfile B:\TEST.PAS not saved. Save (Y/N)? N
```

The user may save the workfile manually at any time by selecting **S** for the Save function on the main Turbo menu. When an existing file is loaded and then saved, the original file is saved with the filename extension of ".BAK" and the modified file is saved with the original filename extension (normally ".PAS").

The active subdirectory may be changed with the **A** command. The **D** command will display the directory of the current drive for all files matching the specified "dir mask;" (i.e., *.*, *.PAS, etc.). The directories of other drives can be viewed by entering the drive letter for the "dir mask" (i.e., A:, B:, C:).

The **R** or Run command will compile and run the current file in memory (or just run it if it has not been modified since it was last run or compiled in this session). The **C** or Compile command will compile the current file.

Other menu features will be covered in a later chapter.

2.2 The Turbo Pascal Compiler

The Turbo Compiler will quickly compile Pascal programs into native machine code residing in memory (for debugging) or into executable, stand-alone program (.COM or .CMD) files which can be run directly from the operating system. The demo version included with this book only allows compiling to memory. Later commercial versions of the Compiler allow the use of chain files (.CHN), Include files, and overlay files (.000) as well.

The Turbo Pascal compiler is extremely easy to use. Just load a program file from disk with the **W** command (or type in the program with the Turbo Editor). To start the compiler, enter **C** at the main menu prompt:

)C

The compiler will show the source program line numbers as the compilation process proceeds. If an error is detected, the line number, error code, and error message will be displayed on the screen in this form:

```
Compiling
   XX lines
Error YY. Error Message. Press ⟨ESC⟩
```

To enter the Turbo Editor at the point in the program where the error was detected, press ⟨Esc⟩. Simply correct the error, press ⟨Ctrl-K⟩⟨D⟩ to return to the menu, and select **C** again to restart the compiler.

Try this process now. A sample program is included on the WORK work disk. From the Turbo main menu, press **W**. (If the program asks about saving the TEST.PAS file, answer "N.") Enter the workfile name "SAMPLE." Now press **C** to compile the program. You will see:

```
Compiling

   8 lines

Error 1. ';' expected. Press ⟨ESC⟩
```

Now press ⟨Esc⟩. The program will be displayed on the screen with the edit cursor (flashing line) at the location of the detected error. In this case, the error is a simple one. There is a semicolon missing and the error was detected at the start of the following line. First move the cursor to the end of the previous line by pressing ⟨Ctrl-A⟩, then insert the semicolon (";") at the cursor location, then press ⟨Ctrl-K⟩⟨D⟩ to return to the Turbo menu. Now press **C** again to recompile the corrected program. This time it should compile without error. Now, run the SAMPLE program by pressing **R**. You should see the message:

```
Welcome...

to PROGRAMMING with TURBO PASCAL

This is a sample Pascal program

that displays text on the screen.
```

Here is what the corrected SAMPLE.PAS program looks like:

```
program sample;
begin
    Writeln('Welcome...');
    Writeln('to PROGRAMMING with TURBO PASCAL');
    Writeln;
    Writeln(' This is a sample Pascal program ');
    Writeln('that displays text on the screen.');
end.
```

The Turbo Pascal compile-time error detection and location feature automatically activates the Turbo Editor with the cursor placed at the location of the error *in the source program text*, making the error correction process almost painless. During program development, programs can be compiled in memory and run to take advantage of a similar error location capability in Turbo Pascal's run-time system.

The many advanced compiler features of Turbo Pascal will be covered in a later chapter.

2.3 The Turbo Pascal Editor

The Turbo Pascal full-screen editor allows easy input and modification of Pascal programs, and supports a number of powerful features. The editor is based on the commands and features of the popular WordStar word processing program familiar to many microcomputer users. The keyboard commands recognized by the editor may be changed with the TINST installation program included with the commercial versions of Turbo Pascal.

The Turbo Pascal Editor is an easy-to-use, high-quality, full-screen text editor. The Turbo Editor supports a useful subset of the WordStar command set, and the commercial version allows all of the editing commands to be redefined by the user. There are minor differences between the capabilities of the various commercial versions of the Turbo Editor, primarily that later versions of the editor include more features and commands.

For those readers who are familiar with WordStar, we will summarize the major differences between the Turbo Editor and WordStar.

With the Turbo Editor:

1. The entire file to be edited must fit in available memory and is limited to a maximum size of 64K bytes or characters;
2. A screen "indent" command has been added, which aids structured program formatting by automatically setting the margin to the first character of the preceding line;

3. Deleted line restore ("undelete") capability has been added;
4. Single words may be marked as blocks with a single keyboard command instead of two commands;
5. "Tabs" are automatically set to the first character of each word on the preceding line;
6. "Tab" (⟨Ctrl-I⟩) characters in the file are displayed but are not used for screen formatting;
7. Control characters in a file are displayed in the opposite mode to text (i.e.,low intensity if text is high intensity, and vice-versa);
8. The cursor may be moved anywhere on the screen, without regard to blanks, nulls, or spaces (except past the last line of text);
9. Trailing spaces are automatically deleted from each line;
10. Block markers are not displayed on the screen;
11. All editor keyboard commands are installed initially using the WordStar command structure, but they may be redefined by the user with the Turbo TINST installation program.

   The Turbo Editor differs from WordStar in that the entire text in a source file to be edited by the Turbo Editor must fit in memory, in a block limited to a maximum of 64K bytes (or characters) in size. This is not a major limitation, as the compiler Include directive allows programs to specify external "source modules" stored in disk files to be included during the compilation process. A side benefit of the memory-based editor is that the time-consuming disk file accesses to "page" text segments in and out of memory are eliminated.
   The text buffer will be slightly smaller (about 62K bytes) if the Turbo compiler error message text file is loaded into memory. The optional loading of the message file is controlled by a question each time Turbo is run.

EDITOR SCREEN

The Turbo Editor screen reserves the top line to display status information for the user. This information includes the current line and column number, the status of the INSERT and INDENT modes and the current workfile name. Other messages will appear in this area as required.

Line 1   Col 1   Insert   Indent   C:TEST.PAS

Figure 2-2 Turbo Editor Status Display.

   On systems with a CGA and color monitor, the editor displays text in yellow, with highlighted text in gray (dim white). Error messages are displayed in red.
   The Turbo Editor handles the screen display in a slightly different manner

than WordStar. The entire screen is available for cursor movement without regard to spaces, nulls, or blank areas, except for areas beyond the current last line of the text.

The Turbo editor has been improved with each release of Turbo Pascal to make it faster, to add more commands, and to prevent screen flashing during updates. Version 3.0 now provides almost instantaneous screen updates with no visible flicker.

Editor Commands

A full-screen text editor displays the text "as it looks" on the screen, and allows a pointer, or cursor to be moved throughout the displayed text, indicating where changes or additions are to be made. Because the screen can show only 24 lines of 80 characters each, the editor displays only a small "window" into the text file at any time. The cursor and this window can be moved around to display and work with any part of the text file.

The Turbo Editor will handle lines of up to 127 characters in length. If the cursor is moved past the right border, the screen window will begin to scroll to the right (and the text will move off screen to the left). When the cursor is moved back to the left border, the text will begin to scroll onto the screen again, moving to the right. If a file contains lines of over 127 characters in length, they will be broken at the 127th character and displayed on two lines.

Cursor Movement

The edit cursor (flashing line) indicates where the next editing action will take place. The cursor can be easily moved around the screen using the standard WordStar control commands based on this diamond-shaped set of keyboard keys:

```
           W    E    R
Ctrl     A    S    D    F
           Z    X    C
```

These keys are grouped so that a typist can easily control the screen display without moving his/her hand away from the main keyboard. When pressed with the Ctrl key each of the keys in the "inner" diamond moves the cursor on a character-by-character or line-by-line basis.

```
      E
  S    D    =    ◄  ▲  ►
      X              ▼
```

Thus, ⟨Ctrl-E⟩ will move the cursor up one line, ⟨Ctrl-D⟩ moves it right one character, ⟨Ctrl-X⟩ moves it down one line, and ⟨Ctrl-S⟩ moves it left one character. The outer keys, ⟨Ctrl-A⟩ and ⟨Ctrl-F⟩ move the cursor left and right one word. The ⟨Ctrl-R⟩ and ⟨Ctrl-C⟩ keys move the cursor up and down one page of text at a time.

The editor's "window" onto the text (the portion of the text displayed on the screen) may be moved up and down or *scrolled* without changing the cursor's relative position in the text with the ⟨Ctrl-W⟩ and ⟨Ctrl-X⟩ keys. Of course, since the cursor always remains on the screen, if the text containing the cursor is scrolled off the top or bottom of the screen, the cursor's relative position will be changed.

Here is a summary of the basic cursor movement commands:

	⟨Ctrl-S⟩ or	
	⟨BackSpace⟩	Cursor left one character
	⟨Ctrl-D⟩	Cursor right one character
	⟨Ctrl-I⟩ or ⟨TAB⟩	Cursor right to next tab or back to left margin (TABS are set to the beginning of each word in the previous line)
	⟨Ctrl-E⟩	Cursor up one line
	⟨Ctrl-X⟩	Cursor down one line
	⟨Ctrl-A⟩	Cursor left one word
	⟨Ctrl-F⟩	Cursor right one word
#	⟨Ctrl-W⟩	Scroll screen up one line
#	⟨Ctrl-Z⟩	Scroll screen down one line
	⟨Ctrl-R⟩	Cursor up one screen page of text
	⟨Ctrl-C⟩	Cursor down one screen page of text
	⟨Enter⟩	Insert new line and move cursor down one line and to left margin or first TAB position

(Note: Commands marked with # are only available in Turbo 2.0 and later versions.)

Figure 2-3 Basic Cursor Commands.

Later versions of the Turbo Editor also support the keyboard cursor-control pad on the right side of the IBM PC keyboard. These keys include Home, End, Pg Up, Pg Dn, the four cursor movement arrows, and the INSert and DELete keys.

Unlike WordStar, the ⟨Ctrl-S⟩ and ⟨Ctrl-D⟩ commands do not work across line breaks—you must use ⟨Ctrl-E⟩, ⟨Ctrl-X⟩, ⟨Ctrl- A⟩, or ⟨Ctrl-F⟩ to move the cursor from one line to another.

The Turbo Editor also includes several two key-sequences for extended cursor movement commands. (Note: In all two key-sequences, the second key may be entered as shifted (upper case), unshifted (lower case), or as a control character (with Ctrl).)

The extended cursor movement commands are:

	⟨Ctrl-Q⟩	⟨S⟩	To left on line
	⟨Ctrl-Q⟩	⟨D⟩	To right on line
#	⟨Ctrl-Q⟩	⟨E⟩	To top of screen
#	⟨Ctrl-Q⟩	⟨X⟩	To bottom of screen
	⟨Ctrl-Q⟩	⟨R⟩	To top of file
	⟨Ctrl-Q⟩	⟨C⟩	To bottom of file
#	⟨Ctrl-Q⟩	⟨B⟩	To beginning of marked block
#	⟨Ctrl-Q⟩	⟨K⟩	To end of marked block
	⟨Ctrl-Q⟩	⟨P⟩	To last (previous) cursor position

(Note: Commands marked with # are only available in Turbo 2.0 and later versions.)

Figure 2-4 Extended Cursor Commands.

Insert and Delete Commands

Of course, an editor would be of little use if it was not possible to insert new material and delete existing text. Several commands are included to allow easy editing:

⟨Ctrl-G⟩		Delete character at cursor
⟨Ctrl-T⟩		Delete word right at cursor
⟨Ctrl-Y⟩		Delete line at cursor
⟨Ctrl-Q⟩	⟨Y⟩	Delete from cursor to end of line
⟨Ctrl-N⟩		Insert new line after cursor position
⟨Ctrl-P⟩	⟨Ctrl-char⟩	Insert control character— note: displays in dim on screen

Figure 2-5 Insert & Delete Editor Commands.

Find and Replace Commands

One of the most powerful features of any editor is a *global search and replace* command. The ability to search for a text string and optionally replace it with another string (or nothing) can make complex editing tasks easy. For example, if you wished to change all occurrences of the word "TEXTFILE" in a program to "DATAFILE," you could do so using just one command in the Turbo editor—⟨Ctrl-Q⟩⟨A⟩, followed by the two strings (the find string and the replacement string) and any desired options.

The Turbo editor provides two global search commands—the find command and the find and replace command. The find command is handy to quickly move to a certain location in the edit file, while the find and replace command is used as described in the example above.

Some hints: Be sure to use the **W** option (whole words only) if your find string may also be embedded in larger words. Since the find command is case-sensitive, use the **U** (ignore case) option if you aren't sure or if you wish to find mixed case occurrences of the search string.

Here is a list of the find and replace commands and their options:

⟨Ctrl-Q⟩	⟨F⟩	Find a given string
	Options:	B: Find backwards—from the current cursor position to the beginning of the text.
		G: Global search, use entire text regardless of current cursor position.
		n: n = any number. Find the n'th occurrence of the search string, beginning at the current cursor position.
		U: Ignore upper/lower case when matching.
		W: Find whole words only, skip matching patterns embedded in other words.
		?: Show command options.
⟨Ctrl-Q⟩	⟨A⟩	Find a given string and replace it with the specified value
	Options:	B: Find and replace backwards—from the current cursor position to the beginning of the text.
		G: Global find and replace, use entire text regardless of current cursor position.
		n: n = any number. Find and replace n occurrences beginning at the current cursor position.
		N: Replace without asking for confirmation.

U: Ignore upper/lower case when
matching.
W: Find and replace whole words only,
skip matching patterns embedded in other
words.
?: Show command options.

Figure 2-6 Find & Replace Editor Commands.

Block Commands

The block commands are used to work with a large section of text at one time.
All block commands are composed of a two-key sequence beginning with ⟨Ctrl-
K⟩. They are:

	⟨Ctrl-K⟩	⟨B⟩	Mark beginning of block
	⟨Ctrl-K⟩	⟨K⟩	Mark end of block
@	⟨Ctrl-K⟩	⟨T⟩	Mark single word
	⟨Ctrl-K⟩	⟨Y⟩	Delete block
#	⟨Ctrl-K⟩	⟨H⟩	Hide block
	⟨Ctrl-K⟩	⟨C⟩	Copy block to current cursor position
	⟨Ctrl-K⟩	⟨V⟩	Move block to current cursor position
	⟨Ctrl-K⟩	⟨W⟩	Write block to disk file
	⟨Ctrl-K⟩	⟨R⟩	Read block from disk file to current cursor position

(Note: Commands marked with @ are not available in WordStar. Commands
marked with # are available only in Turbo 2.0 and later versions.)

Figure 2-7 Block Editor Commands.

On the IBM PC with a CGA and a color or monochrome monitor, blocks
are shown in low intensity or in white (on a color display). The Hide Block
command turns lowlighting on and off in version 2.0 and later. Block markers
are not displayed on the screen, but the beginning and end of a block may be
located by the lowlighted area of text or by using the extended cursor movement
commands ⟨Ctrl-Q⟩⟨B⟩ and ⟨Ctrl-Q⟩⟨K⟩. The block may be manipulated only
when it is displayed, but the extended cursor movement commands ⟨Ctrl-Q⟩⟨B⟩
and ⟨Ctrl-Q⟩⟨K⟩ will still work when the block is not displayed.

Blocks may be turned off in the demo Turbo compiler/editor by inserting a
⟨Ctrl-K⟩⟨K⟩ (end block) at the beginning of the block.

Miscellaneous Commands

The remaining Turbo editor commands affect all operations. ⟨Ctrl-L⟩ will repeat the last find or find and replace command. ⟨Ctrl-V⟩ will toggle the insert mode to control whether new text entries will overwrite existing text or insert new text and move existing text to the right. ⟨Ctrl-Q⟩⟨I⟩ will toggle the auto indent mode on and off. The ⟨Ctrl-U⟩ command will interrupt other commands in progress and the ⟨CTRL-Q⟩⟨L⟩ command will undo the effects of most delete type editing commands. ⟨Ctrl-K⟩⟨D⟩ ends an edit session and returns to the main Turbo menu.

These commands are summarized below:

	⟨Ctrl-L⟩		Repeat the last find or find-and-replace operation (or continue from last find).
	⟨Ctrl-U⟩		Abort command in progress
	⟨Ctrl-V⟩		Toggle insert mode on/off
@	⟨Ctrl-Q⟩	⟨I⟩	Toggle auto indentation on/off
@	⟨Ctrl-Q⟩	⟨L⟩	Undo—restores line to its previous contents as long as the cursor has not been moved from the line
*	⟨Ctrl-K⟩	⟨D⟩	End edit—Return to main Turbo Menu- file remains in memory, command does not save file—use main menu Save command!

(Note: Commands marked with @ are not available in WordStar. Commands marked with * have different effects than similar WordStar commands.)

Figure 2-8 Miscellaneous Editor Commands.

2.4 Demonstration Turbo Pascal

Programming with Turbo Pascal includes a demonstration version of the Turbo Pascal compiler and editor on diskette called TURBODE.COM. This program enables you to input, edit, compile in memory, debug, and run short Turbo Pascal programs. It may be used to run and modify most of the example programs in the book, which are also included on the diskette.

The demonstration version is limited to files of 3490 bytes or less when error messages are included and 4803 bytes if the error message file is not included on the work diskette. This version does not permit compiling programs to COM or CHN files or using Include files. Programs can be compiled and run only in memory.

The demonstration system is based on Turbo Pascal version 1.0. It does not support any of the IBM PC screen display enhancements provided in later versions of Turbo Pascal, but it is a complete working Turbo compiler.

The demonstration Turbo editor install program included in this version does not provide the capability of reassigning editor command keys. The demonstration Turbo Editor does not support the use of the cursor control keypad on the IBM keyboard.

- -
TURBO Pascal *DEMO system*   PC-DOS Serial No. $$$$$$$$$$$$
Copyright (C) 1983,1984 by BORLAND International Inc.
- -

Default display mode

Loading TURBOMSG.OVR

Figure 2-9 Demo Compiler Sign-on Screen.

Logged drive: A
Work file:
Edit   Compile Run Save
Dir   Quit
Text: 0 bytes
Free: 3490 bytes
)

Figure 2-10 Demo Compiler Menu.

2.5 On-line Help Program

The diskette provided with this text includes a special memory resident on-line help program for MS/PC-DOS Turbo Pascal. Once it is loaded into memory, the help program provides a complete menu-driven reference guide to Turbo Pascal features, editor commands, and language definitions on your screen at any time just by pressing a two-key command—even while using another program (like the Turbo compiler).

TURBO Pascal Help Ver 3.0
Programming with Turbo Pascal

MAIN MENU

⟨1⟩	Edit Commands
⟨2⟩	Syntax Structure
⟨3⟩	Standard Procedures/Functions
⟨4⟩	Compiler Directives
⟨5⟩	Runtime Errors
⟨6⟩	I/O Errors
⟨7⟩	Standard Identifiers
⟨8⟩	Version 2.0 Additions
⟨9⟩	Version 3.0 Additions

Figure 2-11 TURBOHLP Main Menu.

The TURBOHLP program is loaded in the memory of the computer at the beginning of a session and is activated by pressing ⟨Alt-H⟩ at any time while running any version of the Turbo Pascal compiler/editor (or many other programs). Once loaded, the TURBOHLP program will remain in memory until the system is re-booted or the power is turned off. TURBOHLP may be reinstalled for your display type using the TURBOINS install program on the demonstration diskette.

The TURBOHLP program is loaded at the start of a session by typing

A⟩ **TURBOHLP**

After TURBOHLP is loaded, the main HELP menu may be called up by pressing ⟨Alt-H⟩ while running almost any program that uses the standard MS/PC-DOS keyboard interrupt BIOS interface. To return to previous menu levels press ⟨Esc⟩. To return to the previously active program and restore the previous screen contents, press ⟨Esc⟩ from the main menu. If the TURBOHLP install program is inadvertently run again after it has been loaded, or if another memory resident program is already using the same user interrupt, the message

"CAN'T INSTALL HELP—INTERRUPT IN USE"

will appear and the loading process will be aborted. The TURBOHLP program takes up about 30K bytes of memory and will run with the Turbo compiler without problems on 128K and larger systems.

If you would like DOS to automatically load the TURBOHLP program when your system is booted from the Turbo work disk, this simple AUTOEXEC.BAT file can be included on your work diskette or added to your existing AUTOEXEC file:

```
DATE
TIME
MODE BW80      ← optional
TURBOHLP
TURBODE
```

This file can be created with your Turbo editor and should be named AU-
TOEXEC.BAT. It will execute the listed functions automatically each time your
system is booted up from your work diskette.

Although TURBOHLP is operationally similar to the Borland program
SideKick, the program included with this book is generally based on the public
domain programs "LASTCOM.PAS" by Stephen R. Davis and "THELP.PAS"
by J. Glen Wood and is included with their permission. It is written in Turbo
Pascal, and source code for the public domain version "THELP.PAS" is available
on the Borland SIG on CompuServe, on many IBM PC bulletin board systems,
and directly from the author.

2.6 Utility Programs

Two utility programs are also included on the demonstration compiler distribution diskette provided with this book—TURBOLST.COM and TUR-
BOXRF.COM. The first utility program, TURBOLST, will list a Pascal source
file to the system printer and provide some limited page formatting. The second
program (TURBOXRF) will create a sorted cross-reference listing of all identifiers used in a Pascal source program. The display type for these programs can
be changed by using the TURBOINS install program on the demonstration
diskette.

2.7 Example Pascal Programs

The source code for the example Pascal programs used in the text is included
on the diskette provided with *Programming with Turbo Pascal*. The programs
may be loaded into the compiler from diskette and need not be typed in. After
setting up the work diskette as suggested in Chapter 1, all the example programs
will be on the work diskette. Due to limitations of the demonstration compiler,
a few example programs that cannot be compiled to memory due to size or
other reasons are also included in compiled form on the disk. Because the
PC-DOS system, Turbo compiler, help and utility programs are all on the work
diskette, you may use the work diskette for the entire book.

Example program filenames may be located by their assigned program identifier in the text (the first line in the program). For example, the program beginning: program hello; would be found under the file name "HELLO.PAS" on the diskette.

## CHAPTER THREE

Introduction to Computer Programming

If you've never programmed a computer before, or programmed only interpreted BASIC (e.g., BASIC or BASICA included on your PC-DOS disk), you may wish to read this chapter closely to gain some additional background on the field of computer programming.

3.1 Computer Programs

Computer programs are lists of instructions that tell a computer how to perform a specific task. Much like a recipe tells a cook how to bake a cake using a list of ingredients, a computer program "tells" a computer how to produce a specific output (result) by processing certain input data items. Just as a cook follows the directions in a recipe, the computer performs or *executes* the instructions in a program, running through them one at a time—hence the terms "executing" or "running" a program.

Program instructions are processed by a computer *sequentially* (in order), unless an instruction is encountered which directs the computer to "jump" to another part of the program and continue processing from that point. Programs do not change while the computer is executing them—they remain static in the computer's memory. However, programs can include alternate sets of instructions to be carried out based on decisions or tests made during execution of the program, thus giving the appearance of dynamic activity. All of the alternatives for each decision must be predefined in the program before it is run or an error will result.

Computer programs are designed and written by programmers to perform specific tasks. If a program performs the task it was designed for and produces the proper results from the input data, then it is considered to be a *correct program*. However, proving that a program is correct is another story. The variety of data which may be input to any given program is virtually infinite. Proving that a complex program will respond properly to every possible set of

33

input data is not practical. The concepts and techniques of *top-down design* and *structured programming* were created to aid in the development of correct programs.

These concepts are based on the idea of breaking down each task into its smallest parts and then programming each part as a simple *module* that is itself "correct." Logically, it follows that if each module in a program is correct, the whole program will be correct.

3.2 Machine Language

Machine language is the set of codes or instructions that are understood by the central processing unit of a given computer. Instruction codes are written in numeric form—in binary, octal, hexadecimal, or decimal numbers—much like the binary numbers actually used inside the computer. These codes represent hardware-related instructions like "add the contents of two registers," "subtract the contents of two registers," "move a byte or word of data from memory to a register" or conversely "move a byte or word of data from a register to memory," "jump to an address" (i.e., continue execution at a different part of the program), etc.

Early computers required that programs be written in their native "machine language" made up of numeric instruction codes, because that was all that the computer could "understand." Programmers worked out their programs on paper, then translated them by hand into the numeric machine instruction codes. You can imagine how tiring and error-prone programming was when programs were made up of thousands of groups of binary numbers like:

```
101 001 001 010 101 111 000 110
110 100 000 110 110 001 110 111
101 111 100 011 111 000 101 001
```

Even today, some specialized computers still accept only hand-coded machine language programs.

3.3 Symbolic Assembly Code

It didn't take too long before someone realized that the tedious process of translating programs from the programmer's notes to the numeric codes required by the computer could be best performed by the computer itself. *Assembler programs* were developed that could translate more easily remembered mnemonic instruction codes like ADD, SUB, JMP, and MOV into the obscure numeric codes of the computer.

The process of automating program coding was further aided when *symbolic assembler programs* were developed, which allowed programmers to use symbolic names or *labels* instead of absolute or relative memory addresses to refer to data and jump locations in their programs. The symbolic assembler keeps track of the labels and the memory locations they refer to. Now programmers could write:

```
    LDA NUM1

    ADD NUM2

    STA RESULT

      . . .

NUM1: DS 0003

NUM2: DS 0004

RESULT: DS 0000
```

3.4 Machine Independence

As computer hardware improved and new computers were developed, a problem soon became apparent. Assembly language is *machine specific*. Because each assembly language is designed around the machine codes and architecture of a given CPU, the assembly programs written for one machine won't run on another. The closer a language is related to the structure of a specific computer, the less *portable* programs written in the language are (i.e., the more difficult it is to translate programs to operate on another type of computer). It is desirable to use most application programs on as many types of computers as possible, to justify their development cost. Thus, the job of translating software from one machine to another became a monumental task.

3.5 High-Level Languages

The level of a computer language indicates how specific or generalized it is in relation to the computer hardware. A low-level language is directly related to the machine—usually involving a one-to-one ratio between the low-level language's instruction set and the computer's machine code. Machine and assembly language are low-level languages.

A programming language that is more removed from the computer's operation and that generates several low-level instructions for each source instruction is called a high-level language. High-level computer languages are often written in a form similar to English, with commands like READ, PRINT, and WRITE.

Many high-level languages recognize familiar algebraic operators like + (add), -(subtract), / (divide), * (multiply), and = (equals). These languages are called *procedure-oriented languages*. Some of these high-level languages used on computers today are FORTRAN, ALGOL, PL/I, Pascal, C, Modula-2, and BASIC.

High-level languages were developed to fill several needs: to allow applications to be easily transported from one machine to another without rewriting, to allow programs to be written by those who were not computer hardware experts, to eliminate the repetitive coding of commonly used functions (input/output, trigonometric functions, real numbers, etc.), to make programs more understandable, and to make programmers more productive and programs more reliable and maintainable.

Programs written in a high-level language must be converted into a form usable by a particular computer before they can be "run" on it. This is done by a compiler or an interpreter program written for each specific computer type. If compilers for a given language are available for several different computers, the same high-level program *source code* can be compiled to run on all of the computers with few (if any) changes.

COMPILERS

High-level programs are usually translated or compiled into low-level code by a *compiler*. The compiler program inputs the high-level program source code file and generates a program in machine, assembly, or intermediate (pseudo) code. Once converted to machine code, the program can be run independently of the compiler. There are several types of compilers; each is named for the type of output code it generates.

Pseudo-Code Compilers

Pseudo-Code compilers generate an intermediate code output made up of "universal" machine level instructions. This intermediate code or "Pseudo-Code" (P-Code) is then executed by a "run-time" *interpreter* program. P-code programs require the run-time program to be used each time the program is run. UCSD Pascal is perhaps the best known P-Code compiler. The steps for using a P-code compiler are:

1. Load compiler/editor
2. Code program
3. Compile program

4. Load runtime program
5. Execute/Debug

Native Code Compilers

Native code compilers generate stand-alone machine language programs that are directly executable by the target computer, without requiring the use of an assembler. They have the advantage of one-step compilation, fast execution, and small compiled code size. Assembly code modules are not easy to link, hand optimization (i.e., manually improving the generated code for speed or efficiency) is not usually possible, and programs must be totally recompiled when changes are made. Turbo Pascal is a native code compiler. The steps for using a native code compiler are:

1. Load compiler/editor
2. Code program
3. Compile program
4. Execute/debug

INTERPRETERS

Interpreters translate the source code file directly on the target computer, interpreting the high-level program "on the fly" as it is executed and calling appropriate library routines as required. BASIC is typically an interpreted high-level language. Interpreters are easy to use and allow quick program development, because the program can be entered into the interpreter's interactive line editor and run without any intermediate steps. However, interpreters have several weaknesses:

—the interpreter program must be present in memory to run the program (many BASIC interpreter programs are built into the computer hardware in ROM chips) and can take up 30-60K bytes;

—an interpreter is usually much slower than compiled code because it must decode each high level statement as it encounters it—this time adds up, especially in loops;

—application source code must (usually) be distributed to end users and is hard to protect;

—interpreters encourage poor programming habits; it is too easy to sit down at the terminal and write code without proper design or planning.

The steps for using an interpreter like BASIC are:

1. Load interpreter
2. Code program
3. Execute/debug

3.6 Structured Programming

The term *structured programming* has become a catch-all phrase used to describe several methodologies used to improve programmer productivity and reduce errors in program development. The concepts of structured programming as a scientific approach to computer programming were introduced by E. W. Dijkstra and C. A. R. Hoare in the late 1960s. Through mathematical analysis of the structure of programs, they showed that many program design errors could be prevented by using a systematic approach to programming.

Data structures are organized collections of data that are processed or manipulated by computer programs. The design and use of efficient data structures in programs is considered an important element in structured programming, contributing to program efficiency and maintainability.

Other concepts of structured programming include:

1. Control Structures
2. Modular composition
3. Program format
4. Comments
5. Readability versus efficiency
6. Stepwise refinement (top-down design)
7. Program verification (correctness)

Figure 3-1 Structured Programming Principles.

Structured programs use a limited number of well understood *control structures* to reduce complexity and simplify the program design process. Program code is designed to execute inline, without jumps or GOTOs, if possible. Conditional and repetitive control structures have only one entrance point and one exit.

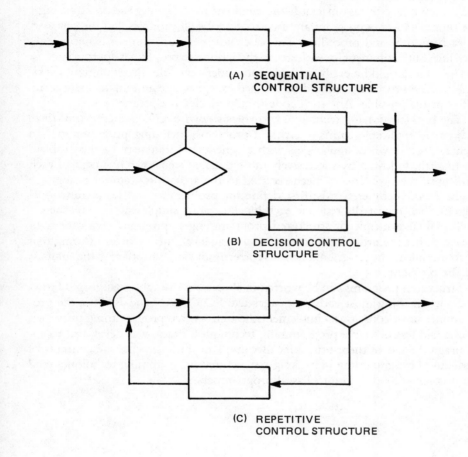

(A) SEQUENTIAL
     CONTROL STRUCTURE

(B) DECISION CONTROL
     STRUCTURE

(C) REPETITIVE
     CONTROL STRUCTURE

Figure 3-2 Control Structures.

Code segments are broken down by functional unit, leading to modularization of programs. In this way, small, easy-to-understand *modules* are used to construct larger, more complex programs. Each module is a functional unit that performs a specific task. Modules are made as independent as possible by using the concept of *local variables* (i.e., variables that exist only within the context of their module and which *cannot* be accessed from other modules). Control of program flow is maintained by providing only one entry point and one exit point in each module.

Programs are formatted in a logical style similar to English outline and sentence structure using indentation to form "paragraphs" that clearly show iteration, decision, and nested structures. Each module is kept to an understandable size—usually less than one page in length—to eliminate page flipping and backtracking.

Comments in the program are used to describe all variables and the purpose of each module and procedure. This does not mean a comment is needed on each line, but a comment for each step in the action of a program is appropriate.

The code should be easily readable and understandable. Programming tricks and obscure procedures should be avoided except where a dramatic increase in efficiency is possible. Any such code should be clearly documented.

The problem-solving technique known as *stepwise refinement* (or *top-down design*) is applicable to many types of problems, including programming. In general, top-down design begins with a generalized statement of the problem in English, followed by successively more detailed steps of refinement of each task until the problem has been reduced to the actual programming language to be used. In other words, first define the problem as a series of functional blocks, then repeatedly redefine each block until its simplest level is reached.

The final principle of structured programming is program *verification*, or proving that the program is correct. At a basic level, this involves insuring that each module in the program functions correctly and is appropriate to the solution of the problem.

Structured programs can be written in almost any computer language. However, when using most early languages like FORTRAN and BASIC, the programmer must consciously implement these structured programming principles and avoid less desirable programming techniques. Pascal was developed to encourage the use of these principles. Because Pascal implements the concepts of structured programming in its design, structured programming techniques tend to become second nature to Pascal programmers.

## CHAPTER FOUR

The Turbo Pascal Language

This chapter presents the elements and symbols which make up the Turbo Pascal language. Computer languages must have a precisely defined *syntax* or set of rules for forming all legal statements so that compilers can interpret them unambiguously. The programmer must also understand and respect the defined syntax or errors will result.

Just as the English language is made up of a specific set of *elements* or components (the upper and lower case letters A-Z and certain punctuation marks), a computer programming language is likewise made up of elements. Meaningful *language symbols* are constructed using the elements of the language —upper and lower case characters, numbers, punctuation, and special characters.

The Turbo Pascal language consists of a basic set of these symbols—a *vocabulary*—including punctuation, logical and arithmetic operators (constructed from a single character or a pair of characters), and reserved words (called keywords or commands in some other languages).

In addition, another set of symbols—called identifiers —are used to represent *objects* like programs, labels, constants, types, variables, procedures, and functions. Some of these identifiers are predeclared and builtin to the language (standard identifiers), while others are declared or defined by the user (user-defined identifiers) in the program. An object is anything referred to by an identifier. All objects in Pascal must be specifically declared in the program unless they are predeclared in a particular Pascal compiler implementation.

4.1 Basic Elements

The Turbo Pascal language is constructed with the upper and lower case letters ("A"-"Z," "a"-"z") and underscore ("_"), the digits ("0"-"9"), and the following special symbols:

    + - * / = ⟨ ⟩ ( ) [ ] { } . , : ; ' # $ ^

Upper and lower case characters are treated alike by Turbo Pascal. Most operators and delimiters are single symbols, but some operators and delimiters are defined as combinations of two special symbols.

The single character operators and delimiters are:

Addition, concatenation:	+
Negation, Subtraction:	-
Multiplication:	*
Division:	/
Declaration, relational equals:	=
Pointer type, control char prefix:	^
Relational less than:	<
Relational greater than:	>
Precedence, parameter:	(and)
Array or set element:	[and]
Comment delimiters:	{ and }
End of program, decimal:	.
List separator:	,
Type declaration:	:
Statement separator	;
String literal delimiter	'
ASCII literal ordinal prefix	#
Hexadecimal integer prefix	$

The two character operators and delimiters are:

Assignment:	:=	
Relational inequality:	< >	
Relational greater than or equal:	> =	
Relational less than or equal:	< =	
Set or subtype range	..	
Brackets (alternate):	(. and .)	for [and]
Comments (alternate):	(* and *)	for { and }

4.2 Reserved Words

Turbo Pascal includes 43 reserved words which cannot be redefined (i.e., reserved words cannot be used as user-declared identifiers). These reserved words are:

* absolute	* external	nil	* shr
and	file	not	* string
array	for	of	then

begin	forward	or	to
case	function	packed	type
const	goto	procedure	until
div	if	program	var
do	in	record	while
downto	*inline	repeat	with
else	label	set	*xor
end	mod	*shl	

Asterisked words are not defined in Standard Pascal.

4.3 Identifiers

Identifiers are symbolic names for objects referred to in Pascal programs. Objects include programs, labels, constants, types, variables, procedures, and functions. Turbo Pascal identifiers consist of a letter or underscore followed by any combination of letters, digits, or underscores. An identifier is limited only by the maximum line length of 127 characters and all characters are significant. Reserved words may be embedded in identifiers without conflict. Turbo Pascal makes no distinction between upper and lower case letters, so upper case, lower case or mixed case letters may be used to add to human readability of long identifiers:

ProgramName	instead of	PROGRAMNAME
InputVariable	instead of	inputvariable

Turbo differs slightly from Standard Pascal in that the underscore character ("_") is permitted within identifiers, making it much easier to write descriptive identifiers like:

Number_of_tries	instead of	NUMBEROFTRIES
Cost_of_living	instead of	costofliving

and allowing a consistent style to be used in the formatting of programs.

PREDEFINED IDENTIFIERS

Turbo Pascal version 3.0 includes over 140 predefined identifiers, including standard types, standard procedures, standard functions, computer and version-specific extensions, and constants. These identifiers may be redefined in a program by the user, but this practice is not recommended because the original meaning and function of the identifier will be lost within that program, and the program's operation can become somewhat confusing to readers.

USER-DEFINED IDENTIFIERS

Almost every high-level computer language allows the programmer to refer to data in memory or to specific program lines by some type of symbolic name. In Pascal, these symbolic names are called *user-defined identifiers*. Identifiers allow transparent access to and manipulation of data elements in memory without regard for their storage format in the computer by referencing the symbolic name assigned to each data element.   Each identifier must be declared in a Pascal program before it is used. The declaration of an identifier includes its data type (INTEGER, REAL, CHAR, BYTE, STRING) if it is a variable or its assigned value if it is a symbolic constant. Other types of declarations are used for statement labels, user-defined data types, and subprograms (procedures and functions).

Declarations and data types will be covered in later sections.

4.4 Meta-language definitions

It is difficult to express the syntax or "rules" for the formation of all possible correct or legal statements in a programming language precisely in sentence form. English is often an ambiguous medium for expressing exact technical concepts. A *meta-language* (i.e., a language for describing the syntax of a programming language) can help solve this problem. A meta-language is used to define all valid sequences of symbols in a programming language, and thus provides the basis for developing a compiler for that language.

In this text, we will use the Backus-Naur Form (BNF) to formally describe the Turbo Pascal language. This method was chosen instead of the popular *"railroad track" syntax diagram* because it corresponds to the method used by Borland in the Turbo Pascal reference manuals. A complete, corrected syntactic description of Turbo Pascal in BNF is included in the Appendix.

BACKUS-NAUR FORM

Although BNF has very few rules and symbols itself, it can be used to define the syntax or form of legal statements for almost any procedural programming language. The semantics of a language (i.e., the meaning of each legal statement) is best defined in written English form.

BNF Rules

Note: The following symbols are meta-symbols belonging to BNF in these definitions and are not a part of the Pascal language.

```
::=        means "is defined as"
|          means "or"
{}         means the contents may be repeated zero or more times
⟨⟩         means the contents are a BNF variable name
           symbols of the language are written in upper case
           concatenation (linking together of elements) is indicated
           by their adjacency
```

To illustrate, here are a few examples from definitions in the previous sections:

⟨digit⟩ ::= 1 | 2 | 3 | 4 | 5 | 6 | 7 | 8 | 9 | 0

⟨unsigned integer⟩ ::= ⟨digit⟩ {⟨digit⟩}

⟨letter⟩ ::= A | B | C | D | E | F | G | H | I | J | K | L | M | N | O | P | Q | R | S | T
         | U | V | W | X | Y | Z | a | b | c | d | e | f | g | h | i | j | k | l | m | n | o | p |
         q | r | s | t | u | v | w | x | y | z | _

⟨letter-or-digit⟩ ::= ⟨letter⟩ | ⟨digit⟩

⟨identifier⟩ ::= ⟨letter⟩ {⟨letter-or-digit⟩}

In this way, the simplest to the most complex expressions can be precisely defined by using a step-by-step building-block approach. We will include the BNF form for Turbo Pascal statements as they are defined in the text.

## CHAPTER FIVE

Pascal Program Structure

A Pascal program is a sequence of instructions implementing the algorithm or method of solution for a given problem. This chapter discusses the structure of Pascal programs (i.e., what goes where in a Pascal program). Pascal is a highly *structured* language and has a rigidly defined yet flexible program structure. Each section or part of a Pascal program must appear in the proper sequence and be syntactically correct, or it will generate an error. This structure allows Pascal compilers to perform extensive error checking at both compile-time and run-time.

On the other hand, in Pascal there are no specific rules for the use of spaces, line breaks, or indentation, so statements may be written *free-format* in almost any style the programmer wishes to use. This is both good and bad, because it leaves the visual design or layout of the program up to the programmer. It is therefore the programmer's responsibility to be consistent and clear in his style.

In this text, Pascal programs will be presented in lower case, with reserved words in UPPER CASE or **bold** and each "block" of statements indented. Turbo Pascal procedure and function identifiers are presented in lower case.

5.1 Standard Pascal

The International Standards Organization has developed a formal specification for ISO Standard Pascal, which is a somewhat more formal definition than the original Pascal defined by Jensen and Wirth in the *Report*. In this book, we will refer to Turbo Pascal differences and extensions in terms of the ISO Standard Pascal definition.

As was mentioned earlier, Pascal was originally designed for teaching introductory computer programming courses. It is intentionally a very simple programming language to learn and use. Pascal has been called "sparse"—referring to the small number of "required" commands, functions, and procedures defined by Wirth in the original Pascal.

Standard Pascal defines only 36 reserved words (commands), five data types,

20 required functions, and 15 required procedures. Turbo Pascal supports virtually all of the features of Standard Pascal with the exception of some advanced data file input/output commands, and includes many powerful extensions to Standard Pascal in the form of built-in procedures and functions.

5.2 Simple Programs

One of the simplest Pascal programs that actually does something looks like this:

```pascal
program hello;
begin
    writeln('Hello world.');
end.
```

To run this program, load Turbo Pascal, select the Turbo Editor by typing **E**, name the workfile "HELLO," and load or type in the program. (Refer to Chapters 1 and 2 if you have problems starting Turbo.) Now return to the main menu by pressing ⟨Ctrl-K⟩⟨D⟩ and type **C** to compile your program. It should compile without error.

(NOTE: Watch out for the single quotes (') and semicolons (;) and the period (.) at the end. Incorrect punctuation is one of the most common errors in programming.)

Next, run your program by pressing **R**. The program will display "Hello world," on the screen and then return to the Turbo ")" menu prompt.

Most computer programs contain two types of instructions—information for use by the translation program (in this case the compiler) and actual instructions that specify actions for the computer to perform. Out of four lines of program instructions in our simple program, the only one that actually produces an action by the computer is the simple procedure statement:

```pascal
writeln('Hello world.');
```

which calls the standard Pascal "built-in" subprogram or *procedure* to "write a line" of data to the terminal or computer screen. The other instructions are necessary to provide the information and the program structure required by the Pascal compiler.

This simple program illustrates two of the major components of Pascal program structure—the program heading and the main program block. All Standard Pascal programs consist of a program heading followed by a main block and terminated with a period. In BNF, the formal definition of a Pascal program is:

```
⟨program⟩ ::= ⟨program-heading⟩ ⟨block⟩.
```

(If the meaning of this BNF definition is unclear, review the section on BNF in the previous chapter.) To understand this definition, we need to also define the ⟨program-heading⟩ and ⟨block⟩ BNF variables.

⟨program-heading⟩ ::= ⟨empty⟩ | **program** ⟨program-identifier⟩
⟨file-identifier-list⟩ ;

⟨block⟩ ::= ⟨label declaration part⟩ ⟨constant definition part⟩
⟨type definition part⟩ ⟨variable declaration part⟩
⟨procedure and function declaration part⟩
⟨statement part⟩

Now, as you can see, we need still more definitions to complete our original definition. (A complete set of BNF definitions for Turbo Pascal may be found in the Appendix.) This process of progressive definition in more and more detail is an example of *step-wise refinement* or *top-down* definition. In this way, we can reach a clear and exact definition of each component.

We will cover each of the above items as we discuss Turbo Pascal program structure in the following sections. First, however, we will review a few basic BNF definitions:

⟨digit⟩ ::= 1 | 2 | 3 | 4 | 5 | 6 | 7 | 8 | 9 | 0

⟨sign⟩ ::= + | -

⟨unsigned integer⟩ ::= ⟨digit⟩ {⟨digit⟩}

⟨unsigned real⟩ ::= ⟨unsigned integer⟩ . ⟨digit⟩ {⟨digit⟩} |
⟨unsigned integer⟩ . ⟨digit⟩ {⟨digit⟩} E ⟨scale factor⟩ |
⟨unsigned integer⟩ E ⟨scale factor⟩

⟨scale factor⟩ ::= ⟨unsigned integer⟩ | ⟨sign⟩ ⟨unsigned integer⟩

⟨letter⟩ ::= A | B | C | D | E | F | G | H | I | J | K | L | M | N | O | P | Q | R | S | T
| U | V | W | X | Y | Z | a | b | c | d | e | f | g | h | i | j | k | l | m | n |
o | p | q | r | s | t | u | v | w | x | y | z | _

⟨letter-or-digit⟩ ::= ⟨letter⟩ | ⟨digit⟩

⟨identifier⟩ ::= ⟨letter⟩ {⟨letter-or-digit⟩}

⟨special character⟩ ::= ⟨space⟩ | ! | " | # | $ | % | & | (|) | * | + | , | - | . | / |
: | ; | ⟨| = |⟩ | ? | @ | [| \ |] | ^ | ` | { | } | ~ | ⟨vertical line⟩ |

⟨character⟩ ::= ⟨letter-or-digit⟩ | ⟨special character⟩

⟨control character⟩ ::= # ⟨unsigned integer⟩ | ^⟨character⟩

⟨string component⟩ ::= ' ⟨character⟩ {⟨character⟩} ' |
                       {⟨control character⟩} | '⟨empty⟩'

⟨string⟩ ::= ⟨string component⟩ {⟨String component⟩}

Figure 5-1 Basic BNF Definitions.

The following figure shows an outline of the basic structure of a Pascal program. The *block* structure is defined in the following section.

```
PROGRAM ⟨identifier⟩ (file identifiers);
        ⟨block⟩.
```

Figure 5-2 Outline Diagram of Pascal Program Structure.

Pascal programs are made up of one or more block structures. Each block, including the main program block itself, may contain any number of parts (zero or more) in its declaration section, followed by the body of the block, delimited by the reserved words **begin** and **end**.

In Standard Pascal, each of the declaration parts must appear exactly zero or one times and in the specific order shown. In Turbo Pascal each of the declaration parts may appear zero or more times and in any order, as long as they precede the program body.

```
LABEL ⟨identifier⟩;                    ⟨⟨DECLARATION SECTION BEGINS⟩⟩
CONST ⟨identifier⟩ = ⟨constant⟩;
TYPE ⟨identifier⟩ = ⟨type⟩;
VAR ⟨identifier⟩ : ⟨type⟩;
PROCEDURE ⟨identifier⟩ (⟨parameters⟩);
   ⟨block⟩;
FUNCTION ⟨identifier⟩ (⟨parameters⟩) : ⟨result type⟩;
   ⟨block⟩;
BEGIN                                  ⟨⟨BLOCK BODY BEGINS⟩⟩
   ⟨simple or structured statements⟩;
END
```

Figure 5-3 Outline Diagram of Pascal Block Structure.

5.3 Program Structure

The preceding two figures illustrate Pascal program and block structures in a simple outline format (not BNF). As with some other syntax definitions, the block structure definition shown here is self-defining or recursive, in that the block is defined in terms of itself. This implies that blocks can be contained or "nested" within other blocks.

Blocks

Pascal is a *block-structured* language. Block program structure allows related declarations and statements to be grouped together. Block structure provides two major functions:

1) It allows a sequence of statements to be grouped together into a single *compound* statement.

2) It provides control over the allocation of storage to variables (declaration) and the ability to refer to variables in various parts of the program (scope).

Blocks may contain declarations, program statements, and other, nested, blocks. Much like sections of an outline are used to organize a document, blocks are used to organize a Pascal program.

Each block begins with the declaration of all user-defined objects that are local or internal to the block (and any included blocks), including labels, types, constants and variables, as well as other subprogram blocks (procedures and functions). These declarations (if any) are followed by one or more program statements contained within the reserved words **begin** and **end** as delimiters.

In well-designed programs, each block performs a specific process and has clearly defined input and output data. Objects defined within a block are local to the block—they are invisible outside of the block, and, in fact, do not exist outside of the block. Of course, objects defined within a given block are global to other blocks nested or included within the containing block.

Block structure also allows flow of control to be clearly defined. In Pascal, control is transferred to blocks (procedures and functions) with an inline reference in much the same way as a subroutine is called in BASIC or FORTRAN. This means that Pascal blocks have only one entry point and one exit point.

Procedure and function blocks may be nested in Pascal, allowing a library of standard procedures and functions to be written whose internal operation can be ignored by the programmer.

All components of the block are optional except for a heading to declare the type of block, the **begin** and **end** delimiters, and zero or more action components (statements or other, included, blocks of statements). Since the Pascal language includes an empty or null statement, null action components are legal. The following is a valid null program:

```
program null;
begin
end.
```

If you enter and compile this program, it will run, but the computer won't do anything. (The screen clearing action is a built-in operation in some versions of the Turbo compiler.) This is because the program does not specify any "actions" to be performed by the computer.

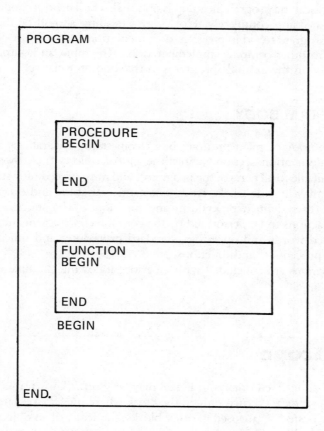

Figure 5-4 Pascal Program Structure

PROGRAM HEADING

Every Standard Pascal program begins with the *program heading*, in the format:

program programname (input, output);

The *arguments* or parameters after the program name are used in Standard Pascal to list the input and output files used by the program, through which the program communicates with the environment. The predefined variables, input and output are used to indicate the standard text input and output files, usually the screen display and the keyboard.

In Turbo Pascal the program heading is optional. The Turbo compiler ignores the program heading completely. However, a heading should be included in every Pascal program to aid in program documentation and to insure portability of programs to other compiler implementations. The input and output file list will be omitted in the example programs in this book for clarity.

PROGRAM BODY

The *program body* or main program block consists of declarations and statements. The declaration section defines the *global objects* (i.e., those objects which are available to all parts of the program), and must precede any statements. Declarations may include labels, types, constants, variables, and other subprogram blocks (user defined procedures and functions). The statement section specifies the actions to be performed by the computer. Statements may include Pascal reserved words and operators, standard procedures and functions, and user defined procedures and functions.

Pascal programs are concluded with a period, following the final **end** block delimiter.

5.4 Scope

The *scope* of declared objects in Pascal may be *global* (known in all parts of the program) or *local* (known only in the block where they are declared). Since blocks can be *nested* or enclosed in other blocks, the scope of an object includes the block in which it is declared and continues down through all nested blocks. In Pascal, all objects have a scope, including labels, constants, types, variables, procedures, and functions.

Objects defined in the main program block are global in scope—that is, they exist in the main program block and in all lower level or nested blocks.

5.5 Declarations

Pascal requires that all *objects* be declared before they are referenced in a program. Objects are programs, labels, types, constants, variables, and subprograms (procedures and functions)—in short anything that can be named. The declaration section is located after the block heading and before any statements in each block structure.

Standard Pascal requires that each part of the declaration section appear in a specific order, but Turbo Pascal has relaxed this requirement. The declarations still must appear before any statements in the block, however.

The six parts of the declaration section are:

1. LABEL - labels used for line references;
2. CONST - symbolic or "named" constants whose values cannot be changed during program execution;
3. TYPE - programmer-defined data types and structures;
4. VAR - variable-type declarations (e.g. REAL, INTEGER);
5. PROCEDURE - programmer-defined sub-programs;
6. FUNCTION - programmer-defined functions.

LABELS

Labels are used to identify points within a program so control can be transferred to them with the GOTO statement. Standard Pascal requires labels to be unsigned integers of four digits or less, but Turbo Pascal permits either unsigned integers or any legal identifier to be used as a label. The BNF definition of a Turbo Pascal label is:

⟨label⟩ ::= ⟨letter-or-digit⟩ {⟨letter-or-digit⟩}

A statement label is followed by a colon (":") as:

error_exit: **end;**

The label declaration part of a block has the BNF form:

⟨label declaration part⟩ ::= ⟨empty⟩ |
    label ⟨label⟩ {, ⟨label⟩} ;

The following is an example of a label declaration part:

label
    error_exit, user_exit;

CONSTANTS

Constants are objects whose value does not change during program execution. They may be of any data type. The type of a constant is implied by the format of its assigned or literal value. The BNF definition of a constant is:

⟨constant⟩ ::= ⟨literal constant⟩ | ⟨symbolic constant⟩

A constant identifier is a legal identifier that has been previously defined as a symbolic constant:

⟨constant identifier⟩ ::= ⟨identifier⟩

Literal constants are actual values included in programs. They are used primarily to initialize named constants and variables, in relational (comparison) expressions, in output statements, and as index limits. The BNF definition of a literal constant is:

⟨literal constant⟩ ::= ⟨unsigned number⟩ |
   ⟨sign⟩ ⟨unsigned number⟩ | ⟨string⟩

Symbolic constants are objects whose identifier and value are defined in a CONST section. The BNF definition of a constant definition is:

⟨constant definition⟩ ::= ⟨identifier⟩ = ⟨constant⟩

Symbolic constants may be initialized only by other constants (symbolic or literal). Symbolic constants are used for values which may be changed when a program is updated or modified. Their use also improves program readability. The BNF definition of a symbolic constant is:

⟨symbolic constant⟩ ::= ⟨constant identifier⟩ |
   ⟨sign⟩ ⟨constant identifier⟩

The constant definition part of a block has the BNF form:

⟨constant definition part⟩ ::= empty |
   const ⟨constant definition⟩ {, ⟨constant definition⟩} ;

This is an example of a constant definition part:

const
   maxcount   = 25;
   date   = 'Jan. 1, 1986';
   version   = '12.2';
   cost_ratio   = 1.22;
   bell_char   = $^\wedge$G;

TYPES

Pascal allows the programmer to define data types and structures in addition to the Turbo Pascal standard scalar types REAL, INTEGER, BOOLEAN, CHAR, BYTE, and STRING. The concept of data types and structures will be discussed in more detail in later sections. A type definition has the BNF form:

   ⟨type definition⟩ ::= ⟨identifier⟩ = ⟨type⟩

The type definition part of a block has the BNF form:

   ⟨type definition part⟩ ::= ⟨empty⟩ |
     type ⟨type definition⟩ {, ⟨type definition⟩} ;

This is an example of a type definition part:

   type
    file_id = string[20];

VARIABLES

Variables are named objects whose value may change during program execution. The data *type* of each variable must be explicitly declared before it can be used in a program. Pascal variables are not automatically initialized to a value when they are declared and therefore a variable is undefined until a value is explicitly assigned to it. Variable declarations have the BNF form:

   ⟨variable declaration⟩ ::= ⟨identifier⟩
    {, ⟨identifier⟩} : ⟨type⟩

The variable declaration part of a block has the BNF form:

⟨variable declaration part⟩ ::= ⟨empty⟩ |
   var ⟨variable declaration⟩ {, ⟨variable declaration⟩}

This is an example of a variable declaration part:

```
var
   ch          : char;
   price       : real;
   index1,
   index2,
   count       : integer;
   name        : string[30];
   file1       : file_id;
   chval       : byte;
```

PROCEDURES

Procedures are *subprogram* blocks which perform a specific set of actions. Procedures are activated by a *procedure statement* containing the *procedure identifier* or name and any parameters. Values or *parameters* may be passed to the called procedure as arguments in the procedure statement. When processing in a procedure is completed, program execution resumes at the statement following the activating procedure statement.

Turbo Pascal includes a number of *built-in* procedures which perform operations like input and output, string handling, screen operations, and file handling. These procedures are covered in detail in later chapters.

User-defined procedures are declared much the same as other objects. A procedure declaration begins with the procedure heading, followed by the procedure block.

```
procedure title (page : integer);
begin
   writeln('This is a title Page #', page);
end;
```

The procedure block may contain declarations of additional objects, including labels, constants, types, variables, functions and procedures. These objects will be local in scope to the procedure and its nested blocks. Procedures will be covered in more detail in Chapter 8.

FUNCTIONS

Functions are also named subprograms, but functions are activated when an expression containing a function reference is evaluated. Unlike procedures, functions normally return a value to the calling expression. Functions are often used to perform a mathematical or logical *algorithm* by using the passed parameters and returning a result.

Turbo Pascal includes a number of *built-in* functions which perform calculations and return a value, like math and trigonometric functions, conversions, and providing data from the operating system. These functions are covered in detail in later sections.

Functions are declared much the same as other objects. A function declaration begins with the function heading, followed by the function block. The function block may contain declarations of additional objects, including labels, constants, types, variables, functions and procedures. These objects will be local in scope to the function and its nested blocks. The result value of a function is set by assigning a value to the function identifier within the function itself.

```
function square (parm : integer) : integer
begin
   square := parm * parm;
end;
```

Functions will be covered in more detail in Chapter 8.

5.6 Statements

Statements describe the actions to be performed by the computer. Statements are placed in the body of program and subprogram blocks. Pascal has both simple and structured statements. Simple statements include the assignment statement, the empty statement, the procedure statement, and GOTO statement. Turbo also provides the INLINE statement for including machine code in Pascal programs. Here are some example Pascal statements:

```
total := 5 + index;
writeln('Total = ',total);
```

Structured statements include the compound statement, the conditional statement, the repetitive statement, and the WITH statement. Statements and expressions will be covered in more detail in Chapter 7.

5.7 Format and Style

Pascal is a free-format language. Blanks and line breaks are not significant except where they are required to keep identifiers and reserved words unique, or in string literal constants. Statements may be broken at any point for clarity of structure, but programmers must remember that the compiler does not consider physical program format when interpreting the source program. Turbo Pascal allows source program lines of up to 127 characters in length.

This means that the textual format of a Pascal program is up to the programmer. The source program format chosen by a Pascal programmer should clearly indicate the structure of a program's design for easy readability, maintenance, and reliability. One format commonly used in Pascal (and in this text) is to indent the beginning of each new control level or program block (and its subsequent statements) by two characters and to move to the left by a like amount upon completion of each structure. Not only is this format attractive and understandable, but it also allows visual checking of nested structures.

Most Pascal procedures and functions should be limited to a maximum of about one page in length. This serves both as a rule-of-thumb to guide program formatting and to keep subprograms to an understandable size. If subprograms are broken down into individual functional modules, this goal should be achievable in most cases.

5.8 Punctuation

Pascal programs use three primary types of punctuation—the comma (,), the semicolon (;), and the period (.).

The comma is used to separate items in a list, much like English. Thus the declaration

```
var
   counter, index, value : integer;
```

will define each of the three identifiers as type INTEGER variables.

The semicolon is a statement separator— not a statement terminator. This is perhaps one of the most confusing concepts for new Pascal programmers and will be discussed in more detail in later sections.

The period is used after the final **end** statement in a program to indicate the last statement in the program. This allows the compiler to check that all **begin** delimiters have a matching **end** delimiter.

5.9 Comments

Programmer comments may appear anywhere in a Pascal program, as long as they are enclosed in comment delimiters "{" and "}" or the alternate delimiters "(*" and "*)." Note that comments may not be nested (contain other comments) because any beginning comment delimiters "{" or "(*" (after the first) contained inside a comment will be ignored by the compiler, and the first ending comment delimiter of the same type "}" or "*)" as the beginning delimiter will end the comment field. Here is an example of a comment:

writeln(a,b,c); { output totals to screen }

If comments are included in a section of code which must be "commented out" (i.e. temporarily removed for debugging purposes), use the alternate comment delimiter. Thus, if the existing comment is delimited with "{" and "}"—use "(*" and "*)" to force the compiler to ignore the code section which includes the comment. The embedded "}" in this case will be ignored because it does not match the inserted beginning delimiter "(*."

## CHAPTER SIX

Data Types

Pascal is a "strongly typed" language. This means that all objects (i.e., labels, data types, named constants, variables, and subprograms) must be declared (defined) in a Pascal program before they are used. A variety of simple and complex data types and structures may be defined in Pascal, making programs virtually self-documenting and more easily understood. The predefinition of all data components in a program simplifies compiler design considerably and enables Pascal compilers to perform extensive error checking during compilation and execution with minimal overhead penalty.

6.1 Data and Computers

There are two types of data used in computer programs, both easily remembered by their descriptive names—constants and variables. Constants may either be literals (i.e., representations of the actual data value) or symbolically named objects which are declared and assigned a value at the start of a program and which do not change value as the program runs. Variables, on the other hand, can change value as the program runs, and are used to hold input values, flag values, indexes, intermediate results, and output values.

In Pascal programs, variables are "typed" by explicit declaration and may only be assigned values which match their data type (e.g., INTEGER, REAL, CHAR, BYTE, STRING). Constants are typed by implication based on the format of their assigned data value. Turbo Pascal also allows a unique "typed constant" which may be used in some ways like a variable. Most Pascal operators and functions are also type sensitive. However, values may be exchanged between dissimilar types by using type conversion functions.

Digital computers store all data in the form of binary codes in memory or in external data files. The amount of space allocated for each data item depends on its type and the particular Pascal compiler implementation and computer used. In most cases, the storage of data is transparent to the programmer since data items are referred to by their identifiers and the compiler handles data transfer automatically, but it is important to realize the limitations of each data type. There are two primary numeric data types in Pascal—integers and real numbers.

INTEGER NUMBERS

Integer numbers are the positive and negative whole numbers, including zero. In mathematics, the set of integers includes all positive and negative whole numbers from negative infinity to positive infinity and zero. This set is represented by a set of points on the number line:

⟨· |· ⟩
− ∞   0   + ∞

The largest positive and smallest negative integer which may be represented in Pascal is dependent upon the particular computer hardware and compiler implementation used. Typically, the maximum integer size is based on the largest signed binary number (MAXINT) which will fit the compiler's basic word size.

⟨//////|· |· ·|//////⟩
− ∞   -(MAXINT + 1)   0   MAXINT   +∞

The Turbo Pascal compiler uses a 16-bit word size for integers, which allows 15 bits for the data value and one sign bit for its INTEGER types. Thus, in Turbo Pascal programs, INTEGER types have 2^15 (or 32768) possible positive values (from 0 to 32767) and the same number of possible negative values (from -1 to -32768).

Turbo Pascal also provides an INTEGER subtype of BYTE, which uses 8 bits (one byte) for storage and has 2^8 (or 256) possible whole number values from 0 to 255.

⟨//////////////////////////////////|· · · · · · · · · · · |////////////////////⟩
− ∞   0   255   + ∞

REAL NUMBERS

Real numbers include all the positive and negative numbers including fractions and zero. In mathematics, real numbers may have an infinite number of values, from negative infinity to positive infinity, as represented by the continuous number line:

⟨————————————————————————|————————————————————⟩
− ∞   0   + ∞

As with integers, there are practical limits on the values and precision of real numbers which can be handled by a particular computer and Pascal compiler. These limits are determined by the format and amount of storage allocated for each real value. Thus, the range of real values which may be represented in a given system are limited by the maximum and minimum real values which can be stored in the real number format selected. The real number range available on most computers is depicted by the number line:

```
←///////|——————————|///// | //////|——————————|///////→
 - ∞        -maxreal        -minreal  0   minreal      maxreal      + ∞
```

Note: Includes zero.

As you can see, very large absolute values (close to infinity) and very small absolute values (close to zero) cannot be represented.

EXPONENTIAL FORMAT

Real numbers are usually represented in what is termed *scientific, exponential,* or *normalized floating point* format comprised of two parts—a *mantissa* and an integer power-of-ten exponent or *characteristic* in the mathematical form:

$$x = m * 10^c \quad \text{as} \quad -3.59 * 10^2$$

or the exponential form:

$$x = mEc \quad \text{as} \quad -3.5900000000E + 02$$

in Turbo Pascal programs. The mantissa contains the significant digits of real number x automatically normalized by the computer to a fractional value in the range $1 \langle = |x| \langle = 10$. The exponent c is a positive or negative integer value. Thus, in Turbo Pascal

10.45 is represented as $0.1045 * 10^{+2}$	or $1.0450000000E + 02$
0.00056993 is represented as $0.56993 * 10^{-3}$	or $5.6993000000E-03$
-245.0 is represented as $-0.245 * 10^{+3}$	or $-2.4500000000E + 03$
0.1 is represented as $0.1 * 10^0$	or $1.0000000000E-01$

ACCURACY AND PRECISION

The values of real numbers which can be represented by a given computer language are limited by two factors—the exponent range supported and the precision or number of binary or decimal digits of accuracy of the mantissa. In practice, the mantissa of a real number is rounded or truncated to a given number of decimal digits precision.

6.2 Standard Data Types

Standard Pascal provides several predefined or standard data types for variables and constants—INTEGER, REAL, CHARacter, BOOLEAN, and TEXT. Turbo Pascal has two additional predefined types—BYTE and STRING. The actual ranges and storage used for these data types are dependent on the particular compiler implementation and computer system used, but files containing similar data types are transportable between Turbo Pascal systems.

A literal constant is an actual value included in program code—usually in assignment or comparison expressions. For example, the following objects are literals:

Object	Data Type
1	integer or byte
-2488	integer
1.0	real
-13.6	real
0.653	real
-1.2345678901E + 12	real expressed in exponent (E) notation
$FA39	integer expressed in hexadecimal
'John'	string
'145'	string
TRUE	boolean
'Y'	char
'2'	char

Symbolic or declared constants are assigned a value in a CONST declaration section. The value of a constant cannot be reassigned during execution of a program.

INTEGER TYPE

Constants and variables of INTEGER data type may be assigned positive and negative whole number values between MaxInt and -(MaxInt + 1). MaxInt is a system dependent predefined constant for the maximum INTEGER value available in a specific compiler implementation. In Turbo Pascal, MaxInt is 32767, and INTEGER type variables may be assigned values ranging from 32767 to -32768. INTEGER types in Turbo Pascal use two bytes (16 bits) of memory for storage. INTEGER literals are written without a decimal point.

INTEGER and BYTE values may also be expressed in hexadecimal notation in Turbo Pascal. Hexadecimal constants are written with a leading $ and one to four hex characters (0 . . F) like:

$4A01
$A0
$FFCD

Turbo Pascal's hexadecimal notation provides a convenient way to express machine-related values like absolute memory addresses without using negative integers (e.g., $8000 = -32768 and $FFFF = -1).

Overflows in integer expressions may be caused by large intermediate results from arithmetic operations like multiplication. These overflows will not produce compile or run-time error messages—just incorrect results. INTEGER type expressions should be carefully designed to preclude overflows, or real variables should be used.

BYTE TYPE

The BYTE data type in Turbo Pascal is a subrange of the type INTEGER and may be assigned whole number values between 0 and 255. As a subrange of the type INTEGER, BYTE types may be used where INTEGER types are expected and vice-versa. BYTE type variables are stored in one byte (8 bits) of memory. BYTE type literals are written without a decimal point or in two-digit hexadecimal notation.

REAL TYPE

Constants and variables of REAL data type may be assigned positive and negative real numbers (including decimal fractions) within the range and accuracy provided by a particular compiler implementation and computer system. Standard Turbo Pascal handles reals with a range of $1.0E-38$ to $1.0E+38$ with a mantissa of 11 significant digits. Real variables use 6 bytes of memory in Turbo Pascal. Real constants, including zero, are written with a decimal point in the form:

    0.0
    1.0
    0.223

Note that the leading digit is required. Reals may also be written in exponential notation as:

    $1.467E+03 = 1467.0$

Turbo Pascal supports other types of real numbers in two optional versions of the 16-bit compiler.

The 8087 math co-processor version of Turbo Pascal supports Real types in the range of 4.19E-307 to 1.67E + 308 with 16 digits of accuracy. The 8087 REAL type is stored in 8 bytes of memory. This version is designed primarily for scientific and other applications requiring high-speed calculation and accuracy over a wide range of values.

The BCD Arithmetic version of Turbo Pascal 3.0 supports REAL types with 18 digits of precision in the range 1.0E-63 to 1.0E + 63. BCD Real variables require 10 bytes of storage in memory. The BCD version of Turbo is designed primarily for business and financial applications requiring absolute accuracy with no rounding errors in computations involving large numbers.

The binary formats for storing real data values in files are not interchangeable among the three versions of Turbo Pascal, but data files may be shared by storing and retrieving the values as ASCII strings in files instead of using the standard binary data formats.

CHAR (CHARACTER) TYPE

The Standard Pascal type CHAR is used for single character values. Characters are written in single quotes as:

'A' 'B' 'c' 'd' '&' '?' ' ' (space or blank)

Characters are represented internally as a binary code. When characters are compared, it is their codes that are actually tested. Because character coding is system dependent (ASCII, EBCDIC, etc.), Standard Pascal does not define any particular character set as standard. Some character codes (like EBCDIC) do not map characters contiguously to their ordinal values (codes), and so programs which depend on one-to-one correspondence between a range of characters and their equivalent ordinal values will not be completely portable.

An ordinal number is the "place" number of a specific object in a set of objects of the same scalar (counting) type. For example, the ordinal value of the character 'A' is 65—'A' is the 66th member of the set of CHAR in the ASCII character set (ordinal counting begins with the "0th" element of a set). The ordinal value of the character 'B' is 66, and so on. Refer to the ASCII character chart in the Appendix for more information on the ordinal values of ASCII characters.

In Turbo Pascal, variables and constants of type CHAR (character) may be assigned any character in the extended ASCII character set ranging in ordinal value from 0 to 255. This extended ASCII set allows the programmer to access the special graphics display characters available in the IBM PC and similar computers. (Refer to the IBM PC character table in the Appendix.) CHAR type values may be assigned by using literals written in single quotes or by using the chr() function. A CHAR value occupies one byte in memory.

BOOLEAN TYPE

Variables of type BOOLEAN may be assigned a value of either TRUE or FALSE. The results of *logical* (relational) expressions are of type BOOLEAN. Logical expressions with BOOLEAN values are used in conditional statements to enable the program to "make decisions" based on testing the value of variables in the program.

A BOOLEAN type requires one byte of memory for storage. Pascal provides the predefined constants TRUE and FALSE for use in logical expressions.

STRING TYPE

The predefined STRING type variable in Turbo Pascal may be thought of as a sequential series of individual characters. This data structure is similar to an array. The first (0th) element of the array contains a byte value equal to the current length (0 ⟨= length ⟨= 255) of the string. This value changes as different length objects are assigned to the string variable.

Storage for STRING type variables is allocated when they are declared.

```
var
    name : string[maxlength];
```

The length of any object assigned to a string must not exceed its maximum allocated storage. Strings may be thought of as arrays defined as follows:

```
String type[maxlength] = ARRAY [0 .. maxlength] of CHAR
```

A STRING type occupies (*maxlength* + *1*) bytes of memory.

6.3 Scalar and Subrange Types

The basic data types in Pascal are scalar types. Each scalar type is made up of a distinct, linear ordered set of values. The scalar types include INTEGER, REAL, BOOLEAN, CHAR, and BYTE. The type REAL is included as a scalar type although it does not fit the scalar definition. Thus, REALs may not always be used in the same ways as other scalar types.

SCALAR TYPE

Pascal supports both the standard scalar types (INTEGER, REAL, BOOLEAN, CHAR, and Turbo's BYTE) and user-defined (or declared) scalar types. Declared scalar types are useful when used with subrange and complex data types to form data structures.

A declared scalar type may be any finite set of ordered values. This type is defined by declaring *all* of its possible values, in place order. The values of the declared type are represented by identifiers which are literal constants of the new type.

The following are examples of declared scalar types:

type
    Day   =   (Mon, Tues, Wed, Thurs, Fri, Sat, Sun);
    Month   =   (Jan, Feb, Mar, Apr, May, Jun, Jul, Aug, Sep, Oct, Nov, Dec)
    Season =   (Spring, Summer, Fall, Winter);

Note that single quotes are NOT used to declare scalar types.

Each of the values of a scalar type has an ordinal (positional) value beginning with 0, which is used to resolve relational expressions. The relational operators are $=$, $\langle\rangle$ (not equal), $\rangle$, $\langle$, $\rangle=$, and $\langle=$. They may be applied to all scalar types. However, both operands must be of the same scalar type (except that REALs and INTEGERs may be mixed). Thus, with INTEGER types, the statement:

    $1 \langle 2 \langle 3 \langle 4$

is true. Similarly, using the definitions above:

    Jan $\langle$ Feb $\langle$ Mar $\langle$ April

is true and

    Spring $\rangle$ Fall

is false.

Note that no more than one relational operator may be used in an actual logical expression in Pascal without using a logical operator like AND, OR or XOR. Thus in a program the statement:

    $1 \langle 2 \langle 3 \langle 4$

is written as:

    $(1 \langle 2)$ **and** $(2 \langle 3)$ **and** $(3 \langle 4)$

Pascal provides three standard functions for manipulating scalar values:

    Succ(summer)   The successor of Summer is Fall
    Pred(Summer)   The predecessor of Summer is Spring
    Ord(Summer)   The ordinal value of Summer is 1

Turbo Pascal also allows *retyping* scalar types by using the type identifier as a function designator followed by one scalar-type parameter in parentheses. Thus,

    Season(1) = Summer

SUBRANGE TYPE

A subrange type is a subset of previously defined ordinal *host* type. Subrange types are used to improve the clarity of a program and to provide additional range checking during program compilation or execution. In some implementations, certain subrange types (e.g., BYTE vs. INTEGER) may save storage space in the computer. Turbo Pascal will allocate only one byte of memory for declared scalar and subrange-type variables with less than 256 possible elements.

Subrange types may be used wherever the host type is legal and have the same characteristics as the host type, with the exception of their range of legal values.

Subrange types are defined by specifying the smallest and largest value in the subrange, in order, with the range symbol ".." as part of a type definition. For example, the type BYTE is a subrange of the type INTEGER, and could be defined as follows:

```
type
    BYTE = 0 .. 255;
```

Other possible subrange definitions include:

```
type
    WesternStates  =  (CA, OR, WA, ID, NV, AZ); {type definition}
    PacificStates  =  CA .. WA;
    Upper case     =  'A' .. 'Z';
    Lower case     =  'a' .. 'z';
    Cardinal       =  1 .. 32767;
    PrintingChar   =  '' .. '~';
    Degrees        =  0 .. 359;
```

Subranges of type REAL are not permitted.

RANGE CHECKING

As mentioned above, one of the benefits of using scalar and subrange types is that they allow extensive range checking to be performed by the compiler and the run-time code. However, inclusion of these tests can slow down program execution and increase compiled code size. Therefore, the Turbo Pascal compiler allows the user to enable or disable the generation of run-time range checking code with the compiler directive *R*. Inclusion of the directive {R+} will enable the feature while {R-} will disable the feature. The default setting is {R-}.

Range checking should normally be used until the program is completely tested and debugged.

6.4 Type Conversion

While most procedures and functions require their parameters (and results) to be of a specific defined type, some operators perform automatic type conversion and in effect allow mixed operands in expressions. The result types of automatic conversion of mixed expressions are defined in the next chapter.

Turbo Pascal also provides several standard functions for type conversion. These include the required Standard Pascal functions:

```
trunc()  round()  ord()  chr()
```

as well as the Turbo Pascal functions:

```
int()  frac()  val()  str()
```

These functions will be discussed in detail in a later chapter.

The unique Turbo Pascal *retype* facility mentioned earlier allows reversing the *ord()* function for scalar types other than CHAR (for which the *chr()* function is available). Retyping allows the extraction of the original scalar values from a scalar variable by specifying its ordinal value. (Remember that ordinal values begin counting with 0.) Using the type definitions above:

```
Month(4)     = May
Season(2)    = Fall
Upper(3)     = 'D'
Day(6)       = Sun
```

6.5 Typed Constants

From a programming point of view, literals and declared constants require more compiled code than do variables, because variables are stored only once in the compiled code while literal and declared constant values are included in the compiled code each time they are referenced.

Turbo Pascal provides the *typed constant* to solve this problem. A typed constant may be thought of as an "initialized variable." Here is an example of typed constant declarations:

```
const
    MaxLoops : Integer = 127;
    PoundExchangeRate : Real = 3.54;
    Title : string[23] = 'Data Conversion Program';
    Response : Boolean = True;
```

Typed constants may be used in place of variables in expressions and as parameters, but their values cannot be changed.

6.6 Literals

As noted earlier, a literal is an object that represents itself, usually a number or a string of characters. Literals are constants without names or identifiers. Literals are used in programs to initialize variables to a specific constant value, as index parameters, in relational expressions, in set definitions, and in output statements. Here are examples of some literals:

```
1.0
0
-3.456E + 13
37000
'5/16/85'
'Y'
```

Good programming practice encourages the use of symbolic (i.e., declared) constants or initialized variables instead of literals in program statements wherever practical to simplify program modification and improve the readability of programs. This is especially true for minimum and maximum ranges, installation dependent constants, version numbers and dates, and other global values which may need to be changed from time to time. For example, if the HELLO program above included a date, it could be written as:

```
program hello_world;
begin
    writeln('Hello world. Jan. 1, 1986');
end.
```

or as:

```
program hello_world;
const
    date = 'Jan. 1, 1986';
begin
    writeln('Hello world. ',date);
end.
```

In a larger program, the second form would be preferred, because the symbolic constant "date" can be easily located and updated whenever necessary without searching the code for each occurrence of the literal.

The data type of a literal is implied by its format (just like the type of a symbolic constant is implied by its assigned value) and is discussed in the next two sections.

NUMERIC LITERALS

INTEGER and BYTE type literal constants are written as numbers without a decimal point. They may also be expressed in hexadecimal notation as discussed earlier in this chapter. These are examples of INTEGER and BYTE literal constants:

1	INTEGER or BYTE
-337	INTEGER
0	INTEGER or BYTE
$F3B2	INTEGER
27645	INTEGER
244	INTEGER or BYTE

REAL type literal constants must be in decimal or exponent format. REAL types require a digit (or zero) on both sides of the decimal point:

```
1.0
0.021
0.0
-5.34
111.5E + 17
-2.311E-3
-13E12
```

STRING LITERALS

String literal constants are one or more displayable ASCII characters enclosed in single quotes. String literals containing only one character are type CHAR while those containing more than one character are type STRING. This type difference has little effect as Turbo Pascal allows CHAR and STRING types to be used interchangeably.

Turbo Pascal allows control characters to be embedded in any string literal by using either of two special forms of notation. ASCII control characters may be written by prefixing the control letter with a "^" symbol as

```
⟨Ctrl-C⟩        = ^C
⟨Ctrl-G⟩        = ^g (note lower case may be used)
⟨Ctrl-Z⟩        = ^Z
```

or by prefixing the ordinal value of the character (between 0 and 255—see ASCII character chart in Appendix) with the "#" symbol as

```
⟨Ctrl-C⟩        = #03
⟨Ctrl-G⟩        = #07
⟨Ctrl-Z⟩        = #26 or # $1F (hexadecimal notation)
```

In either case, the control characters must be placed OUTSIDE the literal's quotes, and must be written without separators or spaces between individual control characters and the literal.

For example, the control character ⟨Ctrl-G⟩ or 07 in ASCII code produces a "beep" on the terminal in most computers. The literal string

```
'Operator ERROR! '^G^G^G'Re-enter data. . .'
```

could be used in a *writeln()* procedure statement to display a message on the terminal and sound three beeps to alert the terminal user to a mistake. The other form of notation (# symbol followed by an integer constant value) could also be used:

```
'Operator ERROR! '#07#07#07'Re-enter data. . .'
```

for the same result, but it is more useful for characters outside the range of ⟨Ctrl-A⟩ to ⟨Ctrl-Z⟩. Note that spaces are not permitted in either form of notation.

```
program input;
var
    ch : char;

begin
    write('Enter any number - '^G);
    readln(ch);
    write('Enter another - '#07);
    readln(ch);
    writeln('- done -')
end.
```

6.7 Error Detection

Data typing allows the compiler to provide extensive error checking both when a program is compiled and when it is run. By comparison, BASIC assumes the type of all variables by the form of their identifiers. In IBM (Microsoft) BASIC, all numeric variables are typed as single precision real unless explicitly declared otherwise, either by the type postfix character (%, !, or #) or with a DEFtype statement. Variables except arrays are automatically declared on their first use in a BASIC program. Some BASICs even automatically declare arrays of ten elements or less.

Because Pascal programmers must declare each identifier before its use, many typographical and other trivial but often obscure errors can be detected by the compiler and corrected without time-consuming debugging. Often, these simple errors are the hardest to find in weakly typed languages like BASIC.

Pascal compilers also check for type mismatches in expressions, providing another level of error detection. Many of the built-in type conversions in BASIC must be specifically requested by using standard-type conversion functions in Pascal.

An added advantage of type declaration is that it allows the Pascal compiler to make the most effective use of storage space—by allotting just enough room for each data type.

## CHAPTER SEVEN

Expressions and Simple Statements

Pascal programs are constructed in structured blocks made up of declarations and statements. Each block in a program is a module containing zero or more declarations and statements.

As was discussed in the previous chapter, declarations are used to define all of the objects in a program with the exception of those standard objects provided as a part of the compiler. All objects in a Pascal program must be defined before they are used in the program, either in specific declarations or in the compiler's standard library.

Pascal *statements* are instructions specifying *actions* to be performed by the computer. Statements are constructed with Pascal keywords and symbols, procedure identifiers, and expressions.

Pascal *expressions* specify a formula for calculating a value. Combinations of Pascal keywords and symbols, constants, variables, functions, and operators are used to form expressions. Expressions have a result value and type when they are evaluated, based on the components of the expression, and an expression of a given result type may be used anywhere in the program that a variable of that type is permitted.

7.1 Operators

Turbo Pascal offers a number of operators for forming various types of expressions. *Arithmetic operators* are used to form numeric expressions using integers and reals. *Bitwise operators* are used to perform bit-oriented operations on integer values. *Logical operators* include boolean operators and relational operators. *Boolean operators* are used to combine logical or relational expressions. *Relational operators* are used to logically evaluate the relationship between two expressions. Some additional specialized operators are provided for manipulating strings and sets.

PRECEDENCE

Operators in Pascal have an *order of precedence*, or sequence in which expressions are evaluated. Precedence in Pascal is designed to follow the familiar rules of algebraic operators. If two operators in an expression have the same level of precedence, then the expression is evaluated from left to right. Portions of an expression within parentheses are evaluated before the rest of the expression without regard to any preceding and succeeding operators, with the contents of the innermost parentheses being resolved first.

Turbo Pascal groups operators by their internal class of operation, which relates to their order of precedence. In Turbo Pascal, operators have one of six levels of precedence, listed in order of evaluation as follows:

1. Expressions within parentheses ( )
2. Unary minus or negation
3. **not** operator
4. Multiplying operators: *, /, **div, mod, and, shl, shr**
5. Adding operators: +, -, **or, xor**
6. Relational operators: =, $\langle \rangle$, $\langle$, $\rangle$, $\langle =$, $\rangle =$, **in**

ARITHMETIC OPERATORS

Pascal provides six arithmetic operators: +, -, *, /, **div, mod**. These operators represent the familiar algebraic operations of addition, subtraction and negation, multiplication, real and integer division, and remaindering, and are used to form arithmetic expressions. They are written in a similar way to algebraic expressions, with operators between operands:

⟨operand⟩ ⟨operator⟩ ⟨operand⟩ {⟨operator⟩ ⟨operand⟩}

Several operators may be used to form a single expression.

An exponential operator ("to the power of") is not provided in Pascal, but if such an operator is required, the programmer may choose to provide his own function to compute integer or real powers. Two examples are provided in later chapters.

Integer Operators

Integer operators are used to form expressions with INTEGER and BYTE operands only. The result type of integer expressions is always INTEGER (with the exception of real division "/ ").

The integer operations in Pascal are +, -, *, **div, mod**.

+	for addition of integers;
-	for subtraction of integers, and for negation;
*	for multiplication of integers;
/	for division with a real result; both reals and integers may be operands;
div	for division with an integer result; operands must be both integer;
mod	for the remainder of an integer division; operands must be both integer.

Care must be taken to avoid integer overflow in expressions. This topic is discussed in more detail in the "Overflow Errors" section later in this chapter.

Real Operators

Real operators are used to form expressions containing REAL type operands only and also those containing reals mixed with INTEGER types. The result type of real or mixed expressions is always real.

+	for addition of both reals and integers;
-	for subtraction of both reals and integers, and for negation;
*	for multiplication of both reals and integers;
/	for division with a real result; both reals and integers may be operands.

Bitwise Operators

Turbo Pascal provides a set of bitwise operators for manipulating individual bits in integer and byte values. These operators are used to perform bit-oriented operations, facilitating direct, machine-level interface. Although it is beyond the scope of this book to provide an introduction to binary arithmetic and its uses, an example will be presented for each operator using decimal, hexadecimal, and binary values:

NOT	bit by bit negation:
	not 0 = -1
	not $0000 = $FFFF
	not (0000 0000 0000 0000) = (1111 1111 1111 1111)
AND	arithmetic and:
	55 **and** 11 = 3
	$37 **and** $B = $3
	(0011 0111) **and** (0000 1011) = (0000 0011)

OR	arithmetic or:
	55 **or** 11 = 63
	$37 **or** $B = $3F
	(0011 0111) OR (0000 1011) = (0011 1111)
XOR	arithmetic xor (exclusive or):
	55 **xor** 11 = 60
	$37 **xor** $B = $3C
	(0011 0111) **xor** (0000 1011) = (0011 1100)
SHR	shift right n bits:
	55 **shr** 3 = 6
	$37 **shr** 3 = $6
	(0011 0111) **shr** 3 = (0000 0110)
SHL	shift left n bits:
	55 **shl** 3 = 184
	$37 **shl** 3 = $B8
	(0011 0111) **shl** 3 = (1011 1000)

The operands of bitwise operators must be type INTEGER or BYTE and the result will be type INTEGER.

A short discussion of binary and hexadecimal numbers is provided in the Appendix.

LOGICAL OPERATORS

The logical operators include the boolean operators and the relational operators. Boolean operators require operands of the type BOOLEAN (i.e., with values of TRUE or FALSE). Relational operators require operands of the same scalar (ordered) type (REAL types are permitted).

Boolean Operators

The boolean operators NOT, AND, OR, and XOR are used to combine logical (boolean) expressions. XOR is not provided in Standard Pascal. The boolean operators are listed in order of precedence:

NOT	- inverts the boolean value of the logical expression following it -
	not true = false
AND	- an AND expression is true if both operands are true -
	true **and** false = false
OR	- an OR expression is true if either operand is true -
	true **or** false = true
XOR	- an XOR expression is true if only one operand is true -
	true **xor** false = true

The *truth table* (below) shows the results of each boolean operator, with the given values for logical expressions A and B:

A	B	**not** A	**not** B	A **and** B	A **or** B	A **xor** B
true	true	false	false	true	true	false
true	false	false	true	false	true	true
false	true	true	false	false	true	true
false	false	true	true	false	false	false

Relational Operators

The relational operators may be used for all standard scalar types: REAL, IN-TEGER, BOOLEAN, CHAR, and BYTE. Operands of type INTEGER, REAL and BYTE may be mixed. Other ordered scalar types may be used as well. The type of the result is always BOOLEAN (i.e., TRUE or FALSE). The relational operators available in Turbo Pascal are as follows:

=	equal to
⟨ ⟩	not equal to
⟩	greater than
⟨	less than
⟩ =	greater than or equal to
⟨ =	less than or equal to

Here are some examples:

A = B	is true if A is equal to B.
A ⟨⟩ B	is true if A is not equal to B.
A ⟩ B	is true if A is greater than B.
A ⟨ B	is true if A is less than B.
A ⟩ = B	is true is A is greater than or equal to B.
A ⟨ = B	is true if A is less than or equal to B.

Note that only one relational operator may be used in each relational expression, and that complex relations **must** be expressed by using the boolean operators (AND, OR, XOR, NOT) to combine relational expressions.

Because the order of precedence of the boolean operators is higher than that of the relational operators, parentheses should **always** be used when writing a complex logical expression. For example:

    (A ⟩ B) **or** (B = C)

Set Operators

A group of operators is provided in Turbo Pascal for manipulating and evaluating set structures. These operators will be discussed in Chapter 13.

String Operators

The only string operator is the *concatenation* operator (" + ") which is used to combine two or more strings sequentially. Its operation is identical with the Concat function described in Chapter 12. For example:

'ABCDE' + 'GHI' = 'ABCDEGHI'

The length of the resulting string may not exceed 255 characters or a run-time error will occur.

The relational operators may also be used with string operands. Relational operators are lower in precedence than the concatenation operator. The results depend on the following rules:

1. Single characters in the two strings are compared from left to right according to their ASCII ordinal values.
2. If the two strings are of different length but equal through and including the last character of the shortest string, the shorter string is "less than" the longer string.
3. Strings are equal only if their lengths and contents (including trailing blanks) are identical.

RESULT TYPES

The data type of the result of a given arithmetic operation depends on the operation and the type(s) of its operands. For example, the result of the multiplication of a REAL and an INTEGER type will be type REAL. In general, the result type of an expression may be determined by its operands:

Operands	Result Type
REAL - REAL	REAL
REAL - INTEGER	REAL
INTEGER - INTEGER	INTEGER (except real division "/ ")

Overflow Errors

It is important to realize that each portion of a complex expression generates an intermediate result as the expression is evaluated. This intermediate result may exceed the values permitted for the expression type, causing underflow or overflow errors.

In integer expressions, intermediate results may cause undetected overflows which will cause the expression to yield an incorrect value when it is evaluated. This is due to the way signed integer numbers "wrap-around" from positive to negative values. The following program will illustrate this problem:

```
program overflow;
var
  ans : integer;
begin
  ans := 32767 + 1;
  writeln(ans);
end.
```

Running this program does not yield the expected result of 32768 in variable *ans*. Instead, the result is -32768. To understand what has happened, recall the series of points on the number line representing the set of integers available on a computer system.

```
⟨//////|.............................|.........................|//////⟩
-∞      |                            |                         |      +∞
     -(MAXINT + 1)                   0                      MAXINT
```

In the case of Turbo Pascal, MAXINT is 32767, the largest signed 16-bit binary number.

```
⟨//////|............................|.........................|//////⟩
-∞     |                            |                         |      +∞
    -32768                         -1 0 1                   32767
    ($8000)                    ($FFFF) ($0001)              ($7FFF)
```

Referring to the equivalent hexadecimal values in the diagram above, it is easier to see what happened when the program added "1" to "32767":

decimal	hexadecimal	binary
32767	$7FFF	0111 1111 1111 1111
+ 1	+ $0001	+ 0000 0000 0000 0001
-32768	$8000	1000 0000 0000 0000

The overflow was carried into the 16th or sign bit of the integer value.

Integer overflow errors are not detected by Turbo Pascal. INTEGER type expressions should be carefully designed to preclude this possibility or a REAL type expression should be used.

Underflows and overflows in real expressions are also possible, but are much less likely due to the larger range of reals. Such situations in real expressions will usually be obvious—yielding results of 0.0E-38 (or 0.0E-39) or generating a run-time error.

Multiplying Operators

Operator	Operation	Type of operands	Type of result
*	multiplication	Real	Real
*	multiplication	Integer	Integer
*	multiplication	Real, Integer	Real
/	division	Real, Integer	Real
/	division	Integer	Real
/	division	Real	Real
div	Integer division	Integer	Integer
mod	modulus	Integer	Integer
and	arithmetic and	Integer	Integer
and	logical and	Boolean	Boolean
shl	shift left	Integer	Integer
shr	shift right	Integer	Integer

Adding Operators

Operator	Operation	Type of operands	Type of result
+	addition	Real	Real
+	addition	Integer	Integer
+	addition	Real, Integer	Real
-	subtraction	Real	Real
-	subtraction	Integer	Integer
-	subtraction	Real, Integer	Real
or	arithmetic or	Integer	Integer
or	logical or	Boolean	Boolean
xor	arithmetic xor	Integer	Integer
xor	logical xor	Boolean	Boolean

7.2 Expressions

Expressions define the method for computing a value. Expressions are constructed of constants, variables, functions, and operators. If the form and operands of an expression are valid when it is evaluated, a resulting value and type will be computed. This value may be assigned to a variable or used in place of a variable anywhere that the result type is appropriate.

Given the following assumptions:

```
type
    a, b : real;
    num, val : integer;
    name : string[20];
    flag : boolean;
    ch : char;
```

Here are a few examples of Turbo Pascal expressions and their types:

EXPRESSION	RESULT TYPE
a / num	Real
num + val	Integer
height ⟨ width	Boolean
(b * a) / num	Real
ch in ['A'..'Z']	Boolean
ord('A')	Integer
day = 1	Boolean
name[3]	Character
(day = 1) and (month ⟨ 6)	Boolean

7.3 Functions in Expressions

Function designators with or without parameter lists may be used in expressions. When an expression containing a function designator is evaluated, the corresponding function is activated and the parameters (if any) are passed to it. Functions return a single result value to the activating expression by assigning a value to the function identifier. Standard Pascal provides 20 standard functions, and Turbo Pascal includes many more. User-defined functions must be declared in the program before the expression which activates them.

The standard arithmetic functions in Turbo Pascal include:

FUNCTION	USE	PARAMETER TYPE	RESULT TYPE
Abs()	Absolute Value	Integer	Integer
Abs()	Absolute Value	Real	Real
ArcTan()	ArcTangent	Real	Real
Cos()	Cosine	Real	Real
Exp()	Exponential	Real	Real
Frac()	Fractional part	Real	Real
Int()	Integer part	Real	Real
Ln()	Natural logarithm	Real	Real
Sin()	Sine	Real	Real
Sqr()	Square	Integer	Integer
Sqr()	Square	Real	Real
Sqrt()	Square root	Real	Real

The standard scalar functions in Turbo Pascal include:

FUNCTION	USE	PARAMETER TYPE	RESULT TYPE
Pred()	Predecessor	Scalar	Scalar
Succ()	Successor	Scalar	Scalar
Odd()	Test for odd	Integer	Boolean

The standard transfer functions in Turbo Pascal include:

FUNCTION	USE	PARAMETER TYPE	RESULT TYPE
Chr()	ordinal to char	Integer	Char
Ord()	scalar to ordinal	Scalar	Integer
Round()	Rounding	Real	Integer
Trunc()	Truncating	Real	Integer

7.4 Statements

The part of a Pascal program which does the actual work is the program statement. Statements specify actions to be taken by the computer. They instruct the computer to perform a particular *process* like evaluating an expression and assigning the result to a variable, comparing two expressions and making a decision, repeating a process a given number of times, activating a procedure, performing a Pascal command, or a combination of these tasks.

Statements consist of expressions, Pascal reserved keywords and symbols, operators, procedures, and functions. An expression alone does not form a complete statement, but must be used with one or more keyword(s) or symbols, the assignment operator, or a procedure identifier.

Pascal supports both simple and structured statements. Simple statements include the assignment, procedure, empty, and GOTO statements. Structured statements will be discussed in later chapters and include compound, conditional, repetitive, and WITH statements.

ASSIGNMENT STATEMENT

The assignment statement is used in Pascal to assign a value to a variable identifier. When an assignment statement is executed, the expression on the right hand side of the assignment operator is evaluated and its value is assigned to the variable on the left. In Pascal, the symbol pair ":=" is defined as the assignment operator. Here is an example:

```
TOTAL := (COST * 1.3) + (INDIRECT * 0.8)
```

Other languages, like BASIC and FORTRAN, use the equals symbol ("=") for both assignment and relational operations. This practice often creates confusion between the concept of "equals" and "assignment." Unlike the equals symbol ("=") in mathematics, in computer programs assignment is a "one-way" process. The value on the right is "assigned" to the variable on the left. This means that statements like:

```
X := X + 1;
```

are perfectly valid, and should be read as "variable X is assigned the value of variable X plus one," not "X equals X plus one." If this concept is confusing, mentally replacing the assignment operator with a left arrow shows what is really happening:

```
X ← X + 1;
```

What actually happens inside the computer? The value in the storage location assigned to variable X is read into the computer's central processor, the constant value "1" is added to it, and the result is replaced in the storage location assigned to variable X. It is important to remember that variable identifiers like "X" represent storage locations in the computer's memory, not actual values.

Assignments are generally valid only between expressions and variables of the same type. An exception is made in the case of an INTEGER expression assigned to a REAL variable, where an *implicit type conversion* is done, converting the INTEGER expression's result to REAL for assignment to the REAL variable.

The BNF definition of the assignment statement is:

⟨assignment statement⟩ ::= ⟨variable⟩ := ⟨expression⟩ |
    ⟨function-identifier⟩ := ⟨expression⟩

Note that in a function, the function's identifier may be assigned the value of an expression, allowing the function to return a value to the expression that activated it.

PROCEDURE STATEMENT

The procedure statement is a statement containing a procedure identifier and any arguments or parameters to be passed to the procedure. When the computer executes a procedure statement, program control is passed to the named procedure block in much the same way as a subroutine is called in BASIC or FORTRAN. In Pascal, this process is called *activation* of the procedure. When processing in the procedure block is completed, control is returned to the statement immediately following the activating procedure statement. This allows procedures to be treated as "black-box" processes with specified inputs and results. Procedures do not return a value to the activating statement, but they may change the value of a passed variable parameter under certain conditions.

Procedures are discussed in more detail in Chapter 8.

EMPTY STATEMENT

The empty or null statement is allowed in Pascal as a programmer convenience. The empty statement does not specify any action to be performed by the computer.

The empty statement is a statement which contains no symbols and which has no effect. Blanks are not symbols. For example, a sequence of two statement separators (";") without a statement between them is an empty statement, even if the separators appear on different lines:

        ; ;

or

        ;
        ;

Empty statements are often created by including an "extra" separator where one is not required—usually in a compound statement, just before the closing END statement as shown in this example:

```
begin
   a := 1 + c;
   d := a - index;
   j := index + 1; ← extra separator
                    ← empty statement
end;
```

GOTO STATEMENT

The GOTO statement transfers program control to a specific program line beginning with a previously declared label:

```
procedure test;
label error_exit;
var
   error : boolean;
begin
       .
       .
       .
   if (error = true) then
      goto error_exit;
       .
       .
       .
error_exit: end;        {procedure ends}
```

Although Pascal includes the GOTO statement, most advocates of structured programming agree that it should be used rarely, if at all. A typical use of the GOTO is to exit a control structure upon detection of an error, without completing execution of the structure.

In Turbo Pascal, GOTO statements may not reference labels outside the current block. Turbo Pascal allows the use of any alphanumeric identifier as a label while Standard Pascal restricts label identifiers to unsigned numbers of up to four digits.

## CHAPTER EIGHT

Procedures and Functions

Any program may be written in dozens or hundreds of different ways, and still work correctly. However, some program designs are preferable to others. Up to this point, we have seen only simple programs written using a single program block which contains all of the program statements.

We have used a few of Turbo Pascal's *built-in* functions and procedures, like *length(string)* and *writeln(data)*, but the concepts behind these procedures and functions have not yet been explained in detail.

A particular task (like inputting data or calculating a value) performed by a group of statements must often be executed several times within a program. We can either include the required statements each time they are needed within the main program block, or we can declare them in a block as a *subprogram* (or subroutine). Subprograms are called or *activated* from other parts of the program, and when their task is completed, execution will resume immediately following the calling statement.

Pascal provides two types of subprograms—*procedures* and *functions*. They may be included in the compiler implementation as built-in or *standard* features or may be defined by the user's program. User-defined procedures and functions are contained in separate blocks in a program and may have their own variable, type, and other data and subprogram definitions. Procedures are used to perform specific operations while functions usually perform a calculation and return a value to the calling expression. A *procedure name or identifier* may be used instead of a statement and a *function name or identifier* may be used in place of a variable in an expression.

Subprograms in Pascal and their declared objects (variables, constants, types, and other subprograms) have a specific *scope* or range of visibility in programs. Scope is discussed in more detail later in this chapter, but for now we can state that some objects are available throughout the program, while others exist only during execution of their containing subprogram block. Objects which exist only within a given subprogram block are known as *local objects*. These objects are effectively "hidden" in their respective subprograms, isolating them from other program units.

In addition to eliminating the duplication of often used program segments, the use of procedures and functions can improve the clarity of programs, aid in debugging, and ease program maintenance and modification. Another advantage of generalized subprograms is the elimination of program-specific routines—allowing libraries of commonly used procedures and functions to be updated without concern for all of the specific requirements of a particular program. Libraries of procedures and functions may be developed and used in many different programs. Tasks like opening a file, computing a power, displaying a menu, evaluating a complex formula, centering a text string, and drawing graphic figures are some typical subprograms.

8.1 Procedures

Procedure blocks are actually miniature "programs-within-programs" and are written just like a main program block—with the exception that a semicolon is used after the final END rather than a period. A procedure identifier (parameter list) or name defines the block of statements to be executed whenever it is specified in the program.

PROCEDURE DECLARATION

All procedures must be declared, either in the compiler implementation as built-in procedures or by the programmer as user-defined procedures.

Procedures are declared in the declarations section of a main program block or another procedure or function block and typically follow the LABEL, CONST, TYPE, and VAR declarations (if any). The general form of a procedure block is:

```
procedure IDENTIFIER    (parameter list);
const                   {local constants, if any}
type                    {local types, if any}
var                     {local variables, if any}
procedure               {local procedures, if any}
function                {local functions, if any}
begin                   {procedure}
   statement(s);
end;                    {procedure}
```

As can be seen, a procedure block is organized in much the same way as a Pascal program block.

USING PROCEDURES

A procedure identifier may be used anywhere a statement may be used and is called a *procedure statement*. The procedure statement may have a parameter list, but it must match the "dummy" parameters or *formal parameter list* in the procedure declaration. When the procedure statement is encountered, the corresponding procedure is "activated" and execution is transferred to the first statement in the procedure. When the last **end** in the procedure block is reached, processing resumes in the previous program section, immediately after the activating procedure statement. This process is similar to the "GOSUB" and "RETURN" used for subroutine calls in the BASIC and FORTRAN languages.

Here is an example of the use of a simple procedure to center a string of text on the screen:

```
program center;
type
   tex = string[80];

var
   instr : tex;

procedure write_center (texstr : tex);
const
   spaces = '                    '; {40 spaces}
begin
   writeln(concat(copy(spaces,1,((79-length(texstr)) div 2))),texstr)
end; {write_center}

begin
   writeln('Center a user input string on the screen');
   writeln;
   writeln('Enter string to center on the next line—');
   readln(instr);
   writeln;
   writeln;
   write_center(instr);
   writeln;
   write_center('- done -');
end. {center}
```

8.2 Functions

Function blocks have almost the same structure as procedure blocks, with the exception that the function name (or identifier) is typed and is used to return a value to the activating expression. As with procedure blocks, function blocks are like miniature programs, with declared constants, types, variables, procedures, and functions. A semicolon is used after the final **end** in a function, too.

A function identifier or name defines the block of statements to be executed whenever it is specified in an expression. To allow the function to return a value to the calling expression, the function MUST include an assignment of the returned value to the function's identifier, which acts as a variable. The type of the function identifier is specified in the function heading:

```
function IDENTIFIER (parameter list) : type;
```

Because the function identifier is typed, functions are sometimes called typed procedures.

FUNCTION DECLARATION

All functions must be declared, either in the compiler implementation as built-in functions or by the programmer as user-defined functions.

Functions are declared in the declarations section of a main program block or another function or procedure block and typically follow the LABEL, CONST, TYPE, and VAR declarations (if any). The general form of a function block is:

```
function IDENTIFIER (parameter list) : type; {note typing of IDENTIFIER}
const                  {local constants, if any}
type                   {local types, if any}
var                    {local variables, if any}
procedure              {local procedures, if any}
function               {local functions, if any}
begin                  {function}
  statement(s)
  IDENTIFIER := value;  {assignment of value to be returned}
                       {by function}
end;                   {function}
```

USING FUNCTIONS

Function identifiers are used in the same way as a variable in an expression, and return a value to the activating expression upon completion of the function.

Functions may optionally include a parameter list. The declared function type must match the expected type in the expression or an error will occur.

Pascal functions are similar to functions in BASIC and FORTRAN, with the major difference that Pascal functions can include a complete subprogram with a number of statements as well as the evaluation of the function equation, if any. Functions in most other languages are limited to a single statement.

As Pascal does not provide an exponential function, one good use for a user-defined function is a natural number (positive integer) exponential routine. The next program uses a function to calculate the natural power of a real number. It is based on an example by Niklaus Wirth in the *Report*:

```
program powers;
var
  w, x : real;
  y : integer;

function expon(u : real ; e : integer) : real;
var
z : real;

begin
  z := 1;
  while e > 0 do
  begin
    e := e - 1;
    z := z * u;
  end;
  expon := z;
end; {expon}

begin
  writeln('Calculate the natural power of a real number');
  writeln;
  write('Enter real number: ');
  readln(x);
  write('Enter integer power: ');
  readln(y);
  writeln;
  w := expon(x,y);
  write('The answer is: ');
  writeln(w);
  writeln('- done -');
end. {powers}
```

Note that the variable *w* in the above example is actually unnecessary—the *expon* function could also be written in the parameter list of the writeln statement as:

writeln(expon(x,y));

8.3 Standard Procedures and Functions

Turbo Pascal has a rich assortment of *standard* procedures and functions, including most of the Standard Pascal "required" procedures and functions.

It is important to note all identifiers (except keywords)—even the standard "built-in" subprogram names—can be redeclared in Pascal. If a standard identifier is redeclared in a program, that standard procedure or function will no longer be available to the program (and some confusion may result), so care should be taken to avoid using any of the more than 150 standard identifiers in Turbo Pascal as user-declared objects. A complete list of Turbo Pascal standard identifiers is included in the Appendix.

Turbo Pascal's subprograms may be classified as:

1. Arithmetic
2. Terminal (screen) control
3. String handling
4. Misc. standard procedures
5. Input/Output
6. File
7. Dynamic memory allocation
8. Screen/graphics/sound—machine specific to IBM-PC

The features available in Turbo Pascal are listed in detail in specific chapters and in the Appendix, but a summary of the basic procedures and functions available in all versions is provided for easy reference, in much the same form as provided by the Borland *Turbo Pascal Reference Manual.*

Some of these standard procedures and functions will be discussed later in this chapter, after we explore the procedure concept further.

8.4 Parameters

Both procedures and functions may be "sent" values as *parameters* from the calling statement or expression. This allows a subprogram to use different data each time it is activated, making the procedure or function more versatile and easier to test as a stand-alone program unit.

Parameters to be transferred to a subprogram from an activating statement or expression are *actual parameters*, while the parameters specified in the subprogram declaration are called *formal parameters*. The transfer of data from the actual parameters in the activating statement or expression to the formal parameters in the subprogram is called *parameter passing*.

The *parameter list* in each subprogram reference in the program must exactly match the formal parameters of the subprogram declaration or an error will occur. For example, if we have declared a procedure as:

```
procedure count(m,n,o : integer);
```

then each time we reference procedure *count*, we must include exactly three integer parameters, either constants or variables:

```
count(1,2,3);
count(max, min, num);
```

PARAMETER PASSING

In Pascal, parameters may be passed either by value or by reference. In the first case, when parameters are passed by value to a subprogram, the current *value* of the "actual" parameter(s) in the calling statement or expression is assigned to the "formal" parameter(s) in the subprogram. Thus, any operations on the "formal" parameters in the subprogram have no effect on the original "actual" parameters in the calling expression or statement. This is similar to assigning the value of a variable to a temporary variable in a program—modifying the temporary variable has no effect on the original variable. The following example will clarify this concept:

```
program parm1;
var
    a,b,c : integer;

procedure count(m,n,o : integer);
begin
    m := m + n + o;
    writeln('Total = ',m);
end;

begin
    a := 5;
    b := 7;
    c := 3;
    count(a,b,c);
    writeln('a = ',a,' b = ',b,' c = ',c);
end.
```

The result of running this program will be:

```
Total = 15
a = 5 b = 7 c = 3
```

In this case, note that the actual paramater a was not affected by the procedure's operation.

When parameters are passed by reference, the *address* or location of the "actual" parameter in memory is passed to the subprogram, and the subprogram (in effect) actually uses the original object (often with a different local identifier) in its operations. Parameters passed by reference are called *variable parameters*. In this case, the value of the actual parameter in the calling statement or expression *may be changed* by the operation of the subprogram. In this way, a subprogram can modify a variable and return results to the rest of the program. This is similar to using a variable in a program.

```
program parm2;
var
  a,b,c : integer;

procedure count(var m,n,o : integer);
begin
  m := m + n + o;
  writeln('Total = ',m);
end;

begin
  a := 5;
  b := 7;
  c := 3;
  count(a,b,c);
  writeln('a = ',a,' b = ',b,' c = ',c);
end.
```

The result of running this program will be:

```
Total = 15
a = 15 b = 7 c = 3
```

In this case, note that the actual parameter a was modifed by the procedure.

The subprogram heading controls whether a parameter is passed by value or reference. In the previously discussed form for a subprogram heading:

```
procedure count(m,n,o : integer);
```

the parameters are passed by value. To specify that one or more parameters are to be passed by reference, include the reserved word VAR before the parameter in the subprogram heading:

procedure count(**var** m,n,o : integer);

In the above example heading, all three parameters m, n, o are to be passed by reference to procedure count. Here is an example of a mixture of parameters:

procedure complement(**var** i : integer; a : real; **var** b : real);

In this example, integer i is passed by reference, real a is passed by value, and real b is passed by reference.

PARAMETER TYPES

In Standard Pascal, parameters may be variables, constants, procedures, or functions. However, Turbo Pascal does not permit procedures and functions to be passed as parameters. Actual parameters passed by value may be either constants or variables, but actual parameters passed by reference MUST be variables.

Complex type constructs are not allowed in subprogram parameter lists. This means that simple types like INTEGER, BYTE, CHAR, REAL, and BOOLEAN may be used directly in parameter list declarations, but complex types like STRINGS, ARRAYS, and RECORDS must be declared elsewhere and the corresponding type identifier used instead. In this example:

procedure uppercase(**var** list : **string**[80]);

the complex type STRING is not allowed and will generate a compiler error, but the following is permitted:

type
  bigstr = **string**[80];
  . . .
procedure uppercase(**var** list : bigstr);

Normally, when using variable parameters in Turbo Pascal, the formal and actual parameters must match exactly. STRING type formal parameters must be the same length as the actual passed data items or an error will occur. However, the V compiler directive (default active or {$V +}) enables variable parameter type checking to be disabled ({$V-}), and allows a STRING type of any length to be passed to the formal parameter in a subprogram.

Turbo Pascal allows parameters of subprograms to be *untyped*, that is to be listed without a type specification in the subprogram heading declaration. Untyped parameters have limited usefulness, as they are not compatible with any other type of data, but they may be used in limited applications where the type of data is not significant—for example as a parameter to Addr, BlockRead/ BlockWrite, FillChar, or Move or as the address specification of absolute variables (see Chapter 17).

8.5 Scope

As mentioned earlier, one major feature of Pascal is that all *objects* (subprograms, variables, constants, types, etc.) have a *scope* or range of visibility. This means that some objects are visible or *known* in all parts of the program—these objects are declared in the main program block. Other objects exist only while their *containing* subprogram block is active (being executed)—these objects are *local* to their containing block. An object which is visible to a block, but external to it is a *global* object to that block.

Scope applies not only to variables and constants, but also to objects like types, procedures, and functions. Scope allows processes and intermediate results to be "hidden" from the rest of the program, and provides a method of isolating program parts from the effects of other elements.

Scope may be thought of as a sort of "downward" visibility. The general rule is that objects are visible in the block in which they are declared, and in all blocks contained in that block. Thus, an object declared in the main program block is known throughout the program, while an object declared in a subprogram is local to that subprogram and its contained subprograms.

If a global object's identifier is redeclared (i.e., reused) in a contained subprogram block, the global object becomes "hidden" and the new object exists in the subprogram and its contained blocks.

The keyboard shared by the IBM PC and XT. Photo courtesy of IBM.

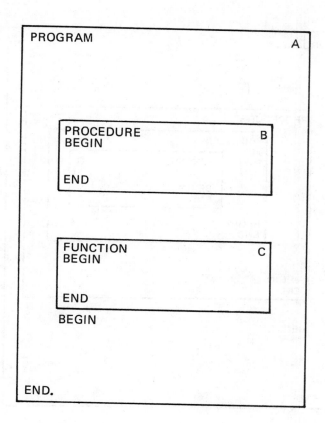

Figure 8-1 Local and Global Scope.

Figure 8-1 shows the organization and scope of a simple Pascal program with a main program block (*A*), one procedure block (*B*), and one function block (*C*). Objects declared in the main program block *A* are *global* to the whole program and are available in *B* and *C*. However, objects declared in *B* are *local* to *B* and are not available in *A* or *C*, and objects declared in *C* are *local* to *C* and are not available to in *A* or *B*.

If a local object declared in *B* or *C* has the same name as a global object declared in *A*, the local object "overrides" the global one in the block(s) in which it is known.

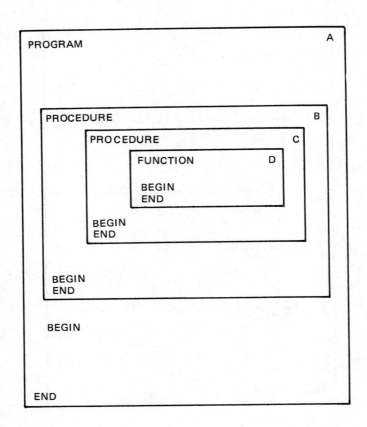

Figure 8-2 Nested Scope.

Figure 8-2 shows a group of nested subprogram blocks *B*, *C*, and *D* in program block *A*. Recall that the scope of an object operates in a "downward" fashion, "into" the nested blocks. Thus, an object declared in *A* is known in *B*, *C*, and *D*, while an object declared in *D* is only known (or local to *D*.

Figure 8-3 shows a more complex scope problem, much like those often encountered in real-world programs. Even here, the scope of variables becomes obvious after a few minutes study. Whenever you are confused by the scope of objects, just draw a box diagram like those above and the answer should jump out at you.

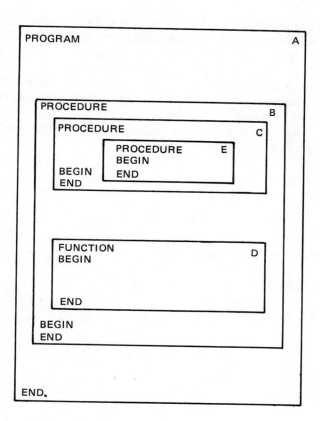

Figure 8-3 Complex Scope.

8.6 Side Effects

In ideal Pascal programs, subprograms are completely isolated from variables in other parts of the program, with all data passed through the parameter list or function identifier. This is not always practical in the real world, but a major effort should be made to avoid *modifying* external variables which are not in the subprogram's parameter list. Unexpected, hard-to-debug *side effects* can appear when procedures and functions change variables not formally passed to them. In fact, the use of global variables to pass data to a subprogram should be avoided entirely if possible.

8.7 Recursion

Recursion is the process of a subprogram calling itself. In many mathematical problems, a recursive solution is much simpler and more "natural" or intuitive than a repetitive or iterative one. Many high-level languages do not provide the capability for a subprogram to call itself, but Pascal does.

Although recursion can provide elegant algorithms, it can also be costly in terms of system resources, because each time the subprogram is called additional memory space is required.

Here is an example of a recursive function for computing the positive or negative integer power of a real number:

```
program powers2;
var
   i : integer;
   a : real;

function power(x:real; n:integer) : real;
begin
   if x = 0.0 then power := 0.0
   else
     if n = 0 then power := 1.0
     else
       if n < 0 then power := power(x,n+1)/x
       else
         power := power(x,n-1)*x
end; {power}

begin
   writeln('Power program 2');
   writeln;
   write('Enter real number - ');
   readln(a);
   write('Enter integer exponent (power) - ');
   readln(i);
   write('Answer: ',a:10:4,' ^ ',i,' = ',power(a,i):10:4);
   writeln;
   writeln(' - done -');
end. {powers2}
```

8.8 Forward References

Pascal requires that *all* identifiers be declared before they are referenced. This includes procedures and functions. But what happens if two or more functions or procedures include references to each other? Which comes first, the chicken or the egg? In this case, Pascal provides the ability to declare a *forward reference* which tells the compiler that there is a subprogram with a specific heading later on in the program in the same declaration section. The compiler can then reserve space for the *forward* subprogram and the error will be eliminated.

The forward reference consists of the complete subprogram heading (including parameters) followed by the reserved word FORWARD, like this example:

```
function evaluate(var a : real) : integer; forward;
```

Later in the declaration section, the subprogram is declared as it normally would be, with the exception that the heading includes only the subprogram name, because the parameter list has already been declared:

```
function evaluate;
```

8.9 External Subprograms

All commercial versions of Turbo Pascal allow the use of external subprograms—compiled or assembled binary files which may be called from a compiled Turbo Pascal program. They are declared as EXTERNAL procedures or functions and are loaded from external files during compilation. The general format for an external subprogram is:

```
procedure IDENTIFIER (parameters);
external 'FILENAME.EXT'
```

or

```
function IDENTIFIER (parameters) : type;
external 'FILENAME.EXT';
```

Additional information on external subprograms is available in the Borland *Turbo Pascal Reference Manual*.

8.10 Basic Standard Procedures

The basic standard procedures in Turbo Pascal that are not specifically discussed in other chapters are listed here.

TERMINAL (SCREEN) CONTROL PROCEDURES

Turbo Pascal allows the user to "install" the compiler for the type of computer and terminal (screen) it will be used on. In addition, utility programs are available (in Borland's *Turbo Toolbox* and in the public domain) which allow reinstallation of a compiled program for a new type of terminal. This process is usually required only in the CP/M-80 versions of Turbo Pascal, but may be necessary to run compiled programs on some MS-DOS computers that do not support IBM PC compatible screen functions or with IBM compatibles with monochrome composite monitors.

Once installed properly, Turbo Pascal "knows" how to control the screen functions of the computer it is used on. Turbo includes a number of powerful "screen handling" procedures common to all versions which are described in this section. Up to this point, we have not used these functions in the example programs. However, they allow the creation of complex screen displays and will be used in some advanced examples.

Later versions of Turbo Pascal for the IBM PC include a number of additional procedures and functions for windows, graphics, and color that are discussed briefly in a later chapter.

In the following descriptions, the *cursor* is the blinking or solid box or line on your screen which shows where the next character will be placed.

CLREOL

Procedure ClrEol clears all characters from the cursor to the end of the current line, without changing the cursor position.

CLRSCR

Procedure ClrScr clears the screen of all characters and returns the cursor to "home" position at the upper left corner of the screen.

CRTINIT

Procedure CrtInit initializes the terminal by sending the predefined terminal initialization string to the screen.

CRTEXIT

Procedure CrtExit sends the predefined terminal reset string to the screen.

DELLINE

Procedure DelLine deletes the line at the cursor position and moves all lines below up one line, inserting a blank line at the bottom of the screen.

INSLINE

Procedure InsLine inserts a blank line at the cursor position. All lines below are moved down one line, and the last line is lost.

GOTOXY(Xpos,Ypos)

Procedure GotoXY() moves the cursor to the position on the screen specified by the integer parameters *Xpos* and *Ypos* for the horizontal position or column (between 1 and 80) and the vertical position or row (between 1 and 25). The upper left corner or "home position" is (1,1) and the lower right corner is (80,25) on the IBM PC screen.

LOWVIDEO

Procedure LowVideo sets the screen to the predefined low intensity video mode.

NORMVIDEO

Procedure NormVideo sets the screen to the predefined normal video mode.

MISCELLANEOUS PROCEDURES

The following procedures are provided by Turbo Pascal to perform special functions not normally available to the programmer.

DELAY(num)

Procedure Delay() produces a program delay of approximately *num* milliseconds by executing a loop. Test this procedure to calibrate it for a particular machine.

EXIT (Turbo 3.0 only)

The EXIT procedure exits the current block. In a subprogram, EXIT will cause the subprogram to terminate and return. In the main program, it causes the program to terminate. This procedure is available in Turbo Pascal 3.0 and later versions only, but it is included here to insure that this identifier is not used in programs for upward compatibility.

HALT (Turbo 3.0 only)

The HALT procedure causes the program to terminate and control to return to the operating system. In PC/MS-DOS systems, if an optional parameter is included in the HALT statement, it is returned as an error code to the operating system. If no parameter is included, a 0 code is returned. This procedure is available in Turbo Pascal 3.0 and later versions only, but it is included here to insure that this identifier is not used in programs for upward compatibility.

RANDOMIZE

Procedure Randomize initializes the random number generator with a random value.

The RANDOMIZE procedure is not functional in Turbo 1.0 and 2.0 versions. The book *Turbo Tutor* from Borland provides a method for "seeding" the random number generator to replace the RANDOMIZE procedure.

MOVE(var1, var2, num)

Procedure Move() does a direct memory copy of a block of *num* bytes from the block beginning at the first byte of *var1* to the block beginning at the first byte of *var2*. This procedure is useful for copying arrays of data quickly.

FILLCHAR(var, num, value)

Procedure FillChar fills an area of *num* bytes of memory beginning at the first byte of *var* with *value*. Argument *var* is a variable of any type, *num* must be a type INTEGER, and *value* is either type BYTE or CHAR.

BASIC STANDARD FUNCTIONS

Standard Pascal includes almost all of the transcendental and arithmetic functions found in other languages with the exception of exponention or raising a number "to the N power." Pascal also has standard scalar and transfer (or conversion) functions. Turbo Pascal includes a number of miscellaneous functions as well.

ARITHMETIC FUNCTIONS

Many angular functions use values expressed in radians. For those who may not be familiar with this unit, here are the conversions to degrees:

```
1 degree = pi/180.0 radians (about 0.0175 radians)
1 radian = 180.0/pi degrees (about 57.3 degrees)
```

Other formulas which might be of use include:

```
ARCCOS(num) = pi/2.0—ARCTAN(num/SQRT(1.0-(SQR(num))))
ARCSIN(num) = ARCTAN(num/SQRT(1.0-(SQR(num))))
TAN(angle) = SIN(angle)/COS(angle) {angle in radians}
num ^ b = EXP(LN(num) * b)
```

ABS(num)

The absolute value of *num* is returned by function Abs(). This function accepts either real or integer arguments. The result type is the same as the type of argument *num*.

ARCTAN(num)

The tangent of angle *num*, in radians, is returned by function ARCTAN(). This function accepts either real or integer arguments and returns a real result.

COS(num)

The cosine of angle *num* expressed in radians, is returned by function COS(). This function accepts either real or integer arguments and returns a real result.

EXP(num)

The exponential of *num* (i.e. *enum*) is returned by function EXP(). This function accepts either real or integer arguments and returns a real result.

FRAC(num)

The fractional part (less than 1.0) of *num* (i.e. frac(num) = num - int(num)) is returned by function FRAC(). This function accepts either real or integer arguments and returns a real result.

INT(num)

The integer (whole number) part of *num* (i.e. (i.e. the greatest integer number less than or equal to *num*, if *num* $\rangle$= 0, or the smallest integer number greater than of equal to *num*, if *num* $\langle$ 0) is returned by function INT(). This function accepts either real or integer arguments and returns a real result.

LN(num)

The natural logarithm of *num* is returned by function LN(). This function accepts either real or integer arguments and returns a real result.

SIN(num)

The sine of angle *num* expressed in radians is returned by function SIN(). This function accepts either real or integer arguments. The result type is the same as the type of argument *num*.

SQR(num)

The square of *num* (i.e. *num* * *num*) is returned by function SQR(). This function accepts either real or integer arguments and returns a real result.

SQRT(num)

The square root of *num* is returned by function SQRT(). This function accepts either real or integer arguments and returns a real result.

SCALAR FUNCTIONS

Scalar functions are used to manipulate and test scalar type variables (both standard and user-defined. Standard scalar types which may be used with these functions include INTEGER, BYTE, BOOLEAN and CHAR.

PRED(num)

The predecessor of *num* (if it exists) is returned by function Pred(). Argument *num* is of any scalar type.

SUCC(num)

The successor of *num* (if it exists) is returned by function Succ(). Argument *num* is of any scalar type.

ODD(num)

If *num* is an odd number, function odd() returns boolean TRUE and FALSE if *num* is even. The argument *num* must be of type INTEGER. Equivalent to the formula ODD := (ABS(num mod 2) = 1).

TRANSFER FUNCTIONS

Transfer functions are used to convert data of one type to another. The Standard Pascal transfer functions are discussed in this section, but Turbo Pascal also includes other types of transfer functions for STRING types.

CHR(num)

Function Chr() returns the ASCII character with the ordinal number corresponding to *num*. Argument *num* must be an INTEGER type. The result is type CHAR.

ORD(variable)

Function Ord() returns the ordinal number of any scalar type (excluding reals). The result is type INTEGER.

ROUND(num)

Function Round() returns the value of *num* rounded to the nearest integer according to the following rules:

if *num* $>=$ 0 then ROUND(num) = Trunc(num + 0.5);
if *num* $<$ 0 then ROUND(num) = Trunc(num - 0.5).

Argument *num* must be type REAL and the result is type INTEGER.

TRUNC(num)

Function Trunc() returns the truncated integer value of *num* according to the following rules:

if *num* $\rangle$= 0 then TRUNC(num) is equal to the greatest integer less than or equal to *num*;
if *num* $\langle$ 0 then TRUNC(num) is equal to the smallest integer greater than or equal to *num*.

Argument *num* must be type REAL and the result is type INTEGER.

MISCELLANEOUS FUNCTIONS

The following functions are provided by Turbo Pascal to perform special machine level operations not normally available to the Pascal programmer.

HI(num)

Function Hi() returns the value of the high order byte (bits 4 through 7) of integer expression *num* in the low order byte of the result. The high order byte of the result is zero. Equivalent to the operation (*num* **shr** 4).

LO(num)

Function Lo() returns the value of the low order byte (bits 0 through 3) of integer expression *num* in the low order byte of the result. The high order byte of the result is zero. Equivalent to the operation (*num* **and** $0F).

KEYPRESSED

Function KeyPressed returns boolean TRUE if a key has been pressed on the console keyboard, and FALSE if no key has been pressed. Useful for testing for the presence of data before attempting to input from the keyboard—somewhat like the INKEY$ statement in BASIC.

RANDOM

Function Random (without a parameter) returns a random number value greater than or equal to zero and less than one. The result is type REAL.

RANDOM(NUM)

Function Random() (with a parameter) returns a random number value greater than or equal to zero and less than *num*. Both *num* and the result are type INTEGER.

SIZEOF(name)

Function SizeOf() returns the number of bytes in memory occupied by variable or type *name*. The result is type INTEGER.

SWAP(num)

Function Swap(num) returns the value of integer *num* with the high and low order bytes exchanged. The result is type INTEGER. For example, *swap*($0123) returns $2301. This function is useful for generating address values in the "reversed" form expected by many processors.

UPCASE(ch)

Function UpCase() returns the upper case alphabetic character equal to *ch*. If *ch* is not a lower case alphabetic character *ch* is returned unchanged. Both the argument and result are type CHAR.

## CHAPTER NINE

Terminal Input and Output

We have now covered almost all of the elements required to write simple Pascal programs—language elements, program structure, data types, operators, expressions, simple statements, and subprograms (i.e., procedures and functions). The remaining ingredient is program input and output or I/O. This chapter will cover the basic terminal (keyboard and screen) I/O procedures built into Turbo Pascal. Other types of I/O will be covered in Chapter 15.

Every functional program requires some form of input and output. In other words, it must communicate with its environment. A program which cannot impart the result of its operation is pointless. Every useful program requires at least one output statement. When a program is executed, input data is manipulated or processed by the program according to whatever algorithm is used and some type of result is produced and output.

In the few simple examples presented earlier, the input data was contained in the program itself. This is *internal data*. Output was displayed using the *writeln()* procedure. Recall our simple *hello* program:

```
program hello;
begin
    writeln('Hello world.');
end.
```

In this example, the input data is actually a literal constant in the program—the string 'Hello world.' The purpose of the program is to display this data on the screen.

9.1 Write and Writeln Procedures

The simplest or default form of the *write()* and *writeln()* built-in procedures allows programs to display almost any type of data on the terminal or screen. The general form of these procedures is:

```
write(data, data, data);
writeln(data, data, data);
```

where there may be zero or more data items, separated by commas.

The *writeln* procedure displays the data items in its parameter list on the screen at the current cursor position and then moves the cursor to the beginning of the next line (scrolling the screen up if necessary). The *write* procedure just displays the data, leaving the cursor at the point on the screen where the data terminates. Here is an example program which shows how these procedures work:

```
program output;

procedure example1;
begin
   writeln(1,2.0,' 3');
   writeln(1);
   writeln(2.0);
   writeln(' 3');
end;

procedure example2;
begin
   write(1,2.0,' 3');
   write(1);
   write(2.0);
   write(' 3');
end;

procedure example3;
begin
   write(1,2.0,' 3');
   writeln;
   write(1);
   writeln;
   write(2.0);
   writeln;
   write(' 3');
   writeln;
end;
```

```
begin
    writeln('Example 1 - Writeln procedure:');
    writeln;
    example1;
    writeln;
    writeln('Example 2 - Write procedure:');
    writeln;
    example2;
    writeln;
    writeln('Example 3 - Write and writeln procedures:');
    writeln;
    example3;
    writeln;
    writeln('- end -');
end.
```

This program simply writes three types of literal data (INTEGER, REAL, and CHAR) to the screen using both the *writeln* and the *write* procedures. Notice how the program uses three user-defined procedures to improve clarity and make the purpose of the program more obvious. The program's output looks like this:

```
Example 1 - Writeln procedure:
1 2.0000000000E + 00 3
1
   2.0000000000E + 00
 3


Example 2 - Write procedure:
1 2.0000000000E + 00 31    2.0000000000E + 00 3

Example 3 - Write and writeln procedures:
1 2.0000000000E + 00 3
1
   2.0000000000E + 00
 3
- end -
```

This test program illustrates several things about how these procedures work. First, if several parameters are provided, they are all displayed on the same line. Second, each data type has a different display format and spacing. Third, the *writeln* procedure can be used without parameters to provide a blank line. Finally, the sequence:

```
write(data);
writeln;
```

is equivalent to the statement:

```
writeln(data);
```

Similar results are obtained by using variables instead of constants in the parameter list, as in this example:

```
program output2;
var
  a : integer;
  b : real;
  c : char;
  d : boolean;
  e : string[15];
begin
  a := 45;
  b := 1.33;
  c := 'x';
  d := false;
  e := 'Turbo Pascal';
  writeln(a,b,c,d,e);
  writeln(a,' ',b,' ',c,' ',d,' ',e);
end.
```

The output of this program is:

```
45 1.3300000000E + 00xFALSETurbo Pascal
45 1.3300000000E + 00 x FALSE Turbo Pascal
```

Note that the format of the second line is easier to read and more attractive than the first line. The parameter list of second *writeln* procedure statement includes literal space characters (' ') in the parameter list between each output parameter to improve readability.

DEFAULT OUTPUT FORMATS

As can be seen from the preceding examples, Turbo Pascal has certain default rules for the formatting of each type of output data. These default formatting rules can be summarized as follows:

The following symbols are used for clarity:
b = blank, d = digit, s = sign (+ or -)

Integer: An integer number is output without leading or trailing blanks -
  ddddd
Integer literals are written without a decimal point.

Real: The real number R is output in a field 18 characters wide, using
floating point (exponential) format -
  R ⟩= 0.0: bbd.ddddddddddEsdd or
  R ⟨   0.0: b-d.ddddddddddEsdd
Real literals are written with a decimal point in either exponential or
decimal fraction form.

Char: A character is output without leading or trailing blanks. Literal
characters are written within single quotes or apostrophes (').

Boolean: The value TRUE or FALSE is output without leading or trailing
blanks. Boolean literals may be written in upper, mixed, or lower case.

String: A string (or character array in string format) is output without
addition of leading or trailing blanks. Literal strings are written within
single quotes or apostrophes (').

SPECIFYING OUTPUT FORMATS

Although the default data output formats are useful for some simple programs,
most applications require more flexibility in controlling the output format to
produce an attractive display. The default display format for all data types may
be changed by specifying the output field width to be used.

The field width is controlled by adding a colon followed by an integer value
(for the field width specification) (i.e. ":5") to the variable or constant parameter
in the *write* or *writeln* procedure statement. For all types except reals, the
specified field width must *exceed* the default width to be effective. In this way,
Pascal "protects" the programmer by displaying data that is larger than the
specified format, rather than truncating or cutting it off. Any rounding or
truncating of data must be specifically done in the program before the data is
output.

An exception is the number of decimal places displayed in real decimal and
exponential fractions, which may be controlled by the formatting commands.
Reals may be specified with either a single or double format suffix. Reals with
a single suffix $(R:n)$ are displayed in exponential format in the specified field
width (minimum width is 7 characters). Reals with a double suffix $(R:n:m)$ are
displayed as decimal fractions, with the first suffix (n) specifying the total field

width and the second suffix (m) specifying the number of digits in the fractional portion ($0 \langle= m \langle= 24$).

If n is less than or equal to the number of digits in the whole number portion of R plus m plus 1, all digits of R to the left of the decimal, plus the decimal, plus m digits to the right of the decimal are displayed anyway. The specified field width n becomes effective only if it is greater than that required to display the whole portion of R plus any specified fractional portion. If $m = 0$, no decimal point or fractional portion is displayed. If m is less than the number of significant digits in the fractional portion of R, the displayed portion is rounded up or down.

In the following example program, several field widths are specified for REAL type data items in both decimal fraction and exponential formats:

```
program output3;
var
    n,m : integer;
    r : real;
begin
    r := 66666.66666;
    m := 3;
    n := 1;
    writeln(n:2,' ',r:n:m,' ',r:n);
    n := 2;
    writeln(n:2,' ',r:n:m,' ',r:n);
    n := 3;
    writeln(n:2,' ',r:n:m,' ',r:n);
    n := 4;
    writeln(n:2,' ',r:n:m,' ',r:n);
    n := 5;
    writeln(n:2,' ',r:n:m,' ',r:n);
    n := 6;
    writeln(n:2,' ',r:n:m,' ',r:n);
    n := 7;
    writeln(n:2,' ',r:n:m,' ',r:n);
    n := 8;
    writeln(n:2,' ',r:n:m,' ',r:n);
    n := 9;
    writeln(n:2,' ',r:n:m,' ',r:n);
    n := 10;
    writeln(n:2,' ',r:n:m,' ',r:n);
    n := 11;
    writeln(n:2,' ',r:n:m,' ',r:n);
    n := 12;
    writeln(n:2,' ',r:n:m,' ',r:n);
end.
```

The output of this program is:

n R:n:m   R:n R = 66666.66666 or 6.666666666E + 04, m = 3

```
1 66666.667 6.7E + 04
2 66666.667 6.7E + 04
3 66666.667 6.7E + 04
4 66666.667 6.7E + 04
5 66666.667 6.7E + 04
6 66666.667 6.7E + 04
7 66666.667 6.7E + 04
8 66666.667 6.67E + 04
9 66666.667 6.667E + 04
10 66666.667 6.6667E + 04
11 66666.667 6.66667E + 04
12 66666.667 6.666667E + 04
```

The first column is the value of n, the field width. The number of fractional digits m is set to 3 (for the second column). Since the number of digits in the whole portion of r (the real number 66666.66666) is 5, the field width specification has no effect until it exceeds $(5 + 3 + 1)$ or 9 characters. In a similar way, the field specification for the exponential form has no effect until it is wider than 7 characters. Note the rounding up of the least significant digit in both forms.

The last displayed digit will be incremented by one (rounded up) if the following digit to the right is five or greater $(5 . . 9)$. If it is four or less $(0 . . 4)$, the last displayed digit will be unchanged. Rounding occurs from right to left, starting with the least significant digit and ending with the least significant displayed digit.

The following program shows the effects of rounding :

```
program output4;
var
    n,m : integer;
    r : real;
begin
    r := 1.23456789;
    n := 12;
    m := 0;
    writeln(m:2,' ',r:n:m);
    m := 1;
    writeln(m:2,' ',r:n:m);
    m := 2;
    writeln(m:2,' ',r:n:m);
    m := 3;
```

```
   writeln(m:2,' ',r:n:m);
   m := 4;
   writeln(m:2,' ',r:n:m);
   m := 5;
   writeln(m:2,' ',r:n:m);
   m := 6;
   writeln(m:2,' ',r:n:m);
   m := 7;
   writeln(m:2,' ',r:n:m);
   m := 8;
   writeln(m:2,' ',r:n:m);
   m := 9;
   writeln(m:2,' ',r:n:m);
   m := 10;
   writeln(m:2,' ',r:n:m);
   m := 11;
   writeln(m:2,' ',r:n:m);
end.
```

The output of this program shows the effects of rounding very clearly:

m	R:n:m	R = 1.23456789, n = 12
0	1	(next digit 2 ⟨ 5 = no round up)
1	1.2	(next digit 3 ⟨ 5 = no round up)
2	1.23	(next digit 4 ⟨ 5 = no round up)
3	1.235	(next digit 5 not ⟨ 5 = round up)
4	1.2346	(next digit 6 not ⟨ 5 = round up)
5	1.23457	(next digit 7 not ⟨ 5 = round up)
6	1.234568	(next digit 8 not ⟨ 5 = round up)
7	1.2345679	(next digit 9 not ⟨ 5 = round up)
8	1.23456789	(next digit 0 ⟨ 5 = no round up)
9	1.234567890	(next digit 0 ⟨ 5 = no round up)
10	1.2345678900	(next digit 0 ⟨ 5 = no round up)
11	1.23456789000	(next digit 0 ⟨ 5 = no round up)

Note that in the last example ($m = 11$), the format changes because field width (n) is set to 12, and 1 (R) left digits + 1 decimal + 11 (m) right digits = 13, forcing the specified format width to be ignored.

Display formats for constants and literals may also be specified:

```
writeln(134.3356:12:3);
```

will display as:

bbbbb134.336 (b = blank)

Output formats can be used when a number of spaces are required in an output:

write(' ':n)

where *n* is the number of spaces required. This technique works because if a format width is specified for a STRING type value, the string is right adjusted in a field of width *n*, and the string is preceded by *n - length(string)* spaces. In this case, the result is *n* spaces.

WRITE PARAMETERS

The arguments in *write* and *writeln* procedure parameter lists may be of any the standard types (INTEGER, REAL, BYTE, BOOLEAN, CHAR, STRING). They may be literal constants, declared constants, variables, functions, or expressions—in fact, anything that evaluates to a value. The following are some examples of legal *writeln()* arguments:

```pascal
program output5;
var
    a,b : real;
    c,d : integer;

begin
    a := 3.5;
    b := 4.2;
    c := 9;
    d := 2;
    writeln('The ordinal value of "A" = ', ord('A'));
    writeln('The total of a + b = ', (a + b):4:1);
    writeln('The difference of c - d = ', c - d);
    writeln('The square root of ', c, ' = ', sqrt(c):6:3);
end.
```

The output of this program is:

```
The ordinal value of "A" = 65
The total of a + b = 7.7
The difference of c - d = 7
The square root of 9 = 3.000
```

9.2 Terminal Control Procedures

In the preceding chapter, the nine standard terminal control procedures provided in all versions of Turbo Pascal were listed. These procedures allow easy manipulation of screen data and the creation of attractive screen displays. The most useful of these procedures are:

CLRSCR—clear the screen and home cursor
CLREOL—clear from cursor to end of line
GOTOXY(Xpos,Ypos)—move cursor to Xpos,Ypos (home = 1,1)
LOWVIDEO—set "dim" or low video intensity mode
NORMVIDEO—set normal or "high" intensity mode

Version 2.0 and later of Turbo Pascal for the IBM PC provides a number of added features for screen handling, including setting color, text and graphics modes, manipulating screen windows, and a number of standard and "Turtle" graphics functions.

9.3 Read and Readln Procedures

Although some programs are designed that just use data contained within the program for input, they have very limited application and must be recompiled each time the data changes. Programs which accept input data from an external source are both flexible and versatile.

The easiest method of inputting data is usually typing it on the keyboard, and then visually verifying it on the screen. Turbo Pascal supports console (echoed keyboard) input as the default mode for the standard *read* and *readln* procedures.

The general form for these procedures is:

read(data, data, data);
readln(data, data, data);

where there may be zero or more data items in the parameter list, separated by commas.

The console input line buffer will handle a maximum of 127 characters. This length may be lowered by assigning a new value between 0 and 127 to the predefined variable *BufLen*.

When using keyboard input, each *read* or *readln* procedure is terminated by pressing the ⟨Enter⟩ key. If fewer values are entered than are contained in the parameter list, any remaining variables will be bypassed—character variables will be set to ⟨Ctrl-Z⟩, numerics will be unchanged, and strings will be empty. If more values are entered than required, the excess data will be ignored.

When used for keyboard input, the *read* and *readln* procedures are identical, with the exception that when the ⟨Enter⟩ key is pressed to end a console input, *read* does not echo the carriage return (CR) character to the screen, while *readln* echoes the CR and adds a line feed (LF), moving the cursor to the beginning of a new line. This feature allows the programmer additional control over the cursor position and screen display (e.g., the ability to display text on the same line following an input operation).

The Turbo Pascal *read* and *readln* procedures allow limited editing of keyboard input data—**before** the ⟨Enter⟩ key is pressed. Pressing the ⟨BACKSPACE⟩ key, usually marked ← will backspace the cursor one character position and delete the character there. The entire input line may be erased by pressing ⟨Ctrl-X⟩, and the data may be re-entered.

INPUT DATA TYPES

Like the write procedures, the *read* and *readln* procedures have specific rules for their operation with various types of variables. Console input is handled as text character input in Turbo Pascal. Each data input item must match the type format for the corresponding variable in the read/readln parameter list or a run-time error will occur. (Note: Integer input will be converted to type REAL if required.)

Type	Action
char	reads one character;
string	reads characters up to maximum length defined for the string or until a CR (End of Line—Eoln) or ⟨Ctrl-Z⟩ (End of File—Eof) is entered;
numeric- (integer or real)	reads up to 30 characters in proper numeric format terminated by a blank, a TAB, a CR, or a Ctrl-Z. Leading blanks, TABs, CRs, or LFs (line feeds) are skipped;
boolean	input of this type not allowed.

If a CR (i.e. ⟨Enter⟩) is input at the beginning of a numeric data item, no new value is assigned to the variable—it remains unchanged. This is different from BASIC, where a null input assigns zero (0) to a numeric variable.

From the above rules, we can generalize that an input list of numeric data items may be separated by a blank or TAB. This differs from BASIC, where input data items in a list are separated by commas. Typically, only one string may be entered per *read/readln*, because strings must be ended with a CR (which also concludes the *read/readln* procedure), unless the input string exactly matches the defined length of the matching string variable.

The Turbo Pascal keyboard input procedures are somewhat more complicated to use than the equivalent INPUT statements in BASIC. Therefore, in our example programs, we will use only one input variable per keyboard *read/readln* procedure to simplify input and enhance program clarity.

This is an example of using the *readln* procedure to read three variables:

```
program input1;
var
   a: integer;
   b: real;
   c: real;

begin
   readln(a);
   readln(b);
   readln(c);
   writeln('a = ',a,' b = ',b,' c = ',c);
end.
```

Recall that if additional data is entered, it will be ignored. In this example, we enter one number on the first line, two numbers on the second line (the second entry is ignored), then the fourth entry on the third line:

10⟨Enter⟩

20.0 30.0⟨Enter⟩

40.0⟨Enter⟩

Here is the program output:

```
10
20.0 30.0
40.0
a = 10 b = 2.0000000000E + 01 c = 4.0000000000E + 01
```

PROMPTING INPUTS

In the previous example, the program waits for input, but the user has no idea of what to do. Keyboard read and readln statements should always be preceded by a *prompt* or request for input from the user. In some versions of BASIC, this may be done as part of the INPUT statement. In Pascal all display output is done with the write or writeln statements. The usual method is to use a write (which does not move the cursor to a new line) followed by a readln in this general form:

```
write('Prompt: ');
readln(data);
```

In the following example, we have modified the preceding program to prompt the user for each input. The program is now clearer and there is less possibility for user error:

```
program input2;
var
   a: integer;
   b: real;
   c: real;

begin
   write('Enter integer value for "a" - ');
   readln(a);
   write('Enter real value for "b" - ');
   readln(b);
   write('Enter real value for "c" - ');
   readln(c);
   writeln;
   writeln('a = ',a,' b = ',b,' c = ',c);
end.
```

HEADINGS AND TITLES

In the examples presented so far, there have been no headings or titles displayed in programs. Now that you are familiar with the use of the *write* and *writeln* procedures we will begin to use them to produce clear, attractive displays. Data labels (like in the output line in the two preceding examples—

a = 10 b = 2.0000000000E+01 c = 4.0000000000E+01

will also be used regularly from this point on.

BOOLEAN INPUT

As mentioned above, boolean types are not permitted for input, but this is easily worked around by assigning the value of a relational expression to the boolean variable:

```
program boolean1;
var
```

```
     a : char;
     b : boolean;
begin
     write('Input T for TRUE or F for FALSE - ');
     readln(a);
     b := ('T' = a);
     writeln;
     writeln(b);
end.
```

Note that in this program *any* input other than capital "T" will produce a result of FALSE. In the later chapters, we will see how programs can be made more immune to data input errors. We will also discuss other forms of input and output. First, however, we will design some simple programs.

CHAPTER TEN

Simple Programs

We now have enough tools to write some simple Pascal programs that will actually do something practical, besides just inputting or displaying a data value. Up to this point we have covered language elements, program structure, data types, operators, expressions, simple statements, subprograms (i.e., procedures and functions), and console I/O.

In this section, we will design some simple Pascal programs. We will also discuss the use of several commonly used built-in procedures and functions.

In the unlikely event any program "hangs" or does not operate properly, it can be aborted by pressing ⟨Ctrl-C⟩, which will stop execution and activate Turbo's run-time error-detection system.

10.1 Average Program

Almost everyone is familiar with the method for computing an arithmetic average. Add a group of values, and then divide the sum by the number of values. Mathematically, this process can be expressed as:

$$\text{Average} = (S1 + S2 + S3 + \ldots + Sn)/n$$

This is our *algorithm*. At this point, we have no way to make decisions in our programs, so all conditions (like the number of values to sum) must be fixed in the program. Let's assume we wish to average 5 numbers. Should they be real or integer types? For the most flexibility, we will make them real types, because integer inputs will be converted to reals automatically.

```
program average;
const
   num = 5;
var
   av : real;
```

124

```
procedure get_data;
var
   a1,a2,a3,a4,a5,total : real;

begin
   write('Enter #1 - ');
   readln(a1);
   write('Enter #2 - ');
   readln(a2);
   write('Enter #3 - ');
   readln(a3);
   write('Enter #4 - ');
   readln(a4);
   write('Enter #5 - ');
   readln(a5);
   total := a1 + a2 + a3 + a4 + a5;
   av := total / num;
end;

begin
   writeln('Average Program ');
   writeln;
   writeln('Input five values and their average will be displayed.');
   writeln;
   get_data;
   writeln;
   writeln('The average of the five numbers is ',av:8:3);
   writeln;
   writeln('- done -');
end.
```

Here is a sample run of the AVERAGE program:

```
Average Program

Input five values and their average will be displayed.

Enter #1 - 3
Enter #2 - 4
Enter #3 - 5
Enter #4 - 6
Enter #5 - 7

The average of the five numbers is        5.000

- done -
```

Notice that the five input values and their total are *local* variables—that is, they are only available inside the procedure get_data. Variable *av* is a *global* variable and is available throughout the program. The "- done -" is displayed at the end of the program run to indicate normal termination of the program.

10.2 Square and Square Root Program

For our next problem, we will compute the square and the square root of a number input by the user. Everyone knows that the square of a number is that number multiplied by itself. The square root of a positive number *a* is the positive value *x*, which when squared equals *a*. Pascal provides standard functions for both of these computations. Recall that when an expression containing a function is evaluated, the function is activated and (usually) returns a value to the expression.

```
program squares;
var
   a : real;

begin
   writeln('Square and square root program.');
   writeln;
   write('Enter value - ');
   readln(a);
   writeln;
   writeln('input = ',a:10:3);
   writeln('square = ',sqr(a):10:3);
   writeln('square root = ',sqrt(a):10:3);
   writeln;
   writeln('- done -');
end.
```

The output of this program looks like this:

```
Square and square root program.

Enter value - 33

input = 33.000
square = 1089.000
square root = 5.745

- done -
```

10.3 String Length Program

These two simple programs will request the input of a string of characters and then display its length. The first uses the *length()* function and the second uses the *ord()* function to determine the length of the string.

```
program string1;
var
   a : string[80];
begin
   writeln('String length program #1');
   writeln;
   writeln('Enter string on the following line:');
   writeln;
   readln(a);
   writeln;
   writeln('String length is ',length(a),' characters.');
   writeln;
   writeln('- done -');
end.
```

```
program string2;
var
   a : string[80];
begin
   writeln('String length program #2');
   writeln;
   writeln('Enter string on the following line:');
   writeln;
   readln(a);
   writeln;
   writeln('String length is ',ord(a[0]),' characters.');
   writeln;
   writeln('- done -');
end.
```

The second example shows that the 0th element of a string contains its length, which must be converted from CHAR type to INTEGER with the *ord()* function before it can be used as a numeric value.

10.4 Character Compare Program

```pascal
program compare;
var
  a, b : char;

procedure compute;
var
  less,
  equal,
  greater : boolean;

begin
  less := a < b;
  equal := a = b;
  greater := a > b;
  writeln('First character is less than second - ',less);
  writeln('First character is equal to second - ',equal);
  writeln('First character is greater than second - ',greater);
end;

begin
  writeln('Character compare program.');
  writeln;
  write('Enter first character: ');
  readln(a);
  write('Enter second character: ');
  readln(b);
  writeln;
  compute;
  writeln;
  writeln('- done -');
end.
```

10.5 Mileage Program

This simple program will compute your car's MPG rating if you keep track of the miles driven between fill-ups and the amount of gas purchased.

```pascal
program mileage;
var
```

```
    miles, mpg, gallons : real;
begin
    writeln('Car mpg computation program.');
    writeln;
    write('Enter number of miles since last fill-up - ');
    readln(miles);
    write('Enter gallons of fuel purchased - ');
    readln(gallons);
    mpg := miles / gallons;
    writeln('MPG rating for car = ',mpg:6:1);
    writeln;
    writeln('- done -');
end.
```

Here is a sample run of the MILEAGE program:

```
Car mpg computation program.

Enter number of miles since last fill-up - 425
Enter fuel purchased - 35
MPG rating for car =  12.1

- done -
```

## CHAPTER ELEVEN

Decision Statements

The examples in the preceding chapter show that some useful straight-line (i.e., sequentially executed) programs can be constructed with the basic elements of Pascal that we have covered so far, but more complex problems require one more tool. We have not yet discussed the most powerful feature of computer programs—the decision statement. This chapter will discuss Pascal's structured decision statements, which can control the sequence in which statements are executed in a program (and whether they are executed at all).

A *structured statement* in Pascal is a group of statements constructed with a specific organization and having a distinctly defined function. Pascal includes four types of structured statements: the compound statement, the conditional statement, the repetitive statement, and the WITH statement. The WITH statement will be discussed in Chapter 13.

The first three kinds of structured statements are used to build *control structures*, that is, statements which modify a program's normal sequential flow-of-control. Since these statements are made up of several parts, usually placed on different program lines, they are termed *structures*.

A control structure evaluates an expression and selects one or more predefined actions based on the resulting value or repeatedly executes a group of statements a specified number of times. In this way, the control structure can actually change the way a program operates while it is running.

11.1 Compound Statements

A *compound statement* is a structure containing a grouping of statements which are executed in sequential order. Compound statements are made up of one or more valid statements delimited by the reserved words **begin** and **end**. Compound statements may include other nested compound statements. Pascal treats a compound statement exactly the same as a single statement, so compound statements may be used wherever a single statement is valid.

The general form of the compound statement is:

```
begin
    statement 1;
    statement 2;

        .
        .
        .

    statement n
end
```

Note that semicolons (";") are used as statement *separators* in Pascal, not as statement terminators. Semicolons are placed between each statement in a compound statement (just like in a program). There is no semicolon separating the **begin** and the first statement or the last statement and the **end** in a compound statement because **begin** and **end** are *delimiters*, not statements. The entire compound statement is considered a single statement in Pascal, and so a semicolon separator is normally used after the **end** delimiter, unless the compound statement forms an intermediate part of another structure.

In most cases, placing an extra semicolon before the **end** will not cause any problem because Pascal allows a helpful construct called the *empty statement*. The empty statement is often hard to spot, because it is invisible. Here is an example program which illustrates this situation:

```
program empty;
var
    sum, a, b : integer;
begin
  begin
    writeln('Sum two numbers program');
    writeln;
    write('Enter first number - ');
    readln(a);
    writeln;
    write('Enter second number - ');
    readln(b);
    writeln;
    sum := a + b;
    writeln('The sum of a and b is - ',sum); { ← the empty statement is here}
  end
end.
```

Even though this program does not conform exactly to the syntax rules of Pascal, it will execute properly because the empty statement (after the last writeln statement) is allowed. In spite of the help provided by the empty statement, there are still occasions when misplaced semicolons can cause problems, particularly in some control structures. Note that there is no semicolon needed between the first **end** and the second **end** as they are both *delimiters,* not statements. In this text, semicolons are used after almost all statements, whether or not their use will create an "empty" statement. This allows easy modification and expansion of programs without having to correct numerous "; expected" compiler errors.

Compound statements are fairly simple—just a group of statements bracketed by **begin** and **end**. At first glance, it may seem that compound statements have little purpose. After all, if the statements in a compound statement are executed sequentially, just like those in the rest of the program, then why bother with them at all? The key to their value is the rule that a compound statement is *exactly the same as a single statement* in Pascal, and is valid wherever a single statement is valid.

We will see shortly that all but one of the control structures provided in Pascal call for a *single statement* as the controlled object of the structure. The compound statement allows the use of several statements in place of just one in these cases. In the following sections, we will see that compound statements are most often used to expand the object of a control structure from a single statement to a group of statements.

The BNF definition of the compound statement is:

⟨compound-statement⟩ ::= **begin** ⟨statement⟩ {; ⟨statement⟩} **end**

11.2 Decision and Repetition

Program execution in a computer program normally proceeds in the order in which statements appear (that is, sequentially). As we have seen, straight-line or sequentially executed programs can be used to solve very simple problems requiring the input of data and the computation and output of a result. However, if any portion of such a program must be executed more than once, the instructions for that portion must also appear in the program more than once. The program must be designed exactly to fit the number of items in the input data, and only very simple algorithms may be coded. Errors can usually be reported, but not acted upon.

Programs made up only of sequentially executed statements can accomplish a few well-defined computational tasks, but most programming problems require the ability dynamically to change which program instructions are executed or how many times they are executed based on input data or calculated results. It is this decision-making capability that makes digital computers so powerful.

Sequential structures (programs, procedures, functions, and compound statements) are made up of blocks of statements which are executed in order. *Conditional structures* allow a statement or group of statements to be executed or bypassed based on the boolean (logical) value of a control expression. *Repetitive structures* perform a sequence of one or more statements again and again until a specified test condition is met.

The single or compound statement which is either executed or bypassed in a conditional structure is the *object statement* of the structure. Some conditional structures may have more than one object statement; however, only one (or none) of the objects may be selected and executed each time the structure is executed.

11.3 Boolean Expressions

Boolean expressions (also called logical expressions) have one of two values, either TRUE or FALSE. In conditional control structures, they form the *control condition* or expression that is tested. The control structure's object statement(s) will be executed *if* or *as long as* or *until* the control condition has a boolean value of TRUE, depending on the particular kind of structure.

11.4 Conditional Statements

Conditional statements are used to make a decision based on the result of evaluating a control condition and thereby select from one or more possible actions (statements) to be performed by the computer. In other words, a conditional statement will take one course of action if the control condition is TRUE and another if the condition is FALSE when it is evaluated.

Conditional statements are executed sequentially, although portions of a conditional control structure may be bypassed based on the value of the controlling expression. In Pascal, they are not normally used by themselves to create repetitive structures.

IF STATEMENT

One of the simplest and most intuitive logical concepts is the IF *A* IS TRUE THEN DO *B* construct. The IF statement is the basic control structure in almost every programming language. It provides the ability to execute a single or compound statement if a given control condition is TRUE. Although the other Pascal control structures can be constructed using the IF statement, they are provided in Pascal for programmer convenience, overall program clarity, and to avoid using the GOTO statement.

The general form of the IF statement is:

    IF condition THEN statement

The BNF form of the IF statement is:

⟨if-statement⟩ ::= **if** ⟨boolean-expression⟩ **then** ⟨statement⟩

The flow diagram for the IF structure shows clearly how it operates. The diamond-shaped box indicates a decision statement.

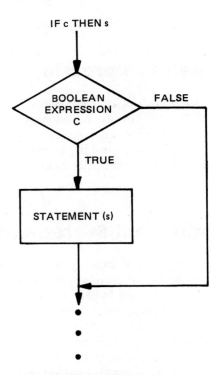

Figure 11-1 Flow Diagram of IF Structure.

Here is an example of the COMPARE program using the IF statement:

```
program compare2;
var
    a,b : real;
begin
    writeln('Comparison program #2');
    writeln;
    write('Enter first value - ');
    readln(a);
    writeln;
    write('Enter second value - ');
```

```
    readln(b);
    writeln;
    if (a < b) then
        writeln('First value is less than second.');
    if (a = b) then
        writeln('First value is equal to second.');
    if (a > b) then
        writeln('First value is greater than second.');
    writeln;
    writeln('- done -');
end.
```

Note that when using a sequence of simple IF statements as in the example above to select one (and only one) of several possible actions, it is important to insure that the control conditions specified are *mutually exclusive*, that is, that only one of the conditions can be TRUE at a time. If the conditions in the example above had been stated as:

$$(a <= b), (a = b), \text{ and } (a >= b)$$

the case where $a = b$ would be TRUE for all three expressions, and in this example would have produced incorrect results.

The possibility of this situation can be eliminated by using either the IF . . . ELSE or the CASE structures described in the following sections.

IF . . . ELSE STATEMENT

The IF . . . ELSE control structure is an expansion of the basic IF statement which provides additional program clarity and eliminates the need for GOTOs and paired IF/IF NOT structures in decisions between two alternative courses of action. Multiple nested IF . . . ELSE structures may also be used to select from alternative courses of action.

The general form of the IF . . . ELSE statement is:

```
IF condition THEN statement 1
ELSE statement 2
```

The BNF definition of the IF . . . ELSE statement is:

⟨if-else-statement⟩ ::= **if** ⟨expression⟩ **then** ⟨statement⟩ **else** ⟨statement⟩

The IF . . . ELSE structure is equivalent to the following two IF statements:

```
IF condition
    THEN statement 1
IF NOT condition
    THEN statement 2
```

The example from the preceding section has been revised to take advantage of the IF . . . ELSE structure, to insure that all conditions are mutually exclusive.

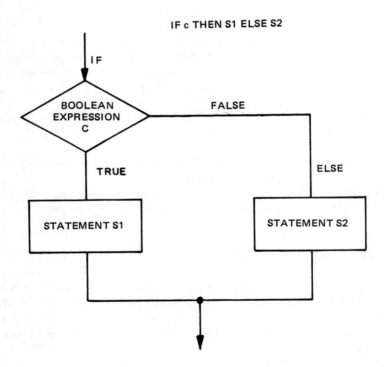

Figure 11-2 Flow Diagram of IF . . . ELSE Structure.

```
program compare3;
var
    a,b : real;
begin
    writeln('Comparison program #3');
    writeln;
    write('Enter first value - ');
```

```
readln(a);
writeln;
write('Enter second value - ');
readln(b);
writeln;
if (a < b) then
    writeln('First value is less than second.')
else
  if (a = b) then
      writeln('First value is equal to second.')
  else
    if (a > b) then
            writeln('First value is greater than second.');
writeln;
writeln('- done -');
end.
```

Note that the tests are performed in the order of the nested IFs, and later tests are only performed if the preceding condition is FALSE.

Standard Pascal is ambiguous regarding the evaluation of the following nested IF structure:

```
IF condition1 THEN
IF condition2 THEN
    statement1
ELSE
    statement2
```

When is the ELSE clause (*statement2*) executed? When *condition1* is FALSE or when *condition2* is FALSE? Turbo Pascal resolves this problem by interpreting each ELSE clause as belonging to the last preceding IF statement without an ELSE part. Our example is interpreted as if a compound statement were used as follows:

```
IF condition1 THEN
  begin
    IF condition2 THEN
      statement1
    ELSE
      statement2
  end
```

In general, it is helpful to write such confusing conditional statements by using a compound statement, even though it may not be required. It is also much easier to expand the statement if necessary in subsequent program revisions.

CASE STATEMENT

The CASE statement is a specialized application of the IF. . . ELSE structure which allows the selection of a single statement to be executed out of a group of statements. The control expression must evaluate to a scalar type (other than REAL). The value of the control expression is compared to each of the *case list* constants for a match. If a match is found, the corresponding statement is executed. If no match is found, the condition is undefined in Standard Pascal. In Turbo Pascal, if no match is found all object statements are bypassed and the CASE structure terminates.

Each item, list, or range in the constant list must be of the same scalar type as the control expression. The following are examples of possible constant list forms and their meanings:

form:	match value for control expression:
1 :	(integer 1)
1, 2, 3 :	(integers 1, 2 or 3)
1 .. 6 :	(range of integers 1 through 6)
'A' .. 'C' :	(range of characters 'A' to 'C')
' + ' :	(character ' + ')

The general form of the CASE statement is:

```
CASE expression OF
   constant list 1 : statement 1;
   . . .
   constant list n : statement n
END
```

Of course, the object statements of the CASE structure may be either single or compound statements.

The equivalent IF . . . ELSE structure for the case statement is:

```
IF expression = constant 1 THEN statement 1
   ELSE IF expression = constant 2 THEN statement 2
   . . .
      ELSE IF expression = constant n THEN statement n
```

The BNF definition of the CASE statement is:

⟨case-list-element⟩ ::= ⟨constant⟩ | ⟨constant⟩ .. ⟨constant⟩
⟨case-list⟩ ::= ⟨case-list-element⟩ {, ⟨case-list-element⟩}
⟨case-element⟩ ::= ⟨case-list⟩ : ⟨statement⟩
⟨case-statement⟩ ::= **case** ⟨expression⟩ **of** ⟨case-element⟩ {; ⟨case-element⟩} **end**

Case structures are used most often to select from among several possible options. They are very handy for creating menu-driven programs. Here is an example of the use of the CASE structure:

```
program calc1;
var
   choice : integer;
   a,b, result : real;
begin
   writeln('Simple calculator program #1');
   writeln;
   writeln('This program calculates the result of a');
   writeln('mathematical operation on two values.');
```

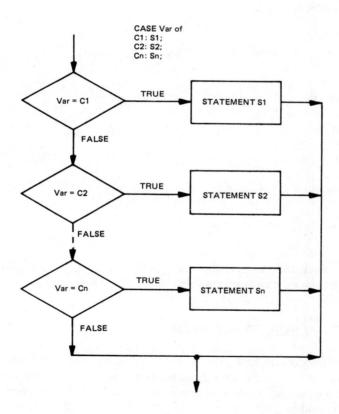

Figure 11-3 Flow Diagram of CASE Structure.

```
writeln;
write('Enter first value - ');
readln(a);
writeln;
write('Enter second value - ');
readln(b);
writeln;
writeln;
writeln('Choose one of the following options -');
writeln;
writeln('1. Add the two values.');
writeln('2. Subtract the second value from the first value.');
writeln('3. Multiply the two values.');
writeln('4. Divide the first value by the second value.');
writeln;
write('Enter selection - ');
repeat
   read(choice)
until ((1 <= choice) and (choice <= 4));
writeln;
writeln;
case choice of
   1 : result := a + b;
   2 : result := a - b;
   3 : result := a * b;
   4 : result := a / b
end;
writeln('The result is ',result:10:2);
writeln;
writeln('- done -');
end.
```

You can see from the example that the CASE structure is much clearer and more straightforward than the equivalent IF . . . ELSE statements.

CASE . . . ELSE STATEMENT

Turbo Pascal resolves the ambiguity in the CASE statement definition provided by Jensen and Wirth in the *Report*. It is unclear what should happen if there are NO matches in the alternatives provided with the CASE statement. Besides defining this condition (see above), Turbo Pascal provides the CASE . . . ELSE structure to handle this eventuality. If no matches in the provided CASE constant lists are found, the statements in the ELSE structure are executed. Since the

ELSE structure is delimited by **else** and **end**, multiple statements are allowed without the need for a compound statement.

The BNF definition of the CASE .. ELSE statement is:

⟨case-statement⟩ ::= **case** ⟨expression⟩ **of** ⟨case-element⟩ {; ⟨case-element⟩}
   else ⟨statement⟩ {; ⟨statement⟩} **end**

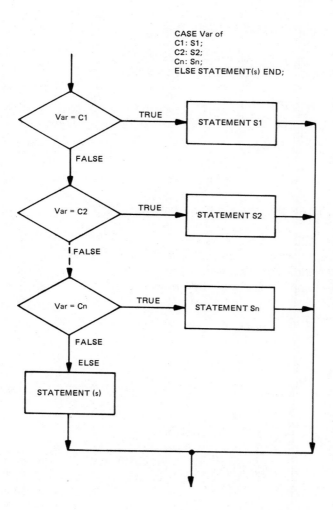

Figure 11-4 Flow Diagram of CASE . . . ELSE Structure.

Here is a revised example of the CALCULATOR program above, making use of the CASE . . . ELSE structure. This program uses the actual symbols to select the requested operation. This form of menu might be useful in applications where the user is not allowed to re-enter his selection.

```pascal
program calc2;
var
   choice : char;
   a,b, result : real;
begin
   writeln('Simple calculator program #2');
   writeln;
   writeln('This program calculates the result of a');
   writeln('mathematical operation on two values.');
   writeln;
   write('Enter first value - ');
   readln(a);
   writeln;
   write('Enter second value - ');
   readln(b);
   writeln;
   writeln;
   writeln('Choose one of the following options -');
   writeln;
   writeln(' + Add the two values.');
   writeln('- Subtract the second value from the first value.');
   writeln('* Multiply the two values.');
   writeln('/ Divide the first value by the second value.');
   writeln;
   write('Enter selection - ');
   read(choice);
   writeln;
   writeln;
   case choice of
      '+' : result := a + b;
      '-' : result   := a - b;
      '*' : result   := a * b;
      '/' : result   := a / b
   else
      writeln('Selection undefined. ');
      result :=  0.0
   end;
   writeln('The result is ',result:10:2);
   writeln;
   writeln('- done -');
end.
```

11.5 Repetitive (Loop) Statements

Another of the basic requirements for writing programs is the ability to repeat a sequence of operations while some logical expression (condition) is TRUE, until a logical expression becomes TRUE, or a given number of times. These three processes are provided by the WHILE, REPEAT . . . UNTIL, and FOR repetitive control structures, often called *loops*.

WHILE STATEMENT

The WHILE control structure allows a single or compound statement to be repeatedly executed as long as the control condition is TRUE. Because the test is performed before executing the object statement, the WHILE structure will be executed zero or more times, depending on the logical value of the control condition.

The general form of the WHILE statement is:

```
WHILE condition DO
    statement
```

The BNF definition of the WHILE statement is:

⟨while-statement⟩ ::= **while** ⟨expression⟩ **do** ⟨statement⟩

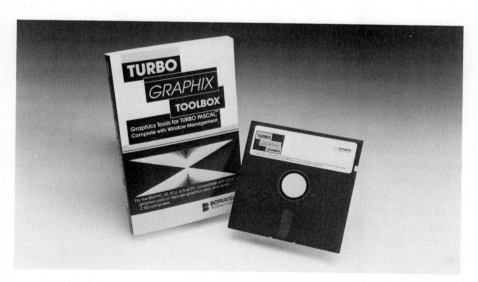

The Turbo Graphix Toolbox adds exciting graphics capability to Turbo Pascal. Photo courtesy of Borland International.

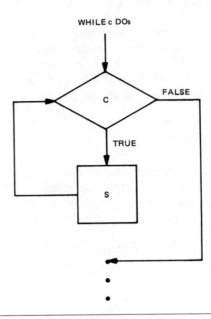

Figure 11-5 Flow Diagram of WHILE Structure.

It is important to note that the value of the control condition in a WHILE structure *must* be modified by the object statement(s) of the structure, or the WHILE clause will continue to be executed forever (the program will be in an *infinite loop*). Of course, if the control expression is initially FALSE, the object statement will not be executed even once. (Note that the condition may also be changed by outside action as well (e.g., the system real time clock).

Another important consideration in avoiding infinite WHILE loops is that the programmer must carefully design the test to insure that the test condition *will* become FALSE at some point.

In the following example program, if the value entered exceeds the *limit* value (20) or if an odd integer (1, 3, 5, 7, etc.) is entered, the WHILE loop will not terminate—the program must be stopped with a user interrupt (by pressing ⟨Ctrl-C⟩):

```
program loop1;
const
   limit = 20;
var
   k : integer;
begin
   writeln('Loop program #1');
```

```
    writeln;
    write('Enter starting value (less than ',k,') - ');
    readln(k);
    while (k ⟨⟩ limit) do
       begin
       k := k + 2;
       writeln(k)
       end;
    writeln;
    writeln('- done -');
end.
```

In this case, the possibility of error could be eliminated by testing for "less than" (*k* ⟨ *limit*) instead of "not equal to" (*k* ⟨⟩ *limit*), insuring that the loop will terminate in any case if *limit* is reached *or* exceeded. It is normally considered poor programming practice to compare for a single matching value when the range of input test values is not under program control.

Here is another example of the use of the WHILE structure:

```
program average1;
var
    count,
    items : integer;
    data,
    sum,
    average : real;
begin
    writeln('Average program #1');
    writeln;
    write('Enter number of items to average - ');
    readln(items);
    count := 1;
    sum := 0.0;
    while (count ⟨= items) do
    begin
       write('Enter value #',count,' - ');
       readln(data);
       sum := sum + data;
       count := count + 1
    end;
    writeln;
    average := sum / items;
    writeln('Average = ', average:8:2);
    writeln;
    writeln('- done -');
end.
```

REPEAT . . . UNTIL STATEMENT

The REPEAT . . . UNTIL structure allows one or more statements to be repeatedly executed *until* a specified condition becomes TRUE. The statement(s) in the structure will always be executed at least once, regardless of the initial value of the control condition, because the test is performed at the end, rather than the beginning of the structure.

The general form of the REPEAT statement is:

```
REPEAT
  statement(s)
UNTIL condition
```

The BNF definition of the REPEAT statement is:

⟨repeat-statement⟩ ::= **repeat** ⟨statement⟩ {; ⟨statement⟩} **until** ⟨expression⟩

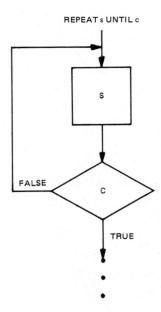

Figure 11-6 Flow Diagram of REPEAT . . . UNTIL Structure.

The REPEAT . . . UNTIL structure specifically permits the use of more than one statement as its object. This structure does not require the use of the compound statement for this purpose because the object statements are delimited by the reserved words **repeat** and **until**.

In the following example program, if the value entered exceeds (*limit* - 2) or 18 in this case, or if an odd integer (1, 3, 5, 7, etc.) is entered, the REPEAT .. UNTIL loop will not terminate—the program must be stopped with a user interrupt (by pressing ⟨Ctrl-C⟩):

```
program loop2;
const
   limit = 20;
var
   k : integer;
begin
   writeln('Loop program #2');
   writeln;
   write('Enter starting value (less than ',k,') - ');
   readln(k);
   repeat
      k := k + 2;
      writeln(k)
   until (k = limit);
   writeln;
   writeln('- done -');
end.
```

Note that the loop is always executed at least once, *before the test,* so the maximum correct input value is 18, not 20. Also, the test expression for a REPEAT . . . UNTIL loop is the logical inverse of that for the equivalent WHILE loop.

In this case, the possibility of input error could be eliminated by testing for "greater than" ($k >= limit$) instead of "equal to" ($k = limit$), insuring that the loop will terminate in any case if *limit* is reached *or* exceeded.

Here is another example of the REPEAT . . . UNTIL structure:

```
program average2;
var
   count,
   items : integer;
   data,
   sum,
   average : real;
begin
   writeln('Average program #2');
   writeln;
   write('Enter number of items to average - ');
```

```
readln(items);
count := 0;
sum := 0.0;
repeat
   count := count + 1;
   write('Enter value #',count,' - ');
   readln(data);
   sum := sum + data;
until (count >= items);
writeln;
average := sum / items;
writeln('Average = ', average:8:2);
writeln;
writeln('- done -');
end.
```

The REPEAT . . . UNTIL structure is often used for keyboard input qualification, to insure that values fall in a given range:

```
program keyin;
var
   count : integer;
   data : real;
begin
   writeln('Keyboard input program');
   writeln;
   count := 0;
   repeat
      write('Enter a real number between 1.0 and 10.0 - ');
      readln(data);
      count := count + 1
   until ((data >= 1.0) and (data <= 10.0));
   writeln;
   writeln('After ',count,' tries, you finally entered ',data:6:2);
   writeln;
   writeln('- done -');
end.
```

FOR STATEMENT

The FOR statement allows a statement or block of statements to be repeated a specified number of times. A control variable is incremented or decremented from an *initial* value TO or DOWNTO a *final* value. The value of the control variable must not be modified by other statements within the FOR structure.

The general form of the FOR statement is:

FOR control-variable := expression1 TO expression2 DO statement
        -or-
FOR control-variable := expression1 DOWNTO expression2 DO statement

The BNF definition of the FOR statement is:

⟨for-statement⟩ ::= **for** ⟨control-variable⟩ :=
      ⟨initial-value⟩ **to** ⟨final-value⟩ **do** ⟨statement⟩ |
      for ⟨control-variable⟩ :=
      ⟨initial-value⟩ **downto** ⟨final-value⟩ **do** ⟨statement⟩

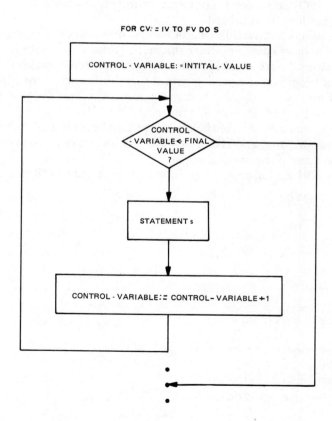

Figure 11-7 Flow Diagram of FOR Structure.

The FOR structure is typically used where the number of iterations (i.e., repetitions) of the loop is established *before* the program begins to execute the loop.

An equivalent expression is:

```
control variable := expression1;
while control variable <= expression2 do
   begin
      statement;
      control variable := control variable + 1
   end;
```

On each pass through the loop, the FOR control variable is *always* incremented or decremented by 1. This differs from similar FOR structures in other languages. The loop is terminated when the control variable is greater than (TO) or less than (DOWNTO) expression2. The target control expressions are only evaluated once, when the loop is initialized.

Although the control variable of a FOR structure is undefined after the loop is terminated in most Pascal implementations, in Turbo it retains the last assigned value (the value of expression2 if the loop was terminated normally). To insure portability of programs, it is recommended that this feature be avoided. Assign the value of the control variable to another variable within the loop instead if the value must be used later outside the loop.

A FOR structure may be exited before completion by using a GOTO; however, it is recommended that a WHILE or REPEAT structure be used in place of the FOR structure if this is necessary.

Here is the AVERAGE program again, this time using the FOR structure:

```
program average3;
var
   count,
   items : integer;
   data,
   sum,
   average : real;
begin
   writeln('Average program #3');
   writeln;
   write('Enter number of items to average - ');
   readln(items);
   sum := 0.0;
   for count := 1 to items do
   begin
      write('Enter value #',count,' - ');
      readln(data);
      sum := sum + data
```

```
  end;
  writeln;
  average := sum / items;
  writeln('Average = ', average:8:2);
  writeln;
  writeln('- done -');
end.
```

11.6 Sample Program

The following example is a character counting program which uses several of
the control structures discussed in this chapter. The program keeps track of the
number of occurrences of each of the vowels A, E, I, O, U as well as the total
number of numerals, spaces, and other characters in a line of text.

```
program charcnt;
var
  textline : string[80];
  ch : char;
  indx,
  len,
  count_a,
  count_e,
  count_i,
  count_o,
  count_u,
  count_char,
  count_num,
  count_space : integer;
begin
  textline := ' ';
  count_a := 0;
  count_e := 0;
  count_i := 0;
  count_o := 0;
  count_u := 0;
  count_char := 0;
  count_num := 0;
  count_space := 0;
  writeln('Character count program #1');
  writeln;
  writeln('This program counts all the characters in a line of text');
  writeln('and keeps track of the vowels A, E, I, O, U.');
```

```
writeln;
writeln('Enter line of text to analyze (no more than 75 chars) - '); writeln;
repeat
   write('-> ');
   read(textline)
until length(textline) < 76;
writeln;
len := length(textline);
for indx := 1 to len do
begin
   ch := UpCase(textline[indx]);
   case ch of
      'A' : count_a := count_a + 1;
      'E' : count_e := count_e + 1;
      'I' : count_i := count_i + 1;
      'O' : count_o := count_o + 1;
      'U' : count_u := count_u + 1;
      '0'.. '9' : count_num := count_num + 1;
      ' ' : count_space := count_space + 1;
   else
      count_char := count_char + 1;
   end
end;
writeln('The results are: ');
writeln;
writeln('Line length = ', len);
writeln('Character A = ', count_a);
writeln('Character E = ', count_e);
writeln('Character I = ', count_i);
writeln('Character O = ', count_o);
writeln('Character U = ', count_u);
writeln('Numerals    = ', count_num);
writeln('Spaces    = ', count_space);
writeln('Other characters = ', count_char);
writeln;
writeln('- done -');
end.
```

## CHAPTER TWELVE

Data Structures
Part I. Arrays and Strings

While *algorithms* (i.e., the methods or procedures for solving a problem) are a major factor in the design of programs, the organization of the data manipulated by programs plays an equally important role. A *data structure* is an organized set of data. Niklaus Wirth put it succinctly when he titled his 1976 book on program design: *Algorithms + Data Structures = Programs.*

The structure of the data indicates how the elements in the data set are related to each other, or organized. The method of representing data can affect the choice of algorithms and design of the program, not to mention its efficiency. In fact, there are usually a large number of possible data structures which may be used in a given situation, unless the data structure is pre-existing.

Standard Pascal provides four predefined data structures—the array, the record, the set, and the file. Turbo Pascal also includes the STRING which is a specialized case of the ARRAY structure. These data structures are *static*—once defined in a program, their structure may not be changed. This chapter will discuss arrays and strings. Records and sets will be covered in the next chapter and files will be covered in Chapter 15.

Other advanced data structures like the stack, linked list, or tree may be created using the ARRAY and RECORD structures, but must be of fixed size and order, and must exist for the duration of the program. Pascal also allows such structures to be defined by the programmer using unallocated memory in the *heap.* These are *dynamic* structures and may be created, expanded, changed, or deleted under program control. Dynamic structures will be covered in Chapter 14.

12.1 Arrays

The array is perhaps the best known data structure because it is available in almost every high level language, including FORTRAN, ALGOL 60, BASIC, C, PL/I, and Pascal. In many languages, it is the only available predefined data structure. An array is a collection of elements of the same type, each of which may be directly accessed. In Turbo Pascal, it is possible to have an array of simple types like INTEGER, REAL, CHAR (character), BYTE, STRING, or BOOLEAN values. Although all elements in an array must be of the same type, complex arrays containing more than one simple type of data may be created using the RECORD type discussed in the next chapter.

An array can be thought of as a group of numbered containers or cells, each of which can hold one data item. A specific item in an array is accessed by referring to its cell number or *index value*. The index to an array may be any scalar type. The declaration of an array includes the *index type* or the range of allowable values for the index. Array index values may be any positive or negative integer or scalar value within the declared index range. The index type also defines the maximum size of the array.

Commercial versions of Turbo Pascal allow arrays of any integer size, limited by the 64K byte maximum data area in memory for variable storage. This means that four 16K arrays of type BYTE (or two 16K arrays of type INTEGER) will use up all of the memory space available for program variables. Large data structures should use the *heap*, which is limited only by the total amount of unallocated memory available.

The demonstration compiler is limited to a total data area of 8K bytes (variables and heap combined). This means that about 7.4K bytes are actually available for variable storage, including arrays.

ARRAY DECLARATION

Like other data types, arrays may be declared in the CONST, TYPE or VAR section of a block. When an array is declared, both its index type and the type of its elements are declared:

```
var
    numlist : array [1..9] of integer;
```

The index type or range for the array is written in square brackets immediately after the reserved word *array* in the variable declaration.

The elements of a variable array are *not* initialized when the array is declared. Therefore, it is important to initialize each element of an array at the start of the program. A constant array may be declared as a typed constant to avoid the requirement for program initialization, but all values must be defined in the declaration.

Arrays may also be declared as types:

type
   code = **array** [1..26] **of** char;
var
   filter_list : code;

Individual array elements are accessed by explicit reference to their index. The statement:

   numlist[3] := 7;

will assign the value 7 to the third element in the array *numlist* previously declared above.

MULTIDIMENSIONAL ARRAYS

Arrays may be multidimensional, in which case their elements may be thought of as a data matrix. Pascal allows specifying an array of arrays, which is actually the same thing as a single multidimensional array. The number of indices required to access a specific element corresponds to the number of dimensions of the array. Thus, the following two array declarations are equivalent:

   table = **array**[row] **of array** [column] **of** integer;

and

   table = **array**[row,column] **of** integer;

A simple two-dimensional array may be thought of as a table with numbered rows and columns of data, like the following example:

ROWS	COLUMNS					
	1	2	3	4	5	6
1	33	7	22	2	9	31
2	20	11	3	60	37	3
3	3	57	0	26	16	10
4	22	54	4	6	1	76
5	65	12	3	2	11	34
6	13	9	43	61	20	25
7	2	58	68	17	4	0
8	1	4	31	6	55	29
9	11	5	12	72	36	18

This array could be specified as

```
type
    row = 1 .. 9;
    col = 1 .. 6;
var
    table : array [row, col] of integer;
```

If we assume that the array has been initialized with the above values, then we can access any specific element by its row and column indices. Here are some examples:

```
table[1,1] = 33
table[9,6] = 18
table[6,5] = 20
```

Arrays are often used to manipulate lists of data. They can facilitate input, output, and processing operations on a series of data items. They can also be used for searches, sorts, and other list operations.

CHARACTER ARRAYS

Standard Pascal uses the *array of char* to handle a series of text characters. Such an array might be used to hold a phrase, a sentence, or a line of text. In this case, each element in the array is one character of text. Because characters are "strung together," one after the other, this structure is often informally referred to as a *string of characters* or just a *string*. Note that the formal Turbo Pascal STRING type is similar to an array of characters, but is defined and handled differently.

Using arrays for text handling can be quite complex as is shown in the following example program which *parses* or analyses a sentence and breaks it into its component words. Here is the example:

```
program parse1;
{$B-} {Compiler directive to use Standard Pascal I/O mode}
const
    max_line_length = 80;
    space = ' ';
    cr = 13;
type
    linetype = array [1..max_line_length] of char;
var
    line : linetype;
    index : integer
```

```
procedure get_line;
var
   ch : char;
begin
   index := 0;
   ch := ' ';
   while not (ch = chr(cr)) and (index < max_line_length) do
   begin
      index := index + 1;
      read(ch);
      line[index] := ch;
   end; {while}
end; {get_line}

procedure parse_line;
var
   index1,
   index2,
   counter : integer;
   phrase : linetype;
   ch : char;

begin
   index1 := 0;
   index2 := 0;
   repeat
      index1 := index1 + 1;
      ch := line[index1];
      if (ch = space) or (index1 >= index) then
      begin
         for counter := 1 to index2 do
         write(phrase[counter]);
         writeln;
         index2 := 0;
      end {if}
      else
      begin
         index2 := index2 + 1;
         phrase[index2] := ch;
      end; {else}
   until index1 >= index;
end; {parse_line}

begin {parse1}
   writeln('Parse program #1');
```

```
    writeln;
    writeln('Enter text string to parse:');
    get_line;
    writeln;
    writeln;
    parse_line;
    writeln;
    writeln('- done -');
end. {parse1}
```

MANAGING ARRAY ELEMENTS

Since the length of a data list in an array can vary, some method is needed to detect the current end of valid data. One possible approach is to use a counter variable to hold the current number of valid elements in the array (as opposed to the maximum declared number of elements in the array).

```
program average4;
const
    maxitems = 20;
var
    maxno,
    minno,
    over,
    less,
    equal,
    items : integer;
    max,
    min,
    sum,
    average : real;
    list : array [1..maxitems] of real;

procedure enter;
var
    data : real;
begin
    repeat
        items := items + 1;
        if items ) maxitems then
            data := -1 {terminate input}
        else
        begin
            write('Item # ',items,' - ');
```

```pascal
        readln(data);
        list[items] := data;
      end;
    until (data < 0);
    items := items - 1;
end; {enter}

procedure calc;
var
  count : integer;
begin
  for count := 1 to items do
    sum := sum + list[count];
  average := sum / items;
  for count := 1 to items do
    if list[count] > average then
      over := over + 1
    else if list[count] < average then
      less := less + 1
    else if list[count] = average then
      equal := equal + 1;
  for count := 1 to items do
  begin
    if list[count] > max then
      begin
        max := list[count];
        maxno := count;
      end;
    if list[count] < min then
      begin
        min := list[count];
        minno := count;
      end;
  end;
end; {calc}


begin {average4}
  writeln('Average program #4');
  writeln;
  sum := 0.0;
  items := 0;
  over := 0;
  less := 0;
  equal := 0;
  max := 0;
```

```
    min := maxint;
    writeln('Enter up to ',maxitems, ' items to average ');
    writeln('or a negative value to end entries - ');
    writeln;
    enter;
    calc;
    writeln;
    writeln('Average = ', average:8:2);
    writeln;
    writeln('Items greater than average - ', over);
    writeln('Items equal to average - ', equal);
    writeln('Items less than average - ', less);
    writeln;
    writeln('Largest item is #', maxno,' = ',max:8:2);
    writeln('Smallest item is #',minno,' = ',min:8:2);
    writeln;
    writeln('- done -');
end. {average4}
```

Another way to manage arrays is to place a marker in the array element immediately following the end of the current data. Such a marker must be distinct from the possible range of data values. For example, if characters are used in the array, either a null or an end-of-line character (carriage return or line feed) could be used as a marker. If data items are positive integers or zero, a negative number could be used to mark the end of the list. For most applications, however, the counter method is the most reliable.

ARRAY FUNCTIONS

Arrays may also be used as translation functions to convert one scalar value to another based on a fixed interrelationship or cross-mapping of values. For example, it is possible to convert a byte (8-bit) value to its two-digit hexadecimal (base 16) equivalent by using an array as a function.

```
program convhex1;
var
    hex : array[0..15] of char;
    hbyte,
    lbyte,
    indat : byte;
begin
    hex[0] := '0';
    hex[1] := '1';
```

```
hex[2] := '2';
hex[3] := '3';
hex[4] := '4';
hex[5] := '5';
hex[6] := '6';
hex[7] := '7';
hex[8] := '8';
hex[9] := '9';
hex[10] := 'A';
hex[11] := 'B';
hex[12] := 'C';
hex[13] := 'D';
hex[14] := 'E';
hex[15] := 'F';
writeln('Hexadecimal conversion program #1');
writeln;
write('Enter byte value (0 - 255) to convert to hexadecimal: ');
readln(indat);
hbyte := indat div 16; {get high 4 bits}
lbyte := indat mod 16; {get low 4 bits}
writeln;
write('Input value ',indat, ' = ');
writeln(hex[hbyte],hex[lbyte], ' in hexadecimal.');
writeln;
writeln('- done -');
end. {convhex1}
```

TYPED ARRAY CONSTANT

Although the above technique can be quite useful, the initialization of a large data structure (like an array) is one of the least elegant operations in Pascal. As mentioned in an earlier chapter, Turbo Pascal provides the *typed constant* which may be used with both unstructured and structured data types to solve the initialization problem. The general form of Turbo Pascal's typed constant declaration is:

```
TYPE
    identifier :type = constant
```

The typed constant is actually a variable with a constant value, and so it cannot be used to define other constants or types. The following revision of our previous example shows how much easier the initialization is when a typed constant array is used:

```
program convhex2;
const
    hex : array[0..15] of char = '0123456789ABCDEF';
var
    hbyte,
    lbyte,
    indat : byte;
begin
    writeln('Hexadecimal conversion program #2');
    writeln;
    write('Enter byte value (0 - 255) to convert to hexadecimal: '); readln(indat);
    hbyte := indat div 16; {get high 4 bits}
    lbyte := indat mod 16; {get low 4 bits}
    writeln;
    write('Input value ',indat, ' = ');
    writeln(hex[hbyte],hex[lbyte], ' in hexadecimal.');
    writeln;
    writeln('- done -');
end. {convhex2}
```

Character array constants can be specified either as strings or individual characters. The above typed array constant could also be defined in this format, by specifying the individual elements of the array:

```
const hex : array[0..15] of char =
('0','1','2','3','4','5','6','7',
'8','9','A','B','C','D','E','F');
```

The values of typed constants are fixed like any other constant, so they cannot be changed in the program as can the values of initialized variables. In many applications this will not present a problem. Note that *all* elements of the specified array must be defined or a compiler error will result.

User-defined types can also be used in typed constant specifications:

```
type
    table = array[0..15] of char;

const
    hex : table = '0123456789ABCDEF';
```

Initializing multidimensional array constants is slightly more complex. The constants of each dimension are enclosed in separate sets of parentheses, separated by commas. The innermost constants correspond to the rightmost dimension. Here is an example of the two-dimensional data table presented earlier:

```
program matrix1;
const
   maxrow = 9;
   maxcol = 6;
   table : array[1..maxrow,1..maxcol] of byte =
      ((33,7,22,2,9,31),
       (20,11,3,60,37,3),
       (3,57,0,26,16,10),
       (22,54,4,6,1,76),
       (65,12,3,2,11,34),
       (13,9,43,61,20,25),
       (2,58,68,17,4,0),
       (1,4,31,6,55,29),
       (11,5,12,72,36,18));
var
   row,
   column : integer;
begin
   writeln('Matrix display program #1');
   writeln;
   for row := 1 to maxrow do
      for column := 1 to maxcol do
         writeln('table[',row,',',column,'] = ',table[row,column]);
   writeln;
   writeln('- done -');
end. {matrix1}
```

Note that the memory requirements for this table are halved by using BYTE rather than INTEGER type values in the array. This is possible because all elements are between 0 and 256 and this is a constant array.

```
program matrix2;
const
   maxrow = 9;
   maxcol = 6;
   table : array[1..maxrow,1..maxcol] of byte =
      ((33,7,22,2,9,31),
       (20,11,3,60,37,3),
       (3,57,0,26,16,10),
       (22,54,4,6,1,76),
       (65,12,3,2,11,34),
       (13,9,43,61,20,25),
       (2,58,68,17,4,0),
       (1,4,31,6,55,29),
       (11,5,12,72,36,18));
```

```
var
  row,
  column : integer;
  quit : boolean;
  answer : string[4];
begin
  quit := false;
  while not quit do
  begin
    ClrScr;
    writeln('Matrix display program #2');
    writeln;
    repeat
      write('Enter table row - ');
      readln(row);
    until (row > 0) and (row <= maxrow);
    repeat
      write('Enter table column - ');
      readln(column);
    until (column > 0) and (column <= maxcol);
    writeln;
    writeln;
    writeln('table[',row,',',column,'] = ',table[row,column]);
    writeln;
    write('Look up another value? (Y/N) - ');
    readln(answer);
    quit := (answer <> 'Y') and (answer <> 'y');
  end;
  writeln;
  writeln('- done -');
end. {matrix2}
```

PACKED DATA TYPES

Standard Pascal may be implemented on many different types of computers
with different "natural" word sizes. To use memory space efficiently, Standard
Pascal allows arrays of characters (and some other types) to be *packed* and
unpacked. A special data type of **packed** is used in declaring packed arrays. For
example, on a large computer with a 32-bit word size, only one (8-bit) character
would normally be stored in each word. After the array is packed, however,
four characters would be stored in each memory word. Turbo Pascal performs
automatic packing and unpacking, and the *pack* and *unpack* procedures are not
implemented. The reserved word **packed** is allowed in Turbo Pascal, but has
no effect.

12.2 Strings

When Pascal was designed, most programs were written to operate in a *batch processing* environment on mainframe computers. Programs were prepared on a *deck* of punched cards and submitted to a large computer with other programs in a batch for processing. Program output was primarily in the form of printouts or magnetic tape files. These types of programs required minimal text handling capabilities because there was no "direct" user interaction with the operating program, and fixed length ARRAYs of characters were adequate for most applications. Today, most microcomputer programs communicate *interactively* with the user via the keyboard and video screen. This change in the programming environment has shown the need for more flexible text handling and processing capability in Pascal than is afforded by the CHAR type and ARRAY of CHAR structure in Standard Pascal.

Turbo Pascal provides the useful predefined STRING data type for working with arrays of characters as an extension to the Standard Pascal required types. The Turbo STRING type is similar to the character string types found in BASIC and other high-level languages, and allows easy manipulation of variable-length strings of characters.

In the preceding examples in this book, we have made use of the STRING type with only a brief introduction. This chapter will provide a more detailed discussion of the STRING type.

STRINGS VS. ARRAYS

A string can be thought of as an array [0..maxlength] of type CHAR, with the first element containing the current string length. The maximum length reserved for a STRING type can be in the range of 1 to 255 characters. The STRING type is compatible with the CHAR type and with ARRAYs of CHAR. ARRAYs of CHAR may be assigned to STRING types of equal or greater length.

STRING DECLARATION

STRING types and variables are declared in much the same way as ARRAYs in Turbo Pascal:

```
type
   strtype = string[14];
var
   answer : string[20];
```

with the value in square brackets indicating the *maximum* length of the string.

STRING type variables cannot exceed 255 characters in length or a run-time error will occur. If a STRING variable is assigned a string value which exceeds its declared length, the string value will be truncated.

STRINGS AND CHARACTERS

Elements of STRING types (i.e., individual characters) may be addressed like elements of ARRAYs by using array notation. For example, the following program:

```
program string_test1;
var
    name : string[20]; {reserves space for up to 20 chars}
begin
    name := 'John Q. Smith';            {assign literal to string}
    writeln(name);                      {display string}
    writeln(ord(name[0]));              {display string length}
    writeln(name[1]);                   {display 1st character of string}
    writeln(name[2]);                   {display 2nd character of string}
    writeln(name[3]);                   {display 3rd character of string}
    writeln(name[4]);                   {display 4th character of string}
    name := 'Bugs Bunny';               {assign literal to string}
    writeln(name);                      {display string}
    writeln(ord(name[0]));              {display string length}
end.    {string_test}
```

print the string "*name*," its current length, and the first four characters of the string on separate lines on the screen, like this:

```
John Q. Smith
13
J
o
h
n
```

followed by printing the second string and its length. Note that the *current* length of the string changes when the new assignment is made.

Since each element of the string is of type CHAR, the element containing the current string length (*name[0]*) must be converted to an INTEGER type with the *ord()* function before printing. To make this easier, Turbo Pascal provides the built-in function *length(String)* that returns the length of a string as an integer result. Note that the string length is the actual length of the current contents of the string, not the maximum length (space reserved) as defined in the VAR declaration.

STRING CONSTANTS

In Turbo Pascal, CONST declarations of character strings in single quotes are stored in STRING types by default. The statement:

```
const
    hex = '0123456789ABCDEF';
```

will create a constant compatible with STRING types. However, the elements (characters) of the constant cannot be individually accessed as the Turbo Pascal compiler will not permit indexing a string constant. The constant must be assigned to a STRING type variable first, or declared as a typed constant.

If a constant ARRAY of CHAR is required (as for indexing purposes), a typed constant must be used to declare it:

```
const
    hex : array [0..15] of char = '0123456789ABCDEF';
```

Of course, STRING types may be declared as typed constants as well:

```
const
    hex : string [16] = '0123456789ABCDEF';
```

and typed STRING constant elements may be accessed like STRING type variables. Note, however, that indexes for strings MUST start at 1, while array indexes may start at zero or any other integer or scalar value as defined in the array declaration.

Just like a normal constant, typed constants may not be assigned a new value in a program.

STRING EXPRESSIONS

Turbo Pascal string expressions are used to work with string values. String expressions are made up of string constants, string variables, the results of string functions, string literals, and operators. String expressions may compare string values using the relational operators with a result of type BOOLEAN (true or false) or may manipulate string values using the string functions and the string concatenation operator ("+"), with a result of type STRING. Concatenated strings may not exceed 255 characters in length or a run-time error will occur.

The relational operators are lower in precedence than the string concatenation operator in Turbo Pascal. The shortest of two similar strings of different lengths in relational expressions will be evaluated as the lowest value.

Thus, in the following example, the string 'Turbo' is "less than" the string 'Turbo Pascal' because it is shorter in length:

```
program string3;
begin
  writeln(' "Turbo" ⟨ "Turbo Pascal" ');
  if 'Turbo' ⟨ 'Turbo Pascal' then
    writeln('TRUE')
  else
    writeln('FALSE');
end. {string3}
```

Note also that string comparisons are based on each individual ASCII character value, and upper case letters are "less" than the same lower case letters (see ASCII character chart in the Appendix). Therefore, the following program will display TRUE on the screen because the string 'TURBO PASCAL' is "less than" the string 'Turbo Pascal':

```
program string4;
begin
  writeln(' "TURBO PASCAL" ⟨ 'Turbo Pascal" ');
  if 'TURBO PASCAL' ⟨ 'Turbo Pascal' then
    writeln('TRUE')
  else
    writeln('FALSE');
end. {string4}
```

Of course, comparisons can also be made on string variables in the same way as on literal constants:

```
program strcomp;
var
  answer1,
  answer2 : string[255];

begin
  writeln('String comparison program #1');
  writeln;
  writeln('Enter two strings to compare - ');
  write(' #1: ');
  readln(answer1);
  write(' #2: ');
  readln(answer2);
  writeln;
  if answer1 ⟨ answer2 then
    writeln('String #1 is less than string #2.')
  else if answer1 ⟩ answer2 then
    writeln('String #1 is greater than string #2.')
```

```
   else writeln('String #1 is equal to string #2.');
   writeln;
   writeln(' - done - ');
end. {strcomp}
```

If it is necessary to compare two strings and ignore their case, a lower case to upper case string conversion function using the Turbo Pascal transfer function *upcase()* is useful:

```
program strcomp2;
type
   strtype = string[255];

var
   answer1,
   answer2 : strtype;

function uppercase(instr : strtype) : strtype;
var
   index : byte;
begin
   for index := 1 to length(instr) do
      instr[index] := upcase(instr[index]);
   uppercase := instr;
end; {uppercase}

begin {strcomp2}
   writeln('String comparison program #2');
   writeln('Case is ignored in comparison');
   writeln;
   writeln('Enter two strings to compare - ');
   write(' #1: ');
   readln(answer1);
   write(' #2: ');
   readln(answer2);
   writeln;
   answer1 := uppercase(answer1);
   answer2 := uppercase(answer2);
   if answer1 < answer2 then
      writeln(answer1,' is less than ',answer2,'.')
   else if answer1 > answer2 then
      writeln(answer1, ' is greater than ',answer2,'.')
   else writeln(answer1,' is equal to ',answer2,'.');
   writeln;
   writeln(' - done - ');
end. {strcomp2}
```

STRING ASSIGNMENT

String constants, variables, the results of string functions, and literals may be assigned to other STRING type variables using the Pascal assignment operator (: =). String assignments in Turbo Pascal are also compatible with both CHAR types and ARRAYs of CHAR.

As mentioned above, if the length of the string value assigned to a variable exceeds the declared maximum length of the variable, the excess characters to the right will be ignored. The only operator supported in string assignments is the concatenation operator (+) which may be used to combine two or more string or character values.

For example, the following simple program demonstrates the use of the string concatenation and assignment operators:

```
program string5;
const
  ver = '3.0';
  space = ' ';
var
  product : string[20];
begin
  product := 'Turbo' + ' ' + 'Pascal' + space + ver;
  writeln(product);
end. {string5}
```

The program will display "Turbo Pascal 3.0" on the screen.

STRING PROCEDURES AND FUNCTIONS

Turbo Pascal includes a number of specialized procedures and functions for manipulating strings. They provide many powerful string handling capabilities, which are summarized here.

PROCEDURES

Turbo Pascal string procedures are used to modify strings and to transfer numeric values between STRING and numeric types.

DELETE

The DELETE procedure removes a number of characters from the target string beginning at the position specified. The general form of the DELETE procedure is:

DELETE(st,pos,num)

DELETE will remove *num* characters from string *st* beginning at position *pos*. If *num* + *pos* is greater than the length of the string only characters within the string are deleted. *Pos* must be in the range of 1 to 255 or a run-time error will occur.

INSERT

The INSERT procedure inserts a substring expression into the target string at the position specified. The general form of the INSERT procedure is:

INSERT(OBJECT,st,pos)

INSERT will insert the *object* string into string *st* beginning at position *pos*. If *pos* is greater than the current length of string *st*, the *object* string is concatenated to string *st*. If the result is greater than the declared length of string *st* the excess characters on the right end of the string are deleted. *Pos* must be in the range of 1 to 255 or a run-time error will occur.

STR

The STR procedure transfers a numeric value to a STRING type variable. The general form of the STR procedure is:

STR(val,st)

Parameter *val* is a *write parameter* of type INTEGER or type REAL. Write parameters may include formatting codes like those used in the WRITE procedure (i.e. INT:3 or REALNUM:3:1) and are discussed in detail in Chapter 9. Parameter *st* is a string variable.

Note that it is possible to use the identifier STR as a string variable in programs. If this happens, procedure STR will no longer be available to your program. Here is a short program that demonstrates this situation—run it and it will flag a compile error:

```
program strtest2;
var
  str : string[80];
  i : integer;
  ans : string[80];

begin
```

```
    i := 100;
    str(i:5,ans);
    writeln(ans);
end. {strtest2}
```

Now, change the identifier of variable *str* to *stri* in the declaration section. The program now compiles properly and runs. This same warning applies to other built-in procedures and functions as well.

VAL

The VAL procedure transfers a string expression containing numeric information to a numeric-type variable (INTEGER or REAL). The general form of the VAL procedure is:

```
    VAL(st,var,code)
```

The VAL procedure will convert the numeric string *st* to a REAL or INTEGER type and store the result in *var*. String *st* must be a string expressing a numeric value following the format conventions for INTEGERs or REALs. If no error is encountered, *code* will be set to 0, otherwise, *code* will be set to the position of the first character in *st* which caused the error.

FUNCTIONS

Turbo Pascal string functions return a result to the calling expression.

COPY

The COPY function extracts a substring from a string expression and returns it to the calling expression. The general form of the COPY function is:

```
    COPY(st,pos,num)
```

It returns the number *num* characters of string *st* beginning at position *pos*. If *pos* + *num* is greater than the length of the string, only characters within the string are returned. If *pos* is greater than the length of the string, a run-time error will occur.

CONCAT

The CONCAT function performs the same operation as the string concatenation operator (" + "). It will combine any number of string expressions in the order in which they are specified and return the result to the calling expression. If the total length of the resulting string is greater than 255, a run-time error will occur. The general form of the CONCAT function is:

CONCAT(st1,st2{,stn})

Length

The LENGTH function has been discussed in earlier examples. The general form of the LENGTH function is:

LENGTH(st)

It returns the length of string *st* as an integer value to the calling expression. It is equivalent to the expression *ord(st[0])*.

POS

The POS function returns the position (if any) of a string expression within a target string. The general form of the POS function is:

POS(object,st)

POS returns an integer value to the calling expression denoting the position of the first character of the string expression *object* within the string expression *st*, or 0 if not found.

A NOTE ON FILLING STRINGS

Often it is necessary to initialize a string variable with a repetitive value (i.e., spaces or graphics characters). A simple FOR loop can be used to successively build such a string by concatenating the string and character to itself:

```
program dashes;
const
  len = 40;
var
  indx : byte;
  dash : string [80];
```

```
begin
  dash := '';
  for indx := 1 to len do
    dash := dash + '-';
  writeln(dash);
end. {dashes}
```

This method works well and automatically keeps track of the correct string length. There may be a temptation to use the expression:

```
for indx := 1 to len do
  dash[indx] := '-';
```

This method also works, but it does not set the string length byte (element 0 of the string) to the correct length. The statement:

```
dash[0] := chr(len);
```

must be included to set the string length.

Another method of filling strings (or other variables) is also available in Turbo Pascal—the FILLCHAR procedure. The general form of the FILLCHAR procedure is:

```
FILLCHAR(var,num,value)
```

This method has the advantage of being very fast (as when initializing an ARRAY of STRINGs), but suffers from the same problem as the second FOR example above—it does not set the string length.

Here is an example program using the FILLCHAR procedure—run it immediately after running the first FOR example above to show an interesting usage problem with FILLCHAR and strings:

```
program pluses;
const
  len = 40;
var
  indx : byte; {dummy variable to match DASHES.PAS file}
  plus : string [80];

begin
  pluses := ''; {dummy statement to match DASHES.PAS file}
  fillchar(plus,len,' + ');
  plus[0] := chr(len);
  writeln(plus);
end. {pluses}
```

(NOTE: Do not include the above comments in the program file or it will not match the DASHES.PAS file size for this demonstration.)

Because Turbo Pascal always assigns data storage in the same order, the two programs DASHES and PLUSES) are the same code size, and Turbo Pascal does not automatically initialize variables, the string PLUS in this example uses the same memory locations as the string DASH in the previous example, and at the beginning of the program has the same value. If you run the two programs in order, your screen will display:

+ +-

or 39 pluses and one dash. This is because FILLCHAR fills the *entire* variable with the value specified. STRING type variables begin with element 0 (the length byte), so FILLCHAR filled the string *plus* from *plus[0]* to *plus[39]*. The dash at *plus[40]* is "leftover" from the variable DASH in the previous program. To correct the problem, the FILLCHAR *num* value must be one more than the actual length needed when used with strings. Thus, the corrected FILLCHAR statement becomes:

```
fillchar(plus,len + 1,' + ');
```

and the program will work properly. *Note: This example does not work with some versions of the Turbo Compiler.*

TESTING STRING ELEMENTS

The ability to access string elements individually allows tests to be made on characters in specific positions in a string. However, it is important to remember that the contents of a string past the current length of the string are not valid data, and in fact can either be uninitialized "garbage" or the previous contents of the string. If tests are made on individual string elements, like:

if st[pos] **in** ['A'..'Z'] **then**

care must be taken also to check that the current length of the string is greater than or equal to the position being tested:

if (st[pos] **in** ['A'..'Z']) **and** (length(st))= pos) **then**

Now the test is correct under all conditions.

Note also that complex relational expressions should always use parentheses to insure correct evaluation of the logical values, because boolean operators have a higher precedence than relational operators.

APPLICATION EXAMPLES

Here are some programs that show some of the power of the Turbo Pascal STRING type and related functions. They should provide the basis for further understanding of string operations.

The following program will remove excess spaces from a line of text by copying the source string to an output string, checking if each character is a space and then copying only the first space in each sequence of spaces to the output string.

```pascal
program spaces1;
const
  space = ' ';
var
  answer,
  answer1 : string[80];
  quit : boolean;

procedure strip;
var
  indx : byte;
  flag : boolean;
begin
  answer1 := '';
  flag := true;
  for indx := 1 to length(answer) do
  begin
    if (answer[indx] = space) then
    begin
      if not flag then
       begin
         flag := true;
         answer1 := answer1 + answer[indx];
       end;
    end
    else
    begin
      flag := false;
      answer1 := answer1 + answer[indx];
    end;
  end;
end; {strip}

begin
  quit := false;
  writeln('Space removal program - Version 1');
```

```
    writeln;
    writeln;
    writeln('Enter a line of text with excess spaces between words,');
    writeln('or ENTER to quit');
    writeln;
    repeat
      readln(answer);
      quit := length(answer) = 0;
      if not quit then
      begin
        strip;
        writeln(answer1);
      end;
    until quit;
    writeln(' - done - ');
end. {spaces1}
```

The above program works, but it can be improved by using the *delete* function so the input string itself is stripped of spaces and by making the procedure a generalized one that can be used with more than one input string. The string is now passed as a VAR parameter to the procedure. Here's the improved version:

```
program spaces2;
const
  space = ' ';
type
  txtstr = string[80];
var
  answer : txtstr;
  quit : boolean;

procedure strip_space (var ans:txtstr);
var
  indx : byte;
  sp_flag : boolean;
begin
  sp_flag := true;
  indx := 1;
  repeat
    if (ans[indx] = space) then
    begin
      if not sp_flag then
      begin
        sp_flag := true;
        indx := indx + 1;
```

```
            end
            else
                delete(ans,indx,1);
        end
        else
        begin
            sp_flag := false;
            indx := indx + 1;
        end;
    until indx > length(ans);
end; {strip_space}

begin
    quit := false;
    writeln('Space removal program - Version 2');
    writeln;
    writeln;
    writeln('Enter a line of text with excess spaces between words,');
    writeln('or ENTER to quit');
    writeln;
    repeat
        readln(answer);
        quit := length(answer) = 0;
        if not quit then
        begin
            strip_space(answer);
            writeln(answer);
        end;
    until quit;
    writeln('- done -');
end. {spaces1}
```

The last program in this chapter is a simple text input filter for keyboard input to the screen. This program cannot backspace and does not display a word until it is completely entered, using spaces for delimiters. A more complex version of this simple "typer" would be possible using the the Turbo screen functions of the computer by using either the IBM PC version of Turbo Pascal or accessing the BIOS functions of the machine (see Chapter 17).

```
program textin;
var
    ch : char;
    word,
    text1,
```

```
  text2 : string[255];
  maxonline,
  curlinelen,
  indx1,
  indx2 : integer;

begin
  writeln('Text input program ');
  writeln;
  repeat
    write('Enter maximum line length (1-79) - ');
    readln(maxonline);
  until maxonline in [1..79];
  writeln;
  writeln('Enter text, ENTER to end -');
  writeln;
  indx1 := 1;
  word := '';
  curlinelen := 0;
  repeat
    read(kbd,ch);
    if ch in ['A'..'Z','0'..'9','a'..'z','.',',',] then
      word := word + ch;
    if ch in [' ',chr(13)] then
      if length(word) > 0 then
      begin
        if length(word) + curlinelen > maxonline then
        begin
          writeln;
          curlinelen := 0;
        end;
        curlinelen := curlinelen + length(word) + 1;
        write(word,' ');
        word := '';
      end;
  until ch = chr(13);
end.
```

## CHAPTER THIRTEEN

Data Structures: Part II. Records and Sets

Pascal provides two additional predefined data structures to handle data with more complex organization—the RECORD and the SET. The RECORD structure allows a number of different types of data related to a common subject to be accessed together. The SET structure allows a number of similar data elements to be evaluated as a single unit.

13.1 Records

While the ARRAY is a very useful data structure, it is limited because all elements of a given array must be of the same data type. In some cases however, it is necessary to deal with related data items of different types. In languages like FORTRAN and BASIC, which do not support data structures more complex than simple arrays, this can be done by declaring different arrays for each type of data, with the indices of each array used to relate the various elements. This can become quite a complex programming task.

Pascal provides a powerful data structure known as the *RECORD* type which can be used to link related data elements of different types together. A record is much like a file folder of information, with all of its data items concerning a single *subject*, and each component individually defined. Niklaus Wirth stated in the *User Manual* that "The record types are perhaps the most flexible of data constructs." An example of this is an array of customer information in which each element contains data about a single customer, like NAME, ADDRESS, PHONE NUMBER, CONTACT NAME, CUSTOMER NUMBER, SALES-MAN, DISTRICT, DISCOUNT SCHEDULE, LAST PURCHASE DATE, and so on. Although all the data concerns a common *subject*, the customer, the record structure can contain many different *types* of data—strings, numbers, characters, etc.

Records are often used to define the structure of the data in an array or a file. Files of data are discussed in Chapter 15.

RECORD DEFINITION

The RECORD type enables the programmer to define the various data items or *fields* which make up each record. The RECORD type may be used in either the TYPE or VAR sections to declare a record.

```
type
name              =    record
                            first_name : string[20];
                            middle_initial : string[20];
                            last_name : string[20];
                       end;
address           =    record
                            street : string[20];
                            city : string[15];
                            state : string[2];
                            zip : string[5];
                       end;
date              =    record
                            month : 1 .. 12;
                            day : 1 .. 31;
                            year : 1900 .. 2100;
                       end;
cust_rec          =    record
                            cust_name : string[40];
                            addr : address;
                            phone : string[12];
                            contact : name;
                            customer_no : 1 .. 9999;
                            salesman_no : 1 .. 99;
                            district_no : 1 .. 10;
                            discount_sched : 'A' .. 'Z';
                            last_purch_date : date;
                       end;
```

As can be seen from the example, each field in the record may be of any type, including type record. The general format for a RECORD type declaration is:

```
TYPE
   identifier = RECORD
               ⟨declarations⟩
               END
```

The reserved delimiters **record** and **end** bracket the record component (field) declaration list.

With the example type definitions above, it is possible to declare a single record-type variable as:

```
var
    cust_list : cust_rec;
```

If a number of customer data records were contained in an array in memory, it could be defined as:

```
var
    cust_array : array[1..maxcust] of cust_rec;
```

ACCESSING RECORD COMPONENTS

Individual record components are designated by the following special notation:

```
record-identifier.field-identifier{.field-identifier}
```

For example, using the record defined above, a value could be assigned to the customer name component by:

```
cust_list.cust_name := 'Johnson Industries, Inc.';
```

and the customer zip code could be accessed by:

```
writeln(cust_list.addr.zip);
```

Any string or array index is placed immediately after the appropriate record variable, as:

```
cust_array[index].addr.zip := '95609';
```

To access only the first character of the zip code string in an array of records, this is one possible method:

```
zipchar := cust_array[index].addr.zip[1]
```

As you can imagine, when a program requires a large number of references to complex records, the record variable notation can become somewhat tiresome.

WITH STATEMENT

Pascal provides an easier method for operating on a number of record fields, to avoid repeating record names over and over. The WITH structured statement defines the record variable(s) to use with the object statements contained within the WITH block, allowing operations on those records using only their field identifiers. The general form of the WITH statement is:

WITH record-variable{, record-variable} DO statement

Notice that the WITH statement predefines *record variables* to be assumed in the block. This means that WITH statements may be nested as required.

The earlier examples could be simplified as follows:

```
with cust_list do
begin
    cust_name := 'Johnson Industries, Inc.';
    writeln(addr.zip);
end;
```

To illustrate the use of an array of records, we will present a simple example program for a "little black book" which contains the following data items:

1. Name
2. Address
   a. Street address
   b. City
   c. State
   d. Zip code
3. Telephone number

Here is the example program which will maintain a phone book in an array in memory:

```
program contact;
const
    maxlist = 10;
type
    addr        =   record
                        street : string[20];
                        city : string[15];
                        state : string[2];
                        zip : string[5];
                    end;
    list_rec    =   record
                        name : string[40];
                        address : addr;
                        telephone : string[12];
                    end;
```

```pascal
var
   contact_list : array [1..maxlist] of list_rec;
   index : integer;
   quit : boolean;
   answer : string[4];
   ch : char;

procedure enter;
begin
   index := 0;
   repeat
      ClrScr;
      index := index + 1;
      writeln('Record #',index);
      with contact_list[index] do
      begin
         write('Enter name: ');
         readln(name);
         write('Enter street address: ');
         readln(address.street);
         write('Enter city: ');
         readln(address.city);
         write('Enter 2 letter state code: ');
         readln(address.state);
         write('Enter 5 digit zip code: ');
         readln(address.zip);
         write('Enter telephone number: ');
         readln(telephone);
         writeln;
      end;
      write('Enter another record? (Y/N) - ');
      readln(answer);
      quit := (answer <> 'Y') and (answer <> 'y');
   until (index = maxlist) or quit;
end; {enter}

procedure retrieve;
var
   index1,
   index2 : integer;
begin
   repeat
      repeat
         ClrScr;
         writeln('Records available are:');
```

```
        for index1 := 1 to index do
          writeln(index1,'. ',contact_list[index1].name);
        writeln;
        write('Enter record # to retrieve: ');
        readln(index2);
      until (index2 > 0) and (index2 <= index);
      ClrScr;
      writeln('Record #',index2);
      with contact_list[index2] do
      begin
        writeln('Name: ',name);
        with address do
        begin
          writeln('Street address: ',street);
          writeln('City: ',city);
          writeln('State code: ',state);
          writeln('Zip: ',zip);
        end;
        writeln('Telephone number: ',telephone);
        writeln;
      end;
      write('Find another record? (Y/N) - ');
      readln(answer);
      quit := (answer <> 'Y') and (answer <> 'y');
    until quit;
end; {retrieve}

begin {contact}
  writeln('Contact list record array program');
  writeln;
  write('Enter Q to quit or any other character to continue - '); read(kbd,ch);
  writeln;
  if not (ch in ['Q','q']) then
  begin
    quit := false;
    enter;
    retrieve;
    writeln;
    writeln('- done -');
  end
  else
    writeln('Program terminated');
end. {contact}
```

Note that this is a demonstration program. All entered data resides in an array in memory and is lost when the program terminates. Each time the program is run, the data must be completely re-entered. As each record takes 100 bytes of variable memory, there is only room for about 70 records when using the demonstration Turbo Pascal compiler. We will develop a more practical version of this program using disk files in Chapter 15.

In the *enter* procedure of the example program, the *address* variables were specified with the record-variable format, while in the *retrieve* procedure, the *address* variables are specified in a WITH block.

In the "directory" list portion, the record array is accessed as a single record variable:

        contact_list[index1].name

while in the input and output portions, the array index is part of the WITH block:

        with contact_list[index] **do**

VARIANT RECORDS

So far, we have explored fixed record structures, which always have the same form. Pascal also allows records with *variant* parts which, may have different structures based on various conditions encountered in the program.

In Turbo Pascal, only one variant part is allowed in a record and it must follow any fixed parts. Here is an example of a variant record:

```
type
name              =    record
                           first_name : string[20];
                           middle_initial : string[20];
                           last_name : string[20];
                       end;
date              =    record
                           month : 1 .. 12;
                           day : 1 .. 31;
                           year : 1900 .. 2100;
                       end;
gender            =    (male, female);
marital           =    (single, married);
applicant         =    record
                           person : name;
                           birthdate : date;
                           sex : gender;
                           case status : marital of
```

```
            single : ( );
            married : (children : byte)
      end;
```

In the common form of the variant record (like the example above), the *active* fields of a variant part are selected based on the value of a *tag-field* defined in the record, much like the CASE statement. This type of variant record, using a tag-field, is known as a *discriminated union*, in other words, a preselection is made between alternative variant parts of the record based on the tag-field value. The *tag-type* following the tag-field must be a previously declared scalar type, and unlike the record field types, it may *not* include a type definition.

It is the programmer's responsibility to insure that in discriminated union variants only active variant fields (as determined by the value of the tag-field) are accessed. If an inactive field in the variant part is referenced, its value is undefined.

A second type of variant record is also legal in Turbo Pascal, called the *free union*. It is similar to the variant record structure in the C language. In this type of variant, the tag-field is omitted. The tag-type may be any previously defined scalar type as above.

In a free union variant record, a field is selected "automatically" when its identifier is referenced. This type of variant is often used to reference a single set of machine-level memory or register values as either integer or byte values:

```
type
  regpack = record
              case integer of
                1: (ax,bx,cx,dx,bp,si,di,ds,es,flags : integer);
                2: (al,ah,bl,bh,cl,ch,dl,dh :   byte)
              end;
```

Since no tag-field is specified in the above example, the variant field to be used will be selected by reference—both groups of fields refer to the same data—in other words, byte fields *al* and *ah* refer to the lower and upper bytes of integer field *ax*, and so on.

The free union variant record can also be used to bypass Pascal's strong typing rules. For example, the actual address contained in a pointer variable can be determined by using the above technique. However, Turbo Pascal provides the *seg()* and *ofs()* functions to return addresses, which can be used to perform the same operation.

13.2 Sets

In Pascal, a *set* is a collection of like elements. Unlike other data structures, sets may be manipulated as a single unit. Sets are possibly the least understood

structure in Pascal, perhaps because of the limited access allowed to set members
in Pascal, or the limited size of sets in most Pascal implementations. Permissible
set size may range from 16, to 256, to thousands of elements or members (on
some mainframes). Turbo Pascal sets may contain up to 256 elements.

A set can consist of zero or more elements of the same *base type*. The base
type must be a simple type, that is, any scalar type except REAL. Sets are useful
in tests and comparisons, particularly of text values.

Sets which do not have any elements are said to contain the *empty set*, signified
by a pair of brackets—[].

Sets can be thought of as existing in a "limited universe" of like elements as
declared by the scalar or set type. A real-world example of this might be the
200 male members of the Senior Class of a small high school. This "superset"
or *type* is made up of a specific group of individuals we will call *male_seniors*.
Now from this "limited universe," some members are football players, some are
basketball players, some play baseball, some are in track, and so on. Participants
in each of these sports form separate groups or *sets* of the type *male_seniors*.
If no one turns out for a sport, then it constitutes an *empty set*. Because the
sports are played during different seasons, some boys will be included in more
than one set, and because not everyone plays sports, some will not be included
in any set except *male_seniors*.

Although this example illustrates the concept of sets, it is not very useful
because Pascal does not allow the members of sets to be input or output. Sets
can be used only to *test* scalar values and this makes large-scale use of set
operations impractical in Pascal. Most set operations are done on character,
integer and byte values.

SET DEFINITION

Set types must be declared before use, except for predefined scalar types like
CHAR and INTEGER. In Turbo Pascal, when each element in a set is declared,
it is assigned an ordinal value beginning at 0 and increasing to 255. This value
is used internally to represent a particular element, much like the ASCII character
set has equivalent ordinal values for each character.

The general form of the set type declaration is:

```
TYPE
    type-name = SET OF base-type;
```

Note that the range operator (. .) may be used, or members making up the
base-type may be individually listed.

```
type
    cats = set of (Common, Persian, Manx, Siamese, Abyssinian, Angora,);
    hex_values = set of 0 .. 15;
    upcase_letters = set of 'A'..'Z';
```

Set variables are declared in much the same way as set types. Set variables must be of a base type like CHAR or INTEGER, or of a previously declared set type.

The following example shows an INCORRECT set type declaration—all type declarations must be simple types, and the two constructs in the set type declaration will cause a compiler error.

```
type
    hex = set of '0'..'9','A'..'F';
var
    hexchar : hex;
```

Instead, use this form to declare a complex set:

```
var
    hexchar : set of char;
begin
    hexchar := ['0'..'9','A'..'F'];
{balance of program}
end.
```

SET CONSTRUCTIONS

A *set construction* specifies elements used in a set expression. Set constructions consist or one or more set elements or ranges of elements of the base type of the set, enclosed by square brackets ([and]). A range is a *contiguous* group of elements, in order, specified by listing the beginning and ending element separated by the range symbol of two periods (. .).

[ ] Set Constructor

. . Contiguous Range of set elements

The following are examples of set constructions:

[1,3,5,7,9]	Integers 1, 3, 5, 7, and 9
[0..5] or [0,1,2,3,4,5]	Integers 0 to 5
['A'..'Z']	ASCII upper case letters
['0'..'9','A'..'Z','a'..'z']	ASCII letters and numbers
[' '..'~']	All printing ASCII characters
['Y','y','N','n']	ASCII letters Y, y, N, and n
[]	The empty set has no members

SET OPERATORS

Set operators are used with set constructions to form set expressions. Set constructions, variables, and combinational set expressions may be assigned by the set assignment operator (": =") to other set variables of the same base type or used in place of a set expression of the same base type. Relational set expressions may be assigned to a boolean variable or used in place of a boolean expression.

The combinational set operators allow manipulation of sets to determine set intersection, set union, and set difference. The *intersection* of two sets (written A * B) is the set whose members are in *both* A and B. The *union* of two sets (written A + B) is the set whose members are in *either* A or B. The *difference* of two sets (written A - B) is the set whose members are in A and *not* in B.

A + B	Set Union	means in either A or B
A - B	Set Difference	means in A and not B
A * B	Set Intersection	means in both A and B
A : = B	Set Assignment	assign the elements of B to A

The relational set operators allow testing the relationship between set constructions or between sets.

A = B	Set Equality	means all members in both sets
A ⟨⟩ B	Set Inequality	means all or some members not in both sets
A ⟨= B	Set Inclusion	means all members of B in A
	or	
A ⟩= B	Set Inclusion	means all members of A in B
A in B	Set Membership	elements of base expression A in set B

Although there is no operator for set inclusion (no elements of A in B), the expression (A * B = []) can be used for this logical test.

Set expressions in Pascal derive most of their usefulness from the IN operator, which allows comparisons between set expressions and variables of the same base (i.e., scalar) type (CHAR, INTEGER, BYTE, etc.) as the set. The IN operator provides an elegant alternative to complex (and confusing) boolean expressions in conditional statements. For example, the program segment:

```
repeat
    read(kbd,response);
until (response = 'Y') or
      (response = 'y') or
      (response = 'N') or
      (response = 'n');
```

can be recoded more simply using the IN operator as:

```
repeat
```

```
      read(kbd,response);
   until response in ['Y','y','N','n'];
```

(Assuming in both examples that *response* is a CHAR type variable.) Similarly, the following program shows the use of the IN operator for prequalifying variables for the CASE statement:

```
program select;
var
   ch : char;
begin
   writeln('Selection demonstration');
   writeln;
   write('Pick a number between 0 and 9 - ');
   repeat
      read(kbd,ch);
   until ch in ['0'..'9'];
   writeln(ch);
   writeln;
   case ord(ch)-48 of
      0 : writeln('You picked zero!');
      1 : writeln('You picked one!');
      2 : writeln('You picked two!');
      3 : writeln('You picked three!');
      4 : writeln('You picked four!');
      5 : writeln('You picked five!');
      6 : writeln('You picked six!');
      7 : writeln('You picked seven!');
      8 : writeln('You picked eight!');
      9 : writeln('You picked nine!');
   end;
   writeln;
   writeln('- done -');
end.
```

It is important to prequalify the range of user input in interactive programs to insure the program cannot be "crashed" by improper entries. In the above example, the input variable is a CHAR type to allow any keyboard input, but the input REPEAT..UNTIL loop will accept only the range of values specified in the set. The *ord()* function converts the accepted ASCII character between '0' and '9' to its ordinal value, in this case an integer in the range of 48 to 57, and subtracting 48 from this value yields the required integer in the range of 0 to 9 for the CASE statement.

(The CASE statement could also have used the CHAR value without conversion simply by changing the CASE specifiers from integer to character constants.)

## CHAPTER FOURTEEN

Pointers and Dynamic Data Structures

Pascal is a powerful and flexible language that supports many different simple and complex data structures. However, all of the data structures we have discussed up to this point have one main restriction—they are fixed in size and order. In the array structure, element one always comes before element two, and so on. The order may be modified by moving existing data and inserting new data into the structure or by copying the structure in a different sequence. However, the size of an array is fixed when it is declared. It can NEVER exceed the maximum declared size, and it always takes up all of the declared maximum memory space. Once declared, the space is committed and cannot be released. A significant factor in the design of large Turbo Pascal programs on the IBM PC is the limitation of the combined program stack and variable data space to one segment of memory or 64K bytes. Each variable in a program or subprogram is allotted space for the duration of the program. As was mentioned earlier, four 16K arrays of type BYTE or two 16K arrays of type INTEGER, or *one* 10K array of type REAL can use up *all* available variable space. More complex arrays of record types can use up space even faster.

Some programs require the ability to *dynamically* allocate data storage, allotting storage when needed and recovering it when a process is completed. Others may require large amounts of memory (i.e., greater than 64K bytes) for data table storage or manipulation. Pascal supports these *dynamic data structures* through the use of the *heap* and *pointer variables*.

14.1 The Heap and Pointers

In Turbo Pascal on the IBM PC, the *heap* is all unallocated memory in the system—that is, the memory which is not used by DOS, by memory resident programs (like SideKick), by the Turbo program (up to 64K bytes), and by its internal stack and its variables in the data segment (also up to 64K bytes). On an IBM PC with 512K bytes installed, approximately 256K bytes of memory are available for use in the heap for dynamic structures. This is about four times the space available for other types of variables in a Turbo Pascal program, and this area can be used and reused as needed during the program's execution.

The heap is a stack structure in memory which begins at the lowest free byte in memory (when the program starts) and grows toward the top of memory as dynamic variables are added to it. A *heap pointer* is maintained which indicates the current "top of the heap" location. As variables are added to the heap, the heap pointer is increased by the number of bytes required for that variable type.

The heap space is accessed by using *pointer variables* which contain the location or *address* of a data item in the heap. Pointer variables are stored in the regular Turbo Pascal variable area or in the heap. So how is the heap useful?

First, pointer variables and the heap can be used to conserve the available 64K bytes of available memory space for Turbo Pascal variables. On the IBM PC, a pointer takes up four bytes of memory—enough to contain a segment and offset address to access any portion of the IBM PC's memory space. If pointers were used to point to a series of INTEGER type values (two bytes each), this type of structure would be quite inefficient—using a four-byte pointer to access a two-byte value. However, suppose pointers were used to access a record-type data structure stored in the heap containing 100 bytes of information per record; in this case we have saved 96 bytes of variable space for *each* record in the structure compared to using an ARRAY of RECORDS.

Second, heap memory space can be allocated and deallocated under program control. Recall that static data structures like ARRAYs remain allocated for the life of the program. Thus, if one program process needs to modify and copy a large structure, and another process needs to sort a similar structure, both segments can reuse the same heap space.

Third, pointer variables can be used to build advanced data structures like *linked lists* and *trees*, and to add, insert, move, and delete elements of the structure *without copying them*, saving execution time and memory space. The form and size of these structures can be dynamically changed by the program as required.

Finally, components of a data structure in the heap need not be physically located sequentially or contiguously in memory. This means that the structure can be sorted by sorting its pointers instead of the data elements, a much faster operation than sorting a large structure itself.

14.2 Using Pointers

Pointer variable types and their objects are identified by the special pointer symbol "^" (also called a carat, circumflex, or up-arrow). Pointer types are declared in the form:

```
TYPE
    typename = ^ base-type;
```

Once defined, a pointer type may be used to declare pointer variables which point to components of the base-type (and size). Thus, a pointer to a group of strings of length 80 could be defined as:

```
type
    strtype = string[80];
    ptrtype = ^strtype;
var
    ptr : ptrtype;
begin
    ptr := nil;
```

A special pointer value, represented by the reserved word **nil**, is used to indicate a pointer is not currently pointing to a valid variable.

Pointer values may be assigned to other pointers of the same base-type. Any other assignment is invalid. Thus after the statements:

```
var
    ptr1,ptr2 : ptrtype;
begin
.......
ptr1 := ptr2;
```

both pointers will point to the same object—whatever PTR2 originally pointed to and both will return the same value. The object PTR1 was pointing to has been lost.

```
ptr1 *→
                        object (data)

ptr2 *→
```

However, the statement:

```
ptr1^ := ptr2^;
```

has a different result. In this case, the *value* of the object pointed to by PTR2 has been assigned to the *object* pointed to by PTR1. Now both pointers will return the same *value*, but they are pointing to different *objects* (i.e., different memory locations containing the same value) since we have copied the value pointed to by PTR2 to the object pointed to by PTR1.

ptr1 *→ | data1 (now has same value as data2)
             ↑
ptr2 *→ | data2

Heap space is allocated to a dynamic variable by the NEW procedure, in the form:

NEW(PtrVar)

Space for the object type of PtrVar is allocated on the heap and the address of the object in the heap is assigned to PtrVar.

14.3 Array of Pointers

The simplest way to use pointers is to create an array of pointers to the data structure contained in the heap. This structure is easy to design and has the advantage that only four bytes of the variable data area are used for each entry, no matter what the size of the structure in the heap.

In our previous phone book list example program we used an array of records. If you compare that program with the following example, you will note only a few modifications are required to use an array of pointers instead. The changed lines are marked by comments.

When run with the demonstration compiler, this program is also limited to a maximum of about 70 entries due to the small data area available. Maxlist is set to 10 entries in the example. All data will be lost when the program is terminated.

```
program contact2;
const
  maxlist = 10;
type
  list_pointer = ^ list_rec;                    {change}

  addr          =    record
                       street : string[20];
                       city : string[15];
                       state : string[2];
                       zip : string[5];
                     end;

  list_rec      =    record
                       name : string[40];
```

```pascal
                                address : addr;
                                telephone : string[12];
                        end;

var
contact_list : array [1..maxlist] of list_pointer;        {change}
    index : integer;
    quit : boolean;
    answer : string[4];
    ch : char;

procedure enter;
begin
    index := 0;
    repeat
        ClrScr;
        index := index + 1;
        writeln('Record #',index);
        new(contact_list[index]);                        {change}
        with contact_list[index]^ do                      {change}
        begin
            write('Enter name: ');
            readln(name);
            write('Enter street address: ');
            readln(address.street);
            write('Enter city: ');
            readln(address.city);
            write('Enter 2 letter state code: ');
            readln(address.state);
            write('Enter 5 digit zip code: ');
            readln(address.zip);
            write('Enter telephone number: ');
            readln(telephone);
            writeln;
        end;
        write('Enter another record? (Y/N) - ');
        readln(answer);
        quit := (answer <> 'Y') and (answer <> 'y');
    until (index = maxlist) or quit;
end; {enter}

procedure retrieve;
var
    index1,
    index2 : integer;
```

```
begin
  repeat
    repeat
      ClrScr;
      writeln('Records available are:');
      for index1 := 1 to index do
        writeln(index1,'. ',contact_list[index1]^.name);          {change}
      writeln;
      write('Enter record # to retrieve: ');
      readln(index2);
    until (index2 > 0) and (index2 <= index);
    ClrScr;
    writeln('Record #',index2);
    with contact_list[index2]^ do                                 {change}
    begin
      writeln('Name: ',name);
      with address do
      begin
        writeln('Street address: ',street);
        writeln('City: ',city);
        writeln('State code: ',state);
        writeln('Zip: ',zip);
      end;
      writeln('Telephone number: ',telephone);
      writeln;
    end;
    write('Find another record? (Y/N) - ');
    readln(answer);
    quit := (answer <> 'Y') and (answer <> 'y');
  until quit;
end; {retrieve}

begin {contact2}
  writeln('Contact list record program - Version 2');
  writeln('Using array of pointers and dynamic data structure');
  writeln;
  write('Press any key to start - ');
  read(kbd,ch);
  quit := false;
  enter;
  retrieve;
  writeln;
  writeln('- done -');
end. {contact2}
```

14.4 Pointers and Advanced Data Structures

Pointers are most often used with data structures known as *lists* or *trees*. A list structure is made up of records which contain one or more elements specifying the location of (or a pointer to) its successor and sometimes its predecessor components. A tree structure is similar to a list, but it may have more than one successor component.

1st item	next item	last item
data | ptr *→	data | ptr *→	data | ptr *→ nil

Figure 14-1 Simple List Structure.

Here is a simple list structure:

```
type
    dataitem = record
                    data : datatype;
                    nextitem : ptrtype;
               end;
```

It is easy to see that each component contains a pointer to the next component in the list. Now we can declare the pointer type—or can we?

```
type
    ptrtype = ^dataitem;
    dataitem = record
                    nextitem : ptrtype;
                    data : datatype;
               end;
```

How can we declare a pointer to an as yet undeclared object? Or an object containing an undeclared pointer? The answer is that Pascal allows the declaration of a pointer type before its object type to resolve this problem. The above declaration is correct.

As an example of the list structure, here is our old friend the phone book program, implemented using pointers to a dynamic linked-list structure. Keep in mind that the data area in the demonstration compiler is still limited to about 70 entries. Changes from the previous version are marked with comments.

```
program contact3;
const
```

```pascal
    maxlist = 10;
type
  list_pointer = ^ list_rec;

  addr            =    record
                          street : string[20];
                          city : string[15];
                          state : string[2];
                          zip : string[5];
                       end;

  list_rec        =    record
                          name : string[40];
                          address : addr;
                          telephone : string[12];
                          next : list_pointer;                {change}
                       end;

var
  firstentry,
  newentry,
  nextentry,
  lastentry : list_pointer;                        {change}
  index : integer;
  quit : boolean;
  answer : string[4];
  ch : char;

procedure enter;
begin
  index := 0;
  firstentry := nil;                               {change}
  repeat
    ClrScr;
    index := index + 1;
    writeln('Record #',index);
    new(newentry);                                 {change}
    with newentry ^ do                             {change}
    begin
      write('Enter name: ');
      readln(name);
      write('Enter street address: ');
      readln(address.street);
      write('Enter city: ');
      readln(address.city);
      write('Enter 2 letter state code: ');
```

```
      readln(address.state);
      write('Enter 5 digit zip code: ');
      readln(address.zip);
      write('Enter telephone number: ');
      readln(telephone);
      writeln;
    end;

    if firstentry = nil then                {change}
      firstentry := newentry
    else
      lastentry^.next := newentry;
    lastentry := newentry;                  {change}
    lastentry^.next := nil;                 {change}
    write('Enter another record? (Y/N) - ');
    readln(answer);
    quit := (answer <> 'Y') and (answer <> 'y');
  until (index = maxlist) or quit;
end; {enter}

procedure retrieve;
var
  index1,
  index2 : integer;
begin
  repeat
    repeat
      ClrScr;
      writeln('Records available are:');
      index1 := 0;
      nextentry := firstentry;             {change}
      while nextentry <> nil do            {change}
      with nextentry^ do                   {change}
      begin
        index1 := index1 + 1;
        writeln(index1,'. ',name);
        nextentry := next;                 {change}
      end;
      writeln;
      write('Enter record # to retrieve: ');
      readln(index2);
    until (index2 > 0) and (index2 <= index);
    ClrScr;
    writeln('Record #',index2);
    index1 := 1;                           {change}
```

```
      nextentry := firstentry;                        {change}
      while (index1 < index2) and (nextentry <> nil) do   {change}
      with nextentry^ do                              {change}
      begin
        index1 := index1 + 1;
        nextentry := next;
      end;

      if nextentry <> nil then                        {change}
      with nextentry^ do                              {change}
      begin
        writeln('Name: ',name);
        with address do
        begin
          writeln('Street address: ',street);
          writeln('City: ',city);
          writeln('State code: ',state);
          writeln('Zip: ',zip);
        end;
        writeln('Telephone number: ',telephone);
        writeln;
      end
      else
        writeln('Record not found');
      write('Find another record? (Y/N) - ');
      readln(answer);
      quit := (answer <> 'Y') and (answer <> 'y');
    until quit;
end; {retrieve}


begin {contact3}
  writeln('Contact list record program - Version 3');
  writeln('Using pointers and linked list dynamic data structure');
  writeln;
  write('Press any key to start - ');
  read(kbd,ch);
  quit := false;
  enter;
  retrieve;
  writeln;
  writeln('- done -');
end. {contact3}
```

It is beyond the scope of this book to discuss the use of advanced data structures in more detail, but one additional example is included at the end of this chapter. Also, the source code as well as the compiled version of the Turbo Pascal cross-reference utility is included on the accompanying disk—it may be compiled with a commercial version of Turbo Pascal or it can be studied to provide a larger example of the use of pointers.

14.5 Allocating Heap Space

Heap space may be allocated as each new variable is created or in programmer-controlled blocks. The NEW procedure allocates heap space for a single variable and the procedure GETMEM allocates blocks of heap space.

NEW

The Standard Pascal procedure NEW is used to allocate space on the heap for a new variable. The general form of the New procedure is:

NEW(PVar)

where PVar is a pointer variable of some object type. The NEW procedure automatically allocates enough space for a new variable of the object type of the pointer variable on the heap, and assigns its location to *PVar*.

GETMEM

The procedure GetMem is also used to allocate space on the heap. Unlike NEW, which allocates as much space as is required by the type of the object pointed to, GetMem allows the programmer to control the amount of space allocated. The general form of the procedure call is:

GetMem(PVar, I)

where *PVar* is any pointer variable and *I* is an integer expression specifying the number of bytes to be allocated.

14.6 Reclaiming Heap Space

Turbo Pascal provides the MARK and RELEASE procedures (as used in UCSD Pascal) for reclaiming heap space. Turbo Pascal Version 2.0 and later also includes the Standard Pascal DISPOSE procedure. Either MARK and RE-LEASE *or* DISPOSE may be used in a given program, but not both.

MARK AND RELEASE

The MARK procedure is used with the RELEASE procedure to free heap space. The MARK procedure assigns the current value of the heap pointer to a pointer variable. RELEASE sets the heap pointer to the value of its argument (a pointer variable set by MARK). Thus, RELEASE discards all dynamic variables above this address. The general form for these procedures is:

    MARK(PVar)
    RELEASE(PVar)

where *PVar* is a pointer variable set to a heap pointer value by MARK. RELEASE cannot free space in the middle of the heap without losing all variables above the RELEASE address.

DISPOSE (TURBO 2.0 AND LATER)

The Standard Pascal procedure DISPOSE is used to reclaim space on the heap. DISPOSE will reclaim the memory used by a specific dynamic variable for new use. The general form of the DISPOSE procedure is:

    DISPOSE(PVar)

when *PVar* is a specific pointer variable.

FREEMEM (TURBO 2.0 AND LATER)

The procedure FreeMem performs the opposite operation to GetMem—it releases a block of space on the heap. The general form of the procedure call is:

    FreeMem(PVar, I)

where *PVar* is any pointer variable and I is an integer expression specifying the number of bytes to be deallocated—which must match EXACTLY the number of bytes previously allocated by GetMem.

MEMAVAIL

On the IBM-PC, MemAvail returns an integer value indicating the number of paragraphs available in the heap at any given time. A paragraph of memory is 16 bytes.

MAXAVAIL (TURBO 2.0 AND LATER)

On the IBM PC, the MaxAvail function returns an integer value indicating the number of free paragraphs available in the largest contiguous block of space on the heap. A paragraph is equal to 16 bytes.

USING POINTERS

The following two example programs illustrate the use of the MARK/RELEASE and the DISPOSE procedures in Turbo Pascal. Note that RELEASE can be used to free memory above and including a given pointer variable, or a special variable (like *top*) can be used with MARK.

The program keeps track of a name and phone list, but the data in the record can easily be expanded to any size allowed by available memory. The beginning and current free memory values are shown above the menu after each operation.

```
program pointer1;

{This program illustrates the use of Mark and Release for heap management. It
will work with the Demo compiler if the error messages are not loaded.}

const
    maxlist = 10;


type
    list_pointer = ^ list_rec;
    strtype = string[10];
    ptrtype = list_pointer;

    list_rec = record
                    name : string[40];
                    phone : string[20];
                    next : list_pointer;
               end;
var
    free : real;
    top,
    firstentry,
```

```
    newentry,
    nextentry,
    lastentry,
    lastentry1 : list_pointer;
    index : integer;
    quit : boolean;
    answer : string[4];
    ch : char;

(* {$I RELEASE.INC } *) {Use with Turbo 2.0 only}

procedure enter;
var
    quit0 : boolean;
begin
    quit0 := false;
    repeat
      ClrScr;
      index := index + 1;
      writeln('Record #',index);
      new(newentry);
      with newentry^ do
      begin
        write('Enter name: ');
        readln(name);
        write('Enter phone: ');
        readln(phone);
        writeln;
      end;

      if firstentry = nil then
      begin
        firstentry := newentry;    {set root}
      end
      else
      begin
        lastentry^.next := newentry;
      end;
      lastentry := newentry;
      lastentry^.next := nil;

      write('Enter another record? (Y/N) - ');
      repeat
        read(kbd,ch);
      until upcase(ch) in ['Y','N'];
```

```
      quit0 := upcase(ch) = 'N';
   until (index = maxlist) or quit0;
end; {enter}

function find(str1:strtype):integer;
var
   index1,
   index2 : integer;

begin
   repeat
      ClrScr;
      writeln('Records available are:');
      index1 := 0;
      nextentry := firstentry;
      while nextentry <> nil do
      with nextentry ^ do
      begin
         index1 := index1 + 1;
         writeln(index1,'. ',name);
         nextentry := next;
      end;
      writeln;
      write('Enter record # to ',str1,' - 0 to quit: ');
      readln(index2);
   until (index2 >= 0) and (index2 <= index);

   if index2 > 0 then
   begin
      ClrScr;
      writeln('Searching for Record #',index2);
      index1 := 1;
      nextentry := firstentry;
      while (index1 < index2) and (nextentry <> nil) do
      with nextentry ^ do
      begin
         index1 := index1 + 1;
         lastentry1 := nextentry;
         nextentry := next;
      end;
   end;
   find := index2;
end; {find}
```

```
procedure retrieve;
var
   quit1 : boolean;
   xx : string[40];
   newindex : integer;
begin
   quit1 := false;
   repeat
     newindex := find('retrieve');
      if newindex > 0 then
      begin
        if nextentry <> nil then
        with nextentry ^ do
        begin
          writeln('NAME      PHONE');
          writeln(name,' ',phone);
          writeln;
        end
        else
          writeln('Record not found');
        write('Find another record? (Y/N) - ');
        repeat
          read(kbd,ch);
        until upcase(ch) in ['Y','N'];
        quit1 := upcase(ch) = 'N';
      end
      else
          quit1 := true;
   until quit1;
end; {retrieve}

procedure clearall;
begin
   release(top);           {use variable set with MARK as marker}
   nextentry := nil;
   index := 0;
   firstentry := nil;
end;

procedure menu;
var
   ch : char;
begin
   repeat
     clrscr;
```

```
    gotoxy(25,3);
    write('Initial free memory = ',free:8:0);
    gotoxy(25,5);
    write('Current free memory = ',(memavail*16.0):8:0);
    gotoxy(38,10);
    write('MENU');
    gotoxy(30,13);
    write('1. Enter data.');
    gotoxy(30,14);
    write('2. Retrieve data.');
    gotoxy(30,15);
    write('3. Clear all data items.');
    gotoxy(30,19);
    write('Q. Quit - all data lost.');
    gotoxy(32,22);
    write('Selection: ');
    repeat
      read(kbd,ch);
    until upcase(ch) in ['1'..'3','Q'];
    case upcase(ch) of
      '1' : enter;
      '2' : retrieve;
      '3' : clearall;
      'Q' : quit := true;
    end;
  until quit;
end;   {menu}


begin {pointer1}
  writeln('Name list record program - Version 1');
  writeln('Using pointers and linked list ');
  writeln('dynamic data structure with the Mark and Release procedures');
  writeln;
  write('Press any key to start - ');
  read(kbd,ch);
  quit := false;
  index := 0;
  mark(top);        {set variable for RELEASE() of all heap}
  firstentry := nil;
  free := memavail * 16.0;
  menu;
  writeln;
  writeln('- done -');
end. {pointer1}
```

Note: Pointer 2 program is on the disk for use with the full Turbo Pascal.

## CHAPTER FIFTEEN

Device and File I/O

Although we have developed some interesting programs in Turbo Pascal up to this point, they all share the same limitation—the input data must come from the keyboard or be included in the program code and the program results must be output to the computer screen. This approach is fine for short applications, but most useful computer programs output results to the system printer or use *text and/or data files* for their input and output. This chapter will discuss device and file I/O operations in Turbo Pascal.

Using a computer to solve a problem and then copying the results to a piece of paper by hand doesn't make too much sense. Computer systems today usually include a system printer which can print the results of a problem quickly and accurately. In fact, the printer can also be used to list a source program to paper for easier analysis and debugging. A program is included in the next chapter that will format and list your Turbo Pascal programs on the printer.

Files are used to store and recall data in a form usable by the computer without requiring re-entry of data. Files of data may be input, processed, and output much faster than manually entered data. Of course, almost all data must be manually entered the first time, but once stored in a text or data file, it may be manipulated, listed, revised, and added to easily.

A file is the basic unit of information handled by the computer's disk operating system. Files of data are stored on a floppy diskette or hard disk drive, and are accessed by a specific file name, like "PAYROLL.DAT." The file name may also contain a disk drive specification like "A:" or "C:" which indicates which drive the file is located on. Application programs are used to access the data contained in files.

Pascal supports two basic types of files—data files and text files. Data files contain information stored in a format similar to that used internally in the computer and are not directly displayable on the screen. Data files are also called binary files, because the data is not stored as ASCII characters. Files are made up of like units of data called *records*. This means that all of the records in a file must be of the same TYPE. Files are declared as a FILE of TYPE. A file record may contain one or more data element or *field* of data, and in this case, the file type must be specified as a RECORD type. File records with more than one field are compatible with the RECORD data structure used in Pascal, and

RECORD structures are used to specify the data format of files with multiple-field records.

Text files are handled as a stream of characters in the form of lines of text. Text files include two special non-printing ASCII markers—end-of-line or EOLN (consisting of a CR and a LF character) and end-of-file or EOF (consisting of a ⟨Ctrl-Z⟩ character). Text files are declared using the special type TEXT which is the same as a FILE of CHAR. Note that some early releases of Turbo Pascal 3.0 have a bug which prevents the ⟨Ctrl-Z⟩ EOF marker from being inserted at the end of a TEXT output file. With these versions, the program must write a ⟨Ctrl-Z⟩ character (ASCII 26) before closing an output text file to maintain compatibility with other software.

Files used in a program must be declared like other objects. Before a file is used, it must be *opened*, or linked to the program. When processing is completed, each file must be *closed* to insure that all the data is transferred from the operating system buffer area in memory to the actual file. If a program terminates without closing all its files, some or all of the data may be lost.

15.1 Standard Pascal I/O

Pascal includes the two pre-defined files INPUT and OUTPUT for use as the "standard" or default text input and output files—on microcomputers these files are normally the keyboard (INPUT) and screen (OUTPUT) which together are also called the console or terminal device. In Standard Pascal, files used by a program must be declared in the program heading (including INPUT and OUTPUT).

Standard Pascal treats all input and output devices as files of data, and requires all I/O devices used by a program to be opened and closed—just like files. The standard files (or devices) INPUT and OUTPUT are opened automatically when they are referenced.

Standard Pascal supports streams of data—in other words, files are read or written from beginning to end using *sequential access*, one record after another. If the 20th record in a file must be accessed, the first 19 records must be read first. Sequential access is the only mode of file access available in Standard Pascal.

Text devices and files in Standard Pascal are are accessed using the standard procedures READ, READLN, WRITE, and WRITELN in much the same way as Turbo Pascal's console I/O discussed earlier in Chapter 9. If a device or file is used other than the default INPUT and OUTPUT files, the file variable must be the first parameter in the READ or WRITE parameter list.

Data files are accessed using a *pointer* to the current data element. (Refer to Chapter 14 for more on the use of pointers.) The standard procedures GET and PUT are used to actually transfer data to and from the file. Because Turbo Pascal does not use GET or PUT or I/O pointers, they will not be discussed here. However, an example is included later in this chapter to aid in converting Standard Pascal I/O routines to Turbo Pascal.

15.2 Turbo Pascal I/O

Turbo Pascal differs significantly from Standard Pascal in the area of input and output. Turbo Pascal includes a number of extensions to Standard Pascal as well as a number of incompatible differences.

Unlike Standard Pascal, Turbo Pascal does not use parameters in the program heading to specify files used by the program—in fact, the Turbo Pascal compiler ignores the program heading completely. Instead, Turbo uses *standard files*, *logical devices*, and assignment of declared file variables to direct input and output data streams.

15.3 Using Files

The Turbo Pascal file access system is similar to the file system used in BASIC. Files are opened, accessed, and closed, just like in BASIC, and Turbo requires that a *file variable* be assigned to the actual operating system file name and that the file variable be used to represent the file whenever it is referenced. This is similar in some ways to the way the file number is used in BASIC. The file variable indicates the data structure to be used when accessing the file.

Here are two skeleton programs for opening a new file and writing a byte of data and for opening an existing file and reading the first byte of data:

```
program filetst1;
var
   outfname : string[14];
   i : byte;
   outfile : file of byte;


begin
   writeln('Write a byte of data to a new file');
   writeln('WARNING! ');
   writeln('This program will erase and rewrite an existing file ');
   writeln('without further notice - choose the file name carefully.');
   writeln;
   write('Enter output file name: ');
   readln(outfname);
   assign(outfile,outfname);
   rewrite(outfile); {open a new file}
   write('Enter a byte value to write to ',outfname,': ');
   readln(i)
   write(outfile,i);
   close(outfile);
end.
```

```pascal
program filetst2;
var
   infname : string[14];
   i : byte;
   infile : file of byte;
begin
   writeln('Read a byte of data from a file');
   writeln;
   write('Enter input file name: ');
   readln(infname);
   assign(infile,infname);
   reset(infile); {open an existing file}
   read(infile, i);
   writeln('The first byte of ',infname,' is ',i:3);
   close(infile);
end.
```

The example above uses several I/O procedures to set-up and access the file. Before using a file, the *Assign()* procedure must be called to assign the file name to a file variable. Before input and/or output operations are performed, the file must be opened with a call to *Rewrite()* or *Reset()*. The file is closed with the *Close()* procedure.

The techniques shown above are quick and easy, but provide no checking for the existence of the file to be opened. The section on I/O result checking later in this chapter shows a better method for opening files.

15.4 File Variables

A file variable is used to specify the file (or device) to be used for an I/O operation. File types and variables are declared with the words FILE OF followed by the component type of the file. File variables can be also be declared as using a previously defined file type.

```pascal
type
   dataset = record
                name : string [20];
                address : string [30];
                phone : string [14];
                age : integer;
             end;
   intfile = file of integer;
var
   infile1 : file of char;
```

```
infile2 : file of integer;
infile3 : text; {TEXT is pre-defined type FILE of CHAR}
infile4 : file of dataset;
infile5 : intfile;
```

The component type of a file may be any type, except a file type. File variables may not appear in either assignments or expressions.

15.5 Using Text I/O

Text I/O in Turbo Pascal is convenient—easy to use. Many applications like text processing programs do not require using binary file I/O, and text I/O will work well. As mentioned earlier, text I/O deals only with characters of data in line format, every item is stored as a sequence of characters, no matter what its type in your program. Thus, if you write data in the form:

```
writeln(outfile, 'Now is the time');
writeln(outfile, 'for all good people');
```

it will be stored in the file as:

```
Now is the time⟨EOLN⟩
for all good people⟨EOLN⟩
⟨EOF⟩
```

If you write numeric data (integer or real) to the file as in this code segment:

```
i := 365;
x := 2.654343;
writeln(outfile,i,' ',x:9:6);
```

the values will also be written to the file in *character* format, just as they would appear on the screen:

```
365 2.65343⟨EOLN⟩
⟨EOF⟩
```

To access the numeric data in a text file, the data must be read into a string, and then converted into the correct numeric type with a string transfer function. Text files are compatible with BASIC text files, word processors, etc.

In Chapter 9 we discussed the the READ, READLN, WRITE, and WRITELN procedures and their use for text input and output operations with the console. In addition to standard console I/O, these procedures can be used to access other standard external devices attached to your computer, like the printer or a communications modem. They are also used to read and write data to text files.

To access other devices and text files an additional parameter must be specified with text I/O procedures—the standard file or file variable to be used with the operation. If the file variable is not specified, the standard (default) files INPUT and OUTPUT are assumed.

Thus, acceptable forms for the WRITELN procedure are actually any of the following:

```
WRITELN(data{, data}); { defaults to standard OUTPUT }
              or
WRITELN(stdfile{, data});
              or
WRITELN(filvar{, data});
```

and similarly the other I/O procedures will accept a standard file or file variable specification as well.

Text I/O operations are compatible with STRING, CHAR, and ARRAY of CHAR type data. Each line in a text file is stored as a sequence of characters followed by an EOLN marker. The end of the file is marked with an EOF character. These may be tested with two boolean functions *eoln(filvar)* and *eof(filvar)* which return TRUE if the EOLN or EOF character is the *next* character in the file.

Text files can only be processed sequentially. A text file cannot be used for input and output simultaneously.

15.6 Logical Devices

In Turbo Pascal, the external I/O devices connected to the computer, such as terminals, printers, and modems are regarded as logical devices and may be accessed by using their logical device name. Turbo Pascal allows assigning a legal device name (ending in a colon, like "CON:") to a file type variable, and then the device can be used just like a text file. The following logical devices are available:

CON: The console device. Output is sent to the operating system's console output device, usually the CRT, and input is obtained from the console input device, usually the keyboard. Contrary to the TRM: device (see below), the CON: device provides buffered input. In short, this means that each Read and Readln from the textfile assigned to the CON: device will input an entire line into a line buffer, and that the operator is provided with a set editing facilities during line input.

TRM: The terminal device. Output is sent to the operating system's console output device, usually the CRT. and input is obtained from the console input device, usually the keyboard. Input characters are echoed, unless they are control characters. The only control character echoed is a carriage return (CR), which is echoed as CR/LF.

KBD: The keyboard device (input only). Input is obtained from the operating system's console input device, usually the keyboard. Input is not echoed.

LST: The list device (output only). Output is sent to the operating system's list device, usually the line printer, LPT1:.

AUX: The auxiliary device. Output is sent to the operating system's punch device and input is obtained from the system's reader device. Usually the punch and reader devices refer to a modem. On the IBM-PC, the AUX: device is serial port COM1:.

15.7 Standard Files

As an alternative to assigning text files to logical devices as described above, Turbo Pascal offers a number of pre-declared text files which have already been assigned to specific logical devices and prepared for processing. Thus, the programmer is saved the assign, reset/rewrite, and close processes, and the use of these standard files further saves code:

Input – The primary input file. This file is assigned to either the CON: device or to the TRM: device, depending on the B compiler option. The default selection is {$B +} or CON: device.

Output – The primary output file. This file is assigned to either the CON: device or to the TRM: device, depending on the B compiler option. The default selection is {$B +} or CON: device.

Con – Assigned to the console device (CON:).
Trm – Assigned to the terminal device (TRM:).
Kbd – Assigned to the keyboard device (KBD:).
Lst – Assigned to the list device (LST:).
Aux – Assigned to the auxiliary device (AUX:).
Usr – Assigned to the user device (USR:).

As the standard files INPUT and OUTPUT are used very frequently, they are chosen by default when no file identifier is explicitly stated. The following list shows some default text file operations and their equivalents:

Write(Ch)	=	Write(Output,Ch)
Read(Ch)	=	Read(Input,Ch)
Writeln	=	Writeln(Output)
Readln	=	Readln(Input)
Eof	=	Eof(Input)
Eoln	=	Eoln(Input)

One use of these standard files is to control the input from the keyboard. Here is a useful keyboard input screening process using the KBD standard file (input without screen echo) which will await the correct input data:

```
write('Enter response (Y/N) - ');
repeat
   read(kbd,ch)                    {get character from keyboard w/o echo}
until ch in ['Y','y','N','n'];
writeln(ch);                       {display character inputted}
```

ALT sequences, function keys and cursor keys require a special input technique because they generate "extended scan-codes," These values require two reads. If the first value read is ESC or ASCII 27, then the next value will be an extended scan-code. The scan-codes are listed in the appendix. These special keyboard inputs may be tested and inputted by the following routine based on a code fragment by Borland:

```
procedure getkey (var Data, FuncKey:boolean;var ch : char);
begin
   FuncKey := False;
   Data := False;
   if KeyPressed then
   begin
      Data := True;
      Read(kbd,ch);
      if (ch = #27) and Keypressed then
      begin
         Read(kbd,ch);
         FuncKey := True;
      end
   end
end;
```

This procedure will return DATA = TRUE if a key was pressed, FUNCKEY = TRUE if the code is an extended code, and CH equal to the input value.

15.8 Random Files

Turbo Pascal allows the use of *random access* on data files as well as the sequential access method normally available for text and data files. This means that data file components may be selected or accessed directly by record number instead of having to read all the components prior to the desired record one-by-one. Random access can not be used with TEXT files.

Random access allows data to be read or written anywhere within the file. However, the file can only be expanded by adding components to the end of the file. The statement

    Seek(filvar, FileSize(filvar));

will move the *record pointer* to the end of the file, then data components may be added sequentially. The RESET procedure moves the file pointer to the beginning of the file.

The Seek and FileSize routines use values representing multiples of the basic component size of the file. All components of a Pascal file must be of the same component type (INTEGER, REAL, BYTE, CHAR, STRING, ARRAY, RECORD). The RECORD type must be used to define a complex file component type.

15.9 File Procedures

The following sections describe the procedures available for file handling. The identifier *FilVar* used throughout denotes a file variable identifier declared as described above.

ASSIGN(FilVar,Str)

Str is a string expression yielding any legal file name. This file name is assigned to the file variable *FilVar*, and all further operation on *FilVar* will operate on the disk file *Str*. Assign should never be used on a file which is in use.

REWRITE(FilVar)

A new disk file of the name assigned to the file variable *FilVar* is created and prepared for processing, and the file pointer is set to the beginning of the file (i.e. component no. 0). Any previously existing file with the same name is erased. A disk file created by rewrite is initially empty, i.e. it contains no elements.

RESET(FilVar)

The disk file of the name assigned to the file variable *FilVar* is prepared for processing, and the file pointer is set to the beginning of the file, i.e. component no. 0. *FilVar* must name an existing file, otherwise an I/O error occurs.

READ(FilVar,Var)

Var denotes one or more variables of the component type of *FilVar*, separated by commas. Each variable is read from the disk file, and following each read operation, the file pointer is advanced to the next component.

WRITE(FilVar,Var)

Var denotes one or more variables of the component type of *FilVar*, separated by commas. Each variable is written to the disk file, and following each write operation, the file pointer is advanced to the next component.

SEEK(FilVar,n)

Seek moves the file pointer to the $(n+1)$'th component of the file denoted by *FilVar*. Argument n is an integer expression. The position of the first component is 0. Note that in order to expand a file it is possible to seek one component beyond the last component. The statement

    Seek(FilVar, FileSize(FilVar))

thus places the file pointer at the end of the file ·(FileSize returns the number of components in the file, and as the components are numbered from zero, the returned number is the one greater than the number of the last component.)

FLUSH(FilVar)

Flush empties the internal sector buffer of the disk file *FilVar*, and thus assures that the sector buffer is written to the disk if any write operations have taken place since the last disk update. Flush also insures that the next read operation will actually perform a physical read from the disk file. Flush should never be used on a closed file.

CLOSE(FilVar)

The disk file associated with *FilVar* is closed, and the disk directory is updated to reflect the new status of the file. Notice that in multi-user environments it is often necessary to Close a file, even if it has only been read from.

ERASE(FilVar)

The disk file associated with *FilVar* is erased. If the file is open, i.e. if the file has been reset or rewritten but not closed, it is good programming practice to close the file before erasing it.

RENAME(FilVar,Str)

The disk file associated with *FilVar* is renamed to a new name given by the string expression *Str*. The disk directory is updated to show the new name of the file, and further operations on *FilVar* will operate on the new file with the new name. Rename should never be used on an open file.

Notice that it is the programmer's responsibility to assure that the file is named by *Str* does not already exist. If it does, multiple occurrences of the same name may result. The following function returns TRUE if the filename passed as a parameter exists, otherwise it returns FALSE:

```
function Exist(FileName : Name) : boolean;
Var
   Fil : file;
begin
   Assign(Fil,FileName);
   {SI -}
   Reset(Fil);
   {SI +}
   Exist := (IOresult = 0)
end;
```

15.10 File Standard Functions

The following standard functions are applicable to files:

EOF(FilVar):BOOLEAN

A boolean function which returns True if the file pointer is positioned at the end of the disk file, i.e. beyond the last component of the file. If not, EOF returns False.

FILEPOS(FilVar):INTEGER

An integer function which returns the current position of the file pointer. The first component of a file is 0.

FILESIZE(FilVar):INTEGER

An integer function which returns the size of the disk file expressed as the number of components (data records) in the file. If FileSize(*FilVar*) is zero, the file is empty.

15.11 I/O Result Checking

Because the programmer has no control over which files will be present on a diskette, or on the file name which may be entered by a user, it is highly recommended that the routines used for opening files include I/O result checking. The standard variable IOResult will contain a value after each I/O operation which indicates the result of that operation. To use this feature, you must disable I/O checking with the {$I-} compiler directive, RESET the file in question, then enable I/O checking with {$I + }. An IOResult value of 0 indicates the file exists, a value not equal to 0 indicates the file does not exist. A list of IOResult codes is provided in the Appendix. Here is a sample routine which can be used to open files for sequential input:

```pascal
var
  infile : file of
  quit : boolean;

procedure open_file;
const
  bell = 07;
var
  infname : string[14];
  goodfile : boolean;
```

```
begin
  quit := false;
  goodfile := false;
  repeat
    write ('Input filename -) ');
    readln (infname);
    if length(infname) = 0 then
      quit := true
    else
    begin
      assign(infile,infname);
      {$I-} reset(infile) {$I+};              {try to open file}
      goodfile := (IOresult = 0);      {if file exists, OK}
      if not goodfile then
      begin
        write (chr(bell));
        writeln ('FILE ',infname,' NOT FOUND');
        delay(3000)
      end
    end;
  until goodfile or quit;
end;
```

Here is a similar routine for opening a file for sequential output—the selected file will be overwritten if it exists.

```
var
  outfile : file of byte;
  quit : boolean;

procedure open_file2;
const
  bell = 07;
var
  outfname : string[14];
  goodfile : boolean;

begin
  quit := false;
  goodfile := false;
  repeat
    write('Output filename —) ');
    readln(outfname);
    if length(outfname) = 0 then
      quit := true
```

```
      else
      begin
         assign (outfile,outfname);
         {$I-} reset(outfile) {$I+};          {try to open file}
         goodfile := (IOresult <> 0);         {if file exists, check}
         if not goodfile then
         begin
            write (chr(bell));
            write ('FILE ',outfname,' EXISTS, OVERWRITE? (y/n) ');
            readln (ans);
            goodfile := (UpCase(ans[1]) = 'Y')
         end
      end;
   until goodfile or quit;
   if not quit then rewrite(outfile) {delete and open file}
end;
```

15.12 Untyped Files

Turbo Pascal allows the use of *untyped files* for a special high speed mode of access to disk files of any type in 128-byte records. Because no additional sector buffer is required, untyped files are the fastest mode of file access and require less memory that other modes of access. This mode is useful also when using the ERASE, RENAME, and other non-input/output file operations.

Untyped files are declared as follows:

```
var
   infile : file;
```

All the standard data file I/O functions and procedures may be used with untyped files except READ and WRITE. Instead, the special procedures BlockRead and BlockWrite are provided. Their syntax is as follows:

```
BlockRead(FilVar,Var,recs)
BlockWrite(FilVar,Var,recs)
```

where *FilVar* is the file variable of an untyped file, *Var* is any variable, and *recs* is the number of 128-byte records to be transferred between the disk file and the file variable. The transfer begins at the first byte of *Var*. *Var* must be large enough to hold the data transferred. All of the file operations on untyped files are in terms of the record size of 128-bytes.

15.13 Converting Standard Pascal I/O to Turbo

A large body of programs exist written in various implementations of Standard Pascal. Most programs will run in Turbo Pascal with few changes. However, file access in Turbo is somewhat different from most other Pascals. This section will discuss converting programs using Standard Pascal I/O to Turbo Pascal.

Text file I/O in Standard Pascal is almost identical to Turbo Pascal. A few simple changes will get most programs using Standard Pascal text I/O up and running in Turbo Pascal.

Standard Pascal programs use the program heading to link files used in a program to the operating system. Turbo Pascal uses the ASSIGN procedure. All files (except for standard pre-defined files like INPUT and OUTPUT) used in a Turbo Pascal program must be linked to a file variable using ASSIGN. Files also must be CLOSEd after they are used. If these two changes are made, programs using TEXT files should work properly in Turbo.

The differences between data file I/O in Standard Pascal and Turbo Pascal can make program conversion difficult. Be advised that some elegantly simple uses of pointer driven I/O in Standard Pascal programs can be quite complex to rewrite in Turbo Pascal. If you encounter problems, refer to a Standard Pascal text.

As with text files, data files must be ASSIGNed and CLOSEd in Turbo Pascal. In addition, Standard Pascal uses the following general form for writing to a data file:

```
program fileout (input, output, outfile);
  var
    outfile : file of integer;
    element : integer;
  begin
    rewrite(outfile);
    write('Enter data: ');
    readln(element);
    while element <> 0 do
    begin
      outfile^ := element;
      put(outfile);
      write('Enter data: ');
      readln(element);
    end;
end.
```

Here is the companion example to read the data file generated by the first program in Standard Pascal:

```pascal
program filein (output, infile)
  var
      infile : file of integer;
      element : integer;
  begin
      reset(infile);
      while not eof(infile) do
      begin
        element := infile ^;
        get(infile);
        writeln('Data: ',element);
      end;
  END.
```

Now, here are the same programs in Turbo Pascal for comparison:

```pascal
program fileout;
var
   outfname : string[14];
   outfile : file of integer;
   element : integer;
begin
   outfname := 'outfile.dat';
   assign(outfile,outfname);
   rewrite(outfile);
   write('Enter data: ');
   readln(element);
   while element ⟨⟩ 0 do
   begin
      write(outfile, element);
      write('Enter data: ');
      readln(element);
   end;
   close(outfile);
end.
```

Here is the companion example to read the data file generated by the first program in Turbo Pascal:

```pascal
program filein;
var
   infname : string[14];
   infile : file of integer;
   element : integer;
begin
```

```
    infname := 'infile.dat';
    assign(infile,infname);
    reset(infile);
    while not eof(infile) do
    begin
        read(infile,element);
        writeln('Data: ',element);
    end;
    close(infile);
end.
```

Well, that's not so bad, is it? Unfortunately, you will find that not all conversion problems are this simple. Just keep in mind that in Standard Pascal the file pointer starts out set to the first element of the file, and it is updated to the next element each time the GET or PUT statement is executed. Data is not transferred from a file until the GET statement is executed or to a file until the PUT statement is executed, then the pointer is set to the next position to be read or written in the file. Good luck.

## CHAPTER SIXTEEN

Advanced Programs

This chapter provides some useful example application programs which make use of disk files as discussed in the previous chapter. These programs can be used "as-is" or as a basis for building more complex programs.

The following programs provide some examples of simple file I/O operations.

16.1 File Typer

This program functions in a similar manner to the DOS TYPE command and will list a text file to the screen.

```
program type1;
const
   bell = 07;

var
   infile : text;
   infname : string[20];
   goodfile : boolean;

procedure open_file;
begin
   repeat
      write ('Input filename → ');
      readln (infname);
      assign(infile,infname);
      {$I-} reset(infile) {$I+};
      goodfile := (IOresult = 0);
      if not goodfile then
```

```
    begin
      write (chr(bell));
      writeln ('FILE ',infname,' NOT FOUND');
      delay(3000)
    end;
  until goodfile;
end; {open_file}

procedure display;
var
  ch : char;
begin
  while not eof(infile) do
    begin
    read(infile,ch);
    ch := chr(ord(ch) and 127); {reset hi bit for WordStar files}
    write(ch);
    end;
end; {display}


begin
  ClrScr;
  writeln('Type File to Screen');
  writeln;
  open_file;
  display;
  close(infile);
end. {type1}
```

16.2 File Lister

This program will list a text file to the system printer device. It prints a heading with the file name and page number on each page.

```
program tlist1;
const
  lines_per_page = 66;
  chars_per_line = 79;
  bottom_margin = 8;
var
  infile : text;
  infname : string[20];
  max_lines : integer;
```

```
procedure open_file;
const
   bell = 07;
var
   ans : string[10];
   goodfile : boolean;

begin
   repeat
      write('Enter input file: ');
      readln(infname);
      assign(infile,infname);
      {$I-} reset(infile) {$I+};
      goodfile := (IOresult = 0);
      if not goodfile then
      begin
         write (chr(bell));
         writeln ('FILE ',infname,' NOT FOUND');
         delay(2000)
      end;
   until goodfile;
end; {open_file}


procedure list;
var
   p,
   line : integer;
   txtline,
   printline : string[255];

procedure print_heading(page:integer);
const
   space = ' ';
begin
   if page <> 1 then writeln(lst,chr(12));
   write(lst,'File: ',infname,space:(60-(5+length(infname))));
   writeln(lst,'Page #',page:3);
   writeln(lst);
   writeln(lst);
end; {print_heading}


begin {list}
   p := 0;
   while not eof(infile) do
   begin
```

```
        p := p + 1;
        print_heading(p);
        line := 4;
        while (not eof(infile)) and (line < max_lines) do
        begin
          readln(infile,txtline);
          writeln(lst,txtline);
          line := line + 1;
        end;
      end;
    writeln(lst,chr(12));
  end; {list}


begin {tlist1}
    max_lines := lines_per_page - bottom_margin;
    writeln('Turbo Pascal Program Lister - Version 1');
    writeln('Formats and lists files to the printer (LPT1:) device');
    writeln;
    open_file;
    list;
    close(infile);
    writeln;
    writeln('- done -');
end. {tlist1}
```

16.3 File Lister #2

This program will list a Turbo Pascal program or other file to the system list
device. It is similar to the previous program except that input lines over 79
characters long are broken into multiple lines for printing on 8½ by 11-inch
paper. It illustrates how a Pascal program can be expanded easily by adding
procedures to the basic structure (as above).

```
program tlist2;
const
    lines_per_page = 66;
    chars_per_line = 79;
    bottom_margin = 8;
var
    infile : text;
    infname : string[20];
    max_lines : integer;
```

```pascal
procedure open_file;
const
   bell = 07;
var
   ans : string[10];
   goodfile : boolean;

begin
  repeat
     write('Enter input file: ');
     readln(infname);
     assign(infile,infname);
     {$I-} reset(infile) {$I+};
     goodfile := (IOresult = 0);
     if not goodfile then
     begin
        write (chr(bell));
        writeln ('FILE ',infname,' NOT FOUND');
        delay(2000)
     end;
   until goodfile;
end; {open_file}

procedure list;
var
   p,
   line : integer;
   txtline,
   printline : string[255];

procedure print_heading(page:integer);
const
   space = ' ';
begin
   if page <> 1 then writeln(lst,chr(12));                {form feed}
   write(lst,'File: ',infname,space:(60-(5+length(infname))));
   writeln(lst,'Page #',page:3);
   writeln(lst);
   writeln(lst);
end; {print_heading}

procedure break_line;
var
   work_str,
   new_str : string[255];
```

```
      indx,
      len : integer;
      ch : char;
   begin
      work_str := txtline;
      repeat
         ch := chr(0);
         len := length(work_str);
         if len > chars_per_line then
         begin
            indx := chars_per_line + 1;
            while (ch <> ' ') and (indx > 0) do
            begin
               indx := indx - 1;
               ch := work_str[indx];
            end;
            new_str := copy(work_str,1,indx);
            delete(work_str,1,indx);
         end
         else
            new_str := work_str;
         writeln(lst,new_str);
         line := line + 1;
         if line >= max_lines then
         begin
            p := p + 1;
            print_heading(p);
            line := 4;
         end;
      until len <= chars_per_line;
   end; {break_line}

begin {list}
   p := 0;
   while not eof(infile) do
   begin
      p := p + 1;
      print_heading(p);
      line := 4;
      while (not eof(infile)) and (line < max_lines) do
      begin
         readln(infile,txtline);
         if length(txtline) < chars_per_line then
         begin
            writeln(lst,txtline);
```

```
            line := line + 1;
        end
        else
            break_line;
    end;
  end;
  writeln(lst,chr(12));
end; {list}


begin {tlist2}
    max_lines := lines_per_page - bottom_margin;
    writeln('Turbo Pascal Program Lister - Version 2');
    writeln('Formats and lists files to the printer (LPT1:) device');
    writeln;
    open_file;
    list;
    close(infile);
    writeln;
    writeln('- done -');
end. {tlist2}
```

16.4 File Dump

This program will dump the contents of a file in both HEX and ASCII to the screen. It can be used to display the contents of any file. The file may also be listed to the printer by pressing 〈Ctrl-P〉 before starting the program.

```
program dump;
const
    bell = 07;
    version = '12';


type
    datstr = string[20];
    datafile = file of byte;


var
    infile : datafile;
    infname : string[20];
    asciitext : string[20];
    sec : real;
    sec1 : real;
    col : byte;
```

```pascal
    dat : byte;        code
    msec : byte;
    hsec : byte;       high
    lsec : byte;       low
    inch : char;
    quit : boolean;

procedure trans(indat:byte);
var
    ch : char;

function xlt(bdat: byte) : char;
begin
    case bdat of
        0..9 : xlt := chr(bdat + ord('0'));
        10..15 : xlt := chr(bdat + ord('A')-10);
    end;
end; {xlt}

begin {trans}
    ch := xlt(indat div 16);      left
    write(ch);
    ch := xlt(indat mod 16);      right
    write(ch);
end; {trans}

procedure uppercase(var str : datstr);
var
    indx,len : integer;

begin
    len := length(str);
    for indx := 1 to len do
        str[indx] := upcase(str[indx])
end; {uppercase}

procedure open_file;
var
    goodfile : boolean;


begin
    repeat
        write ('Input filename → ');
        readln (infname);
```

```
    if length(infname) > 0 then
    begin
      assign(infile,infname);
      {$I-} reset(infile) {$I+};
      goodfile := (IOresult = 0);
      if not goodfile then
      begin
        write (chr(bell));
        writeln ('FILE ',infname,' NOT FOUND');
        delay(3000)
      end;
    end
    else
      quit := true;
  until goodfile or quit;
end; {open_file}

procedure write_header;
begin
  write('Address 00 01 02 03 04 05 06 07 08 09 0A 0B 0C 0D 0E 0F ');
  writeln('      ASCII TEXT');
  writeln;
end;

procedure process;
begin
  msec := trunc(sec / 65536.0);
  trans(msec);
  write(' ');
  sec1 := sec - (msec * 65536.0);
  hsec := trunc(sec1 / 256);
  lsec := trunc(sec1 - (hsec * 256.0));
  trans(hsec);
  trans(lsec);
  write(' ');
  for col := 1 to 16 do
  begin
    if not eof(infile) then
    begin
      read(infile,dat);
      trans(dat);
      if dat in [32..126] then
        asciitext[col] := chr(dat)
      else
        asciitext[col] := '.';
```

```
      end
      else
      begin
         write(' ');
         dat := 0;
         asciitext[col] := ' ';
      end;
      write(' ');
      if col = 8 then write(' ');
    end;
    writeln(' *',asciitext,'*');
    if lsec = 240 then {end of screen page}
    begin
       write('Hit any key to continue.');
       read(kbd,inch);
       write(chr(13));
       writeln('      ');
       writeln;
       write_header;
    end;
    sec := sec + 16;
end; {process}

begin {dump}
   asciitext[0] := chr(16);
   sec := 256;
   quit := false;
   ClrScr;
   writeln;
   writeln('File HEX and ASCII DUMP program Version ',version);
   writeln;
   open_file;
   if not quit then
   begin
      uppercase(infname);
      if (pos('.COM',infname)=0) then sec := 0;
      ClrScr;
      write_header;
      while not eof(infile) do
         process;
      close(infile);
   end;
   if not quit then
   begin
      writeln;
```

```
        writeln('- eof -');
    end;
end. {dump}
```

16.5 Upper to Lower case File Conversion

This program will convert a Turbo Pascal program file to all lower case, except for literal strings and comments. The program is broken into procedure blocks and uses the correct method of I/O result checking when opening files.

```
program lower;
var
    infile : text;
    outfile : text;

procedure open_files;
const
    bell = 07;
var
    infname : string[20];
    outfname : string[20];
    ans : string[10];
    goodfile : boolean;

begin
    repeat
        write('Enter input file: ');
        readln(infname);
        assign(infile,infname);
        {SI-} reset(infile) {SI+};
        goodfile := (IOresult = 0);
        if not goodfile then
        begin
            write (chr(bell));
            writeln ('FILE ',infname,' NOT FOUND');
            delay(2000)
        end;
    until goodfile;
    repeat
        write('Enter output file: ');
        readln(outfname);
```

```pascal
      assign (outfile,outfname);
      {Sl-} reset(outfile) {Sl+};
      goodfile := (IOresult <> 0);
      if not goodfile then
      begin
         write (chr(bell));
         write ('FILE ',outfname,' EXISTS, OVERWRITE? (y/n) ');
         readln (ans);
         goodfile := (UpCase(ans[1]) = 'Y')
      end;
   until goodfile;
   rewrite(outfile)
end; {open_files}

procedure process;
var
   ch : char;
   lastch : char;
   flagbrace : boolean;
   flagquote : boolean;
   flagcom : boolean;
begin
   flagbrace := false;
   flagquote := false;
   flagcom := false;
   lastch := ' ';
   while not eof(infile) do
   begin
      read(infile,ch);
      case ch of
         '{' : flagbrace := true;
         '}' : flagbrace := false;
      end;

   if (lastch = '(') and (ch = '*') then flagcom := true;
   if (lastch = '*') and (ch = ')') then flagcom := false;

   if (not flagbrace) and (not flagcom) then
      if ch = chr(39) then flagquote := not flagquote;

   if (not flagbrace) and (not flagquote) and (not flagcom) and
         (ch in ['A'..'Z']) then
      ch := chr(ord(ch) - ord('A') + ord('a'));
   write(outfile,ch);
   lastch := ch;
```

```
   end;
   writeln(outfile);
end; {process}

begin {lower}
   writeln('Text file upper to lower case change program);
   writeln('Program ignores all text within single quotes, "*)" and braces');
   writeln;
   open_files;
   process;
   close(infile);
   close(outfile)
   writeln;
   writeln(' - done -');
end. {lower}
```

16.6 File Detab

This program will remove any ASCII TAB characters from a Turbo Pascal source file and replace them with the correct number of spaces to maintain the intended format. This is appropriate for files imported from other Pascals, as the Turbo Editor will not use imbedded tabs when displaying a program file on the screen.

```
program detab;
const
   null = 00;
   tab = 09;
   lf = 10;
   ff = 12;
   cr = 13;
   space = 32;
   tabsize = 8; {set tab stops}

var
   infile : text;
   outfile : text;
   col : integer;
   ch : char;

procedure open_files;
const
   bell = 07;
var
   infname : string[20];
```

```
      outfname : string[20];
      ans : string[10];
      goodfile : boolean;

begin
  repeat
      write('Enter input file: ');
      readln(infname);
      assign(infile,infname);
      {$I-} reset(infile) {$I+};
      goodfile := (IOresult = 0);
      if not goodfile then
      begin
        write (chr(bell));
        writeln ('FILE ',infname,' NOT FOUND');
        delay(2000)
      end;
  until goodfile;
  repeat
      write('Enter output file: ');
      readln(outfname);
      assign (outfile,outfname);
      {$I-} reset(outfile) {$I+};
      goodfile := (IOresult <> 0);
      if not goodfile then
      begin
        write (chr(bell));
        write ('FILE ',outfname,' EXISTS, OVERWRITE? (y/n) ');
        readln (ans);
        goodfile := (UpCase(ans[1]) = 'Y')
      end;
  until goodfile;
  rewrite(outfile)
end; {open_files}


procedure process;
begin
  col := 0;
  while not eof(infile) do
  begin
      read(infile,ch);
      case ord(ch) of
      cr,ff : begin
                col := 0;
                write(outfile,ch);
```

```
            end;
      If   : write(outfile,ch);
      tab : repeat
                  col := col + 1;
                  write(outfile,chr(space))
            until (col mod tabsize = 0);

            else
              if ord(ch) <> null then
              begin
                col := col + 1;
                write(outfile,ch);
              end;
            end;
          end;
        writeln(outfile);
      end; {process}

begin {detab}
  writeln;
  writeln('Text file detabify program');
  writeln;
  open_files;
  process;
  close(infile);
  close(outfile)
  writeln;
  writeln('- done -');
end. {detab}
```

16.7 Filter

This program is an example of a simple text file filter which will reset the eighth
bit of all characters in a text file to zero, so that WordStar files can be used as
standard ASCII files. It is written in modular fashion to allow easy addition of
more features as needed.

```
program filter;
{Converts WordStar files to ASCII text files }
const
  nummax = 200; {Maximum input line length}
  null = 00;
  bell = 07;
```

```
  lf  =  10;
  ff  =  12;
  cr  =  13;
  space  =  32;

var
  infile : text;
  outfile : text;
  numlist : array[1..nummax] of byte;
  cnt : integer;
  quit : boolean;
procedure open_files;
var
  infname : string[20];
  outfname : string[20];
  ans : string[10];
  goodfile : boolean;

begin
  repeat
    write('Enter input file: ');
    readln(infname);
    assign(infile,infname);
    {$I-} reset(infile) {$I+   };
    goodfile := (IOresult = 0);
    if not goodfile then
    begin
      write (chr(bell));
      writeln ('FILE ',infname,' NOT FOUND');
      delay(2000)
    end;
  until goodfile;
  repeat
    write('Enter output file: ');
    readln(outfname);
    assign (outfile,outfname);
    {$I-} reset(outfile) {$I+};
    goodfile := (IOresult <> 0);
    if not goodfile then
    begin
      write (chr(bell));
      write ('FILE ',outfname,' EXISTS, OVERWRITE? (y/n) ');
      readln (ans);
      goodfile := (UpCase(ans[1]) = 'Y')
    end;
```

```pascal
    until goodfile;
    rewrite(outfile)
end; {open_files}

procedure get_line;
var
    ch : char;
    num : byte;
    lonum : byte;

begin
    lonum:=0;
    cnt:=0;
    while not eof(infile) and (lonum()lf) do
    begin
        cnt:=cnt+1;
        read(infile,ch);
        num:=ord(ch);
        lonum:=(num and 127);
        numlist[cnt]:=num;
    end
end; {get_line}

procedure translate_line;
var
    indx1 : integer;
    chnum : byte;
begin
    for indx1:=1 to cnt do
    begin
        chnum:=numlist[indx1] and 127;
        if chnum () null then
        write (outfile, chr(chnum));
    end
end; {translate_line}

procedure process;
begin
    while not eof(infile) do
    begin
        get_line;
        translate_line;
    end
end; {process}
```

```
procedure exit1;
begin
   ClrScr;
   writeln('Translation completed!');
   writeln(outfile);
   close(infile);
   close(outfile)
end; {exit1}

begin {filter}
   ClrScr;
   writeln;
   writeln('WordStar to ASCII Filter Program');
   writeln;
   begin
      open_files;
      process;
      exit1
   end
end. {filter}
```

16.8 File Comparison

This program performs a simple file comparison between two files and reports the differences found. It is mainly useful for comparing similar files of about the same length.

```
program filecomp;
const
   bell = 07;

type
   datstr = string[14];
   datafile = file of byte;

var
   infile1,
   infile2 : datafile;
   infname1,
   infname2 : datstr;
   ans : char;
   quit,
   prnt : boolean;
```

```
procedure trans(indat:byte); {convert to hexadecimal}
var
   ch : char;

function xlt(bdat: byte) : char;
begin
   case bdat of
   0..9 : xlt := chr(bdat + ord('0'));
   10..15 : xlt := chr(bdat + ord('A')-10);
   end;
end; {xlt}

begin {trans}
     ch := xlt(indat div 16);
     write(ch);
     ch := xlt(indat mod 16);
     write(ch);
end; {trans}

procedure uppercase(var str : datstr);
{change a string to all uppercase chars}
var
   indx,len : Integer;
begin
   len := length(str);
   for indx := 1 to len do
     str[indx] := upcase(str[indx])
end; {uppercase}

procedure open_files;
var
   goodfile : boolean;
begin
  repeat
     write ('Input filename #1 f13l ');
     readln (infname1);
     if length(infname1) > 0 then
     begin
        assign(infile1,infname1);
        {$I-} reset(infile1) {$I+};
        goodfile := (IOresult = 0);
        if not goodfile then
        begin
           write (chr(bell));
           writeln ('FILE ',infname1,' NOT FOUND');
```

```
             delay(3000)
         end;
      end
      else
         quit := true;
   until goodfile or quit;
   repeat
      write ('Input filename #2 f13l ');
      readln (infname2);
      if length(infname2) ) 0 then
      begin
         assign(infile2,infname2);
         {SI-} reset(infile2) {SI+};
         goodfile := (IOresult = 0);
         if not goodfile then
         begin
            write (chr(bell));
            writeln ('FILE ',infname2,' NOT FOUND');
            delay(3000)
         end;
      end
      else
         quit := true;
   until goodfile or quit;
end; {open_files}

procedure process;
var
   sec,
   sec1 : real;
   col,
   dat1,
   dat2,
   msec,
   hsec,
   lsec : byte;
   ch1,
   ch2 : char;

begin
   sec := 256;
   uppercase(infname1);
   if (pos('.COM',infname1)=0) then sec := 0;
   while (not eof(infile1)) and not eof(infile2)) do
   begin
```

```
    begin
      read(infile1,dat1);
      read(infile2,dat2);
      if (dat1 () dat2) or prnt then
      begin
        msec := trunc(sec / 65536.0)·
        trans(msec);
        write(' ');
        sec1 := sec - (msec * 65536.0);
        hsec := trunc(sec1 / 256);
        lsec := trunc(sec1 - (hsec * 256.0));
        trans(hsec);
        trans(lsec);
        write(' ');
        trans(dat1);
        if dat1 in [32..126] then
          ch1 := chr(dat1)
        else
          ch1 := '.';
        write(' ',ch1,' ');
        trans(dat2);
        if dat2 in [32..126] then
          ch2 := chr(dat2)
        else
          ch2 := '.';
        writeln(' ',ch2);
      end;
    end;
    sec := sec + 1;
  end;
end; {process}

begin {filecomp}
  quit := false;
  ClrScr;
  writeln;
  writeln('File HEX and ASCII COMPARE program ');
  writeln;
  open_files;
  if not quit then
  begin
    writeln;
    write('Print all bytes? (y/n) - ');
    readln(ans);
    prnt := Upcase(ans) = 'Y';
```

```
      process;
      close(infile1);
      close(infile2);
   end;
   if not quit then
   begin
      writeln;
      writeln('- eof -');
   end;
end. {filecomp}
```

16.9 Phone Book

This program is an expanded version of the array-based phone book program presented earlier. Maxlist may be expanded to about 70 entries when using the demonstration compiler. The top limit is much higher (depending on your installed memory) when using a commercial version of Turbo Pascal.

The reader may wish to add the ability to edit individual entries in the data base. (See examples POINTER1.PAS and POINTER2.PAS in Chapter 14.)

```
program contact4;
const
   maxlist = 10;

type
   addr = record
                street : string[20];
                city : string[15];
                state : string[2];
                zip : string[5];
           end;
   list_rec = record
                  name : string[40];
                  address : addr;
                  telephone : string[12];
              end;
   list_array_type = array [1..maxlist] of list_rec;
   data_rec = record
                  rec_count : integer;
                  data_list : list_array_type;
              end;

var
   contact_list : data_rec;
```

```pascal
    quit : boolean;
    answer : string[4];
    ch : char;
    outfile : file of data_rec;
    newfile : boolean;

procedure open_file;
const
  bell = 07;

var
  outfname : string[20];
  ans : string[10];

begin
  write('Enter work filename: ');
  readln(outfname);
  assign (outfile,outfname);
  {$I-} reset(outfile) {$I+};
  newfile := (IOresult <> 0);
  if not newfile then
  begin
    write (chr(bell));
    write ('File ',outfname,' exists, Overwrite or Use data? (o/u ')
    readln (ans);
    if (UpCase(ans[1]) = 'O') then
    begin
      rewrite(outfile);
      newfile := true;
    end;
  end
  else
    rewrite(outfile);
end; {open_file}


procedure enter;
var
  index : integer;

begin
  index := 0;
  repeat
    ClrScr;
    index := index + 1;
    writeln('Record #',index);
```

```pascal
      with contact_list.data_  list[index] do
      begin
        write('Enter name: ');
        readln(name);
        write('Enter street address: ');
        readln(address.street);
        write('Enter city: ');
        readln(address.city);
        write('Enter 2 letter state code: ');
        readln(address.state);
        write('Enter 5 digit zip code: ');
        readln(address.zip);
        write('Enter telephone number: ');
        readln(telephone);
        writeln;
      end;
      write('Enter another record? (Y/N) - ');
      readln(answer);
      quit := (answer <> 'Y') and (answer <> 'y');
    until (index = maxlist) or quit;
    contact_list.rec_count := index;
end; {enter}


procedure load;
begin
  read(outfile,contact_list);
end; {load}


procedure retrieve;
var
  index,
  index1,
  index2 : integer;

begin
  index := contact_list.rec_count;
  repeat
    repeat
      ClrScr;
      writeln('Records available are:');
      for index1 := 1 to index do
        writeln(index1,'. ',contact_list.data_list[index1].name);
      writeln;
      write('Enter record # to retrieve: ');
      readln(index2);
```

```
      until (index2 > 0) and (index2 <= index);
      ClrScr;
      writeln('Record #',index2);
      with contact_list.data_list[index2] do
      begin
         writeln('Name: ',name);
         with address do
         begin
            writeln('Street address: ',street);
            writeln('City: ',city);
            writeln('State code: ',state);
            writeln('Zip: ',zip);
         end;
         writeln('Telephone number: ',telephone);
         writeln;
      end;
      write('Find another record? (Y/N) - ');
      readln(answer);
      quit := (answer <> 'Y') and (answer <> 'y');
   until quit;
end; {retrieve}

procedure save;
begin
   close(outfile);
   rewrite(outfile);
   write(outfile,contact_list);
end; {save}

begin {contact4}
   writeln('Contact list file program - Version 4');
   writeln;
   write('Enter Q to quit or any other character to continue - ');
   read(kbd,ch);
   writeln;
   if not (ch in ['Q','q']) then
   begin
      quit := false;
      open_file;
      if newfile then
      begin
         enter;
         retrieve;
         save;
      end
```

```
      else
      begin
        load;
        retrieve;
      end;
      close(outfile);
      writeln;
      writeln('- done -');
    end
  else
    writeln('Program terminated');
end. {contact4}
```

## CHAPTER SEVENTEEN

Machine Level Interface

Turbo Pascal is somewhat unique among high-level languages in that it provides a powerful set of built-in tools for interfacing Pascal programs to machine (hardware) level operations. In this chapter we will briefly describe these tools in the IBM PC version of Turbo Pascal. The use of these advanced machine level operations is beyond the scope of this book, and so only reference information is included in this chapter.

Although a detailed knowledge of assembly language and the BIOS and DOS functions in the IBM PC is helpful, it is not absolutely required. However, a good 8088 assembly language book and the DOS technical manuals are recommended for those who wish to explore this topic in depth.

Turbo Pascal includes the capability for bit manipulation of integer variables with the SHL and SHR operators which have been discussed in earlier sections. These operators will not be discussed further here. A reference on binary and hexadecimal numbers is included in the Appendix.

17.1 Absolute Address Operations

Turbo Pascal allows variables to be declared to reside at absolute machine addresses. A number of functions are provided for absolute address operations. Predefined arrays are also provided for working with hardware registers, memory, and ports directly. Pointers may be set to specific locations as well.

ABSOLUTE LOCATIONS

The reserved word ABSOLUTE is used to place a variable at a specific location in memory. The general form is:

var
    num : integer **absolute** $0000:$0100;

where the two constants are the segment base address and the offset within the segment. The standard functions CSEG (code segment) and DSEG (data segment) may be used in place of the current segment base address as:

var
    num : integer **absolute** CSEG:$0100;

ABSOLUTE FUNCTIONS

The following functions are provided to return information about variable addresses and system pointers.

Addr(name)

ADDR returns the address in memory of the first byte of a variable with identifier *name* as a 32-bit pointer. Array and record elements may be specified.

Ofs(name)

OFS returns the integer value of the offset in the segment of the first byte of the object with the identifier *name*.

Seg(name)

SEG returns the integer value of the segment containing the first byte of the object with the identifier *name*.

Cseg

CSEG returns the base value of the current **code** segment as an integer.

Dseg

DSEG returns the base value of the current **data** segment as an integer.

Sseg

SSEG returns the base value of the current **stack** segment as an integer.

17.2 Inline Code

Turbo Pascal allows actual machine object code to be included in Turbo programs as INLINE code. Such programs can be called as procedures, functions, or blocks. Variable identifiers are allowed in INLINE code segments.

The general form of the INLINE statement is:

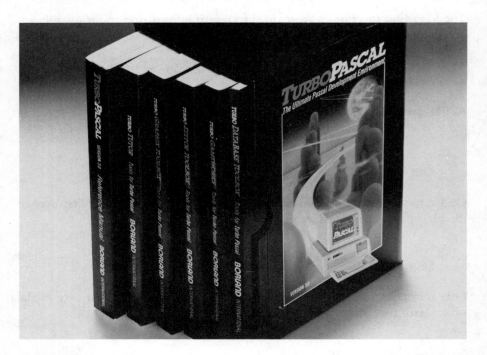

The complete Turbo Pascal product line, conveniently packaged. Photo courtesy of Borland International.

inline
```
( $00/ $00/ $00/ $00/
$00/data/ $00/ $00);
```

and the code is generally in the form of assembled HEX like that produced by the MS-DOS DEBUG line assembler program.

17.3 Software Interrupts

Turbo Pascal provides the procedure INTR to preset the CPU registers and generate a software interrupt, and then return the resulting register values to the calling process at the completion of the interrupt. The INTR procedure is useful for accessing the built-in BIOS and DOS routines in the IBM PC and compatible computers. Refer to the *IBM PC Technical Reference Manual* for information on the BIOS functions available and the *DOS Technical Reference Manual* for information on the DOS functions available.

The procedure INTR uses a special record representing the 8088 CPU registers of the type:

This is what started it all—the Turbo Pascal Compiler/Editor package. Photo courtesy of Borland International.

```
type
    reg_type = record
                   ax,bx,cx,dx,bp,si,di,ds,es,flags: integer;
               end;
var
    regs : reg_type;
```

Of course, a free union variant record may be used to avoid conversions of the integer (16-bit) register values to the byte (8-bit) half register values used in some interrupt calls:

```
type
    regpack = record
                    case integer of
                        1: (ax,bx,cx,dx,bp,si,di,ds,es,flags: integer);
                        2: (al,ah,bl,bh,cl,ch,dl,dh       : byte)
              end;
var
    regs : regpack;
```

In this case, the variant case is selected based on the variable identifier referred to.
    The general form of the INTR procedure is:

```
INTR(InterruptNo, regs)
```

Required register values are set in variable *regs* before the INTR call, and when
the interrupt terminates, *regs* will contain any values returned by the interrupt
service routine.
    The MSDOS procedure is a special "shorthand" form of the INTR procedure
used for accessing the operating system functions in PC-DOS and MS-DOS.
This procedure allows easy access to the full power of the operating system. It
operates similarly to the INTR procedure and generates an INT $21 (invoke
DOS function). This procedure has the form:

```
MSDOS(regs);
```

and is identical in effect to the procedure statement:

```
INTR($21,regs);
```

Of course, the required register values must be properly initialized before the
call to DOS. Returned values are available in the register variables upon completion of the call. To use the DOS functions, the requested DOS function number
is placed in the high byte of the AX register (AH) before the call. Refer to the
MS-DOS or PC-DOS *Technical Reference Manual* for detailed information on
each DOS function.

17.4 DOS Interface Examples

This section includes several examples of programs which interface to DOS
functions. Some familiarity with DOS functions and assembly language are
assumed, but the programs may be used as presented as a basis for learning
more about the machine level interface of Turbo Pascal.

SYSTEM TIME AND DATE

These two programs get the current system time and date from DOS. Note that the high and low bytes of the 16-bit register values are extracted using this technique:

```
hr := cx shr 8;              { get high byte }
min := cx mod 256;           { get low byte }
```

Turbo Pascal functions HI() and LO() could also be used:

```
hr := hi(cx);
min := lo(cx);
```

or the free union variant record described above could be used:

```
hr := ch;
min := cl;
```

but watch out for using "ch" as a character variable in the same program.

```
program systime;
type
  strtime = string[11];

function time : strtime;
type
  registers = record
                ax,bx,cx,dx,bp,si,ds,es,flags: integer;
              end;
var
  regrec            : registers;
  hour, minute, second,
  hundredth         : string[2];
  cx , dx           : integer;

begin
  with regrec do
  begin
    ax := $2C00; { DOS get time function }
  end;
  msdos(regrec);
  with regrec do
  begin
```

```
      str(cx shr 8, hour);                    { convert byte values to strings }
      str(cx mod 256, minute);                { for easy output formatting }
      str(dx shr 8, second);
      str(dx mod 256, hundredth);
   end;
   if length(hour) = 1 then insert(' ',hour ,1);
   if length(minute) = 1 then insert('0',minute,1);
   if length(second) = 1 then insert('0',second,1);
   if length(hundredth) = 1 then insert('0',hundredth,1);
   time := hour + ':' + minute + ':' + second + '.' + hundredth
end; {time}


begin {systime}
   writeln;
   write('The current system time is ',time,'.');
end. {systime}



program sysdate;
type
   strdate = string[10];


function date : strdate;
type
   registers = record
                   ax,bx,cx,dx,bp,si,ds,es,flags: integer;
               end;
var
   regrec : registers;
   month , day : string[2];
   year : string[4];
   cx , dx : integer;


begin
   with regrec do
   begin
      ax := $2A00; { DOS get date function }
   end;
   msdos(regrec);
   with regrec do
   begin
      str(cx, year);
      str(dx mod 256, day);
      str(dx shr 8, month);
   end;
```

```
   if length(month) = 1 then insert(' ',month,1);
   if length(day ) = 1 then insert('0',day,1 );
   date := month + '-' + day + '-' + year;
end; {date}


begin {sysdate}
  writeln;
  write('The current system date is ',date,'.');
end. {sysdate}
```

EVENT TIMER

The event timer program can be used to time program operations (with only
a few modifications) or to time real world events. Not counting user reaction
time, it should be accurate to a hundredth of a second.

```
program timer;
var
  ans : char;
  hr1, hr2, hr3,
  min1,min2,min3,
  sec1, sec2, sec3,
  hun1, hun2, hun3 : integer;


procedure get_time (var hr,min,sec,hund:integer);
type
  registers = record
                  ax,bx,cx,dx,bp,si,ds,es,flags: integer;
              end;
var
  regrec              : registers;
  cx , dx             : integer;
begin
  with regrec do
  begin
    ax := $2C shl 8; {system clock DOS call}          {$2C00}
  end;
  msdos(regrec);
  with regrec do
  begin
    hr := cx shr 8;
    min := cx mod 256;
    sec := dx shr 8;
    hund := dx mod 256;
```

```pascal
    end;
end; {get_time}

procedure display_time (hr,min,sec,hund:integer);
type
    strtime = string[11];
var
    time : strtime;
    hour,minute,
    second, hundredth : string[2];
begin
    str(hr,hour);                 {convert integer values to strings}
    str(min,minute);             {for easy output formatting }
    str(sec,second);
    str(hund,hundredth);

    if length(hour) = 1 then insert(' ',hour ,1);
    if length(minute) = 1 then insert('0',minute,1);
    if length(second) = 1 then insert('0',second,1);
    if length(hundredth) = 1 then insert('0',hundredth,1);
    time := hour + ':' + minute + ':' + second + '.' + hundredth;
    writeln(time);
end; {display_time}

procedure calc_time;
begin
    hun3 := hun2 - hun1;
    if hun3 < 0 then
    begin
        hun3 := hun3 + 100;
        sec1 := sec1 + 1;
    end;
    sec3 := sec2 - sec1;
    if sec3 < 0 then
    begin
        sec3 := sec3 + 60;
        min1 := min1 + 1;
    end;
    min3 := min2 - min1;
    if min3 < 0 then
    begin
        min3 := min3 + 60;
        hr1 := hr1 + 1;
    end;
    hr3 := hr2 - hr1;
```

```
    if hr3 < 0 then
    begin
        hr3 := hr3 + 24;
    end;
end; {calc_time}

begin {timer}
    writeln('Event timer program');
    writeln;
    write('Hit any key to start timer, and again to stop');
    read(kbd,ans);
    get_time(hr1,min1,sec1,hun1);
    writeln;
    writeln;
    write('Start time: ');
    display_time(hr1,min1,sec1,hun1);
    read(kbd,ans);
    get_time(hr2,min2,sec2,hun2);
    write('Stop time: ');
    display_time(hr2,min2,sec2,hun2);
    writeln;
    calc_time;
    write('Total time: ');
    display_time(hr3,min3,sec3,hun3);
    writeln;
    writeln('- done -');
end. {timer}
```

DIRECTORY ACCESS

MS-DOS and PC-DOS versions 2.0 and later provide two methods for accessing the directory information on a disk. The first method is compatible with older DOS versions 1.0 and 1.1, while the second method using file handles is not. Here is a simple example of the first method:

```
program direct;

{This program displays the default directory. It works with MS-DOS (or PC-DOS)
versions 1 and 2. }

type
    regpack = record
                    case integer of
                        1: (ax,bx,cx,dx,bp,si,di,ds,es,flags: integer);
```

```pascal
                     2: (al,ah,bl,bh,cl,ch,dl,dh : byte)
           end;

  fcbarray = array[0..36] of char;
const
  getdta = $1a; {DOS calls - set Disk Transfer Address }
  get1stdir = $11; { - get 1st dir entry }
  getnextdir = $12; { - get next dir entry }

var
  filestr,
  filename: string[14];
  dfcb,
  dta: fcbarray;

procedure callDTA; {set Disk Transfer Address}
var
  regs: regpack;

begin
  with regs do begin
    ah := getdta;
    ds := seg(dta);
    dx := ofs(dta);
    MsDos(regs)
  end
end; {callDTA}

procedure calldir(calltype : byte; var errflag : byte);
var
  regs: regpack;

begin
  with regs do begin
    ah := calltype;
    cx := 0;
    ds := seg(dfcb);
    dx := ofs(dfcb);
    MsDos(regs);
    errflag:= al
  end
end; {calldir}

procedure directory;
var
```

```
      i,
      err: byte;

begin
      clrscr;
      dfcb[0]:= chr(0);                             { set default drive }
      for i:= 1 to 11 do dfcb[i]:= '?';            { set search mask to ????????????}
      callDTA;                                      { set Disk Transfer Address }
      calldir(get1stdir, err);                      { get first entry matching mask }
      while err = 0 do
      begin
        filename:= '';
        for i:= 1 to 11 do
        begin
          filename := filename + dta[i];
          if i = 8 then filename := filename + '.';
        end;
        writeln(filename);
        calldir(getnextdir, err) { get next entry }
      end;
      writeln;
end; {directory}

begin {direct}
   directory
end {direct}
```

COMMAND LINE ARGUMENTS

The command tail, or the information typed after a program name on the command line at the DOS prompt ("A)") can be recovered for use by *compiled* Turbo Pascal programs. As there is no way to enter command line arguments for programs run in memory in Turbo versions 1.0 and 2.0, only compiled programs can demonstrate this technique. (Turbo 3.0 allows "setting" dummy command line parameters in the compiler options menu to enable the use of this feature in programs compiled to memory.) The command line parameters (up to 127 bytes) are located at ABSOLUTE CSEG:$80 at the beginning of the program. This data *must* be assigned to a variable immediately as the first operation of the program, or all but 32 characters will be lost.

Included here is a version of the simple file typer program presented earlier. This version makes use of command line parameters (if entered) to select the file to type, just like the DOS TYPE command. The compiled version of the program is also included (TYPE2.COM) to allow those readers without a commercial version of the Turbo compiler to run the program.

```
program type2;
const
   bell = 07;
   version = '3.1';
   date = 'Sept. 12, 1985';

type
   comstr = string[127];

var
   buffer : comstr;
   comline : comstr absolute cseg:$80;
   infile : text;

procedure open_file;
var
   indx : byte;
   infname : string[20];
   goodfile : boolean;
begin
   goodfile := false;
   if (pos('*',buffer) = 0) and          {check for wild card "*"}
      (pos('?',buffer) = 0) and          {check for wild card "?"}
      (length(buffer) > 0) then          {check for command line entry}
   begin
      indx := 1;
      while (ord(buffer[indx]) = $20) and (indx <= length(buffer)) do
      indx := indx + 1;
      infname := copy(buffer,indx,11);
      assign(infile,infname);
      {$I-} reset(infile) {$I+};
      goodfile := (IOresult = 0);
   end;
   if not goodfile then {ask for manual entry}
      repeat
         write ('Input filename -);
         readln (infname);
         assign(infile,infname);
         {$I-} reset(infile) {$I+};
         goodfile := (IOresult = 0);
         if not goodfile then
         begin
            write (chr(bell));
            writeln ('FILE ',infname,' NOT FOUND');
            delay(3000)
```

```
        end;
      until goodfile;
    writeln('File: ',infname);
    writeln;
  end; {open_file}


procedure display;
var
  ch : char;
begin
  while not eof(infile) do
    begin
      read(infile,ch);
      write(ch);
    end;
end; {display}


begin {type2}
  buffer := comline; {this must be done first!}
  ClrScr;
  writeln('Type File to Screen');
  writeln('Version ',version,' of ',date);
  writeln;
  open_file;
  display;
  close(infile);
end. {type2}
```

WILD CARDS

Accessing a group of files in Turbo Pascal is slightly more complex than accessing just one. The basic technique is the same as in the directory program presented earlier. However, the DTA variable used by the directory calls *getfirst* and *getnext* to store the search parameters MUST be preserved if other disk accesses are done between directory calls. This is accomplished by using two DTA variables and switching between them. Then any required disk operations may be done by the routines, which process each file found without destroying the directory search data.

The following example program is a combination of the list program and the directory program already presented. It will format and list all ".PAS" files on the default drive to the system printer.

The directory search mask is "hard coded" in, but the reader may wish to improve this program by adding user file specification capability including parsing, using both the "*" and "?" wild cards, and allowing other drive specifications.

Input could be either on the command line or by direct program entry. (Hint—use DOS function $29 to parse the user input search mask string.)

```
program listwild;

{This program lists files using wild cards. It works with MS-DOS (or PC-DOS)
versions 1 and 2. }

type
  regpack = record
                    case integer of
                          1: (ax,bx,cx,dx,bp,si,di,ds,es,flags: integer);
                          2: (al,ah,bl,bh,c,ch,dl,dh : byte)
              end;

  fcbarray = array[0..36] of char;
  strtype = string [14];

const
  getdta = $1a;
  get1stdir = $11;
  getnextdir = $12;

var
  inch : char;
  filestr,
  filename: strtype;
  dfcb,
  dta,
  dta2 : fcbarray;

function listproc(fname:strtype) : byte;

const
  lines_per_page = 66;
  chars_per_line = 79;
  bottom_margin = 8;

var
  infile : text;
  time1,
  date1 : string[8];
  infname : string[20];
  max_lines : integer;
  goodfile : boolean;
```

```pascal
type
  datetimetype = string[8];

function date: datetimetype;
  { returns current date in form '08/31/84'. }

var
  reg: regpack;
    y,m,d,w: datetimetype;
    i: integer;

begin
  reg.ah:= $2A;
  MSDOS(reg);
  str(reg.cx:4,y);
  delete(y,1,2);
  str(hi(reg.dx):2,m);
  str(lo(reg.dx):2,d);
  w:= m + '/' + d + '/' + y;
  for i:= 1 to length(w) do
    if w[i] = ' ' then w[i]:= '0';
  date:= w
end; {date}

function time: datetimetype;          { returns current time in form '08:13:59'. }
var
  reg: regpack;
    h,m,s,w: datetimetype;
    i: integer;

begin
  reg.ah:= $2C;
  MSDOS(reg);
  str(hi(reg.cx):2,h);
  str(lo(reg.cx):2,m);
  str(hi(reg.dx):2,s);
  w:= h + ':' + m + ':' + s;
  for i:= 1 to length(w) do
  if w[i] = ' ' then w[i]:= '0';
  time:= w;
end; {time}

procedure open_file;
const
  bell = 07;
```

```pascal
begin
   infname := fname;
   assign(infile,infname);
   {SI-} reset(infile) {SI+};
   goodfile := (IOresult = 0);
   if not goodfile then
   begin
      write (chr(bell));
      writeln ('FILE ',infname,' NOT FOUND');
      delay(2000)
   end;
end; {open_file}

procedure list;
var
   p,
   line : integer;
   txtline,
   printline : string[255];

procedure print_heading(page:integer);
const
   space = ' ';

var
   xx : integer;

begin
   if page <> 1 then writeln(lst,chr(12));                    {form feed}
   xx := (5+length(infname));
   write(lst,'File: ',infname,space:(25-xx));
   write(lst,date1,' ',time1);
   write(lst,space:20);
   writeln(lst,'Page #',page:3);
   writeln(lst);
   writeln(lst);
end; {print_heading}

procedure break_line;
var
   work_str,
   new_str : string[255];
   indx,
   len : integer;
   ch : char;
```

```
begin
   work_str := txtline;
   repeat
      ch := chr(0);
      len := length(work_str);
      if len > chars_per_line then
      begin
         indx := chars_per_line + 1;
         while (ch <> ' ') and (indx > 0) do
         begin
            indx := indx - 1;
            ch := work_str[indx];
         end;
         new_str := copy(work_str,1,indx);
         delete(work_str,1,indx);
      end
      else
         new_str := work_str;
      writeln(lst,new_str);
      line := line + 1;
      if line >= max_lines then
      begin
         p := p + 1;
         print_heading(p);
         line := 4;
      end;
   until len <= chars_per_line;
end; {break_line}

begin {list}
   p := 0;
   while not eof(infile) do
   begin
      p := p + 1;
      print_heading(p);
      line := 4;
      while (not eof(infile)) and (line < max_lines) do
      begin
         readln(infile,txtline);
         if length(txtline) < chars_per_line then
         begin
            writeln(lst,txtline);
            line := line + 1;
         end
         else
```

```
            break_line;
      end;
   end;
   writeln(lst,chr(12));
end; {list}                                    {form feed}

begin {list_proc}
   max_lines := lines_per_page - bottom_margin;
   open_file;
   if goodfile then
   begin
      time1 := time;
      date1 := date;
      list;
      close(infile);
      listproc := 0;
      writeln;
   writeln('- listing done -');
   end
   else
      listproc := 1;
end; {list_proc}


procedure setDTA(num:byte);                    {set Disk Transfer Address}
var
   regs: regpack;

begin
   with regs do begin
      ah := getdta;
      case num of
      1: begin
         ds := seg(dta);
         dx := ofs(dta);
        end;
      2: begin
         ds := seg(dta2);
         dx := ofs(dta2);
        end;
      end;
      MSDOS(regs)
   end
end; {setDTA}
```

```
procedure calldir(calltype : byte; var errflag : byte);
var
   regs: regpack;

begin
   with regs do begin
     ah := calltype;
     cx := 0;
     ds := seg(dfcb);
     dx := ofs(dfcb);
     MSDOS(regs);
     errflag:= al
   end
end; {calldir}

procedure find;
const
   space = ' ';
   period = '.';

var
   i,
   err: byte;
   mask : string[11];

begin
   mask := '????????PAS';                        { set mask to '*.pas'}
   dfcb[0]:= chr(0);                              { set default drive }
   for i:= 1 to 11 do dfcb[i]:= mask[i];          { set search mask }
   setDTA(1);                                     { set DTA }
   calldir(get1stdir, err);                       { get first entry matching mask }
   while err = 0 do
   begin
     filename:= '';
     for i:= 1 to 11 do
     begin
       if dta[i] <> space then
           filename := filename + dta[i];
       if i = 8 then filename := filename + period;
     end;
     writeln(filename);
     setDTA(2);
     err := listproc(filename);
     if err = 0 then
     begin
```

```
        setDTA(1);
        calldir(getnextdir, err); { get next entry }
    end;
  end;
  writeln;
end; {find}

begin {listwild}
  writeln('Wild card program lister');
  writeln('This program formats and lists all ".PAS" files on the');
  writeln('default drive to the system printer.');
  writeln;
  write('Press Q to stop, any other key to continue: ');
  readln(inch);
  if not (inch in ['Q','q']) then
    find
  else
    writeln('Program terminated');
end. {listwild}
```

## CHAPTER EIGHTEEN

Advanced Compiler Topics

Most of the following advanced topics apply only to commercial versions of the Turbo Pascal compiler, and can be reviewed in more detail in the *Turbo Pascal Reference Manual* supplied by Borland with the commercial versions of Turbo Pascal.

18.1 Main File

(commercial versions only)

The **M** or Main file is the name of the master file which contains any Include file {I$} compiler directives. The Work File can then be set to any of the Include files for editing. When a compilation is begun and the Work file name is different from the Main file name, the Work file is saved and the Main file is loaded into memory for compilation.

18.2 Compiler Directives

The Turbo compiler supports a number of compile-time options which are selected by including *compiler directives* in the source program file. These compiler directives are written inside comment delimiters [{ } or (* *)] and begin with a dollar ($) symbol. Several directives may be placed in a group, prefaced by a single dollar symbol and enclosed in one set of comment delimiters.

273

A plus sign (+) indicates the feature is enabled and a minus sign (-) indicates it is disabled. No spaces are allowed either before or after the dollar symbol. Here are some examples of valid directives:

```
{SB + }
{SI-,V-,R + }
(* SX-*)
{SI INCLUDE.FIL }
```

COMMON DIRECTIVES

The following directives (except for Include) are common to all versions of Turbo Pascal, including the demonstration version.

B -   I/O Mode Selection   Default B +
The B directive selects the default console I/O mode to be used for the standard INPUT and OUTPUT text files. When active, the CON: device is assigned to the standard files. When inactive, the TRM: device is used. See Chapter 15 for more details. This directive is global to an entire program block and cannot be redefined in the program.

C -   Control S and C   Default C +
The C directive allows the control characters CTRL-C and CTRL-S to interrupt I/O operations. When it is active, CTRL-C will interrupt program execution and CTRL-S will stop and restart screen output. The CTRL characters are only detected during console I/O operations. When inactive, the control characters are ignored. The checking slows screen I/O somewhat, so the feature should be disabled when display speed is important. This directive is global to an entire program block and cannot be redefined in the program.

I -   I/O Error Handling   Default I +
The I directive enables I/O error handling. When enabled all I/O operations are checked for errors and the program is halted if an error is detected. When disabled, the programmer is responsible for error detection and handling, using the IO Result function.

I -   Include Files
The I directive followed by a file name will cause the named file to be included in the compilation process at the location of the directive. Included files may not be nested—that is, they must not contain Include directives. A space should be placed before the closing comment delimiter to insure the file name is correctly interpreted by the compiler, as in this example:

{SI FILEIO.INC }

The filetype ".INC" is often used to identify include files and differentiate them from ".PAS" program files.

R -   Index Range Check   Default R-
The R directive enables run-time index checks. When active, all array indexing operations are checked to insure they are within defined bounds, and all assignments to scalar and subrange variables are checked to be within range. When inactive, no checks are performed. This feature should be used during program development; however, it does slow program execution.

V -   Var-parameter Type Checking   Default V +
The V directive controls type checking on strings passed as VAR parameters. When active, strict type checking is performed (i.e., the lengths of actual and formal parameters MUST match). When passive, lengths need not match.

U -   User Interrupt   Default U-
The U directive enables the CTRL-C user interrupt at ANY time during program execution (not just during console I/O as with the C directive). Use of this feature significantly slows program execution.

PC-DOS, MS-DOS, CP/M-86 DIRECTIVE

K -   Stack Checking   Default K +
The K directive controls checking for available stack space before each subprogram call, to prevent stack collisions. When passive, no checks are made.

TURBO 3.0 PC-DOS/MS-DOS 2.0 DIRECTIVES

The following directives are only available in PC-DOS and MS-DOS Turbo Pascal Version 3.0 and later. They control the use of DOS 2.0 and later file handles and are beyond the scope of this book.

G	Input File Buffer	Default G0
P	Output File Buffer	Default P0
D	Device Checking	Default D +
F	Number of Open Files	Default F16

CP/M 80 DIRECTIVES

The following directives are only available in CP/M 80 versions of Turbo Pascal. They control the type of code generated and the use of system memory and are beyond the scope of this book.

A	Absolute Code (non-recursive)	Default A+
W	Nesting of WITH Statements	Default W2
X	Array Optimization	Default X+

18.3 Compiler Options

(commercial versions only)

The compiler Options menu (selected by pressing **O** at the master menu) allows selection of the compiler mode (Memory, Com-file, or cHn-file), any "dummy" command line Parameters for testing in memory mode (Turbo 3.0 only), and Finding run-time errors in memory-compiled programs.

---

compile → **M**emory
             Com-file
             c**H**n-file

command line **P**arameters:

Find run-time error **Q**uit

〉

Figure 18-1 Turbo 3.0 Options Menu.

When the COM file option is selected, the compiler parameters will be displayed with the Options menu. These parameters may be changed to provide memory space for CHN files and externally linked routines.

             Memory
compile → **C**om-file
             c**H**n-file

minimum c**O**de segment size: 0000 (max 0D34 paragraphs)
minimum **D**ata segment size: 0000 (max 0FDC paragraphs)
m**I**nimum free dynamic memory: 0400 paragraphs
m**A**ximum free dynamic memory: A000 paragraphs

Find run-time error **Q**uit

)C

Figure 18-2 Turbo 3.0 Options Menu—COM file parameters.

Once the Options parameters are set, the user may return to the main menu by selecting **Q** for Quit Options Menu.

18.4 Include Files

(commercial versions only)

Turbo Pascal allows separate files containing declarations, procedures, or functions to be automatically included with the code in memory during compilation by use of the Include compiler directive. Included files may not be nested—that is, they may not contain Include directives. The general form of the Include directive is:

    {SI FILENAME.TYP }

NOTE that a space should always be provided after the file name and type to insure that it is interpreted correctly by the compiler.

18.5 Chain Programs

(commercial versions only)

Chain programs are compiled program files identical to regular Turbo Pascal compiled programs, except that the 8K byte run-time library is not included at the beginning of the file. When chain programs are loaded by the CHAIN(Filename) command, the run-time library is preserved and processing resumes in the chained program. The chained program overwrites the calling program in memory, but if identical objects are declared at the beginning of each of the programs, constants, types, and variables may be transferred between main and chained programs. This is because Turbo Pascal does not initialize variables at run-time.

18.6 Error Message File

To prevent the error message file from being loaded (and thus provide more room in the demo compiler for larger programs), make a copy of your work disk and ERASE the TURBOMSG.OVR file from the new work disk. The available workspace of the demo compiler will increase from 3490 to 4803 bytes. Of course, if errors are present in your file, you must look up the displayed error code in the Appendix, as the text error messages will no longer be displayed on the screen.

An alternative method to making a new work disk is to place a system disk in drive A and the work disk with the compiler in drive B, and then type:

```
A) B:TURBODE
```

The compiler will be loaded from drive B, but the message file will be searched for on drive A, and as it is not present there, the compiler will proceed as above with the added workspace. Once the compiler is running, you can change the Logged drive to B and continue.

18.7 Differences from Standard Pascal

Turbo Pascal does not support the Standard Pascal get/put buffered file I/O procedures which are replaced by the read/write procedures. The Standard Pascal pack/unpack procedures are not supported by Turbo because all data types are automatically packed. Turbo requires that DOS file names be assigned to file type variables with the ASSIGN() procedure and the file variable be used in all file references in the program.

Any input and output declarations in the program heading are ignored by the Turbo Pascal compiler. Input/output files other than the default terminal devices (keyboard and screen) must be assigned with the ASSIGN and RESET/ REWRITE procedures, or be specified in read and write statements by using Turbo's standard predeclared file variables.

Turbo Pascal does not allow procedures and functions to be passed as parameters. Goto statements may not reference labels outside the current block.

Only one variant part is allowed in a record. Dynamic variant records cannot be created with the NEW procedure.

18.8 Turbo Pascal Extensions

As a part of their commitment to provide a constantly improved product, Borland International has released two new versions of Turbo Pascal since the original product was released in October, 1983. The limited compiler included with this book is based on the original Turbo Pascal version 1.0 for the IBM PC, so these extensions do not apply to the demo compiler.

TURBO PASCAL VERSION 2.0

Turbo Pascal version 2.0 was released in 1984, and included several enhancements. The additions to the IBM PC version of Turbo 2.0 will be outlined briefly in this section.

Program Overlays

The capability to generate program overlays allows a segment of program memory to be reserved for one or more program overlay files which are loaded one at a time from disk. This allows several functional sections of code to be loaded as required, all occupying the same memory space. This method allows much larger programs to be written and is simpler (and faster) to use than CHAINed programs. Overlays are declared by the prefix OVERLAY before the procedure or function heading.

Dynamic Allocation

The Standard Pascal DISPOSE procedure allows individual dynamic variables to be deallocated and the memory they use made available for reuse. (See Chapter 16.)

IBM PC Screen and I/O Interface

A number of procedures allows control of the IBM PC screen display, including text and graphics mode, colors, cursor location, and graphics commands. Screen procedures to generate and control windows are also provided.

Math Coprocessor Support

An optional version of Turbo Pascal version 2.0 allows the use of the 8087 math coprocessor chip if installed in the IBM PC. Accuracy is improved and the speed of all real number math functions is dramatically increased. This version is intended primarily for scientific and other "number crunching" applications.

TURBO PASCAL VERSION 3.0

Turbo Pascal version 3.0 was released by Borland in 1985 and is the only version available for sale as of this writing (November 1985). Turbo Pascal version 3.0 includes several added procedures and functions, and in IBM PC versions, includes Turtle Graphics, advanced graphics routines, and PC-DOS 2.0 and later file handling features. The run-time library has been somewhat enhanced for real number operations (according to some benchmark tests). The compiler itself is almost exactly twice as fast as the Version 2.0 compiler. Turbo Pascal Version 3.0 cannot be used with any version of MS-DOS or PC-DOS earlier than version 2.0.

Added Procedures and Functions

Turbo Pascal now includes the EXIT and HALT procedures, which allow improved control of loop structures and the ability to create error exits without elaborate and verbose logical structures.

A number of other standard subprograms have also been added to the new version, including several text file functions, and procedures for parsing the command line parameters.

MS/PC-DOS 2.0 + Support

The Turbo Pascal 3.0 file system was completely rewritten to allow the use of the new DOS 2.0 file system. Turbo now supports tree directories, and includes commands for subdirectory manipulation. The system now uses DOS 2.0 file handles instead of the older FCB method of file access, and will no longer work with DOS versions earlier than 2.0.

The new techniques allow more flexibility in file access, including paths, and are significantly faster. I/O buffer size may now be specified, allowing the programmer to optimize his application.

File I/O Additions

The APPEND procedure has been added to the available TEXT file I/O operations, allowing the addition of data to the end of a text file.

Turtle Graphics

Version 3.0 for the IBM PC includes a number of procedures and functions for implementing Turtle graphics (originally used in the UCSD version). Turtle graphics can be used to draw and create advanced graphics figures using simple commands. It is valuable for educational and graphic applications. Turtle graphics was a forerunner of the Logo graphics language.

BCD Arithmetic

An optional version of Turbo Pascal 3.0 allows the use of BCD representation of real numbers, significantly increasing the accuracy of real computations. This version is intended primarily for financial and business applications.

Appendix A:
Turbo Compiler Directives

Common Directives:

B	I/O Mode Selection	Default B +
C	Control S and C	Default C +
I	I/O Error Handling	Default I +
I	Include Files	
R	Index Range Check	Default R-
V	Var-parameter Type Checking	Default V +
U	User Interrupt	Default U-

PC-DOS, MS-DOS, CP/M-86 Directive

K	Stack Checking	Default K +

Turbo 3.0 PC-DOS/MS-DOS 2.0 Directives

G	Input File Buffer	Default G0
P	Output File Buffer	Default P0
D	Device Checking	Default D +
F	Number of Open Files	Default F16

CP/M 80 Directives

A	Absolute Code (non-recursive)	Default A +
W	Nesting of WITH Statements	Default W2
X	Array Optimization	Default X +

Directives are enclosed in comments { } and preceded by a "$", use + and - suffix for on and off.

    {-,V-}
    {$I FILENAME.TYP }

Appendix B:
Turbo Editor Commands

Cursor movement commands:

	⟨Ctrl-S⟩	Cursor left one character
	⟨Ctrl-D⟩	Cursor right one character
	⟨Ctrl-I⟩ or ⟨TAB⟩	cursor right to next tab or back to left margin (TABS are set to the beginning of each word in the previous line)
	⟨Ctrl-E⟩	Cursor up one line
	⟨Ctrl-X⟩	Cursor down one line
	⟨Ctrl-A⟩	Cursor left one word
	⟨Ctrl-F⟩	Cursor right one word
#	⟨Ctrl-W⟩	Scroll screen up one line
#	⟨Ctrl-Z⟩	Scroll screen down one line
	⟨Ctrl-R⟩	Cursor up one screen page of text
	⟨Ctrl-C⟩	Cursor down one screen page of text

The extended cursor movement commands are:

	⟨Ctrl-Q⟩ ⟨S⟩	To left on line
	⟨Ctrl-Q⟩ ⟨D⟩	To right on line
#	⟨Ctrl-Q⟩ ⟨E⟩	To top of screen
#	⟨Ctrl-Q⟩ ⟨X⟩	To bottom of screen
	⟨Ctrl-Q⟩ ⟨R⟩	To top of file
	⟨Ctrl-Q⟩ ⟨C⟩	To bottom of file
#	⟨Ctrl-Q⟩ ⟨B⟩	To beginning of marked block
#	⟨Ctrl-Q⟩ ⟨K⟩	To end of marked block
	⟨Ctrl-Q⟩ ⟨P⟩	To last (previous) cursor position

Insert and Delete Commands

⟨Ctrl-G⟩	Delete character at cursor
⟨Ctrl-T⟩	Delete word right at cursor
⟨Ctrl-Y⟩	Delete line at cursor
⟨Ctrl-Q⟩ ⟨Y⟩	Delete from cursor to end of line
⟨Ctrl-N⟩	Insert line break at cursor position
⟨Ctrl-P⟩⟨Ctrl-char⟩	Insert control character—note: displays in dim on screen

Find and Replace Commands

⟨Ctrl-Q⟩ ⟨F⟩   Find a given string

Options: B: Find backwards - from the current cursor position to the beginning of the text.

G: Global search, use entire text regardless of current cursor position.

n: n = any number. Find the n'th occurrence of the search string, beginning at the current cursor position.

U: Ignore upper/lower case when matching.

W: Find whole words only, skip matching patterns embedded in other words.

?: Show command options.

⟨Ctrl-Q⟩ ⟨A⟩   Find a given string and replace it with the specified value

Options: B: Find and replace backwards—from the current cursor position to the beginning of the text.

G: Global find and replace, use entire text regardless of current cursor position.

n: n = any number. Find and replace n occurrences beginning at the current cursor position.

N: Replace without asking for confirmation.

U: Ignore upper/lower case when matching.

W: Find and replace whole words only, skip matching patterns embedded in other words.

?: Show command options.

Block Commands

⟨Ctrl-K⟩ ⟨B⟩   Mark beginning of block

	⟨Ctrl-K⟩ ⟨K⟩	Mark end of block
@	⟨Ctrl-K⟩ ⟨T⟩	Mark single word
	⟨Ctrl-K⟩ ⟨Y⟩	Delete block
#	⟨Ctrl-K⟩ ⟨H⟩	Hide block
	⟨Ctrl-K⟩ ⟨C⟩	Copy block to current cursor position
	⟨Ctrl-K⟩ ⟨V⟩	Move block to current cursor position
	⟨Ctrl-K⟩ ⟨W⟩	Write block to disk file
	⟨Ctrl-K⟩ ⟨R⟩	Read block from disk file to current cursor position

Miscellaneous Commands

	⟨Ctrl-L⟩	Repeat the last find or find-and-replace operation (or continue from last find).
	⟨Ctrl-U⟩	Abort command in progress
	⟨Ctrl-V⟩	Toggle insert mode on/off
@	⟨Ctrl-Q⟩ ⟨I⟩	Toggle auto indentation on/off
@	⟨Ctrl-Q⟩ ⟨L⟩	Undo—restores line to its previous contents as long as the cursor has not be moved from the line
*	⟨Ctrl-K⟩ ⟨D⟩	End edit—Return to main Turbo Menu—file remains in memory, command does not save file—use main menu Save command!

Note: Commands marked with * have different effects than similar WordStar commands.
Those marked with @ do not exist in WordStar.
Those marked with # are only available in Turbo 2.0 and later versions.

Appendix C:
Turbo Pascal Reference Guide

C.1 Reserved Words

Turbo Pascal includes 43 reserved words which cannot be redefined (i.e., reserved words cannot be used as user declared identifiers). These reserved words are:

* absolute	* external	nil	* shr
and	file	not	* string
array	for	of	then

begin	forward	or	to
case	function	packed	type
const	goto	procedure	until
div	if	program	var
do	in	record	while
downto	* inline	repeat	with
else	label	set	* xor
end	mod	* shl	

Asterisked words are not defined in Standard Pascal.

C.2 Operators

The following table summarizes all operators of Turbo Pascal. The operators are grouped in order of descending precedence. Where "Type of Operand" is indicated as Integer, Real, the result is as follows:

Operands	Result
Integer, Integer	Integer
Real, Real	Real
Real, Integer	Real

Operator	Function	Operand Types	Result Type
Unary Operators			
+ unary	sign identity	Integer, Real	as operand
- unary	sign inversion	Integer, Real	as operand
Not Operator			
not	negation	Integer, Boolean	as operand
Multiplying Operators			
*	multiplication	Integer, Real	Integer, Real
	set intersection	any set type	as operand
/	division	Integer, Real	Real
div	Integer division	Integer	Integer
mod	modulus	Integer	Integer
and	arithmetic and	Integer	Integer
	logical and	Boolean	Boolean
shl	shift left	Integer	Integer

shr	shift right	Integer	Integer

Adding Operators

+	addition	Integer, Real	Integer, Real
	concatenation	String	string
	set union	any set type	as operand
-	subtraction	Integer, Real	Integer, Real
	set difference	any set type	as operand
or	arithmetic or	Integer	Integer
	logical or	Boolean	Boolean
xor	arithmetic xor	Integer	Integer
	logical xor	Boolean	Boolean

Relational Operators

=	equality	any scalar type	Boolean
	equality	string	Boolean
	equality	any set type	Boolean
	equality	any pointer type	Boolean
⟨⟩	inequality	any scalar type	Boolean
	inequality	string	Boolean
	inequality	any set type	Boolean
	inequality	any pointer type	Boolean
⟩=	greater or equal	any scalar type	Boolean
	greater or equal	string	Boolean
	set inclusion	any set type	Boolean
⟨=	less or equal	any scalar type	Boolean
	less or equal	string	Boolean
	set inclusion	any set type	Boolean
⟩	greater than	any scalar type	Boolean
	greater than	string	Boolean
⟨	less than	any scalar type	Boolean
	less than	string	Boolean
in	set membership	* see note below	Boolean

* Note: The first operand of the **in** operator may be of any scalar type, and the second operand must a set of that type.

C.3 Turbo 3.0 for IBM-PC—Standard Identifiers

ABSOLUTE	EXP	MARK	SQRT
AND	EXTERNAL	MAXAVAIL	STR
ARCTAN	FALSE	MAXINT	STRING
ARRAY	FILE	MEM	SUCC
ASSIGN	FILEPOS	MEMAVAIL	SWAP

AUX	FILESIZE	MEMW	TEXT
AUXINPTR	FILLCHAR	MOD	TEXT-BACKGROUND
AUXOUTPTR	FLUSH	MOVE	TEXTCOLOR
BEGIN	FOR	NEW	TEXTMODE
BLACK	FORWARD	NIL	THEN
BLUE	FRAC	NORMVIDEO	TO
BLOCKREAD	FREEMEM	NOSOUND	TRM
BLOCKWRITE	FUNCTION	NOT	TRUE
BOOLEAN	GETMEM	ODD	TRUNC
BROWN	GOTO	OF	TYPE
BUFLEN	GOTOXY	OR	UNTIL
BYTE	GRAPH-BACKGROUND	ORD	UPCASE
CASE	GRAPH-COLORMODE	OUTPUT	USR
CHAIN	GRAPHMODE	OVERLAY	USRINPTR
CHAR	GRAPH-WINDOW	PACKED	USROUTPTR
CHR	GREEN	PALETTE	VAL
CLOSE	HALT	PI	VAR
CLREOL	HEAPPTR	PLOT	WHEREX
CLRSCR	HI	PORT	WHEREY
CON	HIRES	POS	WHILE
CONCAT	HIRESCOLOR	PRED	WHITE
CONINPTR	IF	PROCEDURE	WINDOW
CONOUTPTR	IN	PROGRAM	WITH
CONST	INLINE	PTR	WRITE
CONSTPTR	INPUT	RANDOM	WRITELN
COPY	INSERT	RANDOMIZE	XOR
COS	INSLINE	READ	YELLOW
CRTEXIT	INT	READLN	
CRTINIT	INTEGER	REAL	
CYAN	ORESULT	RECORD	
DARKGRAY	KBD	RED	
DELAY	KEYPRESSED	RELEASE	
DELETE	LABEL	RENAME	
DELLINE	LENGTH	REPEAT	
DISPOSE	LIGHTBLUE	RESET	
DIV	LIGHTCYAN	REWRITE	
DO	LIGHTGRAY	ROUND	
DOWNTO	LIGHTGREEN	SEEK	
DRAW	LIGHT-MAGENTA	SET	
ELSE	LIGHTRED	SHL	

END	LN	SHR
EOF	LO	SIN
EOLN	LOWVIDEO	SIZEOF
ERASE	LST	SOUND
EXECUTE	LSTOUTPTR	SQR
EXIT	MAGENTA	SQRT

Appendix D.
Turbo Pascal Syntax

The syntax of the TURBO Pascal language is presented here using the Backus-Naur Form (BNF). The following symbols are metasymbols belonging to the BNF formalism, and not symbols of the Turbo Pascal language:

::=	Means "is defined as"
		Means "or"
{}	means the contents may be repeated zero or more times
⟨⟩	means the contents are a BNF syntactic construct

All other symbols are part of the language. Each syntactic construct is printed in angle brackets, e.g.: ⟨block⟩ and ⟨case-element⟩. Pascal reserved words are printed in **bold**.

⟨actual-parameter⟩ ::= ⟨expression⟩ | ⟨variable⟩
⟨adding-operator⟩ ::= + | - | **or** | **xor**

⟨array-constant⟩ ::= (⟨structured-constant⟩ {, ⟨structured-constant⟩})

⟨array-type⟩ ::= **array** [⟨index-type⟩ {, ⟨index-type⟩}] **of** ⟨component-type⟩

⟨array-variable⟩ ::= ⟨variable⟩

⟨assignment-statement⟩ ::= ⟨variable⟩ := ⟨expression⟩ |
    ⟨function-identifier⟩ := ⟨expression⟩

⟨base-type⟩ ::= ⟨simple-type⟩

⟨block⟩ ::= ⟨declaration-part⟩ ⟨statement-part⟩

⟨case-element⟩ ::= ⟨case-list⟩ : ⟨statement⟩

⟨case-label⟩ ::= ⟨constant⟩

⟨case-label-list⟩ ::= ⟨case-label⟩ {, ⟨case-label⟩}

⟨case-list⟩ ::= ⟨case-list-element⟩ {, ⟨case-list-element⟩}

⟨case-list-element⟩ ::= ⟨constant⟩ | ⟨constant⟩. .⟨constant⟩

⟨case-statement⟩ ::= **case** ⟨expression⟩ **of** ⟨case-element⟩
    {; ⟨case-element⟩} **end** |
    case ⟨expression⟩ **of** ⟨case-element⟩ {; ⟨case-element⟩}
    else ⟨statement⟩ {; ⟨statement⟩ } **end**

⟨character⟩::= ⟨letter-or-digit⟩ | ⟨special character⟩

⟨complemented-factor⟩ ::= ⟨signed-factor⟩ | **not** ⟨signed-factor⟩

⟨component-type⟩ ::= ⟨type⟩

⟨component-variable⟩ ::= ⟨indexed-variable⟩ | ⟨field-designator⟩

⟨compound-statement⟩ ::= **begin** ⟨statement⟩ {; ⟨statement⟩} **end**

⟨conditional-statement⟩ ::= ⟨if-statement⟩ | ⟨case-statement⟩

⟨constant⟩ ::= ⟨unsigned-number⟩ | ⟨sign⟩ ⟨unsigned-number⟩ |
    ⟨constant-identifier⟩ | ⟨sign⟩ ⟨constant-identifier⟩ | ⟨string⟩

⟨constant-definition-part⟩ ::= **const** ⟨constant-definition⟩
    {; ⟨constant-definition⟩} ;

⟨constant-definition⟩ ::= ⟨untyped-constant-definition⟩ |
    ⟨typed-constant-definition⟩

⟨constant-identifier⟩ ::= ⟨identifier⟩

⟨control-character⟩ ::= # ⟨unsigned-integer⟩ | ∧ ⟨character⟩

⟨control-variable⟩ ::= ⟨variable-identifier⟩

⟨declaration-part⟩ ::= {⟨declaration-section⟩}

⟨declaration-section⟩ ::= ⟨label-declaration-part⟩ |
    ⟨constant-definition-part⟩ | ⟨type-definition-part⟩ |
    ⟨variable-declaration-part⟩ |

⟨procedure-and-function-declaration-part⟩

⟨digit⟩ ::= 0|1|2|3|4|5|6|7|8|9

⟨digit-sequence⟩ ::= ⟨digit⟩{⟨digit⟩}

⟨empty⟩ ::=

⟨empty-statement⟩ ::= ⟨empty⟩ ;

⟨entire-variable⟩ ::= ⟨variable-identifier⟩ | ⟨typed-constant-identifier⟩

⟨expression⟩ ::= ⟨simple-expression⟩
    {⟨relational-operator⟩ ⟨simple-expression⟩}

⟨factor⟩ ::= ⟨variable⟩ | ⟨unsigned-constant⟩ | |⟨expression⟩| |
    ⟨function-designator⟩ | ⟨set⟩

⟨field-designator⟩ ::= ⟨record-variable⟩ . ⟨field-identifier⟩

⟨field-identifier⟩ ::= ⟨identifier⟩

⟨field-list⟩ ::= ⟨fixed-part⟩ | ⟨fixed-part⟩ ; ⟨variant-part⟩ |
    ⟨variant-part⟩

⟨file-identifier⟩ ::= ⟨identifier⟩

⟨file-identifier-list⟩ ::= ⟨empty⟩ | (⟨file-identifier⟩ {, ⟨file-identifier⟩})

⟨file-type⟩ ::= **file of** ⟨type⟩

⟨final-value⟩ ::= ⟨expression⟩

⟨fixed-part⟩ ::= ⟨record-section⟩ {; ⟨record-section⟩}

⟨for-list⟩ ::= ⟨initial-value⟩ **to** ⟨final-value⟩ |
    ⟨initial-value⟩ **downto** ⟨final-value⟩

⟨for-statement⟩ ::= **for** ⟨control-variable⟩ := ⟨for-list⟩ **do** ⟨statement⟩

⟨formal-parameter-section⟩ ::= ⟨parameter-group⟩ | **var** ⟨parameter-group⟩

⟨function-declaration⟩ ::= ⟨function-heading⟩ ⟨block⟩ ;

⟨function-designator⟩ ::= ⟨function-identifier⟩ | ⟨function-identifier⟩

⟨⟨actual-parameter⟩ {, ⟨actual parameter⟩ })

⟨function-heading⟩ ::= **function** ⟨identifier⟩ : ⟨result-type⟩ ; |
    function ⟨identifier⟩ (⟨formal-parameter-section⟩
    {, ⟨formal-parameter-section⟩}) : ⟨result-type⟩ ;

⟨function-identifier⟩ ::= ⟨identifier⟩

⟨goto-statement⟩ ::= **goto** ⟨label⟩

⟨hexdigit⟩ ::= ⟨digit⟩ | A | B | C | D | E | F

⟨hexdigit-sequence⟩ ::= ⟨hexdigit⟩ {}hexdigit)}

⟨identifier⟩ ::= ⟨letter⟩ {⟨letter-or-digit⟩}

⟨identifier-list⟩ ::= ⟨identifier⟩ {, ⟨identifier⟩}

⟨if-statement⟩ ::= **if** ⟨expression⟩ **then** ⟨statement⟩ {**else** ⟨statement⟩}

⟨index-type⟩ ::= ⟨simple-type⟩

⟨indexed-variable⟩ ::= ⟨array-variable⟩ [⟨expression⟩ {⟨expression⟩}]

⟨initial-value⟩ ::= ⟨expression⟩

⟨inline-list-element⟩ ::= ⟨unsigned-integer⟩ | ⟨constant-identifier⟩ |
    ⟨variable-identifier⟩ | ⟨location-counter-reference⟩

⟨inline-statement⟩ ::= **inline** ⟨inline-list-element⟩ {, ⟨inline-list-element⟩} ;

⟨label⟩ ::= ⟨letter-or-digit⟩ {⟨letter-or-digit⟩}

⟨label-declaration-part⟩ ::= **label** ⟨label⟩ {, ⟨label⟩} ;

⟨labeled-statement⟩ ::= ⟨label⟩ : ⟨statement⟩

⟨letter⟩ ::= A|B|C|D|E|F|G|H|I|J|K|L|M|N|O|P|Q|R|S|T|U|V|
W|X|Y|Z|a|b|c|d|e|f|g|h|i|j|k|l|m|n|o|p|q|r|s|t|u|v|w|x|y|z|_

⟨letter-or-digit⟩ ::= ⟨letter⟩ | ⟨digit⟩

⟨location-counter-reference⟩ ::= * | * ⟨sign⟩ ⟨constant⟩

⟨multiplying-operator⟩ ::= * | / | **div** | **mod** | **and** | **shl** | **shr**

⟨parameter-group⟩ ::= ⟨identifier-list⟩ : ⟨type-identifier⟩

⟨pointer-type⟩ ::= ^ ⟨type-identifier⟩

⟨pointer-variable⟩ ::= ⟨variable⟩

⟨procedure-and-function-declaration-part⟩ ::=
    {⟨procedure-or-function-declaration⟩}

⟨procedure-declaration⟩ ::= ⟨procedure-heading⟩ ⟨block⟩ ;

⟨procedure-heading⟩ ::= **procedure** ⟨identifier⟩ ;| **procedure**
⟨identifier⟩
    (⟨formal-parameter-section⟩ {, ⟨formal-parameter-section⟩}) ;

⟨procedure-or-function-declaration⟩ ::= ⟨procedure-declaration⟩ |
    ⟨function-declaration⟩

⟨procedure-statement⟩ ::= ⟨procedure-identifier⟩ | ⟨procedure-identifier⟩
    (⟨actual-parameter⟩ {, ⟨actual-parameter⟩})

⟨program-heading⟩ ::= ⟨empty⟩ | program ⟨program-identifier⟩
    ⟨file-identifier-list⟩ ;

⟨program⟩ ::= ⟨program-heading⟩ ⟨block⟩ .

⟨program-identifier⟩ ::= ⟨identifier⟩

⟨record-constant⟩ ::= (⟨record-constant-element⟩
    {; ⟨record-constant-element⟩})

⟨record-constant-element⟩ ::= ⟨field-identifier⟩ : ⟨structured-constant⟩

⟨record-section⟩ ::= ⟨empty⟩ |
    ⟨field-identifier⟩ {, ⟨field-identifier⟩} : ⟨type⟩

⟨record-type⟩ ::= **record** ⟨field-list⟩ **end**

⟨record-variable⟩ ::= ⟨variable⟩

⟨record-variable-list⟩ ::= ⟨record-variable⟩ {, ⟨record-variable⟩}

⟨referenced-variable⟩ ::= ⟨pointer-variable⟩ ^

⟨relational-operator⟩ ::= ⟨⟩ | = | ⟨= | ⟩= | ⟨ | ⟩ | **in**

⟨repeat-statement⟩ ::= **repeat** ⟨statement⟩ {; ⟨statement⟩} **until** ⟨expression⟩

⟨repetitive-statement⟩ ::= ⟨while-statement⟩ | ⟨repeat-statement⟩ |
    ⟨for-statement⟩

⟨result-type⟩ ::= ⟨type-identifier⟩

⟨scalar-type⟩ ::= (⟨identifier⟩ {, ⟨identifier⟩})

⟨scale-factor⟩ ::= ⟨digit-sequence⟩ | ⟨sign⟩ ⟨digit-sequence⟩

⟨set⟩ ::= [{⟨set-element⟩}]

⟨set-constant-element⟩ ::= ⟨constant⟩ | ⟨constant..constant⟩

⟨set-element⟩ ::= ⟨expression⟩ | ⟨expression⟩..⟨expression⟩

⟨set-type⟩ ::= **set of** ⟨base-type⟩

⟨sign⟩ ::= + | -

⟨signed-factor⟩ ::= ⟨factor⟩ | ⟨sign⟩ ⟨factor⟩

⟨simple-expression⟩ ::= ⟨term⟩ {⟨adding-operator⟩ ⟨term⟩}

⟨simple-statement⟩ ::= ⟨assignment-statement⟩ | ⟨procedure-statement⟩ |
    ⟨goto-statement⟩ | ⟨inline-statement⟩ | ⟨empty-statement⟩

⟨simple-type⟩ ::= ⟨scalar-type⟩ | ⟨subrange-type⟩ | ⟨type-identifier⟩

⟨special character⟩ ::= ⟨space⟩ | ! | " | # | $ | % | & | (|) | * | + | , | - | . | / | : | ; | ⟨ | = | ⟩
    | ? | @ | [| \ |] | ∧ | ` | { | } | ~ | ⟨vertical line⟩ |

⟨statement⟩ ::= ⟨simple-statement⟩ | ⟨structured-statement⟩

⟨statement-part⟩ ::= ⟨compound-statement⟩

⟨string⟩ ::= {⟨string-element⟩}

⟨string-element⟩ ::= ⟨text-string⟩ | ⟨control-character⟩

⟨string-type⟩ ::= ⟨string⟩ [⟨constant⟩]

⟨structured-constant⟩ ::= ⟨constant⟩ | ⟨array-constant⟩ | ⟨record-constant⟩ |
    ⟨set-constant⟩

⟨structured-constant-definition⟩ ::=
    ⟨identifier⟩ : ⟨type⟩ = ⟨structured-constant⟩

⟨structured-statement⟩ ::= ⟨compound-statement⟩ | ⟨conditional-statement⟩ |
    ⟨repetitive-statement⟩ | ⟨with-statement⟩

⟨structured-type⟩ ::= ⟨unpacked-structured-type⟩ |
    packed ⟨unpacked-structure-type⟩

⟨subrange-type⟩ ::= ⟨constant⟩..⟨constant⟩

⟨tag-field⟩ ::= ⟨empty⟩ | ⟨field-identifier⟩

⟨term⟩ ::= ⟨complemented-factor⟩ {⟨multiplying-operator⟩
    ⟨complemented-factor⟩}

⟨text-string⟩ ::= '{⟨character⟩}'

⟨type-definition⟩ ::= ⟨identifier⟩ = ⟨type⟩
⟨type-definition-part⟩ ::= **type** ⟨type-definition⟩ {; ⟨type-definition⟩} ;

⟨type-identifier⟩ ::= ⟨identifier⟩

⟨type⟩ ::= ⟨simple-type⟩ | ⟨structured-type⟩ | ⟨pointer-type⟩

⟨type-constant-identifier⟩ ::= ⟨identifier⟩

⟨unpacked-structure-type⟩ ::= ⟨string-type⟩ | ⟨array-type⟩ | ⟨record-type⟩ |
    ⟨set-type⟩ | ⟨file-type⟩

⟨unsigned-constant⟩ ::= ⟨unsigned-number⟩ | ⟨string⟩ |
    ⟨constant-identifier⟩ | **nil**

⟨unsigned-integer⟩ ::= ⟨digit-sequence⟩ | $ ⟨hexdigit-sequence⟩

⟨unsigned-number⟩ ::= ⟨unsigned-integer⟩ | ⟨unsigned-real⟩

⟨unsigned-real⟩ ::= ⟨digit-sequence⟩ . ⟨digit-sequence⟩ |
    ⟨digit-sequence⟩ . ⟨digit-sequence⟩ E ⟨scale-factor⟩ |
    ⟨digit-sequence⟩ E ⟨scale-factor⟩

⟨untyped-constant-definition⟩ ::= ⟨identifier⟩ = ⟨constant⟩

⟨variable⟩ ::= ⟨entire-variable⟩ | ⟨component-variable⟩ |
    ⟨referenced-variable⟩

⟨variable-declaration⟩ ::= ⟨identifier-list⟩ : ⟨type⟩ |
    ⟨identifier-list⟩ : ⟨type⟩ absolute ⟨constant⟩

⟨variable-declaration-part⟩ ::= **var** ⟨variable-declaration⟩
    {; ⟨variable-declaration⟩} ;

⟨variable-identifier⟩ ::= ⟨identifier⟩

⟨variant⟩ ::= ⟨empty⟩ | ⟨case-label-list⟩ : ⟨field-list⟩

⟨variant-part⟩ ::= **case** ⟨tag-field⟩ ⟨type-identifier⟩ **of** ⟨variant⟩
    {; ⟨variant⟩}

⟨while-statement⟩ ::= **while** ⟨expression⟩ **do** ⟨statement⟩

⟨with-statement⟩ ::= **with** ⟨record-variable-list⟩ **do** ⟨statement⟩

Appendix E.
Compiler Error Messages

01 ';' expected
02 ':' expected
03 ',' expected
04 '(' expected
05 ')' expected
06 '=' expected
07 ':=' expected
08 '[' expected
09 ']' expected
10 '.' expected
11 '..' expected
12 BEGIN expected
13 DO expected
14 END expected
15 OF expected
17 THEN expected
18 TO or DOWNTO expected
20 Boolean expression expected
21 File variable expected
22 Integer constant expected
23 Integer expression expected
24 Integer variable expected

25	Integer or real constant expected
26	Integer or real expression expected
27	Integer or real variable expected
28	Pointer variable expected
29	Record variable expected
30	Simple type expected
31	Simple expression expected
32	String constant expected
33	String expression expected
34	String variable expected
35	Textfile expected
36	Type Identifier expected
37	Untyped file expected
40	Undefined label
41	Unknown identifier or syntax error
42	Undefined pointer type in preceding type definitions
43	Duplicate identifier or label
44	Type mismatch
45	Constant out of range
46	Constant and CASE selector type does not match
47	Operand type(s) does not match operator
48	Invalid result type
49	Invalid string length
50	String constant length does not match type
51	Invalid subrange base type
52	Lower bound) upper bound
53	Reserved word
54	Illegal assignment
55	String constant exceeds line
56	Error in integer constant
57	Error in real constant
58	Illegal character in identifier
60	Constants are not allowed here
61	Files and pointers are not allowed here
62	Structured variables are not allowed here
63	Textfiles are not allowed here
64	Textfiles and untyped files are not allowed here
65	Untyped files are not allowed here
66	I/O not allowed here
67	Files must be VAR parameters
68	File components may not be files
69	Invalid ordering of fields
70	Set base type out of range
71	Invalid GOTO
72	Label not within current block

73   Unidentified FORWARD procedure(s)
74   INLINE error
75   Illegal use of ABSOLUTE
90   File not found
91   Unexpected end of source
97   Too many nested WITHs
98   Memory overflow
99   Compiler overflow

Appendix F:
Run-Time Errors

01   Floating point overflow.
02   Division by zero attempted.
03   Sqrt argument error.
04   Ln argument error.
10   String length error.
11   Invalid string index.
90   Index out of range.
91   Scalar or subrange out of range.
92   Out of integer range.
F0   Overlay file not found.
FF   Heap/stack collision.

Appendix G:
I/O Errors

01   File does not exist.
02   File not open for input.
03   File not open for output.
04   File not open.
10   Error in numeric format.
20   Operation not allowed on a logical device.
21   Not allowed in direct mode.
22   Assign to std files not allowed.
90   Record length mismatch.
91   Seek beyond end-of-file.
99   Unexpected end-of-file.

F0   Disk write error.
F1   Directory is full.
F2   File size overflow.
F3   Too many open files.
FF   File disappeared.

Appendix H:
Binary and Hexadecimal Numbers

Today's microcomputers can only understand two things—on and off, "1" or "0", yes or no. Unlike humans, who use the ten digits from "0" to "9" to represent values, computers operate entirely with the *binary* number system, based on the two digits "1" and "0". You can imagine a computer's problem in counting to ten! The binary (or base 2) number system is the computer's counterpart to our *decimal* (or base 10) number system. Due to the electrical nature of the computer, it can best represent numbers in binary by a "1" value (on) or a "0" value (off). We humans use ten values in our decimal system: "0", "1", "2", "3", "4", "5", "6", "7", "8", and "9".

As computers have evolved in the past 20 years, computer engineers and programmers have come up with a better ways of writing binary numbers—all those 1s and 0s—over and over. Not only are the long strings of numbers hard to write accurately, they also are difficult for humans to interpret, remember, and understand. So, various forms of shorthand have become popular over the years, related to the physical hardware design of the computers in use at the time. One of the number systems popular on large computers a few years ago was the *octal* or base 8 number system. The octal number system counts "0", "1", "2", "3", "4", "5", "6", and "7". Octal numbers can conveniently represent three binary bits of data, and as many computers of the time used 24 bit words, their data could be easily represented by eight octal digits (8 digits times 3 bits = 24 bits).

010	110	011	100	000	110	101	111	(24 bit word)
2	6	3	4	0	6	5	7	octal number

When 8 bit microcomputers became popular, octal notation dropped out of common use because octal numbers are most efficient for bit lengths evenly divisible by 3 (like 24 or 12) (since each digit represents three binary bits). Octal was replaced by *hexadecimal* or base 16 notation which represents groups of four binary bits. Hexadecimal or "hex" as it is called, uses the digits "0", "1", "2", "3", "4", "5", "6", "7", "8", and "9" just like our decimal system plus six more symbols - "A", "B", "C", "D", "E", and "F" for the six added values in the hexadecimal notation system.

Two hex digits can represent one byte or 8 bits of data. In the 16 bit computer world, two bytes of data make up a word or 16 bits. A 16 bit data word can be represented by four hexadecimal digits. For example:

```
1101 1001 0110 1111     (16 bit word)
 D    9    6    F        (hex value)
```

The hexadecimal number D96F is certainly simpler to write and remember than the binary number 1101100101101111, isn't it?

Here is a simple table which lists the values from one to sixteen in decimal, binary, octal, and hexadecimal:

Decimal	Binary	Octal	Hexadecimal
0	0	0	0
1	1	1	1
2	10	2	2
3	11	3	3
4	100	4	4
5	101	5	5
6	110	6	6
7	111	7	7
8	1000	10	8
9	1001	11	9
10	1010	12	A
11	1011	13	B
12	1100	14	C
13	1101	15	D
14	1110	16	E
15	1111	17	F
16	10000	20	10

Appendix I:
Keyboard Return Codes

The following table specifies the codes generated for "special" and function keys on the IBM PC. These special codes are indicated by detection of an ESC (ASCII 27) code with a second character in the keyboard buffer. This character may be detected with the KeyPressed function. If a second character is present, it is a special code and the first character is discarded, if it is not present, the code is ESC. Other codes are also shown below.

Key	Unshift	Shift	Ctrl	Alt
F1	27 59	27 84	27 94	27 104
F2	27 60	27 85	27 95	27 105
F3	27 61	27 86	27 96	27 106
F4	27 62	27 87	27 97	27 107
F5	27 63	27 88	27 98	27 108
F6	27 64	27 89	27 99	27 109
F7	27 65	27 90	27 100	27 110
F8	27 66	27 91	27 101	27 111
F9	27 67	27 92	27 102	27 112
F10	27 68	27 93	27 103	27 113
LArr	27 75	52	27 115	27 178
RArr	27 77	54	27 116	27 180
UArr	27 72	56	27 160	27 175
DArr	27 80	50	27 164	27 183
Home	27 71	55		27 174
End	27 79	49	27 117	27 182
PgUp	27 73	57	27 132	27 176
PgDn	27 81	51	27 118	27 184
Ins	27 82	48	27 165	27 185
Del	27 83	46	27 166	17 186
Esc	27	27	27	
BackSp	8	8	127	
Tab	9	27 15		
Enter	13	13	10	
a-A	97	65	1	27-30
b-B	98	66	2	27-48
c-C	99	67	3	27-46
d-D	100	68	4	27-32
e-E	101	69	5	27-18
f-F	102	70	6	27-33
g-G	103	71	7	27-34
h-H	104	72	8	27-35
i-I	105	73	9	27-23
j-J	106	74	10	27-36
k-K	107	75	11	27-37
l-L	108	76	12	27-38
m-M	109	77	13	27-50
n-N	110	78	14	27-49
o-O	111	79	15	27-24
p-P	112	80	16	27-25

Key U-S	Unshift	Shift	Ctrl	Alt
q-Q	113	81	17	27-16
r-R	114	82	18	27-19
s-S	115	83	19	27-31
t-T	116	84	20	27-20
u-U	117	85	21	27-22
v-V	118	86	22	27-47
w-W	119	87	23	27-17
x-X	120	88	24	27-45
y-Y	121	89	25	27-21
z-Z	122	90	26	27-44
[{	91	123	27	
|	92	124	28	
]}	93	125	29	
;:	59	58		
'"	39	34		
`~	96	126		
0)	48	41		27 129
1 !	49	33		27 120
2 @	50	64	27 3	27 121
3 #	51	35		27 122
4 $	52	36		27 123
5 %	53	37		27 124
6 ∧	54	94	30	27 125
7 &	55	38		27 126
8 *	56	42		27 127
9 (	57	40		27 128
-_	45	95	31	27 130
= +	61	43		27 131
,<	44	60		
.>	46	62		
/?	47	63		
*	42		27 114	
+	43	43		
-	45	45		

Appendix J:
IBM PC Character Set

ASCII value	Character	Control character	ASCII value	Character
000	(null)	NUL	034	"
001	☺	SOH	035	#
002	☻	STX	036	$
003	♥	ETX	037	%
004	♦	EOT	038	&
005	♣	ENQ	039	'
006	♠	ACK	040	(
007	(beep)	BEL	041	)
008	◘	BS	042	*
009	(tab)	HT	043	+
010	(line feed)	LF	044	,
011	(home)	VT	045	-
012	(form feed)	FF	046	.
013	(carriage return)	CR	047	/
014	♫	SO	048	0
015	☼	SI	049	1
016	►	DLE	050	2
017	◄	DC1	051	3
018	↕	DC2	052	4
019	‼	DC3	053	5
020	¶	DC4	054	6
021	§	NAK	055	7
022	▬	SYN	056	8
023	↨	ETB	057	9
024	↑	CAN	058	:
025	↓	EM	059	;
026	→	SUB	060	<
027	←	ESC	061	=
028	(cursor right)	FS	062	>
029	(cursor left)	GS	063	?
030	(cursor up)	RS	064	@
031	(cursor down)	US	065	A
032	(space)		066	B
033	!		067	C

Reprinted courtesy of IBM Corporation.

ASCII value	Character	ASCII value	Character	ASCII value	Character
068	D	107	k	146	Æ
069	E	108	l	147	ô
070	F	109	m	148	ö
071	G	110	n	149	ò
072	H	111	o	150	û
073	I	112	p	151	ù
074	J	113	q	152	ÿ
075	K	114	r	153	Ö
076	L	115	s	154	Ü
077	M	116	t	155	¢
078	N	117	u	156	£
079	O	118	v	157	¥
080	P	119	w	158	Pt
081	Q	120	x	159	ƒ
082	R	121	y	160	á
083	S	122	z	161	í
084	T	123	{	162	ó
085	U	124	¦	163	ú
086	V	125	}	164	ñ
087	W	126	~	165	Ñ
088	X	127	⌂	166	ª
089	Y	128	Ç	167	º
090	Z	129	ü	168	¿
091	[	130	é	169	⌐
092	\	131	â	170	¬
093	]	132	ä	171	½
094	∧	133	à	172	¼
095	—	134	å	173	¡
096	'	135	ç	174	«
097	a	136	ê	175	»
098	b	137	ë	176	░
099	c	138	è	177	▒
100	d	139	ï	178	▓
101	e	140	î	179	│
102	f	141	ì	180	┤
103	g	142	Ä	181	╡
104	h	143	Å	182	╢
105	i	144	É	183	╖
106	j	145	æ	184	╕

ASCII value	Character	ASCII value	Character	ASCII value	Character
185	╣	209	╤	233	⊖
186	║	210	╥	234	Ω
187	╗	211	╙	235	δ
188	╝	212	╘	236	∞
189	╜	213	╒	237	∅
190	╛	214	╓	238	∈
191	┐	215	╫	239	∩
192	└	216	╪	240	≡
193	┴	217	┘	241	±
194	┬	218	┌	242	≥
195	├	219	█	243	≤
196	─	220	▄	244	⌠
197	┼	221	▌	245	⌡
198	╞	222	▐	246	÷
199	╟	223	▀	247	≈
200	╚	224	α	248	°
201	╔	225	β	249	•
202	╩	226	Γ	250	·
203	╦	227	π	251	√
204	╠	228	Σ	252	ⁿ
205	═	229	σ	253	²
206	╬	230	μ	254	■
207	╧	231	τ	255	(blank 'FF')
208	╨	232	Φ		

Appendix K:
Turbo Pascal Public Domain Library

The author has collected and maintains a library of over 600 public domain Turbo Pascal programs available on disk. They include applications, utilities, and tools. These programs are available for a copying charge of $15.00 per diskette. A catalog describing all of the programs in the library is available for $1.00.

David W. Carroll
P.O. Box 699
Pine Grove, CA 95665

Appendix L
Bibliography

This bibliography is not all-encompassing, but it does provide a number of good source books for further study for the serious Pascal programmer. As are most writers, I am in debt to those who have gone before. The most complete Pascal bibliography I have found is in Daniel R. McGlynn's book, *Fundamentals of Microcomputer Programming including Pascal.*

Reference Works

Turbo Pascal Version 1.0 Reference Manual, Borland International, 1983, 1984.
Turbo Pascal: Addendum to Reference Manual, Version 2.0 and 8087 Supplement, Borland International, 1984.
Turbo Pascal Version 2.0 Reference Manual, Borland International, 1983, 1984.
Turbo Pascal Version 3.0 Reference Manual, Borland International, 1983, 1984, 1985.
Turbo Tutor, Borland International, 1984.
Turbo Toolbox, Borland International, 1984.
Turbo Graphix Toolbox, Borland International, 1985.
Encyclopedia of Computer Science and Engineering, Second Ed., Van Nostrand Reinhold Co., 1976, 1983.
The VNR Concise Encyclopedia of Mathematics, Van Nostrand Reinhold Co., 1977.
Jensen, K., and Wirth, N., *Pascal User Manual and Report*, Springer-Verlag, 1974, 1978.
Cooper, D., *Standard Pascal User Reference Manual*, Norton, 1983.
   Gleaves, R., *Modula-2 for Pascal Programmers*, Springer-Verlag, 1984.
   Wirth, N., *Programming in Modula-2*, Springer-Verlag, 1983.

Programming Texts

Anderson, R., *From Basic to Pascal*, TAB Books, 1982.
Bowles, K., *Problem Solving Using Pascal*, Springer-Verlag, 1977.
Chirlian, P., *Pascal*, Matrix Publishers, 1980.
Conway, R., Gries, D., and Zimmerman, E., *A Primer on Pascal*, Winthrop, 1976.

Dahlquist, G., Bjorck, A., Anderson, N., *Numerical Methods*, Prentice-Hall, 1974, translated from the Swedish edition published in 1969.

Grogono, P., *Programming in Pascal*, Addison-Wesley, 1978, 1980.

Horowitz, E., and Sahni, S., *Fundamentals of Data Structures in Pascal*, Computer Science Press, 1976 rev 1984.

Hergert, R., and Hergert D., *Doing Business with Pascal*, Sybex, 1983.

Kernighan, B., and Plauger, P., *The Elements of Programming Style*, McGraw Hill, 1974, 1978.

Kernighan, B., and Plauger, P., *Software Tools in Pascal*, Addison Wesley, 1981.

Knuth, D., *The Art of Computer Programming*, (Vols. 1, 2, and 3), Addison Wesley, 1973.

Lecarme, O., and Nebut, J., *Pascal for Programmers*, McGraw Hill, 1984.

Ledgard, H, and Nagin, P., *Pascal with Style: Programming Proverbs*, Hayden, 1979.

Ledgard, H, and Singer, A., *Elementry Pascal*, Vintage, 1982.

Liffick, B. (Editor), *The Byte Book of Pascal*, BYTE, 1979.

McGlynn, D. R., *Fundamentals of Microcomputer Programming, Including Pascal*, Wiley-Interscience, 1982.

Miller, A., *Pascal Programs for Scientists and Engineers*, Sybex, 1981.

Moffat, D., *Common Algorithms in Pascal*, Prentice-Hall, 1984.

Tiberghien, J., *The Pascal Handbook*, Sybex, 1981.

Sand, P., *Advanced Pascal Programming Techniques*, Osborne/McGraw-Hill, 1984.

Schneider, G., Weingart, S., and Perlman, D., *An Introduction to Programming and Problem Solving with Pascal*, Wiley, 1977.

Sedgewick, R., *Algorithms*, Addison Wesley, 1983 rev 1984.

Vick, C. R., and Ramamoorthy, C. V. (editors), *Handbook of Software Engineering*, Van Nostrand Reinhold Co., 1984.

Vile Jr., R. C., *Programming Your Own Adventure Games in Pascal*, TAB Books, 1984.

Wirth, N., *Algorithms + Data Structures = Programs*, Prentice-Hall, 1976.

Wirth, N., *Systematic Programming: An Introduction*, Prentice-Hall, 1973.

Zaks, R., *Introduction to Pascal including UCSD Pascal*, Sybex, 1981.

Index

absolute address operations, 252-254
advanced data structures, 198-202
arrays, 153-164
    array declaration, 154-155
    array functions, 160-161
    character arrays, 156-158
    managing array elements, 158-160
    multidimensional arrays, 155-156
    packed data types, 164
    typed array constant, 161-164

Backus-Naur form, 44-45
basic standard procedures, 102-109
    arithmetic functions, 105-106
    miscellaneous functions, 108-109
    scalar functions, 106-107
    standard functions, 104-105
    terminal control, 102-103
    transfer functions, 108-109
binary numbers, 299-300
boolean expressions, 133

chain programs, 277-278
character counting program, 128
character counting program (sample), 151-152
compiler directives, 273-276
compiler error messages, 296-298
compiler options, 276
compound statements, 130-132
computer programs, 33-34
conditional statements, 133-142
converting Standard to Turbo, 223-225

data and computers, 60-62
decision and repetition, 132-133
Demonstration Turbo, 28-29
differences from Standard, 278
DOS interface examples, 256-272
    command line arguments, 263-265
    directory access, 261-263
    event timer, 259-261
    system time and date, 257-259
    wild cards, 265-272

error detection, 73
error message files, 278
example programs, 31-32
expressions, 82
    functions in, 82-83
external subprograms, 101

File Comparison, 243-247
File Conversion, 237-238
File Detab, 238-240
File Dump, 232-236
File Lister, 227-232
File Typer, 226-227
files, 211
    procedures, 217-219
    standard functions, 219-220
    untyped, 222
    use of, 211-212
    variables, 212-213
Filter, 240-243
formatting, 11-12
forward references, 101

functions, 90-92
  declaration, 90
  use of, 90-92

hard-disk users, 11
heap, 192-193
  allocating heap space, 202
  reclaiming heap space, 202-204
hexadecimal numbers, 299-300

IBM PC, 4
  basics, 3
  character set, 303-305
identifiers, 43-44
Include files, 277
INLINE code, 255
input/output errors, 298-299
input/output result checking, 220-222
installing Turbo Pascal, 13-15
integer numbers, 61

keyboard layout, 4-5
keyboard notation, 5-7
keyboard return codes, 300-302

literals, 70-72
  numeric, 71
  string, 71
logical devices, 214-215

machine independence, 35
machine language, 34
Main file, 273
menu, 17-19
meta-language definitions, 44-45
mileage program, 129

operators, 74-81
  arithmetic operators, 75-77
  logical operators, 77-79
  precedence, 75
  result types, 79-81

parameters, 92-96

passing, 93-95
types, 95-96
Pascal programs, 47-49
  comments, 59
  declarations, 53-57
  format and style, 58
  program scope, 52
  punctuation, 58
  statements, 57

random files, 217
read procedures, 119-123
  boolean input, 122-123
  headings and titles, 122
  input data types, 120-121
  prompting inputs, 121-122
real numbers, 61-62
records, 180-187
  accessing components, 182
  definition, 181-182
  variant records, 186-187
  WITH statement, 182-186
recursion, 100
reference guide, 285-289
repetitive statements, 143-151
reserved words, 42-43
run-time errors, 298

scalar and subrange types, 66-68
scope, 96-98
sets, 187-191
  constructions, 189
  definition, 188-189
operators, 190-191
side effects, 99
software interrupts, 255-256
square root program, 126
standard files, 215-216
Standard data types, 63-66
Standard Pascal, 46-47
  input/output, 210
standard procedures, 92
starting Turbo Pascal, 15
statements, 83-85
  assignments, 84-85

empty, 85-86
GOTO, 86
procedure, 84-85

string length program, 127
strings, 165-179
    application examples, 176-179
    characters, 166
    constants, 167
    declarations, 165-166
    expressions, 167-173
    filling, 173-174
    strings vs. arrays, 165
    testing elements, 175
structural programming, 38-40
symbolic assembly code, 34-35
syntax, 289-296
system requirements, 3

terminal control procedures, 119
text input/output, 213
Turbo Compiler, 19-21
    directives, 282
Turbo Editor, 21-28
    commands, 283-285
Turbo Help program, 29-31
Turbo language basics, 41-42
Turbo Pascal extensions, 279-281
Turbo Pascal input/output, 211
type conversion, 69
typed constants, 69-70

utility programs, 31

writer procedures, 111-118
    default output formats, 113-114
    specifying output formats, 114-118
    writer parameters, 118

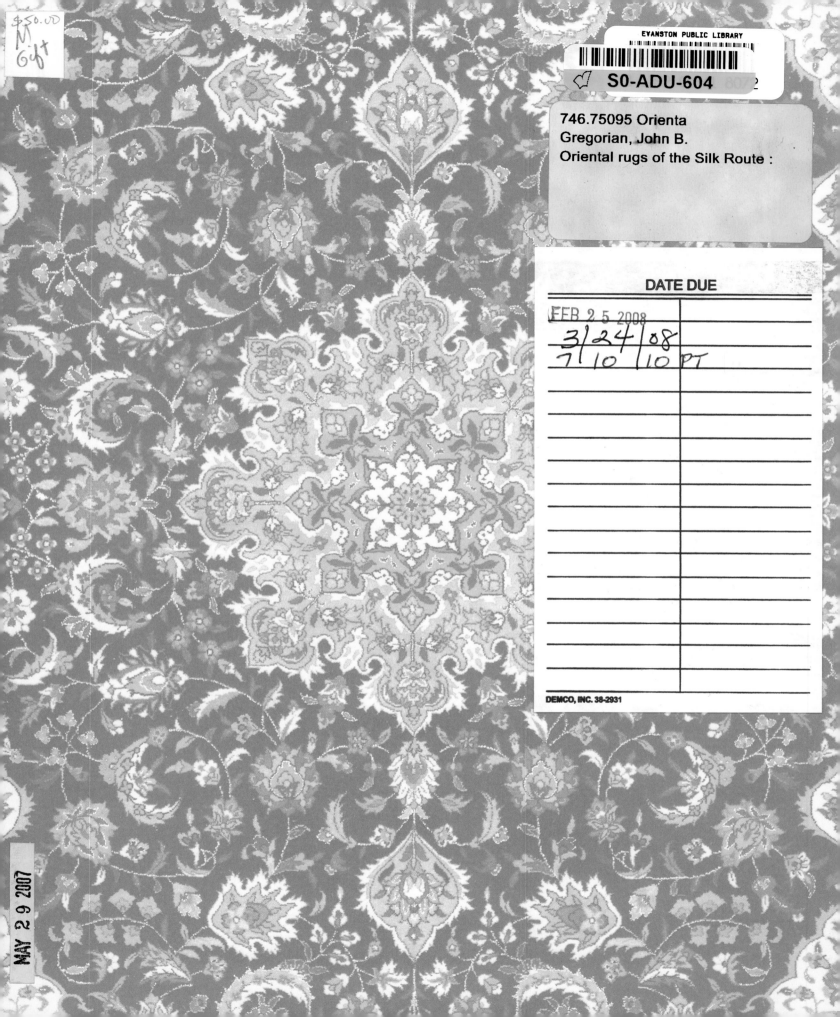

Oriental Rugs of the Silk Route

ORIENTAL RUGS OF THE SILK ROUTE

CULTURE, PROCESS, AND SELECTION

✛

JOHN B. GREGORIAN

RIZZOLI
NEW YORK

First published in the United States of America in 2000 by

RIZZIOLI INTERNATIONAL PUBLICATIONS, INC.

300 Park Avenue South

New York, NY 10010

ISBN 0-8478-2221-4

Library of Congress Cataloging-in-Publication Data 99 75983

Art Director: Galen Smith

Designers: Galen Smith & Lynne Yeamans

Printed and bound in Italy

To my loving, supportive wife Judy, and my three wonderful children, Scott, Melissa, and Jennifer; Sarah and Paul, most welcome additions to our family; my precious grandson, Andrew Paul; my mother, Phebe; and most especially, my father, Arthur, who introduced me to his passion for oriental rugs and the mysteries of the Middle East.

✠

ACKNOWLEDGMENTS

I wish to thank my friend Dick Pirozzolo for his tireless research and input; my nephew, Douglas Christian, enthusiastic and talented photographer and travel companion; Izy Yurmartaci, my Turkish supplier and extraordinarily knowledgeable and hospitable guide; Mr. Shree Dhar Misra and his son, Anoop, for their open door and hospitality; and my old friend, Lotfy Ben Levi, and his son, Marti.

I would also like to thank those whose homes appear in this book: Gerry and Imaging Spence, Mr. and Mrs. Jay Cassell, Lawrence DeRubbo, Glenn and Darci Brown, and Oddvar and Karen Nygaard.

CONTENTS

✦

INTRODUCTION   10

CHAPTER ONE   The Silk Route   14

CHAPTER TWO   Cultural Patterns in Oriental Rugs   30

CHAPTER THREE   A Simple Method of Rug Classification   52

CHAPTER FOUR   Understanding Dyes   60

CHAPTER FIVE   Travels Back in Time: Urmia and Isfahan, Iran   70

CHAPTER SIX   The Gateway to the Silk Route: Turkey   86

CHAPTER SEVEN   Searching the Subcontinent: India   108

CHAPTER EIGHT   The Art of Negotiation   140

CHAPTER NINE   Decorating with Oriental Rugs   150

APPENDIX   Cleaning Oriental Rugs ▪ Repairing Oriental Rugs   164

GLOSSARY   168

BIBLIOGRAPHY   170

PHOTOGRAPHY CREDITS   171

INDEX   172

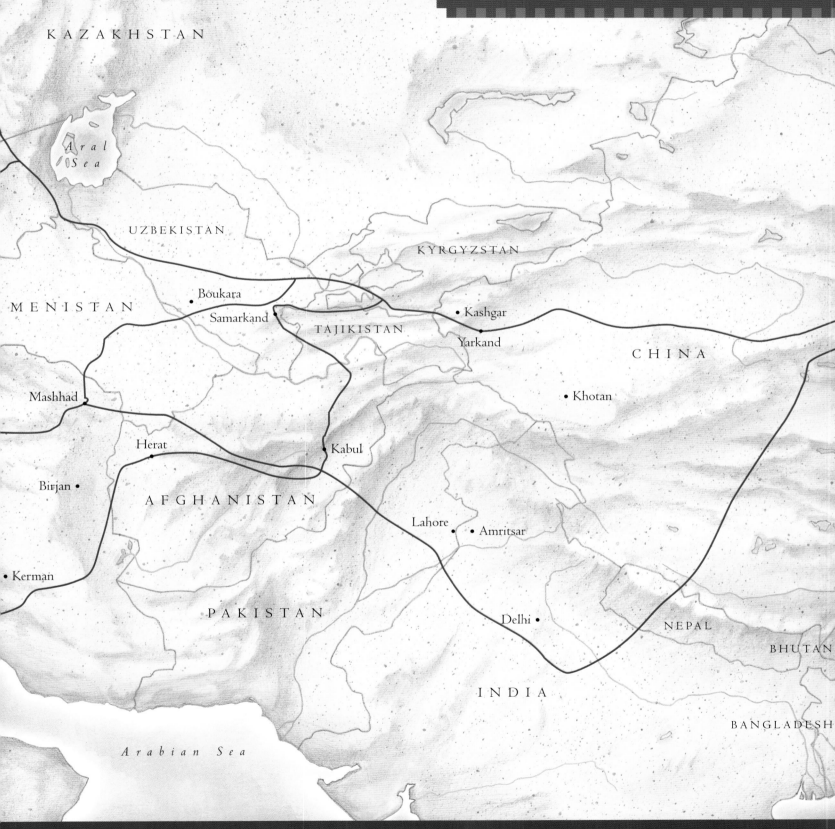

KAZAKHSTAN

Aral Sea

UZBEKISTAN

KYRGYZSTAN

MENISTAN

• Boukara

Samarkand •

TAJIKISTAN

• Kashgar

Yarkand •

CHINA

Mashhad •

• Khotan

Herat •

• Kabul

Birjan •

AFGHANISTAN

Lahore • Amritsar

• Kerman

PAKISTAN

Delhi •

NEPAL

BHUTAN

INDIA

Arabian Sea

BANGLADESH

INTRODUCTION

✛

When a merchant unrolls an oriental rug at a dusty bazaar at one of the trading centers along the famed Silk Route, he is revealing the result of a centuries-old tradition of weaving. Hidden within the symmetries of that rug—and every other—are variations in design and symbols introduced by the weaver that make each rug unique and defy Western interpretation.

The art, the mystery, and the history of oriental rugs make the search for them very intoxicating—and bring me back to the Silk Route year after year.

My first experience along the Silk Route occurred in the summer of 1959. I was seventeen years old and had just finished my junior year in high school. I was also about to begin one of the most exciting experiences of my life. My father and I were going to Turkey and Iran in search of oriental rugs. My father, Arthur, had not been back to Iran since 1918, when, at the age of nine, he fled his homeland before raiding Kurds and Turks during the outbreak of World War I. (The country was called Persia until 1927, when it was renamed Iran—the terms are used interchangeably throughout this book.) For the next three years my father lived as a refugee in Baghdad, emigrating to the United States in 1921. He settled in New Britain, Connecticut, where he

met my mother, Phebe Ballou, a Yankee girl from Westminster, Massachusetts. Upon graduation from high school in 1932, my father followed my mother to Wellesley, Massachusetts, where she attended Wellesley College.

For the next two years, my father worked for various rug dealers in the area, then opened his own oriental rug business during the depression in 1934 in a small, below-street-level shop in Wellesley Hills, with no money, no rugs, and no customers, but lots of determination. By 1959, his business was prospering and he decided that after forty years it was time to find his roots again under the guise of buying rugs, and in doing so would have the opportunity to introduce me to the world of his youth.

We encountered a couple of stumbling blocks prior to our departure. First, just before our trip, we visited my father's terminally ill mother, who implored him not to take me back to their village. All she could remember of the town was the terror of the constant raiding parties, death, and her family's flight nearly forty years earlier. Fortunately, my father assured her that it was safe for us to return.

Secondly, there was a more serious problem that we had to resolve before our departure. Since my father had been

born in Iran, he was considered an Iranian by their government, even though he had become an American citizen many years prior. If he were to travel on an Iranian passport with me, his son, I could be subject to the Iranian military draft. To prevent this, my father contacted the Iranian embassy, where Ambassador Ali Ardilan, who, with the American State Department, managed to arrange for my father to travel on an American passport and prepared numerous letters of introduction to the many provincial governors in Iran asking for safe passage and protection for us.

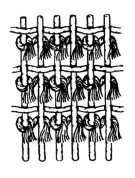

We left New York aboard a Swedish airline on a hot, early July afternoon—this was my first time on an airplane. Our first stop was Scotland, and the trip took twelve hours, as our plane was propeller-driven. The time it took for us to get there had its advantages, though, as the attendants fed us lots of new and unusual continental food. We landed in Glasgow Airport, a World War II airfield with a small barnlike building that served as the terminal. I will always remember vividly a sign that hung there: "Haste ye back to Scotland."

We departed Scotland nonetheless, and many long hours later, we landed at Yeşilköy Airport in Istanbul, Turkey. We arrived in the middle of the night and were met by our hosts: Arça, a young woman who had studied in the United States with my older sister, Lynda, and had become a member of our family, and her father. They were very hospitable and couldn't seem to do enough to make our stay comfortable.

We bought rugs tentatively in Turkey, as we did not yet know any shipping agents there whom we could trust. Many of the Turks with whom we dealt with at that time did not look favorably on Armenians, and, in fact, preferred to call us Mr. John and Mr. Arthur, rather than by our Armenian last name. We did find that the Istanbul bazaar still had a very good number of older Turkish village rugs that were generally in short supply and very much in demand at home.

When we left Turkey for Iran, we took the new French jet "The Caravelle." We landed at Mehrabad Airport in Teheran, and as was typical in Iran and the Middle East in general at the time, everything was chaotic. At passport control, the agents looked at our passports as if they had never seen passports before, chatting to each other and passing them around like rare specimens. Finally, we got our passports back, but were then faced with a similar situation regarding our health cards. Each official scrutinized the documents, trying to ascertain what shots and immunizations we had had. But this lengthy process was easy compared to trying to find our luggage!

Newly arrived passengers were literally climbing over each other trying to find their bags and boxes. I also remember the contrast of seeing, in this relatively contemporary terminal, a poor desert family squatted around a charcoal brazier making tea. When we found all of our luggage, several airport porters appeared and offered their help, which we accepted gladly. Despite the fact that each porter wore a sign on his chest that read "no tipping" in several languages, each insisted on a tip. All I could think was "What a country!"—and what a country it was!

We finally arrived at the Park Hotel—a French–built establishment that attempted to be very continental in spite of its Iranian ambience—and were shown to our room. The furnishings were comfortable, but the room was stuffy and hot, as air conditioning had not yet come to Iran. I spent the night outside on the balcony in nearly 100-degree (Fahrenheit) heat. Teheran is 6,000 feet above sea level, and in the summer the air is extremely hot, but fortunately quite dry.

My trip to Persia had begun. My father had told me stories about Iran since I was a little boy, and in 1959, the country was still an undeveloped, genteel place. Oil had been discovered, but was not yet subject to the extensive international politicking we know today. The path we were taking in our quest for oriental rugs was the ancient Silk Route— a caravan route that not only crisscrossed all of the Middle East and Asia, but also contributed to the exchange of both goods and ideas between the East and West.

After my initial visit, I returned to Iran every year until the 1979 revolution resulted in closing the country to foreign travelers. Today, I continue to visit Turkey, India, and Pakistan in search of oriental rugs, my Holy Grail.

THE SILK ROUTE

OUR SEARCH FOR

oriental rugs begins on the easternmost

shore of the Mediterranean in historic Istanbul—a city at the

crossroads of eastern and western culture and the gateway to the famous silk trading road,

known as the Silk Route. ✤ Though the Silk Route was popularized by the travels of Marco Polo and the cru-

saders, there is ample evidence in Egyptian tapestries to suggest that information and goods traversed this trading road

four thousand years ago. In the fourth century A.D., the Romans used this network of highways and nautical routes that

traversed the Black Sea to acquire silk from China. The roads from the west stretched from the Golden Horn in present-

day Istanbul to Chinese seaports, crisscrossing the Caucasus, Iran (Persia), Afghanistan, and Central Asia. The route, in

fact, looked somewhat like—and had the same economic impact as—the railway system that opened the United States to

trade. By making all sorts of goods available, the railroads improved the standard of living for Americans during the 1860s.

✤ Similarly, the Silk Route influenced life and played an economic role in European incursion into the Middle East and

Asia throughout history. From the seventh century onward, silk was shipped from China to Constantinople, and from

there transported to trading centers in Greece, Italy, Spain, and France. Many of the cocoons went to Bursa in what is

now northwest Turkey, a city still famous as that country's center for silk production. An old story told by Turkish silk

merchants recounts how two Byzantine monks smuggled silk worms hidden inside their hollowed out walking sticks

into Bursa; in Byzantine art, monks are often depicted spinning silk. ✤ In the thirteenth century, Marco Polo

made the Silk Route famous as an early trading caravan route stretching from Europe

to China. This route became the lifeline for Central Asian, Middle

Eastern, and Far Eastern peoples to acquire

European goods.

CHAPTER ONE

SEAT OF MANY
NATIONS

The civilization of Istanbul dates back to 667 B.C., when the ancient Greeks founded Byzantium on the site. In the fourth century A.D., the Emperor Constantine renamed the city Constantinople as the seat of the Byzantine or Eastern Roman Empire. In 1453, Constantinople was taken by the Ottomans and made the new capital of their empire, a position it held until World War I, when the national government convened in Ankara (1919) and finally proclaimed the republic of Turkey in 1923.

SEAT OF MANY NATIONS

. . . .

The civilization of Istanbul dates back to 667 B.C., when the ancient Greeks founded Byzantium on the site. In the fourth century A.D., the Emperor Constantine renamed the city Constantinople as the seat of the Byzantine or Eastern Roman Empire. In 1453, Constantinople was taken by the Ottomans and made the new capital of their empire, a position it held until World War I, when the national government convened in Ankara (1919) and finally proclaimed the republic of Turkey in 1923.

These commercial goods, along with fir, timber, and wax, were exchanged for indigenous items such as silk, spices, and hand-knotted rugs. One of the least known or understood items, these hand-knotted rugs, although beautiful and exotic, were not plentiful and therefore were originally a commerically insignificant trade item for Europeans.

Throughout the nineteenth century, trade along the Silk Route flourished. At the seaports in China, trade items from the Silk Route were loaded onto ships headed to America and Europe (hence the name "oriental" rugs) at the other end of the Silk Route.

At the same time, native weavers placed no significant monetary value on their rugs; they were simply fashioned into utilitarian objects such as beds, bags, horse covers, tent doors, and trappings. As caravan traders sought out examples of this newly discovered art form, village weavers along the Silk Route began making rugs to meet demand. As a result, the quality and workmanship suffered. By the end of the nineteenth century, the wonderful rugs of the Silk Route slipped quietly into a new area of decline.

✦   ✦   ✦

Oriental rugs represent the varied religious and cultural traditions of the peoples living along the Silk Route. Rug weaving was always considered an Islamic art form, but we know that Christian Armenians in Armenia and Karabaugh in the Caucasus wove Islamic-style oriental rugs for themselves and their churches beginning around 1850, incorporating crosses and other Christian motifs into their designs. At about the same time, Hindus, influenced by Islamic-woven Persian court rug styles, began to weave rugs with designs of large native Indian beasts—such as elephants, lions, and tigers—fighting savagely with each other. Moslem weavers seldom incorporated human or animal representations in their sophisticated rugs, but folk-art or village rugs abound with childlike stick figures, people, and animals.

Present-day oriental rug merchants and collectors continue to journey the Silk Route in the tradition of those early trade caravans. There are numerous areas along the Silk Route whose indigenous rug-weaving styles and customs are practiced even today. Such examples could and can be found

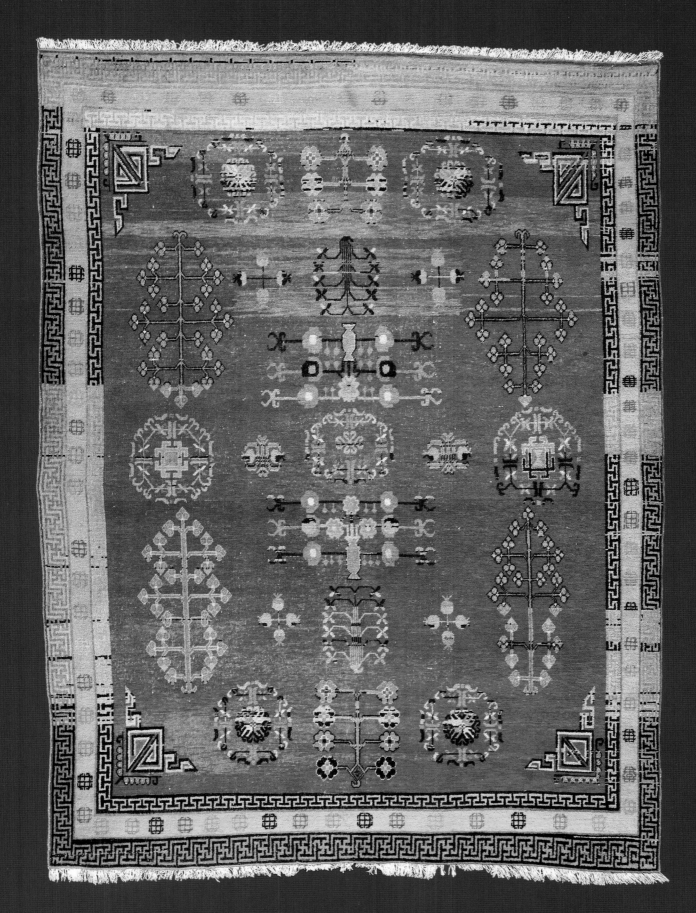

PAGE 20 ▪ *This Caucasian Daghestan, 4'3" x 5' (129 x 152cm), circa 1890, has a field filled with the stylized Persian* boteh *paisley design that swept Europe with the introduction of programmable looms. Despite the fact that no two of the repeated*

patterns are the same size, the design has a uniform effect.

PAGE 21 ▪ *This nineteenth-century Kashgar, 5'8" x 7'8" (176 x 234cm), features Chinese iconography and design motifs. This rug was created by Turkestan weavers in western China—*

ancestral homeland of a people who migrated throughout Turkey, the Caucasus, northern Afghanistan, and parts of Persia.

BELOW ▪ *In addition to making rugs, nomadic tribes used the same technique to create utilitarian objects such as these bags.*

OPPOSITE ▪ *This wonderful example of an early twentieth-century Bidjar, 7'2" x 11'4" (218 x 345cm), features an open field and madder rust color. The medallion and the border incorporates the traditional fish and turtle design.*

all along the route, in places like the Caucasus where rug making today is practically extinct, and in Afghanistan, with its distinctive Boukara (large polygon) designs and somber palates of dark reds and blues with very little ivory.

Prior to 1979, Persia (Iran) was the oriental rug-weaving and trading center of the world, and the term "Persian" was used to describe rugs woven only in Iran. Now, for most people, "Persian" rugs and "oriental" rugs are synonymous, generic names referring to a specific style of handwoven carpet.

When the Shah of Iran was deposed in 1979, the Iranian rug-weaving and exportation industry came to a virtual halt and foreign access to rugs woven in Iran was reduced drastically. Westerners began to attribute an unrealistically high value to all rugs woven in Iran because of the diminished supply, and many inferior

Iranian-made rugs commanded premium prices. Dealers reasoned that since the rugs were made in Keshan, Kerman, Bidjar, and of course, the cultural and artistic city of Isfahan (one of Iran's major rug-trading centers), they were genuine and valuable, regardless of quality.

There are many fine rugs being woven in Iran today, notably folk-art or village rugs, and some top-quality intricate rugs from urban centers. However, a few Iranian weavers—once critical of Indian weavers for copying Persian styles—are now basing their court rugs on the carefully designed and expertly colored rugs from India. Iran, once the industry leader and most celebrated producer of oriental rugs, now has some very formidable competition. In the history of rug buying, the 1990s will be noted as the most advantageous to the rug buyer in terms of quantity, selection, and price.

THE GREGORIAN FAMILY COLLECTION

As a child, I learned about Marco Polo, the grandeur of Constantinople and the wealth of Venice, where fortunes rose on the spice and silk trade, and the romantic cities of Baghdad and Tehran, not from school books, but through the rugs my father had collected, the stories he told about them, and our adventures along the Silk Route. Although my father opened his shop during the Great Depression, he still had the foresight to set aside and preserve a few antique rugs from the late ninteenth and early twentieth century that were superb examples of a particular category of rug or had an interesting history. The rugs he collected are nearly impossible to find today, and in many cases, if one could find a similar rug, the cost would be prohibitive. My father continued his efforts through the early 1950s, and the collection, which he eventually titled *Oriental Rugs of the Silk Route*, grew in size, scope, and stature.

He first showed the collection to groups of vistors at his shop and later to museum goers. I marveled at his gift for teaching and for spinning yarns that were as intriguing as the places he visited and as complex as the patterns in the rugs. I remember how he would ask me to demonstrate the way Moslem worshippers used prayer rugs in daily devotions, and it was a chance to play-act a role that I would later re-enact many times over.

Over the years, I played a more significant role as curator of the collection and immersed myself in researching

individual rugs. What fascinates me is that not only is each rug in the collection a superb example of weaving and art, but that the collection as a whole chronicles the ebb and flow of ideas across a vast region that spans from China to Venice.

In the collection, you can see how diverse cultures passed aesthetic values from generation to generation in tiny villages, and how new ideas flowed across cultures from East to West and back. As an example, one of the more unusual rugs in the collection depicts animals and plant life

OPPOSITE ▪ *One of the most recognized names in oriental rugs is Kerman, and this nineteenth-century rug, 5' x 7'6" (152 x 229cm), is a masterpiece of Kerman craftsmanship. With more than a half million knots, the rug has sharp details and soft and beautifully blended colors. Note how the use of different dye lots of blue is apparent throughout the piece. The treatment of the landscape, the gazelles, and pheasants is delightfully imaginative.*

RIGHT ▪ *The inscription on this Kerman Ravar, 4'7" x 8' (140 x 243cm), circa 1890, was made by an* ustad, *or "master craftsman," Mohammed Zad Kermani. In terms of its detail, this rug is on a par with the finest Persian miniature paintings, for it is filled with intricate floral patterns, including two cypress trees and two rose bushes that meander about and decoratively entwine all of the top. At the bottom of the main field is a plant whose daisylike flowers mimic a peacock tail. Such rugs were made by master weavers who ran schools that instructed students in this fine art form. Ravar is a small town near Kerman in southwestern Iran.*

in a flat medieval perspective that is neither part of the local weavers' environment, nor their aesthetic sense. What the rug demonstrates is that these weavers picked up clues from Europeans passing through and created in their own minds an image of what they thought these Westen travelers would buy as souvenirs. Though the example we have in the collection dates back to the turn of the century, the weaver of this rug was probably not unlike the operator of a modern souvenir shop who tries to anticipate what the tourists will buy.

Another rug in the collection, a Yarkand, incorporates Turkoman concepts in the central field, Mongolian yellow and coral colors and design motifs in the border, and even Persianate trees and blossoms—all in one rug. This rug is a fine example of the syntheses of ideas that took place along the Silk Route. Other rugs cover a spectrum of design themes that embrace local cultures, outside ideas and, in a number of cases, commercial demands. The collection also includes utilitarian prayer rugs as well as oddities that would not normally be seen in rug shops, such as samplers which were woven to showcase the skills of the weaver (these would not be regarded as having any commercial or interior decor value).

In 1948, the public got its first glimpse of *Oriental Rugs of the Silk Route* at The Everhart Museum of Natural History, Science and Art in Scranton, Pennsylvania. Since its debut, the collection has grown and has been exhibited at over seventy museums, colleges, and universities worldwide. The collection continues to be exhibited, and is an ideal way for

OPPOSITE ▪ *This Sarouk, 4'4" x 6'6" (142 x 197cm), a rug from late nineteenth-century Persia comes from a small isolated village whose only access is a road that ends at the village gates. In this example, the best wools and dyes were used and the nap was clipped low to create a firm texture. Despite Sarouk's isolation, older Sarouk rugs of floral design rank with the most sophisticated floral rugs woven in Persia's major cities.*

BELOW ▪ *This Bakshaish, 5'4" x 7'6" (162 x 228cm), circa 1870, from Persia was added to the collection because it is a stunning example of the tree of life design. Its directionality indicates that it has a prayer rug as its roots—a classic rug of the Silk Route that arrived in the West during the heyday of oriental-rug popularity during the nineteenth century.*

TOP, LEFT ▪ *This is a primitive Armenian Kazak, 5' x 6'7" (152 x 201cm), with cross-shaped finials on both the inner and outer medallions. The emptiness of the field is relatively unusual for Armenian weaving.*

BOTTOM, LEFT ▪ *This nineteenth-century Persian Ardebil village rug, 4'8" x 6'10" (142 x 208cm), demonstrates how this design can be easily mistaken for a Tabriz rug. Note the primitive floral pattern in the center is on the same cultural level as most weavers in this area, but with a further similarity to Tabriz design in the border. Overall, however, the treatment is a bit more geometrical than one would find in a true Tabriz.*

OPPOSITE ▪ *A one-of-a-kind masterpiece, this Keshan rug, 4'6" x 7'9" (137 x 236cm), was woven of silk and silver in nineteenth-century Persia. Its intricacy rivals earlier seventeenth- and eighteenth-century carpets made of silk, silver, and gold that were intended as gifts among royalty. The embossed effect is created by two sculptured levels of silk contrasting with a flat weave of silver-wrapped threads. In keeping with the exquisite craftsmanship is the choice of subtle colors and the quality of the silk. Despite its age, the rug glows with fresh color and cleanly-etched patterning. The main border, with its miniature scenes of Persian palaces and gardens, offer additional interest.*

the neophyte or veteran rug lover to see so many examples from vastly diverse cultures at one time.

Of course, the collection occupies a special place in my heart. Every time I open a rug in the collection, the patina, the feel, even the aroma of that rug, takes me instantly back to my childhood and the many times I sat on a pile of rugs in my father's shop and listened to those wonderful tales of ancient lands.

CULTURAL PATTERNS IN ORIENTAL RUGS

Islamic

fatalism

strongly influences the Middle

Eastern rug weaver's craft: since one's

actions have already been decreed by God, the passage of time

has little consequence; without this belief, oriental rugs requir-

ing months and months of labor would probably not exist. As Westerners, we appreciate

artistic and design concepts that make little sense to these artisans. For example, when a

Western painter uses the wrong color or stroke, he wipes off the mistake and starts over, repainting the image until

it looks "perfect." To the Moslem weaver, there is no such thing as perfection on earth: only Allah is perfect, so trying to achieve perfection

would be considered arrogant. ✦ Many Middle Eastern peoples accept mistakes as part of life. If a family is weaving a rug and dyes wool

as needed, with the result being that the colors do not match or age in the same way ultimately, they do not consider this to be an error. The

rug is simply the way it is. In fact, to say "the color changed" is a perfectly acceptable and logical explanation. ✦ A

Persian story about a scorpion who wanted to cross the Euphrates River illustrates this unique sense of logic. Since

the scorpion could not swim, it found a turtle and asked the turtle to ferry it across the

river on its back. "Oh, no," protested the turtle, "If I do as you ask, halfway across the river,

you'll sting me and I'll drown." That is crazy," replied the scor-

pion, "If I sting you, I will drown because I cannot swim." This

sounded logical to the turtle, so it told

the scorpion to climb up on its

back and off

they went.

CHAPTER TWO

Halfway across the river, the scorpion stung the turtle. As the turtle floundered and was about to die, it said, "Now I will die and you will drown. It doesn't make any sense." The scorpion simply responded, "Because this is the Middle East, it doesn't have to make sense."

The "this-is-the-way-it-is" view of life is so pervasive in the Middle East that even rugs knotted according to a predetermined pattern have enormous variation—what Westerners would call errors. But in fact, much of the charm of an oriental rug, and the fact that its appeal grows the longer it is out on the floor, can be traced to the little inconsistencies hidden throughout the pattern.

I once had a customer who called me very excitedly. While vacuuming her rug, she noticed an animal that she had never seen before. That rug, in all its individuality, had become like a child to her—a member of the family.

THE ROLE OF WOMEN IN WEAVING

Rug making is generally a woman's art and craft. This does not mean that you will never see a man at the loom, but, by far, there are many more women weavers. The exception to this rule is in India, where men do most of the weaving. Sometimes, children assist their mothers and grandmothers, so as to eventually learn this high-paying trade.

Children weaving at their parents' side takes place throughout the Middle East and is a time-honored tradition. Weaving is not a full-time occupation for the child and is not to be considered child labor. This passing on of knowledge and skill regarding indigenous crafts is much the same the world over, be it Middle Eastern rug weaving, Scandinavian knitting, or Native American stone carving. Although child labor

was in evidence during the fifties and sixties, I have not witnessed such abuse in my thirty-five years of travel since then. Such abusive behavior is well hidden if it does exist, and most reliable dealers—including myself and all of our suppliers—would not buy from manufacturers exploiting children.

In most villages, women do the lion's share of the domestic chores. Rug weaving is what is done after all the other work for one's home, family, and village is completed. Like the quilting bees or barn raisings of days gone by, rug weaving is a time of relaxation, gossip, social intercourse, and creativity.

SYMMETRY AND SYMBOLISM

At first glance, most oriental rugs look perfectly symmetrical, but closer examination reveals that they are far from balanced. A flower may appear on the upper right-hand corner of a design, while in the corresponding location on the upper left-hand side a comb is depicted. Why? The comb is a symbol of personal neatness, and the rug weaver felt compelled to include it at that juncture in her life. The work may not be symmetrical technically, but when viewed as a whole it is perfectly balanced.

Other variations appear randomly among rugs created by several weavers following the instructions of a chanter who calls out the colors and design in a singsong cadence: "One red, two blue, three green." As work progresses, mistakes are made throughout—but in keeping with the Middle Eastern philosophy of life, no one would consider correcting the error.

In rural communities in Iran and other Islamic countries in the Middle East, the idea of symmetrical perfection as we define it in the West is generally not understood. The concept makes no sense to simple village people. In today's increasingly technological and commercial society, however, we find rugs being designed on a computer, especially in urban centers. In these cases, computer screens are even mounted on looms to guide the weaver in creating the design and determining which colors to use (the designs are dictated by the owners of the looms, who are influenced by Western traders). Nonetheless, the weaver uses more than her eyes and hands to create a rug—the design is also influenced by her heart, her mind, and the cultural traditions of her people. Happily, it will take many more years before the weavers' traditions are erased from their weaving—if ever.

A rug weaver may use a symbol as an identifying "signature" or at times, incorporate an icon or good luck symbol into the most formal of designs as a way to express her own individuality— or just how she happens to be feeling at that moment. This is not unlike the way we bring in our own coffee mug and display pictures of our family and pets at our offices in order to personalize our workspaces.

No matter how hard one tries to keep an open mind, it is tempting to look at an oriental rug and attribute meaning to symbols and numbers that may or may not be necessarily accurate. In his book, *Oriental Carpet Design: A Guide to Traditional Motifs, Patterns and Symbols*, P. R. J. Ford aptly points out that one of the most reviled symbols in Western culture, the swastika—which the Nazis adopted as their emblem—is a mystic design of ancient origin that is viewed as a talisman in eastern oriental rug designs. In India, the swastika is woven into the rug as an auspicious omen, while in China, it symbolizes "ten thousand happinesses" and the "heart of Buddha." Dates, which occasionally

appear in oriental rugs, can also be misleading. A date can accurately indicate when a rug was woven; however, many rug weavers are not literate. Even if the only literate person in a village writes down the date as a guidepost, the weaver may reverse or invert the numerals so that they make little sense.

In other cases, dates are utilized by the weaver in a whimsical way with unbridled artistic license. I once witnessed a comparable example of such license during a visit to Tabriz. One day, I noticed a letter writer who had set up shop on the sidewalk with a small desk and paper. This is quite common and provides employment for poorer literate individuals in areas where access to schools and learning is scant. A villager, perhaps a shepherd or farmer, was telling the writer his story and the writer was busily writing away. Shortly, the villager stopped talking, but the writer continued on making obvious editorial additions to the letter. The villager did not seem to mind—he assumed that the added words were fact, because the scribe had written them down—so the letter was finished, stamped, and sealed.

When I appraise a rug, I look at the construction, design, and color for dating purposes—not necessarily the

date woven into the design. "There have been several occasions on which very specific scientific examinations have helped to date carpets; one carpet from the Victoria and Albert Museum in London was bought in 1933 as a Turkish carpet dating from the late seventeenth century. In 1962 samples of the dyes were analyzed and the results indicated the presence of brilliant purpurin 10 B, invented in 1867, and a fusion of chrysophenine, which was invented in 1885. It now seems that the carpet was woven in Eastern Europe, most likely in Romania, shortly before its purchase by the Victoria and Albert Museum, London."

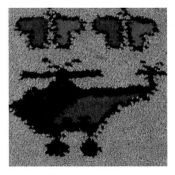

I have a rug from Russia that was woven circa 1920. In the middle of it, the weaver has emblazoned "1999" in large numerals. I presume the weaver meant 1922—or lived in another dimension.

TYPES OF RUGS

WAR RUGS

As the art of oriental rug weaving spread throughout the Persian empire to India, Pakistan, and elsewhere,

new generations of weavers learned the ancient Persian patterns—integrating personal, political, and cultural symbolism into their designs. The inscribed Armenian rugs that my father, Arthur, collected for over fifty years and donated to the Armenian Library and Museum in Watertown, Massachusetts, show how the Armenians attempted to preserve their cultural identity during a time of enormous strife. These rugs were woven by Christian Armenians of the Ottoman Empire, who lived in a Moslem-dominated culture prior to World War I, and endured the Armenian

OPPOSITE ▪ *This three-medallion Kazak, 5'11" × 9' (183 × 274cm), inscribed with "Asak P." and "ARP. 1911 TIV," commemorates the wedding of Arpen, as his name is followed by the Greek P—the initial letter of the Armenian word* pesa, *or bridegroom.*

The weaver has permitted herself a little free expression by including a pair of crested birds in the first medallion. As with most rugs of this tradition, color balance is superb. Note how the ornate crosses throughout the field variegate the large expanse, adding interest.

PAGE 42 ▪ *This huge Bakhtiari or "Bibibaft," 15'7" × 19'9" (475 × 588cm), was woven circa 1900. "Bibi" refers to the first or most proficient wife, whose skills at the loom bring in family income as she weaves such rugs for wealthy customers.*

PAGE 43 ▪ *This is a latter nineteenth-century Mohtashem Keshan, 4'6" × 6'9" (132 × 206cm). Mohtashem was a famous master weaver; his rugs were respected the world over for their fine weave and soft colors.*

massacre of 1915–1918. They depict numerous Christian symbols in an effort to establish the unique Christian identity of a people who had lost their homeland.

Today, war continues to play a role in rug design with rugs from Afghanistan known as "War Rugs," made by the Belouchis, a nomadic tribe of Afghanistan and southern China. The weavers depict stylized tanks, airplanes, and artillery pieces, using the same geometric approach once reserved for the depiction of barnyard animals and flowers.

BAKHTIARI RUGS

Until the latter half of the twentieth century, the Bakhtiaris of Iran were a semimigratory tribe of nomads. In the winter they lived in southern Iran to tend their flocks of sheep, moving north in the summer to meager mountainous pastures in search of grazing land. Although the Bakhtiaris are no longer nomadic, they are still a fiercely independent people. Today the Bakhtiaris are no longer nomadic, but live in villages around Isfahan in central Iran.

Bakhtiari weavers use a charming vernacular of visual metaphor to represent human emotion and circumstance: a weeping willow tree symbolizes sorrow, while a solid, upright juniper tree signifies elegance or arrogance. Prosperity is indicated by an ear of corn or a sheaf of wheat. Each of these individual images is framed within its own square or rectangular panel, the panels alternating gracefully throughout the design. In some of the more elaborate rugs, the weaver will often divide the rug into four sections, each representing a seasonal landscape: winter, with snowy hills; spring, with tiny flowers sprinkling the Persian countryside; summer, with trees in blossom; and autumn, with a harvest scene. These rugs are enchanting works of art as well as pictographic narratives about a way of life.

PRAYER RUGS

In Islamic countries, prayer rugs are neither rarities nor sacred objects; their sole purpose is to keep the faithful clean and protected from the ground on which the rug is spread. They are woven in the same manner as other rugs, but made to a standard size—usually two to three feet wide

OPPOSITE ▪ *This Kazak prayer rug, 3'2" x 5'5" (96 x 165cm), is a striking example of the primitive rug weaving found in the remote Caucuses. It is the product of tribal people who love simple design, large shapes, and strong colors.*

BELOW ▪ *This Ardebil prayer rug, 4'8" x 7'2" (142 x 218cm), was woven in l960 for export, as its large size makes it impractical to use as a prayer rug. This prayer rug motif was used for its design value only.*

by four to five feet long. The chief identifying feature is a pointed or rounded pattern at one end that resembles a doorway or the entrance to a mosque, called a "prayer point," or *mihrab*, whose shape is determined by the ability of the weaver and her heritage. Belouchi (Afghan) prayer points are often simple blunted tips whereas Keshan (Iranian) points are usually highly embellished and domelike in appearance; both indicate which end to point towards Mecca during prayer. Often, the direction to Mecca is open to individual interpretation; it is not unusual to see peasants in the fields praying, each prayer rug pointing in a different direction.

Other symbols that appear in prayer rugs include the tree of life, representing the supplicant's belief in immortality (for more on the tree of life, see "Common Rug Patterns," on the following page), and outstretched hands, indicating where to place one's palms while kneeling on the rug. Very often a little rake-shaped comb will be woven into the design to show that the one who prays upon the rug is a pious person, for the comb indicates cleanliness, a Moslem virtue.

Symbols are also used to express the weaver's individuality: Armenian Christians from the Caucasus who weave prayer rugs for the Moslem trade employ traditional Islamic prayer motifs but often will subtly insert small crosses within the design, symbols of their Christian faith.

OPPOSITE ▪ *This Kohi*
Sultan from Pakistan, 9' x 12'2"
(274 x 370cm), is a contemporary
version of the tree of life design.
The rug is executed in an extremely
fine weave, with tremendous detail
and numerous colors. Its size and
intricacy make it most desirable.

COMMON RUG PATTERNS

TREE OF LIFE (*DRAKHTI*)

The tree of life—the Persian symbol for immortality—is a prevalent pattern in oriental rug design. Some rugs are entirely covered with one enormous stylized tree springing from one end of the rug and filling the whole field, while others are dotted with repeated series of small trees. Nomadic weavers abstract the tree, reducing the image to two leaves springing from a straight stem with a rosette at the top. To illustrate the solid reality of life on earth, trees of life are usually represented with their roots firmly fixed in the ground. The Persians also believe that the tree is a metaphor for humanity, because man is erect, upright, and life-giving, like a tree. A weeping willow connotes sadness and can signify death.

THE ROSE (*GUL-FERANG*)

An even older Persian allegory likens human life to a rose, inferring that life is beautiful, yet has its thorny predicaments. The wild rose bush is a very common pattern in almost all older Sarouk (Iran), Keshan, and many other con-

temporary rugs (*gul-ferang* means "foreign flower" in Farsi). Usually the vines emanate from the corners of the rug, twisting and turning gracefully across the field until whole sections are covered in foliage. Cut flowers, usually roses in a vase, symbolize the transience of life; quite often this image is used as a main field pattern.

FISH AND TURTLE DESIGN (*HERATI*)

The ancient Persians thought the world was flat and that it rested upon the back of a huge turtle which held it up from the ocean depths (this idea is still believed by those living in rural Iranian villages). In the water surrounding the earth were two huge fish which swam around and around the flat earth as if chasing each other; the momentum of their movement made the earth rotate, causing day and night, seasonal change, and all other earthly phenomena. In Iran, hardly a month goes by that one does not feel seismic activity, which only strengthens the belief in this old tale. If the two fish were ever to catch each other or if the turtle were to be upset, the legend holds that the world would end.

In Iran, the Persian New Year (*Nou Ruz*) is observed on March 21, the vernal equinox. At midnight, celebrants try

BELOW ▪ *This rugged Belouch prayer rug, 2'10" × 5' (86cm × 152cm), from Afghanistan, circa 1940, is typical of the craftsmanship created by these seminomadic peoples whose ancestral grazing lands are now divided among Russia, Iran, Pakistan, and Afghanistan.*

to balance a raw egg on its end momentarily. When the egg falls over, they say the turtle has turned around and another year has begun.

Herati literally means "fish and turtle design" in Farsi. While the turtle image is strikingly clear in rugs from the Iranian towns of Fereghan, Saraband, and Bidjar, it is suggested by a mere outline in nomadic weaving and by Azerbaijani weavers from Northwest Iran and the bordering Azerbaijan Republic. Over the years, this icon has been continually ab-stracted so that one cannot say whether it resembles two fish encircling the globe or a blossom encircled by two leaves. Regardless of its exact form, this icon is a symbol of hope signifying that life, death, and rebirth are an infinite circle.

THE EVIL EYE: SUPERSTITION AND RUG MAKING

Supernatural phenomena is used to explain many daily events in the Persian world. Calamity, illness, and mis-fortune are all caused by the "evil eye," or retribution for sinning. Despite the revival of Islamic fundamental-ism in Iran, old-fashioned superstition prevails; the evil eye is still a powerful force there—just as it was througout Europe during the Middle Ages.

Belief in the evil eye is not confined to the primitive nomads, who can neither read nor write, for well-educated city dwellers with access to tel-evision and computers fear it as well. Wherever you go in Islamic Iran, Pakistan, Afghanistan, and Turkey, you see

BELOW ▪ *This contemporary Sultanana, 8'3" x 10' (251 x 304cm), from Turkey is based on traditional designs and colors, is of superb quality, and is available worldwide, thanks to* *an effort to keep the craft of rug weaving alive and highly competitive in a nation whose escalating wages outstrip those of other rug-weaving countries such as India and Pakistan.*

people taking steps to overcome the effects of the evil eye. It is not in good taste, for example, to remark on the beauty of a child in the presence of its parents, for if that child were to contract measles or small pox, the well-wisher would be blamed because his envious spirit cast the evil eye upon the child. In many other cultures, the first person to visit one's home on New Year's Day sets the life course for the entire year and is responsible for every fortune or misfortune to befall the host.

My father, a Christian Armenian, often told me stories of his childhood in Persia, all of which were centered around elaborate schemes to avoid the perils of one evil or another. There was a common belief in his village that a colony of malevolent spirits lived under the bridge that spanned a small nearby river. When it came time for his family's cattle to cross this bridge as they returned at sunset from grazing, my father's grandmother used to meet the cattle to tie burlap around the cows' udders to protect the milk from the spirits' sour thoughts as they crossed the bridge.

My father's mother sewed blue beads on his clothing—a practice that continues in Iran today—to ward off evil spirits that might endanger him, influence him, or creep into his system and cause him to die. These magical blue beads are also strung and tied on to automobile visors, mirrors, and dashboards. Since my father continued to lecture on oriental rugs into his nineties, perhaps the blue beads actually work.

Iranian rugs woven in the style of Shiraz, Bakhtiari, Belouchistan, and Boukara—as well as many Turkish village rugs—sometimes have a decorative string of blue beads sewn along the edges or on the rug itself so that the weaver will not be cursed when someone shows envious admiration of her work. Nor are blue beads the only device used by rug weavers to protect themselves and their families from the evil eye. Shiraz, Saraband, Fereghan, Bidjar, Senna, and many other rugs conceal tiny roosters or even stylized rooster combs within their designs to ward off the evil eye. The custom stems from a Persian belief that roosters are inherently evil, so they can protect against other and presumably greater evil.

Another superstitious tradition dictates that if a woman is working at her loom weaving a particularly striking rug, and someone in her family is taken ill, all labor on the rug must stop at once. The thought is that a visitor admired the rug,

thereby casting the evil eye upon the weaver's family. No further work can be done on the rug until the person recovers or dies. In either case, the spell is then broken.

In 1977, my family had an exhibit of antique oriental rugs at the New Hampshire Historical Society in Concord. One day we received a telephone call from the Society that one of the small antique Kazak prayer rugs had been stolen. The Associated Press got hold of the story and called my father. Whimsically, he told them of the curse this stolen prayer rug carried, and that it was now considered *haram*, or "unclean"—who knew what ill could befall either the person who stole the rug or his family? This article outlining the curse appeared nationwide. Two days later the rug was found—it had been thrown onto the steps of the police station. I always wondered if anything unfortunate happened to the thief or his family.

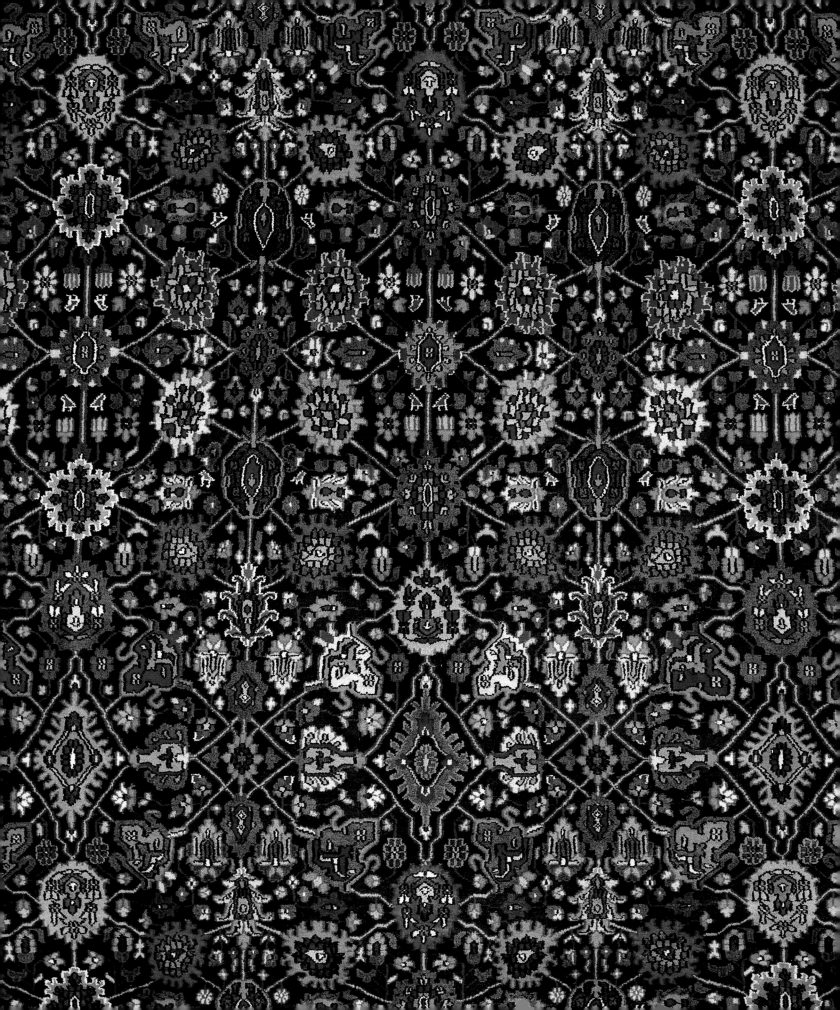

A SIMPLE METHOD OF RUG CLASSIFICATION

For centuries, Persians have been masters of design, evolving a highly stylized art form that was shaped by the Empire's expansion east and west, and in turn influenced artists throughout Europe and Asia. Despite the vast differences between Western and Persian culture and philosophy, Persian art has come down to Westerners as part of our own heritage. Its sensibility is apparent in a wide range of our art forms, including painting and textile design. For example, during the eighteenth and nineteenth centuries, painters in Europe began to include images of oriental rugs in their work; one can see echoes of the blossom motif on Persian rugs from Senna, Saraband, and Qum in the paisley designs produced by the French Jacquard loom. ✦ The hand-knotted oriental rugs sold today come from a variety of rug-making countries and often replicate designs found in prerevolutionary Iran. As weavers along the Silk Route become more adept at recreating the style and look of these old Persian rugs, it will become increasingly difficult for oriental rug appraisers to determine a rug's country of origin. Therefore, the following discussion of rug classification focuses on basic design patterns instead. ✦ The many types of oriental rugs can be classified into three distinct groups: geometric design, floral design, and all-over design. Applying this simple system of rug identification allows one to understand a weaver's background and the forces that influenced his or her life.

✦

CHAPTER THREE

PAGE 52 ▪ *Many Indian rugs such as this contemporary piece are based on old Persian garden patterns that incorporate roses, other flowers, and tree branches.* BELOW ▪ *This is a detail of the evil eye shown in the rug on the opposite page. Still much in evidence in modern Turkey, the evil eye wards off harmful spirits and even hangs in the vestibules of modern Turkish airliners.* OPPOSITE ▪ *This highly textured Çanakkeli from a village south of Istanbul shows how superstitions among contemporary weavers remain strong, for this rug still has the original evil eye beads attached to it.*

GEOMETRIC DESIGNS

Bold, geometric patterns are favored by Central Asian and Middle Eastern nomadic peoples—sheep herders who follow the same pattern of life their ancestors did long ago.

A nomad owns few possessions and measures his wealth by the the number of livestock in his herd. The nomadic existence is one of austerity and hardship, heightened by a belief in supernatural forces. All of these factors coalesce in the striking nomadic rugs, woven chiefly by female tribe members. Today, many nomadic tribes are now settled in villages, yet each tribe retains its own laws, customs, and culture. Although there are dozens of names to distinguish the various tribes who produce these rugs, all of the rugs within this classification have similar characteristics.

A nomadic rug is instantly recognizable by its simple pattern. This pattern is composed of a series of medallions,

large or small, but always strictly geometrical, sharp, and angular. The colors are bright and bold, reflecting the weaver's wild, bold existence. For example, nearly every rug that comes out of Afghanistan, land of the Boukara and Belouchi rugs, is woven with some shade of red as the dominant background color. Most Kazak rugs are from the Caucasus or Central Asia and are woven with brilliant reds, blues, and some natural whites. The local sheep are dark brown and this wool is impossible to dye in light colors. In fact, natural white wool is rare in this region and either comes from belly wool or is imported from other areas. In the nomadic Bakhtiari rugs discussed earlier, bright yellows, greens, and reds predominate. Descendants of some of the ancient Seljuk Turkish tribes now living a settled life in Anatolia still weave in the traditional nomadic style of their ancestors, using primarily chemically made colors.

OPPOSITE AND BELOW •

This classic Indian rug, 4' x 6' (121 x 182cm), is representative of the gul-ferang, or "foreign flower," design, a pattern woven by people who tried to replicate what they perceived as being the more sophisticated floral fabrics and clothing they observed being worn or carried as luggage by European traders.

Nomadic tribes are constantly moving from one location to another, their journeys dictated by the forces of nature. Consequently, tribal rugs tend to develop without much preplanning or grand design. Medallions can be repeated many times to make a long runner, or the work can be terminated after two

or three medallions have been woven and the rug will be complete. The need to relocate perpetually also influences size: smaller rugs are more portable, so most of these rugs measure eight-by-eleven feet or smaller.

FLORAL DESIGN Contrasting with the rugged beauty of geometric rugs are carpets of intricate floral patterns. The Persian aristocracy once commissioned floral rugs to adorn their ancestral palaces and elegant homes in larger cities such as Tabriz, Teheran, Meshed,

Kerman, Qum, Isfahan, and Keshan. Now these court rugs are woven throughout the Middle East, China, and Central Asia, often by urban weavers who are fairly prosperous. The subtle color blending and intricately detailed designs of floral rugs mirror the cultured lifestyle of the city dweller.

Whereas a nomadic weaver tends to repeat one red hue throughout a design, a sophisticated city weaver may use the whole spectrum of red, from pale pink to crimson. The floral rug represents the garden with its intertwining vines, flowers, trees, and streams of gently flowing water. These woven gardens bring nature inside and help brighten both dried-mud village homes and urban abodes. In the Middle East today it is not unusual to see colored lightbulbs hung between buildings or alleys in villages and cities, because of the gaiety they create. The use of colorful curvilinear designs in the floral rug creates the same feeling of excitement and movement.

A classic Persian rug, 4' x 6'2"
(122 x 185cm), is exemplary of the
herati, *or fish and turtle, pattern.*
Though the imagery is highly stylized
and sometimes represented obscurely,
the herati *pattern is a symbol of life's*
whimsical nature.

Floral rugs vary greatly in color from region to region. Thus the city weavers of Iran, India, China, and northern Pakistan prefer pastel rose, blue, and ivory, while others, such as Afghan, Belouchi, and Caucasian weavers, show a decided preference for reds, deep blues, and gold. It is interesting to note that the slight irregularities inherent in all oriental rugs are concealed by the floral weavers while they are flaunted by the nomads.

weavers are visionary and capable artists who interpret their ideas through rhythmic, repetitive patterns indicative of the cyclical nature of the farming lifestyle. Covered-field designs are composed of repeated, noncontiguous, individual motifs with no central medallion. Rural Hindu weavers favor traditional Persian *mir* designs, for example, which repeat a distinctive *badam,* or paisley patterns row after row.

❖   ❖   ❖

This quick review of oriental rug classification does not attempt to catalog individual rugs, but rather place them in a cultural context. How does an amateur determine whether a rug is a masterpiece or a poor specimen? Unless the rug can be appraised by an expert, the best strategy is to rely on personal preference. No single type of rug is superior to any other, and in every class of rug there are superior and inferior examples.

ALL-OVER DESIGNS

The third class of oriental rugs is the all-over, or "covered field" design, typical of weavers in farming communities, where weaving rugs by the light of a sputtering castor-oil lamp occupies families during the long winter months. In spite of this humble existence, the

UNDERSTANDING DYES

✚

MUCH HAS

been written on the quality of

natural dyes versus man-made dyes. Both products are

excellent for rug dyeing, yet each offers the dyer and consumer dif-

ferent properties and benefits. For instance, indigo blue, a rich

color long associated with royalty and one of the most popular

colors for dyeing rugs, was originally derived from the indigo

plant. It was used to dye wool (which yielded a rich blue) and

occasionally silk or cotton (which produced a lighter blue).

Harvesting the plant and preparing the dye was once a cottage

industry, but today there are simply not enough indi-

go plants to meet consumer

demand.

✚

CHAPTER FOUR

SYNTHETIC DYES

According to Susan C. Druding, an expert on textile dyeing, "The big shift to chemical dyes began in 1834, when Runge, a German chemist, noticed that distilling coal tar or aniline resulted in a bright blue-violet color if treated with bleaching powder." Runge's discovery helped to pave the way to the development of other aniline dyes.

In 1856, Sir William Henry Perkin created the color mauve using an aniline dye while searching for a cure for malaria, thus creating the first synthetic commercial dye. His color, a brilliant fuchsia, faded easily, so today our idea of mauve is not the same as the original version. But his distinctive mauve color became very fashionable in Germany during the height of its industrial revolution. Unfortunately, the original aniline dyes made fabrics stiff and dry, and the colors bled.

About 1870, synthetic dyes made their way to the coastal regions of Turkey. They became a popular trade item on the Silk Route, and eventually found their way to the nomadic peoples of the Caucasus and Iran. Particularly for shades of red, the new aniline dyes proved more economical to use than natural dyes, allowing rug makers to speed up production and meet increasing product demand. These dyes also afforded greater control of color from one lot to the next, an attractive characteristic in light of the belief that Western buyers wanted a more uniformly dyed rug.

However, the early aniline dyes had limited success. Village dyers were given bags of powdered dye and a recipe. As in baking a cake, closely following the recipe was necessary for a successful outcome. Unfortunately, most villagers could not read or understand the scientific directions—which were often written in a foreign language to make matters worse—and were used to measuring in handfuls. Given these obstacles, it was almost impossible for the dyers to mix usable colors. In addition, these early aniline dyes faded and, in some cases, changed color completely over time.

Conversely, natural dyes tend to mellow softly with age. Natural dyes were distilled from a variety of sources,

according to Druding: "In Kerman, in the 1890s, madder roots, grape juice, shell fish, indigo, buckthorn, cochineal, onion skins, husk of green walnuts, milk, turmeric, henna, larkspur, and mulberry were all used either singly or in combination to produce the lasting and beautiful shades."

At the turn-of-the century, Mozaffer ed Din, Shah of Persia, issued an edict prohibiting the use of aniline dyes, as they were viewed as being detrimental to the integrity of the rug industry. All aniline dyes were seized and burned publicly. Penalties for use included jail and a fine equal to double the value of the merchandise. Smuggling, however, prevented the strict application of these laws. Eventually, the laws were modified with an export tax levied on rugs with artificially dyed threads.

In the 1940s, chrome dyes were developed using potassium bicarbonate, which allowed for a wide range of rich, colorfast hues that were not harmful to wool. Over the years synthetic dye formulations have been created that provide as interesting and sensitive a palette as any vegetable dye can offer. In fact, my private family collection of oriental rugs includes rugs dyed with early aniline dyes that have stood up to the rigors of time.

Regarding the relationship of the use of synthetic dyes and fiber damage, it is my opinion that synthetic dyes do not cause rug fiber disintegration. This issue must be considered in terms of the rug's history and the quality of the material from which it was woven: for example, at one time there was a custom of buying existing oriental rugs, bleaching their color, then redyeing them to meet consumer demand for specific colors. The bleaching agents, not the dyes, destroyed the fibers in poorer-quality rugs. The most famous of these rugs, called Painted Sarouks, were created in the 1920s; but bleaching seldom weakened these rugs' fibers due to the strength of the wool used in weaving them.

NATURAL DYES   The craft of creating natural dyes is a fascinating and an ancient art that is over four thousand years old. Prior to the twentieth century, traditional plant- and insect-based dyes

were produced according to recipes handed down from generation to generation.

One of the most important coloring agents was madder, a common plant that grows wild throughout the Middle East and provides the basis for the red so common in oriental rugs. The root of the madder plant yields dye for various shades of red, pink, and purple. When combined with a mixture of milk and fermented grape juice, the madder root renders a violet dye. Other bluish reds come from the cochineal and kermes insects that live in the bark of oak trees.

Wild saffron makes a reddish-yellow dye, while cultivated saffron offers a pure yellow. A lighter yellow comes from the root of turmeric, while a fungus of the mulberry bush provides a greenish-yellow dye.

Indigo is the most valued color of all and is derived from soaking and fermenting the Indigo plant. The name is derived from India, where the plant was first used commercially. The plant's blue color is responsible for the English word, "dungarees," named for the Indian city Dungaree whose indigo was used to dye American gold miners' blue jeans in 1848. Synthetic indigo is one of the few dyes used today that is chemically indistinguishable from its plant-derived counterpart.

Dark brown dyes usually come from walnut husks soaked with iron oxide, and were the only dyes to contain mineral fixatives, or "mordants." However, the resulting acidic substance had a corrosive effect on wool. If you run your hands over a fifty-year-old rug that was colored with these dyes, the pile can be very depressed where there is dark brown wool. Brown dyes are also made by mixing madder with yellow or from the shells of green walnuts, gall nuts, and valonia (the acorn cups of an oak). These brown dyes sometimes have a tendency to dull with age.

NOBLE RUGS

Some of the choicest rugs are used by the nobility purely as items of prestige, especially in Iran. The rugs are always hung on the wall or rolled up and stored away except for times of great celebration, when they are brought out for display. During outdoor festivals and parades, these fancy carpets are hung out on the veranda. The fineness of one's rugs and the number of pieces in one's collection are subtle indications of a family's wealth.

Sometimes such rugs are woven entirely of silk or wool with a silk outline, and sometimes certain parts of the pattern incorporate gold or silver threads. Even more extravagant are rugs illustrating trees with hanging fruits made of precious or semiprecious stones. For the celebration of happy occasions—hunting parties and sporting events—rugs that portray joyful scenes are displayed. If the time is one of mourning, it is customary to hang rugs picturing weeping willow trees or grape clusters, both emblematic of tears and sorrow. The grapes may be represented beautifully by series of matched rubies.

When you visit a Middle Eastern rug merchant, his explanations for the many little symbols, figures, designs, and colors in an oriental rug simply may be whimsical tales he created to add value to his product—it is often difficult to tell truth from fiction. In either case, the designs and the stories that accompany these rugs make them come alive and bring the artistry and philosophy of another culture into our lives. Remember, too, that technical fineness is only an indication of the weaver's technique; it is not necessarily an indication of value.

OPPOSITE ▪ *This pattern evokes a sense of spring coming into bloom in a riot of color.* BELOW ▪ *Why is one rug store mundane or even unsettling, and another a pleasurable feast for the senses? The difference is usually in the shop owner's eye for color and willingness to make sure that the rugs are produced in colors that coordinate with contemporary decor and regional tastes.*

PIGMENTATION AND CULTURE

The most successful and widely used colors in oriental rugs are reds, blues, and ivories. Red and blue are favorites of Persian and Afghan weavers, while yellow and green are used extensively in Turkish carpets. Green is seldom seen in old Persian rugs as it was considered a holy Moslem color; more importantly, it is also a difficult color to make naturally and often has a yellowish cast. This lighter yellowish-green is found almost exclusively in antique Turkish rugs, as green was a culturally acceptable color for use in Turkey. Today, green hues—from palest celadon to forest green—are common due to the standardization and availability of synthetic dyes, the decorative nature of oriental rugs, and western color demands.

In the past, yarn was often not dyed in the skein. Instead, each long strand was plunged into the dye (in some rural villages, this method is still practiced). The yarn was then dried in the open air and slowly exposed to sun and dust. This system imparted an endless number of color gradations to the different strands, and made a woven carpet vibrantly come to life. The term for this nuanced color change is *abrash*, an Arabic word describing "change in dye lots or color."

In many villages there was a dye master who produced a very particular color. Customers would bring him five skeins of wool to dye his special hue; he would dye the wool, return three or four skeins to them, and keep the rest for payment. The dye master proudly wore his color splashed over his clothing. His arms were permanently dyed up to the elbow—this was his badge of honor, and he was highly respected in the community. The dyer would pass on his treasured recipe to his son or male heir. If there was no trusted male heir, the recipe was often lost forever. As a result of this practice, I am sure many wonderful natural hues have vanished over the years.

TRAVELS BACK IN TIME
URMIA AND
ISFAHAN, IRAN

WHEN I

first visited

Urmia in 1959 with my father, I began

to better understand how living in a

place where time stands still and a cultural acceptance of life as

it is in the moment influences the rug weaver's art. When I look

over my family's decades-old collection of photographs and films of our visits there, I am

often struck by the lack of change in traditional garb, homes, and the four-legged mode of

transportation. Except for fading, the photographs we took in the 1950s are identical to those we took very

recently. ✚ Our trip in 1959 marked my father's first return to the village since his departure in 1918, when he fled

with his parents, grandmother, and two brothers. As we entered the village, he spied a man working in the field. Although my father was only

nine years old when he left, he immediately recognized the old man from his childhood and remembered his name, Ali. My father asked the

driver to stop and went out to greet the old man. Despite the fact that nearly four decades had passed and his advanc-

ing age, Ali, too, remembered my father. After they spoke for a bit, Ali accepted our offer of a ride into the village,

whereupon the timelessness of life in Urmia became evident again as the old man reached

the car—he had no idea how to open the door, for he had never ridden in an automobile.

✚ Once we were further into the village, we visited the home

where my father was born. The house was made of sun-dried

mud, and we had to duck down to get

inside the doorway. I was surprised

to see that in

this land of

CHAPTER FIVE

oriental rugs, where you can buy any size rug you want, there were two rugs on the floor about two feet too long; the excess was curled up against the wall. When I asked why, our host informed us that "the price had been right." The fact that the rugs were the wrong size never came into question—after all, life is what it is.

As word spread of our visit, relatives and neighbors crowded into the home. Our host—a distant relative—took out an old tobacco pouch with a letter inside written in English and asked my father to read it aloud in Armenian. The letter was from a relative who lived in Philadelphia and had once visited the village. She thanked everyone (mentioning how nice it was to have seen them all) for their hospitality and told of a snowstorm in Philadelphia that day. She acknowledged many of the villagers by name. As my father read each name, the people gathered in the house would smile, nod, and comment excitedly. The date on the letter was 1934 and had no doubt been read and reread dozens of times over the past twenty-five years! I was awed by the villagers' simple

pleasure in hearing the words of this old letter time and again. Their joy in the moment explained how several people could spend years creating a room-size rug of extraordinary beauty and grace and then sell it, giving little thought to the hours spent creating such a masterpiece. In the Middle East, the concept of time is so far removed from our hurried, time-is-money Western culture that we can barely fathom the villagers' view.

Isfahan is the place where I learned about the artistry of oriental rugs and the close relationship between the rug weaver's art and the culture of the Middle East, including the elaborate oriental rug-trading customs and traditions which are more theater than business—a theater that utilizes an ancient script and formalized dramatic gestures. To describe the beauty of pre–1979 Isfahan is impossible. The Persians say "Half the world is Isfahan," for Isfahan was the artistic and cultural center of the Middle-Eastern world. Today, despite the damage from the revolution, it is still a place of great culture and artistry.

TRADING AT THE BAZAAR

Until Iran was closed to Americans in 1979, I visited Isfahan and the surrounding rug-weaving centers regularly with my father. For centuries, Isfahan has been a cultural melting pot filled with merchants and artists, Armenians, Moslems, and Jews, all of whom play out elaborate roles at the bazaar. At an Isfahanian bazaar, a half-truth or misleading statement about the value or provenance of a particular rug is not called a lie—it is simply viewed as cleverness.

My father and I once bought a rug that was quite attractive, with a floral pattern and an ivory background. When the rug arrived in the United States, we discovered that it had been switched with one of lesser quality. Six months later, when we went back to speak to the merchant who sold us the rug, he denied that he had made the switch. However, when we bought the original rug, I happened to have photographed him selling it to my father. When I showed the merchant this incriminating photograph, he simply called my camera the devil, and although he was angry (probably more with himself than with us),

he threw up his hands and became very solicitous, never thinking for a moment that we would terminate our business relationship over what he saw as a bit of clever dealing. In fact, we even bought more rugs from him, which he sold to us at a very good price. Over the years, we continued to do business with him, and our mutual respect grew. The incident was never mentioned again.

In another instance, a merchant once sold us a rug at the Teheran bazaar and soon afterwards ran after us crying, "I've made a terrible mistake. I gave you the rug at my cost, not the selling price. I need more money!" Of course, my father had seen this ruse played out many times before. He politely expressed great concern for the poor merchant's plight and, not wanting him to suffer such a devastating loss, offered to make good by returning the rug to him. "Oh no," the merchant proclaimed, not wanting to give the money back, "I could not do that. I have made a bargain. I will accept your price," and sped off.

During our rug-buying ventures, we always work with a local agent who does the recordkeeping, and at the end of each day we reconcile our figures with him. If

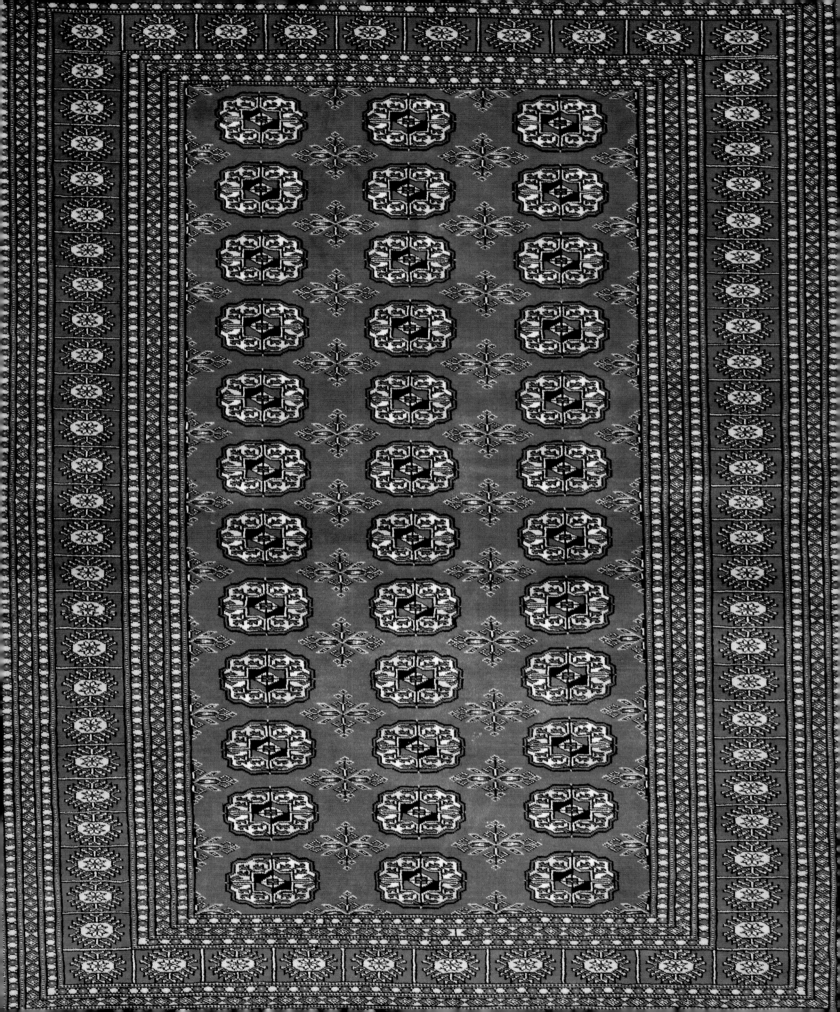

both sets of numbers agree, we give him checks and he distributes the money to the merchants. The agent not only helps us speed the process along by allowing us to concentrate on selecting rugs and bargaining for price, but he also plays a vital

role in maintaining various proprieties: for example, it is not advisable—and usually impossible—to buy rugs from the weavers, as they may set prices based on their time and effort instead of the actual market value. One cannot bargain with weavers. But an agent knows the correct market value of saleable rugs, helps dealers to avoid uncomfortable situations, and arranges beneficial agreements between merchants and buyers; again, as an example, the predominantly Moslem merchants will discuss a business deal with me and my father—because we are Armenians—but will only actually do business (that is, accept a check) with another male Moslem.

The only exception to this custom that I have ever witnessed was when my sister, Joyce, complained to my father that she was not being respected by any of the merchants. Whenever there was a conversation about the rugs, all the discussion was directed to me or my father—the two males. Although Joyce was an important merchant, she was a woman in a male-dominated society. My father said, "I'll fix this," and he gave the checkbook to Joyce and had her make the payments. Instantaneously, the merchants found it most agreeable to deal directly with "Miss Joyce." Power gains respect.

TECHNIQUE AND QUALITY

While there is no single style of rug that can be called Isfahan, there are some interesting similarities shared by the Isfahan family of rugs. Many rugs from this area are woven using the Senna knot which, because of its fineness, enables the weaver to create curvilinear designs and more intricate patterns. Thus Isfahan rugs are often associated with rugs that have leaves, vines, and delicate floral patterns.

The fine, tight weave that allows for intricate motifs is, however, only a technique, and does not in itself signify value. The quality of the wool must also be good, the col-

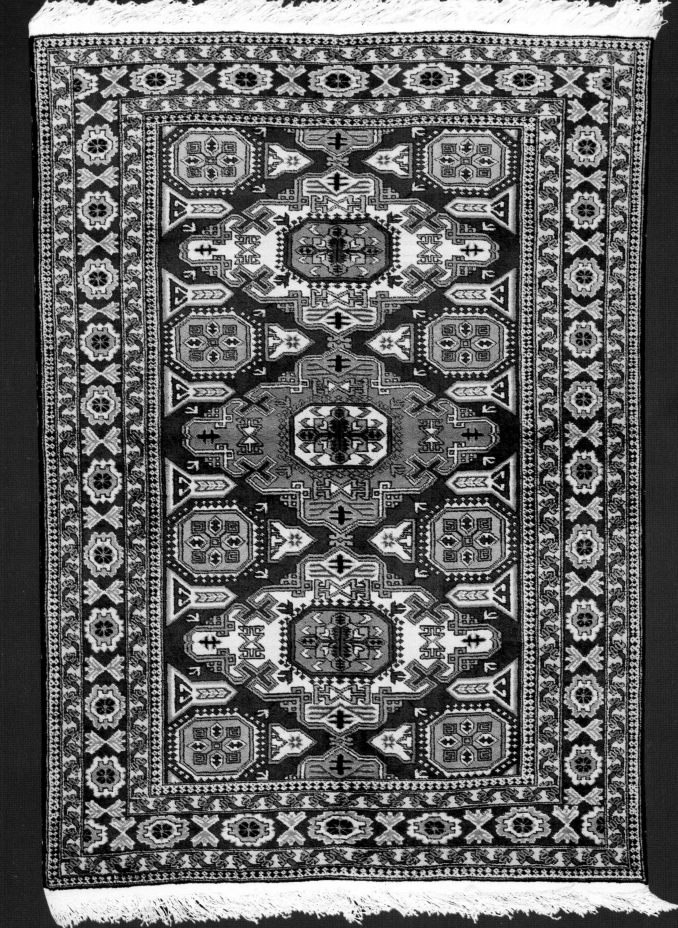

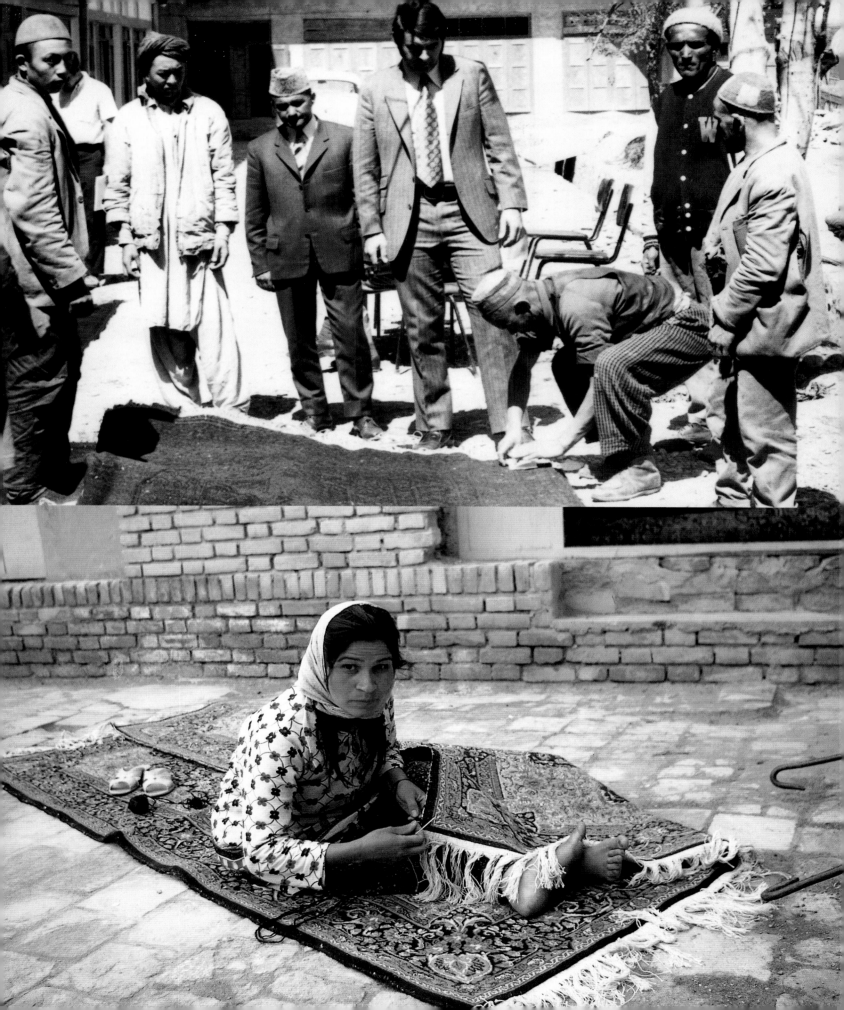

ors true, and most importantly, the overall effect must be pleasing to the eye. One should not judge the quality of a painting by its number of brush strokes, nor a rug by the number of knots or technical quality.

There are many other Iranian rug-weaving peoples such as the Bakhtiari and Afshar, who live south of Isfahan and do much of their trading in the local bazaar. When the Ayatollah Khomeini came to power in Iran in 1979, the first prime minister of the new Republic was a man named Bakhtiar, a French-educated member of the powerful Bakhtiaris. This group of people has left quite a sizable imprint on Persian culture, most especially through the symbols of their garden-pattern rugs (for more information, see pages 40-41). Bakhtiari weavers employ the heavier and more common Ghordi (symmetrical) knot.

RUG TRADE IN IRAN TODAY

In postrevolution Iran, rug weaving is still practiced in many villages and urban areas. Iran is banned from trading with the United States because of the trade embargo, but does continue to trade with Europe, Canada, Australia, and the rest of the world. Weaving in Iran was an indigenous craft, independent of American and European fashions. Unfortunately, the Persian rug is now a minor commodity in the oriental carpet industry. To survive in today's competitive environment, members of the rug industry must keep pace to meet Western design demands. As a result of the Iranian revolution, India, Turkey, and to a lesser degree, China and Pakistan, have dominated the market. China, especially, with its cheap labor force, is poised to become a major rug producer.

THE GATEWAY TO THE SILK ROUTE:
TURKEY

IN HIS WELL-KNOWN BOOK, *ORIENTAL RUGS*, John Kimberly Mumford wrote in reference to rug making in the twentieth century that "the next generation will have lost the magic of its forbears and the fabrics (oriental rugs) . . . will have become mere matters of history." ✦ Every generation seems to predict the demise of oriental rug production, bemoaning the inferior quality of rugs woven "today" as compared to those of the past. Despite the naysayers, Turkey is actively preserving its unique rug-weaving heritage, doing so with a passion that borders on national policy. What better place to begin our search for oriental rugs of the Silk Route than in Turkey, a country whose biggest city, Istanbul, is the hub of the Silk Route. ✦ Although I have been to Turkey many times, during my most recent trips I was struck by the profusion of cellular telephones and satellite dishes. Almost everyone on the street and in restaurants seems to have a cellular phone on their ear or poised for action by their plates. Restaurants have become quite noisy with the ring of these phones and the ensuing loud conversations, but no one seems to mind the intrusion of technology. Even in remote mountain villages, satellite dishes transmit CNN and daily soap operas, while villagers sit with their eyes glued to their television screens. This addiction to mass media is a serious threat to the old way of life, including rug weaving and dyeing, the craft of which is passed down from generation to generation. ✦ One person interested in reviving the old traditions is Dr. Harald Böhmer, an important German chemist working in Turkey. In 1978, he began analyzing plant and other organic dyes used in old Turkish rugs, comparing them to available plant sources. Unlike his secretive forerunners, Dr. Böhmer shared the results of his research with Turkish weavers and guided them in the formation of a profit-sharing cooperative known as the Natural Dye Research

✦

CHAPTER SIX

and Development Project, or DOBAG (the acronym for the Turkish name). The DOBAG Project now supports about four hundred families in western Turkey.

Though DOBAG represents only one aesthetic standard, and many rug experts disagree with Dr. Böhmer's findings, he did gain international recognition for Turkey as a modern rug-weaving center specializing in traditional designs and natural dyes. In addition to DOBAG, Turkey now offers programs at four universities where students can earn bachelor's degrees in order to become qualified managers in Turkey's rug-weaving industry.

Turkish weavers and dyers receive higher wages than their counterparts in India, China, and Pakistan. Rug manufacturers offset this costly labor expenditure by raising the cost of the final merchandise, but ensure customer value by enforcing high production standards and artistic excellence. They do so with an uncanny design sense that combines Turkey's rug-weaving heritage with an understanding of contemporary home decor in North America, Europe, and Australia.

GOLDEN HALI

Golden Hali is one of the new breed of influential rug-weaving companies keeping Turkey at the forefront of the industry. These companies are marrying traditional hand rug weaving with contemporary inventory and quality control methods, market research, and systematic production methods. They are also centralizing the trimming, finishing, and washing of rugs in modern, clean, and efficiently run facilities.

Golden Hali is based in Izmir, Turkey's third largest city, and a jumping-off point for vacationers heading to Aegean seaside resorts or the ancient city of Ephesus—one of the most extensive Greco-Roman archaeological destinations in the world. Izak Yumartaci, better known as Izy, runs Golden Hali with two other partners. Izy is an unassuming intellectual who speaks three languages and regales visitors with his historical knowledge of the ancient Greeks and Romans, the Ottomans, and the Byzantine Empire. On a recent trip he entertained us with the story of the Trojan War, which took place in what is now modern Turkey. Izy is as comfortable in Izmir or a

WEAVING AND
COURTSHIP

. . . .

During a recent trip to the small mountain village of Kulalar, my wife noticed an interesting bit of courtship one late afternoon. Some young men, having completed their work for the day, lined up outside a weaver's house to watch her work. The men were enthralled by the weaver's beauty and her ability to bring in hard currency to her future family.

After a bit of flirtation with the weaver, the men retired to their club, where the proprietor made endless cups of tea served in tulip glasses. A television sat in one corner, and in the winter a simple wood stove warms its one common room.

It's interesting to note that the only other significant cash earned by these villagers is from raising tobacco, a subsidized crop that seasonally draws men, as well as female weavers, into the fields. The men rely on the women to be the breadwinners—marrying a good weaver ensures a man enough money to buy a car (oriental rugs are often used as floor mats) and spend time in the city or local tea house.

OPPOSITE · *In this photograph, the weaver (far left) was so proud of her work that she posed in front of it with her entire family.*

BELOW · *In Istanbul's crowded markets, human power—men fitted with saddles—transport heavy loads to this day.*

mountain village as he is in New York City. He maintains an apartment in the United States and is a student of archaeology, which he says he will pursue full time when he retires.

Golden Hali has developed relationships with weavers in surrounding mountain villages, all of

which are within a three-hour drive of Izmir. Golden Hali provides each weaver with a design, and in a plastic bag, all the wool necessary to complete one rug. In exchange for the labor, Golden Hali pays a weekly wage based on knot count—the criteria for one day's work equals about 6,000 knots. This takes a competent weaver about six to eight hours; faster weavers seldom opt for staying late to earn extra money.

The 6,000 knots per day comes to 30,000 knots in a five-day work week, or 120,000 knots per month, or 1,440,000 per year, which earns a weaver a better lifestyle

and more status than would be possible working at a clerical job in the city. While the repetitious nature of rug weaving is undeniable, there is a relationship between the product and the weaver that is tangible and unlike strictly rote work. Though the designs are specified in advance, the weavers make choices as they proceed, and they voice their opinions by improvising the design. But with satellite dishes sprouting from nearly every roof, interest in the outside world has increased, while a desire to make rugs has surely waned. Competition for expert weavers will no doubt grow more fierce in the future.

When Golden Hali first comes to a rug-weaving village, the company tries to attract weavers with good pay and benefits. In the remote mountain village of Kulalar, all the weavers work exclusively for Golden Hali. (Each of the weaving villages has a company manager who stores the

TURKISH HOSPITALITY

. . . .

One afternoon in Kulalar my wife and I were invited to the village manager's home for lunch. His wife, wearing the modest head scarf that symbolizes Moslem female modesty, greeted us openly and warmly. Her wrists were adorned with the heavy, eighteen-carat gold bangles that denote status and wealth in Middle-Eastern cultures. Their home had a clean coat of white paint inside and out, and we were entertained in the living room, which was transformed into a dining room for a delicious luncheon of village bread baked in the village's central oven, green lentil soup, rice, and a stew of chicken and tomatoes with greens. Dining with us were several men of the village plus the manager and my wife, the only woman at the table (women traditionally eat separately in the kitchen).

It was a lively gathering, and the villagers were welcoming in the spirit of Turkish hospitality.

As in many Turkish village homes, an outside passage led to the bathroom, and the sink was outside on an open balcony. There was an extra parlor—furnished in bamboo-framed sofas and chairs upholstered in an ivory cotton fabric—that looked like it was used only for special gatherings.

One note: if you are planning to visit this area in the winter, be warned that in snow or rain the roads are impassable by anything but a tractor or draft animal. Of the town's two cars, one was a late model Toyota with a small oriental rug as a driver's seat cushion and the other, an old sedan. There was also an old beat-up motorcycle with a side car.

OPPOSITE ▪ *Though she is clad in Moslem garb, this village manager's wife dresses her son in brilliant Benetton colors, demonstrating how modern trends and tradition are synthesized in Turkish culture.*

BELOW ▪ *At Golden Hali, the computer is an everyday design tool used to create rugs whose colors and motifs must keep up with home decor trends.*

BOTTOM ▪ *A weaver's home has an area set aside specifically for work that is separate from the living area, but it must be near the center of family activity so she can perform her domestic duties.*

wool, assigns the work, and warehouses the completed rugs in an area beneath the living quarters of his home.) The company struggles to maintain a positive relationship with the workers so that other rug companies will be kept at bay in the competition for labor—the biggest problem facing the oriental rug industry in Turkey. "You have to pay on time, you have to provide the wool on time, and you have to take care of all the family problems that crop up, from health care to funerals—whatever," Izy explains. "Once we tried to set up a central workshop for the weavers, but no one showed up. They prefer to set aside a place in their own homes rather than leave to go to work."

DESIGNING AND WEAVING RUGS

The creation of a new oriental rug begins in the factory's design department, where computers are used to create designs for a craft whose execution has gone unchanged for centuries. Most of the designs emanating from Turkey today have roots in the antique village rugs of Anatolia and the Caucasus and ornate city rugs. On a recent visit, the design team was working on a Kazak (Caucasian) design noted for its bold geometric patterns, many medallions, farm animal icons, and muted tones that mimic the subtle hues of vegetable dyes.

Design production is a team effort involving aesthetic decisions as well as market research. Izy interviews hundreds of stateside retailers to find out what colors will be "in" next season and how his oriental rugs can be designed to complement the latest styles and trends in interior decorating. The designers also pore over auction catalogs from Christie's and Sotheby's looking for inspiration.

Many traditionalists remonstrate against computer-generated design specifications and accounting for knots on graph paper blueprints called "cartoons," but Izy argues that the weavers maintain their freedom of expression: "They have to stick to the design, but we know they will be at least 10 percent off, substituting colors and changing patterns

PAGE 94 ▪ *The matriarch of Kulalar navigates the rocky streets of her remote mountain village as she observes the rare foreign visitors.*
PAGE 95 ▪ *The patterns of this Visse, Iran rug, circa 1960, 6'8" × 10'2" (203 × 309cm), are often recreated in Turkey to keep such patterns*

alive and available to the world's rug lovers. The open design is reminiscent of Caucasian and Central Asian rugs.
BELOW ▪ *Here a Turkish woman prepares to hand-spin wool on a picturesque hillside.* **OPPOSITE** ▪ *Outside major cities such as Istanbul, animals haul goods to market.*

here and there—we expect the variations. In fact, this is what gives a rug its character—its soul. The same rug woven in China, for example, may well be identical from rug to rug—too perfect, lacking character, with no personality."

The village weavers are fiercely individualistic, and one can see why by taking a trip to Kulalar, an arduous three-

and-one-half-hour drive by car from Izmir. The roads up the mountain are winding and steep, and the drive is edged with highway barriers where the pavement has collapsed—I have never dared to look over the barriers to see how many rusty hulks litter the valleys below! The view is picturesque and the panorama of mountains and valleys is breathtaking. However much Izy values the weavers'

independent streak, he does not want them to stray too far from the planned format: "If a four-by-six rug comes out too small in an effort to finish the product and move on to another rug, we'll point out the problem."

Golden Hali weavers create row after row of Ghordi knots at dizzying speed. The weaver uses her left hand to grab the end of the yarn and pull the strand through the warp threads (the yarn running vertically on the loom); an instant later her right hand, holding a plastic-handled knife, brings down the blade in a counterclockwise motion to sever the yarn. It happens too fast to perceive (I have tried my hand at the process—creating one knot is painfully slow!).

Golden Hali likes to assign complex designs with as many as fourteen colors, since these are more interesting and are sought after by customers, although the weavers prefer simpler designs with fewer colors that can be completed more quickly. Weavers also like to work on approximately two and one-half feet of the rug's width, so they don't have to slide back and forth along the bench.

After each row is completed, the weaver pulls a weft thread (the cord running horizontally on the loom) through alternating warp strands. Then, using a *tarak*, an instrument that looks like a metal rake, she pounds down the row of knots, making the metal loom twang rhythmically (care must be taken not to pound the knots too

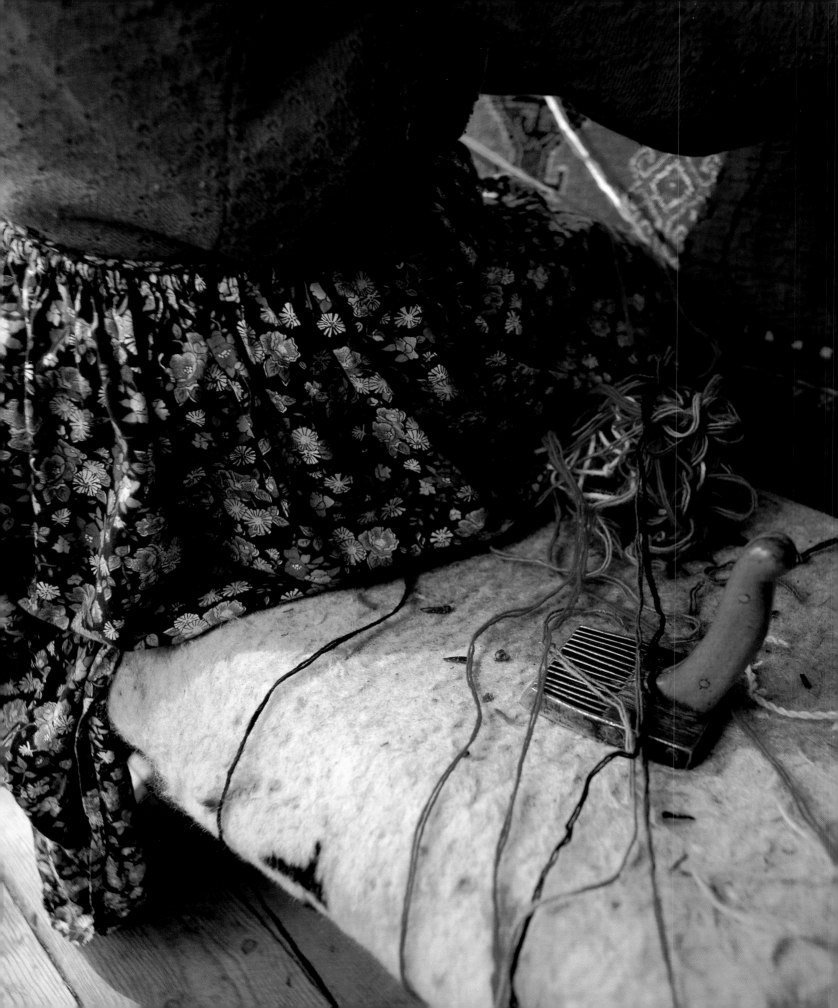

strongly, or the rug will be unsaleable). After the weaver completes about an inch or so of the rug, she guides a pair of heavy duty scissors along the surface to shear the face of the carpet: miraculously, the design begins to emerge.

While one might expect a rug to be done when it comes off the loom, the process is only two-thirds complete. When the weaver's work is finished, the rug is then picked up along with any unused yarn, which is weighed and categorized so next time the amount needed for that particular design can be determined more accurately. Once the rug reaches the warehouse, it goes through a succession of finishing processes. It is sheared to create a flat surface that makes the design more vivid. The fuzz on the back is burned off with a huge blowtorch—probably the most difficult and highly paid job in the factory. It takes a certain skill to know how much burning is enough without damaging the rug, and a strong constitution to withstand the terrible odor from the process. Finally, every rug is washed, blocked flat, and inspected for any defect in weaving or finishing.

Rejected rugs are sent to the bazaar to be sold to tourists; rugs that pass inspection are exported. Generally, rejected rugs are still suitable for purchase, containing only slight irregularities.

RUG SHOPPING IN ISTANBUL

Our next stop is Istanbul, a city renowned for its Grand Bazaar, a labyrinth of sixty-five covered pedestrian streets first erected in 1461 for international trade. The present bazaar was rebuilt in 1780, and in addition to its thirty-three hundred shops selling fabric, leather, antiques, ceramics, jewelry—and, of course, oriental rugs—the bazaar also contains coffeehouses, restaurants, a mosque, and even a truncated minaret from which the faithful can be called to prayer. (If you want to go to the bazaar by hired car, have your hotel concierge specify a particular gate number for your driver to drop you off at, as there are eighteen entrances.) In the tradition of the bazaar, bargaining for all but the most modest purchases is a way of life in Turkey.

On one of my recent trips I stayed at the Pera Palas, the fabled hotel that was home to Mata Hari and is best known as the hotel of choice for travelers disembarking on the last stop of the Orient Express. The hotel is where Agatha Christie wrote *Murder on the Orient Express*, and where Kemal Atatürk, the national hero, often stayed during his presidency in the 1920s and 1930s. His rooms are a miniature museum, and have not changed since he last spent the night. Nor has the entire hotel for that matter!

The lobby displays a sedan chair that was once used to ferry guests from the railroad station to the hotel, and the metal-caged wooden elevator with its cut-glass windows is operated by an elevator man. Unfortunately, the hotel is run by a government agency that has not restored the property to its turn-of-the-century splendor. Hot water is sporadic and not available at night, although dinner service is elegant. A night's stay is an experience, if you like adventure and history.

When it comes to rug shopping in Istanbul, go to the Grand Bazaar. But be forewarned: the rug merchants rank from respected dealers in old and new carpets to prevaricators with little or no knowledge of rug weaving. One of the latter merchants told us he would sell us a rug that would be worth three thousand dollars in the States for only eight hundred dollars. He called it a "rare and beautiful example of Turkish weaving." In actuality, the piece would sell for about a hundred dollars (clearly, he intended to retire early by selling us the rug!). He also insisted that several of his rugs were dyed with the cochineal "plant." When challenged, he readily admitted that he must have been mistaken—as cochineal is, of course, derived from an insect. Another fallacy perpetuated on rug buyers by this particular merchant are vague references to country of origin. Rugs from Afghanistan are fobbed off as originating in Turkey, not a big point for an inexpensive decorative piece, but unfair to the art. Most of the rugs offered for sale in the bazaar are of Turkish origin.

Another bit of misrepresentation is taking place now as well. This dealer and many others claim that all wool rugs must have at least 25 percent nylon in the fiber for strength. This is simply not true, and I puzzle over this stinting on quality. The weaving is the same, the finishing is the same, and marketing costs are the same. How much money can be saved by using inferior wool that needs to be reinforced with nylon? The answer is that the savings are negligible, and worse, such dealers cast suspicion on those who strive to manufacture new rugs to superb standards. It does not seem sensible—remember the story of the scorpion crossing the river in Chapter Two?

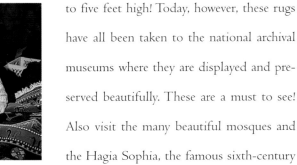

Of course, there are numerous trustworthy shops in the bazaar. One fine example is Sisko Osman Halicilik, which specializes in older carpets. Osman usually invites us to sit in one of his numerous galleries while he sends a runner to fetch apple tea served in tulip glasses. He presents his wares honestly and his prices reflect decent value—his rugs are of the same quality or higher as compared to any reputable rug shop in North America or Europe. He has wonderful old rugs, but is quick to tell us that under Turkish law every antique rug he wishes to sell must be examined and approved for sale by museum inspectors.

It is interesting to note that until the 1970s one could see exquisite antique rugs dating as far back as the thirteenth century in mosques, laid on top of each other in piles four to five feet high! Today, however, these rugs have all been taken to the national archival museums where they are displayed and preserved beautifully. These are a must to see! Also visit the many beautiful mosques and the Hagia Sophia, the famous sixth-century

OPPOSITE ▪ *One of the smart*
shops beneath the Ciragan Palace, home
of the last Sultan of Turkey and now
a world-class international luxury
hotel, is the Koleksiyon Auction House,
a respected emporium offering fabulous
high-quality Turkish rugs.

Byzantine cathedral, but be aware that the mosques are filled with machine-made copies of Turkish rugs.

Another well-respected dealer found at the Grand Bazaar is Sengor, who prides himself on having shown carpets to Hillary Rodham Clinton at her hotel during an official visit. I'm sure that years from now he will still trade on that meeting and use it as his calling card. Sengor offers good-quality, well-designed carpets that he represents honestly, but there is a catch: his prices are comparable to those in major European and North American cities. Sengor does offer a nice merchandizing touch: any rug purchased at his shop is packaged in a wheeled tote bag—a very convenient way to make your way through the bazaar with your new possession.

If you want to view rugs in splendor there are elegant shops, and none is more elegant than Koleksiyon Auction House in the shopping mall beneath the Ciragan Palace Hotel. And nothing soothes jangled nerves acquired at the bazaar like afternoon tea accompanied by a harpist at the Ciragan Palace Gazebo Room overlooking the Bosphorus. The hotel is joined to the Ciragon Palace, an early twentieth-century residence.

If you are tempted to buy a large rug in Turkey or in any other rug-producing country, I recommend that you exert caution. If you are not sure that the dealer is reputable, consider buying a small, inexpensive souvenir of your trip—not your living-room rug. (But if you do fall in love with a larger rug, please refer to Chapter Eight for negotiating guidelines.) Your choices will be limited, though, because you will only see rugs made in the country you are in, and you may be at the mercy of clever merchants who misrepresent their rugs. I have known many people—even those who know the rug-buying markets abroad—who have bought a rug, had it shipped home, and realized that the colors were unsuitable or the size wrong or the price too high! Many people buy a rug while abroad, have it shipped home, and realize that the colors are unsuitable or the size is wrong or the price too high! Buying close to home gives one the advantage of a much wider selection, lower prices, and the opportunity to try a rug before making a purchase.

That said, I encourage you to buy at least a small rug as a memento of your trip and to experience bargaining with the very best. Your trip will be enriched by your rug-buying experience and perhaps give you insight into this centuries-old art form.

SEARCHING THE SUBCONTINENT

INDIA

INDIA IS A NATION

of tremendous motion, energy, and deter-

mination, yet it is also a nation of contrast, with eternal ties to

the past. During a recent trip to northern India's rug-weaving centers, including

Varanasi, Agra, and Jaipur, we stayed overnight in New Delhi. There, in the country's capital, where the roads

were so superbly designed by the British in the 1920s that they can still accommodate modern-day traffic—along

with sacred cows, human-powered carts, and fume-spewing auto-rickshaws—I visited a bookstore near Embassy

Row. When I asked the proprietor for books on oriental rugs he solemnly pulled down a single, dusty copy of

Oriental Rugs and the Stories They Tell, a book my father had written and published in 1967! ✤ A sense of unchanging

time pervades India's rug-weaving industry, which employs mostly inexpensive human labor for such functions as

washing, trimming, and inventory control. In India and Turkey, most of the yarn is spun from local sheep and mixed

with yarn from mills in New Zealand, while in western Turkey, wool for quality rugs is almost exclusively import-

ed from New Zealand and spun on power looms in central factories. Similarly, Turkey has brought modern western

production management and inventory control to every aspect of rug weaving. Finishing and washing are central-

ized and are accomplished indoors. ✤ In both western Turkey and India, larger manufacturers have turned to com-

puter programs to design and color rugs, although in India many more designs are done by hand. The use of

computers has been a boon to manufacturers of program rugs, those who produce the same design in sizes

from two-by-three feet to twelve-by-eighteen feet. The computer can quickly and easily

adjust the size of each design component in the rug. Many

aspects of the rug-weaving industry are

labor intensive.

CHAPTER SEVEN

PAGE 108 ▪ *This Indian rug, 6' x 9' (182 x 274cm), echoes the famous* herati *pattern.* **BELOW** ▪ *A lone Indian designer paints a cartoon whose design was inspired by Mughal rulers from Persia.*

OPPOSITE, TOP AND BOTTOM ▪ *A genuine antique Agra rug woven in shadow of the Taj Mahal commands an extraordinarily high price at auction, and no visit to India is complete without a visit this world-famous tomb.*

This is because labor is plentiful and inexpensive in India, so more people are involved in the process.

Despite the differences, there remains an astonishing similarity between rug weaving in Turkey, Iran, Pakistan, and India—once you cross the threshold of the weaver's home. The loom, the tools, the yarn, and the very the act of hand-knotting an oriental rug are virtually identical to the way rugs were created centuries ago. If you were blindfolded and brought into a weaver's home, the only clue revealing your location would be the weaver's sex: in India and Pakistan, males weave rugs; in Turkey and Iran, this work is done mostly by women.

FOLLOWING THE TRENDS

The rug-weaving industry in India is far more primitive compared to other rug weaving centers, yet when it comes to creating rugs that capture the excitement of leading designers in the North America and Europe, India is producing some of the most trend-setting new designs and colors on the market today. While the rugs of India are rooted in ancient Persian designs, they are also influenced by the latest fashion, fabric, and home decor trends in New York, London, Milan, and other major cities around the world.

Oriental rug dealers, too, must stay abreast of the latest motifs and color combinations in home decor, as well as anticipate upcoming trends. In this way, we can be certain that the rugs coming off the weavers' looms in India a year from now will coordinate with the wall coverings, draperies, and furniture being offered in the home-furnishings markets. Fellow importer Lotfy Ben Levi notes, "In the past the rugs from India were based on ancient designs that came to India from Iran and remained unchanged for decades, but today the rug business is more like the fashion business. Color combinations and designs change as quickly as furniture, wallpaper, and other interior decorating styles. Even clothing styles influence rugs."

In addition to watching new home decor trends like many of my colleagues around the world, I keep a close eye on the important rug auctions held at Christie's and

OPPOSITE ▪ *In northern India, unbearable heat and humidity make dying wool a task reserved for the toughest and strongest.*

BELOW ▪ *Rug merchants who ply northern India's rug-making district begin their quest in Varanasi, where the Hindu faithful gather along the Ganges' many ghats or steps to bathe or cremate their deceased.*

Sotheby's. Doing so helps me develop a sense for which antique oriental rugs are most desirable and which classical patterns are falling out of favor. Rugs based on antique Persian designs, colors, and patterns have always been in demand, and I expect they will remain popular for many years to come. Of late, consumer interest in these types of rugs is spreading, and Indian rug makers are using a variety of washing and dyeing techniques to create rugs that satisfy the demand. In some cases weavers simply dye wool to match the colors found in one-hundred-year-old carpets that have had time to soften and develop a patina. Others use wool of identical colors but of separate dye lots to create variations in the overall look. Another method calls for hand-spinning two shades of wool fibers together to create a variegated look throughout the entire rug. Still others develop their own secret washes using herbs and tea. "It's sort of like the

stonewashed look of jeans, only it's rugs," quips Lotfy Ben Levi's son, Marti.

Whether the designs being produced today are contemporary or traditional, the foundation of India's rug weaving has been to produce rugs that satisfy the tastes of Westerners. This isn't a new idea: records show that rugs were being made to specification by European buyers as early as the early 1600s. All involved in importing rugs from India today agree that the quality has improved markedly, especially during the last decade, with the establishment of new aesthetic and quality standards. *Hali,* the London–based magazine covering antique and new oriental rugs and arbiter of rug trends and styles worldwide, views design trends of the past ten years in a positive light. James Opie, writing for *Hali* on new rugs from India that were unveiled at the International Area Rug Market in Atlanta, Georgia, stated: "Atlanta amply confirmed that

American contributions to the decorative carpet business are central to the current commercial renaissance now in full flower." He called the excitement over these new carpets "palpable" and "genuine." What is more, Opie adds that India is creating new rugs that not only have the look and colors of antique rugs but also their feel—all at "a fifth of the price."

THE MUGHALS

Contributing to the excitement of this particular rug show in Atlanta was the widely acclaimed 1997–98 exhibition *Flowers Underfoot: Indian Carpets of the Mughal Era,* at the Metropolitan Museum of Art in New York, which featured magnificent rugs woven in India between the sixteenth and the eighteenth centuries. India had been threatened by its Islamic neighbors since the eighth century, and by the fifteenth century fell under Moslem rule. In the early sixteenth century, northern India was conquered by the Islamic Mughals, Central Asian descendants of Mongol warriors, and the Mughal era was born. The influence extended to India's art forms. In the *Flowers Underfoot* catalog, Daniel Walker, curator of the department of Islamic Art, observes that the Mughal invaders introduced Islamic art and culture to India, whose native artistic traditions were based on Hindu, Jain, and Buddhist religions. "The abstract, ornamental, and geometric aspects of Islamic art were radically different from the naturalistic, fantastic, and extravagant features of Hindu art. . . However, Hinduism was known for its ability to assimilate new ideas and influences, and Indian artists were especially responsive to the Persian art of manuscript illumination."

During this era, Mughal influence extended, of course, to carpets. Unlike other rug-weaving countries, India's rugs were not essential to the comfort, survival, or religion of its people. In Iran, Anatolia, the Caucasus, and Central Asia, nomadic tribes hand-wove objects including not only rugs, but tent bands, salt bags, and flat-weave kilims that were part of every household. Also, in Moslem

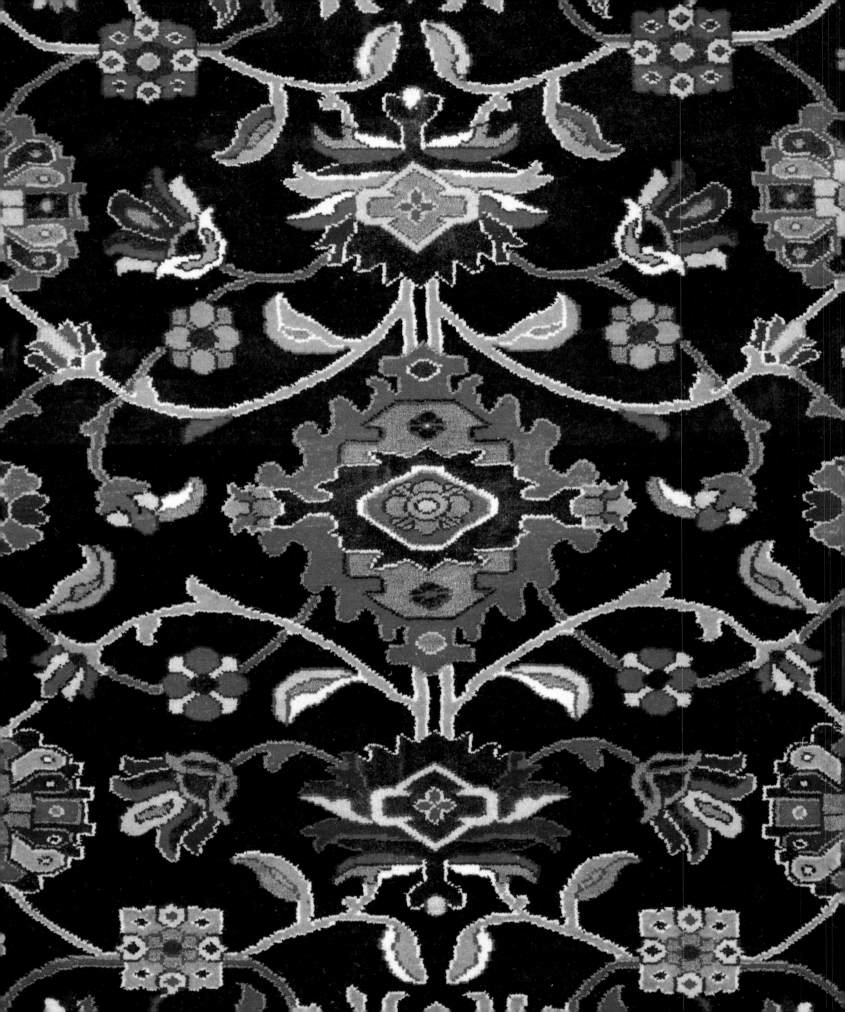

nations prayer rugs are produced for domestic use—this does not occur in predominantly Hindu India.

While the Mughal rulers were setting up carpet-weaving enterprises, European traders were staking their claims in India. By 1600, Great Britain had grabbed a toehold of the market with the creation of the English East India Company, a powerful entity that eventually came to govern India until 1874. The British quickly saw profit potential in exporting oriental rugs. Daniel Walker traces British trade in Indian carpets back to 1611, when the first references to "Turkish carpets" appear, describing carpets manufactured in homes and collected at central warehouses in India by "factors," or agents, for export to other countries.

The term "Turkish carpet" or "Turkey carpet" was a general term used to describe all oriental rugs, regardless of country of origin. For example, at the Captain Robert Bennett Forbes House museum in Milton, Massachusetts, where

my family's private collection has been on exhibit, curators discovered inventories created by Captain Forbes (a nineteenth-century New England trading ship captain) that list "Turkey Rugs" as part of his home furnishings. These were most surely exported by ship from China after traveling for months on eastbound caravans along the Silk Route.

In *Beyond the Fringe,* the newsletter of the New England Rug Society, Julia Bailey, a curator at the Museum of Fine Arts, Boston, highlights evidence of India's early export business: "A spectacularly well-preserved 'Persian-style' carpet ordered in 1630 for the Worshipful Order of Girdlers, a London livery company, is emblazoned with heraldry depicting the order's patron saint, Lawrence, holding the girdler's iron (gridiron, for short) on which he was grilled into martyrdom. Exported in the other direction, a serenely Persianate medallion rug of the 1620s resides in Kyoto, Japan, where for centuries it decorated a float in a yearly parade." To this day, Shinto ritualists bring out this classically designed Kyoto rug as part of an annual citywide celebration known as the Gion Matsuri Procession.

Persian design themes are evident not only in Mughal carpets but also in illustrated folios, art, textile fragments, and architecture. The most famous example is the Taj Mahal, one of the seven wonders of the world in Agra, a major rug-weaving center to this day. The Taj Mahal was built by Mughal emperor Shah Jahan in 1632 as a tomb for his queen, Mumtaz Mahal, who died giving birth to their fourteenth child. The mausoleum and grounds took twenty years to complete, employed twenty thousand workers, and cost forty million rupees. I always urge my rug-loving friends who plan to visit the grandest tomb of all to look for elements of oriental rug design in the detail work of this and other architectural masterpieces in India.

Eventually, conflicts with the British, often instigated by French traders who wanted to establish trade along the Silk Route as well, ended Mughal rule; the final blow was dealt during the Battle of Plassey in 1757. By this time, rug weaving was not only established, but Indian rug designers had refined a leitmotif—scrolling vines, stylized flowers, and other flora often juxtaposed with exotic animals such as elephants, tigers, and various birds—seldom seen in Islamic carpets. As time progressed, the "creatures of the wild" themes gave way to tamer depictions of animal life—presumably few customers wanted animals lunging at one another in their homes.

Collectors consider oriental rugs woven in Agra during the Mughal dynasties to be as prized as any rugs woven within the borders of modern-day Iran. A topic of some debate is whether today's oriental rugs will gain stature as collectible antiques a half-century from now. *Hali* editor Ben Evans, offers his own opinion: "Italy makes a lot of cars but they aren't all Ferraris. What will make a rug produced today a valuable antique art object in the future will be the same factors that make any antique valuable: good quality, well-formulated dyes, and a beautiful design that is well-executed. The biggest differences between today and a century or two ago is that commissioned rugs are much more broadly available. In the past one had to be

BELOW • *Even on the banks of India's holiest of places, the Ganges River, the Coca-Cola logo is evident on buildings and on the many Coca-Cola red tourist boats emblazoned with this world-famous trademark.*

OPPOSITE • *A trip along the Silk Route must include a stop at a silk shop where this Varanasi merchant, Papu, offers silk fabrics in a spectrum of colors and styles. The silks are long enough to sew one sari, and can be used as wall hangings or made into throw pillows.*

very wealthy and powerful and have overseas connections in order to commission a carpet. It certainly was much more elitist then."

When shopping, choose the oriental carpet that most appeals to your aesthetic sensibility. It is impossible to predict trends and artistic values fifty years into the future; enjoy the luxury of your rug today.

MODERN RUG TRADING IN INDIA

Western rug traders have been coming to India for nearly four hundred years. Because of modern transportation, the travel from rug-weaving centers to international rug markets is easier today, and everyone in the rug business in India has fax machines and e-mail access. Even so, rug dealers still visit often to guide the designs, share our knowledge of our countries' tastes, build relationships, as well as seek out and develop new and competing suppliers should there be any dissatisfaction with current suppliers. Yet doing business in India today presents a unique challenge. Despite the

modern conveniences, India is a third-world nation, and the rug industry is still largely nonautomated.

A buying trip starts in Delhi, where even though cows roam freely, one can walk into a McDonald's and enjoy a hamburger (ersatz versions made of mutton or vegetables are available for strict Hindus). Delhi is the jumping-off point to more primitive rug-weaving districts in India, including remote villages around Jaipur, and Agra. Gobiganj, is reached by another flight to its closest airport in Varanasi.

VARANASI

Varanasi, or Benares, "The City of Lights," is the holiest and oldest city in the nation—some say the world. Varanasi attracts three million Hindu faithful who come to bathe in the Ganges each year, descending stone steps, or ghats, to enter the river. The pilgrims believe that by touching or drinking the water, they will be purified of all sins. It is also believed that to achieve immortality, the dead must enter the Ganges as well, so that cremation anywhere along the

THE SILK TRADE:
PAPU'S STORY

. . . .

In addition to being at the center of the hand-knotted rug industry, Varanasi is famed for silk. The town is filled with silk merchants—including a man named Papu, whose nephew runs guided tours of the Ganges. Papu's singular claim to fame is that his tiny twelve-by-twelve-foot shop was visited by comedic actress Goldie Hawn, who purchased several pieces of silk fabric from him and wrote to him when she returned home. A poster-sized photograph of Papu and Goldie graces the walls of his establishment. He keeps a snapshot of the same picture handy so that whenever anyone takes a picture of him, he can hold up the photograph of himself and his famous customer.

The floor of Papu's shop is completely padded with a futon-style mattress covered in white cotton. He displays each silk with a flourish and then removes them one by one, giving the tourist a chance to choose his or her favorite. Papu started his shop with winnings from a lottery, which enabled him to buy a five-story building that includes an apartment for his family as well as the small salesroom. He is about a two-minute walk from the Dasaswamedh Ghat, which is the main ghat, where the pulse of riverside activity is at its most intense.

Ganges is desirable—the remains are scattered into the river.

Away from the banks of the Ganges, Varanasi is a hodgepodge of streets and alleys so confusing that even locals rely on a landmark building called the TV Tower to navigate their way. But every rug merchant passes through Varanasi on his way to Gobiganj, a village known for its rug weavers that is several miles outside the city.

SHREEDHAR & SONS

On the highway to Gobiganj, nothing can prepare the first-time visitor for the heat, confusion, roaming cows and goats, bicycles, cars, mechanized rickshaws, trucks, buses, pedestrians, roadside food stands and animal acts, beggars, and processions of saffron-clad Hindu faithful who share the road. This press of activity is in addition to dozens of carts laden with wool on their way from dyer to weaver, and finished rugs being lugged across the handlebars of ancient Raleigh bicycles. Once, to avoid a collision with a bus, our driver had to make

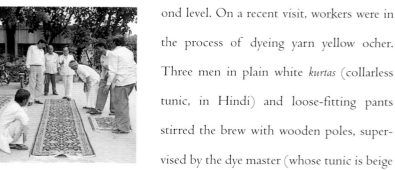

a choice, to either veer towards a cyclist or a cow. He aimed toward the cyclist, forcing him into a ditch, rather than chance harming a sacred animal.

I often travel to Gobiganj expressly to do business with Shreedhar & Sons. Shreedhar operates one of the biggest rug companies in the area. His walled compound is comprised of stucco buildings that house offices, a small warehouse for storing wool and completed carpets, and living quarters for Shreedhar and his wife, as well as apartments for his sons and their families. The courtyard is paved with gray marble tiles and is used to display carpets to merchants.

On a far corner of the compound sits an open, two-story brick structure with charcoal-fired ovens on the first floor that heat metal cauldrons filled with dye on the second level. On a recent visit, workers were in the process of dyeing yarn yellow ocher. Three men in plain white *kurtas* (collarless tunic, in Hindi) and loose-fitting pants stirred the brew with wooden poles, supervised by the dye master (whose tunic is beige

OPPOSITE ▪ *The warp threads on this loom filter the already low light emanating from a doorway and single bare bulb in this weaver's hut.*

BELOW ▪ *The ability to weave rugs is a much-respected skill, one that has more status than skilled clerical worker.*

PAGE 130 ▪ *Notice the stick figure animals and people scattered throughout the field of this Dehaj, Iran rug (4'5" × 6'9" [134 × 205cm]).*

PAGE 131 ▪ *The remarkably vibrant colors of Indian silks have insured them a worldwide market.*

and of a finer quality). Periodically, the dyers dipped into a boiling cauldron, pulled out a few pieces of yarn, wrung them out, and compared them to the dye master's yarn swatch. It took at least three hours of boiling and stirring before they achieved a match. When the dye master gave his approval, the yarn was dyed, removed from the vats, and dried on rows of metal clothesline for three days.

In another building, several workers were assembling and weighing hanks of yarn for distribution to the weavers. Nearby, a woman hand-painted a cartoon for a rug on graph paper, using bottles of colorful tempera and a thin brush. Nearly everyone was barefoot, as there is little distinction between the indoors and the tiled outdoor courtyard.

I also had an opportunity to watch Shreedhar evaluate rugs brought in for inspection and sale. Onlookers, each with a stake in the outcome, gathered around a tree for the review. The master weaver, wearing a red turban and a light gray Punjabi suit, was on hand. He endlessly chews

betel nut mixed with tobacco, an extremely addictive blend that blackens the teeth and turns one's gums and saliva a bright red. Like everyone else in India who chews this mixture, he speaks with his back teeth clenched. It makes him sound like James Cagney with a British accent and Indian cadence!

The loom owner, a very large man, was also present. According to Shreedhar, the loom owner invests close to thirty thousand rupees in a loom which is to be paid back by the weaver at the rate of 10 percent per rug. Certain corrupt loom owners allegedly lend more money to the weavers than they can possibly afford to repay, or even keep up with interest. As a result, a form of indentured servitude or bonded labor has evolved in India, which keeps people shackled to their masters as modern-day serfs. Shreedhar deplores the practice and will not deal with anyone who takes part in it.

Shreedhar also told me that he would have to reject one of the rugs. This always requires a delicate approach: If Shreedhar "scolded" the weavers too harshly and rejected

the rug outright, they would be free to sell it on the open market even though Shreedhar paid for all the wool and provided an advance for the labor. First, Shreedhar pointed out that the rug was not even, and tighter on one end than the other. The master weaver responded by blaming the monsoon weather. He said that if he had woven the rug any tighter it would have placed too much stress on the cotton warp and the rug would pucker when the humidity level dropped.

Everyone watched the exchange of words as if it were a tennis match. Shreedhar acknowledged the truth of the master weaver's statement, thus letting him save face. But still, Shreedhar stressed, the border was too narrow: a serious flaw that did not meet the design specifications of a particular importer. Also, Shreedhar pointed out that the *katen,* the area where the knots of two weavers working side by side come together, was also flawed. He picked up one end of the rug and felt it between his thumb and fingers, finding yet another flaw. The weaver once more defended himself with the monsoon excuse. Ultimately, Shreedhar purchased the rug, ending the verbal confrontation.

Privately, Shreedhar complained to me, "What am I going to do? I cannot ship this rug and without this one piece, the shipping container will not be full. We cannot reject it outright, yet we have supplied him the yarn. If we do reject the rug, then my yarn will be gone. Someone else will see the design and copy it. No. The weaver is a poor man. We will pay for the rug and tell him to do better."

Shreedhar ended up selling the rug on the tourist market for more than he could get for it otherwise.

Over the years, I have watched these discussions take place many times. The buyer always finds flaws in the rug, the weavers protest, and everyone involved wails about the same dire consequences: their children will starve, an entire generation will vanish if this one deal does not go through. But the players know in advance that the deal will be done—the parts they play in this little drama have been scripted in advance by centuries of tradition.

Shreedhar is of course an inveterate bargainer, whose greatest skill is that he pretends that he is not bargaining and has no time for such foolishness. Once, while on the telephone with a customer, he implored, "Why don't we let the deal go through at this price instead of arguing over a few pennies' difference that we are giving to the telephone company?"

"No," immediately replied the customer, adding, "Unless I bargain for a lower price I am not doing my duty to my company. I must bargain. Even if it does not make sense."

BUYING RUGS IN NORTHERN INDIA

Anoop once took me and my traveling companions to a village to inspect several looms that supply his company. Our arrival was an event for the villagers and just about every activity, except the weaving, came to a halt. Men and boys clad in longhis gathered close by. Women and girls wearing silk saris hung back in a group, covering their faces with brightly colored fabrics in yellow, orange, red, and blue.

In contrast to the resplendent clothing, the roads and houses were covered with a sun-bleached tan stucco made from *khākī*

("manure," in Hindi), which is used to harden the walls of the houses and keep the dust down on mud streets. Most of the homes had red-tiled roofs and despite the heat, the interiors stayed surprisingly cool. The entire town was serviced by one electrical outlet, powering a single bulb and a television set—the legacy of Indira Ghandi, who brought universal television to India. Villagers relied on sturdy old Raleigh bicycles (probably in daily use since the British left a half century ago) as the major form of transportation. Water buffalo lolled in a pond to keep out of the heat.

In the Gobiganj area, rug washing and trimming is done in outlying villages where no power machinery exists for shearing the pile after the rug is taken off the loom. This is all done by hand with large scissors that have a place for the thumb and forefinger on the business end to help guide the instrument evenly over the carpet. The only automated machines in most villages are electrically powered irrigation pumps that fill the washing troughs with water.

Tourists might be tempted to wander about northern India, seeking rugs directly from the source. In fact, inferior rugs not woven to specification—and essentially presold to merchants in the United States, Great Britain, and other European countries—are cheap. They are so inexpensive that it is tempting to bring home enough rugs to fill your entire house. But as P. R. J. Ford explains in *Oriental Carpet Design*, general rug production in Kashmir today is of "debased raw materials and crudest colour conceptions." Rugs that are supposedly silk are often made of mercerized cotton or a type of rayon euphemistically called "artsilk" (the "art" is short for artificial, not artistic). Incidentally, a rug woven of pure silk is not more costly because of the material—silk is plentiful and inexpensive—but because of the labor, as silk is much finer than wool and harder to work. On the whole, these modern Kashmiri rugs do not have much appeal to Westerners: their colors and design are based on an Indian concept of what Westerners like, not on any real understanding of contemporary interior design tastes.

Despite such admonitions, it is fun to shop for rugs and get a feeling for the kind of bargaining that goes into making such purchases. Visiting tourist shops and manufacturers in the outlying reaches of Jaipur, the capital of Rajasthan state, allows tourists to see hand weaving, rug washing, and finishing take place without making arduous trips to remote villages.

In Delhi, Rakesh Kumar, owner of the Carpet Palace in the Jor Bagh Market, feels that the tourist trade in rugs has destroyed the livelihood of honest dealers who want to sell quality rugs in India. He explains: "India is famous for handicrafts, and hand-knotted carpets are the king of Indian handicrafts. As a tourist, one would certainly like to pick up such a souvenir. Unfortunately, the sale of carpets is controlled by major organizations that go under innocent sounding-names to make them appear to be little cottage business cooperatives. These companies are, instead, cleverly veiled mass merchandisers with retail outlets in every city that is popular with tourists such as Agra, Jaipur, and Delhi."

BELOW ▪ *An endless stream of rugs ply the streets of Gobiganj, where a bicycle becomes an adaptable mode of transportation.*

OPPOSITE ▪ *An elephant ride to the Red Fort in Jaipur is a major attraction for tourists who visit this rug trading center, where they are invited to watch the making of rugs and other decorative textiles.*

According to Kumar, one such company, Cottage Industries Enterprises (CIE) is so dominant in the tourist trade that it has become the butt of a joke among oriental rug merchants: "The first thing Neil Armstrong saw when he landed on the moon was a sign saying next home of CIE." Kumar also believes that the system of commissions in the tourist trade is a disadvantage to the consumer:

"Guides bring the tourists to these outlets, and everyone blames the guide for limiting their selection to these shops. But all the guides work on a freelance basis and get their assignments from travel agents who have agreements to send tourists to only those outlets that have paid them an annual fee. It used to be the guide who was the boss but now it is the travel agent."

Commissions have to be split among not only the guides and travel agents (who are paid in advance based on potential business they can deliver during the year), but also the bus drivers and tour leaders, who receive 10 percent of the gross as well. With 40 percent going out in commissions, plus the cost of lavish parties to reward the travel people for their loyalty, the quality of the products suffers. "But are they loyal or slaves?" Kumar scoffs, adding, "They are like three people who rob a bank and have the understanding that they will split the profits equally. Afterwards they fight because the driver didn't have as much responsibility as the inside man who had to shoot people during the robbery."

Unfortunately, even tour leaders who come from other countries are inveigled into the scheme by locals and are powerless in terms of taking their groups to merchants outside the circle. Kumar notes, "The tour guide will insist that unless they bring their group to CIE or similar companies, they will be cut off, their children will starve, and so forth."

Warnings aside, I heartily recommend visiting India's rug-weaving centers and making at least a modest purchase. You will come home not only with a rug and wonderful stories, but an appreciation for oriental rugs that cannot be matched. To be sure, those "flowers underfoot" will take on new meaning with every step you take.

THE ART OF NEGOTIATION

FOR MANY

people, nego-

tiating or bargaining is intimidating, as

its practice is not understood or seldom

done well. Bargaining, however, is an ancient and honorable pro-

cedure in the Middle East and Central Asia, which, when exercised

correctly, brings levity and interest to an otherwise static occurrence. ✦ Before traveling and

bargaining for the rug of your dreams, it is helpful to window-shop at home to get an idea of

the type of rugs you like. It is highly probable that the rugs you see will vary greatly from those you discover in your travels;

many of the new colors found in rugs are commissioned for dealers in your country and not displayed in foreign shops. Even in the finest stores in

eastern countries, the owner will show the rugs and colors that he likes—and his taste might not necessarily match yours. However, by window

shopping, you can still get a good overview of styles and prices. ✦ As mentioned in Chapter Six, it is important to consider carefully the pros and

cons of buying a room-size rug during your travels. If you really wish to purchase a large rug, first set a budget and stick

to it, which can be harder to do than you might think. That's because bargaining can be the best part of a transaction.

Adhere to your budget and don't get carried away with impulse buying or succumb to pressure

from the merchants. Also remember that you will only see rugs from the region are visiting

and will be unable to compare styles from different countries. If you

would like to buy a rug for a specific room, make sure to bring exact

floor measurements and take samples of

any dominant colors in the room—paint

and fabric

swatches are

✦

CHAPTER EIGHT

helpful, and photographs of the room and its furnishings can serve as references. The traditional prelude to carpet buying begins with a presentation of tea. (There is a wonderful superstition in the Persian bazaar that when you are given a glass of tea, it is filled to the brim so that the devil can not sit on the edge

and dangle his feet in your drink.) Start the negotiations by keeping everything very personal. A good seller will talk about his children and their need for shoes and other necessary staples of life. A good buyer will say he is buying the rug for his wife or for his living room. Both parties appeal to each other's sense of family and decency. Inwardly, they may be laughing at one another, but they will display a face of humility in public.

Many times, however, the two bargaining people cannot come to terms. In this case, a third party often becomes involved and mediates the deal. It is common for an employee, uncle, or some other person of influence to step in and resolve

family conflicts. I have been fortunate in the past to witness my father bargaining in Afghanistan on several occasions with rug merchants. After a heated negotiation and a lack of agreement, I have seen my father and the merchant grasp hands when an understanding was near and not let go until the deal was struck. Negotiators may also cover their hands with a piece of cloth and make the final deal with their fingers, a process that is very similar to the way one bids at an auction, thus saving face and avoiding exposure to the surrounding crowd.

There are, however, many "rules" that should be observed when negotiating. Bargaining is not an adversarial conflict, for one person wants or needs to buy, and the other wants or needs to sell. In the West, we look at a computer-generated price tag and pay what is marked. In fact, few cashiers in large chain stores ever say thank you—the words are printed on the cash register tape. In the Middle East, a gift is often given along with a purchase, generally for one's wife or children. Usually, the bigger the gift, the better the deal was for the merchant.

Before you begin to negotiate, know the value of what you are bargaining over. The biggest mistake many people make is not knowing the true value of an item and making a ridiculous offer. In Iran it is said "He who speaks first, loses."

When I buy rugs, I spend some time looking around, even if I know what I want and what the price was yesterday. Another Middle Eastern aphorism is pertinent here: "It's a new day and a new deal." Deals not concluded on the same day negotiations are begun often must be totally renegotiated the following day. The seller might not have the same needs today as he did yesterday, and he has also had time to reconsider and change his mind about the price. Other Middle Eastern business practices are puzzling to the Western customer as well: a merchant may close shop early if he has already made a good deal, deciding that he has made enough money and doesn't need to make any more that day.

No merchant has respect for a bargaining buyer who does not know the correct value of what he wants to buy at the time he is buying, so put a little extra time into comparing rugs and values on the day you want to buy. If you travel to a rug-making country such as Turkey or Morocco, you may be taken advantage of by merchants who are familiar with Westerners and their poor bargaining skills.

Sometimes not knowing the language may help. Many years ago I was in Afghanistan with my father. He was not well one day, so I went out alone to look at rugs. I was young and did not know the language. I saw some rugs I liked and offered the only price I knew in Afghan, *yek hazar*, which meant 1,000 afghani. I would have offered more if I knew the words for a larger figure, but I ended up buying several pieces at that price. The next day the merchant told my father what a tough negotiator I was! I was highly respected in the bazaar after that.

A typical negotiation might proceed as follows: you see a rug you admire and the merchant compliments you on your taste. He then quotes a price that reflects his mood more than the true value of the rug. The price does not seem too bad so you offer him half, at which he feigns being stabbed in the heart—you close by splitting the difference. If you wander through the bazaar after making your deal, you will be assailed by other merchants, who will try to sell you rugs almost identical to the one you just purchased for half the price you just paid. So it goes in the rug world.

QUALITY AND PRICING

We all seek quality, but when it comes to oriental rugs, finding it can be an elusive and misunderstood quest. Like beauty, quality is in the eye of the beholder and may be determined by a host of criteria that include color, design, wool, size, knot count, type of dye, the fiber used to create the warp and, most importantly, how all of these individual points function to create a unified whole—a work of art.

In Turkey, for example, the majority of but not all designs are geometric and therefore bold. The colors, too, may range from primary and vivid to soft, pale hues that may in fact be the result of vegetable dyes. Also available are fine, ornate silk rugs, mostly prayer designs, as well as rather harsh floral designs mimicking traditional Persian rugs. When one goes to India, the majority of rugs woven there are floral Persian designs in a spectrum of colors and sizes. There are numerous geometric rugs available as well—reproductions of well-known village tribal rugs of Iran, the Caucasus, Afghanistan, and even Turkey. India and to a large extent Pakistan are adaptable rug-weaving countries; they are able to replicate old carpets and in doing so recreate the most beautiful new designs inspired by trends in other Middle Eastern countries and among demand by Western homeowners and interior design influentials.

Knot count is often said to be the most important factor in determining a quality rug. However, relatively coarse tribal rugs are equally desirable and valuable, often more so than rugs woven with a tight knot count. Using knot count exclusively as a point of consideration is not an accurate way to judge a rug.

Several other features of a rug are critical to determining its quality. First, its colors must be numerous and pleasing, complement each other, and be colorfast. A quick wipe of the rug with a damp white handkerchief tells you if the colors are fast, meaning they will not bleed into each other at the first washing or run into and stain the neutral-colored fringes.

The next element at consider is design, whether the pattern of the rug is pleasing and its lines relatively straight and connected. In certain unsophisticated villages and in tribal rugs, though, this is not important. As mentioned, what Westerners might call mistakes exist in oriental rugs, a quality which gives a rug character. Weavers in India,

BELOW • *As a young man*
inspecting the rugs in an Isfahan
bazaar, I tried out my father's
technique of making sellers wait
for an answer to improve the price.

Pakistan, Turkey, Iran, and Afghanistan today are trying hard to weave rugs that are nearly perfect to the eye, evidence of the influence of Western buyers who want near perfection and a predictable execution of their designs for their clientele.

Another important quality item is wool, the major material used in oriental rugs. The wool must not be too soft yet be pliable to the touch. It should also have an almost creamy feeling, a result of the natural lanolin that remains in the fibers after the rug is completed. Sometimes the oil in wool is washed out of it so that the dyeing will be uniform. This markedly affects the wearing quality of wool, making a poorer oriental rug. The wool should also not feel dry or have a chemical smell. Nearly all wool used in the Middle East is a mixture of New Zealand wool, which is soft and lustrous, and harder local wools to give the pile greater durability.

Oriental rugs come in all price ranges. Once the basic quality criteria are met, a per-square-foot or square-meter price is a good starting point in negotiations. The United States dollar tends to be the currency of the rug industry in the Middle East. In Turkey, a ceiling of about forty U.S. dollars per-square foot or four hundred U.S. dollars per square meter is reasonable. Fine silk rugs and other unusual rugs are priced much higher; as an example, a small silk Hereke rug can cost thousands of dollars. In India, prices range from as low as five to thirty U.S. dollars a square foot (or three hundred dollars per square meter), but the final price depends on the economy, currency, valuation, supply and demand, the look in your eye, or your accent.

Here's a final word about buying at a bazaar. While I have written a great deal about my experiences in the bazaars of

BELOW • *Adding to the intrigue of Istanbul are the many stories of the hapless train travelers being offered drugged tea, then robbed of their wallets and watches and left dazed without a cent to spend. But who can expect any less of a city that inspired* Murder on the Orient Express?

PAGE 148 • *This excellent Khamseh Confederacy tribal weaving, 4'9" x 7'9" (145 x 236cm), uses Persia's famous* boteh *design. Its weaver has shown imagination in creating the* badam, *a small treelike motif with extended branches. The multicolored edging is original, and the ivory field is well covered with detail, giving the background a lacelike composition.*

Iran, Turkey, Afghanistan, India, and Pakistan, my point of view is that of an established professional. I would like to offer a bit of advice for the traveler who is looking for a special rug as a memento of a wonderful and exciting journey to the Middle East.

Make the experience fun, suspend all your Western beliefs about true representation, full disclosure, and consumer protection laws. The stories the merchant at the bazaar tells you about the rug (how it will pay for the weaver's mother's operation, for example) are pure entertainment and should add to your enjoyment as you tell friends about your travel experience.

Above all, don't argue, raise your voice, or challenge the veracity of any statement made by the seller. It is unseemly and in bad taste. Instead, politely say, "I don't like it" and walk away. Any other reason you give will be challenged by the seller and you may weaken just to end an unpleasant situation in a foreign country.

Thinking you can become an instant wholesaler is not good practice, either. The likelihood of selling a rug that you have bought abroad to your local rug store is quite low. Most rug merchants have established relationships with suppliers or have a particular theme to their store and may not be very enthusiastic about purchasing from you at any price.

Again, I am not suggesting that you do not buy a rug on your visit to the rug-weaving world, but that you try to understand the culture there when you do. Travel to this part of the world is exciting and different; oriental rugs conceal within themselves the culture, hopes, fears, and expectations of peoples who live lives quite different than our own. Be wise, have fun, and return home with great stories, and a little rug.

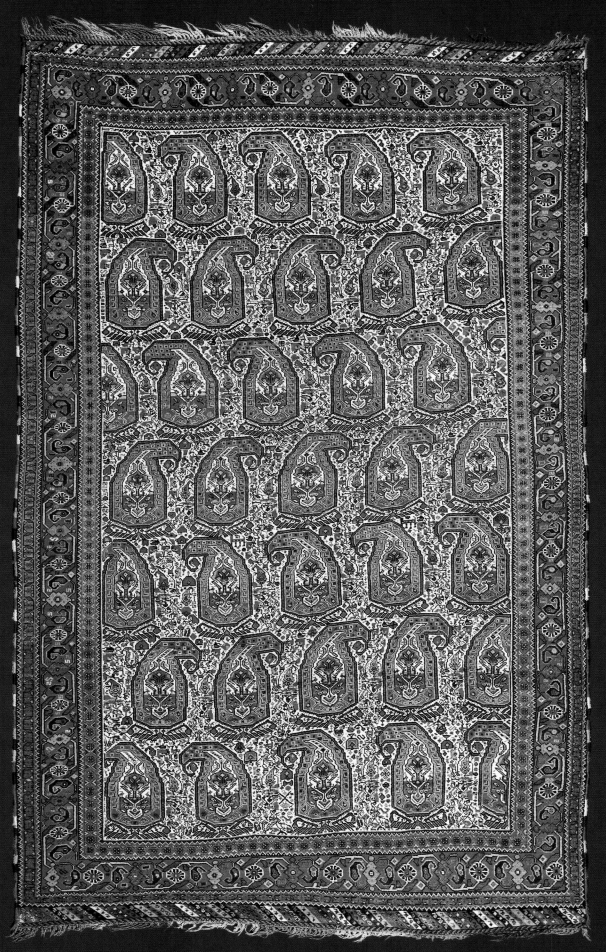

SEARCHING FOR
ANTIQUE RUGS

Collecting antique oriental rugs can offer a great sense of satisfaction and pride, especially if one develops a collection with a theme such as the Silk Route or inscribed Armenian rugs as our family has done for many years. However, don't buy antiques because you expect to get an undiscovered museum-quality masterpiece at a flea-market price, or want to beat the stock market. It just doesn't happen, and anyone who tells you differently is taking your money under false pretenses.

Likewise, don't purchase antiques simply because you feel present-day offerings from Turkey, Pakistan, Afghanistan, and India are inferior. Perhaps a century from now, collectors will be bidding up the price of rugs woven at the end of this century while criticizing the quality of their contemporary pieces.

When it comes to antique rug shopping, it is important to look at a lot of rugs to get a sense for pricing. Overall condition is perhaps the biggest factor to consider and must be taken into account relative to the age of the rug and the quality of any repairs that have been made. The useful life of an oriental rug can be as long as fifty years, so an antique rug that received modest traffic for fifteen years is still considered to be of excellent condition.

To help establish a benchmark, contact auction companies such as Christie's International Auction House and Sotheby's and buy their recent rug auction catalogs. These catalogs include estimated rug values. Following an auction, actual sale prices are sent to those who purchase the catalog. While a particular rug you are looking at can cost more or less than the listed prices, at least you will have a pricing framework. What is more, don't be mislead by size: bigger is not always better. Nine-by-twelve-foot rugs, because they fit more readily into most homes, are in greater demand and command a relatively higher price than larger pieces with a more limited market.

WHEN IT COMES TO SELECTING A RUG FOR YOUR

home, the extraordinary variety of designs and coun-

tries of origin can be overwhelming at first. To begin

the selection process, relax and enjoy the experience of

looking at as many rugs as you can. When selecting an oriental rug, the most important

rule is to use your senses—sight, touch, and smell. Try to take in all the patterns, colors,

and textures you see. Walk on the rug in bare feet, feel the fibers with your hand. Smell it.

A good rug will have a pleasant lanolin smell to it—avoid those that smell harshly of

detergents and chemical treatments or too much like a barnyard. ✦ After a while, you will begin to get a sense of the range of

choices and your preferences — from the traditional floral themes to bold geometric patterns, and many offshoots such as

prayer rugs. Look for a rug that is not too perfect or too programmed without any variance in the design or pattern. The most

enjoyable and gratifying rugs to own are endlessly enigmatic: there is great pleasure in discovering a hidden motif or a pleas-

ing color pattern—even after you've owned the rug for some time. Look for a rug that speaks to your soul. ✦ The first rule

of thumb when it comes to decorating with oriental rugs is that there are no rules, unless, of course, you follow the old rug

merchant's axiom, "Start with the rug and build your decor around its colors and patterns." Although facetious, there is truth

in the jest. Wall coverings, painted surfaces, and window treatments grow tired, fade, and

wear out, but a good oriental rug will not begin to show wear for decades. ✦ In addition

to new rugs, a partially worn antique blends well with natural tones, or can be used to soft-

en the look of a high-tech, no-nonsense kitchen with the latest appliances. Really worn

antique rugs and silk rugs (which should never be used

on the floor) are ideal as wall hangings and offer the

opportunity to have original art on the walls at a very

reasonable price. For more information on evaluating

and buying antique rugs, see "Searching for Antique Rugs," page 149.

There are five critical points to bear in mind in terms of decoration when buying a rug:

✦ Start your room decorating from the floor up if possible. Handmade oriental rugs are most often one-of-a-kind, and probably one of the most expensive items in your room. The carpet you choose for the floor sets the tone for the entire room, too.

✦ Choose carefully. If you're not starting from scratch, make sure you select a rug that works with the color, style, and decorative theme of the area where the rug is to be placed.

✦ Follow your own taste and color preferences. You do not have to be an expert to pick a good rug. No one knows better than you how you live or what you want to live with.

✦ Consider durability. Explain to the dealer your requirements for durability (hard wear at a door, pets, sunlight, and so on) as well as your taste preferences, and look at all of the choices.

✦ Test before you buy. If you buy locally, try taking a few rugs home with you to test. This process should be fun and easy. You should always be able to try a rug without committing to a purchase.

While some people perceive oriental rugs as being formal, this is hardly the case. In fact, the range of rugs on the market today means that you can use an oriental rug to establish just about any look in your home—from Colonial style to Eurocontemporary and everything in between. Before you go off and buy the latest in floor covering, look closely at some of the latest offerings in oriental rugs.

IS THIS THE RIGHT RUG?

. . . .

When choosing an oriental rug, use all your senses—as well consider how the design will integrate with your overall decor.

TAKE A GOOD LOOK

Knot count, whether the rug was dyed with aniline or vegetable dyes, and the country and city of origin are important factors to consider when making a rug purchase. But what matters most is how the design and construction all work together to create a feeling that makes the rug come alive and have a soul. A tribal rug with a bold pattern will not have the same knots-per-inch as an elaborate piece, but that does not mean the tribal rug is less aesthetically pleasing or less valuable. Likewise, aniline-dyed oriental rugs are no less "genuine" than rugs using vegetable dyes. Notice how the light plays off the rug from all directions. Some rugs change dramatically depending on the angle of view.

FEEL THE RUG

Take off your shoes and walk all over the rug to feel it under foot. Stroke the rug with your hand, first one way to raise the nap, then the other way to go with the grain. When going in the direction of the nap, the rug should feel supple; when going against the nap, the rug should have some resistance to it. The rug should not be dry or brittle, but have a certain smoothness, an almost creamy feeling. Different rugs will have a different feel—with some you can even feel the richness of the lanolin. Overall, there should be a sensuousness to the whole process, especially when the natural aroma of the wool reinforces the tactile experience.

SMELL THE RUG

Smell the rug. It should have a rich, pleasant aroma, a combination of wool and lanolin, perhaps with a hint of salt water, if the rug is new. Avoid rugs with an acrid aroma, as this may only intensify after you bring it home.

USE YOUR HEART AND HEAD

Buying an oriental rug requires both emotion and intellect. A rug should appeal to you on an emotional level. Don't be rushed into making a decision; work only with dealers who allow you to bring a rug home for several days before making a decision. Don't be taken in by illegitimate going-out-of-business sales, either, as the majority of these are marketing ploys at best and scams at worst. After all, if you buy a rug from someone who is going out of business, where will you go if you have a problem?

BE DARING

Be daring in your selection, and don't be afraid to suspend all of the design rules when it comes to mixing patterns and colors. Since oriental rugs are based on a Middle-Eastern aesthetic, they aren't always perfectly balanced. Mix boldly patterned window treatments and upholstery with an intricate rug. Try a tribal rug with big geometric shapes in a formal living room. Obviously, the function of the room and the mood you wish to create will play a role in your selection.

For a color boost and an easy way to give a central focus to an otherwise drab interior, an oriental rug can be a quick fix. Oriental rugs allow you to experiment with a bolder look without changing window or wall treatments.

If a room has a vaulted or cathedral ceiling, consider a rug with an ebullient design and vibrant color to "ground" the floor. Mixing textures, patterns, and colors can give a nice balance to an overly spacious room.

Do not feel restricted by tradition when choosing a rug. Placing a rug with unusual color combinations and patterns can be a welcome surprise in an entranceway, by a bed, or a traditionally furnished room.

ORIENTAL RUGS THROUGOUT THE HOME

THE FOYER

Your foyer is not a way station. Like the overture of a Broadway musical, it both welcomes people and sets the tone for what lies ahead. As guests enter through the front door and into the foyer, treat them to a richly colored tribal rug with an exciting pattern, or perhaps a more formal and romantic floral rug. Doing so establishes your home as a friendly, welcoming, and active haven.

By paying special attention to the foyer rug, you will create an entry space that does not have guests feeling as though they have to rush off to another room or take off their dirty shoes. In short, regard your foyer as a room equal in stature and deserving of as much design consideration as any other room in your home. Remember, too, that the foyer is not only the first impression people have of your home, but is their last impression, too.

LIVING ROOMS AND DINING ROOMS

If you want to make an overall statement, be bold in your choice of both rug pattern and furniture pieces in the living and dining room. And by bold, I don't mean wild, but distinctive. First of all, larger furniture is easier to work with as it determines the rest of the room's furnishings and decoration. In the long run, this is a less expensive way to unify a room's decor. The key, though, is to anchor your furniture with a richly patterned oriental rug that makes a statement. Professional designers advocate making a

BELOW AND OPPOSITE ■

*This home was designed with an open
floor plan; boldly patterned and colorful oriental rugs define various living
areas throughout. The contemporary*

*Indian oriental rugs used in the decor
belie the notion that such rugs are formal
and unify the space as well. Note how
the rugs are used to create distinctive
living spaces throughout the home.*

floor plan for a space, then starting the decoration from
the bottom up.

   In a large room, oriental rugs can be used to create
separate seating or conversation areas. One way of empha-
sizing this further is to create two furniture groupings—
one of upholstered furniture, and one using wicker, wood,
or wrought iron—as well. The use of casual wicker or rat-

tan in particular maintains an informal tone and relationship with the outdoors during every season.

   For formal entertainment areas such as the living or
dining room, rugs with an all-over design are ideal, since a
rug with a center medallion may be covered wholly or partially by a table. That said, glass-top dining room tables may
work very well with a medallion rug.

OPPOSITE ▪ *Oriental rugs need not be limited to living rooms and dining rooms. They add color and an interesting design element to a kitchen. Most can also withstand kitchen traffic.*

BELOW ▪ *Small throw rugs are often better for a bedroom, as designs with large central patterns can be lost under the bed. But here the simple all-over symmetry of this rug makes a bold impact and maintains the visual sense of the rug.*

HOME OFFICES

Now that the home office is so much a part of modern home design, many people prefer to decorate this room in a way that clearly sets it apart from the mood of the rest of the house in order to create distinct areas for both work and relaxation. If every other room

in your home has light furniture and informal rugs, you might wish to go with a big mahogany desk and a traditional rug design in dark maroon and deep blues. No matter the design, if the rug says prosperity, your business venture will prosper—that's part of the magic of oriental rugs. If you see clients in your office, whether at home or in a skyscraper with an imposing view of the city, never, ever, consider installing a machine-made or fake oriental rug. If the rug on the floor of your office isn't genuine, then what does that say to clients about your credibility?

THE KITCHEN

Make the kitchen a festive room with an oriental rug. One of the most enjoyable aspects of entertaining is inviting guests into the kitchen to help with cooking. The kitchen is ideal for a rug that you would love to see every day, or for a favorite old rug that may have had its day in the living room, but still has plenty of life left in it. Earlier generations actually turned worn rugs over and let the back side show to extend their longevity.

BEDROOMS

For the master bedroom, I recommend using area rugs around the bed or in open areas. A large room-size rug will unify the room, but much of it will be lost under the bed. In a bedroom, it is the open areas that come alive with colorful oriental rugs. You might want to use smaller rugs, even overlapping them, to create a Middle-Eastern tent look that feels

BELOW ▪ *A pastel Indo-Keshan rug emphasizes the seasonal decor value oriental rugs offer a summer home overlooking the ocean.*

OPPOSITE ▪ *Oriental rugs of different sizes create an unusual but cohesive floor plan in this elegant master bedroom.*

cozy and suggests a respite from the outside world. Small pillows made from old oriental rug scraps and camel bags, a silk rug, or a kilim (flat weave) hung on the wall are all attractive additions to the bedroom as well.

Consider oriental rugs for children's rooms, too. As my father once said, "No one can misbehave in a room with an oriental rug." When it comes to economy, oriental rugs are a bargain because they are so durable that your children will be able to pass down their bedroom rug to their children, even their grandchildren. Look for rugs with an animal or forest motif from India or a whimsical tribal rug from Iran or Turkey in traditional patterns and soft old colors. Don't worry about spillage and excessive dirt, as oriental rugs are quite durable and clean up well. I can tell you from experience that when my children were young, I had the rug in our family room cleaned annually—and the rinse water had nutritional value!

HOMES IN WARMER CLIMATES

Those who first experienced oriental rugs at their grandmother's house often think of them as being in deep maroon tones with center medallions and intricate floral patterns, and associate them with gathering around the table for winter holidays. Thus oriental rugs are often thought of as being austere, reminiscent of cold weather, gray skies, and formal dinners. The truth is, when it comes planning a summer house or home a in warmer climate with lots of glass and vistas of blue skies or the ocean, oriental rugs are a great asset. Walking on no other floor covering barefoot can compare to the comfort and luxurious feeling of lanolin-rich wool.

Many people opt for beige or pastels for a summer home to keep a light look. There are many contemporary oriental rugs woven in pastel colors and with lots of ivory that are available from Pakistan and Iran.

OPPOSITE ▪ *Here, an oriental rug is used to add warmth to this casual space as well as to define a seating area. Wicker and a seafaring mural give this area an outdoor look.*

BELOW ▪ *The combination of boldly designed upholstery fabric and a powerfully patterned rug from central Asia works well to create a comfortable, casual look and feel in this lakeside home.*

SMALL LIVING SPACES

The challenge in decorating a small urban apartment is to make the rooms appear larger. Instead of using a room-sized rug, intersperse small scatter rugs in more spacious areas as accent and interest pieces. A floral rug will bring the feeling of nature indoors, or if your taste is more eclectic, consider a striking tribal or folk-art rug.

✦   ✦   ✦

Imagine the awe European Crusaders felt when they first laid eyes on Constantinople and stood at crossroads of commerce and culture with the East; the incredible journeys of seventeenth-century English merchants who started a brisk trade in custom-made, Persian-inspired rugs acquired through its East India Company in the remote Subcontinent; and the adventures of eighteenth- and nineteenth-century mariners and advances in navigation that made it possible to introduce oriental rugs to Europe, the Americas,

and eventually the rest of the world.

Despite vigorous trade over the centuries and the rapid growth of Moslem populations in Europe and North America, the Middle East still remains an enigma to Westerners. I often think about how easily my father could gather a crowd to watch the silent 16-millimeter movies that he shot on his travels to Iran, Turkey, and India, and listen to his tales. Even though our exposure to these cultures is more frequent today, and travel there is also faster, easier, and safer, the sense of mystery still exists. Go to the Grand Bazaar of old Constantinople, stand quietly in one of its Byzantine corridors, and listen to the sounds of a bargain being struck here, a call to pray there, or the swish of veiled Moslem women passing by. In that solitary moment, you too will experience the same joy, awe, and allure early travelers did when they coursed the Silk Route in search of oriental rugs five centuries ago.

A P P E N D I X

✚

CLEANING ORIENTAL RUGS

If your rug is dirty or needs repair, it should be attended to immediately. A dirty rug not only looks unloved, but will deteriorate more quickly. In fact, the biggest cause of oriental rug deterioration is improper or the total lack of cleaning.

The best way to preserve a rug is to send it to an established oriental rug cleaning company, one that washes the rug on a flat surface with soap and water. An oriental rug should never be cleaned with dry-cleaning solutions or steamed.

You can also clean oriental rugs yourself, but it is best to limit this to very small area rugs, as large rugs become very heavy and unmanageable when wet. It is also best to clean the rug on a warm, sunny day to speed the drying process.

The first step in cleaning an oriental rug is to knock out the grit.

GETTING OUT THE GRIT

My grandmother often used to take a rug outside in the winter after it had just snowed, hang it over the clothesline, beat the grit out, and then rub snow all over the surface. It was very satisfying to see the snow get so dirty, but inadver-

tently, she preserved the rug by knocking the grit out of it. In the Middle East it is not uncommon to see a dirty rug being taken from the home and placed upside down on the road for cars, trucks, and animals to pass over it in order to knock out all the grit!

Grit or sand is the single most important factor in causing the early deterioration of a rug. When grit is trapped in the pile, the constant agitation of walking on the rug can cut the wool pile at its base. At this rate, the rug will never have a chance to wear out!

The first step in cleaning an oriental rug is to knock out the grit while the rug is dry. If the rug becomes wet first, the grit turns into a concretelike substance and will never come out. To knock out the grit properly, vacuum both sides of the rug. Then take the rug outside and knock out any remaining grit by vigorously shaking the rug with a firm snap.

WASHING THE RUG

After knocking out the grit, place the rug on a clean flat surface outdoors (a driveway is a good choice), and wet it thoroughly with a hose. Next, mix up a pail of animal fat or oil-based soap (inquire at your rug dealer if you aren't sure what to use) and water. With a push broom, scrub the rug vigorously on both sides, rinse with a hose, then scrub again. (In the Middle East, a rug is often wet down and scrubbed without soap to brighten and clean the face.)

Rinse the rug again with a hose. When you rinse, it is not necessary to rinse out all the soap, but caution should be taken to prevent the colors in the rug from bleeding into each other. Fixing color is not a concern for modern rugs that use chemical chrome dyes exclusively, but it can be problematic in certain new village and urban rugs woven in Iran, Afghanistan, Turkey, and North Africa, where natural dyes ares in vogue. Generally, older rugs, such as family heirlooms, have been washed so many times that the colors probably will not run. A good way to test the stability of the dyes in your rug is to wet a white cloth or handkerchief and rub it on a small spot of the rug to see if the colors bleed.

To prevent bleeding, it may be necessary to use a color fixative in the final rinse. This keeps certain fugitive dyes from running into the fringes and onto ivory wool on the rug itself. In a pail, mix a handful of alum powder, available at many drugstores, with 10 liters of water, then slosh the solution over the rug. Let the rug stand for five minutes, then rinse with clear water.

Finally, lay the rug flat on a clean outdoors surface, such as driveway, patio, or deck, and leave it in the sun to dry.

✦   ✦   ✦

As a young man, I used to wash rugs in my father's basement. In those days, houses were or had been heated with coal, and everything in the house, including the rugs, was covered with a grimy coal-dust coating. Washing those rugs was amazing—once they were clean again, it was like turning on the lights in a dark room. The colors and shapes were so much sharper. My father's favorite story was about a woman who, when she picked up her rug after cleaning, said, "That's not my rug—it never had such bright colors."

PREVENTING COLORS FROM FADING

The quality of the wool and dyes in a rug make a big difference in its durability. An important factor is the rug's exposure to direct sunlight, which will bleach out and change strong colors.

Examine your rug closely and part the pile, looking towards the base of the knot: you may well find the bleaching is only on the very tip of the pile and that the color is still vibrant below. In this case, if the pile is thick and you wish to revive the original colors, the rug may be shaved a tiny bit in order to remove the faded tips of the pile. I do not generally recommend this, but it can be done. Once a rug has been shaved, it should not be left in strong sunlight again; eventually, you will run out of wool to shave! There is a product on the market that filters ultraviolet light; it is applied to windows in a thin film to reduce color fading.

CLEANING SILK RUGS

A silk pile rug must be cleaned in an entirely different way than a wool rug. Silk, unlike wool, does not spring back to its original shape, and if wet, lies down and becomes flat like a cheap shag carpet. Once this has happened, the pile can not be restored to what it once was.

Silk must be cleaned with a damp rag or sponge and a little soap, stroking the pile in the direction it lays, and not soaking it. Wipe the pile again with a clean, damp sponge (without soap) to remove the residue and let the rug dry. It is critical that you use as little water as possible.

REPAIRING ORIENTAL RUGS

The condition of an unrepaired rug will only worsen if measures are not taken to stop its further erosion. Treasure your rug today, and your children will treasure it tomorrow.

The most perishable part of any rug is the fringe (ends) and edges (sides). The white cotton fringes often become discolored after cleaning, as the grimy rinse water sometimes leaches onto them. Many rug cleaners use a chlorine bleach to whiten the fringe after the rug is cleaned, but if the fringes are bleached and not completely rinsed, they will begin to deteriorate over time.

Fringes are also exposed to other dangers, such as vacuum cleaners—which eat fringes if not properly used—and wear from constant foot traffic. It is good to vacuum an oriental rug, but it is important to push the vacuum cleaner over the fringe and then lift, not drag, it back onto the rug.

Fringe can be fixed. You have three options: 1) Do nothing (which may be fine in an older rug if the edges are otherwise good shape); 2) Have a new machine-made fringe sewn on, an inexpensive solution; or 3) Actually weave in a new fringe that looks exactly like the original.

The other common trouble spot on oriental rugs are the edges, where a number of cords are wrapped with wool much the same color as the rug. Because the wear is on the edges of the wool—not on the tips as is the case with the pile—the cords may break apart. The cords are often easily restored and should in no way be considered a deficiency in the rug.

There are numerous other things that can injure a rug, such as burns, moths, cuts, pet stains, and so forth. Also, don't place potted plants directly on a rug; if you do, the moisture from the plant will eventually eat a nice round hole in the rug right through to the floor! I once had a customer who brought in a rug to see if it could be fixed. It seemed her husband was cleaning his shotgun and he blew one corner of the rug off! Happily, we restored the rug to its former state. (I never heard what happened to either the husband or the shotgun.) Consult your rug dealer about the proper treatment for repairing rug damage.

When I travel, I always try to buy dyed wool in the different districts I visit. This way, I almost always have the proper wool and color for any repair—a bit of quality customer service I learned from my father! You may chose to buy extra wool if your rug has unusual colors.

TREATING AND PREVENTING INFESTATION

Wool moths, rug beetles, and other pests can be very destructive to an oriental rug. These insects find a protected or undisturbed area of a wool rug and nest in it: usually under a piece of furniture or in an area that has been soiled with drinks or food and has nutritional value. Often the infestation goes unnoticed until substantial damage has been done. The good news is that the damage can be rewoven by a skilled restorer so as to be undetectable, but the labor can be time-consuming and costly.

You can protect your rug from pests with commercial moth flakes, by turning your rug, and by cleaning it on a regular basis, depending on the use. An old method that works and that we still use on occasion is to place newspaper under a rug to deter insects. The newspaper ink is a preventative; however, the newspaper needs to be changed about every six months to keep the odor strong.

Overall, the best precaution is to keep rugs out from under furniture, vacuum them regularly, and have them picked up and professionally cleaned with soap (that is as close to pH neutral as possible and preserves the lanolin) and water.

GLOSSARY

✦

ABRASH: Variegated shading of colors in a rug caused by the use of various dye lots or by the oiliness of the wool.

ALL-OVER DESIGN: A pattern that covers the entire surface of a rug. Also referred to as a covered field design.

ANATOLIA: Greek for "Asia Minor."

BAKHTIARI: Tribe living in central Iran, whose name means "the lucky ones."

BADAM DESIGN: Farsi for "paisley design."

BORDER: A design on a rug that frames all of its outside edges.

BLOCKING: A method of reshaping a rug. When a rug is wrinkled, or misshapen due to being wet, the rug must be stretched flat, tacked down, wet again, then allowed to dry to regain its original shape.

BOTEH DESIGN: Farsi for "immature flower" or "palm leaf." A pattern that resembles *badam*.

CARTOON: A schematic illustration, done either by hand or computer, that outlines the various design elements of a rug and is often colored in.

COVERED FIELD: See *All-Over Design*.

DOZAR: A rug measuring about four feet, six inches by seven feet.

DRAKHTI: Farsi for "Tree of Life." See *Tree of Life*.

FIELD: The inner design of a rug, excluding the border. May be a solid color or with a central design of a floral or geometric nature, and contains the dominant rug color. See *Ground*.

FISH AND TURTLE DESIGN: A pattern in which two fish appear to be chasing each other around a globe carried on the back of a turtle. Over the years, this pattern has been continually abstracted so that it may also resemble a blossom encircled by two leaves. See *Herati* and *Mahi*.

FRINGE: The strings, or warp ends, that extend from the end of the rug.

GHORDI KNOT: The most common knot used in rug weaving, it is often called a symmetrical knot or Persian knot.

GIZ (KIZ) KILIM: A kilim woven by a young girl (Giz is Tukish for "girl"), often for her dowry.

GROUND: See *Field*.

GUL: Farsi for "rose" or "flower."

GUL-FERANG: Farsi for "foreign flower."

HALAL: Farsi for an item that is "pure," "clean," or "unstained."

HALI: Turkish for "carpet" or "rug."

HALICILIK: Turkish for "rug seller."

HARAM: Farsi for an item that is "impure," "dirty," or "stained."

HERATI: Farsi for "Fish and Turtle Design." See *Fish and Turtle Design* and *Mahi*.

JUNGAL (F) DESIGN: Refers to the representation of animal in a natural setting or in a forest (jungle).

JUVAL: A handmade bag used to store grain.

JEJIM: See *Kilim*.

KATEN: The area on a rug where the knots of two weavers working side by side come together.

KILIM: Also known as *Jejim*. A flat, woven fabric, usually wool, used as a covering, curtain, or to cover the earthen floor within a tent.

MAHI: See "Fish and Turtle Design" and *Herati*.

MIHRAB: The prayer point of a prayer rug.

MIR: A small all-over paisley design.

OVERCAST: A method of repairing a rug. When the ends of a rug are coming apart, they can be sewn using a concealed whip stitch.

PARDEH: A door or curtain for a tent. Also a rug measuring about five by eight feet.

PILE: The surface of the knots which make up the face of a rug.

POSHTI: A small rug, approximately two by three feet.

PRAYER RUG: A rug or a mat with a directional design that its user points to the east when praying. The mat is also meant to protect the user from the dirty ground while he prays.

SAFAVID DYNASTY: Persian dynasty ruled by Shah Abas from 1587–1628 A.D.

SENNA KNOT: A common knot used in rug weaving. Also referred to as an asymmetrical or Turkish knot.

SOUMAK: A type of flatweave like a kilim, but heavier.

SWASTIKA: A symbol that originated in China that represents "ten thousand happinesses" or the "heart of Buddha" in that culture.

TARAK: A metal, comblike, hand-held tool used to beat down the knots to make the rug knotting tight.

TREE OF LIFE: The Persian symbol for immortality. See *Drahkti*.

VAGIREH: A sampler made by weavers to show their work and from which they take rug orders.

WAR RUGS: These rugs were woven by the Afghan Belouchi people during the Soviet invasion of Afghanistan.

WARP: The foundation thread that runs the length of the rug and becomes the fringe.

WEFT (WOOF): The thread that runs the width of the rug, between the rows of knots, and helps to hold the rug together.

BIBLIOGRAPHY

✤

Bailey, Julia. "Flowers Underfoot: Metropolitan's Mughal Exhibition." *Beyond the Fringe*, published by the New England Rug Society, Volume 4, January 30, 1998, pps. 6–8.

Druding, Susan C. "Dye History from 2,600 B.C. to the Twentieth Century." Paper presented at Convergence 1982, Seattle, Washington.

Evans, Ben. Telephone interview. London, England. March 6, 1998.

Ford, P.J.R. *Oriental Carpet Design: A Guide to Traditional Motifs, Patterns and Symbols.* London: Thames and Hudson, 1992.

Kumar, Rakesh. Interview. Delhi, India. August 6, 1998.

Levi, Lotfy Ben and Levi, Marti Ben. Interview. Seacaucus, New Jersey. January 14, 1999.

Mumford, John Kimberly. *Oriental Rugs.* New York: Charles Scribner's Sons, 1900.

Opie, James. "Marketplace." *Hali*, Issue 97, March 1988, p. 131.

Shreedar, Anoop. Interview. Gobiganj, India. August 7 and 8, 1998.

Victoria and Albert Museum Desk Diary 1998. London: Random House UK, Ltd., 1997.

Walker, Daniel. "Flowers Underfoot." New York: The Metropolitan Museum of Art, 1997.

Yumartaci, Izak. Interviews. Izmir, Turkey: February 15 and 16, 1999; New York: April 5, 1999.

PHOTOGRAPHY CREDITS

✦

All photography by Douglas Christian except:

Gregorian Collection of Antique Oriental Rugs: pps. 14, 17, 21, 23, 24, 25, 26, 27, 28, 29, 34, 42, 43, 44.

Amos Chan: p.148, courtesy Northeastern Log Homes, Kenduskeag, Maine.

Vincent Lisanti, p. 161, courtesy Northeastern Log Homes, Kenduskeag, Maine.

George Riley: p.153, courtesy Classic Post & Beam, York, Maine; pps. 154–155, courtesy Northeastern Log Homes, Westfield, Massachusetts; p.160, courtesy Classic Post & Beam, York, Maine.

Roger Wade: p. 159.

INDEX

A

Abrash, 50, 69, 168
Aesthetic values, 19, 24, 27, 45
Afghanistan
 rug trade in, 22, 48, 83, 85, 147
 rugs from, 41, 45, 54, 58, 69, 104, 144, 149, 165
Agents, role of, 12, 80, 119, 138–139
Agra, 36–37, 109–111, 120, 124
Airports, 12–13
All-over designs, 53, 58, 168
Anatolia, 93, 114, 168
Animal designs, 19, 38–39, 41, 50, 120, 129–130
Antique rugs, 104, 113–144, 149–152
Appraisal techniques, 36, 58
Architecture, 120, 134
Ardebil rugs, 28, 45
Ardilan, Ali, 12
Armenians, 12, 19, 39, 41, 77
Art form
 negotiation based on, 144, 146–147
 oriental rugs as, 19, 22, 24, 53
 passing on skills of, 32, 34, 53, 72
Artsilk, 137
Atatürk, Kemal, 103
Auctions, 93, 106–107, 110, 113, 142, 149
Australia, 85, 88

B

Bachelor degrees, in weaving, 88
Badam design, 58, 147–148, 168
Bags, from rugs, 22, 107, 114, 119–120, 160

Bailey, Julia, 119
Bakhtiari designs, 41–42, 49–50, 54, 85, 168
Bakshaish rug, 26–27
Bazaars
 buying strategies, 143, 146–147
 in Istanbul, 101–103, 107, 163
 trading customs, 72, 77, 80, 137
Beads, 49–50, 54–55, 102–103
Belouchi design, 38–41, 48–50, 54, 58, 72–73
Benares, 124, 126
Bergano rugs, 86, 88
Betel nut, 129
Beyond the Fringe, 119
Bibibaft design, 41–42
Bidjar, 22–23, 34–35, 50, 116, 119, 134
Bleaching agents, 62, 65, 165–166
Blocking, 132–133, 168
Blueprints, graph paper, 93, 129
Böhmer, Harald, 87–88
Borders, 133, 167–168
Bosphorus, 107
Boteh design, 147–148, 168
Boukara design, 16, 19, 22, 49–50, 54, 79–80
Bridegrooms, 40–41
Buddhism, 114
Burning, for finishing, 101
Business practices, 72, 110, 124, 129, 137, 139
 see also Negotiation
Buying strategies, 124, 141–149, 152, 165
Byzantine Empire, 15, 18, 88, 163

C

Cadence callers, 80
Çanakkeli rug, 54–55
Cartoons, 88–89, 93, 110, 129, 168
Cat's paw design, 140, 142
Caucasus region
 rug trade in, 15, 19, 22, 62
 rugs from. *See* Kazak rugs
Celebrations, 40–41, 46, 48–49, 68
Central Asia, 13, 15, 54, 57, 114
Character, of rugs, 96, 144, 146
Child labor, 32, 34
China
 rug trade in, 15, 19, 85, 119
 rugs from, 41, 57–58, 96
Christianity, 19, 39, 41, 45
Christie, Agatha, 103
Cirgan Palace, 106–107
City dweller designs, 57–58
Classification methods, 39–45, 53–58
Cleaning procedures, 113, 132–133, 160, 164–167
Cleanliness, 45, 50
Climate, 13, 160
Coal, 62, 165
Color
 bleeding factors, 62, 144, 164–165
 decorating per, 151–153, 155, 160
 fading factors, 62, 67, 165–166
 in designs, 22, 27, 36, 69
 market research, 69, 88, 93, 129
 trend-setting, 110, 113–114
 use in classifications, 54, 57–58
 see also Dyes

Combs, 35, 45, 50
Commissions, 57, 68, 120, 124, 138–139
Competition sources, 22, 91, 93
Computers, 35, 48, 88–89, 93, 109, 124
Constantinople. *See* Istanbul
Consumer protection laws, 147
Cottage Industries Enterprises (CIE), 137–139
Cotton, 61, 137
Court rugs, 22, 57–58
Courtship, rug-weaving and, 90
Culture, in oriental rugs
 combination strategies, 85, 88
 pattern representations, 31–51, 53–58
 pigmentation representations, 68–69
 trading customs per, 72, 77, 80, 92
 tradition representations, 19, 24, 27, 68, 147
Currency, 88, 91, 101, 143, 146

D

Daghestan rug, 20, 22
Darand, 72–73, 80
Dating techniques, 36, 39
Decorating, with oriental rugs, 151–163
 bedrooms, 159–161
 critical points, 107, 141, 151–153
 current trends, 110, 113–114
 dining rooms, 155–156
 furniture and, 142, 155–156, 159, 162–163
 home offices, 159
 in warmer climates, 160

living rooms, 155–156
small living spaces, 163
the foyer, 154–155
the kitchen, 158–159
Dehaj, 129–130
Delphi, 124, 137
Demand
influences on, 19, 22, 24,
110, 113
negotiation based on, 144,
146
production for, 62, 109,
114
Desmealti rug, 152
Deterioration, 62–67,
64–167
Dozar, 168
Drakhti, 46, 168
Druding, Susan C., 62, 64
Durability factors, 152,
159–160, 165
Dye masters, 67, 69, 98, 101,
126, 129
Dyeing process, 66–69,
112–113, 120, 122,
126, 129
Dyes
as trade item, 62–63, 69
bleeding factors, 62, 144,
164–165
dating techniques with, 39,
69
insect-based, 65, 67,
103–104
natural, 61–62, 64–65,
67–68, 87–88, 144,
165
research on, 62, 69, 87–88
synthetic, 61–62, 64–65,
67, 165
vegetable, 61, 65, 67, 98,
101, 144, 153
see also Color

E

East India Company, 119, 163
Economic factors, 13, 15, 19,
22, 24, 62, 80
Envy, as evil spirit, 49–50
Ephesus, 88
Euphrates River, tale of,
31–32
Europe, 15, 19, 53, 85, 88,
113
Evans, Bob, 120
Evil eye, 48–50, 54–55
Exhibitions, 27–28, 50, 119
Export tax, 64

F

Factors, as agents, 119
Far East, 13, 15, 163
Farmer designs, 58
Feelings
decorating per, 68, 151,
153
in designs, 35–36, 41, 46
Fereghan design, 50
Field, 168
Fingers, deals with, 142
Finishing processes, 101, 109
Fish and turtle design, 46,
48, 56–59, 108, 110,
168
Fixatives, color, 67, 165
Floor mats, 90
Floral designs
as classification method, 53,
57–58
examples, 25, 30, 32, 46,
54, 56–57, 68–69, 120,
168
Flowers Underfoot, 114
Folk-art, 19, 22, 163
Forbes, Robert Bennett, 119
Ford, P. R. J., 137
France, 13, 53, 120
Freelance business, 139
Fringes, 166–168
Full disclosure, in buying,
147
Furniture
decorating per, 142,
155–156, 159, 162–163
market coordination, 92,
110, 133

G

Ganges River, 113, 124–126
Garden-pattern rugs, 41, 85
Geometric designs, 53–57,
144, 153
examples, 12, 60, 62,
84–85, 152
Ghats, of Ganges, 124–125
Gifts, with purchases,
142–143
Gion Matsuri Procession, 120
Gobiganj, 124, 126–134, 138
Golden Hali company, 88, 91,
93, 97, 104
Good luck symbols, 36, 49
Grand Bazaar, 101–103, 107,
163
Great Britain, 119–120
Gregorian collection, 24–28,
50, 119, 149

Grid-iron traditions, 119–120
Guides, freelance, 138–139
Gul, 168
Gul Pagan, rugs from, 76–77
Gul-ferang, 46, 56–57, 168

H

Hagia Sophia cathedral,
18–19, 104, 107
Halal, 168
Hali, 168
Hali, 113, 120
Halicilik, 104, 168
Haram, 50, 168
Head scarfs, 92
Health care issues, 13, 93
Herati, 46, 48, 56–59, 108,
110, 169
Heriz, 84–85
Hinduism, 19, 58, 114, 119
Hotel accommodations, 103,
107, 114–115
Human labor
cost factors, 85, 88, 91, 93,
101, 110
functions of, 101, 109, 134
hours of, 72, 109
indentured, 129
Humanity, in designs, 19, 46
Humility, in negotiations, 142

I

Icons, in designs, 36
Immortality, 45–46
Immunizations, 13
India
Mughal rugs, 114,
119–120, 124
northern region, 109, 114,
134–139
rug trade in, 13, 39, 85,
124–139, 147
rug weaving in, 19, 22,
109–114
rugs from, 58, 67, 144,
149, 160
examples, 104–105, 108,
110, 116, 119–120,
123, 129–130,
134–136, 140, 142
transportation in, 109,
114–115, 120, 124,
126, 134, 138
Indo-Gaba rug, 154–155
Insect infestations, 167
International Area Rug
Market, 113
Inventory control, 109

Iran
New Year in, 46, 48–49
politics of, 12–13, 22, 57,
64, 72, 85
rug trade in, 10, 13, 22, 62,
72, 77, 80, 85, 147
rug weaving in, 83, 85, 110,
114
rugs from, 41, 45–50, 53,
58, 69, 144, 160, 165
examples, 70, 72–81,
84–85, 95–96
Isfahan
rug trade in, 22, 41, 77, 80,
101–107
rugs from, 32–33, 57, 70,
72, 80, 85
Istanbul, 12, 15, 18, 24,
87–88, 163
Izmir, 88, 91, 93, 96

J

Jain religion, 114
Jaipur
Red Fort center, 138–139
rugs from, 50–51, 80–81,
109, 124, 137
Jejim, 169
Jews, influence of, 77
Jor Bagh Market, 137
Joshegan, 78, 80
Jungal design, 169
Juval, 169

K

Kashgar rugs, 21–22
Kashmiri rugs, 137
Katen, 126–127, 133, 169
Kazak rugs
designs in, 54, 58, 93, 114,
144, 152
examples, 28, 36–37,
40–41, 44–45
Kerman rugs, 22, 24–25, 57,
64
Kermani, Mohammed Zad,
25
Keshan, 22, 41, 43, 45–46,
57, 160
Khäki, 119, 134
Khamseh Confederacy tribal
weaving, 147–148
Kilims, 11–12, 114, 160,
168–169
Knots
by hand, 19, 97, 101, 110
center of rug, 126–127,
169

count significance, 80, 85,
91, 93, 144
ghordi, 12, 85, 97, 99–101,
168
senna, 12, 169
Kobi Sultan rug, 44–45
Kulalar, 64–65, 92, 96
Kumar, Rakesh, 137–139
Kurtas, 126
Kyoto, Japan, 119–120

L

Labor issues. *See* Human labor
Landscapes, 41
Language issues, 143
Leitmotifs, 120
Letters and letter writers, 36, 72
Levi, Lotfy Ben, 110, 113
Light bulbs, colored, 57
Literacy, of weavers, 36
Logic, beliefs about, 31
Looms, 12, 109–110, 129,
134

M

Mahi, 169
Malaria, 62
Malevolent spirits, 49
Managers, rug-weaving, 88,
91, 93, 109
Manure, 134
Manuscript illumination, 114,
120, 123
Marasali rug, 14, 19
Market, current
domination of, 85, 88, 110
influences on, 19, 22, 27
research on, 88, 93, 110,
113
Marketing ploys, 107, 137,
149, 153
Mass media, 48, 87, 90–91
Mata Hari, 103
Mecca, 45
Medallions, 40–41, 54,
57–58, 119, 156
Merchants
range of, 103–104
strategies. *See* Business
practices
Metallic threads, 28–29, 68
Metaphors, 41, 46
Middle East
culture of, 31–32, 144
rug trade in, 13, 15, 22,
147, 163
rugs from, 54, 57, 153, 165
Mihrab, 45

Mir, 58, 169
Misrepresentation, during
trading, 77, 80,
103–104, 107, 147
Mistakes, beliefs about, 31,
35, 133, 144, 146
Monsoons, 133
Mordants, 67
Moslems
fatalism of, 31, 48–49
representation of, 19, 31,
41, 45
trading influence, 77, 80,
144
see also Mughal dynasty
Mosques, 104, 107
Mourning, rugs for, 68
Mozaffer ed Din, Shah of
Iran, 64
Mughal dynasty, 30, 32, 110,
114, 119–120, 124
Mumford, John Kimberly, 87
Mumtaz Mahal, 120
Museums, 39, 104, 114, 119

N

Namak dun, 114, 119
Nap, 153
Natural Dye Research and
Development (DOBAG)
Project, 87–88
Negotiation, art of, 77, 82,
85, 101, 104, 107, 134,
141–149
New Delhi, 109, 114–115
Nomad designs, 48, 54, 57,
114, 153
Nou Ruz, 46, 48
Nylon fiber, 104

O

Omens, in designs, 36
Opie, James, 113–114
Opium, role of, 82, 85
Orient Carpet Design, 137
Orient Express, 103
Oriental rugs
demise of, 85, 87
Gregorian collection, 24–28
origins, 19, 22, 24, 53, 119
Ottomans, 18, 39
Overcast, 169

P

Paisley design, 53, 58
Pakistan
rug trade in, 13, 39, 48, 85,
147

rugs from, 46–48, 58,
79–80, 110, 144, 149,
160
Papu, 124–125
Pardeh, 169
Patina, of rugs, 28, 113
Penalties, for dye use, 64
Pera Palas, 103
Perfection
beliefs about, 31, 35, 58,
96
decorating choice and, 151,
153
negotiation based on, 133,
144, 146
Perkin, William Henry, 62
Persia. *See* Iran
Personal preferences, 58,
151–152
Pesa, 40–41
Photographs, for shopping, 142
Pictographic narratives, 41
Pile, 169
Pillows, 124, 160
Plassey, Battle of, 120
Politics, in designs, 39
Polo, Marco, 15, 24
Poshti, 169
Prayer point, 45
Prayer rugs
examples, 44–45, 48,
72–73
Moslem, 114, 119
origins, 22, 27, 41, 45, 169
stolen, 50
Precious stones, 68
Preservation techniques,
164–167
Prices
economics of, 19, 22, 24,
62, 80
for antique rugs, 107, 149
negotiation of, 77,
142–144, 146–147
per design, 80, 85, 144,
146
per knot count, 80, 85, 144
per size, 107, 141, 144,
146–147, 149
per wool, 80, 85, 146
Production factors, 62, 88,
91, 93, 97, 101
see also Human labor
Production process
systematic, 88, 109–110
traditional, 97, 101, 109,
126, 129, 133

Q

Quality
influences on, 19, 22, 35,
64–65
prices per, 137, 144,
146–147
standards for, 77, 113
Quantity, influences on, 19,
22
Qum, 53, 57, 140, 142

R

Rayon, 137
Record keeping, for trades, 77,
80
Red Fort trading center,
138–139
Refugees, role of, 10, 12
Religion, in designs, 19, 24,
114
Reproductions, 53, 58, 107,
114, 144
Restoration options, 166–167
Roman Empire. *See* Byzantine
Empire
Rose designs, 46, 168
Rug designs
all-over, 53, 58, 168
animal, 19, 38–39, 41, 50,
120, 129–130
common, 46–50
computer-generated, 35,
88–89, 93, 109
contemporary, 110,
113–114, 134–137
culture-based. *See* Culture
diversity in, 10, 24, 27–28,
32, 96–97
floral. *See* Floral designs
geometric. *See* Geometric
designs
market research, 88, 93,
110, 113
noble, 57, 68
non-rug applications, 22,
107, 114, 119–120, 160
price based on, 80, 85, 144,
146
reproductions of, 53, 58,
107, 114, 144
symbols in, 31, 35–36, 39
symmetry in, 31, 35–36, 39
trees in, 25, 41, 45–46, 147
see also specific design
Rug trading (shopping)
bans on, 85
customs, 72, 80, 110, 124,
141–149

misrepresentation during, 77, 103–104, 107, 147
see also Negotiation; Prices
Rug weavers
benefits for, 91, 93
children as, 32
city, 57–58
competition for, 91, 93
farmers as, 58
individuality by, 35–36, 39, 45, 91, 93, 96–97
master, 25, 36, 129, 137
men as, 32, 110
nomadic. *See* Nomad designs
of India, 109–110
of Iran, 80, 85
of Turkey, 90–93, 96, 99–100
skills of, 27, 36, 80, 129
wage factors, 88, 91, 101
women as, 32–34, 54, 73, 90, 110
Rug weaving
passing on skill of, 32, 34, 85, 88
speed factors, 62, 91, 97
steps for, 80, 97, 101, 109, 126, 129, 133
tools for, 12, 97, 101, 109–110, 134
traditions of, 10, 19, 31, 34–35, 90, 110
Runge, Friedlieb Ferdinand, 62

S
Safavid dynasty, 169
Sale prices, 149, 153
Samplers, 27
Saraband design, 50, 53
Saris, 118–119, 124, 134
Sarouks, 26–27, 65
Scorpions, tale of, 31–32, 104
Seismic activity, 46
Seljuk tribe, 54
Sengor, 107
Senna design, 12, 50, 53, 80, 169
Senses, choices per, 28, 146, 151, 153
Sexism, 80
Shah Jahan, 120
Shaving, of tips, 166
Shinto religion, 120
Shiraz design, 49–50
Shreedhar & Sons company, 126–139

Signatures, of weavers, 36
Silk Route
economic impact, 13, 15, 19, 22, 120, 163
gateway of, 12, 15, 87–107, 163
oriental rugs of, 19, 22, 24–28, 119, 163
personal exposure, 10, 12–13, 71–72, 124
Silk rugs, 61, 68, 137, 160, 166
Silk, production and trade, 15, 19, 124–125, 129
Sinning, retribution for, 48
Size
decorating and, 141, 160–161, 163–164
influences on, 41, 45, 57
prices per, 72, 107, 141, 144, 146–147, 149
Smuggling, 15, 64
Snake charmers, 137
Soumak, 169
Spinning techniques, 96, 109, 113
Sultanana rug, 49
Supernatural phenomena, 48–50, 54
Superstitions, 48–50, 54–55
Supply factors, 62, 146
see also Wool
Survival objects, 22, 107, 114, 119, 160
Switching, of rugs, 77
Symbolism, 10, 31, 35–36, 39, 68
Symmetry, 31, 35–36, 39

T
Tabriz, 17, 19, 28, 57
Taj Mahal, 110–111, 120
Tales, fictional, 31–32, 68, 104
Tarak, 97, 100–101, 169
Tea, 90, 101, 104, 107, 142, 147
Technology access, 48, 87–88, 90–91, 124, 134
Tent bands, 114
Tests, before buying, 152, 165
Tobacco chewing, 129
Tools, for weaving, 97, 101, 110, 134
Trade embargoes, 85
Traditions
nature of, 71–72, 92, 103
representation of, 19, 24, 49

Transportation
in India, 109, 114–115, 120, 124, 126, 134, 138
in Iran, 77
in Turkey, 91–92, 96–97, 103
Travel considerations, 10, 12–13, 138–139
Tree designs, 25, 41, 45–46, 147
Tree of life, 25, 45–46, 169
Tribal rugs
decorating per, 144, 153, 160, 163
designs of, 41, 48, 54, 57, 168
Trimming techniques, 101, 134
Trustworthiness, 12, 77, 103–104, 147
Turkey
as gateway, 12, 15, 87–107, 163
rug trade in, 10, 12, 85, 101–107, 143, 147
rug weaving in, 21–22, 88–101, 110, 119
rugs from, 39, 49–50, 54, 69, 88–101, 144, 149, 160, 165
examples, 86, 88, 95–96, 104–105
traditions of, 12–13, 18, 48, 92, 103
transportation in, 91–92, 96–97, 103
Turkish carpet, 119
Turkoman design, 60, 62, 79–80
Turtles
in designs. *See* Fish and turtle design
tale of, 31–32
TV Tower, 126

U
Ultraviolet light, 166
Upholstery. *See* Furniture
Urmia, 71–72
Useful life, 149
Ustad, 25, 129

V
Vagireh, 169
Valuation. *See* Prices
Varanasi, 109, 113, 124–126

Village rugs
examples, 28–29, 54–55, 71–72, 124, 126–139
origins, 19, 22, 62, 69
Visse, 95–96

W
Wages, 88, 91, 101
Walker, Daniel, 114, 119
Wall coverings, 110, 151, 155
War rugs, 38–41, 169
Warp, 144, 169
Washing techniques
for cleaning, 132–133, 160, 164–166
in manufacturing, 109, 113, 132–134
Wealth, indications of, 41–42, 57, 68
Wear. *See* Deterioration
Weft (woof), 97, 169
Western traders
design preferences, 27, 32, 35, 53, 85, 88, 110, 113–114
influence of, 15, 24, 62, 124, 137, 142–147, 163
Window treatments, 133, 151, 155
Window-shopping, 141
Wool
coloring of. *See* Dyes
lanolin-rich, 146, 151, 153, 160
New Zealand, 64, 109, 146
prices per, 80, 85, 146
strength factors, 65, 104
supplies, 80, 93, 101, 104, 129, 133, 144, 167
World Wars, 10, 12, 18, 39
Worry beads, 102–103
Worshipful Order of Girdlers, 119
Wum design, 53

Y
Yarn
dyeing, 66–67, 69, 112–113, 120, 122, 126, 129
spinning, 96, 109, 113
Yumartaci, Izy, 88, 91, 93, 96–97

World History

3rd Edition

by Peter Haugen

A Wiley Brand

World History For Dummies®, 3rd Edition

Published by: **John Wiley & Sons, Inc.**, 111 River Street, Hoboken, NJ 07030-5774, www.wiley.com

Copyright © 2022 by John Wiley & Sons, Inc., Hoboken, New Jersey

Published simultaneously in Canada

No part of this publication may be reproduced, stored in a retrieval system or transmitted in any form or by any means, electronic, mechanical, photocopying, recording, scanning or otherwise, except as permitted under Sections 107 or 108 of the 1976 United States Copyright Act, without the prior written permission of the Publisher. Requests to the Publisher for permission should be addressed to the Permissions Department, John Wiley & Sons, Inc., 111 River Street, Hoboken, NJ 07030, (201) 748-6011, fax (201) 748-6008, or online at http://www.wiley.com/go/permissions.

Trademarks: Wiley, For Dummies, the Dummies Man logo, Dummies.com, Making Everything Easier, and related trade dress are trademarks or registered trademarks of John Wiley & Sons, Inc., and may not be used without written permission. All other trademarks are the property of their respective owners. John Wiley & Sons, Inc., is not associated with any product or vendor mentioned in this book.

LIMIT OF LIABILITY/DISCLAIMER OF WARRANTY: WHILE THE PUBLISHER AND AUTHORS HAVE USED THEIR BEST EFFORTS IN PREPARING THIS WORK, THEY MAKE NO REPRESENTATIONS OR WARRANTIES WITH RESPECT TO THE ACCURACY OR COMPLETENESS OF THE CONTENTS OF THIS WORK AND SPECIFICALLY DISCLAIM ALL WARRANTIES, INCLUDING WITHOUT LIMITATION ANY IMPLIED WARRANTIES OF MERCHANTABILITY OR FITNESS FOR A PARTICULAR PURPOSE. NO WARRANTY MAY BE CREATED OR EXTENDED BY SALES REPRESENTATIVES, WRITTEN SALES MATERIALS OR PROMOTIONAL STATEMENTS FOR THIS WORK. THE FACT THAT AN ORGANIZATION, WEBSITE, OR PRODUCT IS REFERRED TO IN THIS WORK AS A CITATION AND/OR POTENTIAL SOURCE OF FURTHER INFORMATION DOES NOT MEAN THAT THE PUBLISHER AND AUTHORS ENDORSE THE INFORMATION OR SERVICES THE ORGANIZATION, WEBSITE, OR PRODUCT MAY PROVIDE OR RECOMMENDATIONS IT MAY MAKE. THIS WORK IS SOLD WITH THE UNDERSTANDING THAT THE PUBLISHER IS NOT ENGAGED IN RENDERING PROFESSIONAL SERVICES. THE ADVICE AND STRATEGIES CONTAINED HEREIN MAY NOT BE SUITABLE FOR YOUR SITUATION. YOU SHOULD CONSULT WITH A SPECIALIST WHERE APPROPRIATE. FURTHER, READERS SHOULD BE AWARE THAT WEBSITES LISTED IN THIS WORK MAY HAVE CHANGED OR DISAPPEARED BETWEEN WHEN THIS WORK WAS WRITTEN AND WHEN IT IS READ. NEITHER THE PUBLISHER NOR AUTHORS SHALL BE LIABLE FOR ANY LOSS OF PROFIT OR ANY OTHER COMMERCIAL DAMAGES, INCLUDING BUT NOT LIMITED TO SPECIAL, INCIDENTAL, CONSEQUENTIAL, OR OTHER DAMAGES.

For general information on our other products and services, please contact our Customer Care Department within the U.S. at 877-762-2974, outside the U.S. at 317-572-3993, or fax 317-572-4002. For technical support, please visit https://hub.wiley.com/community/support/dummies.

Wiley publishes in a variety of print and electronic formats and by print-on-demand. Some material included with standard print versions of this book may not be included in e-books or in print-on-demand. If this book refers to media such as a CD or DVD that is not included in the version you purchased, you may download this material at http://booksupport.wiley.com. For more information about Wiley products, visit www.wiley.com.

Library of Congress Control Number: 2021953351

ISBN 978-1-119-85560-6 (pbk); ISBN 978-1-119-85562-0 (ebk); ISBN 978-1-119-85561-3 (ebk);

SKY10032304_010422

Contents at a Glance

Introduction 1

Part 1: Getting into History 5
CHAPTER 1: Tracing a Path to the Present 7
CHAPTER 2: Digging Up Reality 19
CHAPTER 3: Putting History into Perspective 29

Part 2: Finding Strength in Numbers 41
CHAPTER 4: Getting Civilized 43
CHAPTER 5: Rising and Falling Empires 61
CHAPTER 6: Splitting Eras: The Middle Ages 77
CHAPTER 7: Struggling for Dominance 93
CHAPTER 8: Grabbing the Globe 113
CHAPTER 9: Pulling Empires Together as Subjects Push Back 135

Part 3: Seeking Answers 161
CHAPTER 10: Worshipping through the Ages 163
CHAPTER 11: Loving Wisdom: Philosophy's Impact 185
CHAPTER 12: Being Christian, Thinking Greek 201
CHAPTER 13: Awakening to the Renaissance 211
CHAPTER 14: Breaking Away: The Reformation 229
CHAPTER 15: Opening Up to Science and Enlightenment 251

Part 4: Fighting, Fighting, Fighting 267
CHAPTER 16: Wielding Sticks and Stones: Old-Fashioned War . . . 269
CHAPTER 17: Upgrading the War Machine 283
CHAPTER 18: Modernizing Mayhem 297

Part 5: Meeting the Movers and Shakers 313
CHAPTER 19: Starting Something Legendary 315
CHAPTER 20: Battling Toward Immortality 329
CHAPTER 21: Exploring and "Discovering" 343
CHAPTER 22: Turning Tables: Rebels and Revolutionaries 357

Part 6: The Part of Tens 373
CHAPTER 23: Ten Unforgettable Dates in History 375
CHAPTER 24: Ten Essential Historical Documents 383

Index 393

Table of Contents

INTRODUCTION 1
    About This Book. 1
    Foolish Assumptions. 2
    Icons Used in This Book 3
    Beyond the Book 3
    Where to Go from Here 3

PART 1: GETTING INTO HISTORY 5

CHAPTER 1: **Tracing a Path to the Present** 7
    Firing Up the WABAC Machine 8
    Footpath to Expressway: Building on Humble Beginnings 9
    War! What Is It Good For? Material for History Books,
    That's What. 12
    Appreciating History's Tapestry. 13
        Threading backward 13
        Crossing threads 15
        Weaving home. 15
    Making the Connections. 16
    Tracking the Centuries 17

CHAPTER 2: **Digging Up Reality** 19
    Homing In on Homer 19
        The Troy story 20
        Inspiring archaeological finds 21
    Raising Atlantis. 21
    Reading the Body Language of the Dead. 22
        Frozen in the Alps 23
        Salted away in Asia 24
        Bogged down in northern Europe 24
        Dried and well preserved in the Andes 24
        Preserved pharaohs in Egypt. 26
    Tracking the Centuries 27

CHAPTER 3: **Putting History into Perspective** 29
    Being Human Beings. 30
        Nearing the Neanderthal 31
        Talking like no one had before 32
        Making sense of AD, BC, CE, and BCE. 33

Dividing Time into Eras . . . and Giving Them Names. 34
    Sorting ancient from modern 34
    Telling classical from schmassical. 35
    Bowing to the queens. 35
    Perceiving and avoiding biases 36
Noticing the Noteworthy and the Notorious. 37
    Studying contradictions 38
    Looking at events from different angles 38
    Verifying virtue. 39
Tracking the Centuries 40

PART 2: FINDING STRENGTH IN NUMBERS 41

CHAPTER 4: **Getting Civilized**. 43
Building Jericho's Walls for Mutual Defense .44
Planting Cities along Rivers 45
    Settling between the Tigris and Euphrates 45
    Getting agricultural in Africa 46
    Assembling Egypt 47
    Going up the river into Kush 47
    Giving way as new civilizations rise. 47
    Heading east to the Indus and Yellow Rivers 49
Coming of Age in the Americas. 52
Keeping Records on the Way to Writing and Reading 52
    Planning pyramids. 52
    Laying down laws and love songs. 53
Shaping the World Ever After 54
    Building a Persian Empire 54
    Growing toward Greekness. 54
    Making Alexander great 57
Developing Cultures Abounding 59
Tracking the Centuries 59

CHAPTER 5: **Rising and Falling Empires** 61
Rome's Ascent and Demise 61
    Forming the Roman Republic 62
    Earning citizenship 62
    Expanding the empire. 63
    Crossing the Rubicon 64
    Empowering the emperor 66
    Roaming eastward. 66
    Western empire fades into history 67
    Rome and the Roman Catholic Church 68

Building Empires around the World 70
    Ruling Persia and Parthia 70
    India's empires 71
    Uniting China: Seven into Qin 72
    Flourishing civilizations in the Americas 74
Remembering Far-Flung Cultures 75
Tracking the Centuries 76

CHAPTER 6: **Splitting Eras: The Middle Ages** 77
Building (And Maintaining) the Byzantine Empire 78
Sharing and Imposing Culture 79
    Bearing with barbarians 80
    Traversing Africa with the Bantu 81
    Sailing and settling with the Vikings 81
    Traveling the Silk Road 83
Planting the Seeds of European Nations 84
    Repelling the raiders 84
    Uniting Western Europe: Charlemagne pulls it together 85
    Keeping fledgling nations together 87
Emerging Islamic Fervor 88
Rebounding Guptas in India 89
Rounding Up Developments in Cultures Far to the East
and to the West 90
Tracking the Centuries 91

CHAPTER 7: **Struggling for Dominance** 93
Extending the Arab Empire and Spreading Islam 94
    Taking education and literacy to new heights 94
    Making advances in science and technology 94
    Mastering the Indian Ocean 95
    Assembling and disassembling an empire 96
Excelling in East Asia 97
    Innovating the Chinese way 97
    Traveling the Silk Road for trade and cultural exchange 98
    Sailing away for a spell 99
Developing a Taste for Eastern Goods 100
    Orienting Venice 101
    Controlling trade routes between Europe and the East 102
Mounting the Crusades 103
    Meeting the main players 103
    Looking at the misguided zeal of specific Crusades 104
    Setting a precedent for conquest 105
Growing Trade between East and West 106
Surviving the Black Death 107

Killing relentlessly 108
Doing the math: Fewer folks, more wealth 108
Seeking a Way East and Finding Places to the West. 109
Meeting the Americans who met Columbus 110
Celebrating or ruing "discovery" 110
Training and experience shaped Columbus 110
Stumbling upon the West Indies 111
Tracking the Centuries 112

CHAPTER 8: **Grabbing the Globe** 113
Sailing South to Get East 114
Getting a foothold in Indian trade. 115
Demanding respect. 115
"Discovering" America. 116
How the Aztecs rose and fell 117
Incas grasp greatness and then fall to the Spanish 119
Circling the Planet 120
Ottomans ascend among Eastern empires 121
Founding East India companies 122
Closing the door to Japan. 124
Playing by British East India Company rules 124
Going from Ming to Qing in China 125
Spreading the Slave Trade 126
Perpetuating an evil 127
Developing a new market. 127
Profiting from a contemptible institution .128
Starting Revolutions 129
Bringing in the new 129
Playing with dangerous ideas 130
Rebelling Americans 130
Erupting rage 131
Making a bold bid for freedom in Haiti 132
Tracking the Centuries 133

CHAPTER 9: **Pulling Empires Together as Subjects
Push Back** 135
Managing Unprecedented Empires 136
Britain battles on multiple fronts 136
France rebrands after its revolution. 138
Europe divides Africa 139
Challenging European Dominance 142
Turning against Spanish and Portuguese rule
in Latin America 142
Reclaiming Africa for Africans 145
Uprising in Asia 145

      Unleashing pent-up power in Japan 145

      Ricocheting unrest comes home to Europe 146

   Revolting in Russia 146

      Standing apart up north. 147

      Rushin' toward rebellion. 147

      Taking power in the Soviet Union 148

   Fighting World Wars 151

      Redefining war: World War I 151

      Returning to conflict: World War II 153

   Running Hot and Cold (Wars) 156

      Daring each other to blink in the Cold War 157

      Seeing no end to violent conflicts 157

   Getting it Together and Forming the United Nations 158

   Tracking the Centuries 159

PART 3: SEEKING ANSWERS 161

CHAPTER 10: Worshipping through the Ages 163

   Defining Religion 164

      Divining the role of god(s) 165

      Analyzing the religious impulse. 167

      Distinguishing philosophy from religion 167

   Assessing Animism 167

      Seeking understanding through spirit 168

      Connecting animals to deities 168

   Jotting down Judaism 169

      Awaiting a Messiah 169

      Maintaining Jewish nationalism. 169

   Hammering Out Hinduism. 170

   Biting Off a Bit of Buddhism 172

   Condensing Christianity 172

      Initiating the Roman Catholic Church. 173

      Evaluating the Eastern Orthodox Church 176

      Peeking at the Protestant churches 177

   Investigating Islam. 178

      Honoring the Five Pillars. 179

      Going beyond Mecca and Medina 179

      Clashing cultures 180

   Summarizing Sikhism 182

   Tracking the Centuries 183

CHAPTER 11: Loving Wisdom: Philosophy's Impact 185

   Asking the Big Questions 186

      Founding science in philosophy 186

      Mixing philosophy and religion. 187

Tracing Philosophy's Roots 188
   Living on the edges of Greek society 189
   Drawing inspiration from other cultures 189
   Traveling broadens the mind. 190
Examining Eastern Philosophies 190
Leading to (and from) Socrates 191
   Building a tradition of seeking answers 191
   Thinking for himself: Socrates' legacy. .194
   Building on Socrates: Plato and Aristotle. 195
   Tracing Plato's influence 195
Philosophy in the Age of Alexander and After 196
   Spreading Hellenistic philosophies. 196
   Putting philosophy to practical use 198
Tracking the Centuries 199

CHAPTER 12: **Being Christian, Thinking Greek** 201
The Great Chain of Being 202
Interpreting Christian Theology 203
   Stacking scripture upon scripture. 203
   Replacing Homer with the Bible 204
Establishing Jesus's Divinity 204
Augustine's Influence on Early Christian Thought 205
   Divining the mind of God. 205
   Condoning righteous killing. 205
   Tracing two paths to salvation. 206
The Philosophy of Aquinas. 207
   Keeping scholarship alive. 207
   Coming back to Aristotle 208
   Supporting faith with logic. 208
Embracing Humanism and More 209
   Nothing secular about it. 209
   Tracing humanism's impact. 210
Tracking the Centuries 210

CHAPTER 13: **Awakening to the Renaissance** 211
Realizing the Reach of the Renaissance. 212
Redefining the Human Role. 213
   Flowering in Florence 213
   Spreading the word. 214
   Promoting human potential 214
   Reclaiming the ancients 214
   Presenting the printing press 215
Uniting Flesh and Soul 216
   Inspiring Michelangelo 217
   Living in the material world 217

Returning to Science 219
   Shifting the center of the universe 219
   Studying human anatomy 219
Being All That You Could Be. 220
   Striving for perfection 221
   Stocking up on self-help books 222
Writing for the Masses 223
   Creating new classics 223
   Staging dramas with Classical roots 223
   Packing something to read onboard a ship. 224
Undermining Renaissance Gains with Conflict 224
   Battling for control of Italian city-states. 224
   Spilling outside Italy's borders. 226
Tracking the Centuries 228

CHAPTER 14: Breaking Away: The Reformation 229
Cracks in the Catholic Monopoly. 229
   Losing authority. 230
   Satirizing the Church. 230
Luther Challenges the System. 232
   Selling salvation 232
   Peddling to pay the pope 233
   Insisting on faith 234
A Precarious Holy Roman Empire. 234
   Searching for sources of cash 235
   Fighting crime and inflation. 235
   Setting the stage for dissent 236
Here Luther Stands (Up to the Emperor). 236
Luther Gains a Following 237
   Losing control of the Lutheran movement 238
   Choosing sides. 238
The Empire Strikes Back. 239
   Savoring a bitter victory 239
   Achieving compromise 239
Reform Spreads to England. 240
   Creating the Church of England 240
   Realizing Henry's legacy 243
Along Comes Calvin. 244
   Reforming the Swiss church 244
   Establishing Puritanism 245
   Causing turmoil in France 246
   Sparking rebellion in Holland 246
   Weakening the Holy Roman Empire. 246
   Pushing for Puritanism in England and Scotland 247
   Emigrating to America 248
Tracking the Centuries 248

CHAPTER 15: **Opening Up to Science and Enlightenment** 251

Mingling Science and Philosophy 252
Starting a Scientific Revolution 253
Gazing at the heavens: Astronomy. 253
Advancing the scientific method 255
Waking Up to the Enlightenment 256
Experiencing empiricism 256
Living a "nasty, brutish, and short" life 257
Reasoning to rationalism 257
Expanding to the Encyclopedists. .258
Engineering the Industrial Revolution .258
Dealing with the social fallout 259
Raging against the machines: Luddite uprising 261
Marketing Economics 261
Playing the money game with Adam Smith. 262
Developing capitalism and Marxism. 262
Tracking the Centuries 264

PART 4: FIGHTING, FIGHTING, FIGHTING 267

CHAPTER 16: **Wielding Sticks and Stones:
Old-Fashioned War** 269

Fighting as an Ancient Way of Life 270
Raising Armies 271
Keeping out attackers. 271
Escalating weapons technology: Using metal 272
Riding into battle: Hooves and wheels 272
Avoiding Assyrian Arsenals 272
Assembling the units. 273
Wreaking havoc 273
Farming and Fighting Together in Greece 274
Soldiering shoulder to shoulder 275
Standing up to the Persians. 276
Facing Macedonian ferocity 276
Making War the Roman Way 278
Marching in three ranks 278
Recruiting a standing force 279
Diversifying the legion 280
Returning to riders 281
Tracking the Centuries 281

CHAPTER 17: **Upgrading the War Machine** 283

Reinventing the Cavalry 284
Standing tall and staying astride with stirrups 284
Raiding as a way of life on horseback. 285

Guarding Byzantine borders 285
Battling mounted Moors 286
Charging into chivalry 287
Donning the Steel Suit 287
Wearing metal rings: Chain mail 287
Putting more power into the archer's bow 288
Charging behind the lance 288
Marrying precision to power with the longbow 289
Adding Firepower with Gunpowder 290
Lighting the fire of discovery 290
Spreading explosive news 290
Bringing in the big guns 291
Battering down Constantinople's walls 291
Refining the new weaponry 291
Adapting old strategies for new weapons 293
Floating fortresses on the sea .294
Adapting fortifications to the artillery era 294
Tracking the Centuries 295

CHAPTER 18: **Modernizing Mayhem** 297
Following Three Paths to Modern War .298
Promoting devastation in Prussia 298
Putting technology to deadly uses: The Crimean War 299
Redefining armed conflict: The U.S. Civil War 303
Tying Tactics to Technology in the 20th Century 305
Trapping valor in a trench: World War I 306
Retooling the World War II arsenal 307
Warring On Despite the Nuclear Threat 307
Drawing strength from stealth: Guerilla tactics 308
Wielding the weapon of fear: Terrorism 309
Tracking the Centuries 311

PART 5: MEETING THE MOVERS AND SHAKERS 313

CHAPTER 19: **Starting Something Legendary** 315
Spinning Legends 316
Uniting for Strength 317
Playing for Power 319
Building Bridges 321
Writing Laws 324
Tracking the Centuries 327

CHAPTER 20: **Battling Toward Immortality** 329
Towering Over Their Times 330
Building Empires 332
Launching Attacks 334

Mounting a Defense 335
Devising Tactics 337
Instigating Inspiration. 338
Tracking the Centuries 340

CHAPTER 21: **Exploring and "Discovering"** 343
Famous Pioneers: Arriving Before Their Time. 344
Courageous Couriers: Carrying Messages. 346
Trailblazing Explorers: Seeking New Routes .348
Notorious Conquerors: Bad Company. 350
Famous Firsts 351
Renowned Guides 353
Famous Mavericks: Taking Advantage of Opportunity 354
Tracking the Centuries 355

CHAPTER 22: **Turning Tables: Rebels and Revolutionaries**. 357
Rising from Revolutionaries to Rulers 358
Gaining Support As Charismatic Rebels. 362
Making Ideas Reality 363
Standing Against Authority 365
Changing Rules 366
Living and Dying by the Sword 367
Dying for a Cause 369
Tracking the Centuries 370

PART 6: THE PART OF TENS. 373

CHAPTER 23: **Ten Unforgettable Dates in History** 375
460 BC: Athens Goes Democratic 376
323 BC: Alexander the Great Dies. 376
476: The Western Roman Empire Falls. 377
1066: Normans Conquer England. 377
1095: The First Crusade Commences. 378
1492: Columbus Sails the Ocean Blue 379
1776: Americans Break Away. 379
1807: Britain Bans the Slave Trade 380
1893: Women Start Getting the Vote Around the World. 380
1945: The United States Drops the A-Bomb 381

CHAPTER 24: **Ten Essential Historical Documents** 383
    The Rosetta Stone 384
    Confucian Analects 384
    The Bible 385
    The Quran 386
    The Magna Carta 387
    The Travels of Marco Polo 387
    The Declaration of Independence 388
    The Bill of Rights 389
    Das Kapital 389
    On the Origin of Species 390

INDEX 393

Introduction

The complete history of the world boiled down to 400-some pages and crammed between paperback covers? The idea is preposterous. It's outrageous. I'd be crazy to attempt it. So here goes.

This book doesn't claim to be complete. It can't be. Hundreds of other volumes are devoted to a measly decade or two (the World War II era comes to mind). Plumbing thousands of years in one little book would be impossible. Skimming the surface, however, is another matter.

About This Book

Here, you can find enough information that if you hit on an era, a personality, or a civilization you'd like to know more about, you'll at least know what to look for. There's no lack of places to find out more. You can turn to many far more complete accounts of the history of specific countries (such as the United States), continents (such as Europe), and events (such as the U.S. Civil War). You can find books about all these topics and more in this excellent *For Dummies* series. But if you want a simplified overview, consisting of a collection of easy-to-read glimpses of major players and events that have made the world what it is today, I'm your guide, and *World History For Dummies,* 3rd Edition, is your first-stop reference.

History is like a soap opera that has been running ever since the invention of writing. The show is lurid, full of dirty tricks and murder, romances and sexual deceptions, adventures, and wars and revolutions. (And, yes, treaties and dates.) Or maybe a better analogy is that history is like hundreds of soap operas, with thousands of crossover characters jumping out of one story and into another — too many for even the most devoted fan to keep straight, which is all the more reason for an easy-to-use overview.

The most important thing to remember is that history is fun, or should be. It's not as though this is life-and-death stuff. . . . No, wait. It *is* life-and-death stuff — on a ginormous scale. It's just that so many of the lives and deaths happened long ago. But that's good, because I can pry into private affairs without getting sued. History is full of vintage gossip and antique scandal, peppered heavily with high adventure — swords and spears and cannons and stuff. The more you get into it, the better you'll do when the neighbors drag out the home version of *Jeopardy*. (Renaissance Italy for $500, please.)

Every field from brain surgery to refuse collection has its conventions, a special vocabulary chief among them. History is no exception, but I tried to steer clear of historians-only words and phrases. When such a word is unavoidable, I explain it in reader-friendly terms. As for other technical terms, I usually follow them with definitions and explanations.

You'll find a few Latin and other foreign words and phrases sprinkled throughout the book too. I have to include them because I tell you about cultures and countries where English was unknown. Latin terms show up because this book's subjects include the important, influential Roman Empire, where everybody spoke Latin. I also cover Europe in the Middle Ages, when Latin was the international language. I use other words that may be unfamiliar; those terms are highlighted in italics and defined. Finally, I can't write about world history without covering the enormous influence of the Roman Catholic Church, an institution that for many centuries clung to Latin as its official means of expression. But don't worry. I promise not to use many such terms, and when I do, I'll explain what they mean.

Foolish Assumptions

As I wrote this book, I made some assumptions about you. They may be foolish, but here they are:

>> You've studied at least some history in school. You may even know quite a lot about certain historical topics, but you'd like to find out more about how it all fits together.

>> You've seen movies or read novels set in various historical eras, and you suspect that they'd be more enjoyable if you were better informed about the time periods and the historical peoples featured.

>> At least once in your life, you've encountered an obnoxious history know-it-all, one of those people who spews random facts about ancient Rome or the French Revolution. In the event that it happens again, you want the satisfaction of either keeping up with the conversation or contradicting Smartypants and knowing (at least a little bit) about what you're talking about.

Icons Used in This Book

Throughout this book, icons in the margins highlight certain types of valuable information. Here are the icons you'll encounter and a brief description of each.

Remember icons mark information that's especially important. But it's okay if you forget; just go back and look for the icon. I hope that points you to content that's memorable.

The Technical Stuff icon in this book marks information that's interesting but not essential, so if you want, you can skip it. I like these asides, but you don't have to.

Tip icons are for ideas that you may find helpful, including places to see historical artifacts that can help you feel more in touch with the past. If the artifact is in a museum, you probably won't get to touch it physically, though.

The In Their Words icon marks a quote that makes a point better than I can, although I hate to admit it.

The Warning icon tells you to watch out! In considering history, it's especially important not to assume, to keep an open mind, and to set preconceptions aside.

Beyond the Book

In addition to the abundance of information and guidance related to world history that you can find in this book, you can get access to even more help and information at Dummies.com. Check out this book's online Cheat Sheet. Just go to www.dummies.com and search for "World History For Dummies Cheat Sheet."

Where to Go from Here

You can start with Chapter 1 and read to the end, but that's not required. A great thing about this book is that it's organized so that you can jump in any place you want. As you page through and browse, note that you can look at the same era from different perspectives. Part 3, for example, tells you how philosophy and religion shaped history; there, you can find out about the religious wars that followed the Protestant Reformation. But if you're more interested in the weaponry and strategies of war, jump to Part 4. And if you just want to browse the bios of some historical all-stars, check out Part 5. Not sure what you're looking for? Part 1 is a good place to get a general feel for history. The table of contents and index, along with the part summaries earlier in this introduction, should get you to the pages you need.

1
Getting into History

Follow the threads of cause and effect that weave through every part of human experience. If you want to know how things got to be the way they are today, look to yesterday.

See how myths and artifacts — such as the ruins of once-great cities and even the preserved remains of our ancestors — provide wonderful clues to the realities of the ancient world and the beginnings of what we call history.

Put history and its personalities into perspective and wrap your head around how long humans have been doing a lot of the same things people do today: buying, selling, cooking, falling in love, traveling, and fighting wars.

Chapter **1**

Tracing a Path to the Present

Just two decades into the 21st century, humanity hit a speed bump, in the form of a pandemic. The pandemic was a new viral disease — relatively benign in many patients but deadly in others and wildly unpredictable. Because it was new to our species, nobody had a ready immune response. Highly contagious, it spread rapidly around the world. Immunologists, the scientists who are experts at these things, had to figure out how to fight the disease on the fly.

The World Health Organization called the virus SARS-CoV-2, for severe acute respiratory syndrome coronavirus, version 2 (after a predecessor in 2003). It called the sickness COVID-19, for coronavirus disease 2019, the year it was identified.

The nature of the threat and how it should be dealt with sparked worldwide debate. Some governments took quick, decisive action to contain it, while others decided to go more slowly. The latter approach proved to be ineffective as infection rates soared.

Another point of discussion was why the world was caught unprepared. "Public health experts have predicted we'd be hit by another pandemic for decades," puffed the pundits. "Why didn't leadership have a plan?" asked the journalists.

"Why the heck didn't anybody see this coming?" queried podcasters. "It's all a hoax!" screamed too many conspiracy theorists.

The pandemic changed the world. According to Johns Hopkins University, it killed more than 4 million people worldwide by the middle of 2021, with case rates rising again. It stalled the world economy and influenced the way people did their jobs, as well as where and how they chose to live.

But this book isn't about a 21st-century pandemic any more than it's about the bubonic plague that ravaged Europe and Asia in the 14th century. It isn't about modern epidemiology or economics, either. It's about two broader questions: "How did things get to be like this?" and "Why is the world as it is?"

There have been too many years of human activity on this planet — too many lives lived, too many diseases, technological breakthroughs, migrations, wars, murders, weddings, coronations, revolutions, recessions, natural disasters, and financial meltdowns — to trace humanity's route simply. Too many historians have interpreted events in too many contradictory ways. But what I hope you find in this book is a general view of how human history has gotten you and the world you live in to current reality. To this. To now.

Firing Up the WABAC Machine

If you care about classic TV cartoons, you've heard of the WABAC Machine. Pronounced "way back," the machine was a fictional time-traveling device built and operated by a genius dog named Mr. Peabody. In every episode of the 1960s animated series *Rocky and His Friends*, the professorial pooch and his pet boy, Sherman, transported themselves to a historical setting — say, ancient Rome, revolutionary America, or medieval England — where they interacted with famous people and solved whatever ridiculously absurd dilemma was troubling cartoon Julius Caesar, George Washington, or King Arthur. Thus, Mr. Peabody and Sherman allowed the events we think of as history to take their proper course.

These episodes spoofed a classic science-fiction premise. Storytellers often use time travel as a plot device. American novelist Mark Twain did it in 1889 with *A Connecticut Yankee in King Arthur's Court*. England's H.G. Wells followed suit in 1895 with *The Time Machine*, although he sent his protagonist (identified only as "the Time Traveller") into the future. Other examples include British TV's numerous incarnations of *Doctor Who* to hundreds of novels, graphic novels, plays, films, and videogames.

Often, these stories involve someone going back in time to change something in the present or to prevent the present from being changed in some fashion that will cause a future catastrophe. One tiny interference in the "time continuum," as it's often called, can lead to a monumentally altered chain of events.

Nobody can do that, of course.

REMEMBER

You can, however, understand more about the present if you time travel in your head — that is, think about the ways that yesterday's events shaped today. You can ponder how what happened a decade ago shapes this year and how a single change somewhere in the past could have made today different. Historians scoff at the "what if" game, but it's a tool for getting your head into history.

What if incumbent Donald Trump had won the 2020 U.S. presidential election instead of challenger Joe Biden? Would an angry mob have attacked the U.S. Capitol the following January? How different would American politics have been? How about if voters in the United Kingdom had not chosen, in a 2016 referendum, to withdraw that nation from the European Union? Would that nation's banks or fishing industry be better off or worse today? What about its people?

For that matter, what if Japan had not attacked the U.S. fleet at Pearl Harbor in 1941? Or what if the terrorists who crashed airliners into the World Trade Center and the Pentagon on September 11, 2001, had been stopped before they could board the planes? Think about the lives that would have been saved and the grief that would have been averted. Imagine the years since. What would have been different?

In the case of the World Trade Center, U.S. troops wouldn't have been sent to Afghanistan, for one thing. That invasion turned into a two-decades-long conflict, the United States' longest war. And if the Trade Center had not fallen, would there have been that other U.S. war in the Middle East — the one in Iraq? We can't know for sure, but we know that many lives changed because of that tragic 2001 attack.

Footpath to Expressway: Building on Humble Beginnings

Human beings used to be hunter-gatherers. There may be a slim chance that you're still living that way, getting all your food from the natural world around you. I doubt it, though. Instead, you're a student, an office worker, or perhaps a truck driver. Maybe you write code, or you're an IT specialist. You perform any of thousands of occupations unimagined by early humankind. You use tools like cellphones and GPS navigation — things hardly dreamed of even when I was born in the middle of the 20th century, let alone at the dawn of civilization. Yet here I am, clacking away on a computer keyboard, checking my meager investments online, and listening to my streaming playlist just like a modern human being.

In a way, here too are the people of 30,000 years ago, my ancestors and yours. They may have thought a lot about berries, seeds, insects and grubs, shellfish, and calorie-rich bone marrow from fresh or scavenged kills. But they were endowed with the same basic biological equipment we have today. They were big-brained, tool-using bipeds with opposable thumbs, and after tens of thousands of years living hand to mouth from what they could find or kill, some of them spread across the world.

Either pushed by circumstance (climate change, for example) or inspired by new opportunities, they traveled from the lush forests, savannahs, and seacoasts of Africa to face the harsh challenges of virtually every environment on Earth, including mountains, deserts, frozen steppes, and remote islands. Eventually, they traded in stone spearheads and scrapers for tools and weapons made of copper, then of bronze, and then of iron . . . and ultimately built things like microcircuits and Mars rovers. Those people traveled and adapted and innovated all the way to today. They are you and me. In a weird way, then is now.

Around 12,000 years ago, not very long after the last Ice Age ended, some people whose technology consisted largely of sticks and rocks settled down. They were discovering that if they put seeds in the ground, plants would come up, and that this process worked best if they stuck around to tend the plants. This realization eventually led to farming.

Scholars point to an area they call the Fertile Crescent (see Figure 1-1), as a hotbed of early farming. Shaped like a mangled croissant, the Fertile Crescent stretched from what is now western Iran and the Persian Gulf through the river valleys of today's Iraq and into western Turkey. Then it hooked south along the Mediterranean coast and the Jordan River through Syria, Lebanon, Jordan, Israel, Palestine, and into northern Africa and the Nile Valley of Egypt. The crescent is where archaeologists have found some of the oldest cities in the world.

The chain reaction that starts civilizations goes something like this: Agriculture leads people to stay put in exchange for more food, and ample food enables population growth. When a group's population reaches a certain size, there's little chance of going back to a hunter-gatherer lifestyle, because there wouldn't be enough food for so many people. Ample food also gives the growing population commodities to trade. Trade leads to more trade, which leads to more goods and wealth. Not everybody works in the fields. Some folks can specialize in hauling goods; others can construct buildings or perhaps concentrate on making weapons, used either to protect their own wealth or to take wealth away from others. Artisans create jewelry and turn mundane objects (arrowheads, pots, baskets) into aesthetic statements. Society gets multilayered. Buildings rise. Villages become towns. Cities rise. Trade necessitates keeping track of quantities and values, which necessitates a way to record information. Number systems get invented. Writing follows. Prehistory becomes history.

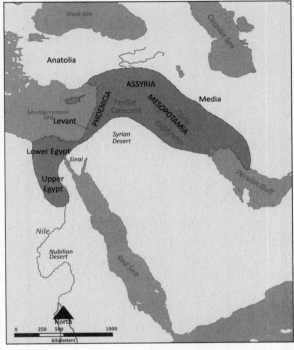

FIGURE 1-1: The Fertile Crescent extended from the Persian Gulf through Iraq and into Turkey, Syria, Lebanon, Jordan, Israel, Palestine, and into the Nile Valley of Egypt.

Next thing you know, an English-speaking woman in Florida, whose various ancestors spoke Spanish, Irish Celtic, and Japanese, is sitting in her South Korean car, stuck in traffic on the expressway, a style of limited-access road invented in Germany. She's sipping a cup of coffee harvested in El Salvador, brewed in the Italian style in a machine manufactured in China to Swiss specifications. On her car's satellite radio, a voice beamed from London is introducing news stories about outbreaks of disease, raging wildfires, floods, and a new tropical storm. The reports come from Greece, Canada, China, and Haiti. She reaches over and switches to a station that features a style of music invented in Jamaica by English-speaking people of African descent.

War! What Is It Good For? Material for History Books, That's What

A view of history that sees only progress — this advance leads to that terrific advance, which leads to another incredible breakthrough, and so on — doesn't account for the fact that people can be awful. Some are ruthless, some are destructive, some are stupid, and many are hateful. More often, people are simply thoughtless and careless. Not you, of course. You're full of compassion and understanding, and capable of doing great things. And we all know or at least know about somebody whose ability to make this world better is off the charts. But the human race also produces bad characters and bad results.

Much of this book deals with war. I wish that weren't so, but for reasons that anthropologists, psychologists, historians, politicians, economists, and many more have never been able to untangle, there's always been somebody who's eager to bash, skewer, shoot, blast, or vaporize somebody else. History is too often an account of how one group of people, under the banner of Persia, Genghis Khan, William of Normandy, imperial Japan, or whatever decided to overrun another group. Many such efforts succeeded, if success can be defined as killing other people and stealing their land, resources, wealth, wives, children, and so on.

IN THEIR WORDS

One of my favorite quotations about war comes from the historian Barbara Tuchman: "War is the unfolding of miscalculations." It underscores two facts: Many decisions made in war turn out to be wrong, and many successful wartime strategies have turned out to be the result of dumb luck.

Historians cite the 20th century as being perhaps the worst ever in terms of war and its toll — not because people were more warlike, but because the weapons had grown so much deadlier and transportation so much faster. During World War I (1914–18) and even more during World War II (1939–45), the machines of destruction reached farther and did more damage than ever before.

Wars since WWII have been somewhat contained to a region or fought with an understanding that neither side would escalate the weaponry too far. During the Vietnam War, a 1960s-'70s conflict between communist North Vietnam and the nationalist government of South Vietnam, each side had allies with deep pockets and nuclear weapons. The Soviet Union and China provided supplies and arms to the North Vietnamese, while the United States sent military advisers and then, starting in 1965, active troops to fight for South Vietnam. The military conflict spread to Cambodia and Thailand, but not around the world. The Americans, though deeply suspicious of and armed against both the Chinese and the Soviets, avoided all-out war with either.

In the 21st century, humankind has far more than enough destructive power to kill everybody on the planet. Keep in mind that there are two kinds of progress: constructive (as in trade, peaceful innovation, medicine, cultural exchange, and the like) and destructive (as in thermonuclear weapons).

Human advances have also been influenced by disasters such as volcanic eruptions, floods, droughts, and disease. The bubonic plague of the 14th century, known as the Black Death, changed history in part because it so drastically reduced the populations of Europe and Asia. So many fewer people meant that their labor was worth more, so there was more wealth. More wealth meant more demand for goods, which in Europe spurred a search for better trade routes, which led Westerners to places such as India, China, and the Americas. The results were good for Europeans but disastrous for the Indians, Chinese, and Native Americans.

Also in the 21st century, the world faces new challenges that may be more immediately dangerous than stockpiles of nuclear weapons. The changing climate — hotter summers, melting glaciers, worse and more-frequent storms, and rising sea levels — will in the not-too-distant future, challenge us all.

Appreciating History's Tapestry

A standard analogy is that human events over the centuries are a "rich tapestry." But many readers and students aren't all that familiar with tapestries, which are decorative fabrics usually hung on a wall to show off their craftsmanship. Made from weaving threads together in such a way that the colors of the thread form recognizable shapes and scenes, tapestries may be called "rich" because people have to be rich to own them. Classic tapestry is hand-woven, taking a lot of time and skill to produce, which makes it expensive. Also, the process is complex. Each thread contributes a tiny percentage of the finished image.

History is like that, even if the threads interweave somewhat randomly and the picture is often hard to figure out. Yet with history, you can follow a thread and see where it crisscrosses and crosscrisses (if you will) other threads to see how the picture formed into what you recognize as the historical present.

Threading backward

History often gets told in chronological order, which makes sense. Much of the content of this book is presented in chronological order, but not all of it. I thought it would be a good idea to break out some of the big influences on how people behave — things like philosophy and religion, styles of warfare, and even individual personalities. Giving these developments their own parts of the book (3, 4, and 5) allows you to come at the same events and eras from different perspectives.

Even when I tell you things in the order in which they happened, though, I sometimes refer to latter-day developments that resulted from long-ago events, or I use modern examples of how things today can work pretty much as they did then (whenever *then* was).

When studying history, it helps to start by thinking about where humanity is now and work backward, asking the questions that the journalists, pundits, and podcasters did when talking about the COVID-19 pandemic: How did we get here? Why are we here now, and not later or before? You don't have to start with now, though. You can work backward from an interesting event that began in, for example, 2003.

Earlier in this chapter I mentioned such an event, the war in Iraq. It started when U.S. planes bombed a bunker where Iraqi President Saddam Hussein was thought to be meeting with top staff. (The raids didn't get him then but were followed up with an invasion that led to his eventual capture and execution.) To trace every thread of that war through time would be too ambitious, but you can follow a few threads. Warm up the WABAC Machine, Sherman.

Among the reasons that U.S. President George W. Bush and his advisers cited for invading Iraq was the need to remove a brutal dictator. Saddam came to power in 1979, when his cousin and predecessor, Ahmed Hassan al-Bakr, stepped down, or (as many people believe) was forced out of office. Al-Bakr's career included ousting two previous military dictators and helping with the overthrow of Iraq's monarchy in 1958.

The monarchy dated to the 1920s, when the United Kingdom (Britain), which ruled Iraq as a colony, installed Faisal I as king. A descendant of the family of the Prophet Mohammed, Faisal was not from Iraq, but from Saudi Arabia, and the British expected him to answer to London. Yet he helped secure Iraq's independence before he died.

The League of Nations, a short-lived predecessor to the United Nations, had cobbled Iraq together after WWI. The body put Britain in charge of Baghdad and Basra, two adjacent parts of the old Ottoman Empire (which fell apart in WWI), and a few years later threw in Mosul to the north.

The Ottomans first conquered that territory in 1535. Baghdad (later Iraq's capital) had been a center of the Islamic world since Arabs conquered the region in the seventh century; before that, it was a province of the Persian Empire. Alexander the Great conquered the region in the fourth century BC. (The designation BC can be confusing. It means before the time of Jesus — in this case, 400 years before. I explain BC, along with AD, BCE and CE, in more detail in Chapter 3.)

In fact, when Alexander died in 323 BC, he was just south of the city of Baghdad, in Babylon, one of the most famous places in the ancient world and one of those early cities that arose in the Fertile Crescent after agriculture took hold. Babylon had been the capital of a kingdom established by a people called the Amorites in the 19th century BC. Archaeologists think it was a much older town that grew to city size by 2400 BC, more than 4,400 years ago.

Crossing threads

Okay, the preceding section has a highly superficial tracing of a thread I'll call "What was Iraq before, and who ruled it?" This discussion is so superficial that I skipped parts in which different conquerors fought over the territory and rule shifted back and forth. The famous Turkish-Mongol conqueror Timur, for example, took over for a while in the 14th century. His thread would take you back to his ancestor Genghis Khan, a great Mongol warrior and ruler. And his thread could take you forward (it works both ways) to Genghis's grandson, Kublai Khan, a 13th-century emperor of China.

But in tracing that one thread back from 21st-century Iraq, I crossed other threads. At one intersection was WWI, which was triggered by a Serbian nationalist rebellion against Austrian rule of Bosnia. That war redrew the map of Europe and brought down not just the Ottoman Empire, but also the Russian, German, and Austro-Hungarian empires.

The overthrow of the Russian Empire led to the establishment of the Soviet Union — a military superpower and archrival to the United States through much of the 20th century. Then there's the fact that WWI ended with the 1919 Treaty of Versailles, whose harsh terms imposed upon Germany have been blamed in part for the rise of Adolf Hitler and WWII. The war also led to the establishment of the League of Nations, which lumped together the group of territories we know as Iraq.

Weaving home

The German Empire was a successor to the Holy Roman Empire. Not to be confused with the earlier Roman Empire, the Holy Roman Empire was a union of Central European territories dating back to Otto the Great in 962 AD. It was considered to be a continuation of the Frankish Empire, established in 800 AD, when Pope Leo III crowned Charlemagne Emperor of the West — essentially naming him the successor to the Roman emperors going back to Augustus, whose rule began in 27 BC.

Follow Leo's popish thread, and you'll get to Pope Urban II, who in 1095 called upon Europe's Christians to make war against the Turks, especially the Seljuk Dynasty, who controlled the city of Jerusalem and the land surrounding it, considered to be the Christian Holy Land.

Urban's war became the First Crusade, followed by at least nine more crusades over several centuries in which Christians from Europe traveled east to conquer territory in western Asia. Not surprisingly, these incursions contributed to enduring hard feelings on the part of many Muslims toward Christians and the West.

You may trace a thread between the Crusades and latter-day anti-U.S. sentiments, such as those held by the notorious terrorist organization called ISIS, for the Islamic State of Iraq and Syria. (Confusingly, it's also called IS, ISIL [for Islamic State of Iraq and the Levant], and Daesh.) That thread also crosses the one in which the United Nations partitioned what had been British Palestine (another post-WWI territory) into Arab and Jewish areas to make way for the modern nation of Israel.

Before the rise of ISIS, another terrorist group, al-Qaeda, attacked the United States on September 11, 2001. The American response was a War on Terror(ism) that included the invasion of Afghanistan, where the leaders of al-Qaeda were supposedly hiding, and then the invasion of Iraq, whose leader was thought to be hiding banned weapons and aiding terrorist groups. That second invasion and war destabilized Iraq for many years, giving ISIS a place to form and grow. And I'm back where I started.

Making the Connections

If you're not thrilled with the tapestry analogy, how about the notion of six degrees of separation, also known as "six degrees of Kevin Bacon" when applied to entertainment figures. The idea is that anybody on Earth can be linked to anybody else in six or fewer interactions. Depending on which interpretation of this idea you like, the interaction could be as simple as a shared acquaintance or a handshake. Some people call it an urban legend, but a few researchers have tried to test the notion, with mixed results.

The game calls for making the connection in six steps or less. Let's see whether I can do that with Alexander the Great, who died in ancient Babylon, and the Iraq War that started in 2003.

1. Alexander's conquests spread Greek influence around the Mediterranean Sea.

2. Romans embraced aspects of Greek religion and philosophy.

3. The Roman Empire eventually adopted Christianity.

4. The Roman Catholic Church preserved ancient writings containing classical (Greek and Roman) ideas through the Middle Ages.

5. Christian scholars rediscovered Greek philosophy, sparking the Renaissance.

Oops. Darn. I'm not there yet.

So historical connections aren't as easy to make as movie-actor connections, but I was on my way. See, the Renaissance led to the Enlightenment, when ideas such as government by consent of the governed took hold. That period led to the American Revolution and modern democracies — the style of government that George W. Bush said he would establish in the Middle East after getting rid of Saddam Hussein by invading Iraq, which helped make room in Iraq and Syria for the rise of ISIS. That's more than six steps, but not bad.

REMEMBER

If you fill in enough steps and make enough connections, you'll begin to see the interconnectedness of virtually everything people do on Earth. Maybe once upon a time, a band of hunter-gatherers in what would later be Yemen or Thailand could live for 1,000 years in ignorance of the rest of the world, and no other band of hunter-gatherers anywhere would have known that those prehistoric Yemeni or Thai people existed. But that moment is long gone. Delve into any bit of human-kind's story now, and you're on a path that reaches far beyond whatever city or village you started in. Each path branches into countless others that together reach around the world and stretch through time to what came before. Everything that ever happened, somebody once said, is still happening. History is now.

Tracking the Centuries

Before 12,000 BC: The Pleistocene Epoch, known today as the last major Ice Age, ends after ice sheets recede northward.

Perhaps 10,000 BC: Agricultural societies develop in an area called the Fertile Crescent in the Middle East.

About 2400 BC: The town of Babylon, between the Tigris and Euphrates Rivers, has grown into a city.

About 323 BC: Alexander the Great dies of a fever in the ancient city of Babylon.

27 BC: Augustus becomes the first Roman emperor.

962 AD: Otto the Great is crowned Holy Roman Emperor in Aix-la-Chapelle, Germany.

1535: Ottoman Turks conquer Baghdad.

1919: The Treaty of Versailles sets out terms of peace to officially end WWI.

1932: The Kingdom of Iraq wins its independence from British rule.

1947: The United Nations partitions what had been British Palestine into Jewish and Arab areas.

1965: The United States escalates its involvement in the Vietnam War by sending troops to fight on the side of the South Vietnamese government.

2001: Nineteen suicide terrorists hijack four commercial airlines and succeed in crashing two of them into New York City's World Trade Center and a third into the Pentagon in Washington, D.C. The fourth plane crashes in Pennsylvania.

2003: The United States and the United Kingdom, along with small contingents of troops from other allied countries, invade Iraq.

2016: The United Kingdom votes in a referendum to separate from the European Union, a move known as Brexit.

2019: A previously unknown viral illness called COVID-19, arises in China, on its way to becoming the fastest-spreading pandemic the world has yet seen.

2021: President Joe Biden withdraws American troops from Afghanistan.

Chapter **2**

Digging Up Reality

I f you think of history as lists of facts, dates, battles, and key civilizations, you may memorize a lot, but you'll never experience the thrill of the past. If, on the other hand, you're able to make the leap to identify with people who are long dead and to imagine what their lives must have been like, you may be among those for whom the past becomes a passion — and perhaps even an addiction.

Maybe you read history, and your imagination brings the stories to life. Or maybe you need help. Hard evidence, the kind you can examine at historic sites or in museums, often works. Seeing what the people of the past left behind — what they made and built, and even their preserved bodies — can bridge the gap between then and now. These things are reminders that real people walked the Earth long ago, carrying within them dreams and fears not so unlike yours.

In this chapter, I look at two "lost" cities and discuss evidence for their actual existence. I also look at mummies and discuss the ways they can bring history alive.

Homing In on Homer

The Iliad and *The Odyssey*, ancient epic poems, tell fantastic stories about a long war between Greeks and Trojans and the journey home from that war. They're *so* fantastic — full of vengeful gods and supernatural peril — that it's hard for modern people to credit any part of them as true.

Yet a kind of history is in these poems. This history became more tantalizing in the late 19th century, when an eccentric German businessman dug up the city of Troy, revealing that it had been a real place, one of many ancient Troys built in just the place the poems describe. Each city rose and fell, and another rose on top of it while the old one was forgotten.

The Troy story

Greeks attacked Troy more than 3,200 years ago, in the 13th century BC. (In the next chapter, I explain BC, AD, CE, and BCE.) The stories about that decade-long war were already ancient by the time of the philosopher Aristotle and Alexander the Great in the fourth century BC. *The Iliad* and *The Odyssey* are supposedly the work of a blind singer–poet called Homer, but nobody knows for sure who he was, when he lived (maybe the ninth century BC), or even *whether* he lived. One widely respected theory is that, long before anybody wrote these stories down, storytellers and singers performed them, often set to music, over and over, each generation teaching the tales to the next.

As centuries and millennia went by, the real Trojan War faded so far into the past that these stories were all that was left — that is, until Heinrich Schliemann, a wealthy German enthusiast, decided to find Troy. With little to go on except his faith in Homer, he dug up not just one but a stack of nine Troys built one on top of another. Then he went to Greece and discovered the mighty civilization of Mycenae, which also figures in Homer's saga.

Sure that *The Iliad's* account of the Trojan War was true, Schliemann fixed on an ancient mound at a place called Hissarlik, on the southwest coast of modern Turkey.

Starting in 1870, Schliemann's workers dug into a promising mound of dirt and rubble. What they couldn't budge, they blasted with explosives. If you've seen documentaries about modern archaeologists painstakingly picking through an archaeological site with dental picks and soft brushes, put that image out of your head. These guys approached excavation with all the delicacy of a dog in a flower bed.

The crew hardly slowed down as they passed through what later archaeologists identified as the probable Troy of the Trojan War (about 1250 BC), only three levels down. Schliemann's workers burrowed to an earlier layer of the ancient city, one from before 2000 BC — maybe 700 years earlier than the Troy in Homer's stories. In 1874, Schliemann found gold artifacts that he erroneously thought had belonged to Priam, the Trojan king in *The Iliad*.

Not satisfied with his Trojan findings, Schliemann went back to Greece to look for the palace of Agamemnon, the leader of the Greeks in *The Iliad*. There, he not only made more finds (in the form of ancient tombs), but again came up with treasure, including a golden burial mask that he declared to be the Mask of Agamemnon. Later archaeologists dated it to about 1600 BC, too early for Agamemnon, and some modern archaeologists even think it's a fake that Shliemann placed in the tomb so that he could "discover" it.

Inspiring archaeological finds

Schliemann's enthusiastic work may not have been fraudulent, but it was clumsy and ill-informed. Yet he stumbled upon discoveries of real value, things found by archaeologists such as Arthur Evans (1851–1941), an Englishman who uncovered the remains of the great Minoan civilization. (The Minoans were a powerful people who thrived on Crete and other Aegean islands between 3000 and 1450 BC.) Such finds reminded both scientists and historians that ancient stories — even fantastical ones —can contain important clues to the foundations of history.

Raising Atlantis

Do Schliemann's discoveries tell us every "lost" civilization was for real? No. I don't think it means scientists or explorers will someday find the sunken nation of Atlantis. Oops. I shouldn't have mentioned Atlantis. There isn't room in this book to delve into even a small fraction of the theories and fantasies about where and what was Atlantis — if anything like it ever existed.

The story describes a land of peace and plenty, destroyed in an overnight cataclysm. It traces back to the writings of Greek philosopher Plato (about 428–347 BC), who used Atlantis to make a point about social order and good government. But Plato's descriptions leave room for interpretation, and people have interpreted wildly for thousands of years.

Plato described Atlantis as in the Atlantic Ocean, just past Gibraltar on your way out of the Mediterranean Sea, but geology seems to dictate that it couldn't have been there. Dueling historians, archaeologists, mystics, and self-appointed prophets have argued vociferously over an alternate site, putting the lost continent everywhere from Britain to Bermuda to Bolivia, from Colorado to the China Sea. One theory claims it was on another planet. Sci-fi movies, comics, and graphic novels depict Atlantis thriving in a giant plexiglass bubble on the ocean floor. Virtually every theory has to make allowances for Plato, who got the story of Atlantis indirectly from the Athenian statesman Solon, who supposedly got it from scholar–priests during a visit to Egypt in about 590 BC. Because Plato wrote his version almost two centuries later, in about 360 BC, details surely changed along the way.

REMEMBER

One of the least outrageous theories is that the story of Atlantis is based on the volcanic disaster that destroyed Santorini, an island in the Mediterranean. Archaeologists and geologists have studied the way the Santorini cataclysm caused a monstrous tsunami, followed by sky-darkening ashfall.

Santorini (also known as Thera) lies about 45 miles north of the Greek island of Crete, which was the center of the Minoan culture. Minoan ruins are plentiful on what's left of Santorini, but they're only a small remnant of what was on the island until about 1600 BC, when the 5,000-foot volcano in its middle exploded and collapsed into the sea. Ever since, the island has been a crescent surrounding a volcanic-crater lagoon. The volcanic eruptions continued for 30 years, building up to a devastating climax: an enormous tidal wave that knocked down buildings on islands throughout the region.

The tsunami decimated the population, and the subsequent rain of volcanic ash probably finished off the Minoan civilization. Nobody knows for sure whether the sinking of Santorini had anything to do with launching a lasting legend of a capsized civilization, but news of such a catastrophic event surely spread around the Mediterranean and in time could have become legend.

Reading the Body Language of the Dead

Some people who lived hundreds or thousands of years ago left more than just their images in sculpture and paintings on stone. Preserved bodies are in-the-flesh evidence of long-ago reality. The mere fact that a human body from thousands of years past is still more or less intact and recognizably like this year's model can help open your mind to the connection between then and now. Something about a mummy helps your imagination bridge all the generations since that puckered flesh was taut, upright, and dancing.

In history books that cover big expanses of time, you have to adjust your perspective so that a century becomes a relatively small unit of history. In this book, you can breeze through a thousand years here and a thousand years there. Thinking of the Byzantine Empire as one civilization, a single station on the history train, is easy to do. Yet the empire grew and receded, changed governments, and restructured policies over centuries — more than five times longer than the United States has been a nation.

When you back up far enough to take that concept in, you may lose sight of individual lives, which flicker past quickly. I find that contemplating mummies is a helpful, if gruesome, tool for hooking into the perspective of a single life span, a single person, so long ago. Strangely, you may be able to identify with a mummy easily, if you don't find the idea too macabre.

Mummies have turned up all over the world. Some were preserved naturally by something in the environment where the body came to rest. Others, as in the celebrated tombs of ancient Egypt, were artfully prepared for their voyage into death.

Frozen in the Alps

In the summer of 1991, German tourists hiking in the Ötzal Alps on the border between Austria and Italy spotted a human body lodged in high-altitude ice. A few days later, a rescue team cut free the corpse of a bearded man dressed in leather. Perhaps he had been a back-to-nature hippie whose 1960s wanderings went tragically awry? No. Other curious details made that scenario unlikely — including the man's flint-bladed knife, flint-tipped arrows, and copper-bladed ax.

Researchers at the University of Innsbruck in Austria first estimated the freeze-dried body to be 4,000 years old. Further examination moved the date of death back by 1,300 years, meaning that Ötzi (as scientists nicknamed him) was journeying over the mountains around 3300 BC when he died and was covered by falling snow.

Ötzi, who resides in Italy's Museo Archologico dell'Alto Adige in Bolzano, is a natural mummy in that his body was preserved by nature. Scientists find out all kinds of things about the ways people lived and died from mummies, especially those that were preserved whole. Ötzi was between age 40 and 50 when he died, and he suffered from several chronic illnesses; his medicine pouch contained herbal prescriptions for what ailed him. He also had a sloe, the fruit of the blackthorn tree, presumably to eat. Probing the mummy's stomach, researchers found that he'd eaten the meat of chamois (a European mountain goat) and deer, as well as grain (possibly in the form of bread) shortly before he died.

Ötzi's mummified body and the things found with it prompted scholars to rethink some assumptions about the roots of European civilization. His copper ax showed that the transition from stone technology to metal happened earlier than archaeologists had previously believed. The rest of his gear — a bow, a quiver of arrows, a waterproof cape woven of grass, even his well-made shoes — show that Ötzi was well equipped for his trek across the mountains. The stress patterns in his leg bones suggest that he made such journeys routinely. At first, scientists theorized that he might have been a shepherd, but further research showed that he had been shot with an arrow and involved in a physical struggle with other men. A blow to the head and blood loss from the arrow wound probably killed him. This man could have been a soldier, perhaps part of a raiding party.

Salted away in Asia

In the dry climate of Chinese Turkestan (between Russia and Mongolia), bodies buried in the salty soil near the towns of Cherchen and Loulan as long as 4,000 years ago turned into mummies rather than rotting away.

Some of the Turkestan mummies have well-preserved blond hair and appear to be of Caucasian ancestry, which challenges latter-day assumptions about the range of ancient ethnic groups. Based on their well-made, colorful clothing, they may have been related to the Celts, whose culture would later flourish all over Europe and whose descendants include the Irish, Scots, and Welsh. The fabrics show weaving techniques similar to those still practiced in rural Ireland. DNA analysis has suggested genetic links ranging from western European to east Asian, which may mean that their home, the Taklimakan Desert basin, was an ancient cross-roads between cultures.

Bogged down in northern Europe

The watery peat bogs of northern Europe also made mummies. Tannins in the peat (partially decayed plant matter) and the cold water preserved bodies in such startlingly good condition that Danish villagers have sometimes mistaken a 2,500-year-old body for that of someone they knew only decades before.

Though discolored by the tannins, the mummies look much as they did when the people died. Some people may have fallen into the bogs, but many were killed and dumped there, perhaps as ritual sacrifices or as victims of another kind of execution. Some mummies of young women wear blindfolds, and other mummies appear to have been drowned alive. There are mummies with ropes around their necks, and some with slit throats.

Most of these peat-bog mummies have intact skin, hair, fingernails, and even facial expressions. And their jewelry and clothing sometimes look unsettlingly like something that could hang in your 21st-century closet.

Dried and well preserved in the Andes

The 500-year-old bodies of Inca children in the Argentine Andes, discovered atop Mount Llullaillaco in the 1990s by archaeologist Johan Reinhard and a team from the National Geographic Society, are among the best-preserved mummies ever found. Apparently killed as a religious ritual sacrifice, the boy and two girls — aged between 8 and 15 — were so perfectly frozen that the scientist said they looked as though they had just drawn their last breaths.

The Argentine discoveries are more than fascinating and informative; they're also terribly sad. The idea of killing an 8-year-old makes me recoil in horror. What could possibly possess a culture to worship gods that must have the blood of innocents? Yet that's another reason why the three preserved bodies are so compelling: They draw you into the past as you struggle to comprehend how these people, who were so startlingly similar to modern people in some ways, could have understood the world so differently.

TECHNICAL STUFF

MUMMIES FOR DUMMIES

If you got a job preparing wealthy and royal Egyptians for the afterlife, how would you go about it? Here's the how-to:

1. To remove the brain, stick a long, narrow bronze probe up one nostril, breaking through the sinus bone into the cranial cavity. Wiggle the tool vigorously, breaking down the tissue until it's the consistency of raw egg. Turn the corpse over to drain the liquefied brain through the nostril. Return the body to a face-up position. Use a funnel to pour boiling-hot tree resin into the cranium to halt decomposition of remaining tissue.

2. Extract the internal organs through a slit in the abdomen wall. (You'll have to reach in with a sharp knife and feel around for them.) Wait! Leave the heart. Egyptians considered the heart to be the control center for thought and action, so they figured they'd need it in the afterlife. What to do with the other organs? Put them in jars decorated with the heads of gods or a likeness of the departed. The jars go in the tomb with the mummy.

3. Bathe the body in spices and palm wine. Cover it with natron salts, a sodium paste found in drying lakebeds, to retard spoilage and dry the skin.

4. When the body is good and dry, stuff rolled-up linen cloths inside, kind of like stuffing a turkey. Try to restore the person's shape to something resembling lifelike.

5. Wrap more linen, cut into neat strips, around the outside of the body to create that creepy, bandaged look that will scare the pants off moviegoers a few millennia later.

6. Put the body in a coffin, preferably a double coffin (one inside another). If you're working on a pharaoh, put the coffin inside a stone sarcophagus inside a hidden tomb.

Preserved pharaohs in Egypt

Perhaps nobody devoted quite so much thought and energy to death and the after-life as the ancient Egyptians. After burying their dead with great care and ceremony since perhaps 4000 BC (Chapter 4 has more on ancient Egypt), the Egyptians began artfully mummifying their pharaohs sometime before the 24th century BC.

By 2300 BC, the practice had spread beyond royalty. Any Egyptian who could afford it was dried and fortified for the trip into the afterlife. The mummy was buried with possessions and even servants for use in the next world.

REMEMBER

Egyptian mummies differ from many others in that researchers can figure out exactly who some of these people were in life. King Tutankhamen's identity is intact thanks to ancient Egyptian pictorial writings called hieroglyphics. Again, writing gives us actual history. British Egyptologist Howard Carter discovered fabulously preserved artifacts in Tutankhamen's tomb in 1922. The discovery made Tutankhamen the most famous pharaoh in our time, although he may not have been that in his own time. Tut took the throne in 1361 BC at about age 9 and reigned for only 9 years.

Carter first gazed by candlelight into the wonders of that tomb, unseen for more than 3,300 years. That moment has been held up ever since as the ideal archaeological breakthrough — completely unlike most great discoveries, which are scratched out of the ancient dust and painstakingly pieced together.

IN THEIR WORDS

Carter said that he stood in front of the tomb for a long time, allowing his eyes to adjust to the gloom. His patron and partner, George Herbert, Earl of Carnarvon, stood behind him in the dark, unable to stand the suspense. "Do you see anything?" asked Carnarvon breathlessly. "Yes," replied Carter in a hushed tone. "Wonderful things."

The discovery made all the papers, and so did Carnarvon's untimely death. The earl died of an infected mosquito bite a few months after he helped Carter find the tomb. Naturally, some people blamed his death on an ancient curse against anyone who disturbed the boy king's eternal rest. (Grave robbers had been the scourge of Egyptian royalty.)

The notion of Tutankhamen's curse may have disappeared if it weren't for a 1932 horror movie called *The Mummy*, which is wrong on every point of archaeology and Egyptian religion but features a compellingly compelling performance by Boris Karloff in the title role. *The Mummy* was successful enough that many remakes and variations followed.

Tracking the Centuries

About 4000 BC: Egyptians begin burying their dead with ritual care.

About 3300 BC: A well-equipped male traveler in the Italian Alps succumbs to an arrow wound and falls face-down into the snow.

About 1600 BC: The volcano on the island of Santorini erupts, destroying the island, wiping out villages, and probably ending a civilization.

1352 BC: Tutankhamen, young king of Egypt, dies and is mummified.

About 1250 BC: A confederation of Greek kings and warriors attacks the city of Troy, in today's Turkey.

Ninth century BC: The bard Homer sings about the Trojan War.

Early fourth century BC: In Athens, the philosopher Plato writes about Atlantis, a land lost under the sea.

1870s: Heinrich Schliemann, a German commodities broker and amateur archaeologist, finds Homer's Troy.

1922: British archaeologist Howard Carter opens Tutankhamen's perfectly preserved tomb.

1991: Hikers in the Italian Alps discover the 5,300-year-old mummy of a well-outfitted traveler. Researchers nickname him Ötzi.

» **Figuring out BC and AD**

» **Accepting the relativity of the names of eras**

» **Embracing contradictory characters**

Chapter **3**

Putting History into Perspective

In several places in this book, I refer to the year 1492, when the explorer Christopher Columbus, sailing under a Spanish flag, landed for the first time on an island in the Bahamas, east of Florida. That year is a big dividing point in history, in that it marks the beginning of European colonialism in the Americas. The Western Hemisphere changed in ways that were devastatingly tragic for the people who had been living there. Diseases from Europe killed them by the millions. The rest of the world, meanwhile, saw changes that ranged from new crops (corn, potatoes, tobacco, peppers, coffee) to population migrations, to new, lucrative markets for slave trading (the most pernicious kind of population migration). A global economy took root once European navigators realized they could sail to new worlds, and soon around the world, in their little wooden ships.

Yet according to *The New York Times,* a survey conducted back in 2008 showed that fewer than half of teenagers in the United States could correctly pick the date of Columbus's discovery from a multiple-choice list. If today's teenagers, or adults, were given the same test, how many would choose the right answer? Many people have trouble putting history and its events into perspective. The history of the world is such a huge topic, covering so many eras, cultures, events, conflicts, ideas, and beliefs, that it's easy to get mixed up. Three common problems that you may have are:

>> Sorting out such terms as ancient, recent, and modern when they're used by historians and other scholars and connecting them with the stretches of time that people have lived on the planet.

>> Getting comfortable with labels such as classical and Victorian that historians use to refer to eras and periods. Often, these labels can seem more cryptic than helpful.

>> Understanding the often-contradictory reasons why certain exceptional people are judged to be worthy of historical study.

In all three cases, I suggest that you relax. The terminology is less important than you may think.

In this chapter, you get a chance to ponder what it means to be human before you plunge into the cavalcade of civilizations that follows in Part 2. If you can work up a healthy sense of awe about our remarkable species and its beginnings, you'll be better able to appreciate the broad sweep of time that people have been around. And you can see that historical language — including relative terms such as ancient and labels for eras such as Classical Greece — is somewhat flexible and may be used differently by different historians. As with any subject matter, there are different ways of looking at history and even different ways of evaluating people in history. Sometimes perspectives conflict, but they can also complement one another.

Being Human Beings

Earth formed about 4.5 billion years ago, or so the astrophysicists say. My mind balks at the thought of such an expanse of time.

I do better starting with recent times, here meaning the many thousands of years that people have lived on Earth. Recent is a relative term. The modern human species — meaning people who are anatomically the same as you — may not be much more than 100,000 years old, although scientific estimates vary. And paleo-anthropologists (human-fossil nerds) say that human beings didn't start acting fully "human" until more recently. Humanity turned a corner roughly 60,000 years ago, when stone tools got more sophisticated, and people began carving patterns into rocks and bones, using charcoal to make exquisite cave paintings, and inventing rafts to cross water. These artistic expressions and engineering tasks mark them as being more like you and less like earlier models of the hominid (human-like) family. Many scholars refer to members of our species who lived 30,000 years ago as being fully modern. In that usage, modern, like recent, is a relative term. Obviously, it doesn't mean people who share TikTok videos. We can take it to mean people who behaved a bit more like us and less like earlier prehistoric humans had.

You've probably seen the familiar illustration showing successive ancestor species marching single file, ever more upright and less hairy, toward modern humanity. Evolution didn't happen that way, however. Evolution is rarely neat. Different kinds of more-or-less humanlike animals lived at the same time. Many were genetic dead ends and died out, although the genetic record reveals that other, related types of humans — including Neanderthals and Denisovans — interbred with our own ancestors, so in that way, they are us. All earlier hominids are extinct . . . unless you buy the idea that Sasquatch (Bigfoot) and Yeti (the Abominable Snowman) are your reclusive country cousins.

REMEMBER

As a species, modern humans are young, and again, I'm speaking relatively. Homo erectus — if not your direct ancestor, at least a close relative — was on Earth much longer than modern people have been here. Homo erectus lived from about 1.7 million years ago to perhaps as recently as 108,000 years ago.

If you think of the entire time since the emergence of hominids, perhaps 4 million years ago, to the present day as a single 24-hour day, Homo erectus lasted more than 8 hours. On that scale, modern humans have been here for about 15 minutes.

Nearing the Neanderthal

Neanderthals lived over a wide area stretching from today's Belgium southward to Spain and eastward around the Mediterranean Sea to Turkey. This big-brained branch of the family arose about 150,000 years ago in Europe. After swapping some genes with our species, Neanderthals died out perhaps as recently as 28,000 years ago.

While Neanderthals were still in their prime, glaciers receded, and anatomically modern folks migrated into the Neanderthal part of the world. The two kinds of humans coexisted for thousands of years, both leaving evidence of their camps among the same hills, valleys, and caves. It's perhaps inevitable that they inter-bred, but nobody knows how well they got along. Did modern humans wipe out their Neanderthal cousins over centuries of brutal genocide? Did the newcomers have better survival skills?

If it bothers you that Neanderthals mated with people like us, it shouldn't. They had big brains — maybe bigger than ours — and they did some rather modern things, such as burying their dead with flowers and ochre (a reddish clay used like body paint). They made tools and art, too, although some researchers argue that they may have borrowed ideas from their more "modern" neighbors.

Neanderthals lived over a wide geographical area, but not as wide as that inhabited in a relatively short time by their successors. Our kind evolved in Africa, where earlier hominids also originated. Then they migrated on their two spindly legs not just into the Mideast and Europe, where the Neanderthals had been coping with ice ages, but over all the other continents except Antarctica.

Talking like no one had before

Before creating counting devices and pictures on rocks, human beings accomplished a more remarkable feat: They talked. Other species communicate with noises, and some (birds and certain monkeys, for example) have complex vocabularies. But no other creature has anything as versatile or expressive as human language.

Scientists don't know when language happened. No one can tell whether the first anatomically modern humans were able to make all the sounds that their descendants do, because soft tissues such as the tongue and larynx rot away, even when bones fossilize. We don't know how well, or even whether, Neanderthals and Denovisans talked. It seems likely that they did. Yet whenever it came about, nuanced language brought huge change. As people gave specific meanings to combinations of vocal sounds, they were devising sound symbols. As with some other species, a noise stood for a thing, an action, or an emotion. But humans got fancy with their noisemaking. They went beyond warning about predators and calling the children to dinner and progressed to sharing more complicated information.

People began to amass knowledge— not just as individuals, but as societies. They could always learn by watching and doing; now they could also understand by being told. The how-to genre was born.

Through language, early humans benefited from the experiences of tribe members who were no longer living. After tribes built lore (a body of shared knowledge), they could embellish it, spinning hunting stories that did more than help successive generations find and kill large prey, for example. Within several generations, tribes surely had more fanciful folktales about ancestors, heroes, creation, spirits, and gods who commanded the stars and the Earth. After writing developed, it was possible for cultures to leave a permanent record of events.

Herodotus the Greek, credited as the father of history, took his subject to the level of intellectual inquiry in the fifth century BC as he gathered 1,000-year-old stories from around the Mediterranean. As the body of oral and written history grew, there came a need to organize it.

Making sense of AD, BC, CE, and BCE

In 1854, scientists studying fossil skulls that were discovered in European caves, decided to name their subject *Homo Neanderthalensis*. Like 1492, when Columbus sailed, 1854 is AD, just like this year. *AD* stands for Anno Domini. That's Latin for "Year of the Lord," referring to the Christian era, or the time since Jesus was thought to have been born. Before that, years are designated as BC, or *Before Christ*. Historians now prefer *CE* (for *Common Era*) instead of *AD* and *BCE* (for *Before the Common Era*) instead of *BC*, for the obvious reason that a lot of non-Christians and non-Christian nations use the system. AD and BC, however, are what most people are used to. They're widely understood and deeply ingrained, so I stick with them.

The years BC are figured by counting backward. That's why the year when 32-year-old Alexander the Great died, 323 BC, is a smaller number than the year when he was born, 356 BC.

Yet Alexander never thought of himself as living in backward-counting years three centuries before Jesus. Our system of counting years didn't come about until 1582, when Pope Gregory XIII decreed it. Popes had that kind of power back then. Gregory's system, called the *Gregorian calendar*, gradually became the one that most of the world uses to track appointments, supplanting older traditional calendars (and there have been many of them) for civil business, if not religious observances. The Gregorian system revised an earlier one named for Roman statesman and general Julius Caesar, which in turn replaced an even older Roman calendar.

In this book, you can assume that a four-digit year without two capital letters following it is AD. So, I may tell you that William the Conqueror, who ruled the kingdom of Normandy, successfully invaded England in 1066. For the years 1–999 AD, I use AD — for example, Norsemen invaded Ireland and began building the city of Dublin around 831 AD. I also include the initials for all the BC years. Examples: Saul was anointed the first king of the Israelites in about 1050 BC, and Julius Caesar was murdered in 44 BC, the year before the calendar named for him took effect. (The reason why I say *around* and *about* for the dates of Dublin's founding and King Saul's coronation is that nobody knows the dates for sure.)

Another thing that may be confusing is the way centuries are named and numbered. When you see a reference to the 1900s, it doesn't mean the same thing as the 19th century. The 1900s are the 20th century. The 20th century was the one in which four-digit year numbers started with 19; the 19th century was the one in which years started with 18, and so on.

You may wonder why this century, the one with 20 starting every year, isn't called the 20th. That's because theoretically, the first century (according to Pope Gregory and his advisers, anyway) began in the year 1. When the numbers got up to 100 (or, technically, 101), we were in the second century, and so on. Figuring the centuries BC works the same way (in reverse, of course): The 21st century BC is the one with years starting with 20, just like the 21st century AD.

Dividing Time into Eras . . . and Giving Them Names

If history teachers told you that medieval means the period between the fall of Rome (476 AD) and the Renaissance (the 14th century), you could have thrown the author H.G. Wells at them.

Not literally, of course. (Let Mr. Wells rest in peace.) Yet it may surprise students of history and certain teachers to find out that historians disagree about when the period called medieval began. Wells (1866–1946) is better remembered today as a pioneering science-fiction writer, author of *The Time Machine* and *War of the Worlds* (1898), but he also wrote a three-volume *Outline of History* (1920). He begins the second volume of this major history of the world, called *Medieval History*, at 300 BC with the rise, not the fall, of Rome's empire.

So what? That's my point. Wells's work is just one illustration of the fact that history is full of periods divided by arbitrary lines etched in the shifting sands of time.

REMEMBER

Historians have points of view. The good ones have really well-informed points of view, but they don't all march in intellectual lockstep.

Sorting ancient from modern

"That's ancient history, Pops." In American movies from the 1930s through the 1950s, a teenage character often says something like that to an adult, thus dismissing an event that the adult remembers as being too long ago to matter. Ancient is another relative term, like recent, modern, and medieval. To a person born in 2021, the teenager in that 1950s movie will seem beyond ancient.

IN THEIR
WORDS

In history, ancient has more specific meanings. Wells defined it as "From the World Before Man to the Rise of the Roman Empire," and he considered the modern period to have begun in 1567.

Telling classical from schmassical

Classical is another historical label that can have different meanings in different contexts. The classical period in European music, for example, was about 1750 to 1820, but people who study the Maya civilization of the Yucatan Peninsula refer to a classical historical period of about 250–900 AD.

One of the best-known uses of the term *classical* applies to the years 479–323 BC in the southern Balkan Peninsula of Eastern Europe. That period was a particularly influential era of Greek culture: Classical Greece (with a capital C).

Traditionally, many historians have hailed the Classical Greeks as being the founders of Western civilization's core values: rationality, freedom of debate, individuality, and democracy. These concepts did arise and gain acceptance during that time, yet the Greece of the time was hardly an ideal society. Greek cities often fought wars against one another, and in addition to creating enduring ideas, they hatched some notions that sound quite peculiar today. In Aristotle's time (the fourth century BC), for example, one could argue that women were "failed men," a lesser rendering of the same biological pattern as males. Yikes!

The Greek city–state Athens is often cited as a model for modern democracies, but there are huge differences between the Greeks' notion of democracy and today's. In Athens, maybe 30 percent of the population at most were citizens, and all citizens were men.

Historians constantly reevaluate the past. As scholars reinterpret the period, the term Classical may no longer be helpful for understanding the years 479–323 BC in Greece. And you know what? That's okay. You can look at the Greeks from any number of angles, and they don't get any less fascinating.

IN THEIR WORDS

As H.G. Wells said of history, "The subject is so splendid a one that no possible treatment . . . can rob it altogether of its sweeping greatness and dignity."

Bowing to the queens

Scholars also name eras and periods for notable events or people, such as Columbus's arrival in the Americas. In the Western Hemisphere, times before that event are frequently called pre-Columbian. A period label is often based on the reign of a monarch, such as England's Elizabeth I (before there was a United Kingdom). Events, fashions, and literature from her reign (1558–1603, a golden age of English culture) carry the designation Elizabethan. A label may cover much longer periods, as when they derive from Chinese dynasties. The Ming Dynasty, for example, ruled from 1368–1644.

For a cinematic depiction of England's Elizabethan era, you can check out 1998's *Elizabeth* and its 2007 sequel, *Elizabeth: The Golden Age,* both starring Cate Blanchett. The movies take liberties with the historical truth (as do all movies based on history), but they also give a vivid visual sense of England in the 16th century. A British "docudrama" miniseries from 2017 titled *Elizabeth I* makes an earnest effort to stay factual.

As with so many of the terms discussed in this chapter, the names of historical periods can lose their meaning with the passage of time. I was born and grew up in the postwar era, but as World War II fades into history and as more recent wars erupt, the term postwar is less widely understood. ("Which war are you talking about, Pops?") Also, some labels can seem more arbitrary than others. Only 16th-century England under the reign of Elizabeth I wears the tag Elizabethan, for example. *Elizabethan* doesn't describe the worlds of late-16th-century China (Ming) or late-16th-century Peru (ruled by the Spanish). Yet Victorian, a term for the period 1837–1901, when Victoria was queen and empress of Britain's vast colonial holdings, applies well outside her sphere, especially to styles and cultural attitudes. Victoria never ruled California, for example, but San Francisco is recognized for its Victorian architecture.

Perceiving and avoiding biases

Some people challenge the very concept of history. "Whose history are we talking about?" they ask. If the victors write history, why do we accept those bullies' tainted point of view as being true? What about the victims? What about the indigenous peoples, such as American Indians and Australian Aborigines? What about women? It's not fair that so much of history is so overwhelmingly about white men.

It's true that history as we know it is slanted. History is people writing about people, so prejudice is built in. You have to factor in the biases of the time in which events happened, the biases of the time when they were written down, and the prejudices of the scholars who turn them over and over again decades and often centuries later. I can't change the fact that so many conquerors, monarchs, politicians, soldiers, explorers, and — yes — historians have been men. It's just as true that conventionally taught world history still spends a disproportionate amount of time on Europe, on how it was shaped and how it shaped the other parts of the world: the Americas, Africa, the Middle East, and Asia.

Are there other stories worth telling, other points of view, and other truths? You bet. You'll find some of them in this book, lightly touched upon, just like everything else here. Where I can, I nod toward the realities of our global society as non-Western countries — most notably China, among many — have become major modern economic and political forces, and developing nations are poised to play ever-larger roles in shaping history.

I try not to repeat historical accounts that lie, saying that something didn't happen when it did. Civilizations and nations have always done terrible things in the name of patriotism, nationalism, racial purity, religious righteousness, security, and most of all greed. Those things should be named and remembered. In 1096, for example, bands of Christians, as they gathered to travel east for the First Crusade (a war against Muslims at the behest of the Pope) waged brutal attacks on Jewish communities in Europe. Does it help anything today to pretend that those attacks never happened? No. Neither does it help to pretend that at least 500,000 members of the Tutsi ethnic minority weren't brutally murdered, largely by militias under the Hutu-majority government in the African nation of Rwanda in 1994. It happened.

During World War I, the Ottoman Empire killed at least 1 million Armenian residents in what is today Turkey and deported many more. The Turkish government denied, and continues to deny today, that the wartime "relocation" of Armenians was an attempted genocide.

A few years after that atrocity, in 1921, a white mob in Tulsa, Oklahoma, attacked a prosperous black business district and destroyed it. The violence left hundreds hospitalized, an undetermined number of dead, and as many as 6,000 black people locked up by the National Guard. Tragically, the Tulsa Race Massacre and other attacks like it happened in many places in the United States in the late 19th and early 20th centuries. Yet 100 years after Tulsa, some Americans vigorously argued that the event should be forgotten, that to recall it was too divisive, that this part of history shouldn't be taught. U.S. President Joe Biden, when he visited the site in June 2021, disagreed, saying, "Some injustices are so heinous, so horrific, so grievous, they cannot be buried, no matter how hard people try."

You may want to change the world. Good. It needs changing. Or you may just want to change the history books. Either way, it helps to know what you're up against.

Noticing the Noteworthy and the Notorious

People are contradictory creatures. Many of the most famous people ever were as much bad as good. A great military leader, for example, can also be a cruel murderer. Furthermore, the way that a person is evaluated in history can change from book to book and historian to historian, depending on the point of view of the author and the subject matter being discussed. One book focusing on a king's private life may depict the ruler as being an abusive husband, whereas another oriented toward his impact on his subjects may show that same man as a resolute champion of social reform.

Studying contradictions

King Henry VIII, who ruled pre-UK England from 1509–1547, provides a particularly colorful example of a contradictory character. If you're reading about the history of Christianity, you'll note Henry's role as founder of the Church of England. In military history, his attention to building a strong navy stands as an important factor leading up to the English fleet's celebrated victory over the mighty Spanish Armada in 1588. If you're interested in his personal life, you'll remember him as being handsome and athletic in his youth, but obese and diseased in later life. You'll certainly remember that the most famous thing about Henry is that he married six times and ordered two of his wives to be beheaded for treason.

Like any other person, Henry changed. He contradicted himself. He had good qualities and bad ones. The bad overwhelmed the good as the king got older, but his life still illustrates how multifaceted a historical figure can be. (You can read more about King Henry VIII in chapters 10, 14, and 22.)

Looking at events from different angles

Some of the most fascinating characters in history are those who appear to be heroes from one perspective and villains from another. An example, also from English history, is Guy Fawkes, the man who tried to blow up King James I and both houses of Parliament in 1605. Fawkes was caught red-handed before he could ignite a massive charge that would have blown apart a meeting of the monarch and parliamentarians. He was executed for his crime and remains a British national villain. In the United Kingdom, people still celebrate Bonfire Night every November 5, the anniversary of his capture, by building bonfires and burning effigies.

Yet Fawkes wasn't merely a villain — not just a mad bomber. He was part of a group of Catholic activists who planned this violent act as a last-ditch effort to overcome repressive and brutal anti-Catholic persecution in officially Protestant England. Viewed from that perspective, many English Catholics of the time considered Fawkes to be a freedom fighter.

In a similar vein, George Washington is viewed as one of the greatest Americans ever — the Father of His Country. But events could have unfolded differently. As an American colonist, Washington was technically a subject of the British Crown. If the American Revolution of the 1770s had failed, the king would have been justified in charging Washington with treason, a hanging offense. Thus, he could have gone down in history as a traitor.

REMEMBER

When complex, self-contradictory personalities clash, history's narrative grows beyond multifaceted and becomes multidimensional, if you will. So, if you want to get comfortable with history, don't try too hard to fit any person into any single category.

Verifying virtue

History celebrates the strong, especially those who wielded military or political power. Sometimes, it seems to be exclusively about those who fought — for territory, for defense, for wealth, and so on. Yet there have also been fighters for ideals. Too often, peaceful idealists are left out of history's stories. The exceptions are idealist leaders whose courage resulted in political or cultural change. Prime examples include the following two men:

>> Mohandas Karamchand Gandhi (1869–1948): Known as the Mahatma, or great soul, he fought discrimination against Indian people in South Africa and then, after returning to his home country, fought for India's independence from Great Britain — without striking a literal blow. Gandhi adopted the idea of nonviolent civil disobedience espoused by American writer Henry David Thoreau (1817–62) and in turn inspired American civil-rights leader Dr. Martin Luther King, Jr.

>> Dr. Martin Luther King, Jr. (1929–68): King was inspired by Mahatma Gandhi to use nonviolent protest against racial discrimination in the United States in the 1950s and 1960s. He played a major role in winning popular support for the landmark Civil Rights Act of 1964, legislation that outlawed segregation by race in schools, in the workplace, and at public facilities.

Gandhi and King brought about change and stirred resistance. Each was human, and humans are flawed. Gandhi has been accused, posthumously, of racism toward blacks during the 21 years that he lived in South Africa before returning to India. While King was still alive, the Federal Bureau of Investigation accused him of having extramarital affairs. Yet each man sought to make the world better, and both arguably succeeded to some extent. Had their efforts been entirely in vain, Gandhi and King may have been seen as ineffectual dreamers. (Turn to Chapter 22 for more about Gandhi and King.)

Tracking the Centuries

About 4.5 billion BC: Earth forms.

Maybe 4 million BC: Early hominids (humanlike ancestors) walk on their hind legs. (Some evidence points to evidence of even earlier apelike bipeds.)

About 700,000 BC: Homo erectus walks out of Africa.

About 60,000 BC: Human beings leave behind early examples of art.

479–323 BC: The Classical Greek era gives rise to democracy.

1605: The Gunpowder Plot against England's King James I is foiled when conspirator Guy Fawkes is caught with explosives below the assembly hall of Parliament.

1789: George Washington is elected president of the United States of America.

1948: An assassin kills Mahatma Gandhi.

1968: An assassin kills Dr. Martin Luther King, Jr.

2
Finding Strength in Numbers

Visit the earliest cities, seeing how ancient people learned to work together for mutual benefit and how defensive alliances, commerce, and conquest spread written language, law, and new ways of thinking.

Follow the rise of the Roman Republic, which grew into an empire whose influence is still felt today, and see how other ancient empires rose and fell.

Discover how the Middle Ages, an unsettled time of migrations and regional conflicts, set the stage for modern nations.

See how the rise of Islam reshaped vast parts of Asia, Africa, and even Europe, and how the Crusades and the Silk Road fed Western appetites for trade with India and East Asia.

Follow new sea routes that enabled a handful of European powers to claim pieces of every other habitable continent as components of worldwide empires and get a glimpse of how colonial residents chafed at foreign control.

Find out about the push and pull of globalism as imperial powers, eventually enabled by technologies such as the steam engine and the telegraph, extended their reach even while subject people fought to break their ties with European overlords.

Chapter **4**

Getting Civilized

Human beings lived without cities — with none of what people today call civilization — much longer than people have lived with cities and civilization. Archaeologists can't find much evidence that anything that could be called a city existed until at least 10,000 years ago, although there are older ruins that show the beginnings of cities. The people of 20,000 years ago may have thought about large permanent settlements as impractical — that is, if the idea ever occurred to them — because the way to get food reliably was to remain mobile. If you wanted to eat, you went where the plants were thriving, where the shellfish clung to the river rocks, and where herds and flocks migrated. You followed food sources season by season, and as you wandered, you took care not to merge your band of wanderers with other bands. It wasn't a good idea to have too many mouths to feed.

But even before they fully adopted agriculture, as early as 11,000 years back, humans got together in great numbers for impressive building projects. The ruins at Göbekli Tepe in southern Turkey give evidence. More than 200 T-shape stone pillars, each about 20 feet high, are arranged in 20 circles. There are no nearby ruins of dwellings, so researchers think the circles may have been a site of worship or ritual burial for a hunter-gatherer society. Ruins at Tel Qarmel, in northern Syria, also include stone towers that may be older than farming. That fact makes such finds more impressive — and more mysterious.

When the practice of farming did get people to settle down, communities followed, and grew — villages to towns, towns to cities. By 10,000 years ago, Jericho, a city on today's Palestinian West Bank, was either welcoming travelers who happened by their oasis or chasing them away with rocks and spears thrown from the town's protective walls and tower.

Archaeologists know quite a bit about early civilizations, especially those that rose along major rivers in Iraq and Egypt. It helps that Iraq and Egypt are also where people invented writing. When the written record began, prehistory could grow into history.

Cities developed not just in the Middle East, but also in Pakistan, India, and China, where great civilizations have risen and receded as they interacted with the rest of the world over 3,000 or 4,000 years. They also arose in the Americas, where Europeans and the diseases they carried wiped out advanced native societies in the 16th century AD.

In this chapter, you can find out about early civilizations and how their ruins teach us about people gathering, collaborating, and trading in greater numbers as they recognized shared needs for safety, sustenance, order, and justice. Forms of law, religion, and philosophy developed and led, by a long, circuitous path, to modern ways of thinking and governing. They developed systems of writing, without which we couldn't study history. The world that you and I know started to take shape in those first urban societies as cities grew into city-states, civilizations, and eventually empires.

Building Jericho's Walls for Mutual Defense

The Bible says that Joshua and the Israelites raised a ruckus that brought down the walls of Jericho, a city in Canaan (today's Palestinian-administered West Bank). Jericho appears to be one of the world's oldest cities; it predates even the early civilizations along the Tigris and Euphrates rivers in modern Iraq. What the Bible doesn't say is that Jericho's walls of perhaps 3,200 years ago were built on top of walls that were built on top of walls. (Maybe that's why those walls toppled so easily when Joshua and his posse arrived.) Scientists date the settlement's earliest buildings to as early as 9000 BC, which is about 11,000 years ago. True, Jericho was abandoned and rebuilt maybe 20 times, but when you're talking about thousands of years, what are 20 do-overs?

Scientists say Jericho's living quarters were first round and then in later levels the style changed to rectangular. Researchers can speculate about the residents' lifestyle based on the stuff found lying around—pottery and animal bones stand up to time rather well. Human skulls fitted with realistic plaster faces, for example, may have been creepy reconstructions of dead loved ones or slain enemies.

Most significantly, the walls and tall stone tower of Jericho tell a story. They show researchers that residents worked together for a common goal: to build civic structures that provided community defense. Working together in such an organized way — whether voluntarily or under the orders of a hard-handed ruler — is a sign of civilization.

Unfortunately, archaeologists don't know the names and stories that passed from generation to generation by word of mouth in the earliest centuries of Jericho. You can assume that people gossiped about romances and affairs. Guys no doubt bragged about the size of the fish they almost caught in the Jordan River. They surely teased and trash talked, especially after a little too much wine. And they must have told stories. But civilization didn't wait for a way to write things down so that later generations could read about its beginnings.

Planting Cities along Rivers

Although Jericho grew at a desert oasis (a prehistoric pit stop, if you will), it wasn't far from the River Jordan. Other early cities, those of the best-known early large-scale civilizations, formed along rivers in Mesopotamia (today's Iraq), Egypt, India, and China.

REMEMBER

River floods spread rich, silt-laden mud. Besides being fun to squish around in, this mud built up over eons and enriched the soil of the valleys where organized human society would first take hold on a large scale. Good soil and readily available water enabled primitive farmers to increase their annual yields and feed ever-larger populations. It follows that early cities, early legal codes, and systems of counting and writing — all elements of civilization — would also arise in these river valleys.

Settling between the Tigris and Euphrates

Mesopotamia, the land between the Tigris and Euphrates rivers, was an inviting place to stop and settle. The lower rivers, as they neared the Persian Gulf, formed a great marsh with plentiful fish, birds, and other wildlife. Late Stone Age people lived there in reed huts. As hunter-gatherers and herders who lived around the swamp and in the hills to the north turned increasingly toward the hot new farming lifestyle (a gradual change that probably took thousands of years), the fertile valley to the northwest of the marshland beckoned.

By about 5000 BC, barley and flax farmers dug networks of irrigation canals from the Tigris and Euphrates rivers and their tributaries and built villages along those canals. These communities fueled a hot real estate market, becoming fashionable neighborhoods that grew into about a dozen impressive cities of the Sumerian civilization, followed after 2000 BC by the great city-state of Babylon and its successive empires. (A city-state is a city that's a nation in itself, like modern-day Singapore and Monaco.)

From about 2700–2300 BC, the leading city-state in southern Mesopotamia was Ur, home to the Bible's Abraham. Like other cities in the region, Ur was built of mud bricks. Besides fertilizing the fields and inspiring epic mud-wrestling battles, the mud of the river valley proved the best building material in an area with little stone or wood.

Getting agricultural in Africa

Northern Africa, where the great Sahara Desert is today, was once fertile grassland with generous rainfall. It was a good place for animals to graze and a great place for nomadic hunters, gatherers, and herders to wander, stop to try a little farming, and establish villages.

REMEMBER

The switch to farming was anything but sudden. From their experience gathering edible grass seeds, tribal people knew that if there was enough rainfall, the ground where they beat or trampled seeds to remove the inedible hulls would eventually become green with new growth of that same grass. Having seen stray seeds sprouting, over time people tried spreading some of the fattest seeds on the ground in the hope of growing more of the same.

FLOODING ON A MYTHIC SCALE

The early cities of Mesopotamia benefitted from rivers and the mud that periodic floods spread over the land. Yet floodwaters could rise disastrously high. Between the ruins of one Sumerian city and the ruins of the city that came before it, 20th-century archaeologists found a deep layer of dried mud — evidence of a terrible flood. To the Sumerians, a flood on that scale — one that swept away cities — must have seemed to be end of their world. Mud tablets (the first books) found in the ruins of the Mesopotamian city of Nineveh contain *The Epic of Gilgamesh*, which includes a story of how the gods decided to wipe out mankind with a flood, but one man named Utnapishtim, his family, and his animals were saved. Is this the same story as the Bible's account of Noah and the Flood? Not exactly, but many scholars think the tale of Utnapishtim may be an earlier version of the same legend.

Farming worked only if the people came back to the places where they planted the seeds to harvest the crop. Eventually, they stuck around. With the promise of a regular food supply, it was easier for nomadic people to stop wandering and establish roots in agricultural villages (pun intended).

TECHNICAL STUFF

Something ironic happened in North Africa over the thousands of years when the agricultural lifestyle was taking hold. The weather slowly changed so that it rained less. Grasslands gave way to sand. Over many generations, fewer seeds sprouted, and fewer sprouts matured; ultimately, villages rose and fell without people being aware of what was happening to the world around them. As the climate changed, more and more folks gathered up the kids (and the goats, assuming that they'd caught onto that crazy new domestic-animal trend) and headed into Asia and the Middle East. In northeastern Africa, they crowded into a sliver of land with a terrific source of water: the Nile.

Assembling Egypt

Villages sprang up in the Nile Valley as early as 5000 BC. A thousand years later, people in the valley were burying their dead with meticulous care and ornamentation, a trend that led to big things, such as Egypt's pyramids. Villages and towns became cities that eventually came together into larger civilizations until the long river valley held just two nations: Upper Egypt and Lower Egypt. Then, around 3100 BC, a great king named Menes (also known as Narmer, although that may have been the name of a slightly later king) united Egypt and built a capital at Memphis. The city in Tennessee is named after it.

Going up the river into Kush

Further up the Nile (or further down in Africa, if you're looking at a map), another culture developed in Upper Nubia, or Kush (where Sudan is today). Influenced by Egypt's culture, the Kushites built pyramid-shaped tombs in the Egyptian style. Egypt ruled the Kushites from 2000–1600 BC and again from 1500–900 BC. Later, in the eighth century BC, the Kushites turned on their northern neighbors and brought down Egypt's ruling dynasty, ruling over Egypt until about 671 BC.

Giving way as new civilizations rise

To the people of early civilizations, their cities must have seemed superior to rural villages and nomadic tribes (plenty of which still wandered the hinterlands), and incredibly powerful and secure. Yet the early civilizations, like every civilization since, faltered, splintered, succumbed, or evolved as political and military fortunes rose and fell.

A good example of an evolving civilization is Babylon, which grew into an empire around 1894 BC as King Sumuabum conquered surrounding cities and villages. His successor, Hammurabi, extended Babylon's lands from the Persian Gulf to parts of Assyria before he died in 1750 BC. Babylon's first empire (another arose 1,000 years later, and I talk about it later in this section) lasted almost 300 years. But in 1595 BC, a fierce neighboring people, the Hittites, conquered the city of Babylon and its lands.

The Hittite Empire spread across Asia Minor, encompassing a huge area of what are today central and eastern Turkey and extending into today's Syria. Then, around 1200 BC, marauders smashed and burned Hittite cities so thoroughly that eventually, nobody remembered who had left carvings such as the twin lions flanking what must have been a grand ceremonial entrance. It took 19th- and 20th-century archaeologists to rediscover these once-mighty people.

The Hittites were major rivals, and later major allies, of Egypt. The two superpowers pitted their armies against each other at the Battle of Kadesh in Northern Syria in 1275 BC. A few decades later, the nations were at peace. Pharaoh Ramses II married a daughter of Hittite King Hattusilis III.

The Assyrians, a common enemy of the Hittites and Egyptians, built a great civilization too, centered on the upper Tigris River. Assyrians ruled much of Mesopotamia between 2600 and 612 BC. These people, or at least their rulers, appear to have been a bloodthirsty lot. Carvings on their palace walls feature scenes of enemies being beheaded. In Assyrian writings, kings boasted about how many captives they crucified, impaled, and skinned alive.

PERILS OF POWER

From the time Egypt became one nation, its increasingly powerful, ever-richer ruler also underwent a transformation. More than a man, the pharaoh was a living god.

Being a god wasn't as great as it sounds, though — at least, not at first. Early kings of unified Egypt had to prove themselves fit to stay on top. A king who failed a rigorous annual physical challenge was considered no longer able to provide for the state and so was killed by priests in ritual sacrifice. Understandably, considering who made the rules, this practice disappeared by about 2650 BC.

Babylon emerged as the center of a new empire in the late seventh century BC, after the Chaldeans — a Semitic people related to Arabs and Jews — moved into the ancient city and conquered lands stretching to the Mediterranean. This territory was the empire ruled by Nebuchadnezzar II (605–562 BC), whose conquest of Jerusalem you can find in Chapter 20. The empire of Babylonia fell in the Persian conquest of 539–538 BC, but the city of Babylon remained an urban center for more than 200 years. (Alexander the Great died there in 323 BC.)

Heading east to the Indus and Yellow Rivers

Early civilization wasn't limited to the lands around the Mediterranean. Just as the Tigris, Euphrates, and Nile rivers gave rise to cities, so the upper Indus River (in lands now divided between Pakistan and India) and the Yellow River in China provided ideal environments for villages to grow into cities in the East.

Plumbing the mysteries of ancient Indus Valley sites

The cities on the Indus River, including sites in modern Pakistan at places such as Harappa and Mohenjo-Daro, surprised archaeologists who found them for a couple of reasons:

» As with the Hittite cities, nobody remembered, for a long time, that the Indus River cities had ever existed. Although the sites have been located, the origin of the people who built and lived there is still uncertain.

» These communities of 2500 BC had streets laid out in a grid of rectangles, like New York City, and houses in Mohenjo-Daro boasted bathrooms and toilets with drains feeding into municipal sewers. Writings found among the ruins indicate that the Indus Valley was home to a literate society that probably spoke an early Dravidian language related to many languages still spoken in parts of South Asia.

At its height, the Indus civilization probably covered an area bigger than Mesopotamia and Egypt put together. (See figure 4-1). Mohenjo-Daro was rebuilt and rebuilt again over the course of what some scientists think were centuries of geologic change that plugged the Indus River, altered its course, and put successive layers of houses underwater. Others say that earthquakes and massive flooding ended the civilization around 1700 BC.

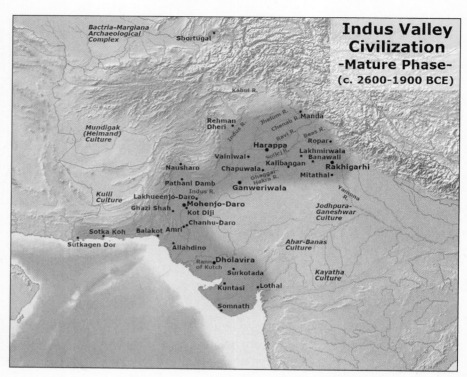

FIGURE 4-1:
The Indus Valley
Civilization was in
what is now India
and Pakistan.

Nomadic herding tribes from the Iranian plateau arrived in northwestern India around then as well, and they seem to have displaced the people of the Indus cities. Raiders eventually destroyed Mohenjo-Daro, by then in steep decline. The newcomers brought an Indo-European language (a distant ancestor of modern India's Hindi, as well as English and many other tongues) and the roots of what became Indian religion and culture.

REMEMBER

Historians have used the term Aryan to mean the people who displaced the Indus River civilization and gave rise to later Indian culture, but Aryan is a widely misunderstood word because of the way German Nazis misused it to refer to light-skinned Caucasians. Properly applied, *Aryan* refers strictly to speakers of long-ago Indo-European languages; it has nothing to do with ethnicity or physical type.

PULLING PREHISTORY FROM A BRICK PILE

Harappa, perhaps the dominant city of the sophisticated Indus Valley Civilization, was a mess when archaeologists started picking through it in 1920, because 19th-century railroad builders had mined the site for bricks to build a roadbed. The engineers knew that the bricks were old, but they couldn't have guessed that they were 4,000 years old. They left the hole in the ground, so local villagers helped themselves to the bricks too.

In 1922, two years after the scientists at Harappa began to understand what the site had been, an Indian archaeologist tackled another mound of brick rubble and river silt 400 miles away. He thought he'd found an abandoned Buddhist monastery. Instead, he unearthed the riches of Mohenjo-Daro, a virtually untouched ruin of great villas, public baths, and dazzlingly sophisticated sculpture. Since then, archaeologists have explored more than 150 Indus Valley sites.

Separating history from myth: China's oldest dynasties

A river also runs through the beginnings of Chinese civilization: the powerful Yellow River. Around 4000 BC, people started farming (first millet and later rice) along this northernmost of China's major rivers. Chinese legends attribute the nation's origins to semimystical, demigod monarchs, including a Yellow Emperor of about 2700 BC, three "Sage Kings" or "August Rulers" (from 2350 BC), and a Hsia Dynasty that lasted until 1766 BC. Because historians have no proof that these figures are anything but legend, they credit the later house of Shang (also called Yin) as being the first dynasty to bring together warring Yellow River city-states in the 16th century BC.

TECHNICAL STUFF

Under the Shang, the early Chinese charted the movement of the sun and stars to predict seasons, kept astronomical records to rival those of the Egyptians, and devised a nifty 12-month calendar. The Shang Dynasty lasted until 1027 BC, when it was succeeded by the Zhou Dynasty.

Isolated from Asia Minor and Africa, where the Sumerians and Egyptians invented writing, the Chinese developed their own kind of pictograph symbols. Archaeologists have found characters on Shang Dynasty artifacts that are essentially the roots of the same writing system that China uses today. China's historical writings outshine the records of any other culture in volume, detail, and continuity. For the BC period, China boasts 26 major official written dynastic histories.

Coming of Age in the Americas

By 2000 BC, good-size communities with public buildings existed in South America, specifically in the Andes mountain range of what's now Peru. Archaeologists have found evidence, for example, that the people near modern Lima irrigated their farmland and built a stone pyramid at nearby El Paraiso around 1800 BC.

In Peru's northern highlands, the Chavín people started building cities around 1000 BC. Their culture thrived for 500 years, but they didn't leave many clues for the ages. The Chavín may have traded with the Olmec, who had even earlier urban centers, dating from about 1200 BC, along the southern Gulf of Mexico in today's Mexican states of Veracruz and Tabasco. The Olmec left huge stone heads that may be portraits of their kings (albeit not very flattering ones). They also seem to have passed down their culture and social structure to later, more elaborate civilizations, such as the Maya (more on them in Chapter 5).

Keeping Records on the Way to Writing and Reading

Just as the practice of farming led to the founding of villages, towns, and then cities, it gave rise to record keeping and disciplines including astronomy and math.

In Egypt, for example, practical scientific and engineering methods arose as ways to keep track of planting seasons. The Nile flooded in predictable annual patterns, so farmers could calculate when the water would rise. They studied the sun and the stars, and over centuries, Egyptians developed an accurate calendar with 365 days in a year. In Mesopotamia, too, practical considerations such as keeping track of seasons, trade transactions, lawmaking, and the invention of that most-treasured aspect of modern life — large-scale government bureaucracy — gave rise to record keeping. Record keeping soon led to more general writing and reading, without which you wouldn't be doing what you're doing right now.

Planning pyramids

Measuring and math came in handy for building Egypt's pyramids, which are mind-boggling feats of engineering. Herodotus the Greek, a historian of more than 2,400 years ago, wrote that 100,000 men worked for 20 years on Egypt's Great Pyramid at Giza. That may be an exaggeration, though, because the Great Pyramid was already more than 2,000 years old when Herodotus wrote about it.

Building pyramids and keeping calendars would be almost impossible without a way to note things. As the Sumerians had a little earlier, the Egyptians developed their own way of recording information in the form of pictures (called pictographic writing), which evolved into a kind of writing called hieroglyphics (medu netcher or "words of the gods" in ancient Egyptian). Then came written stories, recorded history, love poems, and (with a few steps in between) email spam.

An important way for the Egyptians to impose order on their world, hieroglyphics also became the key for much later people to find out about the Egyptians. I tell you about the Rosetta Stone, the modern world's key to deciphering hieroglyphics, in Chapter 24.

Laying down laws and love songs

In Mesopotamia, the Sumerians' pictographs (beginning a bit earlier than the Egyptians') evolved into symbols that represented words, syllables, and eventually even phonetic sounds. Cuneiform, the Mesopotamian way of writing with the sharpened end of a reed in wet mud, spread all over the Middle East.

Also like Egyptian hieroglyphics, cuneiform writing opened new vistas of early history in the 19th century AD, when European scholars figured out how to read cuneiform documents such as royal edicts, business letters, and even love songs.

Cuneiform writings include early codes of laws. Babylonian King Hammurabi enacted one of the best-known in the 18th century BC. Here's a sample: "If the robber is not caught, the man who has been robbed shall make claim . . . and the town and its governor shall give back to him everything that he has lost."

ABCs IN BC

When scribes started using symbols to represent pieces of words — first syllables and then individual sounds — alphabetic writing began. At first, alphabetic writing was a form of shorthand, even though it wasn't actually shorter, just easier to write than the pictograph style, which required a different symbol for every word. With an alphabet, scribes were able to combine fewer symbols to make many words.

Shaping the World Ever After

Throughout this book, you find references to Greeks who lived between about 479 and 323 BC. Their ideas shaped world civilization, leading to modern science, shaping influential schools of philosophy and religion, and setting precedents for democratic government.

Before I get to these Classical Greeks in this section, you need to know about their world, which is ancient but not as ancient as the earliest Mesopotamian and Egyptian civilizations.

Building a Persian Empire

By the seventh and sixth centuries BC, the Middle East had been crawling with civilizations great and small for centuries. Before the Persians rose up and asserted themselves, they were ruled by another conqueror: the Medes. Famous for crack-shot archery, the Medes came from Media. Media (also spelled Medea) was in northern Iran.

In 512 BC, Cyrus, a young Persian king from the Achaemenid family, got tired of paying tribute to his grandfather, the king of the Medes. Cyrus gathered up his troops and turned the tables on Gramps, after which he built the Achaemenid Persian Empire. This empire ruled western Asia for two centuries, taking in an area stretching from western India to North Africa and even into Eastern Europe. Around 500 BC, one of the empire's greatest kings, Darius I, built a 1,500-mile highway from Susa in Iran to Ephesus in Turkey, with stations providing fresh horses on the way for messengers (much as the Pony Express did in America in the 19th century AD).

Also in Turkey, the independent-minded Ionian Greeks in coastal city-states stood up to the Persians. Originally from Greece, across the Aegean Sea, these Ionians spoke Greek; organized their society along Greek lines; and looked to Greece, not Persia, as their homeland. With support from mainland Greek cities such as Athens, they rebelled against Persian rule in 499 BC. Darius I sent an army to punish Athens for helping the revolt, setting off the Persian Wars. Although the Greeks eventually won, bad feelings remained and flared up again more than 150 years later, when Alexander the Great headed the Greek forces.

Growing toward Greekness

Long before the Persian Empire, prehistoric cultures grew and flourished in Greece and on the islands of the Aegean Sea. The Minoans had a complex economy and government on Crete and other islands in the area until about 1450 BC, when Minoan traders suddenly disappeared from Egyptian trade accounts. (For speculation about why, see Chapter 2.) Mycenaeans living in 13th-century BC Greece also had a sophisticated government and culture.

Both civilizations were predecessors and possibly ancestors of the Classical Greeks — called Classical not because of their taste in music (Mozart wouldn't be born for a long, long time), but because so much of what they thought, said, and wrote has survived. Classical Greek ideas, literature, and architecture — not to mention toga parties and those cool letters on the fronts of fraternity and sorority houses — are still around in the 21st century AD.

By routes direct and indirect, the Greeks — especially their philosophical approach to examining the world critically — spread all over the Mediterranean and then down through history, profoundly influencing successive cultures.

Adapting to the lay of the Greek land

Sea and mountains cut up the Greek homeland, separating people instead of bringing widespread populations together. Yet Greek growers gathered for trade, and from marketplaces, they built cities in mainland valleys and on isolated islands. Greek citizens gathered and lived in these independent cities, and they did something unusual for this stage of history: They talked openly about how the independent city-state (called a polis) should be run.

REMEMBER

A city-state is an independent city, not politically part of a larger country. Many city-states, however, ruled broader lands. Athens, one of the best-known Greek city-states, became capital of an empire in the fifth century BC. The Greeks were great sailors who founded new city-states not just in Greece and on the Aegean Islands, as shown in Figure 4-2, but eventually all over the Mediterranean Sea. They settled in places as far away as Sicily and southern Italy. These far-flung city-states were types of colonies in that they preserved and spread Greek language and culture, but they weren't colonial in the political sense. That is, the remote city-states were often independent. If adventurers from the Greek city-state of Corinth founded a city-state hundreds of miles away, that new city-state wasn't necessarily a Corinthian possession.

Greek citizens, whether living in Greece, Turkey, or Italy, were free to an extent unheard of in imperial societies such as Persia's. Most Greek citizens were small farmers for whom freedom meant being able to grow and market their crops without interference. Citizen was far from being a universal status, of course; one had to be a man (never a woman) of Greek parentage and language to be a citizen. (Foreigners who didn't speak Greek, whose languages sounded like so much "bar bar bar" to the Greeks, were dismissed as barbarians.)

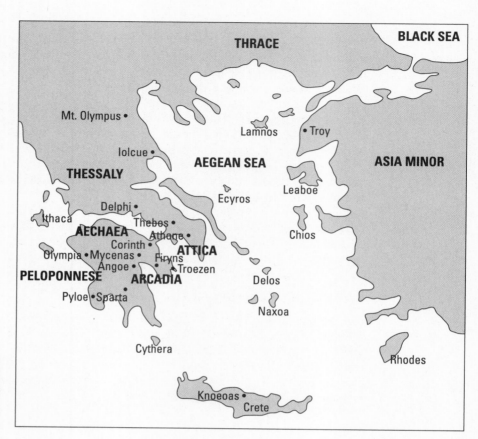

Yet among free Greek citizens, the custom of asking questions — about the way the city was run, about the legends of their gods, or about the way nature works — led to exciting advancements. Inquisitiveness fueled philosophy and thought about nature. Mathematics, astronomy, physics, and even biology became issues to theorize about and problems to solve.

Finding strength in common culture

The Greek city-states built empires based on influence and alliance more than conquest, but they did fight one another. Sparta, famous for single-minded military ferocity, began the long, exhausting Peloponnesian War of 431–404 BC because Spartans objected to what they saw as imperialism on the part of Athens — especially under powerful Athenian leader Pericles. Sparta brought down Athens, center of learning and beauty, and Thebes tamed Sparta. (I talk about the Greek style of fighting in Chapter 16.)

Yet the Athenians, Spartans, Thebans, and others in Greek city-states never forgot that they were Greeks; they spoke dialects of the same language, worshipped the same gods, and grew up hearing the epic poems of Homer. (*The Iliad* and *The Odyssey* were a combination of holy scripture, Star Wars-type saga, and *World History For Dummies* of the time.) Different city-states also gathered for athletic competitions (the original Olympics). When Greeks were threatened by barbarians, as in the wars against the mighty Persian kings Darius I in 490 BC and his son Xerxes I in 480 BC, the city-states worked together, if only temporarily.

The 2006 film *300* introduces elements of fantasy into its depiction of the Battle of Thermopylae in 480 BC, a landmark conflict of the Persian Wars. *300* depicts the king of Sparta and his tiny force of 300 troops standing up to the million-strong Persian army of Xerxes I.

Making Alexander great

The Greeks' fierce, contentious independence made them vulnerable over the period between 359 and 337 BC as a king to their north, Philip of Macedon, used a combination of military force and aggressive diplomacy to muscle in on successive city-states. Macedon (the Macedonian region of modern Greece) wasn't a mighty empire like Persia, but a small, mountainous country. Yet the Greeks failed to unite against Philip. He conquered, coerced, and negotiated peace treaties with individual city-states until he was in position to set himself up as protector of Greece. Philip formed the city-states into a league that helped his son put together the biggest empire yet.

Philip planned to lead the Greeks against Persia as payback for Persia's invasions of more than a century before, but he was murdered before he could mount the expedition. Some historians say that his wife, Olympias, paid the killer so that her son, Alexander, could succeed his dad. Nineteen-year-old Alexander, well educated in war and philosophy (one of his tutors was the Athenian philosopher Aristotle), joined her in killing other candidates for the throne of Macedon.

His power at home secure, Alexander quickly disabused the Greeks of any notion that they would have an easy time resisting him, nearly destroying Thebes in the process (not to be confused with the ancient Egyptian capital also called Thebes).

Director Oliver Stone's 2004 film *Alexander*, starring Colin Farrell in the title role, is an ambitious attempt to trace Alexander the Great's entire life, from his difficult relationship with Philip and his complex feelings for his mother through his greatest conquests and beyond. As always with movies, it's more entertainment than education.

Extending an empire to the farthest reaches

In a career marked by one victory after another, Alexander the Great built an empire beyond the limits of what had been the known world. By the middle of 331 BC, Alexander and his Macedonian-Greek army defeated two great Persian forces, the second led by King Darius III.

Although he was a brilliant, fearless, and inventive warrior, Alexander didn't do it all by force or ingenuity. The Egyptians, conquered earlier by the Persians, gladly chose Alexander as their leader instead. When the young conqueror marched into Mesopotamia, ancient cities opened their gates to him and took him as king. When Darius III was out of the way (murdered by his own men), the Persians fell down before Alexander and made him feel almost as though he were a god. He liked that treatment, but his officers didn't.

Alexander marched on beyond the frontiers of Persia, clashing with Afghan tribes, founding cities, and crossing the Himalayas. In India, his forces prevailed against the battle elephants of King Porus. Finally, his troops refused to go any farther. Returning as far as Babylon, Alexander died of a fever (perhaps malaria) at age 32 in 323 BC.

Leaving a legacy

Alexander's clout didn't die with him. Legend says that his body was preserved in honey while his followers spent more than two years building an ornate funeral wagon. When the wagon was ready, mourners loaded the imperial casket onto it and began a ponderous, 1,500-mile funeral procession to Macedon for burial. They never got there. Alexander's General Ptolemy, appointed governor of Egypt, diverted the procession to Alexandria, one of the cities the conqueror had named for himself. There, the possession of Alexander's corpse gave Ptolemy the status to become ruler in his own right. He founded Egypt's Ptolemaic Dynasty, which continued until his descendant Cleopatra VII died in 30 BC.

REMEMBER

One of Alexander's enduring achievements is that he spread the infectious Greek way of questioning and thinking about the world. He and his largely-Greek forces disseminated Greek attitudes. Alexandria, Egypt, became a center of Hellenistic culture, meaning that Greek-influenced ideas and language networked beyond the widespread Greek city-states and lasted into much later eras.

Rationality, democracy, individualism, citizenship, free debate, and the inquiry born of Greek-style philosophy percolated through other cultures. Some anthropologists, and some historians too, like to call this "cultural diffusion" or "transcultural diffusion." Those terms just mean that ideas — including philosophy, but including technology, cuisine, and fashion — migrate to new places as diverse groups of people come into contact with each other. After Alexander, philosophy became a cornerstone of science, and the scientific approach became a primary tool for interpreting reality. In that way, the Classical Greeks still exert a powerful influence.

Developing Cultures Abounding

Over the thousands of years since the first cities and civilizations rose and spread in the Middle East and Asia, many other cultures in the following areas took significant strides. Here are just a few examples:

>> **Africa:** In what's now northern Nigeria, the Nok people cleared tropical rainforest for farmland, using iron-bladed axes and hoes, around 600 BC. The Nok were also sculptors, making realistic figurines of terra cotta.

>> **Ireland, Scotland, Denmark, France, and Spain:** Hundreds of years before the first pyramids in Egypt, people in Western Europe built communal graves out of stone and earth. Surviving examples date back to 3500 BC; some particularly good ones remain in Orkney, a group of islands off the coast of Scotland, and at Newgrange, Ireland. Europeans of the late Stone Age also left entire villages built of stone. More spectacular yet are the huge stone circles called megaliths (or "big rocks") that these people erected. Stonehenge, the most famous, was raised in southern England between 3000 and 2000 BC.

>> **Japan:** People lived in small villages on the mountainous islands that would become Japan as early as 9000 BC, mostly near the ocean and along rivers. They transitioned from a hunter–gatherer lifestyle to agriculture, first growing vegetables and millet. These people were potters, too, and their cord-pattern pots give the period its name, *Jomon*. By the end of the Jomon era, around 300 BC, Japanese potters showed a broader view of the world as they borrowed Chinese-style decorations. Another Chinese innovation, rice growing, also spread to Japan.

Tracking the Centuries

9000 BC: People live in a walled community at Jericho, a crossroads town at a spring–fed oasis near the Jordan River. It would grow into a city.

About 5000 BC: Barley and flax farmers dig networks of irrigation canals and build villages along those canals between the Tigris and Euphrates rivers in what would become Iraq.

About 3100 BC: King Menes unites Upper Egypt and Lower Egypt into one kingdom with its capital at Memphis.

2000 BC: Egypt conquers the neighboring Kush culture to the south.

About 1700 BC: Earthquakes and sudden mass flooding may be responsible for ending the sophisticated Indus River Valley civilization.

512 BC: Cyrus, a young Persian king, leads troops against his grandfather, king of the Medes.

404 BC: Sparta defeats Athens in the 27-year Peloponnesian War.

323 BC: While staying in Babylon, Alexander the Great comes down with a sudden fever and dies.

» Bringing states together in a united Indian empire

» Uniting and organizing China

» Establishing the Maya and other empires in the Americas

Chapter 5

Rising and Falling Empires

The Roman city-state's origins are obscure and lost to history, if not to legend. But the history of Rome as it grew into one of the greatest empires the world has ever seen is anything but obscure. Even in 20 books this size, I probably wouldn't be able to fit in everything that's known about the Roman Empire and its people — let alone its pervasive legacy.

In this chapter, you'll follow the way Rome grew from a city-state ruled by a king to a republic to a vast empire and how that empire eventually deteriorated into a divided, crumbling political ruin. And you can find out about how Rome left such a history and a lasting mark on the world that sometimes, it almost seems that the Roman Empire was the only great empire of the final century BC and the early centuries AD. But you'll also encounter other powerful empires that rose and fell in the Middle East, Asia, and in the Americas, far away and isolated from the Roman sphere. Imperial expansion dominated much of the world.

Rome's Ascent and Demise

From its legendary beginnings to its fractured demise, the Roman civilization had a certain pizzazz that has captured the imagination of not just historians, but also everybody who's fascinated by human achievement, military adventure, political intrigue, and tragedy. Shakespeare was among those who have been drawn to its stories (see more in the later section "Crossing the Rubicon"), and so am I.

What's the attraction? You can look at Rome's long rise and descent from any number of angles and marvel at the complexity and sophistication, not to mention the cruelty and corruption of this long-lived culture. In the brief glimpses that follow, you can find clues to what fascinates so many of us with the Roman civilization.

Forming the Roman Republic

Roman legend says that the half-god, half-mortal Romulus, a son of the Greek war god Mars, built the city of Rome on the Tiber River in 753 BC and ruled as its first king. The legend also says that a female wolf suckled baby Romulus and his twin brother Remus, whom Romulus later murdered. Historians tend to disagree, especially about the wolf, and put the founding of Rome a bit later, around 645 BC. (For more about Romulus and Remus, see Chapter 19.)

Although he may not have tasted wolf's milk or killed his twin, legend credits Romulus as being the first of seven kings who ruled Rome as a city-state, not unlike the Greek city-states around the Mediterranean (which you can find out about in Chapter 4), until 509 BC. That year was when King Tarquinius Superbus got on the wrong side of his advisory body of citizen-magistrates, the Roman Senate.

The Senate gave Tarquinius Superbus the boot and set up a republican system of government designed to prevent a tyrant from ever misruling Rome again. Two consuls, elected annually, served as administrative executives under the supervision of the Senate. The republic system worked, bringing the stability that Rome needed as it grew. And did it grow.

TECHNICAL STUFF

Rome borrowed freely from other cultures — a pantheon of gods from the Greeks; Athenian-style democracy; and metalworking technology from an older Italian culture, the Etruscans. (I talk about cultural diffusion in Chapter 4.) Yet the Roman civilization did so much with what it borrowed that you can't overestimate its impact, both in its own time and since. You can feel Rome's influence even today. For one thing, the Roman language, Latin, is the foundation of not just Italian, but also of French, Spanish, Portuguese, and Romanian. Latin also left a deep impression on non-Latin languages, such as English. Even after Latin fell out of everyday use, it remained a unifying language of learning, particularly in medicine and science.

Earning citizenship

Romans lived in a stratified society organized by class (see the nearby "Roman class" sidebar for more). Opportunities and employment were strictly defined by birth, just as they were in many other cultures dominated by privileged aristocrats. Yet Roman custom also offered ways for non-citizens to improve their status or that of their children.

Rome allowed foreigners and slaves to become citizens. This opportunity was highly limited when compared to today's standards but progressive for its time. Giving the Roman Empire's lowborn and conquered people a chance at inclusion in society helped win those people's loyalty to Rome, which added greatly to Rome's growth and resilience.

Democratic Athens offered no such opportunities for outsiders. (See more about Athens in chapters 4 and 11.) In a Greek city-state, a slave could be granted freedom, but the best he could hope for was lowly resident-alien status; he was unlikely to develop loyalty to a state that excluded him. (And I do mean him. Women couldn't even dream of citizenship.)

Why so exclusive? Greeks valued Greekness, looking down on those who didn't speak their language and worship their gods. But the exclusion was also economic. The city-states of rocky Greece were usually short of resources, especially good farmland. Granting citizenship meant increasing the number of people who had a direct claim on the food supply. Making slaves citizens was expensive and would have meant increasing the number of voters, which may have caused unwanted power shifts.

In fertile Italy, on the other hand, food was relatively abundant, so shares weren't such an issue. Also, blocks of votes rather than individual votes determined Roman elections, so an extra vote in a block had little potential impact.

REMEMBER

Rome offered slaves the real possibility of earning citizenship, but only in the lowest class of citizenship: plebeian. Plebeians, however, could hope for their children to rise to a higher class. Further, Rome united other cities in its empire by bringing conquered people into the fold. Roman officers propped up local aristocrats in newly taken provinces, making them dependent on Rome's support. The defeated country's men were enlisted in the next conflict and rewarded with part of the profits from the almost-inevitable conquest. Loyalty was lucrative.

Expanding the empire

By the third century BC, Rome had only one major rival for the position of top dog in the western Mediterranean: the city of Carthage, a rich trading port in North Africa.

Before 1000 BC, the Phoenicians sailed out of what is now Lebanon to expand trade opportunities. On the north African coast, in present-day Tunisia, they established the port city of Carthage. Around 600 BC, Carthage became so rich and populous that it cast off Phoenician rule.

ROMAN CLASS

Plebeian, which refers to a lowly person, is a word you may still run across. In Rome, the plebeian belonged to the second-lowest of four social classes. The lowest was the slave, who had no rights. Plebeians were a little better off, in that they were free, but beyond that, they had no clout. Next in the hierarchy were the equestrians, or riders. Equestrians were rich people — rich men, actually — of a class that rode horses when they were called to fight for Rome. They weren't rich enough to have much power, though. For real power, you had to be among the patricians, or nobles. Patrician is a word that still gets used, too. Now, as back then, it's applied to people of wealthy families who are accustomed to having authority.

Carthage and Rome fought three Punic Wars from 264–146 BC. (Punic comes from Punicus, a Latin word for *Phoenician.*) Carthage should have quit while it was ahead. In the first of these wars, Rome won the island of Sicily, its first overseas province. In the second Punic War, Carthage lost the rest of its far-flung territories and became a dependent ally of Rome. The alliance was never sweet, and then it really soured: The third Punic War began, and Rome destroyed Carthage.

To the east, Rome fought the Hellenistic kingdoms, Greek-influenced nations carved out of Alexander's empire. Romans took Macedon, Greece, Asia Minor, and the eastern shore of the Mediterranean, eventually including Judah, founded by the Jewish leader Judas the Maccabee in 168 BC. In 63 BC, the Romans made Jerusalem the capital of Roman Judea.

REMEMBER

The empire pushed north into Gaul, to the Rhine and the Danube rivers, growing so big that administering the vast territory became too difficult for the republic, which had an unwieldy, often-contentious government. Turmoil created the opportunity for a military genius to step forward.

Crossing the Rubicon

Gaius Julius Caesar (better known as Julius Caesar) was a Roman aristocrat and military commander. His far-flung conquests extended Rome's growing dominion, and he was ambitious for himself as well as for his country.

In the first century BC, Rome desperately needed leadership. Decades of uneasy peace, fierce political rivalries, and widespread bitterness had followed a series of civil wars. Quarreling politicians fighting for power rendered the Roman Senate useless. In 60 BC, three leaders formed the First Triumvirate (rule by three) to restore order. The Triumvirate was an unofficial arrangement and kept secret at first, but it dominated Roman politics for most of a decade. The three co-rulers were Marcus Licinius Crassus; Gnaeus Pompeius Magnus (widely remembered as Pompey); and Julius Caesar, the youngest. Caesar was especially feared by politicians who opposed the Triumvirate, in part because he was a nephew of the late Gaius Marius, who had served seven times as consul, the top administrative post in the Roman government. (A consul was a bit like a combination prime minister and attorney general.)

Caesar's victories in the Gallic Wars (58–50 BC) pushed the empire's borders all the way to Europe's Atlantic seaboard. He also led Rome's first incursion into Britain in 55 BC. (The Iron Age tribes he encountered there are remembered as Britons, ancestors of today's Welsh, Scottish and Irish.) While Caesar was away, Crassus died, and the First Triumvirate fell apart. Pompey sought to consolidate his own power, standing as Caesar's rival instead of his ally.

Returning home in 49 BC, Caesar started another civil war by defying a law that said Roman troops had to stay north of the Rubicon River, in today's northern Italy. The law was intended to prevent a military leader from taking over the republic by force. Caesar led his troops across the stream and fought other Roman leaders for the prize of absolute power in battles that continued until 45 BC. (Rubicon has meant *point of no return* ever since.) His rivals defeated, Caesar took the title Dictator for Life.

Caesar wasn't technically an emperor, but his reign marked the end of the Roman Republic and the beginning of the age of emperors. Rome's ruling families didn't take this change lightly. The dictator liked elaborate compliments and formal tributes, making his enemies think he was aiming for not just regal status, but also a kind of imperial divinity. Many Romans were upset by what Caesar was doing to their republic, and they still talked about how the Roman Senate had kicked out Tarquinius Superbus, the last Roman king. Two senators, Brutus and Cassius, plotted Caesar's assassination and carried it out successfully.

England's William Shakespeare wrote a terrific play on the subject of Caesar's downfall 1,600 years after it happened. If you've ever said "Beware the Ides of March" or "Friends, Romans, countrymen, lend me your ears," you've quoted Shakespeare's *Julius Caesar*. Director Joseph L. Mankiewicz made a movie version of the play in 1953, starring 1950s screen sensation Marlon Brando holding his own alongside Shakespearean heavyweight John Gielgud. It's not as much fun as a top-flight stage production of the play, but the movie could be a lot worse.

Many more years of civil war followed Caesar's assassination. Caesar's cousin and general, Marcus Antonius (Mark Antony), was in position to emerge with supreme power. But Antony's formidable rival, Caesar's great-nephew and adopted son, Octavian, came out on top in 31 BC with a win over the combined forces of Antony and his partner (romantic and political), the Egyptian Queen Cleopatra, at Actium off the coast of Greece.

Empowering the emperor

Like his predecessor, Octavian didn't call himself a king or emperor, although that's what he was — the undisputed ruler of the Roman world. Instead, he took the relatively modest title principate (first citizen). His modesty would have seemed sincere if he hadn't also gotten the Senate to rename him Augustus, which means *exalted*. Augustus already bore the family name Caesar. Both Augustus and Caesar became titles handed down to successive Roman emperors.

Augustus cut back the unbridled expansionism of late-republican days and set territorial limits: the Rhine and Danube rivers in Europe and the Euphrates River in Asia. The empire was stable. It annexed no territory until it conquered Britain in 44 AD. Then, in 106 AD, Emperor Trajan took Dacia (modern Romania) and Arabia. Figure 5-1 shows the expanse of the Roman Empire under Emperor Trajan.

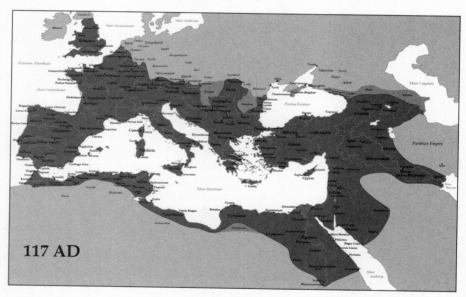

117 AD

FIGURE 5-1: The Roman Empire at its height under the Emperor Trajan. 117 AD.

Roaming eastward

Emperors ran Rome for hundreds of years more as dynasties and factions rose and fell, and as pressure along the far-flung borders demanded vigilance. (For more on Roman defensive strategies, see Chapter 16.) Successive Roman emperors concentrated resources along the eastern frontier formed by the Danube River, which flows from today's Germany to the Black Sea.

In the third century AD, the Emperor Diocletian, a soldier from Croatia who was trying to restore order after a period of internal revolt, tried splitting the empire in two:

>> East: He took the wealthy, relatively healthy eastern lands, which he ruled from a new capital where Izmit, Turkey, is today.

>> West: He tapped the general in charge of Gaul, Maximian, to rule the western half of the Roman Empire from the city of Rome.

Both Diocletian and Maximian had the title Augustus, and two more co-rulers, Constantius and Galerius, received the lesser title Caesar.

When Constantius died, his son, Constantine, later called Constantine the Great, succeeded him and eventually won control of the whole empire. The reunification couldn't last, though, especially considering that Constantine based himself in the east too. He built what he called New Rome at the site of the old seaport of Byzantium on the Bosporus, the channel that connects the Black Sea with the Sea of Marmara and in turn the Mediterranean. Completed in 330 AD, New Rome was renamed Constantinople that year. Today, the city is called Istanbul.

One result of the power shift away from Rome was that the Roman Senate was sometimes relegated to the status of a city council. True, Rome was quite a city for a council to oversee, but the power was where the emperor was (or the emperors were). Rome's western half became less and less an empire and therefore grew more and more vulnerable to invasion by the barbarian tribes from the north: Huns, Vandals, Visigoths, Ostrogoths, and more.

By 400 AD, Theodosius had a senate in Constantinople and a staff of 2,000 bureaucrats. Also around this time, Roman tax collectors could no longer move about Europe without military escorts. The Visigoths sacked Rome in 410 AD.

Western empire fades into history

With its western territory overrun by barbarians and pirates, the Roman Empire was no longer anything like its former self. In 439 AD, Vandals advanced to Roman North Africa, capturing Carthage, the former Phoenician capital that had become one of the major cities of the Western Roman Empire. The once-mighty Western empire was unable to defend this valuable trade center.

While the Western empire declined, the imperial government in Constantinople signaled the changing times by declaring Greek, rather than Latin, to be the official language. Latin was the language of the West, of Rome. Greek was the language of the eastern Mediterranean, the new center of Roman ascendancy. Remembered as the Byzantine Empire, this eastern branch of the Roman Empire would persist for another 1,000 years.

Roman administration in the West struggled on until 476 AD, but without authority. When barbarian leaders closed in on the last emperor to sit on the Roman throne, a poor youngster named Romulus Augustus, a name recalling his great predecessors, they didn't bother to kill him. This emperor (also known by the diminutive Augustulus) wasn't considered to be important enough.

Rome's legacy pervades the Mediterranean, the Middle East, Europe, the Americas, and other far-flung places culturally affected by Europeans — a broad swath that takes in the Philippines, South Africa (and most of the rest of the African continent), Australia, and arguably the whole world.

Rome and the Roman Catholic Church

After Rome was no longer an imperial capital, its name loomed so large and for so long in people's minds that it continued to invoke power and an aura of legitimacy, in part because the Roman Catholic Church remained headquartered there. If you think of Romans as feeding Christians to the lions in the Coliseum, don't forget that the empire later converted to Christianity. The Emperor Constantine, who built his capital in western Turkey, helped bring about a new Roman tolerance toward Christians and became the first Roman emperor to convert to Christianity, in 312 AD. Starting in 331 AD, Constantine also made the Roman Catholic Church rich by

>> Seizing the treasures of pagan temples and spending them on magnificent new Christian churches from Italy to Turkey to Jerusalem.

>> Handing out huge endowments.

>> Authorizing bishops to draw on imperial funds as reparation for the years of enmity.

These moves helped establish the institution's wealth and power for centuries to come. In 391 AD, Constantine's successor, Theodosius I, added a final touch by prohibiting old-style Roman pagan worship, making Christianity the official religion. The empire—both in its western and eastern components—continued to promote, strengthen, and spread that religion in Europe, western Asia, North Africa, and beyond. Two centers of early, state sanctioned Christianity emerged—one in Constantinople and the other in the city of Rome.

Even as the empire shifted its energies away from Rome, it remained Christianity's western headquarters and it is still the center of Roman Catholicism because of what the city had been at its imperial height.

WHATEVER IT'S CALLED, IT'S STILL *THE* CHURCH

When talking about the Christian Church in its early years, I often refer to it simply as the Church. Christianity was a huge cultural force from late Roman times onward. Before the Protestant Reformation of the 16th century, the Catholic Church was the Christian church in Western Europe — virtually the only one. It was the Catholic Church because catholic was still an adjective meaning *universal*. (Spelled with a lowercase *c*, catholic still means *universal* or *wide-ranging*.) After Rome banned pagan worship, and as the old Norse and Celtic beliefs faded, virtually everybody was a Christian, at least nominally. Everybody was also Catholic; there was no such thing as a Protestant. Historians capitalize the word Church when they mean the network of cathedrals, chapels, priories, and so on that looked to the pope in Rome for direction, and so do I in this chapter and in chapters 10 and 14.

In addition to its role as the root of modern romance languages (Italian, French, Spanish, and so on), Latin was the unifying language of the Roman Catholic Church, which to Roman and other European Christians before the 16th century AD was just the Church. Until the middle of the 20th century, Catholic masses worldwide were almost always celebrated in Latin.

REMEMBER

Don't confuse the Roman Empire with the Holy Roman Empire. The Holy Roman Empire was a later group of European principalities and duchies (lesser monarchies) that changed shapes and allegiances over centuries. It started in 800 AD, when Pope Leo III bestowed the new title of Emperor of the West on Charlemagne, king of the Franks (a Germanic tribe) and the first ruler since the original Roman Empire's demise to unite most of Western Europe under a single rule. The title carried with it an understanding that Charlemagne would use his military strength to defend the Church.

Charlie's empire, based where France is today, didn't long survive him, but German King Otto I put together another edition of the Holy Roman Empire in 962 AD, and that one hung on until the 19th century. (For more on the Holy Roman Empire, see Chapters 6 and 14.) Aside from the pope's blessing and his expectation of loyalty, this empire's nominally united lands, largely German and Austrian, and had little to do with Rome. Still, the name Roman smacked of imperial legitimacy.

Other Roman terms endured as well, especially terms for positions of authority. The Russian title czar (or tsar, as it's often spelled) and the later German kaiser both came from the Roman title caesar. The name of a powerful dynastic family, the Romanovs, who ruled Russia from 1613–1917, referred to imperial Rome too. Even in the Islamic world, the name Qaysar — a place name found from Afghanistan to Egypt — comes from Caesar.

Building Empires around the World

After Alexander the Great died of a sudden fever in 323 BC, his vast empire disintegrated. Without Alexander, there was little to unite such widespread, dissimilar places as Macedonia, northern India, and Egypt — all among his territories. Yet the breakup brought about new empires — not as big, but impressive nonetheless. Several of them were founded by Alexander's former military governors.

REMEMBER

Alexander was primarily a conqueror. He couldn't personally rule all the lands he won — especially not while conducting further military campaigns — so he appointed regional viceroys to govern in his name. The word viceroy is similar to *vice president,* with the "roy" part meaning king. These assistant kingships went to some of Alexander's top military commanders.

With Alexander gone, the generals were free to turn their territories, which they had been holding in trust for their boss, into personal kingdoms. Ptolemy, Macedonian governor of conquered Egypt, used Alexander's funeral procession to found his own Egyptian dynasty. Although the Roman Empire, the largest and most influential empire to emerge after Alexander, arose first as a city-state, and although the Mediterranean was sprinkled with successful Greek city-states, imperial might became the model for large-scale government in the late centuries of the BC period and the early centuries of the AD period.

Ruling Persia and Parthia

Seleuces was the Macedonian general whom Alexander the Great left in charge of conquered Persia (largely what's now Iran) in the 330s BC. The Achaeminid Empire, also called the Old Persian Empire, had been immensely powerful at its height, around 480 BC. It was in decline by the time Alexander added it to his collection of kingdoms. Still, there was precedent for imperial government in Persia, and Seleuces took advantage of it by bringing Persian officers and Persian regional officials into his government of Macedonians and Greeks and by using his troops to keep order. He successfully dropped the *vice* and transformed himself into a full-on *roy* (*king*).

Seleuces' descendants, the Seleucid Dynasty, ruled a piece of Asia that stretched from Anatolia (the Asian part of modern Turkey) to Afghanistan. Seleucid rule lasted until a powerful regional rival, the Parthians, conquered Persia in the second century BC.

The rise of the Parthians traces back to 250 BC, when the leader Arsaces, from central Asia, founded Parthia in eastern Persia. His descendant, Mithradates I, went on an empire-building campaign of his own from about 160–140 BC, assembling lands from the Persian Gulf to the Caspian Sea and eastward into India.

Mithradates' goal was to re-create the Achaeminid Empire of more than 300 years earlier. Alexander and his successors had displaced Persian culture with Greek — a change called Hellenization because the Greeks called themselves Hellenes. Mithradates reversed Hellenization and revived all things Persian. The Parthian Empire lasted until 224 AD, when a soldier called Ardashir, a member of a noble Persian family called Sassanid, rebelled against the king and killed him. Like the Parthians, the Sassanid Dynasty was Rome's major rival in the East, lasting until the Muslim Arabs conquered Persia in about 642. (For more about the Arabs, turn to Chapter 6.)

India's empires

The political borders within today's India and Pakistan shifted a few times over the centuries between 300 BC and 400 AD, a time that gave rise to both the Indian subcontinent's first united empire — the Mauryan — and India's golden age under the Gupta Dynasty.

In 322 BC, a nobleman named Chandragupta Maurya (sometimes spelled Candra Gupta Maurya) overturned Alexander the Great's Indian conquest by leading a successful revolt against governors in the Punjab (modern Pakistan and northwest India). He also seized Magadha, the main state in northeast India, and formed the biggest Indian political force yet, the Mauryan Empire. Seleucus, the general who became Persia's king after Alexander died, invaded from the west in 305 BC, but Chandragupta defeated him and won a treaty from him setting an Indian border along the Hindu Kush Mountains. The Hindu Kush, an extension of the Himalayan range, is the barrier that Alexander crossed when he invaded India.

Chandragupta's son and grandson enlarged the empire, especially to the south, but war sickened the grandson, Asoka. After early victories, he became a devout Buddhist, devoted to peace. Instead of troops, he sent missionaries to win over Burma and Sri Lanka.

After Asoka died in 238 BC, his successors proved less able to hold the large territory together, and the Mauryan Empire declined. An ambitious rival from the Sunga family assassinated the last Mauryan king, Birhadratha, in 185 BC, and seized power. The resultant Sunga Dynasty couldn't prevent the subcontinent from breaking into a number of independent kingdoms and republics — something like what would soon happen during the medieval period in Europe.

Another leader, another Chandragupta, united India again about 600 years after the Mauryans did. The new power grew into the Gupta Empire, achieving great wealth through widespread trade and intelligent government, and bringing about the greatest cultural flowering ever to rock India.

Known as Chandragupta I, this conqueror started in the kingdom of Magadha in 320 AD, bringing surrounding kingdoms under his influence by force and persuasion. He revived many of Asoka's principles of humane government. Much as the Romans did, he put local leaders to work for him instead of killing or imprisoning them; he propped up regional authorities and made them dependent on his administration. This model for governing India government worked for a long time. It served the Mughal emperor Akbar in the 16th century and even the British in the 19th century.

Chandragupta had able successors, including his son Samudragupta, who spread the Gupta territory to the north and east. Grandson Chandragupta II, a great patron of the arts, ruled from 376–415 AD, spending tax money to promote architecture, painting, and poetry. The Gupta era gave India glorious temples, palaces, sculpture, music, dance, and poetry.

The Guptas weren't without enemies. Huns from Mongolia and northern China battered the northern frontier of India in the fifth century. In the 480s AD, after the last Gupta king died, Huns took over the north. (For more about the Huns and what they were doing to Europe around the same time, turn to Chapter 6.)

Uniting China: Seven into Qin

Divided into seven warring states, China was in turmoil from 485–221 BC. Then the king of one of those states, a place known as Qin, emerged as the dominant leader. He united China for the first time by beating his rivals and consolidating their territories into greater Qin, calling himself Qin Shi Huang (sometimes written Shi Huangdi), meaning *the First Emperor of Qin*, which suggests that he thought there would be more emperors after him. He was right. From *Qin* (which you also can spell Chi'in) came the name China.

Qin Shihuangdi got things done. He may have been inspired by the great Persian road-builder Darius I, because just as Darius built a 1,500-mile highway, Qin Shihuangdi linked the various defensive walls on China's northern border into one Great Wall. His successors continued to work on the wall until it was more than 2,500 miles long; you can see it in Figure 5-2. Darius also inspired the Parthian empire-builder Mithradates, whom you can read about earlier in this chapter. (For more on Darius, see Chapter 4.)

FIGURE 5-2:
Qin Shihuangdi started linking defense works that became the Great Wall.

Qin Shihuangdi also built roads and canals with a fury, and from his northern power base, he conquered southern China. He got rid of feudalism and disarmed nobles, dividing the country into 36 military districts, each with an administrator who reported to the emperor. He was a firm believer in big government, using his clout to reform weights and measures and to standardize everything from Chinese script to the length of cart axles.

The emperor looked after himself and his entourage, building a palace complex that doubled as a massive barracks, sleeping many thousands. He also linked hundreds of lesser palaces via a covered road network. You may conclude from these facts that he didn't like to be alone, and perhaps this trait accounts for what researchers found when they opened his tomb in 1974: 7,000 warriors, each a distinct individual, sculpted of terra cotta and standing in battle formation as if to protect their king. With painted faces and uniforms, the sculptures still hold real weapons. Terra-cotta drivers man real chariots hitched to terra-cotta horses.

There's nary a hint of historical authenticity in the 2008 action-horror-comedy film *The Mummy: Tomb of the Dragon Warrior*. Still, the filmmakers seem to have been inspired by Qin Shihuangdi's sculpted army. The film features Brendan Fraser battling 10,000 terra-cotta soldiers who answer to an evil, immortal ancient Chinese king.

The first Chinese emperor died in 210 BC, and his dynasty didn't last long, yet the family that emerged as rulers only four years later, in 206 BC, was smart enough not to undo the Qin work. Building on Qin Shihuangdi's reforms, the rulers of the Han Dynasty reigned until 220 AD.

Relatively late in the Han Dynasty, during a time called the Eastern Han, the Chinese invented both paper and porcelain, among other important technological advances that flourished under later dynasties such as the short-lived Sui and the succeeding Tang.

Flourishing civilizations in the Americas

During the Roman era, not all the action was in Europe and Asia. Empires formed in the Americas too.

Sharing with the Maya

The Maya culture took shape in Central America by about 1 AD, rising to prominence around 300 AD and enjoying what historians call its Classic Period until about 900 AD, when it went into a long decline.

In the tropical rainforests on the Yucatan Peninsula, in an area spreading over what's now southern Mexico, Guatemala, northern Belize, and western Honduras, the Maya built on inventions and ideas developed by nearby cultures such as the Olmec (see Chapter 4). The Maya also shared aspects of their culture with the Toltec of northern Mexico, whose great city of Tula (about 40 miles north of present-day Mexico City) covered 13 square miles and was home to as many as 60,000 people. The Toltec predated the Aztecs, who met the Spanish when they arrived in Mexico in 1519. (For more on the Toltec, take a look at Chapter 6.)

The Maya developed astronomy, a sophisticated calendar, and a writing technique similar to Egyptian hieroglyphics. They built terraced cities in neat grids and pyramid temples in ceremonial cities such as Copan, Palenque, and Tikal. Both the cities and temples are now ruins for archaeologists to study and tourists to climb on.

An elite class of priests and nobles ruled the majority, who tended fields cleared from the jungle. Modern experts haven't settled on why the Maya ultimately abandoned their cities, although environmental decline seems to have been a factor.

Building in Peru

Farther south, a culture called the Paracas took root as early as 750 BC on a peninsula jutting from the southern coast of Peru. What's known of the Paracas comes purely from archaeological evidence. Apparently at its height, from the first century BC until as late as the fourth century AD, this farming civilization built extensive canals for irrigation.

The Paracas were skilled at weaving, a fact illustrated by the beautifully embroidered textiles found wrapped around the mummified bodies of their dead. Archaeologists refer to a large seaside complex of Paracas tombs as the Paracas Necropolis, meaning *city of the dead.*

In the dry river valleys inland from the south coast of Peru, the Nazca culture appears to have risen around 200 BC, perhaps as an offshoot of the Paracas. As with the Paracas, most of what's known of the Nazca comes through interpretation of surviving artifacts such as textiles and colorful pottery.

Based on such evidence, archaeologists think the Nazca reached their civilization's height between 200 BC and 500 AD. Their huge-scale earthen etchings, designs that are most visible today from the air, are cited today as evidence of long-ago interplanetary visitors. Theorists say that the figures can't be seen except from the air, so they could have been landing strips for alien spaceships. Archaeologists who study the Nazca, however, point out that the figures can indeed be seen from surrounding hills and that the lines of the drawings are far more likely to have been ritual paths that were part of the Nazca religion.

Arising a little later than the Nazca — in the first century AD — in the fertile valleys inland from the north coast of Peru, the Moche culture may have resembled that of Classical Greece, in that it seems to have consisted of politically independent city-states united by a common language and religion.

Although the Maya had hieroglyphics, the Paracas, Nazca, and Moche people left no evidence of written language.

Remembering Far-Flung Cultures

Over the long stretch of time when the Roman Empire was rising and falling, other cultures around the globe continued to grow and change, too, many beyond the main focus of this chapter, but still important. Just because certain cultures seem so influential to the course of history, you don't have to forget about how many, varied ways that human societies developed and progressed. For example,

>> The Aksum: In northeast Africa, where Ethiopia is now, the Aksum people put together an empire that grew rich after 200 AD by trading with places as far away as India. The Aksum became Christian in the fourth century AD and spread the new religion to neighboring peoples.

>> The Celts: Tribal people with sophisticated metalworking skills but no written language, the Celts kept expanding their European territory from central Europe toward the west and south. By the fifth century BC, they were

dominant in Gaul (modern France), England, Ireland, much of Scotland, and parts of Spain. By the third century BC, the Celts spread through the Balkans. They made beautiful golden jewelry and harness ornaments. In some places, the Celts built large forts atop hills and fought Roman legions as the empire absorbed Europe. Later, the Celts clashed with Romans and other invaders who overran their territory through the early centuries AD.

>> **The Japanese:** Discovering how to mine and smelt iron, the Japanese joined the Iron Age sometime in the third century AD. They buried emperors and other big shots with their weapons and other valuable possessions in mounds made of stone and earth.

Tracking the Centuries

753 BC: According to legend, Romulus, the half-mortal son of a Greek-Roman war god, builds the city of Rome.

About 645 BC: According to historians, people from a group of small settlements in west-central Italy establish the city of Rome on a hilly site along the Tiber River.

509 BC: Romans rise up against King Tarquinius Superbus and drive him into exile. They establish a republic in place of the monarchy.

238 BC: Asoka, emperor of India, dies. His Mauryan Dynasty begins to decline.

221 BC: The First Emperor of Qin unites warring Chinese states.

140 BC: Mithradates I begins a campaign conquest to enlarge the Parthian Empire.

45 BC: Julius Caesar emerges victorious from Roman civil war and takes the title Dictator for Life.

27 BC: Octavian, great-nephew of the assassinated Julius Caesar, accepts the title Augustus, becoming Rome's first emperor.

330 AD: Roman Emperor Constantine completed building his new capital city, Constantinople, in Turkey, far to the east of Rome.

476 AD: Barbarian invaders remove Romulus Augustus, the last Roman emperor of the West, from his throne.

Constantinople

» **Going berserk with barbarians and Vikings**

» **Following the Bantu all over Africa**

» **Uniting Arabs and building empires**

» **Bouncing back in India**

Chapter **6**

Splitting Eras: The Middle Ages

Middle Ages and medieval mean *an age between ages.* The Middle Ages in Western Europe was the period between the collapse of the Western Roman Empire (officially 476 AD, although there wasn't much of the empire left to collapse by then) and the Renaissance in the 14th century. (You can find much more about the Renaissance in Chapter 13.)

Calling this period the Middle Ages doesn't mean that nothing happened in Western Europe between the 5th and 14th centuries, however. There's no such thing as a 900-year span when nothing happened. What it means is that the Middle Ages were sandwiched between two more monumental-seeming eras: the Roman Empire and the Renaissance.

Meanwhile, in what is today's Turkey and a huge surrounding region, history wasn't wedged between two great ages, but smack in the middle of one great age: that of the continuing Eastern Roman Empire, which we tend to call Byzantine. Other empires peaked in those centuries too, as India flowered and Arab armies conquered vast lands, inspired by their new religion, Islam.

In what used to be the Western Roman Empire, however, civil authority became decentralized. Cities weren't as important as they once were, and the economy became more agricultural and local than commercial and trade-based. Authority followed the rules of feudal loyalty; in place of a central imperial hierarchy, local vassals served local lords in return for favor and protection. The exception was the monolithic Roman Catholic Church, which was extremely powerful and still based in Rome.

In this chapter, you'll revisit Rome, or at least its lasting influence. You can check in on the long-lived, relatively stable Byzantine Empire and also meet many of the restless, mobile groups — raiders, conquerors, and refugees — who made this age what it was. You'll glimpse the Huns, Goths, Visigoths, Avars, and others from the Eurasian Steppe (a vast area stretching from Manchuria to Hungary). Descendants of the fighters who brought down Rome, these barbarians' descendants remained in post-Roman Europe, blending and clashing among themselves and with the descendants of earlier Europeans. You'll see how these people joined older European populations to form the beginnings of modern nations by standing up to new waves of raiders from the north (Vikings) and conquerors from the east and south (Arabs and Moors). You'll see how other populations continued to move as well, and not just into Europe. Wave after wave of a people called the Bantu transformed the African continent over a millennium of southern migrations.

The world that emerged at the end of the Middle Ages was vastly different from what it was when Rome fell. So maybe the Middle Ages should be called the Transitional Ages.

Building (And Maintaining) the Byzantine Empire

Roman Emperor Constantine the Great and his successors built the eastern branch of the Roman Empire (the Byzantine Empire) as a continuation of Imperial Rome, except the eastern branch rose as a Christian power rather than a pagan one, and people spoke Greek instead of Latin.

Constantine chose the Greek outpost of Byzantium for his new capital, rebuilding it to fit his concept of a great city and renaming it Constantinople in 330 AD. By the time the western part of the Roman Empire fell apart in the fifth century, Constantinople (today's Istanbul) was a seat of power that rivaled old Rome at its height. The Byzantine emperor had more power than most of his western predecessors, and the Byzantine senate evolved as a sprawling, intricate, and notoriously corrupt bureaucracy.

As a center of government, the Byzantine capital was remarkably stable. It was an urban seat of great power, boasting a high level of literacy and wealth as the result of a commercial economy and extensive lands. Although its boundaries changed many times, the empire was always vast.

Before he died in 565 AD, Justinian, who became emperor in 537 AD, ruled lands on the north and south shores of the Mediterranean Sea, stretching from southern Spain (confusingly well west of Rome, seat of the old Western Empire) all the way east to Persia. Trying to reunite east and west into one Christian Empire, Justinian sent his armies to retake many formerly Roman lands in Europe and North Africa. He even recaptured Italy, establishing a western Byzantine capital at Ravenna. But Justinian couldn't reconcile the eastern and western branches of the Church, which had become bitterly divided. (For more about the early Christian Church, see Chapter 12.)

To last so long as a power center, Constantinople had to endure physically too. The city's location on the Bosporus (the channel that links the Sea of Marmara with the Black Sea) and its heavily fortified walls helped it resist invasion. Although Constantinople took a beating, the Arabs' four-year siege that finally ended in 678 AD failed. (You can read more about Constantinople's strategic advantages in Chapter 17. See the later section "Emerging Islamic Fervor" for more about the Arabs, who quickly became a force to be reckoned with.)

Sharing and Imposing Culture

The so-called Middle Ages were an unsettled time in much of the world as different populations migrated, clashed, and intermingled. Europe continued to feel the influence of the barbarian peoples who had come west from Asia during the late centuries of the Western Roman Empire. Meanwhile, in Africa, the Bantu people spread their languages and cultures southward as subgroups of Bantu migrated down the continent for century upon century. Later in the period, from the 8th to 11th centuries, seafaring raiders called Vikings plagued, conquered, and ultimately settled parts of Europe.

At the same time, cultural influences from China and India began penetrating westward into the Byzantine Empire (Turkey and the eastern Mediterranean), not through population migrations, but through growing trade along an overland route called the Silk Road.

Bearing with barbarians

The hordes of barbarians battering away at the Roman frontiers for centuries brought cultural crosscurrents, although destructive ones. In a way, the barbarians created the Middle Ages, so it pays to understand who they were. It's amazing how many peoples came out of the east and how far and fast they came without expressways or high-speed rail.

To the Romans, a barbarian was an outsider who didn't speak Latin. The term most often applied, however, to members of tribes such as the Goths and Vandals. Seeking lands to settle and eager for plunder, these migrating, warlike folks were a force in northern Europe for a very long time before and after Rome fell.

Many barbarians came from central Asia, and most were nomadic herders before they turned to raiding. The Vandals and Alans wandered north of the Black Sea before they came west, as did some of the other barbarians, although they moved so much that it's difficult to pin down where they started. Once they were in Europe, they sometimes settled in a specific region — the Huns in Hungary, for example, and the Vandals in Denmark. That didn't mean, however, that the groups stayed together or stayed put. The Vandals also built Vandalusia, a kingdom in what is now Spain. (Over time, the *V* fell off; the region is known today as Andalusia.)

When Vandals arrived in Denmark in Roman times, they met, fought, and mingled with people who had been hunting and farming in Scandinavia for thousands of years. The Greek adventurer Pythias of Marseilles, who hung out in Britain for a bit around 350 BC, wrote that he also traveled across water (perhaps the North Sea) to a place he called Thule (maybe Norway). There, he visited friendly blond people who threshed their grain indoors to save it from the damp, cold climate.

TECHNICAL STUFF

Before 500 BC, a prolonged warm spell pervaded the far north of Europe. Archaeological evidence seems to show that for a while the ancient Scandinavians didn't even have to bother with much clothing. But a gradually cooling climate and difficulty raising food provided the northern tribes with the incentive to come south and prey on Celts and Romans who were enjoying the continent's warmer climes. The barbarian incursions went on for centuries, and tracing them to a colder north gives only a small picture (and maybe a distorted one) of the population movements that defined those hundreds of years.

Related to the Mongols, who made China their own, the Huns rode into Europe in the fourth century AD and settled along the River Danube. From there, their leader Attila launched fifth-century attacks on Gaul (modern France) and Italy.

Until about 550 AD, entire populations were constantly migrating, some for thousands of miles, and not just around Europe. Just as it is in the 21st century, migration was often a response to economic hardship and climate changes. When people move, they run into other people. During the Middle Ages, the ones on the move were often warlike and desperate, so the encounters got ugly.

Many barbarians were poor and looking for a better life. If plunder was a way to a better life, they went for it.

Traversing Africa with the Bantu

The barbarians weren't the only populations on the move. Bantu people flowed out of today's Nigeria and north-central Africa, beginning in the last century BC and continuing through the first millennium AD. The Bantu, a group of related peoples who spoke Bantu languages (the largest group of African languages today), were grain farmers and metalworkers who mastered iron-smelting technology long before the rest of Africa.

The Bantu success led to population growth that in turn forced them to seek new lands. So they took their languages and their metalworking technology with them as they overwhelmed indigenous populations all the way to the southern tip of the African continent. Most of the people in Africa today are descendants of Bantu.

Also like the barbarians of Europe, new waves of Bantu continued to move south over successive centuries, overwhelming descendants of earlier waves of Bantu immigrants. In the 12th century, the Bantu founded the powerful Mwenumatapa civilization (in today's Zimbabwe), centered in the city of Great Zimbabwe.

Sailing and settling with the Vikings

In Europe, another wave of invasions from the north, beginning around the year 800 AD, profoundly marked the Middle Ages. The people of Norway, Denmark, and Sweden, thriving through agriculture and sea trade, started running out of good farmland. Naturally, they went to find some more.

A way to find it was to go a viking — adventure and raid as far as their sturdy, maneuverable ships could take them, which was very far indeed. With the advantage of good longboats and experienced navigators, the Vikings raided the coasts of Britain, Ireland, France, Spain, Morocco, and Italy.

The Vikings were opportunists and traders as well as warriors. Like earlier barbarians, Vikings sometimes settled in places they raided. They founded Dublin and Limerick in Ireland, and the Shetland Islands off Scotland remained a Norwegian possession for centuries. In northeast England, the city of York was once a Viking settlement called Yorvig. Viking dynasties also set up Norse kingdoms in diverse parts of Europe from Sicily to Russia to Normandy. The last, a region of France, gets its name from the Northmen who came to raid and stayed to settle.

INVADING ENGLAND'S FORMER INVADERS

The Anglo-Saxon rulers of England fought wave after wave of invading Vikings, yet Anglo-Saxons were invaders in their own time. Angles, Saxons, and Jutes were among the tribal northerners that the Romans called barbarians. (For an explanation of why the name of the Germanic tribe called the Angles becomes Anglo in Anglo-Saxon, see the sidebar in this chapter called "Angling for a kingdom's name.")

From northern Europe (Denmark and Germany), some Germanic tribes had settled in Britain in the fourth century AD. It wasn't until the Romans left the island to its own defenses in the early fifth century, however, that Angles, Saxons, and Jutes poured into Britain in significant numbers. These newcomers overwhelmed the indigenous Celts, or Britons, and drove some of them west to Cornwall and Wales, north to Scotland, and across the water to Brittany (now part of France).

The invaders' medieval descendants were Anglo-Saxons, often called just Saxons, who controlled pieces of Britain for hundreds of years. For a time, Vikings challenged Saxon control and ruled all of northern England, including Yorkshire. But Saxons gained the upper hand in 878 AD when the king of Wessex (or the West Saxon land), Alfred, defeated the Viking ruler Guthrum. He let Guthrum keep the north, called the Danelaw, but Alfred united the Saxon lands and made the Vikings pay him tribute. Saxons ruled much of England for most of the next 200 years, although Vikings reasserted control for a time in the early 11th century. Alfred predated a united England, but he is the only "English" king to be called "the Great."

Carrying on through generations

As with the earlier waves of population movement in Europe, the Vikings' prolonged and successive impacts echoed across the continent in interesting ways. The Viking leader Hrolfr (in French, the much-easier-to-pronounce Rollo), for example, founded the dynasty of Norman kings in the duchy (like a kingdom) of Normandy when he conquered that land in 911 AD.

William the Conqueror was Hrolfr's descendant. Yet when he invaded England and claimed the English throne in 1066, he battled a kingdom that had only recently been under the rule of Vikings from Denmark. Edward the Confessor, of Saxon lineage, had nominated William's rival, Harold II, for the English throne. Edward, however, had gained the throne in 1042 only after a king called Hardicanute, a Dane, failed to leave a successor. Hardicanute's father, Canute (or Cnut), ruled over England, Denmark, and Norway simultaneously. His father, Danish ruler Sweyn Forkbeard, had conquered England in 1013. Whew!

Finding and losing the New World

One place where Vikings had little impact was North America. Norwegians from Greenland landed in Canada around 1000 AD, but after a few years, they lost interest in the new land. The first Norseman to see North America, the trader Bjarni Herjolffson, was trying to get from Iceland (colonized by the Norse in the 860s AD) to recently settled Greenland in the summer of 986 AD. Losing his way in the fog, Herjolffson came to a shoreline, probably that of Labrador, which obviously wasn't where he wanted to go, so he turned around without exploring. About 15 years later, young Leif Eriksson (son of Erik the Red, who colonized Greenland) bought Herjolffson's boat, rounded up a crew, and set out from Greenland to find the new land.

For a short while, parties of Norse explored and even tried settling in the place they called Vinland (today's northeastern Newfoundland). They fought with natives, but unlike the Spanish explorers who came to southern North America 500 years later, the Vikings had no firearms, so they had no huge advantage in battle. As well as fighting them, the newcomers traded with the indigenous people. Some Norsemen (and Norse women) built houses and stayed for a while, but they fought among themselves, undermining their chances to thrive. The voyages west from Greenland soon stopped, and the Vinland settlements faded into memory.

Even if the Norse had taken a keener interest in North America, their discovery was marred by several factors:

>> The climate changed. After 1200, the North Atlantic experienced a mini ice age, which locked ports and closed off Viking settlements in Greenland. No more settlers came; many left.

>> Trade had become less lucrative. Russian furs flooded the European market, and craftsmen clamored for elephant ivory, which was considered to be superior to the walrus tusks that the Greenlanders could offer.

>> Bubonic plague (the Black Death) destroyed Norse Greenland. When the plague arrived in Greenland in the 14th century, it devastated the small remaining Norse population. Norway and Iceland, both hard-hit by the epidemic, no longer had a reason to send ships so far west.

Traveling the Silk Road

Around the second century AD, traveling merchants began moving increasing amounts of trade goods eastward and westward along the Silk Road, a caravan route that followed the Great Wall of China and wound along a natural corridor through the Pamir Mountains and Tajikistan, across Afghanistan and south of the Caspian Sea to the eastern Mediterranean. By the sixth century AD, the Silk Road had reached Constantinople.

A single caravan was unlikely to make the entire journey. Rather, traders operated an improvised relay system, with regional merchants buying and shipping over selected distances. Wool and precious metals were traded eastward; coveted Chinese silk, the luxurious fabric that gave the road its name, was the primary trade good going west. Centuries of trade in silk and spices changed Western tastes and contributed to European-ruled, worldwide empires. (See Chapter 7 for details).

Planting the Seeds of European Nations

In the Middle Ages, the European map looked very little like what you see in a modern atlas. There was no France, Germany, Spain, or Italy. For the sake of convenience, I sometimes refer to these areas by the national names they bear now, but the concept of nationhood was lost on Europe for quite a while after the Roman Empire collapsed.

Yet also in the Middle Ages, people and regions began to come together and to take on identities that would lead to modern nations such as France. The catalyst for this unity came partly from the inside, as feudal leaders sought more power, but it got its biggest push from the outside — from the very raids and invasions that I cover throughout this chapter.

When people in Ireland tired of Viking raids, for example, they looked to a king who would be strong enough to bring regional lords together to mount a defense. In France (then called Gaul), the people known as Franks feared invasion by Arabs and by fierce Magyar raiders from Hungary. The Franks, like the Irish and other Europeans, looked to someone to unite them.

Repelling the raiders

Alfred the Great was the leader who brought Saxons (and Angles and Jutes) together in Britain. You can read more about him in the nearby sidebar "Invading England's former invaders."

In Ireland, a warrior named Brian Boru seized power as high king (one who ruled over lesser kings) and gathered forces strong enough to conquer the Vikings at Clontarf, near Dublin in 1014. He died in that battle, but the Irish won. United under an Irish leader for the first time, Ireland no longer belonged to the Norse.

Uniting Western Europe: Charlemagne pulls it together

The Franks gave rise to the strongest of the new European kings, the only one to forge an empire anything like old Rome's. A Germanic people from the Rhine region, the Franks settled in Gaul (roughly identified with modern France) around 400 AD, and in 451 AD, they helped the Romans repel Attila the Hun at Châlons. By 481 AD, the Romans in Gaul no longer had a Roman Empire to back them up. The king of the Franks, Clovis, overthrew the Romans and took possession of all the land between the Somme and Loire Rivers. Clovis's dynasty, called the Merovingians, gave way to a new Frankish dynasty called the Carolingians in the middle of the eighth century.

ANGLING FOR A KINGDOM'S NAME

England's Anglo-Saxon rulers were called Anglo-Saxon because they descended from Germanic tribes, chief among them the Angles and the Saxons. England means *the Angles' Land*, and regions within England also got their names from these people. That's why there are a Wessex (West Saxon Land), Sussex (South Saxon Land), Essex (East Saxon Land), and East Anglia.

People say "Anglo-Saxon" rather than "Angle-Saxon" because of the influence of Latin on the language. Anglo is a Latinized version of Angle, applied when the word, today often used to mean English or British, is put together with the name of another ethnic or national group, as in an Anglo-Danish business venture or the Anglo-Japanese Alliance of 1902. The *Anglo* part here refers to the United Kingdom as a whole.

French becomes Franco in such combinations, as in a Franco-American trade agreement. Things get crazier when you talk about the Chinese, because political scientists and historians cling to an old Greek word for Chinese and then put the Latin ending on it, which is why you might read about a Sino-Japanese economic conference.

The people of England are English. You can also call them British, but the word doesn't mean the same thing. Properly sorted out, the British are chiefly English, Welsh, Scottish, and Northern Irish. England has long been the largest piece of the United Kingdom, also called Britain. The name *Great Britain* technically refers to the big island containing England, Scotland, and Wales, but it's also used as a blanket term for British people and entities. Still confused? Me too. Try this: In the Olympics, British athletes compete together as Team GB, but in World Cup football, England, Scotland, Wales, and Northern Ireland field their own separate "national" teams.

(continued)

(continued)

The United Kingdom includes

- **England:** The Anglo-Saxon King Æthelstan first united it under one rule in 927 AD.

- **Wales:** England annexed it in the 16th century.

- **Scotland:** Parliaments of both countries voted to join it with England in 1707.

- **Northern Ireland:** Created in the 20th century, it remained part of the United Kingdom after most of Ireland became a republic.

The Arab Empire came out of the Middle East in the seventh century, conquering most of North Africa and then extending northward to Spain. (You can find out more about the Arabs in "Emerging Islamic Fervor" later in this chapter.) In Spain, the Arabs — who were Muslim (followers of the Islamic faith) — and their North African comrades, the Moors, beat Visigoth rulers in 711 AD, taking over most of the Iberian Peninsula (Spain and Portugal). The Visigoths were among the many groups of barbarians who brought down the Roman Empire. From their stronghold in Spain, these Moors (as all Spanish Muslims soon were called) pummeled southern Gaul, gaining a foothold just as the Carolingians came to power later in the eighth century.

In 732 AD, Islamic forces tried to conquer Gaul. The Carolingian king, Charles Martel, stood up to them and turned them away. If he hadn't, historians say that Western Europe could have turned out Islamic. This event would have upset Charles Martel's grandson, Charlemagne, an avowed Christian. Charlemagne (Charles the Great) became king of the western Franks in 768 AD and then ruled all the Franks after his brother Carloman died in 771 AD.

Charlemagne wasn't the kind of Christian who thought that the meek inherit the Earth. To get the Saxons of Germany (yes, they were related to the Saxons of England) converted to the faith, he fought and subjugated them. Instead of waiting for the Moors to try another invasion, he plunged his forces into Spain and attacked the emir of Cordoba. He also smashed the kingdom of Lombardy in northern Italy, among many other conquests that brought most of Western Europe under his rule. The extent of Charlemagne's empire at his death is shown in Figure 6-1.

REMEMBER

Pope Leo III liked Charlemagne's efforts to conquer and convert, especially his 774 AD victory over the Lombards in northern Italy. Another tribe of northern invaders who had come to stay, the Lombards ruled much of Italy and represented a threat to the Papal States (an area ruled directly by the Pope). The grateful pope crowned Charlemagne as Carolus Augustus, emperor of the Romans (or Holy Roman Emperor), in 800 AD, beginning the strange-yet-enduring European entity, the Holy Roman Empire.

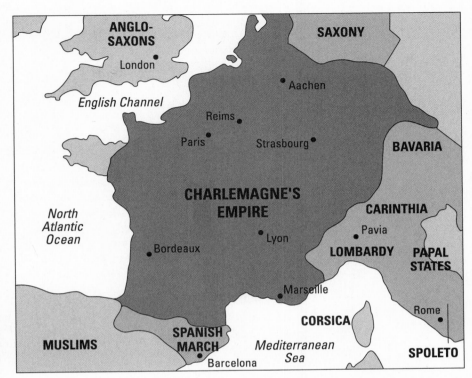

FIGURE 6-1:
Charlemagne's empire as it was when he died in 814 AD.

Charlemagne mellowed in his later years. He built churches and promoted education and the arts, along with Christianity, and sponsored improved agriculture and manufacturing. His stable reign fostered a kind of mini-Renaissance hundreds of years before the big one. After Charlemagne died in 814 AD, his empire deteriorated quickly.

Keeping fledgling nations together

Although strong kings rose to patch together diverse, small principalities and duchies (ruled over by princes and dukes, respectively), consolidated power was difficult to keep. The title of king or even emperor didn't guarantee that lesser lords of the feudal system would remain loyal. Otto I (or Otto the Great) of Germany, who became Holy Roman Emperor in 936 AD, also gained the title King of the Lombards in 951 AD after he rescued Lombardy's Queen Adelaide (imprisoned by a neighboring prince) and married her. Lombardy, still ruled by descendants of the Lombards whom Charlemagne had fought, was in Italy, and Otto's empire, supposedly Roman even though it was based in Germany, included other Italian lands. Yet even after getting Pope John XII to give him an official coronation as emperor in 962 AD, the German king never won Italian support. Italian princes who were officially his vassals (meaning that they had to pay Otto tribute) fought him at every turn.

Emerging Islamic Fervor

People of the ancient Arab ethnicity, which according to tradition dates back to the Biblical figure Ishmael, son of Abraham, are related to the ancient Hebrews and to the Assyrians and Mesopotamians. Originally farmers in the then-fertile region of what is now Yemen, and also nomads and traders throughout the Arabian Peninsula, they get little mention in history up until the seventh century. Arab states rose and fell. Trade flourished, and wealth grew, largely because the Arabs had two valuable substances: frankincense and myrrh, aromatic gum resins refined from the sap of trees (frankincense) and bushes (myrrh). Highly prized for their scent and therapeutic properties, frankincense and myrrh were as valuable as gold.

The Arabs followed many religions, including Greek-style paganism. Judaism gained a foothold, and Christianity won many converts. But all that was before an Arab merchant called Muhammad gave up his business so that he could devote himself to contemplating "the one true god." The name for *God* in Arabic is *Allah*. Things in Muhammad's part of the world would never be the same.

Religion was volatile during the late Roman period and through the Middle Ages as Buddhism spread east from India to China along silk-trading routes and as Christianity became the unifying focus in Europe and beyond. (The Christian faith even spread to the Aksum Empire in northeast Africa.) But perhaps no religion ever had such an immediate and powerful effect as Mohammed's Islam. (For more about religions, see Chapter 10.)

Muhammad, who said the new religion came to him in a vision of the angel Gabriel, became a prophet, but as he gathered followers, he also gained authority in earthly matters. Leaders in his native Mecca saw his power grow and kicked him out. In the city of Medina, however, Muhammad became a lawgiver and judge. Soon, the prophet's Muslim army surged out of Medina to conquer Mecca.

By the time Muhammad died in 632 AD, the Muslims had conquered most of Arabia. His immediate successor, Abu Bakr, finished the job within a couple of years. Then the Muslim Arabs conquered Egypt on their way to expanding westward into Algeria in North Africa, eventually conquering most of Spain and Portugal. Muslims pushed north from Arabia into Iraq and Syria and then west to Persia.

New Islamic dynasties followed this expansion, including the Umayyad Dynasty, founded in 661 AD. From its capital at Damascus, in Syria, the Omayyad Dynasty ruled an empire that stretched from Morocco to India. Although factionalism arose within Islam, and disagreements led to power struggles and war, the Arab world had remarkable continuity. The Abbasid Dynasty, descended from Mohammed's uncle, succeeded the Umayyads, moved the capital to Baghdad, and ruled for 500 years.

Rebounding Guptas in India

Islamic armies surged eastward as well as westward, and new national and ethnic identities formed around the faith and variations within it. Muslims from Afghanistan conquered much of India in 1100.

Yet before Muslims got there, India experienced another flowering similar to that of the Mauryan Dynasty (fourth to second centuries BC). In Chapter 5, I talk about both the Mauryans, the first dynasty to unite most of India, and the Gupta Dynasty, whose stable rule brought an Indian golden age in the arts, architecture, and religion in the mid-fourth to mid-sixth centuries AD.

Hun attacks on India's northern borders eventually caused the Gupta Empire to collapse, just as a western contingent of Huns was among the barbarian people whose attacks brought down Roman authority in Europe, beginning the Middle Ages. As decades passed, the Huns of India became more Indian, adopting local customs and habits.

Assimilating into the general population diffused the Huns' power and helped a Gupta leader named Harsha, descended from the great Gupta kings, reestablish an Indian Empire in 606 AD. Equally good at conquest and administration, and an art lover like his ancestor Chandragupta II of the Gupta Dynasty, Harsha built a glorious capital city, Kanauj, famous for its magnificent buildings, on the Ganges River. Indian culture, thus fortified, spread to Burma, Cambodia, and Sri Lanka. Indian influence over the region continued as the Chola of southeast India conquered much of the country after 880 AD. Savvy merchants and businesspeople, the Chola built up prosperous trade routes with the Arabs to the west and the Chinese to the east. The Chola government style continued the Gupta tradition of allowing local control.

Rounding Up Developments in Cultures Far to the East and to the West

Imagine yourself traveling very rapidly through time and space as we catch up on a sampling of happenings elsewhere in the wide, wide world during Europe's Middle Ages:

>> The Japanese: Japan was deeply influenced by China beginning sometime around the fourth century. By 538 AD, that influence took the form of religious conversion as the Japanese court adopted Buddhism and replaced old temples with new ones. The cultural pendulum began to swing the other way only in the eighth century, when the Chinese-influenced Japanese emperors lost power to a rising warrior class. The warrior leaders, or samurai, were organized by clans and fought among themselves, plunging the island into civil war in the 12th century and giving rise to the imperial office called shogun. Minamoto Yoritomo became shogun in 1192 and used his samurai retainers to impose law and order. Japan was governed this way for centuries.

>> The Khmer: In Southeast Asia, the Khmer people of Cambodia broke away from foreign influence (Chinese and Indian) as they established their first state, called Funan, on the Mekong River. The later Angkorian Dynasty grew into an empire that built a capital at Angkor and ruled until the 14th century.

>> The Maya: In Central America, the Maya civilization lasted from 300 BC–1500 AD, although what was left after 900 AD was a shadow of what had been. Great Mayan cities (actually independent city-states) boasted temples, ball courts, and community housing. In addition to maize (what English-speaking Americans call *corn*), Mayans grew beans, chiles, other vegetables, cocoa, and tobacco. They domesticated bees (although not European honeybees, which had not yet been introduced to the Western Hemisphere), as well as ducks and turkeys. More important, the Maya were the first people in the Americas to use an advanced form of picture writing. Good at mathematics and astronomy, the Maya developed a 365-day calendar. (Find more on the Maya in Chapter 5.)

>> The Polynesians: Between 400 and 800 AD, Polynesian people originally from Southeast Asia spread across thousands of miles of ocean to virtually every island in the Pacific — Hawaii, Tahiti, and Easter Island among them — proving themselves to be some of the most skillful and courageous navigators in the world. Around 1000, when Leif Eriksson was checking out the east coast of Canada, a group of Polynesians made it to New Zealand, where they developed the Maori culture.

>> The Toltecs: Farther north than the Maya, the nomadic Toltecs settled down and farmed central Mexico long before the Aztecs rose in the same region. The Toltecs built the city of Tula. Covering 13 square miles, Tula may have been home to as many as 60,000 people.

Tracking the Centuries

330 AD: Roman Emperor Constantine renames his eastern capital, Byzantium (in today's Turkey), making it Constantinople.

538 AD: The Japanese adopt Chinese Buddhism.

527–565 AD: Justinian, the Byzantine emperor, amasses vast lands stretching west from his capital in Constantinople (today's Istanbul) to encompass much of formerly Roman North Africa and part of Spain, as well as east to Persia.

632 AD: Muhammad, founder of a vigorous new religion called Islam, dies after conquering most of Arabia.

661 AD: The Umayyad Dynasty comes to power over Arab lands, ruling from its capital at Damascus, Syria.

800 AD: Pope Leo III gives the Frankish king, Charlemagne, the new (if anachronistic) title Emperor of the Romans. This event marks the beginning of the Holy Roman Empire.

878 AD: King Alfred of Wessex and his Anglo-Saxon followers defeat the Viking ruler Guthrum, who must then pay tribute to Alfred (later referred to as Alfred the Great).

911 AD: Viking leader Hrolfr (or Rollo) founds a dynasty of Norman kings in Normandy, later part of France.

1000: Leif Eriksson and a party of sailors from Norse Greenland land on the coast of Canada.

1014: Brian Boru, the first high king of Ireland, leads Irish warriors to defeat the Vikings at Clontarf, near Dublin.

» **Expanding trade with the Chinese**

» **Pitting European invaders against Middle Eastern rulers: The Crusades**

» **Following Columbus to Asia via the Americas**

Chapter **7**

Struggling for Dominance

I f you'd been living around the year 1000 AD and were asked which culture you thought would end up dominating most of the globe nine centuries later, you probably wouldn't have picked Western Europe. With its feudal power struggles, confusing divisions between secular and spiritual authority, vulnerability to Viking raids, and backward agricultural practices, the region and its culture had a lot of growing to do.

Your other options would have included the Arabs, who transformed a huge part of the world with amazing zeal and ingenuity in the seventh and eighth centuries, and the Chinese, the most technologically advanced and best-governed civilization on earth. But both of these Eastern cultures had their own character flaws, just like Western Europe. The Chinese leaders of 1,000 years ago were justly proud but complacent, sure that no other country had anything they wanted. And the original Arab Empire fractured into competing sects and contending emirates, united in their Islamic faith but less and less united in international goals.

In this chapter, you get to know these major world players — the Arab Empire, the Far East (especially China), and the countries and cultures of Western Europe — and how each approached global exploration and trade efforts up until the 15th century. You'll also find out what made Europe eager and able to assert itself when it did.

Extending the Arab Empire and Spreading Islam

The Arabs rose to power with incredible swiftness and force in the seventh and early eighth centuries. (You can read more about that rise in Chapter 6.) The empire was inspired by its religion, Islam, which united its people and gave them a fervor that helped them spread both the faith and Islamic law. Simultaneously, it encouraged education and intellectual advances.

Taking education and literacy to new heights

The Abbasid Caliphate, the Muslim dynasty that ruled most of the central Middle East from 750–1258 AD, achieved more widespread literacy than any other culture on Earth at the time. Muhammad, founder of Islam, said that the Angel Gabriel had visited him and imparted revelations, which Muhammad taught his followers to recite and which were later written down as a book, the Quran (also spelled Qur'an or Koran). It serves as the holy centerpiece of the Islamic faith and the guide to proper living. (You can find out more about Islam in Chapter 10 and read why the Quran is one of the most important documents in Chapter 24.) Unlike Christians of the Middle Ages, who left the reading of scripture to priests and monks, Muslims stressed that everybody could and should read the Koran. So good Muslims were encouraged to read. With this holy book as a primer, the Islamic world became a culture of learning and scholarship.

Making advances in science and technology

The Arabs ruled much of what had once been the Hellenized, or Greek-dominated, world and held on to much of ancient Greek literature, including the Greeks' philosophical, scientific, and mathematical foundations. They embraced Roman engineering, which had spread to the Middle East and served the mighty Byzantine Empire of the Middle Ages. Building on those foundations, the Arabs adapted and refined Roman advances in architecture, such as the dome, to which they added the delicately distinctive Islamic minaret. You can see examples of these tall towers, which adorn or adjoin mosques and from which people are called to prayer, in Figure 7-1.

Great astronomers and mathematicians in their own right, the Arabs weren't content to tend the flame of Greek and Roman learning. They adopted useful new notions such as the number system from India, which they passed down as Arabic numerals: 1, 2, 3, and so on. That the words *zero* and *algebra* come to English by way of Arabic is no coincidence.

FIGURE 7-1:
The Blue Mosque
in Istanbul boasts
the distinctive
Middle Eastern
minarets
(towers).

Murat Taner/The Image Bank/Getty Images

The Arabs also were way ahead of the rest of the world in medicine. For centuries, European medical textbooks were actually Persian collections of Arabic knowledge.

Mastering the Indian Ocean

Although their civilization's roots were in the desert, Arabs took to the sea and became innovative sailors. Using technology such as the astrolabe (basically a mechanical model of the sky) first developed by Greek and Roman astronomers, they were excellent navigators who figured out the trade winds and mastered the Indian Ocean before anybody else.

Although no Arab made the voyage to test the theory, the great Muslim scientist Al-Biruni speculated as early as 1000 AD that there must be a sea route south of Africa. When Portuguese explorer Vasco da Gama found such a route and arrived in the northeastern Indian port city of Kozhikode in 1498, becoming the first European to get to India by sea, he did it with Arab help. (You can find out more about da Gama in Chapter 8.)

Arab sailors were especially familiar with the arm of the Indian Ocean called the Arabian Sea, which was notoriously difficult to navigate and virtually unknown to Europeans. Da Gama used the best European navigational science of the time to sail around the tip of Africa, but he might not have made it the rest of the way without the help of the greatest Arab navigator, Ibn Majid, author of the best Arab nautical directory. (You can find out more about Ibn Majid in Chapter 21.)

Assembling and disassembling an empire

The late seventh century proved to be a good time for the Arabs to amass their empire, but they weren't able to hold it together in the 9th and 10th centuries.

Taking advantage of circumstances

Muslim Arabs built on the success of founding prophet Muhammad after his death in 632 AD by completing the conquest of the Arabian Peninsula and then turning their attention to nearby lands. Circumstances favored the Arabs' advances. Older Middle Eastern powers — the Byzantine (Turkey) and Sassanid (Persia) empires — were busy fighting each other and fending off barbarian invasions. The Sassanids had to worry about Huns hammering away at their frontiers, while marauding Avars and Berbers bedeviled the Byzantines. (The Berbers hadn't yet become Islamic themselves but would later.)

The fact that plenty of Byzantine subjects, such as the Egyptians, were fed up with taking orders from Constantinople didn't hurt the Arabs' efforts to grow their empire either. (See Chapter 6 and the section "Excelling in East Asia" later in this chapter to find out more about barbarian invasions.)

Growing apart

Islam remained an extremely important religious, cultural, and political force as the 11th century began, but the Arabs' imperial ascendancy was past its peak by that time.

TECHNICAL STUFF

Arabs fought Arabs as early as 656 AD, when a civil war resulted in the capital's being moved from Muhammad's power base at Medina (in today's Saudi Arabia) to Damascus (in today's Syria). In the 9th and 10th centuries, rival caliphates, or Islamic kingdoms, arose in Arab North Africa and Spain, breaking the empire into pieces that, although still united by faith, were no longer politically joined.

Although the empire fractured mostly over issues of power and local control, the Islamic world also broke into religious factions. The two major branches were majority Sunni and minority Shiite, and they persist to this day. Their differences trace to a disagreement about the succession of leadership from Muhammad. Sunnis, who are by far more numerous, hold a traditional view that Abu Bakr, as the first caliph, was Muhammad's rightful heir. Shiites (or Shia) believe that before the prophet died, he named his son-in-law, Ali ibn Abi Talib, as his successor, and they reserve the title of imam for religious leaders descended from Muhammad's family. Today, the Muslims of Saudi Arabia, Kuwait, Qatar, and Indonesia, among other countries, are largely Sunnis. Iran and Azerbaijan have Shia majorities.

HOLDING ONTO ANCIENT DIFFERENCES

The Shia-Sunni divide remains relevant in the 21st century as a Saudi-led coalition (Sunni) battles Iranian-backed Houthi rebels (largely Shia) in Yemen. According to the non-partisan Council on Foreign Relations, Sunni-Shia enmity has been increasing since at least 2013. In that time, extremist Sunni groups such as al-Qaeda and ISIS (the Islamic State) have directed more acts of violence against other Muslims than against Western targets. In 2015 alone, ISIS bombed Shia worshippers in Kuwait, attacked mosques in Saudi Arabia, and claimed responsibility for suicide bombings that killed more than 40 people in a Shia-majority district of Beirut, Lebanon. Meanwhile, Shia militant groups have gained strength, in response to the growing threat of Sunni extremism.

Too big, too diverse, and too multifaceted, Islamic civilization was unable to sweep so much the world again as a single, overwhelming political force after it fractured in the 9th and 10th centuries.

Excelling in East Asia

Great in both size and cultural achievements, China was so far away and sounded so strange that medieval Europeans could hardly imagine it. Yet China was a well-spring of technological inventions, an economic marvel, and a cultural model for neighboring nations. China's leaders, knowing that they had something special, tended to be a bit smug.

Innovating the Chinese way

The 400-year Han Dynasty (206 BC–220 AD) made amazing advancements and innovations. Following are some examples:

>> Chinese scientists invented the compass and the first accurate grid-based maps.

>> They put efficient rudders on ships back when Romans and barbarians still steered by sticking a big paddle in the water at the back of the boat.

>> They came up with the crossbow, a serious weaponry escalation for its time.

>> They made the world's first paper, which may seem to be trivial until you consider what the world would have been like without it. Predecessors of paper in the Middle East and West included papyrus, which tended to mold and rot in European climates, and parchment, which is tanned animal skin.

The Chinese didn't always use their inventions in seemingly obvious ways. Instead of first using the compass as a navigational device, for example, they found it to be a dandy tool for making sure that temples were built on the proper, sacred alignment.

Innovation didn't stop when the Han Dynasty fell in 221 AD. Successive dynasties originated or embraced more new ideas, including the stirrup, which allowed riders much more control and stability and gave Chinese horsemen the edge in warfare — for a little while, anyway.

Under the T'ang Dynasty, which took over in 618 AD, China developed beautiful things such as porcelain and ingenious things such as movable-type printing, which didn't make it to Europe for hundreds of years. The Chinese invented gunpowder too, and they began to use it in warfare around 1000. There weren't any guns yet, but the Chinese were learning how to blow up stuff with bombs while Europeans were still poking each other with pointy things. (For more about the invention of gunpowder and its early uses, see Chapter 17.)

China's economy and agriculture excelled. During the Han dynasty, China's ability to feed its large population stood as a model of self-sufficiency. The climate, especially in the south, allowed two rice crops a year, which fed many people and therefore permitted China's growth to outpace that of any other region on Earth.

By the early 20th century, Chinese peasants were poised on the edge of starvation after a very long decline in conditions.

Traveling the Silk Road for trade and cultural exchange

Because China had so much that other parts of the world coveted, its leaders rarely cared much about the world far beyond its borders. From the Han Dynasty on, the Chinese believed themselves to be at the center of the world. They certainly were at the cultural center of East Asia and had a profound influence on language, writing, government, and art from Burma to Korea to Japan.

Even if some of their rulers tended toward isolationist policies, Chinese businesspeople certainly traded beyond the Great Wall. From the second century onward, Chinese goods traveled west on the backs of Bactrian camels that trekked the Silk Road (sometimes called the Silk Route). The caravans followed a natural corridor from northern China through remote central Asia, between the peaks of the Pamir Mountains and through the Taklimakan Desert to Persia (now Iran) and the Mediterranean Sea. As a result, Middle Easterners — and some people farther west as well — enjoyed Chinese silk, the finest fabric in the world, along with luxuries such as spices.

The camels carted gold back over the route to China, but the path also fostered cultural interchange. Christian missionaries from the Nestorian Church, a controversial fringe Christian sect, traveled the Silk Road to spread their faith after the Byzantine Empire exiled them in the fifth century.

Yet the Chinese hungered for little that other cultures offered. Under the early Ming Dynasty — founded by the monk-warrior Chu Yuan-chang in 1368 after he drove out the Mongol rulers of the Yuan Dynasty — China's rulers went so far as to forbid ships to leave coastal waters. With long voyages banned, Chinese shipbuilders stopped building big seagoing vessels.

Sailing away for a spell

In the early 15th century, Emperor Yung Lo turned outward — an unusual posture for a Chinese ruler — and sponsored impressive voyages of exploration. Zheng He (sometimes written Chung Ho or Cheng Ho), a Muslim court eunuch who was also an accomplished sea admiral, commanded the ventures. (A eunuch was a male servant, generally a slave, who had been castrated, presumably to make him more docile and to ensure that he wouldn't be tempted by the master's women, or they by him.) Zheng He somehow overcame his lowly status to become an important member of Yung's court.

TECHNICAL STUFF

Zheng sailed seven large, well-financed expeditions. His ships landed in India, navigated the Persian Gulf, and anchored off East Africa. His vessels were larger and faster than Arab and European ships of the time and were equipped with sophisticated bulkheads (walls between sections of the ship's hold), so if one part of the ship sprung a leak or caught fire, the damage could be contained, and the ship wouldn't sink.

BREACHING THE WALL: INVADING CHINA

China endured for such a long time that you may think it was invulnerable, but sometimes, the empire succumbed to invaders.

The Chinese began the Great Wall of China as a string of defensive outposts in the third century BC and then added to this barrier over the course of hundreds of years. But some enemies got past the wall. Around 100 BC, the Xiongnu people challenged the great Han Dynasty. More than 1,000 years later, in the 13th century, a successful Mongol invader breached the wall again. He was Genghis Khan, and his grandson, Kublai Khan, founded China's Yuan dynasty.

(continued)

(continued)

Genghis Khan, whose name means *universal chief,* joined lands from the Pacific Ocean west to the Black Sea. Before he died in 1227, he split his empire into four parts that he called khanates. His Chinese lands made up the easternmost khanate.

Kublai Khan was the first Chinese ruler most Europeans found out about, because the famous Venetian traveler Marco Polo wrote about living and working in Kublai Khan's court. Kublai Khan finished what his grandpa began, making his Mongol capital in Khanbaligh (now Beijing) in 1267 and finally finishing off China's Song (or Sung) Dynasty 12 violent years later.

After Emperor Yung Lo died, the expeditions stopped, and nothing much came of Zheng's voyages — no expanded trade, no extended political influence, and no broadened military influence. But the idea had never been to subdue other parts of the world anyway. In Chinese thinking, China was not just the best state, but also the only sovereign state. The ships were in part a peaceful effort to broadcast the message of Chinese superiority. But to Yung Lo's successors, the rest of the world apparently still wasn't worth the trouble, seeing as they didn't continue exploration efforts.

Developing a Taste for Eastern Goods

Like the Arabs and many other cultures of the 13th through 18th centuries, Europeans fought among themselves, but their competition also took the form of a race for far-flung riches. They knew that vast wealth could be found in trade, especially trade with China. Several factors enhanced the European craving for more Eastern trade. Here's a sampling:

» Some Europeans got a tantalizing preview of Asian luxuries — including fine silks and spices not tasted in the West — thanks to the Crusades, which were hundreds of years of Christian military expeditions that began against Seljuk Turk–controlled Palestine in the 11th century. (If you think spices are no big deal, imagine what European food tasted like before Europeans had them.)

» The Moors in Spain, with their Eastern ties, had trade-route access to Chinese delights. And a vast, Euro-Asian Mongol Empire from the Black Sea to China opened northern trade routes, bringing eastern goods west into the German states.

» *The Travels of Marco Polo,* a book about China written by a 13th-century commercial traveler from the Italian city-state of Venice, drummed up interest in East Asia.

> » Oddly enough, a terrible plague in the 14th century helped create a market for exotic Eastern goods. To find out how that worked, you can skip forward to the section titled, "Doing the math: Fewer folks, more wealth," later in this chapter.

REMEMBER

Before they could supply the growing market and interest in Eastern products, the Europeans needed to get around some serious geographical obstacles. Europeans needed to find ways to bring cargo from faraway India and China. The Byzantine Empire and competing Turkish realms (Seljuk and later the powerful Ottomans) controlled the land routes to the East; besides, only sailing ships could carry the volume of merchandise that European dreamers had in mind. The problem was that nobody in Europe knew how to reach East Asia by sea. The Europeans needed sea routes, and the search for those routes brought about a world crisscrossed by new cultural connections.

Orienting Venice

Venice was a city-state of ambitious traders that started out as an island refuge from barbarians in the fifth century AD. It was part of the Byzantine Empire until the ninth century, and even later, as an independent city-state, Venice enjoyed favored trading status with the Byzantines. This Eastern connection gave Venice an economic advantage that its rulers used to build up a neat little Mediterranean empire, including the Italian cities of Padua, Verona, and Vicenza, along with the strategically placed eastern Mediterranean islands of Crete and Cypress.

Economically and militarily, Venice was oriented toward Constantinople and Asia. The word orient originally meant *east* or *to face eastward.*

Although another seafaring Italian city-state, Genoa, gave Venice some stiff competition, Venice dominated Mediterranean trading. The wealth that Venetians enjoyed because of their access to the East made the rest of Europe sit up and take notice.

Writing the first best-selling travel book

Over the Silk Road to China, shippers and wholesalers customarily traded goods only to the next trader down the way, so no one trader or camel driver covered the entire exhausting route. The father and uncle of 13th century traveler Marco Polo were more ambitious than most other traders in Venice: They traveled all the way from Italy to China in their quest for lucrative deals.

Polo's elders were on their second trip to East Asia when they invited the young man (probably about 19 at the time) to tag along. The trio arrived in Beijing in 1275. According to the book that Polo later wrote, he entered Emperor Kublai Khan's diplomatic service and traveled to other Mongol capitals on official business. (Kublai Khan, though China's emperor, was a Mongol.)

Almost two decades went by. Young Polo, not quite so young anymore, finally left China in 1292 and tried to return to Venice. But the rival city-states were at war, and he was captured. He was in a Genoa prison when he wrote — rather, dictated to a fellow prisoner — the fantastic story of his years abroad.

Many of Polo's contemporaries thought he lied in his book, and some modern scholars think that that he at least exaggerated his story or reported things he'd heard about from other travelers but not actually seen. But his defenders have verified so much of what he wrote as being accurate that it's likely he was telling the truth. Even if he got a few things wrong, those errors wouldn't undercut the impact of his descriptions. Polo's book was about a faraway place, and to Europeans at the turn of the 14th century, it was like a dispatch from outer space. At the very least, Polo's stories spread and fed the perception that China was the trader's mother lode. *The Travels of Marco Polo* was the most influential book of its time.

Fighting for economic advantage

Venice's trade success fueled military conflicts with the rival city-state Genoa and with more remote competitors. Venice was in there swinging when European Christendom launched the Crusades (see "Mounting the Crusades" later in this chapter).

REMEMBER

Any military campaign against those who controlled access to the Silk Road — whether they were Turks or Byzantine Christians (Western Crusaders sacked Constantinople in 1204) — interested the Venetians. They were first in line among Europeans who wanted unimpeded access to the profitable thoroughfare.

Venice declined as the major trading power in the Mediterranean only after the 1571 naval Battle of Lepanto against the Ottoman Turks (successors to the Byzantines). In that conflict, the Venetians were allied with Rome and Spain in the Holy League, created by the pope. Venice won the Battle of Lepanto but lost its colony Cyprus, a crucial trade outpost, and its power slipped.

Controlling trade routes between Europe and the East

Turkish empire-building reached its height in the 15th century, when the Ottomans assembled a humongous collection of lands into the Ottoman Empire. Ottoman power lasted until the 20th century. In its heyday, the empire made significant inroads into Eastern Europe. Animosity between Islamic Bosnians and Christian Serbs, which fueled a war in Bosnia and Herzegovina in the 1990s, is rooted in long-ago Ottoman incursions west.

European traders who lusted after Eastern riches had to take the Ottomans into account, because these Turks blocked the land trade routes. Coupled with

Venice's and Genoa's dominance in the Mediterranean, the Turkish presence made other Europeans wonder whether they could find their own Silk Roads, perhaps by sea. One sailing ship could carry more cargo than many camels could, anyway. The problem was that no one knew yet how to get from Europe to East Asia by water.

Necessity, as the saying goes, became the mother of invention. Or maybe it was greed more than necessity. Either way, this hunger to find a new way to get the treasure of the Far East gave birth to a new age of European empires.

The Portuguese, Dutch, Spanish, and English wanted a piece of the Asian market and began exploring as never before. The first to risk a bold western course toward Asia, Christopher Columbus, didn't find what he was looking for, but he did bump into the Americas, which were soon a lucrative market for the dirty business of selling enslaved people to force them to work raising valuable commodities such as tobacco and sugar. (For more about Columbus, skip ahead to the section "Seeking a Way East and Finding Places to the West.")

Mounting the Crusades

It may seem that 21st-century civilization has become so globally interconnected because of air travel and the digital revolution, especially communications satellites and the Internet. Yet today's worldwide connections, as you can tell by skimming almost any section in this chapter, really started taking shape many centuries back.

The Crusades are perhaps the earliest events that pointed forcefully toward today's world, which is still deeply marked by the European empires of the 16th to 20th centuries. In a nutshell, the Crusades were hundreds of years of sporadic Christian military campaigns. (For more about the marks left on today's world by Europe's second-millennium empires, see the sidebar "Putting cultural dominance in perspective" in this chapter. Don't worry; it's not as stuffy as that title makes it sound.)

Meeting the main players

The Crusades began in 1095, when diverse Europeans, answering a call from the pope and united in religious zeal (or so they said), tried to free the Holy Land, Palestine, from Turkish rulers. They weren't the Ottoman Turks, whose great empire would supplant the Byzantine Empire in the 15th century, but their predecessors in Middle Eastern empire-building, the Seljuk Turks.

The Seljuk Turks were a nomadic and marauding population of barbarians from wild north-central Asia. Barbarians show up in chapters 5 and 6 as well as in this chapter because they kept showing up in successive centuries, riding into lands as diverse and far-flung as China and Spain.

Like the China-conquering Mongols, the Turks called their chiefs by the title khan. In the early centuries of the first millennium, Turks were a subject people, paying tribute (sort of like taxation without representation) to another barbarian group, the Juan-Juan. But as the Arab conquests of the seventh and eighth centuries spread the religion Islam, the Turks converted and adopted the Arab fervor for empire-building.

The Seljuk ascendancy (conquering Asia Minor in the 11th century and beating the armies of the Byzantine Empire) alarmed Christendom all the way back to Rome, where the last straw for Pope Urban II was the Seljuk takeover of Palestine. Western Christians felt possessive about this land because Jesus of Nazareth had lived and died there, and it contained the holiest shrines of Christianity. Meanwhile, nobody asked the people living in 11th-century Palestine whether they wanted to be freed from Turkish rule.

The pope was also angered by reports that Turks were messing with Christian pilgrims on their way to shrines in the Holy Land. As Muslims, the Seljuk rulers had little reason to protect these travelers, who were easy pickings for robbers. The pope got so ticked off that in 1095, he called for a war to make Jerusalem safe for Christians again. The Crusades, the answer to his call, may have started as idealistic religious adventures, but they descended into brutal wars of hatred, greed, and opportunism.

TECHNICAL STUFF

Seljuk Turks, like the Mongols, were superior horsemen; Seljuk warriors could fire accurate arrows at full gallop while standing in their stirrups. This skill helped them wreak havoc on established powers as they swept through Afghanistan and Persia in the 11th century, taking over Jerusalem on their way to Baghdad, the declining capital of an earlier Muslim empire founded by Arabs, to conquer the Middle East.

Looking at the misguided zeal of specific Crusades

Sadly, the thousands of ordinary Europeans who set out for Palestine full of Christian fervor were the Crusaders least likely to survive. They were ignorant and in no way ready for what they'd face. But well-armed nobles and skilled warriors went East too. Here's a rundown of some of the Crusades:

» **First Crusade:** In 1099, the first official European force to reach Jerusalem massacred most of the people it found there before setting up European-ruled Latin Kingdoms, notably the Kingdom of Jerusalem, along the eastern shore of the Mediterranean.

» **People's Crusade:** The People's Crusade was a ragtag part of the First Crusade led by an itinerant preacher from France, a monk called Peter the Hermit. His followers walked into a Seljuk slaughter. (For more about Peter the Hermit and his colleague Walter the Penniless, see Chapter 20.)

» In the build-up to the Second Crusade, which began in 1147, a fanatical French monk, preaching in favor of the expedition, claimed Jews in Germany were not supporting the cause. This inspired mobs, including Crusaders preparing for their adventure. These Crusaders brutally attacked Jewish residents of the Rhine Valley and cities including Cologne and Mainz.

» **Third Crusade:** In 1189, the expeditionary force of the Third Crusade ventured eastward to attack the Kurdish leader Saladin, who had united Syrian and Egyptian Muslim forces and captured the city of Jerusalem from its Christian rulers in 1187. Members of this force included King Richard I (Lionheart) of England, Emperor Frederick I (Barbarossa) of the Holy Roman Empire, and King Philip II of France. The emperor drowned while crossing a stream.

» **Fourth Crusade:** The Fourth Crusade (1202–04) may have been the ugliest of all. Crusaders sacked Constantinople, a Christian city, and then briefly based another Latin Kingdom there (as if the split between the Roman Catholic and Eastern Orthodox churches wasn't already wide enough).

» **Children's Crusade:** The Children's Crusade of 1212 was the most pitiful one. About 50,000 impoverished kids, and many poor adults too, walked southward from France and Germany under the delusion that they could restore Palestine to Christian control yet again. Most of the tots who made it as far as Italy's seaports succeeded only in sailing straight into the Muslim slave markets of North Africa and the Middle East. Few were ever heard from again. Some people say that the story about the Pied Piper of Hamelin is based on the Children's Crusade.

Setting a precedent for conquest

Where did Europeans of the 16th through 19th centuries get the nerve to sail all over the world, claiming chunks of other continents for their kings back home? You could argue that their attitude hearkens back to Rome's imperial habits or that the Europeans, many of barbarian stock (and thus perhaps as much Asian as European), were born to fierce conquest.

You could make those arguments, but you'd be making a stretch. More accurately, you could reach back to the Middle Ages and the need to fight off Viking invaders, and show how that need prompted feudal vassals to rally around strong leaders. This trend began to build nations such as England as it took shape under Saxon kings such as Alfred the Great and Æthelstan. But nation-building was a slow process, and Europeans didn't yet think in terms of political states based on national identity. (For more on the emergence of strong kings and the beginnings of nation-building, see Chapter 6.)

The Crusades shaped a European, Christian outlook on the rest of the world and taught Westerners to assert themselves beyond Europe. Rulers put their resources into an imperial venture in a systematic way, setting a precedent for the exercise of power. Christendom became militant, confident of its ability to stomp other parts of the globe. Militant confidence served Europe's nations well several centuries later, after its navigators arrived at a reasonably accurate idea of what the planet looked like.

Growing Trade between East and West

Early in the 13th century, Genghis Khan and his Mongol clan conquered a huge swath of Asia stretching from the Pacific Ocean all the way to northeastern Europe above the Black Sea. For part of that century, these lands were under one rule, and even after Khan died in 1227, they remained a loose affiliation of allied Mongol powers.

The Mongol Empire cleared northern trade routes between East and West, some of them using the Volga and Dnieper rivers (which feed into the Black Sea) and the Caspian Sea of the Middle East. Vikings and Slavs had used these routes for centuries, and now, thanks to the Mongols, northern Europeans could take advantage of an Eastern trade pipeline that flowed more freely than ever before.

As new goods filtered into northern Europe, towns grew fat. Hamburg flourished on the Elbe River, as did Lubeck on the Baltic Sea. But merchants had a problem: These towns had no reliable, unified government and no source of widely recognized order to defend their shipping routes from robbers and pirates.

In 1241, businesspeople in Hamburg and Lubeck formed a hansa, an association for their mutual protection. Early in the next century, that association grew into the Hanseatic League, a commercial confederation of some 70 towns stretching from Flanders (today Belgium and part of northern France) to Russia. Its interests were purely commercial, but the league performed some governmental functions too. It even went to war in the middle of the 14th century, when Danish King Waldemar IV tried to mess with its trading. In the end, King Waldemar proved to be no match for King Commerce.

PUTTING CULTURAL DOMINANCE IN PERSPECTIVE

Europeans spent several centuries of the second millennium AD venturing out to other parts of the world, subjugating the locals and building empires. The world as you know it — with people speaking English in South Africa and Portuguese in Brazil — still bears the innumerable cultural and economic marks (many people call them scars) of these adventures.

Some people, including some historians (although none recently), treat this European ascendancy as though it were inevitable and even right. This shortsighted view is called Eurocentrism, and you may think you see it shaping the narrative in this book. If so, you're right. One reason is that European dominance has been so recent, relatively speaking, and it continues via Western clothing styles, the English language, Western-style economic systems, and the worldwide popularity of American movies. (It continues despite backlash from certain quarters, such as Islamic extremists who reject Western values. This book is partly an account of how civilization came to this particular point, so it must include the story of how European countries (and their heirs, such as the United States) accomplished what they did.

Throughout this book, I relate how one culture or another always seems to be coming to the forefront, dominating for centuries or even a millennium, and asserting itself as superior. I also point out how great civilizations can disappear so thoroughly that nobody remembers them. (For an example, see information on the Hittites in Chapter 4.) The disappearance of today's worldwide civilization seems to be inconceivable in an age of billionaires in space, cloud computing, and the other snazzy advances that have transformed commerce and daily life, but any study of history shows that civilizations not only rise, but also inevitably fall.

Surviving the Black Death

Europeans in the 14th century were looking at the world in a new way, seeing far-off places as being desirable, worth finding out about, and maybe even worth acquiring. Yet before Europeans really got out and started taking over that world, there had to be enough personal wealth back home to make a decent-size market for foreign luxuries. Oddly, it took a horrible disease and death on a massive scale for that market to find a foothold.

The Black Death (also called the Black Plague) was a devastating epidemic of bubonic plague and its variants that may have started in the foothills of Asia's Himalayan Mountain range. The origin, like that of COVID-19 in 2019, is a matter of debate, but in the 14th century, something happened to make disease spread, and many people have speculated that the culprit was the rise of trade. The disease lived in fleas carried by black rats, and where people go — especially people carrying food — so go rats and their parasites.

When a rat died, its fleas jumped to another rat. When no other rat was handy, the fleas tried less-desirable hosts. When those hosts were human, the people got terribly ill, and most of them died quickly. The blackish bruises that appeared beneath their skin were called buboes, which is where the name *bubonic plague* comes from. (Think of that next time you hear a child call a bruise a "boo-boo.") An even deadlier version of the disease, pneumonic plague, spread through the air from person to person.

Killing relentlessly

In 1333, the plague killed thousands of Chinese and spread west. By 1347, it reached Constantinople, where it was called the Great Dying, and it continued rapidly west through the Balkans, Italy, France, and Spain. Then, year by year, the disease advanced northward. Within a few years, the Black Death reached Russia, Scandinavia, and beyond, following the Viking trade routes to Iceland and wiping out Norse settlements in Greenland. (For more about the Norse in Greenland, refer to Chapter 6.)

As many as 25 million people died of the Black Plague in Europe. Maybe a third of the people in England fell. Periodic outbreaks followed for centuries after, but the Black Death had an impact even beyond the horror and sorrow it inspired. (And don't forget the morbid fascination: Many examples of art from this time focus on disease and death.)

Doing the math: Fewer folks, more wealth

The Black Plague so drastically reduced Europe's population that a smaller labor pool changed the economy. Ironically, this turn of events improved many Europeans' lives by creating disposable income, which in turn spurred a demand for Eastern luxuries and even Eastern ideas. The intellectual and cultural result of this reduction in population and Eastward focus came to be called the Renaissance. You can find out about the Renaissance in Chapter 13.

With so many dead, fewer people were left to work the land. A few workers had the spunk to stand up to the nobles and landowners, pointing out that they weren't about to work more for the same money — not when the supply of workers had become smaller and thus more valuable. The most famous of these uprisings was led by Wat Tyler, an English rabble-rouser who got himself killed for his trouble in 1381.

FALLING DOWN

Folklorists dismiss the idea, and they should know. Yet many history buffs think that the children's rhyme "Ring around the Rosie" may be much older, and much more morbid, than parents realize. They hear in it an echo of plague times, when "rosie" may have meant the rash that appeared as victims first came down with the disease. "Pocket full of posies," then, might refer to the use of flower petals as a defense against the overwhelming smell of death. "Ashes, ashes" is from the funereal Biblical passage "ashes to ashes, dust to dust." And the final line, "All fall down," may have carried the understanding that few victims, if any, would get back up again. The scholars who study oral traditions say there's no written evidence that the rhyme had those particular words until more recent centuries.

Post-plague economics forced some large landholders to split their estates into smaller plots. Instead of remaining mere sharecroppers who turned over the bulk of what they grew to the landlord, some laborers actually began earning pay for their work.

Though there were fewer people overall, more people had land, income, and the potential to buy goods. This condition stimulated the growth of villages into towns and towns into cities. There was an increase in merchants, craftspeople, and skilled traders who could supply goods. Up until that time, you were either rich or poor — usually poor. The plague helped create a middle class.

Seeking a Way East and Finding Places to the West

European nations' hunger for the luxuries possessed by China, India, Japan, Indonesia, and other Eastern cultures — and for the wealth that came to anyone who could import coveted goods such as silk cloth and rare spices — sent many adventurous sea captains of the 15th and 16th centuries in search of navigable sea routes to East Asian ports. (For more on those journeys and their results, see Chapter 8.) One particular navigator stands out from the rest, however, because he was the first we know of to sail westward in search of the lands that lay far to the east of Europe. This navigator was Christopher Columbus.

Columbus didn't find what he sought, but he changed world history in a fundamental way by landing on populated islands in the Caribbean Sea and, later, on mainland South America.

Meeting the Americans who met Columbus

The Arawak and Carib tribes both came to the islands later called the West Indies from northern South America. Before 500 AD, some Arawak migrated to the islands and farmed there for hundreds of years before the Carib followed, around 1000.

The Carib weren't as much into farming. By reputation—rightly or wrongly—they've been called warriors and cannibals who tortured, killed, and ate the men of the tribes they conquered, and turned the women into slave wives. Many latter-day skeptics, including descendants of these indigenous Americans, take exception to this depiction, contending that Columbus and his successors made up the whole cannibalism business as an excuse for Spaniards to enslave these people.

Arriving in the Indies, Columbus probably met some Arawak first and then the more hostile Carib. Full of hope that he was off the coast of Asia, Columbus called all the tribespeople Indians, and the name stuck.

Celebrating or ruing "discovery"

Christopher Columbus's discovery of the Americas, a part of the world unknown to his European contemporaries, opened the way for colonization and trade, bringing great wealth to Spain, the nation that sponsored his four voyages to the Caribbean Sea, and to other imperial European powers. His discovery also began centuries of death and destruction for native populations and their cultures. Although many people of European heritage have in past celebrated Columbus as a hero, more recent evaluations take into account all the negatives — devastating disease, slavery, slaughter, and displacement — that followed his "discovery" in 1492.

Training and experience shaped Columbus

For his part, Columbus never sought to discover a "new world" and went to his grave in 1506 without admitting that he had done so.

Genoa-born in 1471 and reared at sea, Columbus read the ancient Greeks, particularly the astronomer Ptolemy, who lived in Alexandria, Egypt in the 2nd century AD, when it was part of the Roman Empire. Ptolemy envisioned the world as a globe. His influential writings were preserved by the literate Arab culture that later ruled Egypt, and they came to Europe through Arabic translations.

TECHNICAL STUFF

Lisbon, Portugal, the port city where Columbus lived, was a good base for a seafarer because it was the location of Europe's foremost school for navigation, astronomy, and mapmaking (established by Prince Henry the Navigator in the 15th century). Graduates explored Africa's west coast, searching for a way around the continent to the Indies. (You can read more about these explorers and their discoveries in Chapter 8. Henry the Navigator appears in Chapter 21.)

Stumbling upon the West Indies

Columbus proposed to Queen Isabella I of Castile that he could find a sea lane linking Europe and India by sailing west instead of east — the direction that would have occurred to most European sailors. The navigator possessed both the education and the common sense to grasp Earth's general shape, even as he seriously underestimated its circumference. His discoveries paid off for Isabella and her husband, King Ferdinand, whose 1469 marriage had effectively, if not officially, united Spain. But the impact of what he'd done wasn't immediately apparent, and Columbus doggedly refused to face up to the fact that he led Europeans to continents they hadn't previously known about.

After his first voyage to the Caribbean, he kept going back there (it was later, after Columbus died, named after the Carib). He did not return repeatedly because he loved piña coladas and that calypso rhythm (neither of which existed then), but because he couldn't admit that what he'd found was someplace entirely new — to European navigators, anyway.

SMOKIN'

Among the most puzzling things that Columbus brought back from the West Indies were the pungent leaves and seeds of a plant that the Caribbean natives prized. Dried leaves of this kind were among the first presents Native Americans offered the European visitors, who didn't know what to do with them and threw them away. It was just as well for the sailors' lungs that they did because the leaves were tobacco.

A couple of Columbus's colleagues, Rodrigo de Jerez and Luis de Torres, saw natives in Cuba forming the leaves into the shape of a musket with a palm or corn-shuck wrapper, lighting one end on fire, putting the other to their mouths, and drinking the smoke. Jerez tried it, got hooked, and took the habit back to Spain. The smoke billowing from his mouth and nose frightened his neighbors, and they reported him to the Spanish Inquisition. Jerez spent seven years in prison. (And some people think that today's anti-smoking laws are extreme.)

REMEMBER

Columbus wanted the Americas to be East Asia, telling himself and anybody who would listen that these islands were just some obscure part of Indonesia called the Indies. If Cuba wasn't part of mainland Asia, which he made his officers swear it was, he wanted Cuba to be Japan. Who wanted a New World when an old one — China — was the sea trader's big prize?

Tracking the Centuries

618 AD: The T'ang Dynasty takes control of China, beginning a period of technological innovation that includes the invention of printing and gunpowder.

About 1000 AD: Members of the Carib tribe sail from Venezuela to islands in the Caribbean (as it would later be named). Carib people are still there when Columbus arrives 500 years later.

1147: Christian Crusaders and their supporters, preparing to ride eastward to liberate Jerusalem from Muslim rule, join anti-Semitic mobs in Germany's Rhine Valley to massacre resident Jews.

1212: About 50,000 poor people, most of them children, walk from France and Germany toward Italy's seaports. These Crusaders believe that they can free the Holy Land from Muslim rule. Those who don't collapse along the way are sold in the slave markets of North Africa.

1241: Two northern European trading cities, Hamburg and Lubeck, form a hansa that eventually grows into the Hanseatic League, a commercial and quasigovernmental confederation of some 70 towns.

1275: Marco Polo, a young Venetian, arrives in Beijing and takes a job in the diplomatic service of the Chinese emperor.

1347: The Black Death (bubonic plague) reaches Constantinople on its march across Asia to Europe. The Byzantines call the epidemic the Great Dying.

1381: In England, Wat Tyler leads peasants in a revolt against landowners. He dies in the conflict, but the rebellion brings agrarian reforms.

1571: The commercial city-state Venice loses its island colony Cyprus to the Ottoman Empire. Without this Adriatic outpost, Venetian trade and influence begin a steep, permanent decline.

Chapter 8

Grabbing the Globe

When European sailors set out looking for new sea routes in the 15th and 15th centuries, they were in it for the money. Riches beckoned. Some sailors whose voyages changed maps of the world and the world itself include

- » **Christopher Columbus:** A Genoese (from the Italian city-state of Genoa) sailing for Spain, he discovered America in 1492 because he was trying to get to Asia, a source of lucrative trade goods.

- » **Vasco da Gama:** A Portuguese captain who was also looking for a sea route to Asia as he rounded Africa and sailed east, he successfully reached India in 1498.

- » **Ferdinand Magellan:** Also Portuguese, but sailing on behalf of Spain, he set out for Asia's Spice Islands (today's Indonesia) by a different route from da Gama's in 1519.

Magellan died on the voyage, but he proved that it was possible to get from Europe to Asia by sailing west, as Columbus claimed. (You just had to steer south of the

South American mainland first.) He also proved that Europeans could circle the globe. The one surviving ship of his original five rounded Africa from the east and sailed into San Sanlúcar de Barrameda, Spain, in 1522.

Magellan's achievement was a huge step in navigation and a symbolic triumph. Europeans could circle the world by sailing — and soon thereafter by trade and military conquest.

Also in the early 16th century, two Spanish generals conquered the two greatest civilizations in the Americas:

>> Hernan Cortés defeated the Aztecs of Mexico in 1521.

>> Francisco Pizarro brought down the Inca Empire of Peru in 1533.

In this chapter, you'll meet adventurers who introduced the reality of a "New World" to their fellow Europeans. The term referred to the Americas, but in a sense, the entire world was new because it was suddenly within reach — a ripe plum ready to be picked. You'll see how the Spanish and Portuguese, soon joined by the Dutch, English, and French, picked the plum by trading with, conquering, exploiting, and enslaving the indigenous people of the Americas, Africa, and more. You'll also find out about how European sea powers began to face consequences for bringing most of the globe under their influence. Almost as soon as Europeans subdued other peoples, those subjects began fighting to break free. This age of empires became an age of revolutions, and not just in the Americas and other colonial lands. You'll see how freedom fever spread, and how revolution came to Europe as well.

Sailing South to Get East

For Europeans, 1498 seemed an even more monumental year than 1492, when "Columbus sailed the ocean blue." Columbus was trying to reach the rich ports of Asia by sea — a major goal for traders and navigators. Vasco da Gama, sailing for King Manuel I (Manuel the Fortunate) of Portugal, actually did what Columbus failed to do: He found a sea route to the East.

Da Gama found this route by sailing south around the tip of Africa, up that continent's east coast, through the treacherous waters between the big island of Madagascar and the African mainland, and then, with the help of an Arab navigator, across the Indian Ocean. The greatest seafaring venture yet, da Gama's journey made good on its promise of an economic payoff, whereas Columbus's mistaken discovery of bewilderingly wild islands had yet to prove economically rewarding.

Getting a foothold in Indian trade

Vasco da Gama crossed the Arabian Sea and arrived on India's Malabar Coast (the southwestern edge of the subcontinent) in 1498. He docked near the city of Kozhikode (often written as *Calicut*). He was eager for Asian spices but hadn't come well prepared. By custom, the way to honor the Hindu ruler of Kozhikode, called the Samoothiri (or Zamorin), especially if you wanted a favor, was to shower him with gifts. But the Indians weren't impressed by da Gama's offer of washbasins, bolts of cloth, hats, beads, and lumps of sugar. These items went over well on the coast of western Africa, but they were laughable in trade-rich Kozhikode, a well-established commercial port for Arab and Chinese ships and merchants.

Da Gama had to work hard to reach any deal at all. But after three months of appeals, he received approval to do business and was able to buy enough spices to impress the folks back home in Lisbon, even though he hadn't achieved the trade relationship with Kozhikode that he'd sought.

Demanding respect

Vasco da Gama's first voyage to India seemed to point the way toward peaceful trade. Before he returned to Kozhikode, however, the tone of East–West relations turned ugly.

Just two of da Gama's four ships and 55 members of his original crew of 177 survived the first trip to India and back. Those losses were considered reasonable for the time, especially for such a great breakthrough. King Manuel of Portugal sponsored a second expedition, led by Pedro Cabral, in 1500. On his way down the coast of Africa, Cabral veered so far west that he "discovered" Brazil. Cabral claimed it for Portugal, giving King Manuel a piece of the New World in addition to the route to Asia.

On the Malabar Coast, Cabral built on da Gama's work, winning trade privileges by negotiating the kind of treaty that da Gama had wanted. He installed a small community of Portuguese to represent King Manuel's interests and establish a trading post. But members of the region's Arab merchant guild saw the Europeans as unwanted competition. Some Muslim businessmen attacked the Portuguese, killed most of them, and destroyed their trading post.

An enraged King Manuel responded by sending da Gama again, this time in the capacity of enforcer, commanding a well-armed fleet, and with orders to retaliate against the Arabs and their Indian trading partners.

Crossing the Arabian Sea toward India, da Gama intercepted a ship carrying hundreds of Muslims on their pilgrimage to Mecca. He demanded all the treasure on board; locked the crew and passengers belowdecks; and set the ship ablaze, killing everyone onboard, including women and babies.

When da Gama reached India, he demanded satisfaction for the attack on his countrymen, insisting that Muslims be banned from Kozhikode. When local authorities refused, he responded with more brutal violence, mutilating a Hindu priest who served as the ruler's negotiator, harassing Arab ships that were trying to trade at Kozhikode, killing innocent fishermen, and provoking a sea battle against the Hindu ruler.

In the following years, Portugal took control of Kozhikode and used similar tactics to turn other Indian ports into colonies. In addition to being first to sail directly from Europe to South Asia, da Gama had set the violent pattern that Europeans would follow to subdue much of Asia in the following centuries.

"Discovering" America

Columbus didn't think of himself as a discoverer, and you shouldn't either. The whole notion of discovery is insulting to the people who already lived in the Americas and had no inkling that they were undiscovered.

Many kinds of people lived in the Americas before Columbus arrived. He called the people he encountered on Caribbean Islands Indians because he thought he was in Asia, so the original people of the Americas have been lumped together under that label ever since. (Some of them prefer to be called Native Americans, Amerindians, or First Nations.) No matter what you call them, these Americans were never a single culture. They lived in widely differing climates, made their livings in different ways, spoke different languages, and wore different styles of clothes. Even their origins may have been more different than was once thought. Until late in the 20th century, many scholars believed that all the pre-Columbian Americans could be traced to a single crossing of a land bridge that linked Asia with Alaska between 20,000 and 10,000 years ago. Then archaeological finds began to suggest that at least some people were living in the Americas much earlier and that other groups arrived at different times.

By the time the Europeans came, the Americas had seen civilizations rise and fall. The Spanish arrived in time to see the great Maya civilization of Mexico and the Yucatan, although its impressive cities were in deep decline by the 16th century.

In 1519, Spanish military commander Hernan Cortés came across a great city north of the Maya settlements in the highlands of central Mexico. This city, the Aztec capital Tenochtitlán, was at its peak. Spanish soldiers said that Tenochtitlán, with its brightly painted pyramids and broad causeways linking the island city to the mainland, was as magnificent as Rome or Constantinople. The Spaniards went on to wreck it, of course, but nobody ever said that conquest is pretty.

Although pre-Columbian civilizations boasted many accomplishments, they lacked some key advantages that the Spanish invaders enjoyed:

>> **Gunpowder:** This technology had spread all the way from China to Europe but didn't touch the Americas until the Spaniards arrived.

>> **Iron:** Although several American cultures achieved splendid metalworking by the 16th century, none had learned to make harder, more durable iron weapons.

>> **Horses:** Although wild horses had once roamed ancient North America, they'd gone extinct, and there were no horses in the Americas again until the Spanish arrived. (See Chapter 17 for more on the horse's role in warfare.)

>> **Immunities:** The most important reason why Europeans prevailed over natives may be that they brought with them diseases that had never crossed the ocean before. Indigenous Americans had no biological defenses against these diseases.

How the Aztecs rose and fell

Before the Aztecs of Mexico rose to power, they were a conquered people, essentially enslaved. Legend says they followed a prophecy that told them to build their capital, Tenochtitlán, where they saw an eagle sitting on a cactus (ouch!) eating a snake. The cactus happened to be on an island in a big lake (now covered by Mexico City). More credible accounts say that the Aztecs chose the island as a defensive position and hideout from their former masters.

Mexico adopted the image of the eagle, snake, and cactus in its national flag, the detail of which is shown in Figure 8-1.

Becoming masters

The Aztecs (also called the Mexica) founded Tenochtitlán around 1345 and began developing military skills so that other people could no longer enslave them. They built temples, roads, an aqueduct, and causeways over the lake. They also established a hierarchical society in which commoners, although allowed to own land, were expected to pay tribute to and serve nobles, who were believed to have descended from the god Quetzalcoatl. Family lineage determined a person's place within townlike communities. These communities were grouped into territorial states, which were ruled by local chiefs or kings. The Aztec Empire took shape as key states joined in an ever-broader alliance.

FIGURE 8-1:
The Mexican flag commemorates a legend about the Aztecs.

By the 15th century, the Aztecs were strong enough to turn the tables on tribes that had been their former masters. Aztec leaders Itzcóatl and Moctezuma I (or Montezuma) waged wars of conquest throughout the Valley of Mexico and beyond.

Why did they fight? In part, they thought that the Aztec war god, Huitzilopochtli, demanded sacrificial victims. The Aztec religion included the belief that Huitzilo-pochtli especially relished fresh human hearts, preferably from brave victims. At the dedication of a pyramid in 1489, Aztec priests cut up 20,000 captives. Victims of the Aztecs' wars fed Huitzilopochtli.

Believing in the return of Quetzalcóatl

In the 16th century, things went haywire for the Aztecs: Their subject people began to revolt. Their leader was by then Moctezuma II, who tried to restore order, but he was interrupted when a renegade Spanish explorer, Hernan Cortés, showed up in 1519. You may know this Aztec leader and his predecessor by the names "Montezuma I and II," but that Anglicized spelling and pronunciation have fallen out of favor with people who study Mexican history.

REMEMBER

Besides Huitzilopochtli, the Aztecs and their subject peoples feared the white-skinned, bearded deity Quetzalcóatl. According to a widely told myth dating back to the Maya, whose civilization predated the Aztec, Quetzalcóatl had gone across the sea and prophesied that he would return to rule the empire. Shortly after Cortés landed on the coast of the Yucatan Peninsula, he realized that to the locals, he fit this description. Natives thought the Spaniard and his soldiers were more than mere men. To Aztecs, who had never seen a horse, a mounted soldier looked like a two-headed beast.

When Cortés arrived at the Aztec capital, Moctezuma II welcomed him — possibly believing him to be Quetzalcóatl or trying to bribe him into an alliance. Cortés suspected a trap and took Moctezuma II captive. It was too late for the emperor by then anyway, because he had bowed before the Spaniards and lost the respect of his own subjects. When Moctezuma II next attempted to speak before the Aztecs, his audience turned on him and pelted him with stones and arrows, fatally injuring him. In 1521, leaderless Tenochtitlán fell to the Spaniards.

Incas grasp greatness and then fall to the Spanish

Cortés's conquest of the Aztecs in 1521 inspired another Spanish commander, Francisco Pizarro, to invade the greatest South American civilization, the Inca, a decade later. With only 200 troops to subdue an empire of more than a million people, it took him just two years to capture Cuzco, the Inca capital.

Cortés's prize, the Inca Empire, was at its height. Centered in the Andes Mountains of Peru and spread over a territory from northern Chile to Ecuador, the empire encompassed a network of tribes, all subjugated and administered by one dominant culture.

Building an empire like no other

Like the Aztecs to the north, the Inca started as a subject people under the thumb of previous Peruvian empires. Incas started flexing their muscles in the 12th century. In the 1430s, a ruler called Pachacuti repelled an invasion by a neighboring people and went on to increase the size of the Inca Empire until it encompassed parts of today's Chile, Bolivia, and Ecuador.

By the 16th century, Pachacuti's successors controlled more land than any South American people before them. Like the Romans (more on them in Chapter 5), the Incas brought the leadership of the people they conquered into the Inca fold, rewarding those who joined and making cooperation easier than resistance. Also like the Romans, the Incas were wonderful engineers. Inca stonemasons built fortifications of giant granite blocks fitted together so perfectly that a knife blade still won't penetrate a seam today.

Just as remarkably, the Incas maintained a 19,000-mile road system, and the government sent fleet-footed messengers along those roads, with runners stationed every 1½ miles. Using this system, they could send a message 150 miles in a day.

The ruling family held everything together, which proved to be the Inca's undoing. All Pizarro had to do to topple the empire was overcome the royals, which he accomplished in 1532 through base trickery.

Accepting the invaders' invitation

In 1532, Francisco Pizarro invited the king of the Incas, Atahualpa, to a meeting at Cajamarca, a city away from his capital. When the king arrived (along with his enormous royal retinue), Pizarro kidnapped him, surprised his followers, and killed several hundred of them. The victims included the king's family members. Atahualpa tried to ransom himself, but Pizarro wanted to use him as a puppet ruler. The king didn't go along with it, refusing to convert to Christianity, so Pizarro killed him too. Then Pizarro and his troops marched to Cuzco, Atahualpa's capital city, capturing it in 1533.

The Spanish spent about 30 years beating down revolts throughout former Inca lands (and fighting among themselves as they fought Indian rebels), but they were fully in control of the empire by the 1560s. The 1969 film *The Royal Hunt of the Sun* is adapted from a hit British stage play and tells the story of Pizarro and Atahualpa's encounter. Unlike the play, which was revived in London in 2006, the movie, starring Robert Shaw and Christopher Plummer, wasn't a box-office success.

Circling the Planet

Like Vasco da Gama, Ferdinand Magellan was a Portuguese explorer who found a sea route to Asia. Like Christopher Columbus, Magellan was a non-Spanish commander of a Spanish flotilla that tried to reach Asia by sailing west from Europe.

Magellan's expedition was successful in spite of the fact that it lost its captain, four of its five ships, all its officers, and most of its crew on the eventful voyage that went across the Atlantic, through the straits at the southern tip of South America (ever after called the Straits of Magellan), across the Pacific Ocean (Magellan named it), through the coveted ports of the Spice Islands (in today's Indonesia), around Africa from the east, and home.

TECHNICAL STUFF

Although he died on the trip, Magellan (whose name in Portuguese was Fernao de Magalhaes) gets credit for being the first navigator to circle the globe. He made it as far as the Philippines, and as Magellan may have earlier sailed that far east with Portuguese expeditions, you could say that he personally sailed around the world.

Technically, his ship's master (like a chief petty officer on a modern ship), Juan Sebastian del Cano (or de Elcano), was the first commander to circumnavigate the globe, arriving home in Spain in 1522. He took command of the expedition after Philippine natives killed Magellan.

The expedition's success gave Europeans proof that the Americas were more than just an unexplored part of Asia. The vast ocean to the west of the New World confirmed that it really was a new world — to Europeans, anyway. Further, Magellan proved that it was possible to get at Asia from either direction. In 1522, when his one remaining ship and its few sick, emaciated sailors returned to Spain, Asia was still the prize that European traders and their monarchs coveted most.

Ottomans ascend among Eastern empires

Although Europeans were strong and becoming stronger with their worldwide sea routes, they couldn't immediately grab up huge parts of Asia the way Spain and Portugal claimed all of South and Central America in the late 15th and early 16th centuries. This was still a time of Asian empires or, in the case of the Ottoman Empire, of an enormous Asian, African, and European empire.

Amassing a vast area

The Ottoman Empire arose at the end of the 13th century in northern Asia Minor (part of today's Turkey). Related to the Mongols and other nomads, the Turks, a loosely connected group of nomadic peoples from central Asia, were organized into dynastic clans. One such clan was the Seljuk Turks, who were powerful in the Middle East in the 11th century. European crusaders battled the Seljuk Turks in the First Crusade of 1095. The Ottomans, another clan of Turks, captured Constantinople in 1453, ending the Byzantine Empire.

TECHNICAL STUFF

The Ottoman Turks weren't named for a padded footstool; rather, the footstool, adapted from a Middle Eastern style of low, backless chair, was named after these people.

Like the Seljuk Turks before them, as well as Arabs and other people through western Asia, the Ottoman Turks were Muslim. (See Chapter 6 for more about the rise and spread of Islam.) Also like the Arabs, the Ottoman Turks assembled a great empire that, like the Byzantine Empire before it, bridged western Asia and Eastern Europe. Besides stretching from Budapest in Hungary to Baghdad in Iraq to Aswan on the upper Nile, at its height it also encompassed the Mediterranean coast of Africa.

Looking eastward to other Asian empires

Another nomadic people like the Turks, the Mongols came out of Central Asia to build empires. Their greatest warrior-king, Genghis Khan, controlled a huge empire across Asia to northeastern Europe in the 13th century. His grandson, Kublai Khan, conquered China and established a dynasty there in 1280.

The Mongol Empire fell apart in the late 13th century, but descendants of Genghis Khan continued to exert power. One of the most famous, the brutal Timur, came out of Turkestan to bedevil the Persians and Ottomans in the 14th century. Sometimes called Tamerlane or Timur the Lame (because of a pronounced limp), he was an able warrior and merciless conqueror whose acquisitions ranged as far as Moscow, which his troops occupied in the late 1390s. Timur's descendant Babur conquered northern India (including today's Pakistan) in 1526, founding the Mogul Dynasty. The name is a variation on *Mongol*, in reference to Babur's empire-building heritage.

The Mogul Dynasty eventually claimed most of the Indian subcontinent and boasted strong rulers and remarkable stability until the 18th century, when struggles within the royal court weakened central authority. The empire began to crumble as provincial rulers, nominally subject to the Mogul king, claimed more power for themselves. This decline of Mogul rule eased the way in India for trade-hungry European nations. The British abolished the Mogul court in 1857.

European traders moved quickly into the East after the Portuguese opened the sea route around Africa in 1498. Portugal conquered Goa Velha (old Goa), capital of what is now the Indian State of Goa, and sailed on to the Spice Islands (in today's Indonesia). It also claimed Macao, a peninsula jutting from the coast of China near Canton.

The Portuguese built fortified outposts from which they could monopolize the spice trade in the Far East. Commerce paid so well that the Dutch and British couldn't just sit by and watch while Portugal raked in the gold.

Founding East India companies

In 1599, 80 London merchants got together to form the East India Company; Queen Elizabeth I granted them a charter in 1600. The Dutch formed their own East India Company in 1602. The French got in on this action with their East India Company, founded in 1664.

For a short time, the Portuguese enjoyed a trading monopoly as the only European nation with the navigational charts and the trade contacts necessary to transport Asian goods by sea. How did the East India companies get around the Portuguese monopoly? Much the way the Portuguese established that monopoly in the first place: by muscling in. After Britain established its first trading station at Surat, India, in 1612, the British moved on to other Indian ports. In 1639, the British built a fort and trading post at a fishing village called Madrasapattinam (Madras Town), on the Bay of Bengal. This post grew into the city of Madras, for which the plaid fabric Madras is named. Britain's traders built a post at Mumbai in 1688 and founded Calcutta as their Indian headquarters in 1690.

The Dutch captured Jakarta, a city with a fine protected harbor on the north coast of Java (part of today's Indonesia), in 1619 and renamed it Batavia after the Batavii, a Celtic tribe in the Netherlands during Roman times. The Dutch East India Company made Batavia its headquarters. Not until 1949 did a newly independent Indonesia restore the name Jakarta.

In 1638, the Dutch got another exclusive: In an edict banning European traders from Japan's ports, that country's isolationist ruler made them the single exception. In return for the right to stay, the Dutch had to promise not to preach Christianity. The spice trade proved to be a high-risk profession. The Dutch took Amboyna, a base in the Moluccas, away from the Portuguese. Then, when English merchants tried to trade there, the Dutch put the interlopers to death.

TELLING EAST FROM WEST

You may wonder why the British, Dutch, and French trading organizations in Asia were called East India Companies. Yes, India is to the east of Europe. But when the companies were forming, there were those other Indies in the west. When Columbus arrived in the Caribbean in 1492, he wanted desperately for the islands he found there to be part of Asia. He imagined that he was in Indonesia, so he called the Caribbean islands Indies. For more on Columbus, see Chapter 7 and the first few sections of this chapter.

After everybody figured out that Columbus was wrong — that the American islands to the west of Europe were different from the Asian islands to the east — they distinguished between the islands by saying West Indies and East Indies. For a while there, every time you headed out from port, you had to specify which Indies you intended to reach.

Closing the door to Japan

Japan was a special case among Asian nations. Isolated by the sea, it had never succumbed to the invasions of nomadic tribes that roamed the rest of East Asia and rose to power as empire-builders (people such as the Mongols, whom I discuss in Chapter 7). Since 1192, power in Japan had been in the hands of a warrior class. Authority was concentrated in the shogun, a warlord nominally appointed by the emperor but in reality far more powerful. The shoguns of the Tokugawa family, which ruled from 1603–1868, were essentially military dictators. Here's a rundown on the first three of these shoguns:

>> Tokugawa Ieyasu, the first Tokugawa shogun, gained office at the end of a series of messy civil wars. He was suspicious of outsiders, especially Europeans. In 1614, he signed an edict banning Christianity, which led to the later expulsion of all missionaries.

>> Tokugawa Hidetada inherited his father Ieyasu's distrust of Christians. Hidetada thought that if the Christians gained too many Japanese converts, Japan's ability to defend itself against a European invasion would be weakened. The shogun persecuted Christians more and more severely; in 1622, his officials in Nagasaki crucified 55 missionaries at the same time.

>> Tokugawa Iemitsu, the next shogun, was the one who finally threw all missionaries and most traders out of Japan during his reign (1623–51). He outlawed foreign travel for Japanese and forbade shipbuilders from building the big vessels needed for long-range voyages. Tokugawa Iemitsu even restricted Buddhism, preferring the Confucian emphasis on loyalty to superiors.

Japan continued to trade with China, Korea, and a small contingent of Dutch, the latter being kept off the mainland most of the time on an island in Nagasaki Bay. The Togugawa family successfully kept Japan closed off from extensive Western trade until the mid-19th century.

Playing by British East India Company rules

The British, shut out of Molucca and Japan, had plenty of other ports to exploit, especially in India. From its headquarters in Calcutta, the British East India Company traded in textiles and expanded its influence. It oversaw the administration of trade, but it also governed British subjects in its trading ports and beyond, becoming a quasi-government.

In the mid-18th century, the British East India Company expanded its role to military power, declaring war on the local Mogul ruler, or nawab. The nawab, Siraj-ud-Daulah, had asked the British to stop fortifying Calcutta. When they refused, he captured the city in 1756, forcing company officials to flee. The nawab's forces captured a garrison of East India Company guards and threw them into a small jail known ever after as the Black Hole of Calcutta. A British survivor claimed that 146 people were thrown into the 18- by 14-foot jail overnight and that all but 23 died. (Later scholarship showed that the number of prisoners was probably 64 to start with.)

The story rallied British popular opinion against Siraj-ud-Daulah and firmed up the East India Company's resolve to fight back. The company's soldiers responded by attacking and defeating a coalition of provincial Muslim rulers allied with the nawab and the Mogul emperor. At war's end, a British trading enterprise had transformed itself into the provincial ruler of the Bengal region of India.

The company's power and profits grew alarmingly, and so did mismanagement and corruption. Irresponsible speculation in company stock contributed to a banking crisis in 1772, and the British government passed a series of laws to reform the East India Company, requiring more direct government supervision of company affairs.

In 1857, a conflict known as the Sepoy Rebellion (or Mutiny) began when Hindu and Muslim rebels massacred British soldiers, and the British responded with overwhelming weaponry and mass executions. The uprising against East India Company rule forced the government in London to reexamine colonial policies again. In 1858, Parliament passed an act requiring the East India Company to hand its powers over to the British Crown.

Going from Ming to Qing in China

The Ming Dynasty ruled China from 1368–1644, a period distinguished by good government, peace, artistic achievements, and prosperity. Ming emperors took an interest in the common people's welfare, going so far as to break up large estates and redistribute them among the poor. Was this some kind of prelude to the socialist government that the Chinese established in the 20th century? Not really, but it was forward-thinking.

China was also fortunate that when the Ming Dynasty finally crumbled in 1644, a ruling family from the province of Manchuria took over, establishing the long-lived Qing (or Chi'ing) Dynasty, which lasted into the 20th century. At its height, the Qing Dynasty gave China some of its ablest emperors and most stable administrations ever.

Kangxi, the Qing emperor from 1736–96, molded himself into the image of the ideal Confucian ruler: a benevolent protector of the people. (Chapter 10 has more on Confucianism.) Kangxi stressed loyalty, traditional morality, and hard work for the common good — especially in farming.

Adequate food production is the greatest common good in a country growing as fast as China was in the 18th century. By 1800, the population was 300 million, double what it was a century before. Under successive Qing emperors, the Chinese developed fast-maturing varieties of rice so that they could produce multiple harvests within a single growing season.

The Qing Dynasty traded successfully, even importing foods such as corn and sweet potatoes from the Americas. (With 300 million mouths to feed, why not?) But China was still suspicious of and resistant to most European business overtures, restricting foreign traders to specific ports such as Canton and Shanghai. For most transactions, the Chinese wanted hard currency such as precious metals. The British East India Company had to pay for tea and other Chinese goods with silver. The Brits felt that they were getting the short end of this deal, so they looked for something else the Chinese would take in trade. By the 19th century, they'd found it: opium, from British-ruled India. More and more Chinese, especially in the south, were smoking opium and becoming addicted, to the point that they were willing to pay for it in tea, silks, and even silver (which helped finance British India).

Opium destroyed Chinese lives and damaged the Chinese economy. For both reasons, the Qing emperor sent officials to Canton to burn 20,000 chests of British opium. This kind of thing riles a drug lord even today. The Brits were mad enough to go to war over it — and they won.

After the first Opium War, 1842's Treaty of Nanjing forced the Chinese to cede the island port of Hong Kong to Britain. Hong Kong remained a British Crown Colony through most of the 20th century. Another Opium War followed from 1856–60, with a similar result. China was forced to open more ports to British and other Western traders. (In 1997, Britain restored Hong Kong and adjacent territory to China.)

Spreading the Slave Trade

Slavery is evil. Ownership of human beings by other human beings is among the worst practices ever to blight humankind. Yet much of what is called civilization was built, at least in part, on slavery. In ancient cultures including Sumer, Babylon, ancient Greece, and Rome, slavery was an economic foundation and often considered to be a reasonably tolerable way of life for the poor — preferable to starving, anyway.

Perpetuating an evil

There had been a market in the Middle East for enslaved people from the ancient days of Sumer and Babylon forward. In the Middle Ages, Vikings found a way to get in on it. Although Sweden's western ports are on bodies of water called the Skagerrak and the Kattegat, which are arms of the North Sea, most of that country's seacoast is on the Baltic Sea, facing east. So Vikings from that part of Scandinavia, instead of heading off toward England, France, or Greenland, often sailed eastward. As these Norse adventurers explored harbors in today's Latvia, Lithuania, and Estonia, they began sailing farther up inlets and rivers into Russia. In Russia's northern, inland forests, they found a source of wealth: tribal people whom they captured to sell as slaves.

TECHNICAL STUFF

They carried their human cargo down the Dnieper River, which runs through western Russia, Ukraine, and Belarus on its way to the Black Sea. From there, they could sail to Constantinople. Farther east, the Volga flows south into the Caspian Sea, which borders today's Iran. From the Caspian Sea, the Vikings could reach the slave markets of Baghdad. When Christian missionaries first ventured into Scandinavia, the Norse captured and sold some of them too.

Arabs had long dealt in enslaved people and had sources besides the Viking traders for captives. Since conquering much of North Africa in the sixth and seventh centuries, the Arabs had taken people from that continent. (Find more about the Arab conquests in Chapter 6.)

African wars, like wars in much of the rest of the world since prehistoric times, often involved one tribe or village capturing people from another tribe or village. As Arab traders penetrated the continent, Africans learned that they could trade their captive enemies to these strangers for valuable goods.

The Arab trade created a slave economy in Africa, one that was still in force in the late 15th century. When Portuguese navigators began landing at West African ports, they found local slavers willing to sell them laborers. In 1482, Portuguese traders built their first slave-trading outpost in Ghana. By the early 16th century, the Portuguese were shipping captives to Portugal and to the Azores Islands in the Atlantic, where Portuguese settlers needed laborers. Within a few years, America was a new market for slaves, and the Portuguese were poised to supply that market.

Developing a new market

By the middle of the 16th century, Spanish settlers on Caribbean islands had decided that they needed a new source of forced labor. The local Indians, whom they used as workers, had no immunity to diseases from Europe. Many were sick or weak, and too many died.

The Spaniards began importing Africans, who were less likely to keel over from smallpox. (Smallpox — one of the deadliest diseases among Europeans and far more deadly to Caribbean Indians — was also widespread in Africa, so enslaved Africans carried natural resistance.) The first such captive people were purchased from Portuguese ships around 1530, beginning a trade that escalated sharply through the 16th and 17th centuries and peaked in the 18th century.

Also in the 16th century, the Spanish found that slave labor made cash crops such as sugar, which they could grow on Hispaniola and other Caribbean Islands, highly profitable. So, they bought more people. By 1700, 4,000 enslaved Africans arrived in the Spanish-ruled islands every year.

Portugal brought captured Africans to Brazil in such numbers that by 1800, half the population of that big country was of African heritage.

The English, who founded their first permanent settlement in North America at Jamestown, Virginia, in 1607, didn't wait long to begin importing forced workers. They also had a labor-intensive, profitable crop — tobacco — and needed more people in their fields. In 1619, the White Lion, a British-owned ship flying a Dutch flag, brought around 20 enslaved Africans — originally taken captive by the Portuguese — to Old Point Comfort, in what is today Hampton, Virginia. They were the first of many thousands of Africans purchased by English colonists in North America.

Profiting from a contemptible institution

Trafficking in enslaved people was one of the surest ways to get wealthy in the shipping business from 1500–1800. Europeans joined Arab traders and local African rulers who could also make fortunes in this ugly business. The Spanish, Dutch, British, French, and Danish all competed with the Portuguese by building slaving stations in Africa.

In 1713, Spain granted Britain a monopoly to supply its American colonies with 4,800 enslaved people a year for 30 years. Nobody knows how many were captured and sold, but they numbered perhaps 7 million in the 18th century alone. The numbers are hard to come by, partly because so many people died in transit. Appalling conditions onboard slave ships included packing chained captives into holds a little over 3 feet high. Many died in the filth, disease, and despair of these holds. Sailors dumped the bodies unceremoniously into the sea. Those who survived were sold at auctions.

Starting Revolutions

Many Europeans who came to the Americas wanted to distance themselves from the countries they came from for one reason or another. Often, the reason was economic. The New World offered land to the landless and opportunities to the poor.

Religion also played a part in making the New World a desirable destination. This was the case for separatist Christians from England who landed in North America in 1620 — the people whom many Americans honor as the Pilgrims of Plymouth Colony. In Massachusetts, these immigrants could do more than worship according to their own Puritan beliefs; they could also live and govern themselves by those beliefs. Over the previous century, as the Protestant Reformation flowered in northern Europe, England's state religion had gone from long-engrained Roman Catholicism to a new Church of England, back to Catholicism, and then to Church of England again. (For more about the Reformation, see Chapter 14.) Religious minorities, suffering repression and discrimination, wanted out, and North America represented a refuge. Another sect of Puritans founded Boston and other Massachusetts cities. Catholics came to Maryland, Baptists to Rhode Island, and Quakers to Pennsylvania.

England's religious turmoil in the 16th and 17th century did more than spur religiously-motivated emigration. It also brought political upheaval that pointed ahead to the American and French revolutions that would break out in the late 18th century.

Bringing in the new

Without realizing it, King Charles I of England, Scotland, and Ireland (the United Kingdom wasn't a formal entity quite yet) put himself in peril when in 1640, he convened Parliament to deal with financial matters. Charles, of the House of Stewart (Scottish royalty) had little other use for Parliament. He believed in a concept called the Divine Right of Kings, which stated that members of royalty were God's representatives on Earth, all-powerful within their individual realms.

Way back in 1215, that concept had suffered its first blow in England with the Magna Carta. Dissatisfied barons forced the unpopular King John to sign the document, which guaranteed English people — and especially English nobles — political and civil liberties. The Magna Carta (or Great Charter) was a step toward government by consent of the governed. (For more about the Magna Carta, see Chapter 24.) Not everybody considered the agreement to be binding, of course, especially not Pope Innocent III, who absolved King John of any responsibility to observe it.

Four centuries later, Charles I counted on his ability to convene and dissolve Parliament at will, but this time, the body passed a bill saying that he couldn't dissolve it without Parliament's consent. The members' defiance led to the English Civil War between Parliamentarians, largely supported by Puritans and other religious nonconformists, on one side and Royalists on the other. Ultimately, Charles I was tried and executed. From 1649–60, his former realm became a republic, referred to as the Commonwealth.

The British restored their monarchy in 1660, but late in the next century, two more antiroyalist revolutions appeared to be more likely to cast off the old order for good. The American Revolution of the 1770s and 1780s created the United States of America and spread the idea that colonists could break free of European rule. The French Revolution, beginning in 1789, shocked traditionalists even more deeply by revealing that the old order could be turned on its head right there in Europe. The French Revolution also confirmed that, as in England in 1649, the old order's head — in this case, King Louis XVI's head — could be chopped off and tossed into a bloody basket.

Playing with dangerous ideas

Before the American and French revolutions came an intellectual movement: the Enlightenment.

The revolutions grew out of economic and political issues between people and their rulers, but they also grew out of the ideas of a new crop of philosophers and scientists. The Englishman John Locke (1632–1704) was a pioneer in arguing that the authority of government comes from the governed. Locke's outlook, a major departure from tradition, was surely marked by the English Civil War of 1642–49.

Ideas such as his — that people are free and equal — gained ground among other educated Europeans. In France, the writers François Voltaire and Jean-Jacques Rousseau challenged old ideas about the king's representing God.

The Enlightenment also grew out of scientific thought, as men such as Isaac Newton in England and Antoine Lavoisier in France theorized about, discovered, and proved natural laws such as gravity. (See Chapter 15 for more about the Enlightenment.)

Rebelling Americans

Enlightenment ideas also took hold overseas, where rational science and engineering, including practical agricultural reforms, put people in North

America into a pragmatic, rational frame of mind about government. As independent-minded as many Americans always were, they had little trouble accepting the ideas that men (still just white men, according to the ideas of the time, and not women) were inherently free and that rulers' authority flowed from the people instead of from God.

When the British government imposed a series of taxes on the American colonists to pay for the French and Indian War, colonists didn't take it kindly. "Where is our voice?" they asked. "Who represents our interests in Parliament?" The answers: unheard, and nobody.

In one of the more creative acts of resistance, some Bostonians dressed up as Native Americans and destroyed the cargoes of several tea ships. (That isn't what you'd normally want to do at a tea party, but okay.) Parliament shot back by sending troops and closing Boston Harbor. New Englanders fought old Englanders in two Massachusetts villages, Lexington and Concord, in 1775, beginning the American Revolution. A Continental Congress formed of representatives from 13 British colonies (British Canada didn't participate) declared independence from England the next year in the Declaration of Independence, a document that rings with Enlightenment philosophy. The great shock was that the outnumbered colonists won, but they couldn't have done so without the French, who supplied money, weapons, and troops to help them defeat the English.

Over centuries, the kings of France had taken measures to prevent insurrections. First, a clever cleric, Cardinal Richelieu (1585–1642) set up governmental offices that cut into the power of the French nobles and concentrated the king's authority. He was chief minister to Louis XIII, who was succeeded by Louis XIV (known as the Sun King) in 1643, during the English Civil War. Louis XIV was among the most absolute of absolute monarchs.

Erupting rage

Enlightenment ideas link the American and French revolutions, but so do economics. Just as the English government bred unrest among Americans by raising taxes to pay for the French and Indian War, so the French government bred unrest among the French. King Louis XVI (great-great-great-great grandson of the Sun King) made the situation worse by stretching French finances even farther to support the American patriots.

Louis XVI's generosity toward American revolutionaries made his government all the more vulnerable to the upheaval that rocked France — eventually spilling over into much of Europe — beginning in 1789 with the French Revolution. That was the year when Louis XVI called a meeting of the Estates-General, the French parliament. It was a bold move, considering that the body hadn't met in more than

150 years. A well-meaning fellow and smart enough to know that things must change, Louis was trying not to lose his crown, or his head, in the process. Calling the Estates-General was an attempt to get agreement on necessary reforms.

But when he called the body to session after it had been dormant so long — essentially nonexistent since the mid-17th century — Louis began something he couldn't control. The idea that the king might permit reform of any kind brought forth a flood of pent-up discontent. People were fed up with the privileged classes and high taxes.

On July 14, 1789, an angry Parisian mob stormed the Bastille prison, a symbol of arbitrary injustice, and things didn't settle down for years. Led by some of its most radical members, the Estates-General became the democratic National Assembly, which issued a Declaration of the Rights of Man in 1792, abolishing the constitution and the monarchy. The revolutionary government used the guillotine — a supposedly humane means of execution — to behead Louis XVI early the next year.

Louis' beheading wasn't the end of the turmoil, however — not by a long shot. The Reign of Terror followed in 1793 and 1794. During that period, French nobles could be sentenced to death for looking at somebody cross-eyed.

Within a decade, in a classic case of pendulum swing, the neck-chopping excesses of the raging French Revolution provided an opportunity for the first guy who could restore order to step in. He wasn't exactly waiting in the wings (unless you call invading Italy and Egypt waiting in the wings), but when the opportunistic, bold, and charismatic military officer Napoleon Bonaparte returned to France, the revolutionary era gave way to a dictatorial empire. (You can read more about Napoleon's impact in Chapter 9.)

Making a bold bid for freedom in Haiti

After folks began throwing around Enlightenment ideas in revolutionary France, the ideas took on a life of their own. François-Dominic Toussaint (also called Toussaint Bréda), a slave in Haiti, was inspired by Enlightenment philosophers as well as by the news from Paris.

Changing his name to Toussaint Louverture, he led other slaves against the French authorities in the early 1790s. In 1795, he won control of most of the formerly French-held territory. (Haiti occupies about one-third of the island of Hispaniola.) He abolished slavery there and declared Haiti independent in 1801.

Napoleon tried to put a stop to this business in 1803, when his forces retook the island nation, captured Louverture, and took him to Paris, where he died later that year. But the sparks of liberty aren't always easy to extinguish. Jacques Dessaline soon led the Haitians against the French again and drove them out in 1804. (For more about Louverture, see Chapter 22.)

These events in Haiti were evidence that ideas imported from Europe took root among people, even enslaved people, who would use them, over the next century or two, to shake off Europe's hold.

Tracking the Centuries

About 1345: Aztecs establish their great capital city, Tenochtitlán.

1482: Portuguese in Ghana build their first African slaving outpost.

1522: One surviving ship of Ferdinand Magellan's expedition to Asia completes the voyage around the world by returning to Spain.

1603: Tokugawa Ieyasu founds Japan's anti-Western Tokugawa Dynasty.

1619: Dutch traders capture Jakarta, Indonesia, and rename it Batavia.

1649: English Puritans execute King Charles I of England.

1776: Americans declare their independence from Britain.

1789: Angry Parisians storm the Bastille.

1801: Casting off slavery, Toussaint Louverture leads a revolution in Hispaniola and declares Haitian independence.

1842: China cedes the island port of Hong Kong to Britain.

1949: Batavia, no longer a Dutch possession, regains the name Jakarta.

1997: Britain returns Hong Kong to China.

» Rocking Europe to the revolutionary beat

» Leaping forward in fields of transportation and communication

» Feeling the reverberations of the world wars and the Cold War

» Attempting to avoid more wars: the League of Nations and the United Nations

Chapter 9

Pulling Empires Together as Subjects Push Back

As the 19th century began, the world headed in two directions at the same time: defiantly away from European imperialism and headlong into the most imperialist period ever. The planet was being knit together tighter and tighter by European dominance, global trade routes, and new technologies. At the same time, individual cultures were straining to break free and achieve self-rule. As royalty and the colonial powers pulled ever more tightly on the reins of governance, people who were being governed struggled against those constraints.

After two groundbreaking revolutions — the American rebellion against British rule and the French overthrow of monarchist order — liberation movements rose in colonies such as the Spanish-ruled lands in Latin America and on the European continent. These movements rolled on into the early 20th century, when reform fervor turned the Russian Empire into a new kind of socialist state.

In France, revolutionary spirit faded as Napoleon Bonaparte took over, carving France's European neighbors into another empire. The British joined with Prussia, Russia, and other allies to stop Bonaparte's land grabs. It wasn't that the United Kingdom was opposed to amassing territory or power; it was opposed to competition. Although they lost North American colonies, the British raced to secure an empire that stretched around the world.

Africans, Asians, and other people intent on resisting European control or tossing out their European masters faced a difficult task — especially before Europe's powers clashed in cataclysmic 20th-century conflicts that caught fire throughout their empires, drawing in non-European powers too. World War I and World War II depleted the resources and resolve of colonial powers, forcing them to let go of third-world possessions.

In this chapter, you can see how empires, in addition to making the world more interconnected and feeding European lust for treasure and territory, also bred enmity — leading to monumental wars — and rebellion among the governed. You can find out how people ranging from the French citizenry to South American patriots fought back against mighty powers and disrupted them. And you'll see the way World War I and World War II depleted the resources and resolve of colonial powers, forcing them to let go of third-world possessions.

Managing Unprecedented Empires

Since the Portuguese sailors Magellan and da Gama pioneered sea routes around the world in the late 15th and early 16th centuries, (see Chapter 8), a handful of nations built widespread empires. Russia extended its territory eastward across Asia to the Pacific Ocean, and venturing westward, descendants of Europeans in North America spread to the Pacific.

In 1915, both England and France ruled more people in overseas possessions than they did at home. Africa, much of which hadn't even been explored by Europeans before 1800, had by a century later become a crazy patchwork quilt of colonies held by Germany, Belgium, France, and other colonial powers.

Britain battles on multiple fronts

Britain should have beaten the nankeen britches off the upstart American rebels in the 1770s and 1780s. What were nankeen britches? Also called breeches, they were the khakis of their time — and they're not as beside the point as they seem.

At the time of the American Revolution, Britain was the greatest sea power of the world and a huge trading power. It was on its way to putting together an empire that, at its height, would have made Alexander the Great's eyes pop out of his handsome Macedonian head.

The American setback (although the American Revolution wasn't a setback to the colonists) could be blamed on just how far-flung and thinly spread the British had become. They were busy in other corners of the globe in the late 18th century. British soldiers fought French forces in West Africa and the West Indies and faced Dutch opposition in India. Spain got into the fight, blockading the British colony at Gibraltar. Meanwhile, the East India Company troops plunged into the second of four closely spaced Mysore Wars against the Muslims who ruled south-west India.

British manpower was so overstretched and its wealth great enough that Britain resorted to fighting the American war with hired German mercenaries, the Hessians. (Hesse is a state in Germany.)

In the larger scheme of world domination, Britain's setback in America — even its inability to bring the Americans to their knees in the War of 1812 — amounted to not all that much, compared with its world-spanning sphere of influence. Those popular nankeen britches, for example, evidenced how the empire's global trade shaped Westerners' taste in menswear. They were made of a sturdy, buff-colored cloth from Nanjing, China (then known as Nanking), which gave the trousers their name.

REMEMBER

For colonial powers, progress amounted to blows upon many of the world's indigenous peoples.

Australia, the last habitable continent to receive Europeans, was home to a British penal colony starting in 1788. Voluntary settlers followed. Many Australian Aborigines who had been isolated from most of the world for thousands of years met the same fate as natives in the Americas had: widespread disease that was often fatal. Without immunities against the Europeans' diseases and no weapons to match the Europeans' guns, the entire native population of Tasmania, the large island off Australia's southern shore, died between 1803, when the British built a penal colony there, and 1876. They were wiped out in one lifetime.

IN THEIR WORDS

"Wherever the European has trod," wrote the English biologist Charles Darwin in 1836, "death seems to pursue the aboriginal." Darwin was thinking of Australia, the Americas, Polynesia, and Africa.

By the early 20th century, Britain's empire included some 400 million people, with only 35 million of them in the British Isles (including British-ruled Ireland).

France rebrands after its revolution

Circumstances in Europe forced the British to take other challenges more seriously than they did the American colonists' breakaway. Another rebellion against a king, the French Revolution (see Chapter 8) changed France radically in 1789, but the governments in Paris and London remained more bitterly opposed than ever.

British–French rivalry only intensified as Napoleon Bonaparte seized power in Paris and made much of Europe into his empire. Conquering Spain, Italy, and the Netherlands, Napoleon tried to overtake the entire continent in the early 19th century. Napoleon became so powerful that some of his bitterest opponents, including Austria and Britain, agreed to fragile, short-lived peace agreements that gave economic and territorial concessions to France.

Finally, in 1812, Napoleon made a serious mistake: He invaded Russia, marching a force of 500,000 men over muddy, rutted terrain. The outmatched Russians withdrew so rapidly that the French penetrated all the way to Moscow, trailed by supply wagons that couldn't keep pace and broke down trying. Troops were used to foraging and living off the land while on the march, but Russia — a land of poor, widely spaced farms with meager crops that had already been raided or even burned by the retreating Russians — offered too little sustenance. Napoleon conquered Moscow but then was unable to provision or shelter his troops through the coming Russian winter, especially after a fire of disputed origin devastated the city. Thousands of starving French soldiers froze to death during a desperate trudge back west.

Anti-Bonapartist European nations — Britain, Austria, Prussia, Russia, Sweden, and more — joined in a series of alliances during Napoleon's years of power. Although these countries' leaders often distrusted one another, they distrusted Napoleon more. You may have run across the term "balance of power" in a history classroom somewhere. It means the way nations protect their borders, trade, and political spheres of influence, either by getting more power and territory or by forming alliances with other nations to match or overmatch the power of a competitor. Balance of power has always figured in international alliances. There was a lot of it going on in the Napoleonic era and it has continued since.

After the disaster of the Russian invasion, Napoleon was vulnerable. His foes took advantage of the situation and invaded France in 1814. Armies commanded by Alexander I of Russia removed the self-made French emperor from his throne that year. Napoleon was exiled to the Mediterranean island of Elba, but he escaped, seized power in Paris, and fought the allies again. Britain, Prussia, Russia, and Austria defeated Napoleon one final time at Waterloo, Belgium, on June 18, 1815.

In the French Revolution (and there's more about it in Chapter 7) revolutionaries deposed and beheaded King Louis XVI and his wife, Marie Antoinette. During Napoleon's exile on Elba, another Louis — number XVIII, the former king's brother — took the throne, but he had to skip town when Bonaparte came back. After Waterloo, Louis XVIII donned the crown again and stayed a while.

TECHNICAL STUFF

What happened to Louis XVII? The son of Louis XVI and Marie Antoinette reportedly died in prison without even getting a style of furniture named after him. The fact that he wasn't guillotined led to rumors that he was still alive. Several imposters claiming to be Louis XVII emerged long after the revolution. Some of them won small groups of followers, both in Europe and in the United States, but none were authenticated.

Europe divides Africa

Europeans put their figurative foot in Africa's door in the 15th century. Portugal was both the first European sea power to sail around Africa and the first to establish a slaving station on the continent's west coast, dealing in captured people before 1500.

Other European nations followed the Portuguese into slave trading. Anyone with a working conscience saw this vile trade as unspeakably cruel and ugly, even in those times, but the business was profitable and many ship-owners who dealt callously in denying freedom and dignity to fellow human beings became rich.

Empire builders eventually wanted more from Africa than just its captive labor. In the 19th century, territory-hungry Europeans carved the continent into colonies.

Making gradual inroads

Taking large pieces of African turf took a while for Europeans because for hundreds of years after the Portuguese began landing at African ports, few outsiders were able to penetrate the interior. Dense tropical forests, forbidding deserts, and disease-ridden wetlands made overland journeys difficult. In 1760, Europeans knew no more about Africa beyond Egypt and the Mediterranean than their ancestors had known in Roman times — maybe less.

Scotsmen James Bruce and Mungo Park began changing that limitation with their expeditions — Bruce in Ethiopia and Park in West Africa — in the late 18th century. As more European explorers followed, word got out about the vast resources of Africa's interior.

PRESUMING DR. LIVINGSTONE

In the 1860s, while on an African expedition to settle a dispute about the source of the Nile (Europeans weren't sure where the river started), British explorer, medical doctor, missionary, and popular author Dr. David Livingstone disappeared.

Famous for his earlier African explorations, Livingstone intrigued British and American newspaper readers. Lacking anything to report on the missing doctor, The New York Herald hired another explorer, Henry Morton Stanley, to go after Livingstone. (Stanley had made his reputation writing dispatches from the American West and the Middle East.)

After two rough years of searching, Stanley sent back a story reporting what he said when he found the man: "Dr. Livingstone, I presume?"

Maybe because the public waited so long for news of Livingstone, or because Stanley's greeting was such an understated, civilized conclusion to such a long, difficult search, the phrase struck a nerve. Of course, the only other white man for hundreds of miles around was Dr. Livingstone. "Dr. Livingstone, I presume" became a catchphrase quoted over and over well into the 20th century.

Livingstone was seriously ill and died before he could return to Britain. After finding him, Stanley led another expedition into Africa, and his 1878 book about the trip, *Through the Dark Continent*, was a best seller.

REMEMBER

Europe's Industrial Revolution (see Chapter 15), which began in the 18th century, ate up raw materials. Nineteenth-century Europeans realized that they could mine, cut, and grow needed resources in Africa, so nations began sending armed expeditions to claim rights to one chunk after another of the big, yet-untapped continent.

The keen competition for African colonies and resources threatened a delicate balance of power (there's that phrase again) between nations that German Chancellor Otto von Bismarck prided himself upon maintaining. In the 1880s, Bismarck, a Prussian statesman who had played a big role in putting together the German Empire (the first version of the modern nation of Germany), called representatives from 14 nations to set rules for claiming African territory. In effect, those rules speeded up what was called the "Scramble for Africa."

By the early 20th century, the African map was a jigsaw puzzle, with pieces bearing European names such as French West Africa, Belgian Congo, German South West Africa, British East Africa (Kenya), and Anglo-Egyptian Sudan (British-controlled), as shown in Figure 9-1.

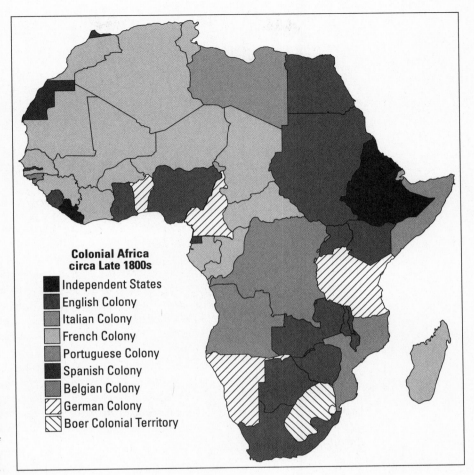

FIGURE 9-1:
By 1900, the African map was a jigsaw puzzle of European conquests.

Colonial Africa circa Late 1800s

- Independent States
- English Colony
- Italian Colony
- French Colony
- Portuguese Colony
- Spanish Colony
- Belgian Colony
- German Colony
- Boer Colonial Territory

Overwhelming Africa's defenders

African peoples such as the Asante and the Zulu tried to resist the Europeans who took over their lands, but the natives were largely outgunned.

Samory (or Samir) Ture emperor of Guinea in West Africa, built an Islamic nation in the region of the upper Niger River and had a large and disciplined, if poorly equipped, army at his command. From 1883, Ture fought hard to keep out Europeans, but squeezed between the French and the British, he had little chance. His army was defeated, and he died in exile in Gabon in 1900.

Only one African nation successfully resisted the Europeans. Ethiopia smashed an invading Italian army of 17,000 at the Battle of Adowa in 1896. Ethiopia was the only independent native African nation left. Then in 1935, Italy, ruled by Fascist dictator Benito Mussolini, returned to conquer Ethiopia, which was liberated by the Allied Powers during World War II.

Challenging European Dominance

By the start of the 20th century, white Europeans and their descendants ruled so much of the world that it's almost easier to say what they hadn't yet grabbed than to list everything they had.

As I mention in the preceding section, Ethiopia was a self-ruled holdout in Africa. Persia and the Ottoman Empire resisted in the Middle East — although the long-lived Ottoman Empire, based in Istanbul and ruled since the 15th century by an Islamic Turkish dynasty, was only a ghost of its mighty former self. Afghanistan, twice invaded in the 19th century by the British, was ruled by dictator Abdur Rahman Khan, who sought British help in keeping out the Russians. To the east, Japan stood apart; so did China, but shakily. Beyond that handful of nations, there was little that Europe (or the descendants of Europeans, as in the United States) didn't control besides poor countries no European power wanted yet.

Even the strongest colonial powers, however, could never take their holdings for granted. They had to fight to keep their trade advantages, as when China resisted European hegemony over its ports. The colonial powers also had to fight uprisings both by colonists and conquered indigenous people, as happened in South America and Africa. And they had to watch for new powers rising to rival them, as Japan did, emerging from a long, self-imposed isolation.

Turning against Spanish and Portuguese rule in Latin America

REMEMBER

Spain's greatest empire was in the Americas. Land claims based on explorations and conquests in the late 15th century brought Spanish rule to much of southern and western North America and most of Central and South America. Under a 1494 agreement with Spain, called the Treaty of Tordesillas, Portugal claimed the part of South America that became Brazil.

Rebels began challenging Spain's authority in South America starting in the late 18th century. In Peru in 1780, Jose Gabriel Condorcanqui rallied workers — descendants of the Inca — against their Spanish bosses. They attacked Cuzco and La Paz in neighboring Bolivia.

Condorcanqui, a rich man of mixed Spanish–Inca heritage, called himself Tupac Amaru II, borrowing the name of a 16th-century emperor. The Spanish caught and killed him and crushed the revolt after two years. But more unrest was on the way.

Confusing leadership in Chile

Spanish authority in the Americas really faltered after Napoleon, self-crowned emperor of France and conqueror of Spain, knocked King Ferdinand VII off the throne back in Madrid. In 1808, Napoleon gave Spain's crown to Joseph Bonaparte, his brother. Two years later in Chile, a Spanish captain-general lost his power to a junta (a political committee), which in turn, was replaced by one republican leader and then another, creating continuous confusion. When Ferdinand regained his Spanish throne in 1814, royalist troops marched to restore authority in Chile, and the military leader who emerged from the republican chaos to fight them was the memorably named Bernardo O'Higgins.

Breaking away with Bolívar

Simón Bolívar, inspired by the North American patriots and the French revolutionaries, believed that all of Spanish South America needed to break free. His revolutionaries took over Venezuela in 1816. Then Bolívar beat the Spanish in Colombia, where he became president. He went back to Venezuela when the Spanish tried to recapture it and drove them out again. Yet Bolívar was far from finished.

Hopping borders with José de San Martín

Down in Argentina, the Spanish-trained soldier José de San Martín led a revolutionary army in that country's fight for independence. Then he joined O'Higgins, who had been driven out of Chile by royalist troops. Together, they beat Spanish forces, and Chile declared independence in 1818. With O'Higgins in charge as supreme director (dictator), San Martín headed to the next spot on the map: Peru.

He beat the Spanish yet again, declaring Peru independent in 1821. He even stayed on for a bit to lead the new government in Lima. After he retired in 1822, the Peruvians replaced him with Simón Bolívar, who drove the remaining Spanish forces out and became dictator in 1824. But Bolívar still wasn't finished. He moved north and founded Bolivia.

Achieving a royal independence for Brazil

As in Spanish-held parts of South America, the Napoleonic Wars also led to independence for Brazil. After Napoleon invaded Portugal in 1807, King João VI sailed away to his colony in Brazil. Then, after the Battle of Waterloo ended the French threat (see the section titled "France rebrands after its revolution," earlier in this chapter), João decided to stay in the Western Hemisphere. He declared a new political entity called the United Kingdom of Portugal, Brazil, and the Algarves. (The Algarves is the southernmost part of what we think of as Portugal.)

To govern this unwieldy realm, he relied on help in Europe from that other United Kingdom, the British. This alliance angered many Portuguese, who wanted the Brits out and their king back. Bowing to pressure, João returned to Lisbon, leaving his son, Prince Dom Pedro, as ruler in Rio de Janeiro.

In 1822, Dom Pedro, trying to calm Brazilian military and civil unrest, declared the nation's independence and founded the Empire of Brazil. After several tumultuous decades, this empire collapsed in a *coup d'état*, and a dictator-led "republic" continued into the 20th century.

Struggling in Mexico

Mexico's struggle to break free of Spain began only a few decades after the United States threw off British rule, but Mexico suffered many setbacks on its way to a stable independent government. Early in the 19th century, Spanish authorities arrested two priests, Miguel Hidalgo y Costilla and Jose Maria Morelos y Pavon, for spreading ideas from the French Revolution (see Chapter 8). Both received the death sentence, but revolutionary fever had taken hold. Augustin de Iturbide broke Mexico free of Spain in 1823, declaring a short-lived Mexican-Guatemalan Empire. The following year, Mexican patriots replaced Iturbide with a constitution based on that of the United States.

The biggest setbacks in Mexico came in quick succession from the 1830s through the 1860s. Still struggling to find its feet after winning independence from Spain, Mexico lost its northeastern state of Texas to an independence movement in 1836. Then Mexico lost huge territories in western North America to the United States in the Mexican-American War of 1846–1848.

France, again ruled by an emperor from the Bonaparte family (Napoleon III) invaded Mexico in 1861. Mexican forces defended the homeland, scoring an improbable and heroic victory on May 5, 1862 (Cinco de Mayo), at Puebla. The Europeans persisted and eventually prevailed, however, and about a year later, Emperor Napoleon III offered the Mexican throne to Ferdinand Maximilian Joseph, archduke of Austria, who belonged to the powerful Habsburg dynasty.

Maximilian didn't last long as emperor of Mexico. Napoleon III withdrew French troops, leaving his puppet unable to maintain authority. Mexican General Benito Juarez defeated and captured Maximilian in May 1867 and ordered the deposed emperor to be executed.

Reclaiming Africa for Africans

Although conquered by Europeans fairly late in the game, Africa didn't wait long to get in on the rebellion business. The people of Zimbabwe rebelled (unsuccessfully) against the British in 1896. Tanzanians rose against their German government in 1905, but that movement too was crushed. Germany's colonial troops burned crops to create a famine and weaken the rebels.

The Herero and Nama people of Namibia suffered incredible losses in their own uprisings against the Germans. The cattle-raising Nama were reduced from a population of 20,000 to less than half that. Of the estimated 80,000 Herero living in central Namibia before the war, only 15,000 were left in 1911.

This struggle finally began to result in self-rule for African nations during the 1950s. In 1948, riots shook Ghana (then called Gold Coast), and the British, whose home nation was impoverished by World War II, realized that they could no longer afford an empire. Other colonial powers also woke up to the same reality during that time; the war had rocked the European empires to their foundations.

Uprising in Asia

In the 1820s, the Dutch rulers of Java (one of the largest islands in Indonesia) fought a Javanese prince, Diponegoro, who tried to liberate his island from the foreigners. The Dutch arrested and exiled him. As in so many colonial holdings, Indonesian independence had to wait until after the turmoil of the world wars loosened the Europeans' hold.

Europe had to fight to hang onto its economic dominance in other parts of East Asia, too. The Chinese went to war against Britain from 1839–1842 and again from 1856–1860 over the issue of illegal British imports of opium from India to China (see Chapter 8). Although China lost the fight and had to allow trading concessions to the British and other European powers as a result, deep-seated resentment lingered.

Unleashing pent-up power in Japan

In Japan, teenage Emperor Meiji inherited the throne in 1867. Simultaneously, the longstanding system of rule by a shogun, a warlord far more powerful than the emperor, crumbled under pressure from nobles and others eager for the long-isolated nation to adopt Western technology. After 700 years of shogunate rule and a short civil war, the last shogun, Tokugawa Yoshinobu, gave up his powers in 1868.

This transition, the Meiji Restoration, freed the emperor to pursue modernization and launch an ambitiously militaristic foreign policy strategy. While many empires of the era fell back or held steady, Japan gained territory from China in the 1890s and from Russia in the Russo-Japanese War of 1904–05 (a humiliating defeat for the Russians). In 1910, Japan seized control of Korea. This empire-building continued long beyond Meiji's death in 1912. In 1932, Japan turned Chinese Manchuria into the Japanese puppet state of Manchukuo.

Ricocheting unrest comes home to Europe

Europe didn't shake the unrest at home after the French Revolution, because the ideas that fueled upheaval in 1789 didn't go away. The French saw another revolution in 1848, although this one didn't involve as much head-chopping. France replaced King Louis Phillipe, a champion of the rich, by electing Louis Napoleon, a nephew of Napoleon I, to a four-year presidency in 1850. Under a banner of law and order, the new president worked to consolidate his power and succeeded in getting the French Senate to declare him Emperor Napoleon III in 1852.

TECHNICAL STUFF

What about Napoleon II? He never got his opportunity. Born in 1811, Napoleon's son was a child when supporters tried to prop him up as an emperor in 1815. The allies who beat his dad at Waterloo discouraged the attempt, and Junior moved to Vienna and stayed out of the way.

France had rebellious company in 1848. Many Europeans were miserable — hungry, out of work, and angry — because the changes that accompanied the agricultural and industrial revolutions didn't benefit everyone. Revolutionary movements broke out in Austria and Hungary, and in many German and Italian states. Revolts also rocked Ireland, Switzerland, and Denmark. The revolutionaries failed to overthrow their governments, but the people made themselves heard. Change was in the air. Most of Europe — especially Western Europe — eventually headed toward democracy, but the road wasn't smooth or easy.

Revolting in Russia

The pressures that erupted into the 1848 revolutions in Europe were much the same as the ones that brought about revolution in Russia a half-century later. In 1905, Russian troops fired on Russian workers marching in the streets of St. Petersburg who were trying to win higher wages and shorter hours in the factories.

Shooting at them didn't work. The surviving demonstrators went on strike and strikes spread from St. Petersburg to other Russian cities. Then the rebellion spread to rural revolts against landlords.

Standing apart up north

Russia had long been a special case among European nations. It was remote, northern, and inland. Russian technology lagged that of Western Europe. Russians lacked the level of craftsmanship and skill that the Germans and British, among others, had achieved in fields ranging from shipbuilding to architecture to weaponry to printing. Peter I (also known as Peter the Great; see Chapter 22), who became sole ruler of Russia in 1696, spent two years traveling in England, France, and the German states, learning about a wide variety of industries. When he returned, he brought experts and teachers with him because he was determined to drag Russians into the 18th century, kicking and screaming if necessary.

REMEMBER

Despite its modernizations, Russia still stood apart. As other nations abolished the old feudal system of serfdom, for example, Russia went the other way, making even more people serfs. Serfs were not little blue cartoon characters from the 1980s (those are Smurfs), but people at the bottom rung of society who had no rights. In Russia, they were essentially slaves. Serfdom disappeared from England in the Middle Ages but continued in many lands on the European continent. France abolished the institution with its revolution of 1789; in Austria and Hungary, serfdom endured until 1848. Russia finally freed its serfs in 1861. (Smurfdom, on the other hand, continues in a long succession of movies and TV series in many parts of the world.)

Rushin' toward rebellion

Perhaps it's not surprising that revolutionary unrest hit Russia hard and went to extremes in the late 19th and early 20th centuries.

You'd think that Russian peasants, having been freed from serfdom, would be better off than they had been, but an unfair land settlement left many without enough soil in which to grow adequate food. High taxes also fueled unrest. Urban professionals and nobles didn't like paying for their government to build an expensive fleet of warships just to see the Japanese sink those ships during the Russo-Japanese War of 1904–05.

Unrest locked up the country. In 1905, rebels elected representatives to the St. Petersburg Soviet of Workers' Deputies, a council to coordinate strikes and demonstrations. Other soviets (councils) soon formed across Russia. In October 1905, Czar Nicholas II agreed to reforms, including the creation of a Russian parliament, the Duma. By giving unhappy Russians a legislative body, Nicholas hoped to provide a safety valve to ease political dissatisfaction — a place for society to air its grievances. But the Duma was doomed from the beginning. On the left, socialist groups boycotted it. On the right, reactionaries in Nicholas's court fought the Duma's efforts to reform tax and farm policies. The czar's advisers persuaded Nicholas to dissolve the legislature every time they didn't like its direction. Between 1905 and 1912, he dissolved the Duma three times.

In 1917, after 5 million Russian soldiers died in World War I, Czar Nicholas faced widespread unrest. Again, he ordered a disobedient Duma to dissolve itself, but the legislators refused his order.

Taking power in the Soviet Union

After forcing Czar Nicholas to abdicate, a broad coalition of representatives — liberals, social democrats, and agrarian socialists, most of them organized into the Russian Democratic Socialist Party — formed the Russian Provisional Government and set up headquarters in the czar's Winter Palace in St. Petersburg. The provisional government held elections for a Constituent Assembly — a representative body to draft a constitution.

The party contained factions. Lenin's followers were called Bolsheviks, which means *majority*, even though they were probably a minority at first. That mislabeling came about because at an organizational meeting years earlier, his partisans had won more votes than a rival faction. That other group came to be called Mensheviks, meaning minority, although they weren't, really. It certainly didn't hurt Lenin's group to give the appearance of outnumbering the other guys. And in 1917, after Bolsheviks achieved actual majorities in the soviets (governmental councils) of Moscow and Petrograd (the post-revolutionary name of St. Petersburg) Lenin was in a powerful position. After allowing the Constituent Assembly to convene in January 1918, he then used soldiers to break it up.

Lenin and his Red Army fought counterrevolutionaries over the next few years, but Russia — renamed the Union of Soviet Socialist Republics (USSR), or the Soviet Union for short — became a very different beast for most of the 20th century.

REMEMBER

Inspired by the writings of Karl Marx, a 19th-century German economic philosopher, Lenin set up a government based on national ownership. Everything belonged to the government, and everybody worked for the government (or, nominally, for "the people"). For the first time ever, a great national power was run by leaders who wanted to overthrow and replace all existing society with communism's new economic model.

As Lenin's successor, Josef Stalin, later proved, a Leninist–Marxist system could bring about rapid industrialization, turning the Soviet Union into one of the two greatest economic and military powers in the world. But on the way toward economic gains, Stalin left many millions of Russians dead. His so-called agricultural reforms caused widespread starvation.

In the 1930s, Stalin brutally eliminated any colleague he perceived as a rival for his power, staging show trials and executions of many men who had stood beside him in 1917. The USSR's Bolshevik veterans were forced to confess to unlikely crimes and sentenced to death by firing squad or sent to a prison camp from which they would never return. From 1934 to 1938, hundreds of thousands of lesser officials also disappeared as victims of Stalin's purges.

Nobody knows exactly how many people Stalin killed and imprisoned but estimates range as high as tens of millions.

By 1991, the Soviet Union was in economic ruin, strained by Cold War military spending, and fell apart. In the 21st century, the Russian Federation reemerged as an important economic and military power.

GETTING PLACES FASTER, THANKS TO TECHNOLOGY

As you get closer to modern times, you find that human civilization quickly becomes more tightly crisscrossed, with more interconnections between peoples and places than ever before. The globalization of trade and political power started when people and information traveled at the speed of a sailing ship. Over the 17th to 21st centuries everything speeded up as machines born of the Industrial Revolution (see Chapter 15) made distances less . . . well, less distancing. Globalization accelerated and events unfolded faster and faster.

Steam ships: Robert Fulton, an American, and Patrick Bell of England built working steamships around 1807. By the 1830s, shippers could keep to schedules as never before because they weren't relying on favorable winds. International commerce boomed. By the 1880s, steam engines powered virtually every kind of vessel.

Railroads: Richard Trevithick, a British engineer, put a steam engine on wheel and steel tracks in 1804. By 1825, England had its first commercial railway and by 1851, there were rail networks in 17 other countries. Before 1900, Russia had built a railroad across Siberia.

(continued)

(continued)

Automobiles: In 1885, German engineer Karl Benz used an internal combustion engine to power a practical motor car. Large-scale automobile manufacturing took off in 1908, when American Henry Ford (1863–1947) began using an assembly line to make cars affordable for the middle class.

Airplanes: in 1903, Orville Wright and his brother Wilbur, Ohio bicycle mechanics, achieved sustained, controlled flight with a self-propelled, heavier-than-air vessel. Commercially built aircraft soon followed, and the airplane became a weapon during World War I.

The telegraph: By the middle of the 19th century, it was possible to send messages over wires by electric current. The technological advance proved only the beginning of a wired-up world. Samuel Finley Breese Morse, an American, invented Morse code in 1837.

The telephone: Scottish–Canadian Alexander Graham Bell (1847–1922) put his interest in sound and communication together with telegraphic technology to build an experimental telephone in 1876. By the early 20th century, the phone was becoming an everyday convenience.

Radio: In 1901, Italian-born inventor Gugliemo Marconi sent a wireless telegraph signal across the Atlantic Ocean from Cornwall, England, to Newfoundland, Canada. He won the Nobel Prize for physics in 1909.

Television: In the 1920s, U.S. inventors came up with devices for sending electronic pictures via radio waves. Philo T. Farnsworth invented an electronic picture scanning system in 1922, and Vladimir K. Zworykin followed with the television camera and picture tube in 1923. By the middle of the 20th century, these devices commanded huge audiences.

Mobile phones: In 1977, the U.S. electronics company Motorola developed a wireless telephone that connected with the public telephone network through a system of short-range radio cells. In the 21st century, personal cellphones evolved into smartphones, essentially merging the communications device with a handheld computer.

The World Wide Web: Physicist Tim Berners-Lee invented Hypertext Markup Language (HTML) as a way for non-specialist Internet users to display data in text, pictures, and sound so that other computer users could access them. In 1991, Berners-Lee put his creation, the World Wide Web, on the Internet. The Web became the place for businesses, political parties, activists, service organizations, and ordinary people to share information.

Fighting World Wars

REMEMBER

Even if you're just skimming this chapter (and by all means, feel free to skim), you may notice that European nations, which had the rest of the world in a bear hug by 1900, seemed to fight an awful lot of wars. From ancient times onward, war was the way to build and keep empires. But with the rise of Europe's global empires of the 19th and early 20th centuries, wars tended (more quickly than ever before) to spill over from one part of the world to another.

An early example of what was to come, the Seven Years' War (1756–1763) had multiple fronts in India, Europe (where Prussia, Hanover, Austria, and Russia sided with Britain and Spain sided with France), and America (the French and Indian War). The trend only got worse — lots worse. By the 20th century, the tendency toward war and the technology to support it led to World War I and World War II.

Advances in travel and communication (see the nearby sidebar "Getting Places Faster, Thanks to Technology") and more efficient weapons, such as the easier-to-load rifles used in the Crimean War and the American Civil War of the mid-19th century, kept right on until in 1945, when one U.S. airplane carrying one bomb destroyed an entire city: Hiroshima. That first nuclear bomb killed 70,000 people instantly and destroyed one-third of the city. Another like it, dropped on the city of Nagasaki, underlined the point that warfare had become vastly more horrible than ever. Soon, leaders had the ability to push a single button and launch a missile attack capable of wiping out all civilization on the planet. (For more on how technology changed war, turn to chapters 16 and 18.)

Redefining war: World War I

At the time, nobody gave the so-called Great War a number, because they weren't planning to have another. One was quite enough, thanks.

Also called the Big One, and later World War I, this conflict proved uglier, costlier, longer, more widespread, and more brutal than many people realized war could be. From 1914 to 1918, two lines of infantry soldiers stretching across northern France and Belgium faced each other month after month, year after year, hunkered down in muddy, rat-infested, soul-killing trenches only a few hundred yards apart.

Mechanized as no war before it had been, World War I took to the skies as airplanes dropped bombs and fought the first-ever air-to-air battles. It also brought about routine submarine warfare. German U-boats (the *U* stood for *underwater*) sank enemy ships without warning. Guns were bigger, faster-firing, longer-range, and more numerous than those of any war before. There were also so-called advances in chemical warfare, such as crippling mustard gas.

Precipitating events and attitudes

You may have learned in school that World War I started in 1914, when a Serbian terrorist shot an Austro-Hungarian archduke in Sarajevo, Bosnia. That's true, but the origins of the war are more complicated. Isn't everything?

TECHNICAL STUFF

For one thing, the Serbians were angry with the Austro-Hungarian Empire (a combination of Austria and Hungary) for annexing Bosnia (even though Bosnia still technically belonged to the Ottoman Empire, which was weakened by its own internal revolt). The Austro-Hungarians worried about the Serbs potentially uniting the Slavs in southeastern Europe, in a mountainous region called the Balkans. Such unification would have threatened the Hungarian part of their empire. Meanwhile, Russian leaders believed that the Balkans, with its largely Slavic population, rightfully belonged in the sphere of influence of the Russian Empire, which was also largely Slavic. Although they had no legal claim, the Russians felt especially protective about Slavic Serbia.

Russia mobilized troops, which provoked the Germans — who were allies of the Austro-Hungarian Empire — to declare war on both Russia and its ally France. The Germans cut through neutral Belgium on the way to attack the French.

Britain had no formal quarrel with Germany, but relations between the two countries were strained by an undeclared race for naval superiority. Starting in the 1890s, Wilhelm II, the German kaiser (meaning *emperor*), aggressively built more and bigger ships. Britain responded by stepping up its own shipbuilding. German troops crossing into Belgium in 1914 solidified anti-German feeling in Britain because the incursion violated international law, giving the British an excuse to mobilize.

Adding combatants to the war

The war grew as more countries entered the fray. The two sides included

>> **The Entente (Allies):** Britain, France, Russia, Japan, Serbia, Italy, Portugal, Romania, China, and the United States. (The United States joined the Allies in 1917 after Germany's submarine blockade of Great Britain began sinking neutral ships.)

>> **The Central Powers:** Germany, Austro-Hungary, and the Ottoman Empire.

Reacting to the carnage

World War I helped create the Soviet Union. Four empires — Russian, Ottoman, German, and Austro-Hungarian — collapsed in that war. Besides rearranging the map, the Great War brought famine, destroyed economies, and demonstrated to a shocked public that war brought little more than widespread disaster. This conflict wasn't the heroic warfare of patriotic songs, but a blight.

A leader in this line of thinking was U.S. President Woodrow Wilson. He worked on the terms of peace in Europe, making sure that the process included the League of Nations — an international body created expressly to prevent future wars.

The League of Nations, established by the Treaty of Versailles in 1919, helped Europe rebuild. Fifty-three nations joined by 1923, including Britain, France, Italy, and Japan. Unfortunately, the League of Nations didn't work, especially not for Wilson. The U.S. Senate refused to approve Wilson's terms or let the United States join the league. Wilson suffered a massive stroke while trying to drum up public support to make the senators change their minds and spent the rest of his term, until early 1921, as an invalid.

Although Germany joined the league in 1926, it withdrew, along with ally Japan, in 1933. Italy withdrew three years later. The organization subsequently proved helpless to stop German, Japanese, and Italian expansionism. By the late 1930s, the world was in for another big one.

Nobody before him ever tried regulating international life the way President Wilson envisioned. Maybe his brainchild was bound to fail, but the League of Nations was a step toward something new.

Returning to conflict: World War II

World War I sowed the seeds for the second one. In Germany, impoverished citizens and resentful leaders alike bitterly opposed the terms of the Treaty of Versailles, which included

>> A war-guilt clause that blamed everything on Germany

>> Severe limits on the size of Germany's military

>> Lost territories, with Alsace-Lorraine returned to France, the Rhineland turned into a demilitarized zone, and most of Germany's overseas colonial holdings going to other empires

>> Cash reparations that the war-ravaged country couldn't pay

Adolf Hitler, the boss of the National Socialists, or Nazis, used this national anger to take over the government. He called his repressive, authoritarian, and fiercely nationalistic administration the Third Reich — heir to the medieval Holy Roman Empire (the first Reich, or empire) and to the German Empire of 1871–1918.

Breaking the treaty: Hitler moves his troops

Hitler secretly rearmed the country in the 1930s and then started moving his troops in direct violation of the Versailles Treaty. He occupied the Rhineland (so much for a demilitarized zone); annexed Austria; and headed for Czechoslovakia, a country that had been created after World War I. He considered himself to be within his rights there because he worked out a deal with the governments of Italy, France, and particularly the United Kingdom.

TECHNICAL STUFF

Hitler asserted that the Sudetenland region of Czechoslovakia rightly belonged to Germany. Italian dictator Benito Mussolini, whose postwar rise was not unlike Hitler's, arranged the meeting in Munich at which Hitler, British Prime Minister Neville Chamberlain (who was bending over backward to avoid another conflict with Germany), Mussolini, and French Prime Minister Édouard Daladier carved up Czechoslovakia without consulting the Czechs.

Hitler also signed the Nazi–Soviet Pact with Josef Stalin, Lenin's successor in Moscow. (There's more about both Lenin and Stalin in the earlier section "Revolting in Russia.") After claiming the Sudetenland, the Nazis plunged into Poland with the idea of dividing that country with the Soviet Union.

Choosing sides

Germany's 1939 invasion of Poland proved to be too much even for peace-seeking Chamberlain. The British woke up to the reality that there was no avoiding conflict, and Britain declared war that year.

Even more nations than in World War I took sides or were overtaken and forced into the fight that became World War II. A majority of the nations of the world participated. Here's an incomplete breakdown:

>> **Axis:** Included Germany, Italy, Japan, Hungary, Slovakia, Bulgaria, Croatia, Finland, Romania, Iraq, Thailand, and many more, notably vast swaths of Asia and Africa controlled by Axis nations.

The Soviets, originally on Germany's side, were forced to switch allegiances abruptly when Hitler violated his pact with Stalin and sent an invasion toward Moscow. Germany overran France in June 1940, after which three-fifths of the country became a puppet state of Germany and the rest a collaborationist regime aligned with the Axis. Many other states also shifted allegiances during the war, often because neutral or pro-Allied governments, as in Norway, Denmark, the Netherlands, and Belgium, were overcome by invading Axis powers.

>> **Allies:** Included the United Kingdom and the worldwide British Empire (notably British India), Canada, Australia, South Africa, New Zealand, France (until June 1940), Poland, the Soviet Union (starting in June of 1941), and later the United States, China, Cuba, the Philippines, Guatemala, Nicaragua, the Dominican Republic, Honduras, Haiti, and more.

When Japan attacked the U.S. fleet in Hawaii in late 1941, the United States was still officially neutral, although leaning strongly toward Britain. Immediately after the attack, the Americans declared war on Japan and its Axis allies.

Assessing the war's damage

Ending in two atomic blasts, World War II killed 15 million military personnel — 2 million of them Soviet prisoners of war. About 6 million of the 35 million civilians killed were Jewish victims of the Holocaust, organized anti-Semite mass murders and concentration camps in Germany and Eastern Europe.

The weapons of this war grew faster, deadlier, and bigger than those in the previous war. Massive bombs devastated many European cities.

REMEMBER

The Allied bombing of Dresden, Germany, in 1945 killed 80,000 civilians in a night. That attack was the work of hundreds of bombers, but later that year, on August 6, 1945, one American plane dropped a single atomic bomb on Hiroshima that demolished everything in a four-mile radius of where it went off. That blast and a second atomic bomb dropped on Nagasaki a few days later remain the only nuclear weapons ever used on people. The first bomb killed about 70,000 people out of a population of 343,000 inhabitants. By the end of that year, more than 100,000 had died, including those injured in the blast and others who suffered radiation poisoning. The second killed 40,000 people instantly. At least 30,000 more would die of injuries and radiation poisoning subsequently. The war ended soon after the Nagasaki blast.

Redrawing the map

World War II rearranged Europe and the world even more than World War I had done. Among the more dramatic changes, Germany emerged as two nations: West Germany, aligned with the United States and other Western powers, and East Germany, a satellite of the Soviet Union.

The war also brought profound changes to Asia and Africa, largely because of the way it drained power and money from the European colonial powers. Britain, on the winning side but nearly ruined, had neither adequate resources nor the will to maintain overseas holdings.

The years after World War II were big for independence movements. Britain withdrew from India in 1947, and France tried for almost two decades to hang on to Algeria before finally letting it go in 1962.

China, at war with Japan from 1937 to 1945 (Japan surrendered on that front too), promptly plunged right back into a civil war between Nationalist and Communist parties. The Communists won, and under the Marxist leader Mao Zedong, the ancient civilization became the People's Republic of China on October 1, 1949.

Running Hot and Cold (Wars)

The years after World War II weren't peaceful, but they didn't erupt into World War III either (knock on wood). For much of the era, major world powers were preoccupied with a game of nuclear standoff.

The major postwar powers turned out to be the United States and the Soviet Union. The United States expected to enjoy its nuclear monopoly for 20 years or more, but the Soviets surprised everyone by developing their own atomic bomb in 1949. Although they were allies on the winning side in World War II, the two nations became bitter rivals.

Soviet foreign policy reflected Josef Stalin's viciously paranoid behavior toward any rival — real or imagined, internal or abroad. (For more about Stalin, see "Taking Power in the Soviet Union" earlier in this chapter.) The Soviet Union became increasingly exclusionary and closed off. Soviet goals included maintaining control over satellite Communist states, several of which were set up in Eastern Europe in the wake of World War II, while keeping out foreign cultural and economic influences.

The United States emerged as leader of the West — meaning Western Europe, the Western Hemisphere, and developed nations anywhere that resisted communism and promoted the private pursuit of profit.

Daring each other to blink in the Cold War

With their nuclear arsenals, the Soviet Union and the United States engaged in the Cold War, a diplomatic, political, and military standoff. Both nations built more and bigger missiles and warheads that could deliver a nuclear bomb from a Nebraska wheat field to downtown Moscow, for example. Both nations developed the tragic ability to blow up the Earth several times over.

This madness was tempered a bit by a Nuclear Test Ban Treaty in 1963, numerous arms talks, and arms-reduction agreements, but the two nations basically kept guns pointed at each other's heads until the economically ruined Soviet Union fell apart in 1991. Along the way, other countries built nuclear arsenals as well — China prominent among them.

Seeing no end to violent conflicts

Despite the ominous threat of nuclear annihilation, regional wars continued raging during and after the Cold War. The United States was embarrassed in one of them — a futile attempt to keep Vietnam, a former French colony in Southeast Asia, from going communist. During the 1980s, the Soviets failed to quash Muslim rebels in Afghanistan.

When the Jewish state Israel was established in 1948 in what had been British Palestine, surrounding Arab nations joined Palestinian Arabs in opposing it. The disagreement turned violent many times from the 1950s on. Subsequent decades were scarred by many terrorist bombings in the region — often motivated by support for the Palestinian cause — that killed many innocent civilians. Then, in the 1990s, Iraq invaded neighboring Kuwait. A U.S.-led international force turned the Iraqis back.

On September 11, 2001, 19 extremist Muslim terrorists, most from Saudi Arabia, hijacked four American passenger jets to use as weapons. They crashed two planes into the World Trade Center in New York City, killing everyone onboard and thousands more in the twin skyscrapers, which were destroyed. A third plane crashed into the Pentagon, headquarters of the U.S. Department of Defense in Washington, D.C. All onboard that plane died, as did 125 people in the building. When they learned about the crashes in New York and D.C., passengers on the fourth jet attacked the hijackers who were flying their plane. The plane crashed in Pennsylvania, killing all 44 people onboard.

The United States responded to this slaughter by invading Afghanistan, where a theocratic Muslim government called the Taliban had harbored the terrorist organization responsible for the attacks, Al Qaeda. In 2003, President George W. Bush followed by ordering an invasion of Iraq, although that country had not been involved in attacking New York. In both Afghanistan and Iraq, U.S. troops ousted the reigning governments, but insurgent violence against U.S. troops and by rival groups among Afghans and Iraqis required long, costly military operations. In 2021, as U.S. troops were pulling out of Afghanistan, Taliban fighters retook the country, including its capital, in a matter of days. The U.S.-aligned Afghan government toppled quickly.

After the breakup of the Soviet Union in 1991, Russia fought against an Islamic independence movement in Chechnya, a region between the Black and Caspian seas. The Soviet collapse also led to the breakup of Yugoslavia, a former Soviet satellite state, which in turn led to an ugly war in Bosnia and Herzegovina (part of the former Yugoslavia) involving Serbs, who were largely Orthodox Christians, and Bosnians, who were mostly Muslims. The war featured indiscriminate shelling of civilian targets; widescale rape; and "ethnic cleansing," a euphemism for genocide against Muslims. Intervention by troops from the North Atlantic Treaty Organization (NATO) helped end the war in 1995. In the summer of 2008, war erupted between Russia and the Republic of Georgia, another former part of the USSR.

Post-Cold War conflicts were by no means confined to a single part of the world either. For example, horrible violence also broke out in Africa, most shockingly in Rwanda, where militias formed mostly of members of the Hutu majority conducted a genocidal mass killing and mutilation of members of the rival Tutsi tribe in 1994. Beginning in 2003 in Sudan, a government-supported militia, the Janjaweed, began a campaign of brutal attacks against farming villages, resulting in hundreds of thousands of civilians being killed and many more displaced and starving. Clearly, humanity has not come close to achieving a world without war.

Getting it Together and Forming the United Nations

So, what happened to Woodrow Wilson's splendid idea of a League of Nations dedicated to preserving international peace and security? The concept is still around. The United Nations emerged during World War II, when 26 nations pledged themselves to continue the fight against the Axis powers. After the war, 51 countries signed a charter creating the United Nations. The League of Nations turned its functions over to the new body.

REMEMBER

The charter defines the United Nations as a world community of independent sovereign states that will protect international peace and take collective action against war, or against forces that threaten war, if necessary. In 2021, the UN's membership total stood at 193 nations, many of them former colonies of European masters.

Its critics see the organization as, at worst, a plot to undermine the sovereignty of individual nations or, at best, as a waste of time and money. The United Nations has been ineffective in many of its attempts to keep international conflicts from turning violent, but it also has scored some moderate successes. As with the League of Nations, this business of internationalism is still new to humankind.

Even as people around the world grow closer together, forces pull us apart. Nationalists and antiglobalists work to maintain and reinforce borders and stress cultural differences.

Western Europe spent the last decades of the 20th century forging closer bonds as the European Union, with ease of trade and travel between member nations, but in 2016, voters in the United Kingdom, a key part of that confederation, voted to get out. Brexit became reality in 2020.

Still, with communications satellites and the Internet, every place is simultaneously in touch with the rest of the world. United Nations or not, European Union with or without the United Kingdom, national sovereignty may ultimately come to mean less as cultural intermingling speeds up. Don't hold your breath, but civilization (whatever that funny word means) may finally become truly global. Whether or not that's a good thing remains to be seen.

Tracking the Centuries

1788: Britain establishes a penal colony in Australia.

1808: Napoleon puts his brother, Joseph Bonaparte, on Spain's throne.

1837: American Samuel Morse invents Morse code.

1848–49: Revolutionary movements sweep Europe.

1890s: Germany's Kaiser Wilhelm II begins an aggressive shipbuilding campaign, alarming Britain, the world's top naval power.

1914: In Sarajevo, Bosnia, a Serbian terrorist assassinates the heir apparent to the Austro-Hungarian throne, triggering World War I.

1939: Germany invades Poland, beginning World War II.

1991: The government of the Soviet Union collapses. Russia reemerges as an independent sovereign state.

2001: Al Qaeda terrorists crash three hijacked airliners into iconic buildings in New York and Washington, D.C., killing thousands. A fourth hijacked plane crashes in Pennsylvania.

2003: The United States invades Iraq and deposes its ruling dictator, Saddam Hussein.

2016: In a referendum election, United Kingdom voters choose to end their nation's membership in the European Union, a separation known as Brexit.

2020: After four years of trying to negotiate favorable terms for Brexit, the U.K. leaves the European Union.

2021: U.S. troops pull out of Afghanistan in a move to end America's longest war. The Taliban, former rulers, immediately retake the country.

3

Seeking Answers

Take a look at the religions that have shaped societies, brought people together, and pitted them against one another since before the rise of civilization, and how religions continue to shape how human beings get along (or don't).

See how philosophy both intersected with and diverged from ancient religions, and how the roots of scientific thinking arose from a love of wisdom.

Follow the unlikely path of Greek philosophical traditions and sometimes conflicting interpretations of them — traditions that became central to European Christianity's ways of understanding reality through the Middle Ages.

Trace Christian humanism, descended from one of those old Greek traditions, and see how it revived an appreciation of worldly beauty and human achievement during the Renaissance.

Find out how growing openness to questioning authority in the 16th century shattered the authority of the once-monolithic Catholic Church in Europe, leading to religious wars, revolutions, migrations, and (of course) Protestant denominations.

Discover how asking questions and seeking answers — in disciplines ranging from astronomy to physics to economics — sparked both the Scientific Revolution, the Industrial Revolution, and political upheaval from the 18th-century Enlightenment right up until the present.

Chapter **10**

Worshipping through the Ages

What does religion have to do with history? Just about everything. Religious belief has both united societies and ripped them apart. Religion played a large and forceful role in creating civilization (see Chapter 4). Belief has also been a primary cause of wars, revolutions, and migrations.

Civilizations were built around belief. For thousands of years, societies raised their rulers to divine status or thought of their royalty as being human descendants of gods or mortal representatives of gods. Egyptians, at least as long ago as 2950 BC (that's 5,000 years ago), considered their kings to be deities. Alexander the Great (356–323 BC) declared himself a god. Rome bestowed divinity on Augustus (27 BC–14 AD), its first emperor (see Chapter 5). And in South America, the Incas of the 15th century AD worshipped their king as Sapa Inca, or Son of the Sun.

Three hundred years ago, many if not most Christians still thought absolute monarchy was the just way for a godly society to be organized. (For more about the divine right of kings, see Chapter 12.) They believed that the king was God's representative, imbued with holy authority, and wanted the world to be run that way.

Most societies through history have been organized around religion, and arguably, most governments until modernity have been theocratic to at least some extent. There was an official religion that everybody was supposed to follow. Even in the 21st century, theocracies continue. Afghanistan under Taliban leadership and Iran are examples of theocratic states. Israel defines itself as being a Jewish and democratic state, and the nation-state of the Jewish people.

The terrorist group Islamic State (ISIS or ISIL) has declared itself to be a worldwide ruling authority over all Muslims. For a few years in the early 21st century, it physically controlled a large area of Syria and Iraq; then it was driven underground in 2019 by an international coalition of military forces, including those of the United States and Russia. Like al-Qaeda, this group uses its interpretation of religion to justify attacks on *soft targets,* such as crowds of civilians, schools, cafés, mosques, churches, and publishing companies.

In this chapter, I discuss the variety of forms a religion can take, because before you can understand religion's impact on civilization, you need to consider what religion is. Then I introduce you to some major religions around the world, explain how they arose, and highlight some ways that they influenced social or political life.

Major religions have the most followers and play the biggest role in history. In this chapter, you'll find them arranged in rough chronology.

REMEMBER

For many people, religion is at the core of everything. It's the basis for determining right from wrong and good from evil, for knowing how to live in the world and prepare for a world yet to come. If religion holds this level of importance for you, I assure you that nothing in this chapter is meant to challenge, undermine, or insult your beliefs. I try to examine each religion in this chapter objectively, which means that I don't give one belief system preference over another. If the prospect of seeing your religion set side by side with other systems of belief and looked at as a piece of human history bothers you in any way, I encourage you to skip this chapter or any part that you think could offend you. If you find that I don't adequately explain the complex system of belief that is your religion, you're right. If I leave out your religion, you have my apologies. I mean no disrespect. This chapter isn't a complete guide or a comprehensive catalog. It is a consideration of the very large role that religion has played in human history, with examples.

Defining Religion

No single definition could sum up the traditions, practices, and ideas lumped together under the general category religion. The word religion refers to publicly shared beliefs, privately held convictions, and ways that people express their faith. Worshipful customs such as regular churchgoing and daily prayer are part of religion. So are dietary rules (as when Muslims fast for Ramadan) and modes of dress (such as a Jewish man's skullcap, called a kippah or yarmulke). It also refers to rituals, from the simple lighting of a candle to human sacrifice.

Divining the role of god(s)

Most religions, but not all, are based on belief in a god or in multiple gods. Buddhism, for example, doesn't require a belief in gods; rather, it concerns itself with reincarnation and freeing the self from desire. Even in schools of Buddhism that venerate certain gods, the gods aren't central to the religion.

TECHNICAL STUFF

Religions that require belief in a god or gods — such as Judaism, Christianity, and Islam — are called theistic religions. Specifically, these three religions are monotheistic, meaning that they're built on belief in a single all-powerful god. Other religions are polytheistic, in that they embrace multiple gods. The religion of ancient Greece was polytheistic, and so was the Norse religion that preceded Christianity in northern Europe.

Worshipping a supreme god

Many religions recognize a supreme god. Some polytheistic religions feature a sky god that reigns above all others; others focus on an earth god or goddess. In the Norse religion, displaced by Christianity about 1,000 years ago, Odin (or Wodin) was the father god and the ruler of Valhalla (a supernatural drinking hall for dead warriors).

The Greeks' Zeus was a father god. In some later forms of Greek religion, Zeus became so supreme and powerful that he was worshipped as virtually the only god. Note that the Greek name Zeus resembles the Latin Deus, for the almighty Christian God. Greeks got the name from Dęus, an older, Indo-European god of the daytime sky.

Monotheistic (one-god) religions center on a single true God, forsaking other, false gods. The second of the Ten Commandments, central to Judaism and Christianity, is "Thou shalt have no other gods before me." The first part of the shahada, the Islamic profession of faith, is "There is no god but God."

Monotheistic religions often originate with, or are reinvigorated or reinvented by, an individual prophet who claims a direct relationship with God. Judaism, Christianity, and Islam all trace their roots to Abraham (or Abram or Ibrahim). Scripture says that this patriarch moved his clan from the Mesopotamian city of Ur (in today's Iraq) to the promised land of Canaan (Israel and Palestine). Later leaders such as Moses, the lawgiver of Judaism and Christianity, and Mohammed the Prophet, founder of Islam, are in the tradition of Abraham.

Not all monotheistic visionaries fall into this Judaic–Christian–Islamic tradition, but religious ideas travel. In the 14th century BC, King Akhenaton of Egypt imposed monotheistic worship of the sun-disk god Aton in place of traditional Egyptian polytheism. After his death, his successors went back to the old ways. Some people wonder whether there's a link between this Egyptian fling with monotheism and other monotheistic movements, particularly Judaism.

Worshipping many gods

Many religions are polytheistic; the cultures that follow them worship a group of divine figures. Ancient Greek polytheism featured lustful, flawed, humanlike gods such as Zeus (often depicted as a buff old guy with a big fluffy beard) and his daughter Athena, the goddess of wisdom. Although the Greek religion arose separately from Egyptian polytheism, it adopted some Egyptian gods, such as the mysterious Isis.

REMEMBER

The Romans adopted Greek polytheism, combining it with early Roman beliefs such as the worship of ancestors. (Many early religions required reverence for ancestors.) But Rome renamed the gods. Zeus became Jupiter, for example, and Athena became Minerva.

Together, the characters in Greek–Roman theology are the pantheon. The gods in the pantheon are still widely known as literary characters. They figure in Homer's epic poems, for example (see Chapter 2). Because Homer (whoever he was or they were) told stories that were partly true, those verses are not just literature, but also a bridge between myth and history; they're about a real war between real ancient Greeks and Trojans. So, these gods are mixed into that history, creating a dilemma for scholars who are trying to winnow the facts out of the legends.

CREATION STORIES

Whether the inspiration was divine or earthly, early people told stories in an effort to understand nature's workings and to explain how the world and its inhabitants came to be. Cultures everywhere have different ways of accounting for the beginning of the world. Folklorists call these stories *creation myths*. Somebody probably told the first one not long after language evolved. (See Chapter 3 for details on the beginnings of language.)

In the ancient Egyptian religion, the creation story starts with a watery chaos called Nun, from which the sun god (Atum or, in his later manifestation, the hawk-headed Re) rose to bring forth air (Shu) and moisture (Tefnut), twin deities who combined to create earth (Geb) and sky (Nut). Geb and Nut also produced other gods.

Playwrights in the ancient world, poets of the European Renaissance, and later writers often based works on Greek and Roman myths, Homer's poems, and Norse legends. Hollywood screenwriters still use these stories as inspiration. Marvel Comics and the Marvel Cinematic Universe employ ancient gods as superhuman characters in their stories.

Analyzing the religious impulse

Scholars sometimes look at religions as being purely human-made phenomena. Anthropologists, archaeologists, and psychologists trace the religious impulse to the human need to understand or to the societal need for authority and an unassailable source of agreed-upon rules. Such theories rarely credit religious beliefs and customs as coming from a supernatural or transcendent truth.

REMEMBER

Most religious people, on the other hand, would argue strongly that the god or gods they worship (or the transcendental reality they seek) existed before humans occupied the Earth and will exist after humankind is gone. Religion, to most who embrace it, is a way to connect with and pay tribute to a power (or the power) greater than earthly existence.

Distinguishing philosophy from religion

Drawing a line between religions and philosophies (ways of explaining and coming to terms with existence; see Chapter 11) can be difficult. The ancient Chinese philosopher widely known as Confucius taught a system of ethics based on responsible behavior and loyalty to family and society. He didn't advocate a religious creed, yet after his death in 479 BC, his teachings became the basis for a long-lasting system of thought, Confucianism, that is often considered to be a religion. (There's more information about Confucius in Chapter 24.)

Assessing Animism

Some thinkers wonder whether the human tendency to project personalities onto inanimate objects, especially among long-ago people eager to explain natural phenomena, may have brought about a form of religion called animism.

My wife's late father once drove a Dodge sedan that he named Brunhilde, after a Valkyrie — a mythical figure from the Norse religion. He called that car "she," and my wife continues to use the feminine pronoun when reminiscing about that car. Did my wife, a science writer, and her father, a scientist, ever really think of

Brunhilde as being anything more than a machine? Not on a rational level, certainly. Yet human beings are often irrational.

Who hasn't named a car or some other possession? Who hasn't thought or said in frustration that some inanimate object "wants" or "doesn't want" to do something? A nail wants to bend rather than be pounded straight into the board, or a jar lid doesn't want to come loose. It doesn't mean that you attribute a will, let alone a soul, to the car, the nail, or the jar lid. Even if you did, you wouldn't worship these objects (unless the car is really expensive). Yet these examples illustrate the human habit of thinking about the world as though it were filled with personalities whose whims shape everyday life.

Seeking understanding through spirit

Prehistoric life was tough. The human ability to see cause and effect was a great survival tool, but it also raised questions. Early people saw patterns in herd migrations and the changing seasons. Their view unencumbered by artificial light, they marveled at the stars. They recognized how vulnerable they were to forces beyond their control, such as floods and storms. Who wouldn't want to understand what made such things happen, and take steps to appease nature and seek fate's favor?

Animism, which occurs in cultures all over the world (from Native American to pre-Islamic Arab), is based on the ideas that rocks, trees, and animals have souls and that these spirits influence events. Some late-19th-century scholars, including the anthropologist Edward Taylor (1832–1917), argued that animism was the earliest form of religion and that other forms of religion sprang from it. More recent anthropologists reject Taylor's view as being too simplistic. (That's too bad for people like me, who like to keep things simple.)

Connecting animals to deities

Simplistic or not, animism probably did give rise to the more discriminating practice of totemism, in which a particular animal or plant bears special significance for a clan or tribe. Some Australian Aborigine tribes have the kangaroo as a totem, for example. The pioneering French sociologist Emile Durkheim (1858–1917) saw totems as being key elements of primitive religions.

Ancient Egypt's religion (see Chapter 4) seems to have arisen from tribal beliefs that a certain animal represented a certain god. As Egyptian society developed, villages and regions adopted specific gods, which appear in paintings and carvings with human bodies and animal heads. The animal wasn't the god but was sacred to the god. The hawk, for example, was sacred to the sun god Re and the sky god Horus.

Jotting down Judaism

The roots of both Christianity and Islam are in early Judaism, which arose sometime after 2000 BC. The God of Abraham revealed himself to his chosen people through a series of prophets. His word is contained in the Hebrew Bible (Christians call it the Old Testament), especially in the first five books, the Torah. The Torah contains hundreds of commandments, including the central Ten Commandments delivered by God to the prophet Moses.

Awaiting a Messiah

Jews believe in Hebrew law, also called Halakh, the collective body of Jewish laws contained in the Torah. They honor *Talmudic laws,* which are civil and ceremonial rules arrived at long ago through discussions among high rabbis (scholars and teachers). Long-standing customs and traditions also come under the heading of Hebrew law. Central among Jewish beliefs are the ideas that the human condition can be improved and that a Messiah (Hebrew for *anointed one*) will someday bring about a state of earthly paradise.

REMEMBER

Modern Jews differ in the ways they interpret the Torah and the Talmud. Orthodox Jews (a diverse category in itself) view the Torah and its commandments as being absolutely binding. Conservative Jews observe Hebrew law but allow for changes to accommodate modern life. Reform Jews concentrate on the ethical content of the Torah and the Talmud rather than on specific laws.

Maintaining Jewish nationalism

The tribal descendants of Abraham united under King Saul in the 11th century BC to create the kingdom of Israel, which split in the late 10th century BC into the separate kingdoms of Israel and Judah (sometimes called Judaea). The land and its people later fell under the rule of others, including the Seleucid Dynasty, the Syrians, and the Roman, Byzantine, Ottoman, and British empires.

Throughout their long history, much of it chronicled in the Scriptures, Jews remained distinct from other people of the region, such as the Canaanites. Jews also spread to other parts of the world. In Europe, Jews were often victims of persecution by Christians. Anti-Semitism culminated in the 1930s and 1940s when the Nazi government of Germany rounded up millions of Jews — along with Roma, (once widely called "Gypsies," which is now considered a derogatory term), homosexuals, and other "undesirables" — and shipped them to concentration camps, where they were systematically killed.

The beliefs that God promised Israel to Abraham and that God restored the homeland to Moses's followers after their slavery in Egypt have had a powerful influence on international relations. The struggle to regain, keep, and control this homeland became part of the religion. The feast of Hanukkah, for example, commemorates the Jews' rededication of the temple at Jerusalem after a victory over the Syrians in 165 BC. The hilltop fortress Masada, where 400 Jewish revolutionaries committed suicide rather than surrender to the Romans in 73 AD, is an important symbol of Jewish solidarity.

The modern Zionist movement started in the late 19th century as an effort to return far-flung Jewish populations to the homeland. With the Balfour Declaration, issued during World War I by Arthur Balfour, U.K. foreign secretary, Britain expressed its support for the cause. After the war Britain took control of the region, which had been part of the Ottoman Empire and encouraged Jewish immigration. After World War II, the U.K. government referred the issue to the United Nations (see Chapter 9), which carved out Israel's territory, against the wishes of Palestinians. As a modern nation, Israel declared its independence in 1948.

REMEMBER

In reaction to the partition and Israel's declaration, fighters attached to the Palestinian Liberation Army (PLO) launched attacks on Israeli targets. They were soon joined by troops from Lebanon, Syria, Iraq, and Egypt (with a contingent from Saudi Arabia fighting alongside the Egyptians). Israel fought off the invaders and later negotiated peace agreements with its Arab neighbors. Yet resentment and hatred between Israelis and Arabs persisted, leading to subsequent armed conflicts and deadly terrorist attacks on Israel and its allies, including the United States and Britain.

Hammering Out Hinduism

Around 1700–1500 BC, nomads from the Iranian plateau filtered into India, bringing with them a culture and language that produced a profound and continuing effect on that part of the world.

The religion practiced by the nomads became the roots of Hinduism. Hindus believe that living beings are reincarnated repeatedly and that the form you take in the next life results from the quality of your actions in this life (your karma). Hindu sacred scriptures, the *Veda*, dating from about 1500 BC, contain hymns, chants, and monastic doctrine. Although Hinduism's polytheism supports numerous Hindu gods, chief among them are the trinity of Brahma the creator, Vishnu the preserver, and Shiva the destroyer. The war god Skanda, son of Shiva, is shown in Figure 10-1.

FIGURE 10-1:
The Hindu god
Skanda is often
depicted atop a
peacock clutching
a cobra.

World History Archive/Alamy Stock Photo

Traditional Hindu belief separates Indian society into castes, with priests, rulers, and warriors at the top and farmers and laborers at the bottom. Under the caste system, marriage outside your own caste is forbidden. Many modern Hindus have rejected the concept of caste, even though it still colors social interaction among Hindus. Sects within the religion practice a wide range of rituals and hold diverse beliefs.

There are about a billion followers of Hinduism worldwide, according to the Pew Research Center; other sources put the number even higher. Most of that population lives in India, where the religion has survived many challenges. The Emperor Asoka established Buddhism as India's state religion in the third century BC, but after Asoka, Hindu beliefs rebounded and spread, withstanding the period from 1526 to 1857, when Muslims ruled most of India as the Mogul Empire.

Religious disagreement has often escalated into violent conflict in India, which is a diverse land of many languages and ways of life. A Hindu extremist assassinated the nationalist leader Mahatma Gandhi in 1948, for example, because Gandhi was trying to stop Hindu–Muslim conflict in the Indian state of Bengal. (For more on Gandhi, see Chapter 1 and Chapter 22.) India's religious conflicts have grown into interregional and even international disputes. The country of Pakistan was carved out of India in 1947 as a separate homeland for India's Muslim minority. Now both countries possess nuclear arms aimed at each other.

Biting Off a Bit of Buddhism

The followers of Siddhartha Gautama, a sixth century BC prince from southern Nepal, believe that through years of meditation he achieved enlightenment by rediscovering an ancient spiritual path to escape the cycle of birth and rebirth that is a central tenant of Hindu belief. They believe that he gathered a community of monks to carry on his teachings, which are built on the Hindu law of karma, and on the Four Noble Truths.

The law of karma says that good and evil deeds result in appropriate reward or punishment in this life or in a succession of rebirths on a path toward Nirvana, or "the blowing out of the fires of all desires." The Four Noble Truths are as follows:

» Existence is a realm of suffering.

» Desire and belief in the importance of oneself cause suffering.

» Achievement of Nirvana ends suffering.

» Nirvana is attained only by meditation and following the righteous path in action, thought, and attitude.

Buddhism has two main traditions. The first, Theravada, follows the teachings of the early Buddhist writings. In the more-liberal second tradition, Mahayana, salvation is easier to attain. Other schools include Zen Buddhism, Lamaism, Tendai, Nichiren, and Soka Gakkai.

In the third century BC, the Indian King Asoka made Buddhism his official state religion. He adopted a policy of dharma (principles of right life) and stopped waging war — a rare instance of a religious principle overcoming dynastic ambition. Buddhism has not always had such a calming influence on the politically ambitious, however. The 14th-century AD Chinese emperor Chu Yuan-chang started out as a Buddhist monk, but he fought his way to power and employed violence to discourage dissent.

Condensing Christianity

Early in the first century AD, Jesus of Nazareth traveled through the Roman vassal state of Judaea (today's Israel and Palestine) teaching a philosophy of mercy and God's redeeming love. His sermons and his reputed ability to heal the sick made him so popular that local leaders thought he threatened their authority, so they arranged to have him nailed to a wooden cross — the painful Roman method of executing criminals.

Christians believe that three days after he died, Jesus left his tomb, and after revealing himself to his followers, he rose bodily, straight into Heaven. His followers considered him to be the Messiah, as promised in the Hebrew Bible. Jesus is also seen as being both God's son and God in human form — ideas hammered out in early theological debates within the Church (see Chapter 12). To Christians, his death is an act of God's love to save believers from eternal condemnation in Hell. Jesus was bestowed the title Christ, from the Greek for *Messiah).*

Four of Jesus's 12 disciples, who were called apostles, told of his words and deeds in the Gospels, which make up a major part of the New Testament. The Old Testament and the New Testament together comprise the Christian Bible.

Initiating the Roman Catholic Church

After Jesus died, some of his apostles continued to preach his message and to organize converts into early Christian congregations. Paul, an early Jewish convert, was especially enthusiastic about spreading the new Christian faith to gentiles (non-Jews); he taught that believers didn't need to abide by Hebrew dietary restrictions and other requirements, such as male circumcision. At first considered to be a heretic sect of Judaism, Christianity grew into one of the most powerful religious, philosophical, and political influences in history.

Others among Jesus's first followers also delivered their teachings to gentiles. Tradition says that the Apostle James traveled to Spain and that the Apostle Peter, toward the end of his life, established a Christian congregation in Rome, where he died a martyr's death.

Historians can't confirm that Peter lived or preached on the Italian peninsula, but the Catholic Church credits him as being the first bishop of Rome, which would make him the first pope. The Church came to be based in Rome, where the successive popes (from the Latin papa, meaning *father)* have been honored as Peter's successors and representatives of God on Earth.

Becoming "the Church"

REMEMBER

Until the Protestant Reformation (discussed later in this chapter and in Chapter 14), the Roman Catholic Church was just the Church — at least in Europe. Spelled with a lowercase *c*, catholic means *universal* or *wide-ranging.* The Roman Catholic Church was everybody's church.

Roman Catholic doctrine (see Chapter 12) centers on the Holy Trinity, in which one god takes the form of three persons: God the Father, God the Son (Jesus), and God the Holy Spirit. Catholics also honor Jesus's mother, St. Mary, believed to have been a virgin when she miraculously gave birth. (Saints are people whose exemplary lives bring about God's miracles and whose virtue, as confirmed by the Church, accords them blessed status.)

Although several Roman emperors persecuted Christians, Emperor Constantine the Great did an about-face in the fourth century AD. Along with his then-co-emperor Licinius, he issued the Edict of Milan in 313 AD. It extended imperial recognition to Christianity and ordered benevolent tolerance of Christians.

Constantine personally became a Christian and made the Church both wealthy and powerful. (You can find more about Constantine in Chapter 5.)

Being a unifying force

After the fall of the Western Roman Empire in the fifth century AD (see chapters 5 and 6), the Church remained the main civilizing, unifying force in Europe. Kings claimed their authority as a right granted by God. The pope was a political as well as spiritual leader.

Pope Leo III (later St. Leo) crowned the Frankish king Charlemagne as Emperor of the West (or Holy Roman Emperor) in 800 AD. Pope Urban II began the Crusades when he called for the liberation of the Holy Lands (Israel and Palestine) from Turkish control in 1095 (see Chapter 7).

Facing dissent and departures

Not everybody agreed, however, about whether a king answered directly to God or to the pope. This debate brought on centuries of power struggles. In 12th-century England, this disagreement led Henry II's soldiers to murder the Archbishop of Canterbury — a public-relations disaster for the king. King Henry denied ordering the hit, but he had complained about the archbishop, Thomas Becket, who was also his former chancellor. The king wished aloud to be rid of the "turbulent priest."

Sometimes, disputes arose about who was the rightful pope. When the Holy Roman Emperor Frederick I disagreed with the choice of Orlando (or Roland) Bandinelli to become Pope Alexander III in 1159, Fred simply appointed his own alternative. Then he appointed another and another — the antipopes. Victor IV, Paschal III, Calistus III, and Innocent III all called themselves pope, but Rome denied them.

Power struggles between the Church and national rulers fueled the Protestant Reformation of the 16th century. The Reformation generated military struggles between Protestants and Catholics, the biggest being the Thirty Years' War. The war started in 1618, when Protestants in Bohemia, part of the Holy Roman Empire, tried to appoint a Protestant king. Spain plunged into that war on the Catholic side, but as if to show that religious wars are often about things other than religion, Catholic France joined the fight on the Protestant side. (The French were worried that the Catholic Habsburg family, which ruled both Spain and the Holy Roman Empire, was getting too powerful.)

Some nominally Protestant–Catholic conflicts raged much later. One especially bitter struggle, which frequently sparked violence over the two decades after the formation of the Provisional Irish Republican Army in 1969, centered on whether Northern Ireland, where the majority of people were Protestant, should remain part of Great Britain or join the Republic of Ireland, a Catholic democracy.

Instigating the Inquisition

Before the German priest Martin Luther touched off the Reformation in 1517, (see Chapter 14), Church officials tried to deal with the widespread and growing perception among Europeans that priests and monks had become corrupt and arrogant. Some cardinals and bishops tried to root out unfit priests; reform efforts had little success except in Spain, which faced different challenges from most of Europe and came up with a rather more rigorous solution.

The Moors, who were Muslim, ruled Spain for hundreds of years. Christians took over the last of Spain's Muslim kingdoms in 1492, the same year that Christopher Columbus set sail. Many Jews lived in Spain too. The Moors of that time had been more tolerant toward Jews than European Christians were, so Jews settled there.

With the Moors out of power, however, and Catholicism restored as the state religion, Muslims and Jews were stuck. They could get out of the country, adopt Christianity, or risk being killed. Many converted, but they were tepid Christians at best. Most hated the Church and everything it stood for, practicing their own religions in secret.

Spanish Christians worried that these new Christians would revolt if Moors from North Africa or Muslim Turks from the east attacked. Church officials also worried that the new Christians' resentment would undermine priestly authority. To alleviate these fears, the co-monarchs Ferdinand and Isabella (see Chapter 19) started the Spanish Inquisition, a campaign to root out and punish heresy. The Inquisition gained a reputation for thoroughness, even-handedness (commoners, nobles, and churchmen were all vulnerable), and cruelty. Operating in secret, using anonymous informers, and making arrests by night, the Inquisition employed solitary confinement and torture to force confessions.

Sentencing was public, however; it involved a gaudy ceremony called an auto-da-fé, with prisoners dressed in special gowns called sanbenitos. Punishments ranged from fines to flogging to death. Foreign sailors dreaded an arrest in Spain for smuggling or piracy, certain that they would be turned over to the Inquisition. They spread stories, some of them exaggerated, about its horrors.

During the Inquisition, the Church in Spain tightened its operations; corrupt priests, monks, and even bishops got the heave-ho. By the time Martin Luther expressed his objections to certain Church practices, sparking the Reformation (see the section "Peeking at the Protestant Churches," in this chapter, and also Chapter 19) Spain was not fertile ground for his ideas to take root. The Inquisition made short work of the few people who were tempted by Protestantism. And just to make sure, the Inquisition kept out notions that were considered to be dangerous by banning foreign books and prohibiting Spaniards from attending foreign universities. As a result, Lutheran and Calvinist ideas never caught on in the Iberian Peninsula.

Maintaining continuity

The Church remained a major civil influence in solidly Catholic countries and their territories in the 16th century and remained powerful in many places for centuries afterward. Priests, who were among the first Spaniards in many parts of the New World, built missions and converted the indigenous population, often by force, establishing Catholicism as the majority religion throughout most of Latin America.

Catholic laws influenced civil law, especially on moral issues such as divorce and birth control. Some dealings in political affairs, however, are contrary to Vatican policy. In the 20th century, for example, the Roman Catholic Church rebuked South American priests for teaching liberation theology and taking part in popular political movements.

Evaluating the Eastern Orthodox Church

Constantine the Great, a Christian, built his new imperial capital far to the east of Rome, at Byzantium. Renamed Constantinople after the emperor, the city was a center of Christianity in its own right, especially after the Western Roman Empire collapsed (see Chapter 5).

Rome's Church had less and less influence over the Eastern faithful between the 5th and 11th centuries. And when Roman Catholic Crusaders sacked Orthodox Christian Constantinople in 1204, the attack by avowed Christians upon brother Christians showed how alienated from each other the two major branches of the faith had become. (For more about the Crusades, turn to Chapter 7.)

The Eastern Orthodox Church evolved into a communion of self-governing churches in Eastern Europe, Greece, Ukraine, Russia, Georgia, and the Middle East. Practitioners honor the leadership of the patriarch of Constantinople, but they don't hold him supreme, as Roman Catholics do the pope. Orthodox doctrine looks to the scriptures as being the source of Christian truth and rejects points of doctrine developed by Church fathers in Rome. Much of the estrangement between the Eastern and Roman churches began in disagreements over basic questions about the nature of God and the relationship between Jesus and God the Father.

The Orthodox Church suffered a serious blow in 1453, when the Ottoman Turks conquered Constantinople. The city became Islamic, and its name was changed to Istanbul. The Turks turned its magnificent domed church, Hagia Sophia (completed in 537 AD), into a mosque. Later, the building was a museum, and in 2020, the conservative Turkish government redesignated it as a mosque.

Grand Prince Vladimir established the Russian Orthodox Church as part of the international community of Eastern Orthodox Christianity in 988 AD. The Russian Orthodox Church remained Russia's state religion until the Revolution of 1917 (see Chapter 9). Communist officials restricted worship and persecuted worshippers through most of the 20th century, but the church endured and began to rebuild itself after the Soviet Union collapsed in 1991.

Relations between the Orthodox churches (which have 218 million members worldwide) and Roman Catholicism have improved since the later decades of the 20th century.

Peeking at the Protestant churches

Protestant is a broad and imprecise term applied to a wide range of churches, most of them the offshoots of rebellion against the Roman Catholic Church or earlier Protestant churches. The word Protestant is related in meaning to protester. At first, Protestant applied to a group of 16th-century German princes siding with the breakaway priest Martin Luther. These princes protested efforts by other German leaders to force them and their subjects back into the Roman Church's fold.

TECHNICAL STUFF

The Protestant Reformation started with an individual act of protest. Luther, a university professor as well as a priest, didn't like the Archbishop of Mainz (in Germany) raising money by sending a friar around to cities and towns selling indulgences. An indulgence was a sort of pass that Christians could buy to get themselves or loved ones into Heaven without so much suffering. If you think that's a gross oversimplification of what an indulgence was, you're right, and you can find more about indulgences (simplified a little less grossly) in Chapter 14. The point is, however, that Luther thought they were wrong.

Luther wrote down almost 100 reasons why he disagreed with the archbishop and the friar, and he stuck the paper to the door of the church in Wittenberg on October 31, 1517. The list is called the 95 Theses (arguments), and its posting is considered to be the start of the Reformation.

The Reformation soon involved Frederick, the Elector of Saxony (who started the University of Wittenberg and thus was Professor Luther's protective boss), and Charles V, the Holy Roman Emperor. The Reformation would quickly touch other kings, nobles, churchmen, and commoners in ways that Luther never could have imagined. Even England, a country in which the king was so fiercely anti-Lutheran that the pope named him Defender of the Faith, became Protestant when that same king (Henry VIII) named himself head of a church that no longer answered to Rome.

A few of the major Protestant denominations are

>> Lutheran (of course)

>> Baptist

>> Church of Christ

>> Church of England and affiliated Episcopalian churches

>> The Reformed Church (an ideological heir to the French moral reformer John Calvin; see Chapter 14)

>> Methodist

>> Presbyterian

Many of these denominations have subgroups, such as the Evangelical Lutheran Church in America (ELCA) and the Southern Baptist Conference.

In the 21st century, many Protestants worship as part of what are called nondenominational congregations; they're unaffiliated with any of the denominations listed here but often are part of a widespread evangelical movement. One sense of the word evangelical is a synonym for Protestant, but the word is often reserved for fundamentalist-style Christianity.

Protestant churches are prominent social forces. In U.S. politics, for example, fundamentalist preachers have gone so far as to endorse candidates and lobby on social and moral issues. Ironically, these Protestants sometimes find that their closest ideological allies — especially on issues such as legalized abortion (which they oppose) — are Catholics.

Investigating Islam

Exploding out of Arabia in the seventh and early eighth centuries AD, Islam was at once a spiritual, political, and military movement. The founder of the faith was Muhammad (often written Mohammed or any of several other spellings). He grew from a religious visionary to a lawgiver, judge, military general, and ruler before his death in 632 AD. (For more about him, see chapters 6 and 19.)

WARNING

This section is about a religion. Throughout this book, including here, you'll find references to enmity — ancient and modern — between some Muslims and some Christians, or between some Muslims and some Jews, or some Muslims and the West, but as with any religion, there is far more to Islam than conflict and strife. For more about terrorist attacks and war, you can skip ahead to the section called "Clashing Cultures." In the meantime, I hope you'll take this opportunity to find out about the beliefs and history of a major and influential faith.

Honoring the Five Pillars

Islam means *submission to God*. Followers worship through the Five Pillars. They are:

>> The shahada, or profession of faith ("There is no god but God, and Mohammed is his Prophet")

>> The salat, or formal prayer, performed five times a day while facing Mecca

>> Zakat, which is purification achieved through sharing wealth by giving alms

>> Saum, which is fasting during the holy month of Ramadan

>> Hajj, which is the pilgrimage to Mecca (Mohammed's birthplace and now the capital of the Hejaz region of Saudi Arabia)

Going beyond Mecca and Medina

Rising out of Mecca, where Mohammed, then a merchant, received the holy vision that commanded him to preach "the true religion," Islam spread quickly during Mohammed's lifetime. Around 610 AD, he began teaching the doctrine of "submission to God" that defines Islam. Followers gathered, to the point that local officials feared the holy man was becoming dangerously influential. They eventually threw him out, but he built a power base 200 miles north in Medina. He later returned and took Mecca by force.

Mohammed's followers united most of the Arabic-speaking peoples behind this new faith in only a few decades, but there was some resistance and backlash from Arab tribes that initially accepted and then renounced Islam. This turnaround resulted in jihad, or holy struggle, to restore the faith — by force, if necessary.

That jihad gathered huge momentum over the century after the prophet's death, sweeping far beyond the traditional Arab lands. Muslims believe that people, societies, and governments should all be obedient to the will of God set forth in the holy book, the *Quran*. The Muslim warriors who waged Jihad were sure that if they died honorably while fighting for Allah, they would reap special heavenly rewards. Their fervor was hard to defend against, especially as the Persian and Byzantine empires were in decline.

The conquests led to an Arab Empire that, at its height, stretched from Spain to the Indus Valley in northwest India. (See Chapter 6 for more about the Arab conquests.) Then the Arab Empire splintered into smaller Islamic kingdoms and empires. Although Arab political unity disintegrated, Islamic beliefs and law maintained a cultural common thread among Muslim countries.

Clashing cultures

Early on, Muslims were rather tolerant toward other religions, especially Judaism and Christianity, because of the kinship among the three faiths. (Muslims see Mohammed as being the ultimate prophet in a line of prophets that began with Abraham, continued through Moses, and included Jesus.) In Syria and Egypt, the Arab conquerors let Christians and Jews keep their faiths as dhimmi, or protected peoples, although they had to pay a tax for the privilege.

Enmity among the Islamic, Jewish, and Christian faiths developed over centuries. The Crusades, which began in the 11th century as European Christian attacks on the Islamic Seljuk Turk rulers of Palestine, left deep bitterness. So did territorial clashes as Christians struggled to take Spain away from its Muslim rulers, the Moors. The Ottoman Turks, also Muslim, clashed for centuries with Christians over territory in Eastern Europe.

Turks were among many non-Arab peoples who embraced Islam, which also spread among non-Arab people in Africa, East Asia, and Southeast Asia. Indonesia is the most populous of the predominantly Muslim countries today; it also has been the site of violent clashes between Muslim and Christian groups.

As Islam spread, sects arose. Two major groups within the faith are the Sunni Muslims, who are the vast majority, and the Shiite Muslims:

>> **Sunni Muslims:** The Sunnis believe that correct religious guidance derives from the *sunna* (teachings) of Mohammed. They recognize the first four caliphs (spiritual leaders) of the Arab Empire as being Mohammed's legitimate successors. They also believe that a just government can be established on the basis of correct Islamic practice.

>> **Shiite Muslims:** The Shiites, who account for about 10 percent of Muslims, believe that only descendants of Mohammed's family are the legitimate leaders of the faith. They recognize only the line of Ali, the fourth caliph and the nephew and son-in-law of Mohammed, as the prophet's legitimate successors.

Among the subgroups of Shiites, the Imamis are the largest. Located in Iran, where Shiism is the state religion, the Imamis believe in 12 imams — charismatic leaders who were infallible sources of spiritual and worldly guidance. Because the last of these imams disappeared in the ninth century, the Imamis believe that holy men called ayatollahs will be in charge until the 12th imam returns.

Much of the fractious politics of the region called the Balkans, in southeastern Europe, results from religious differences. In one late-20th-century flare-up, Serbian (mostly Orthodox Christian) troops drove mostly Sunni Muslim civilians from their homes, killing many in the process and briefly depopulating much of the province of Kosovo.

Muslim–Jewish enmity caught fire in modern times after the United Nations carved up Palestine to create the new nation of Israel in 1948, displacing natives (both Muslim and Christian) and outraging the Arab world.

Shiite revolt brought about the Iranian Revolution of 1978–79. Opposed to what they saw as its Western decadence, Iranians overturned the government of their monarch, Shah Mohammad Reza Pahlavi, while he was in the United States for medical treatment. Demanding that the U.S. government return the shah to face punishment, the revolutionaries occupied the U.S. embassy in Iran and held many of its staff members hostage for more than a year.

Islamic fervor also fed rebellions against the Soviet Union in Afghanistan and against post-Soviet Russia in Chechnya. Pan-Islamic activists, who believe that Muslim identity overrides national borders, have aided these rebellions. Some of these same activists formed the terrorist organization Al-Qaeda, which orchestrated the 2001 attacks on the World Trade Center in New York City and the Pentagon in Arlington, Virginia. Al-Qaeda was based in post-Soviet Afghanistan, which at the time was ruled by a militia called the Taliban. The 2001 attacks resulted in a U.S. invasion and occupation of the country. U.S. troops finally withdrew in 2021, after which Taliban fighters regained control of the country within a few days.

Another pan-Islamic terrorist group, Islamic State (ISIS or ISIL) emerged at the end of the 20th century and declared itself the government of much of western Iraq and eastern Syria until 2017.

REMEMBER

Extremists —including Al-Qaeda and the Islamic State — make up an infinitesimally small, if attention-getting, fraction of the more than 1.3 billion Muslims worldwide.

Summarizing Sikhism

Founded around 1500, Sikhism combines aspects of Hinduism and Islam into what's called the religion of the gurus. Sikhs seek union with God through worship and service.

The Guru Nanak, Hindu by birth and upbringing, was an Indian seeker of spiritual truth who gathered his followers in Kartarpur, Punjab. Nanak wanted to unite Islam with the ancient Brahmanism that was part of the Indian Hindu tradition. He also held pantheistic beliefs, which means that he thought God and the universe are one — an idea that also features in Hinduism and some sects of Buddhism.

In the doctrine of Sikhism, as laid out in the *Adi-Granth*, its sacred scripture, God is the true guru and has spoken to humanity though 10 historical gurus, the first being Nanak. The last of these gurus died in 1708, leaving the Sikh community at large to serve as guru.

Sikhs established their own kingdom in Punjab in the 18th century and fought fiercely in two closely spaced wars between 1845 and 1849 to prevent British conquest of the region. The Sikhs lost that struggle but maintained their devotion to the idea of a Sikh-ruled Punjab. In 1947, Punjab was partitioned between newly independent India, with its Hindu majority, and the newly created Muslim-majority country of Pakistan. Since then, activist Sikhs have continued to call for Punjab independence.

In 1984, a Sikh separatist militant group occupied the Golden Temple, Sikhism's holiest shrine, in the city of Amritsar in the Indian part of Punjab. India's prime minister, Indira Gandhi, ordered army troops to clear the shrine of the activists, resulting in an armed battle estimated to have killed hundreds of militants and as many as 3,000 others, most of them Sikh. The month after this disaster, two of Gandhi's bodyguards, both of them Sikh, assassinated the prime minister.

Tracking the Centuries

1700–1500 BC: Nomads from the Iranian plateau arrive in India, bringing with them the roots of Hindu religious belief.

11th century BC: Tribes descended from the patriarch Abraham unite under King Saul to create the kingdom of Israel.

Third century BC: Asoka, king of India, makes Buddhism his official state religion. He adopts a policy of dharma (principles of right life) and stops conducting wars of conquest against neighboring countries.

About 33 AD: At the request of local Jewish leaders, Roman authorities arrest Jesus of Nazareth. He's sentenced to death and nailed to a cross, where he hangs until pronounced dead.

313 AD: Roman co-emperors Constantine and Licinius jointly issue the Edict of Milan, recognizing Christianity and extending tolerance to its followers.

About 610 AD: The Prophet Mohammed begins teaching "submission to God," or Islam.

About 1500: In Kartarpur, Punjab, the Guru Nanak seeks to unite ancient Brahmanism, part of the Hindu tradition, with Islam. He founds the Sikh religion.

October 31, 1517: Martin Luther, a German priest and university professor, nails his *95 Theses* to a church door, protesting the clerical practice of selling indulgences.

1948: The United Nations carves a new Jewish homeland, the modern nation of Israel, out of what was British-controlled Palestine.

September 11, 2001: Muslim extremists belonging to the terrorist organization Al-Qaeda hijack four American airliners and succeed in crashing three of them, passengers and all, into U.S. targets. The fourth plane also crashes, killing everyone onboard.

2020: In Istanbul, Turkey, Hagia Sophia, built as a palatial Christian church in 537 AD and used as a mosque between 1453 and 1935, reopens again as a mosque after serving for 85 years as a museum.

Chapter **11**

Loving Wisdom: Philosophy's Impact

Philosophy often gets dismissed as mind games — idle speculations cooked up by eccentrics with overactive imaginations. If that's all philosophy were, you wouldn't have to take it into account when considering history. But philosophy keeps bumping into history by getting into religion, politics, and government, and influencing how people conduct their lives. Therefore, any overview of world history includes looking at philosophy and where it comes from.

Traditionally, philosophy is thought to come from the ancient Greeks, although they probably picked up on earlier cultures' philosophical traditions. Wherever they got their inspiration, the Greeks — a culture of thinkers and talkers — made the most of it.

In this chapter, you will meet ancient philosophers and their ideas. You'll be able to follow the way their tradition of pondering the nature of reality led to the traditions rooted in the ideas of Athenian teacher Socrates, his student Plato, Plato's student Aristotle, and Aristotle's student Alexander the Great. You'll see the way that philosophy and the love of wisdom spread through the Hellenistic (Greek) world that carried over into the Roman Empire. And you can consider how enduring and influential the writings of Plato and Aristotle remained for many centuries.

Asking the Big Questions

Philosophy can sound wild, especially when you ponder what the guys trying to practice it more than 2,500 years ago had to say. But they were doing the best they could with the knowledge and tools they had. And most of what they wrote has been lost, which makes it difficult for history to give them a fair shake.

Take Thales, who was born about 625 BC; he said the world floated on water. He also seemed to think that everything was made of water. Actually, he just could have been impressed by how much water there was.

What Thales was talking about with regard to everything being made of water isn't clear. No complete texts of philosophical works from that far back survive. It seems, however, that Thales and the philosophers who followed him — proposing such things as air, fire, and the infinite as being the basis of all matter — were thinking about a reality based on observable phenomena.

REMEMBER

Philosophers tackle the big questions, which include the following:

>> What is the world?

>> Who am I?

>> What am I doing here?

>> Does reality consist of what people see and experience?

>> If not, what is reality?

>> What does reality mean?

Founding science in philosophy

Today's scientists answer questions empirically — based on physical evidence. But before modern scientific methods, scientists were philosophers: They asked questions and thought about possible answers without hard data to back them up.

In Greece almost 3,000 years ago, few tools were available for conducting scientific experiments. Thales couldn't take samples of water, marble, fingernail clippings, and olive oil and then run tests that would show that they weren't all forms of the same thing. So scientist–philosophers did the best they could in formulating theories that seemed to explain the world they observed.

Testing a theory but blowing the methodology

Unlike some early philosophers, Anaximenes, who came along later than Thales (Anaximenes died around 500 BC), conducted experiments. These experiments were flawed, but they had an inkling of scientific method about them.

Anaximenes thought everything was made of air, which could transform into other matter by compression or expansion. He decided that clouds were made of condensed air on its way to becoming more condensed. At a certain point, air would become so condensed that it would turn into water, and even more tightly compressed air, he thought, became mud, earth, and stone — in that order. Fire, he said, was extremely rarified air.

Anaximenes thought he had good evidence for his theory, in that when you purse your lips and blow, a compressed stream of air comes out cold. If you open your mouth wide and breathe out, the air — now rarified rather than condensed — feels hot. Presumably, by extension, if you could open your mouth really, really wide, you could breathe out fire.

Diverging disciplines

TECHNICAL
STUFF

As thinkers figured out more and better ways to test, prove, or disprove their theories about the physical world, sciences split off from philosophy. Philosophers continued to ask questions about the nature of being (called metaphysics), the nature of knowledge (called epistemology), ethics, and morals; they asked questions that couldn't be satisfactorily answered by experiments.

Yet despite this split, philosophy and science overlapped in many ways. Until the 1840s, scientists were called natural philosophers.

Mixing philosophy and religion

Just as philosophy and science intermingled, so did philosophy and religion, as they still do. Religion often means much the same as philosophy — a way of understanding reality. Religion includes publicly shared beliefs, private convictions, and ways that people express faith. (You can find out more about religions in Chapter 10.) The Greek religion focused on the *pantheon* — a group of gods who behaved much as human beings do but existed in a supernatural realm that interacted with and affected mortal affairs.

Early philosophers apparently weren't content with taking creation myths and Greek polytheism (the worship of many gods) at face value. But that doesn't mean they rejected religion, as evidenced by these examples:

>> One early Greek philosopher, Pythagoras (about 580–500 BC), founded a religious community and preached about the transmigration of souls. His followers said he was the son of the god Apollo and that he could appear in two places at once.

>> Xenophanes, a philosopher born around 580 BC, opposed anthropomorphic gods (gods who look and act like people) and polytheism, yet he described a god that he called "the greatest amongst gods and men."

>> Legend says that Empedocles, who thought the universe was made of four elements (fire, air, water, and earth), claimed to be a god himself. To prove it, according to one rumor, he jumped into a live volcano around 430 BC. He couldn't make any more claims after that.

Greeks, and later Romans, worshipped the gods of their pantheon for century after century while philosophical arguments rose, fell out of favor, and rose again. Plotinus, a Greek from Egypt who moved to Rome in 224 AD, mixed popular myths with the ideas of Plato (discussed later in this chapter). Plato, who lived 500 years before Plotinus, said that the world as people experience it is made of imperfect, temporary reflections of perfect, eternal Ideas, or forms. Plotinus also stirred in bits from Aristotle, the Stoics, and the Pythagoreans and came up with Neoplatonism, a school of thought that flourished for a millennium and came back in new Christian forms in the 14th and 15th centuries.

Tracing Philosophy's Roots

Greeks weren't the first to ask basic questions. Supernatural creation stories (see Chapter 10) addressed some of the same things that the first philosophers wondered about, such as what the world is made of, what the sun and moon are, and what place humankind has in nature. Philosophy arose among the Greeks fewer than 3,000 years ago, yet complex sophisticated civilizations existed long before that.

Some scholars argue that the Greeks built on a tradition of inquiry that came from the ancient Hindus. In the sixth century BC, more than a century before Empedocles made the same claim, an Indian philosopher known as Ajita of the Hair Blanket (catchy name, huh?) said the world consisted of earth, air, fire, and water. Did Empedocles get the idea from Ajita? Nobody knows. In the fifth century BC, the Greek Leucippus argued that the world is made up of tiny particles: *atoms.* But Pakudha Kacchayana, an Indian of the sixth century BC, walked that path first.

Sumer and Babylon, both in Mesopotamia, had traditions of literacy that long predated the Greeks. So did Persia. Some scholars point to Africa as the original source of intellectual inquiry. The problem with these claims is that there's no proof. Clues, however, indicate that Greek philosophy benefited from cultural crosscurrents. The first Greek philosophers didn't live in Greece, for example.

Living on the edges of Greek society

Greeks were colonizers. As they sailed around the Aegean Sea and beyond into the wider Mediterranean, they liked to settle and establish city-states like the ones back home. Their colonies produced the Greeks' earliest hotshot thinkers.

TECHNICAL STUFF

Pythagoras was born on an island off the coast of Turkey and moved to Italy. Thales, his student Anaximander, and the younger Anaximenes are called the Milesians or the Ionians because they lived in Miletus, a city-state in Greek Asia. (That part of the world, in present-day Turkey, was called Ionia.) Xenophanes lived in Colophon, near present-day Izmir, Turkey.

Drawing inspiration from other cultures

Greeks of the fifth century BC looked back on an honored past embodied in the works of their poets, especially Homer. Greeks held a traditional regard for wisdom (their word for it was sophia) and for skill with words. They also had a tradition of considering what is right and moral and of questioning how society should function.

TECHNICAL STUFF

Greeks living on the frontiers of their culture surely found their traditions stimulated by the scholarship of adjacent cultures. Mesopotamians used mathematical skill to measure accurately long before the Greeks. In 2017, a team of researchers from an Australian university made headlines with a claim that the cuneiform markings on a bit of a clay tablet from 1800 BC show that the Babylonians already understood that in a right-angled triangle, the square of the longest side is always equal to the sum of the squares of the other two. This idea, called the *Pythagorean theorem*, has been credited to Pythagoras, who lived more than 1,000 years later. Other scholars disagree with the finding.

Babylonians studied the stars and planets for centuries. Also, writings from Persia and probably Egypt — considerations of natural phenomena such as tides and stars — circulated among the learned in Greek society. Some modern scholars say that when the Greeks wrapped their minds around Babylonian astronomy and started talking about the stars as natural phenomena rather than supernatural personalities, science began.

Traveling broadens the mind

Thales, that philosopher of the seventh century BC who was fascinated by water, visited Egypt and came up with a way to measure the height of the Great Pyramid. Standing next to the pyramid as the sun rose in the sky, he watched his own shadow. When his shadow exactly matched his own height, he hurried to mark the length of the pyramid's shadow. By measuring the shadow, he determined the pyramid's height. Was this novel thinking on Thales's part, or did an Egyptian surveyor teach it to him?

Living where they did, Thales and his progeny could have seen Indian poetry or accessed Sumerian texts. Could these guys have just taken older Eastern or African ways of looking at the world and talked them up among their fellow Greeks? Nobody knows for sure.

Examining Eastern Philosophies

China developed philosophical traditions around the same time that the Greeks were creating a name for themselves in the field. Chinese philosophies had a widespread impact throughout East Asia.

Confucius and Lao-tzu, China's most famous early philosophers, were roughly contemporaries of Anaximenes of Miletus (also in this chapter). The teachings of both Chinese philosophers grew into traditions that came to be considered religious as much as philosophical:

>> Confucians stress the importance of cultural heritage, family, and society.

>> Taoists look to the natural world and its underlying path, or *way,* as the route to peace.

Also in China, the School of Names liked to twist concepts around and play with paradoxes. This group of philosophers theorized that if you took a stick and cut it in half every day, you'd never use it all up, because half of any length, no matter how short, is still not zero. This thinking corresponded with the ideas of a fifth-century-BC Greek, Zeno of Elea, who said that to run any distance, you must start by running half that distance. To run that half-distance, you must first run one-quarter the total distance, but first, you must run one-eighth the distance. Carried to extreme, such an argument supposedly proved that you could never run the entire distance.

Another major Chinese tradition, legalism, concerned a ruler's need to bring forth laws, set out rewards and punishments, and build the kingdom's power against its rivals — the basics of civil society then and now.

Leading to (and from) Socrates

People who study philosophy draw a line between Eastern traditions and the Greeks. Scholars also draw a line within the Greek tradition — a line that falls right at Socrates (469–399 BC). Like all such lines, it's arbitrary, but Socrates really did change things.

Socrates began something that his student Plato and Plato's student Aristotle continued: a tradition founded in personal understanding of what is true and what is right.

Unlike the Ionians and other colonial philosophers, Socrates, shown in Figure 11-1, lived smack-dab in the middle of Greek culture — in the great city-state of Athens at its cultural, economic, and military peak.

FIGURE 11-1: Socrates' reputation as a philosopher rests mainly on what Plato wrote about him.

Bridgeman Images

Building a tradition of seeking answers

The philosophers who came before Socrates — men such as Pythagoras, Thales, and Anaximenes — are often lumped together as the pre-Socratics. You can find a few of their ideas (such as Thales's thoughts about water) at the beginning of this chapter. Many pre–Socratic ideas seem weird, even from the perspective of later Greek philosophers who wrote about them. Here are a couple of gems:

>> Anaximander of Miletus thought that the Earth was shaped like a cylinder and that gigantic, tire-shaped rings full of fire surrounded it. The firelight shone out of various holes of different sizes, which people on Earth saw as stars, the moon, and the sun. Anaximander also thought that the first human embryos grew inside fishlike creatures. (He didn't eat fish.)

>> Heraclitus, who lived in Ephesus (present-day Turkey) in the early fifth century BC, thought all things were made of fire. He also said that the soul runs around inside the human body the way a spider patrols its web.

As far-fetched as their ideas seem to be now, the pre–Socratic philosophers were important because they started a tradition of observing, thinking, and questioning that would reject Anaximander's fish embryos and Heraclitus's spiderlike soul, instead hanging on to their insistence on trying to understand.

Leading from the city-state of Athens

Greeks who lived in Miletus and other parts of Asia Minor weren't carefree, even if their theories suggest that they had too much time on their hands. They were on shaky political turf: Persian territory. The Persian Empire had controlled that part of the world since the mid–sixth century BC. Greek residents rebelled in 500 and 499 BC, but Persia's King Darius crushed the rebellion. Then he decided to teach a lesson to those back in the Greek homeland who had supported the rebellion.

Persia attacked Greece, bringing about the Persian Wars, which lasted from 490–449 BC. Over that time, the sometimes-fractious Greek city-states pooled their resources and won. Athens emerged as the leader of a federation of city-states, including those in Ionia. Called the Delian League, the federation amounted to a far–flung Athenian empire.

Training in the art of persuasion

By 460 BC, a democratic Athens was the culmination of hard-won government reforms that began in the late sixth century BC. Athenians chose jurists and even magistrates by lottery. All citizens (a class restricted to free Athenian men as opposed to enslaved or foreign-born men and any woman) were eligible to sit in the popular Assembly, the city-state's main lawmaking body.

Thanks to the democratic proceedings in Athens, it became important for young men to learn how to speak persuasively. For that, Athens needed teachers. Itiner-ant instructors came to be known as sophists, men who were skilled in rhetoric and legal argument. Mostly concerned with teaching privileged youngsters how to plead their cases, sophists were criticized as being more concerned with winning arguments than with truth. Sophistry became known as the art of constructing arguments that sound good despite their flaws.

But some genuine philosophers emerged from among the sophists, paving the way for Socrates by engaging in thoughtful, persuasive dialogues. Still, many Athenians considered Socrates to be just another sophist. The comic playwright Aristophanes made fun of sophists in general and Socrates in particular in his play *The Clouds* (about 423 BC), which depicts the philosopher walking around with his head literally in the clouds.

Living and thinking in a heady time

After the Persian wars, Athens was alive with new ideas. The thinker Anaxagoras moved from Turkey to Athens and talked philosophy with Pericles, leader of the city-state, who became his friend and supporter.

Pericles, who built Athens into a monumental city with architecture to fit its new status as imperial capital, also hobnobbed with the new Athenian playwrights such as Sophocles and Aeschylus, men who were inventing the Western theater. The playwright Euripides also studied with Anaxagoras.

His friendship with Pericles helped make Anaxagoras a VIP around town. The philosopher's ideas also were intriguing on their own: Anaxagoras propounded a kind of proto-Big Bang theory that sounds like modern astrophysics. In his version, everything started out packed inside an infinitely small pebblelike unit that began to spin and expand, throwing out all matter into an ever-expanding universe. He also envisioned an infinite mind (not unlike a god) governing all matter.

Some of what Anaxagoras said was controversial, especially ideas about the sun that contradicted religious orthodoxy. Eventually, the philosopher found himself banished. (Athenian citizens voted every year on whom to ostracize, a word that to them included physical banishment.) Before he left town, Anaxagoras may have taught Socrates.

Another war, this one pitting Athens against the Greek city-state Sparta (which had grown tired of being in Athens's shadow), lasted from 431–404 BC. Early in this conflict, called the Peloponnesian War, Pericles died of a plague and lack of leadership led to Athens defeat. The conflict brought dramatic change to the city as a cultural and political center and figured prominently in Socrates' career and reputation.

Thinking for himself: Socrates' legacy

Already in his late 30s when the Peloponnesian War broke out, Socrates served honorably in the Athenian infantry. Later in the war, he sat as a member of the Assembly when that lawmaking body judged some Athenian generals accused of abandoning warriors after a victorious sea battle. The lost warriors fell overboard in a sea so stormy that the generals decided to let the high winds blow the ships home instead of fighting their way back to seek unlikely survivors. The generals arrived expecting to be hailed as heroes but were tossed in the clink instead.

All but one Assembly member voted for conviction. The holdout was Socrates. Why? For one thing, the law said the generals had to be tried as individuals, not as a group. Everybody else conveniently overlooked this point, but Socrates wasn't one to follow the herd.

REMEMBER

Socrates made up his own mind. He thought it was the individual's responsibility to determine virtue from vice and to act on the resulting knowledge without regard for consequences.

Glimpsing Socrates through Plato's writings

Socrates didn't write about his philosophy. His reputation rests on what other people, especially his student Plato, wrote about him.

Plato depicted Socrates as being intent on persuading his fellow Athenians to reexamine their ideas about right and wrong. Plato's writings describe Socrates using a technique that has been called the Socratic method ever since: Socrates asks the person he's talking to for a definition of a broad concept (such as piety or justice) and then tries to get the person to contradict himself with his answer.

IN THEIR WORDS

What Socrates seems to have believed can be summed up in a quote attributed to him: "There is only one good, knowledge, and one evil, ignorance."

Viewing Socrates as the scapegoat

Socrates lived to question and to pick apart assumptions. During the Peloponnesian War, Athenians' assumptions that they were the best among Greek city-states fell apart just like the city walls that the Spartans pulled down when they finally won the war.

When Athens went looking for a scapegoat after losing the war, its eyes fell on the man who had questioned its earlier ideas about Athenian supremacy. The state charged Socrates with impiety (disrespecting the state religion) and with corrupting the young.

He could have apologized. He could have promised to shut up. He could have saved his own life. But that wasn't Socrates' style. He preferred to submit to Athens's method of execution — drinking a solution prepared from the poisonous herb hemlock — rather than abandon his principles.

Socrates' insistence on making up his own mind based on his own understanding of what's good made him a new kind of hero — not a warrior, but a man of conviction.

Building on Socrates: Plato and Aristotle

While Socrates was alive, Athens lost its imperial greatness. But after Socrates' death, Athens rebuilt itself as a center of learning. After traveling widely, Socrates' student Plato returned to Athens in 387 BC to set up a school (at nearby Academia) that would train generations of thinkers.

Tracing Plato's influence

Plato developed doctrines (including a theory about the immortality of the soul) that would wield incredible influence over philosophers who followed him.

IN THEIR WORDS

The Englishman Alfred North Whitehead, who taught and wrote in the late 19th and early 20th centuries, described the entire tradition of European philosophy as "footnotes to Plato."

Advancing the theory of Ideas

Perhaps the best-known tenet of Platonism is the theory of *Ideas* or Forms. Plato thought that elements of the material world (such as a table, a man, or an acorn) were imperfect reflections or shadows of eternal, perfect Ideas (such as the Idea of a table, a man, or an acorn).

In his book *The Republic*, Plato describes an ideal political state that brings forth philosopher–kings trained in the highest levels of knowledge.

Recognizing Aristotle's advancements

Plato is often seen as the inventor of idealism, whereas Aristotle, his student (born around 384 BC), is seen as a hands-on realist. Aristotle was a naturalist, a marine biologist ahead of his time who gathered knowledge from studying the real world.

Aristotle could be down to earth about seemingly universal matters. When he made his famous statement "Man is by nature a political animal," Aristotle was probably just observing that human beings are more like bees, who live in relation to one another, than like cats, who hunt alone. His ideal state, unlike that in Plato's *The Republic*, was based on the Greek city-state, with traditions such as family and even slavery intact. Aristotle wrote about ethics, morality, politics, and much more, often refining Plato's ideas — which makes sense, considering that Aristotle was Plato's student for 20 years. He had opinions on matters ranging from the nature of being (the word metaphysics comes from the title of one of his works) to earning interest by lending money (which he opposed).

Philosophy in the Age of Alexander and After

If it weren't for Aristotle and a rather special student of his, history may have taken a very different course.

Socrates taught Plato, who taught Aristotle, who taught Alexander the Great, who conquered the world. Okay, not really the world, but Alexander conquered such a large and wide-ranging territory that it seemed like the whole world to the people of his time (see Chapter 4).

Alexander was never a philosopher, but he did collect samples of exotic plants and animals while on his empire-building campaigns. He sent them back to Aristotle so that his old tutor could study them. The philosopher and the emperor later grew apart, especially after Alexander proclaimed himself to be a god. (If you value your philosophy professor's good opinion, don't claim personal divinity.)

The philosophical schools founded by Plato and Aristotle didn't build Alexander's empire, but the thinking they nurtured was at the center of what became the dominant culture of the Mediterranean.

Spreading Hellenistic philosophies

The period after Alexander's conquests is labeled the Hellenistic Age (Greeks were Hellenes) because Hellenistic (Greeklike) philosophies spread and remained influential through the height of the Roman Empire. Some of these philosophies had names that are still recognized today — not just in the philosophy department's faculty lounge, but also in everyday life. You may call somebody a cynic or stoic, for example. You may find yourself skeptical as you read this sentence. Perhaps you're an epicure. These terms, applied to people behaving or thinking in certain ways, emerged from the philosophies of the Hellenistic Age — from the heirs of Plato and Aristotle.

Pleasing yourself: Hedonism

The pleasure principle has been around at least since the fourth century BC, when Aristippus, who studied under Socrates, decided that the sensation of pleasure is the only good. His followers, though they practiced hedonism, were called Cyrenaics after Cyrene in Africa (Aristippus's birthplace).

Hedonism isn't often clearly articulated as a philosophy — at least not by its adherents — because it's not much fun to articulate a philosophy. As a practice, hedonism sometimes figured in social movements, as with the widespread relaxation of social mores in the United States and Western Europe in the 1960s and 1970s.

Looking at original cynicism

If you think everybody's trying to con you, you may have a reputation as a cynic, but that wasn't what cynicism used to be. (No, I'm not trying to con you about this.) Antisthenes, a friend of Socrates, started cynicism with the purpose of getting back to nature, ignoring social conventions, and living simply.

Antisthenes' follower and colleague, Diogenes of Sinope, really got into asceticism — shunning civilization's pleasures and sleeping in a tub. Legend says he walked around Athens in broad daylight carrying a lantern and saying that he was searching for an honest man. If indeed he did this, it was probably his way of commenting on the artificiality of life in the city. Yet the idea stuck that the cynics thought honesty was hard to come by, so cynicism became a word for distrusting everybody and everything.

Indulging in Epicureanism

The meaning of epicure evolved, too. Nowadays, an *epicure* (or *epicurean*) is someone who indulges appetites. But Epicurus, who founded the movement in the early third century BC, believed in moderation.

Epicurus was concerned with logic and physics. He was an atomist, theorizing a universe composed of tiny particles. His name, however, became attached to his teachings about ethics and then to gross distortions of those teachings. He defined pleasure as consisting of peace of mind and freedom from pain.

Epicurus saw excessive desire as an enemy of pleasure, not something to be indulged. His ideas got mixed up with other people's grosser ideas, and the result is Epicureanism, which would have appalled him. Epicureanism flourished in Rome from about 320 BC–200 AD.

Standing together in Stoicism

Around 300 BC, students gathered every day where Zeno of Citium (Cyprus) taught at the painted colonnade in Athens. A *colonnade* is a row of columns. The words for *painted colonnade* were Stoa poikile, so these folks came to be called the *Stoics*.

Zeno's students shared a vision of the world as a benevolent, organic whole. If people see evil, it's because they don't see or know the entire thing. The Stoics thought, as Socrates had, that human virtue is based in knowledge: The more you know, the more you see the good.

Like Aristotle, the Stoics saw reason as an underlying principle of nature, and they thought people should live in harmony with nature. The most famous part of Stoic philosophy is a bit about how pleasure, pain, and even death aren't really relevant to true happiness, and all these things should be borne with equanimity.

Stoicism spread to Rome, where it competed for followers with Epicureanism and skepticism. The Stoics believed in a brotherhood of humans, making Stoicism the philosophy of Roman republicans who opposed a return to monarchy.

Doubting the world: Skepticism

A skeptic is someone who habitually doubts, especially someone who questions accepted assumptions. There was an element of skepticism in the way Socrates rooted out contradictions in conventional wisdom.

Skepticism as a philosophical tradition, however, goes deeper than that, casting doubt on the possibility of any human knowledge at all. Its founder, Pyrrho (360–270 BC), believed that all people are clueless, so it's best to suspend judgment and stay calm. Skepticism had adherents in Rome.

Putting philosophy to practical use

If you get the impression that Greeks after Alexander the Great didn't do anything but philosophize, remember that much of what came under the broad heading philosophy (Greek for *love of wisdom)* would today be called math and science.

Philosophy of the time had practical applications. Geometry, for example, came in handy for surveying and building. Incredible buildings went up during the Hellenistic Age. Among them was a fantastic marble lighthouse in the harbor of Alexandria, Egypt (Figure 11-2).

FIGURE 11-2:
A drawing of the marble lighthouse in the harbor of Alexandria by German archaeologist Prof. H. Thiersch (1909)

German archaeologist Prof. H. Thiersch

Alexandria became a center of Greek-style learning. The library there held 700,000 volumes, and around 255 BC a Greek named Eratosthenes became its librarian. Also a geographer, Eratosthenes worked out a formula for measuring the circumference of the Earth by measuring shadows in Syene, Egypt, and in Alexandria at the same time: at noon on the summer solstice. Then he took the difference between the shadows and multiplied by the distance between the two cities to calculate the planet's size.

Another Greek at Alexandria, the mathematician and inventor Hero, reportedly built a kind of steam turbine, called an aeolipile, although nobody knew what to use it for. That thread of knowledge would be picked up in England quite a few centuries later (see Chapter 15). Hero's more practical inventions included a coin-operated machine for dispensing holy water and a wind-powered organ.

Tracking the Centuries

Sixth century BC: Indian philosopher Ajita of the Hair Blanket says the world consists of four elements: earth, air, fire, and water.

500–499 BC: Greeks in Ionia (today's Turkey) rebel against Persian rule.

449 BC: Athens emerges victorious from the Persian Wars as leader of a federation of city-states, the Delian League.

430 BC: According to legend, the philosopher Empedocles demonstrates his own immortality by jumping into the volcanic crater atop Mount Etna.

423 BC: In his comedy *The Clouds*, playwright Aristophanes makes fun of Socrates, depicting him with his head literally in the clouds.

399 BC: Condemned to death for his teachings, the imprisoned Socrates drinks a poison hemlock potion and dies, surrounded by his followers.

387 BC: Plato returns to Athens to found a school of philosophy.

384 BC: Aristotle is born in Macedon, the son of the king's physician.

Around 300 BC: Zeno of Citium teaches philosophy every day at the painted colonnade, or Stoa poikile, in central Athens.

Around 255 BC: Eratosthenes becomes librarian at Alexandria, Egypt, and is in charge of the largest storehouse of knowledge in the world.

of Being

» **Hammering out beliefs in the early Christian Church**

» **Adapting Platonic thinking**

» **Paving the way to salvation**

» **Bringing Aristotle into the fold**

Chapter **12**

Being Christian, Thinking Greek

In this chapter, you may think you're getting a rerun. If you're reading the book in order of the chapters, that is (and you don't have to), you may well wonder why there's more here about the Christian Church in Western Europe (see Chapter 10) and more about the philosophical traditions of the ancient Greeks and Romans (Chapter 11). But this is not a chapter about a religion or a philosophy as much as it is about the minds of Western Europeans, the people who, right around the time of the Renaissance, began establishing new, long-distance shipping routes, "discovering" other continents, dominating world trade, and extending their political, cultural, economic, scientific, and military power over just about every other part of the world, thus influencing nearly everything nearly everywhere.

At a glance, Christianity and the philosophies of pre-Christian Greeks don't seem to have much to do with each other. Jesus, after all, was a Jew. His followers saw him as the Messiah promised by the Hebrew Scriptures. They considered him to be both the Son of God and that God in human form — a monotheistic God.

By contrast, the Greek philosophers came from a polytheistic tradition. They were unconnected to the Christian message, yet the Greek philosophies didn't go away after Christianity became the dominant faith of the Roman Empire and then post-Roman Europe. If anything, Greek thought — especially the lines of thought founded by Plato and Aristotle — became central to Christian religious contemplations and the way European society was organized. Theologians adapted Aristotelian and Platonic ideas into Church teachings through the Middle Ages and into the Renaissance. In fact, a Christian interpretation of Aristotle's philosophy shaped attitudes that helped bring about both the Renaissance and an era of exploration and conquests.

REMEMBER

So, in this chapter, you can find out how theology and philosophy intermingled and fed what's come to be called a Eurocentric world view. You'll gain perspective on how European rulers and their representatives came to think of themselves as doing God's will. You'll be better prepared to understand how avowed Christians came to consider other lands to be prizes for the taking and perhaps also how they could show different kinds of people — including indigenous Americans, Australians, and Africans — such little regard.

The Great Chain of Being

One Greek idea that hung around into Christian times came to be known as the Great Chain of Being. This way of ordering reality owes its foundation to Platonic thought (see Chapter 11). The Great Chain of Being shaped the way most Christians looked at the world in medieval and Renaissance times.

The Great Chain is an organizational chart of existence, with the richest, most complex grade of existence at the top and the humblest at the bottom. Everything can be ranked by its relative distance from the ultimate, or ideal, reality. This Platonic notion adapted well to Christianity, which put God at the top of the chain. Everybody and everything had a station on the chain, each above and below certain other links in the chain.

REMEMBER

The Great Chain lent itself to the certainty that kings were closer to God than lesser nobles, who were closer to God than commoners were. Serfs, who were essentially enslaved, could be comfortably tucked at the bottom of Christian humanity without worry. Non-Christian humanity, such as those in other parts of the world, hardly figured in the Great Chain, but they might be considered only barely above animals and other life forms. Worms and fleas and such were waaay down there. Thus, differences between levels of human society and between biological species were the same thing — part of the proper, godly order.

The Great Chain of Being was rigidly conservative. It nailed society's institutions — especially class distinctions — in place and went hand in hand with the notion of the divine right of kings, under which doctrine a monarch's authority came from God and a kingdom's obedience to its sovereign reflected Christendom's obedience to the Almighty. To defy the state was to defy God on high.

Kings and would-be kings disagreed all the time about who was God's rightful candidate, of course. Sometimes, *churchmen* — a term meaning not just priests, bishops, cardinals, and popes, but also learned monks — got into these arguments too. (You can find several of their clashes addressed in chapters 7 and 13.) But the overarching principle of the Great Chain hung on through the Middle Ages and beyond.

Interpreting Christian Theology

Based on Jesus's teachings about God's forgiveness and on the miracle of the Resurrection of Christ (see Chapter 10), Christianity gave rise to more than 2,000 years' worth of painstaking theological interpretation and fierce, often violent, disagreements that often grew into wars.

Divergent ideas aren't unusual in religion. Most beliefs evolve with variations on their central themes emerging and breaking off from the original religion. In the case of Christianity, circumstances contributed to early and wide-ranging interpretations.

Stacking scripture upon scripture

Christianity was particularly open to various interpretations in part because it's a religion built on another religion, embracing the writings of the original — Jewish — tradition as its own.

Holy Scripture consists of the much-older Jewish Bible (the Old Testament) and the Christian writings from the first century AD (the New Testament). From the get-go, Christians had to make decisions about how to reconcile this wealth of literature. What did these incredibly rich writings — often seemingly contradictory from one book to another and from Old to New Testaments — really mean?

By necessity, Church fathers based their teachings on interpretations of God's will — interpretations that they didn't always agree upon among themselves. Although Christians revere the Hebrew scriptures, for example, they never followed many Hebrew laws. Saint Paul, a rabbi before his conversion, brought the gospel message to many gentiles (non-Jews) in the first century AD. He taught that Christians who were not Jews by birth could disregard Judaism's dietary restrictions and ritual circumcision, among other Biblical stipulations.

Replacing Homer with the Bible

Furious interpretations and counterinterpretations marked Christianity from the beginning, in part because of the places where Christianity sprang up. Christianity filtered through a world marked by Hellenistic (Greeklike) traditions and teachings that followed Socrates, Plato, Aristotle, and Alexander the Great's empire.

REMEMBER

Early centers of the Church included Alexandria, Egypt, which was a capital of Greek scholarship, and Rome, where many Hellenistic philosophies rubbed up against one another for a long time. The New Testament was written in Greek, and Jesus came to be known by a Greek word meaning *Messiah* or *anointed one*, that word being Christ.

As Greek thought shifted to Christian thought, the Bible took the place of Homer's poems and the Classical pantheon as a general context for philosophical questioning. The pantheon comprises Zeus (the father god), Athena (goddess of wisdom), Apollo (god of the sun), and Dionysus (god of wine and celebration) and so on. When pre-Christian Greeks and Romans talked about abstract concepts such as good, they relied on phrases such as "pleasing to the gods." They used stories about the gods to illustrate points of philosophy.

The intellectual energy from all the Greek-based philosophies of the Hellenistic Age funneled into Christian philosophy. Philosophical thought became the province of *theologians* — people trying to figure out, or at least interpret, God. In the part of the world that embraced Christianity, scholarly priests absorbed and redefined the ideas of the Greeks, channeling those ideas into beliefs about how the Church and the world should be arranged.

Establishing Jesus's Divinity

Constantine the Great and his co-emperor, Licinius, issued the Edict of Milan, which ordered toleration of Christians, in 313 AD. Only 12 years later, after Constantine had defeated and killed Licinius to become sole Roman emperor, he called together the top bishops of the Christian Church. The churchmen met at Nicaea (also spelled Nicea), near Constantine's new Roman capital, Constantinople (today's Istanbul), to hammer out important issues. (Chapter 6 covers Constantine's founding of Constantinople.)

In Nicaea, the bishops sought an official policy about Jesus's divinity: Just how divine was he? In the early centuries of the Church, some priests taught that Jesus, as the Son of God, was subordinate to his father, the Hebrew God. Others thought that Jesus was essentially a mortal and God's greatest prophet but not divine. The bishops disagreed with these ideas and drew up the Nicene Creed, which said that Jesus was God the Son — in essence, the same as God the Father.

The issue of Jesus's divinity wasn't settled easily, however. (It remains a point of departure for some sects even today.) Disagreement about whether Jesus and God the Father were the same or similar separated Christians in Rome from those in Constantinople. And the question of how to regard the third part of the Christian Trinity — the Holy Spirit — was a sore spot between the Western and Eastern branches of the Church and a major cause of their eventual split (see Chapter 10).

Augustine's Influence on Early Christian Thought

The most influential early interpretations of Christian thought come from Saint Augustine, born in 354 AD, in Roman North Africa, in the city of Thagaste (now Souk Ahras, Algeria). Raised by a Christian mother and a pagan father, he did not convert to Christianity himself until he was 31, in 386 AD. Formerly a teacher of rhetoric, he became a priest, and in 395 was appointed Bishop of Hippo (not the pudgy, water-loving animal, but another city in what is today Algeria).

Divining the mind of God

Some of Augustine's early writings adapted Plato's ideas to Christianity. According to Plato, everything you can see and experience is an imperfect reflection of a perfect, eternal Form or Idea. In other words, there is an Idea of a table and an Idea of a woman that are apart from and superior to all actual tables and all actual women. In Augustine's version of Plato's philosophy, these eternal Ideas reside inside a mind: the mind of God. (For more on Plato, flip to Chapter 11.)

Condoning righteous killing

Augustine's teachings affected history powerfully and directly. One example: Although some early Christians were strict pacifists and interpreted the biblical command "Thou shalt not kill" quite literally, Augustine wrote that war isn't wrong if it's conducted on divine authority. He also taught that it's okay to carry out the death penalty in accordance with the laws of the state.

REMEMBER

According to Augustine, a just Christian society has the authority to kill people. This statement opens the moral and ethical door wide, considering that there aren't many societies whose leaders would admit to being unjust.

Tracing two paths to salvation

What does the title of a popular television sitcom from the turn of the 21st century have to do with Christian philosophy? The title of *Will and Grace* (1998–2006, revived 2016–20) may have been a joke on the creators' liberal arts educations, but even that joke reflects how deeply philosophical arguments run into the workings of the world.

Will (as in free will) and *grace* (as in God's grace alone) are two possible paths to salvation in competing Christian philosophies. These paths reflect a debate that began in the writings of Saint Augustine.

Adapting Augustine's ideas

Unlike just about anybody in TV or movies today, Augustine rejected sexual pleasure and things of the flesh. He seems to have picked up this aversion during a youthful fling with Manicheism, a religion founded in Persia (today's Iran) in the third century AD.

Manicheism taught that the material world represents the powers of darkness, which have invaded the realm of light. An ascetic and puritanical religion, Manicheism marked Augustine profoundly, even though he roundly denounced it when he converted to Christianity. Especially as he got older, he became convinced that the whole human race had somehow taken part in the sin of Adam and Eve — an idea called original sin.

In the Bible story of humankind's creation, Eve, under the influence of an evil serpent (widely understood to be Satan), entices Adam to disobey God's order not to eat the fruit of the Tree of Knowledge. God drives Adam and Eve from the Garden of Eden for this act. In Augustine's interpretation, everybody descended from Adam inherited that original sin of disobedience. That's except God in human form, meaning the immaculately conceived Jesus, so the only thing that can save any human soul is God's grace. Further, God awards that grace (and this is the tricky part) without regard for individual merit. That is, you can't earn your way into heaven. Prayer and good deeds won't do it. Salvation or damnation is decided beforehand in what's called predestination, and you have no free will. You can't even hope to understand grace. God is beyond understanding.

As you may imagine, Augustine's theory of predestination proved to be controversial. (And yes, that's a monumental understatement.) Many who rejected his doctrine preferred the view that God gave human beings free will — a mind and the ability to make up that mind — and that with that freedom comes the responsibility to embrace God.

Predestination has been interpreted and argued about in endless ways since Augustine. Some versions embrace fatalism, which is the idea that the future is just as unchangeable as the past. Not all versions of predestination go that far; neither are all versions restricted to Christian thought. In Islam, for example, a person can't oppose God's will but can accept or reject God. If you reject God, you face dire consequences. Much of Christianity took philosophical routes not far from this one.

Promoting other views on predestination

Some leaders of the Protestant Reformation embraced predestination. (For more on this movement, see Chapter 14.) The Frenchman John Calvin, a major force in shaping Protestantism, was especially Augustinian. His version of predestination, called theological determinism, asserts that people can't influence God in the matter of who is saved and who isn't.

In most branches of Christianity that preach a form of predestination, believers are supposed to be good — that is, to do God's will — out of faith, love, and devotion. They're not supposed to behave virtuously just because they're angling for a heavenly payoff or out of fear of eternal punishment. Yet without the spiritual equivalent of a carrot or stick, keeping some people on the narrow path is impossible, so some moralists consider predestination to be a lousy motivator.

The Philosophy of Aquinas

The way Augustine looked at religion, you couldn't understand anything without first believing in God. The last thing you'd want to do would be to try to arrive at belief by way of understanding. Belief, in this medieval tradition of scholarship, was the foundation of understanding.

It was later in the Middle Ages that some Christian scholars — inspired by their reading of Plato's student, Aristotle — began to reason that if God is reflected in material reality, the study of the world can lead to an understanding of God. Chief among these was the Italian priest and author Thomas Aquinas, whose ideas would help spark the Renaissance.

Keeping scholarship alive

The idea of medieval times as the Dark Ages, when everybody in Europe was sunk in ignorance, fails to account for the fact that universities are medieval inventions. The University of Bologna, in Italy, was the first university, founded in the 10th century. Then there were the University of Paris in the 12th century and Oxford in the 13th.

Scholasticism was the intellectual tradition at these universities. Saint Anselm, an archbishop of Canterbury (in England) at the turn of the 12th century and a scholastic himself, described scholasticism as "faith seeking understanding." With that orientation, working out ideas by using Greek philosophy was considered okay.

For early churchmen, Aristotle's line of reasoning caused more trouble than Plato's.

>> In Augustine's faith-based brand of Christian Platonism, you don't have to see and touch and feel objects (things your senses perceive) to find out about the truth. Those things, by definition, aren't true. They may be reflections of the truth, but the truth is in the Idea, which flows from God.

>> In Aristotle's way of looking at the world, you can work your way up to understanding, even to understanding ultimate truth, by using your senses and reason. This approach puts much more responsibility on the sinful human being.

Scholasticism embraced the Aristotelian way of doing things after Aquinas (later Saint Thomas Aquinas) brought Aristotle into the Church in the 13th century.

Coming back to Aristotle

Aquinas wasn't the first medieval European scholar to be drawn to Aristotle. An important predecessor — not a Christian, but a Muslim — was Ibn Rushd, who became known to Latin-speaking European scholars as Averroës. He was an Islamic judge and physician of the 12th century who lived and worked both in Moorish Spain and in North Africa.

Averroës's numerous writings contemplating Aristotle, most of them dating from the 1180s, found their way to a German with the unwieldy name Albertus, Graf von Bollstädt. (Graf von means *count of.*) Also a churchman, he taught at the University of Paris, where he started applying Averroës's arguments to Christian faith and established the study of nature as a legitimate scholarly pursuit. Albertus (better known today as St. Albertus Magnus or St. Albert the Great) passed his interest in Aristotle to his pupil, who was none other than Thomas Aquinas. If it helps you remember him, think of St. Albert as "Big Al." I doubt he'll mind.

Supporting faith with logic

From about 1265 until his death in 1273, Aquinas worked on his major work *Summa Theologica*. It is the book that hooked Aristotelian reasoning to the Church, where it eventually became official Catholic doctrine. Aquinas even used Aristotle's logic to prove the existence of God. How did he do that? Here's an example of his logic:

[W]hat is in motion must be put in motion by another. If that by which it is put in motion be itself put in motion, then this also must needs be put in motion by another, and that by another again. But this cannot go on to infinity, because then there would be no first mover, and consequently, no other mover. . . Therefore it is necessary to arrive at a first mover, put in motion by no other; and this everyone understands to be God.

Arguments such as that one fired scholastics with a passion for using their minds to get at the root of big questions. Universities became places where scholars pursued logic and rhetoric and debated the nature of being (within Christian boundaries).

Embracing Humanism and More

Embracing the human intellect as a tool to confirm faith contributed to big movements in world history, such as the Renaissance (which you can read about in Chapter 13). The focus on intellect also led to a rediscovery of Classical (that is, Greek and Roman) science, which led Europeans to scientific and navigational advances, and that in turn helped make possible the voyages of world exploration that I talk about in Chapter 8.

The reliance on rational thought wasn't a linear path, however. You can point to scholasticism as leading to something called humanism, which focuses on the relationship between God and humans. Yet humanistic thinking arose as a backlash against the scholastics; it was a reaction to the abstract concerns of medieval scholarship (all that logic and analysis and such).

Nothing secular about it

Nowadays, "humanism" usually comes after the word "secular." Secular humanism is often criticized as an anti-religious philosophy, but late medieval and Renaissance humanism was a Christian religious movement. Humanists asked, "What is humankind's place in God's plan?"

That doesn't mean that the humanists broke with all those centuries of reaching back to Greek philosophy. Early humanism is identified with Neoplatonism (see Chapter 11). Humanism didn't embrace Augustine's brand of Platonism, however. Augustine mistrusted the things of the world, which he saw as false reflections of the perfect reality (God). Living in this false, material world, human beings couldn't understand God.

Humanistic Neoplatonism looked at things the other way around, seeing human beings as not just made by God, but also as expressions of godliness. Giovanni, Conte Pico della Mirandola (from Mirandola, Italy), was a Renaissance philosopher who probably expressed this viewpoint best. According to him, the universe — stars, trees, dogs, sausages, and human beings (especially human beings) — reflected God. (For more about Pico della Mirandola, see Chapter 13.) Humans could be understood as being perfect expressions of the ultimate truth and as a small version of God's universe: a *microcosm*. A human being could not only seek God, but also find God within the individual soul. You could look inside your finite self and find infinity.

Tracing humanism's impact

Humanism's concept that people have the ability to find God had everything to do with what happened in Renaissance art, theology, philosophy, science, and even politics. If everything that human beings can think and create, including pre-Christian art and science, reflects God, the door to exploration opens all the way. The Renaissance brought major scientific discoveries, giving rise to the Enlightenment, a rational-humanist philosophical movement that in turn brought forth modern democratic theory. (For more on the Renaissance, continue to Chapter 13.)

Tracking the Centuries

325 AD: Christian bishops gather near Constantinople (in today's Turkey) to hammer out basic theological principles.

354 AD: Aurelius Augustinius, later known as Saint Augustine, is born in the Roman-ruled community of Numidia, North Africa.

386 AD: Augustine becomes a Christian, accepting baptism on Easter Sunday.

1180s: Ibn Rushd, an Islamic judge, physician, and prolific author in Moorish Spain, writes numerous interpretations of the Greek philosopher Aristotle.

Between about 1265 and 1273: Thomas Aquinas writes his *Summa Theologica*, showing Aristotle's thoughts to be compatible with Christian doctrine.

» **Celebrating the physical world through the arts**

» **Spurring a Scientific Revolution**

» **Pursuing personal perfection for God's glory**

» **Warring for control of Italy's greatness**

Chapter **13**

Awakening to the Renaissance

To many people, the word Renaissance means *art*, especially Italian art. If you're one of those people, good. Keep thinking art. Keep thinking Italy.

You can look at Renaissance art — the result of a creative explosion that began in Italy in the early 15th century — and understand not just why the artists saw and depicted the world differently from their predecessors, but also why their vision reflected the world at large.

Renaissance art embodied ideas about the place of humankind in God's universe, reflecting a significant shift in the perception of what being human means. Because of this shift, striving to make the very best of mortal minds and bodies became important. The new thinking said that you could strive to be your best, and should do so, while enhancing rather than imperiling your immortal soul.

Even the Protestant Reformation (see Chapter 14), when all those European Christians broke away from the Roman Catholic Church, becomes easier to grasp if you look at the paintings and sculptures of Masaccio and Michelangelo first. Never heard of Masaccio? Don't worry. I discuss him — and other Renaissance supermen — in this chapter.

In this chapter, you can find out about the ways that economic and political changes, including more wealthy Europeans, spurred a creative revolution that spread all over Europe. You can see how the prosperous ruling families of Italian city-states as well as the Church competed to support artists, writers, and teachers. You can trace the way that aesthetics of Classical Greece and Rome reemerged at the center of European taste. You can follow nobles and courtiers who, like the artists and theologians of the time, sought perfection through self-improvement. And you can see how rivalries between rulers led to conflicts that brought decline to some of the very city-states where the Renaissance had begun.

Realizing the Reach of the Renaissance

By focusing on Renaissance artists, you may wonder whether you risk missing the scope of the Renaissance. You probably realize that this period was about much more.

The Renaissance was about philosophy and religion. It was also about literature, architecture, technology, science, music, political theory, and just about everything else imaginable. The Renaissance was about more than I can possibly do justice to in this chapter. So why mention art? If you're interested in history, it's convenient that the intellectual, spiritual, and even commercial trends of the Renaissance are all reflected in its creative works. A defining world view shows up in the art, so the paintings and sculpture can help you understand what made this era tick.

The Renaissance spread beyond Italy, all over Europe. One reason why it's hard to put dates on the Renaissance is that it was gradual. Different aspects of it hit different parts of Europe at different times — from the 14th through the 16th century and beyond. There's no absolute start-stop date for the era. As I explain in Chapter 3, historians don't all agree about exactly when certain ages started or ended and you shouldn't have to worry about arbitrary dates for such things. No one in the year 1300 said, "Okay! Now it's the Renaissance!" or announced, "It's over!" in 1600. In fact, some historians refer to a "proto-Renaissance," starting as early as 1200. And both the English playwright William Shakespeare and the Spanish novelist Miguel de Cervantes are considered Renaissance writers, though their careers stretched into the 17th century.

The Renaissance spread far beyond Europe as explorers, responding to the same economic and cultural influences that stimulated artists back in Italy, landed in the New World and found sea routes from Europe to Asia in the late 15th century.

One root of all this change was more individual wealth. More Europeans could afford to buy foreign trade goods. And (here I go oversimplifying again) that change came about in part because there were fewer Europeans, at least temporarily. The bubonic plague (see Chapter 7) killed so many people that those who survived had more resources, more land, and even more money. The value of work increased because of the scarcity of workers.

Redefining the Human Role

Chapter 12, which discusses Christian philosophies through medieval times, ends with a focus on humanism — a philosophy that concentrates on God's relationship with humanity. This philosophy was a big deal during the Renaissance (and has been important for most of the time since it appeared). Christian writers started to depict human beings not just as God's creations, but also as symbols of God — little embodiments of divinity. Among the earliest writers to reflect this view were the Italian poets Francesco Petrarcha (1304–74), known as Petrarch, and Giovanni Boccaccio (1313–75).

Flowering in Florence

The humanist shift in thinking got a boost when the chancellor of Florence, Italy, Coluccio Salutati (1331–1406), started promoting his city-state's status as the intellectual capital of Europe. In 1396, he invited Manuel Chrysoloras, a scholar from Constantinople, to teach Greek in Florence. Many more Eastern scholars came west, bringing with them Greek learning and philosophical traditions, after Constantinople fell to the Ottoman Turks in 1453.

The status associated with scholarship wasn't lost on another Florentine leader, the financier, statesman, and philanthropist Cosimo de' Medici (1389–1464). He was a patron of Florence's Platonic Academy (founded by Salutati), where scholars such as Marsilio Ficino (1433–99) and the philosopher Giovanni, Conte Pico della Mirandola (1463–94) worked to reconcile Christianity with newly rediscovered ideas from Greek and Roman philosophy.

In this effort, Pico della Mirandola mixed into his Christian humanism Greek and Roman stoicism (a philosophy that saw the world as being a benevolent, organic whole; see Chapter 11), material from the Jewish Kabbalah (a philosophical and literary tradition rooted in a mystic striving to know the unknowable secrets of existence), and Islamic sources. He thought that all people's intellectual and creative endeavors were part of the same thing: God.

Spreading the word

The Platonic Academy in Florence and other schools like it drew students from far away, and their influence spread humanism all over Europe.

John Colet (1467–1519), for example, came to Florence from Oxford, England. When he returned to England and became a priest, he shared Florentine teachings with prominent Englishmen and the famous Dutch scholar Desiderius Erasmus (1466–1536), who lived in England. Erasmus wrote criticisms of the Church that anticipated the Protestant Reformation, which I discuss in Chapter 14.

Promoting human potential

Why did humanism pack such a wallop? Well, Pico della Mirandola, who best expressed what the early Renaissance was about, wrote that the human being is a perfect expression of the ultimate truth. As a human, he argued, you're a tiny reflection of God's enormous universe. This concept of the human as a microcosm may seem to be less-than-adventurous reasoning today, but it was an enormous change from the way medieval Christians thought about themselves.

REMEMBER

Under the influence of St. Augustine, medieval Christian thinking held that humankind was false, flawed, corrupted, forever marked by Adam's sin, and unable to play an active role in winning redemption (see Chapter 12). Humanism changed that view, making it okay within a Christian context to celebrate human beauty and creativity in ways that no one in Europe had dared to do openly since Roman times.

Reclaiming the ancients

Because the dawn of the Renaissance meant that intellect and creativity reflected God's greatness, the Classical poets and playwrights whose works had been ignored, lost, or both through medieval times could be reclaimed and inducted into the Godliness Hall of Fame (figuratively speaking). Roman playwrights such as Seneca, who wrote comedies, became fit subjects for study and emulation.

Renaissance writers took ideas from Rome and Greece and put new life into them. The word renaissance, in fact, means *rebirth* or *reawakening*. Renaissance scholars woke up to old books that had been kept in monastery libraries — books that monks had copied by hand from still-older books.

Chrysoloras, the Greek who came from Constantinople to teach in Florence, encouraged his students to start collecting ancient Greek manuscripts. (There were no Pokémon cards, so they thought this hobby would be fun.) Well-heeled Florentines even started traveling to Greece to look for books. They came back with literary treasures and began amassing the first private (rather than Church-kept) libraries since the Roman Empire.

Presenting the printing press

In Mainz, Germany, the right technology arrived at a crucial time. Johann Gutenberg, who started his career as a goldsmith, devised a way to print books and pamphlets with movable type. He made a little metal cast of each letter and then arranged the letters, clamped them firmly into place, coated them with ink, and printed as many identical pages of type as he liked before rearranging the letters and printing copies of the second page, then the third, and on and on.

Printing in the 15th century wasn't as easy as clicking a Print icon, but it was much easier and faster than what medieval monks were doing, which was painstakingly lettering every word on every page by hand. Until Gutenberg's advance, every book was a precious, one-of-a-kind artifact. Thanks to Gutenberg, books could be mass-produced.

Printing the Gutenberg Bible

Gutenberg and his financial backer, Johann Fust, built their press around 1450. The Gutenberg Bible, the first mass-produced book, came off that press — or a successor to it — around 1455. (Fust and his son-in-law, Peter Schöffer, completed the Gutenberg Bible after Gutenberg went bankrupt. Unable to repay a loan from Fust, the printer had to surrender ownership of his innovative press.)

Books were suddenly more numerous and cheaper, so more people could afford them. And because books were more widely available, more people learned to read.

Reading other early publications

At first, other Europeans called printing the German art. But technology never respects borders. A merchant named William Caxton learned the new process in Cologne and took it to England around 1473. Caxton's first publications included a history of the Trojan War and a collection of sayings of the philosophers.

In Venice, the scholar Aldo Manuzio (also known by his Latin name, Aldus Manutius) picked up Gutenberg's craft and printed easy-to-read, easy-to-carry editions of Greek and Latin classics at affordable prices. Imagine the change from going to a musty abbey and heaving open a hand-lettered volume so valuable that it was chained to the library shelf to carrying a book in your pocket!

Having an impact on Church authority

Because the pre-Christian authors were now seen as reflections of God's glory, there was a reason to read, admire, and even copy them, and doing so didn't put your faith in jeopardy. But in a subtle, gradual way, the pre-Christian books still undermined the Church's authority. Through medieval times, the Church held the monopoly on wisdom. In the Renaissance, other, older, diverse voices were influencing people throughout Europe as literacy flourished — one of the ways that the Renaissance led to the Reformation.

Uniting Flesh and Soul

Are you still thinking about the Renaissance as a flowering of Italian art? Good, because it's time to turn to Michelangelo's *David*, shown in Figure 13-1. The Renaissance artist sculpted this masterpiece in Florence at the beginning of the 16th century. The white marble statue depicts a perfect, exquisitely rendered male form — lean, muscular, graceful, and nude. *David* is a sculpture of the hunkiest young man that probably anybody in Italy could imagine — sexy in the extreme, but also a representation of a sacred subject, David, the great biblical war hero, Hebrew king, and earthly ancestor of Jesus.

FIGURE 13-1:
Michelangelo's *David*, a holy hunk.

Mark Neal / Pexels.

Michelangelo's masterpiece is flesh and spirit rolled into one. Sex and scripture. Earthly and godly. Flesh, according to the philosophy of humanism, is spirit. Not all Christians were comfortable with this convergence, which is another factor that contributed to the Protestant Reformation.

Inspiring Michelangelo

Michelangelo (1475–1564), whose style may be considered to be the height of Renaissance sculpture, didn't think up his approach all by himself, of course. Pioneers such as the painter Masaccio inspired Michelangelo. Born in Florence in 1401, he was born Tommaso di Giovanni di Simone Guidi but earned the nickname *Masaccio*, which means *clumsy Tommaso,* for his absent-minded, careless approach to life. Focused on his art, he painted biblical scenes of unprecedented drama and sensual richness, exploring the human form in ways that would have seemed sinful a century before. His fleshy, dramatic approach changed sacred art. His influence endured, even though his career was cut short by his early death at age 27.

The sculptor Donatello (in full, Donato di Betto Bardi) was another pioneer and inspiration for Michelangelo. Born around 1386 in Florence, he was the first artist since Classical times to make statues that were independent works of art rather than parts of a building. He also fashioned an anatomically impressive David — this one made of bronze.

Donatello was one of the earliest Renaissance artists to rediscover mathematical perspective, along with Filippo Brunelleschi (1377–1446), who moved on from sculpture to architecture. In art, *perspective* is any method used to achieve the illusion of three-dimensional depth. The ancient Greeks, who were interested in geometry and optics, noticed that objects appear smaller the farther they are from the viewer. What's mathematical about that? An artist with a feel for geometry can give the impression of distance in a drawing or painting by working on a grid of lines (merely imagined or marked and then painted over in the finished work) shaped like an upside-down fan. Such lines seem to project from a point of convergence on the horizon called the vanishing point. (Imagine staring at a straight two-lane highway that you can see all the way to the horizon on a level plain.) Brunelleschi came up with this so-called one-point system around 1420.

Living in the material world

Because Renaissance thinking held that the human form was a reflection of God and that the material world was an aspect of the divine, concentrating on all the angles, curves, contours, and colors of the physical world became positively holy. Artists wanted paintings and sculpture to be lifelike and reflect reality — albeit an idealized reality.

To that end, artists branched out. Artist Leonardo da Vinci (1452–1519) was also a human anatomist, botanist, engineer, architect, writer, musician, and inventor. He was known mostly by his first name, just as Michelangelo and Donatello were, because last names, although beginning to come into fashion, hadn't quite caught on among most Renaissance Italians. Vinci was the name of his home village.

Leonardo da Vinci's knowledge of the physical world informed his art (see Figure 13-2). He and other painters and sculptors ushered in new ways of thinking about the physical world and how its pieces interact. Leonardo da Vinci even drew diagrams of flying machines, although there's no evidence that he ever built one.

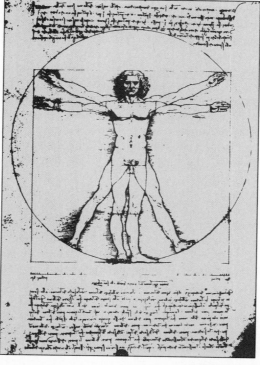

FIGURE 13-2:
In his famous drawing *Vitruvian Man,* Leonardo da Vinci used geometric principles to illustrate ideal human proportions, thus blending art and science.

Barks/Adobe Stock

Leonardo's work in engineering and perspective stimulated and intersected with the work of a new breed of architects and mathematical theoreticians, some of whom built on ancient mathematical disciplines to improve weapons and fortifications.

Returning to Science

The Renaissance planted the seeds of a Scientific Revolution that took off around 1600 with discoveries made by people such as the astronomer Galileo and the physicist Isaac Newton. (Chapter 15 has more information about both men.)

Shifting the center of the universe

Copernicus, a Polish-born, Italian-educated churchman, took a big step toward the Scientific Revolution in 1543, when he published his theories about how the Earth and planets move in relation to the sun. Copernicus said that the sun, not the Earth, was the center around which the universe revolved.

In his book *On the Revolution of Heavenly Spheres*, he also presented the notion that the Earth spins on its axis. His ideas upset traditional astronomers and other churchmen. To claim that God would place His creation on a spinning ball that revolved around another heavenly body struck many people as preposterous, not to mention heretical.

For decades, the Catholic Church dismissed Copernicus's findings as merely hypothetical. But in 1610, Galileo Galilei of Florence published *Sidereus Nuncius* (*Starry Message*), based on his pioneering telescopic observations of the moon, planets, and stars. Galileo and a very few others among a new generation of observational astronomers began to speak of the Copernican, sun-centered system as fact rather than theory, which led the Church to ban Copernicus's book — a prohibition that lasted until 1835. (For more on Galileo, see Chapter 15.)

Studying human anatomy

Whereas Leonardo da Vinci's interest in engineering stimulated and was part of a revival of mathematical theory and Classical architecture, his anatomical studies came just as the field of medicine began to catch the Renaissance spirit.

Medieval physic (as doctoring was called) was based on a theory that the body contained four fluids: blood, yellow bile, black bile, and phlegm. Called the humors, their balance was considered to be essential to good health. People today still sometimes refer to good humor, which is rooted in this theory (although Good Humor brand ice cream treats wouldn't be nearly as appetizing if they made you think of bile).

At the turn of the 14th century, Pope Boniface VIII prohibited the dissection of human cadavers. The idea that human flesh reflected God meant that to cut into and study it was a kind of sacrilege. The pope's decree, however, inconveniently interrupted the work of doctors who thought that there was more to learn about the body than this humors business.

Some maverick researchers conducted dissections in secret. By 1543, this science was out in public again with the publication of *Seven Books on the Structure of the Human Body*, a breakthrough work by Andreas Vesalius, a professor of surgery and anatomy at the University of Padua (Italy). His successor there, Matteo Realdo Colombo, figured out heart–lung circulation, a phenomenon that Michael Servetus of Spain discovered independently. Their work led to the Englishman William Harvey's discovery in the following century of the circulation of the blood throughout the body.

This new focus on the body resulted in medical breakthroughs, including:

>> A theory about microscopic contagion, developed by Girolamo Fracastoro, who practiced medicine in Naples after 1495. He based it on his work with syphilis, typhus, and tuberculosis patients.

>> Plastic surgery, pioneered in Bologna by Gaspare Tagliacozzi (1545–1599), who transplanted skin from his patients' arms to repair noses eaten away by syphilis.

Until these guys came along, surgery was the work of barbers. The anatomist and French Army surgeon Ambroise Paré (1510–90) helped change that arrangement. Among his advances, he was the first to tie off arteries after an amputation. Until Paré, cauterizing a blood vessel with a hot iron was the accepted way to close off the vessel.

Being All That You Could Be

You could think about what happened in the Renaissance as being a kind of philosophical–intellectual feedback loop. The noises that the Renaissance made were more varied than electronic feedback, of course. So were the ideas and the works of art. But the Renaissance movement fed itself, and fed *on* itself; humanism made it not just okay, but also virtuous to both contemplate and pursue human achievement.

Achievements — intellectual, artistic, and physical — amplified and gave glory to the reflection of God. The pursuit of human perfection fed an appreciation for human perfection, which in turn spurred even more pursuit of human perfection.

Striving for perfection

In the Renaissance mindset, everybody had a responsibility to become as perfect as possible by developing all the powers given them by God. "Be all that you can be," a recruiting slogan used by the U.S. Army back in the 20th century, could have been applied to the so-called Renaissance man (see the nearby sidebar).

In pursuit of human potential, artists studied math, architecture, engineering, and even literature. Long before the world thought in terms of interdisciplinary work, all these subjects overlapped, each discipline informing and strengthening the others.

REMEMBER

Renaissance man sounds sexist today, and it is. There's no pretending otherwise. Although human beings — male and female — could be exalted, males were thought to have the godly gifts most worth developing.

Many people think Leonardo da Vinci was the ultimate Renaissance man: engineer, artist, inventor, and so on. But there were many others, including the sculptor-architect Brunelleschi, who was also a goldsmith. The Spanish medical researcher Servetus was a theologian, and Michelangelo, a great painter and greater sculptor, was a poet too.

WHAT A MAN!

One of the most wide-ranging Renaissance men was the architect Leon Battista Alberti (1404–72), from Genoa. He was an artist, poet, physicist, mathematician, and philosopher, as well as one of the finest musicians of his day (he played the organ) and an astonishing athlete. Alberti claimed that he could leap, with his feet together, between the heads of two men standing shoulder to shoulder without touching them.

Alberti's arm would have made him a fortune today as a pro baseball pitcher or football quarterback. He surprised people by throwing an apple over the highest roof in Genoa, and he could chuck the javelin farther than anyone who challenged him. He was also an excellent archer.

Hate him already? Me too, especially after I read that he was always in a good mood — cheerful, unflappable, and uncomplaining, even in terrible weather.

Stocking up on self-help books

Because making the best of what God gave you was so important, self-improvement became a hot topic during the Renaissance.

The best-selling book of 1528, *The Courtier*, by Count Baldassare Castiglione, spelled out rules for what a gentleman ought to be. Among the most desirable qualities: You should be good at everything, but you shouldn't look like you're trying too hard. Even your manners should be easy and natural — courteous, but not polished. *The Courtier* was 16th-century cool.

Castiglione thought that being a courtier, one of those nobles who hang around the castle and wait on the prince or king, was one of the most important things anyone could do. Today, you may look back on courtiers as being yes-men or sycophants, and many of them probably were. But Castiglione saw the courtier's job as both advising the prince and setting a good example for him. Even if the prince was a slobbering clod, the good manners and wisdom of exemplary courtiers were supposed to rub off on him.

Nicolo Machiavelli wrote the most notorious how-to book of the Renaissance, a little volume called *The Prince*. This 1513 publication was and remains controversial because it seems to advocate an amoral pragmatism, a way of operating that came to be known as Machiavellian.

Machiavelli may be remembered as an advocate or as simply the best, most honest reporter of another aspect of all this focus on human achievement. Within the Renaissance focus on humanity, the chase for human perfection often turned to a selfish pursuit of human glory, personal wealth, and especially political power.

In Machiavelli's view, a ruler's end justifies his means. If a prince is successful, he is right. "Cruelties inflicted immediately to secure one's position are well inflicted (if one may speak well of ill)," he wrote. To be feared is more important than to be loved, the author claimed. As for honesty, a prince should keep his word as long as it's useful to do so. Machiavelli's critics call him evil. His defenders say that he was telling it like it was and simply sharing what he learned as a Florentine official and diplomat. Machiavelli placed his work well within the framework of Christian humanism, as he understood it.

"God is not willing to do everything," he wrote, "and thus take away our free will and that share of glory, which belongs to us."

Writing for the Masses

With the development of the Gutenberg press and the spread of printing, language changed. Regional tongues on the way to becoming modern French, English, and Italian took on new vitality and authority. More and more writers began using these languages instead of Latin to write poetry and plays. (See the sidebar "Who killed Latin?" later in this chapter.) The old prejudice that educated people shouldn't write in the vernacular (common) language faded.

The poet Dante Alighieri (1265–1321) wrote his *Divine Comedy* and other works in Italian. London's Geoffrey Chaucer (1343–1400), who traveled in Italy and read Boccaccio, wrote in what's now called Middle English. (It was English, but not yet the language we'd readily recognize.)

Creating new classics

Writing in the vernacular really caught on as printers realized that there was a commercial market for it. William Caxton, who brought printing to England, achieved a best seller in about 1476 when he published Chaucer's comic *Canterbury Tales*.

Many of the new books written in everyday language, given time, proved to be just as classic as the old Latin and Greek books. Here are some examples:

>> Castiglione wrote *The Courtier* in Italian.

>> François Rabelais, a physician and humanist, wrote controversial 16th-century satires in French.

>> In the late 16th and early 17th centuries, William Shakespeare cranked out plays for the popular theater (and the popular press) in English.

>> Shakespeare's contemporary, Miguel de Cervantes, wrote *The Adventures of Don Quixote* in Spanish.

Staging dramas with Classical roots

Shakespeare brought Renaissance drama to its peak, but he built on a tradition that began in the late 13th century, when the Italian Albertino Mussato began writing comedies in the style of Seneca, a Roman. In addition to *The Prince* and other work in political science, Machiavelli wrote stage comedies after the Classical style. The most famous to survive is called *The Mandrake*, which he wrote in 1518.

Shakespeare's plays show how thoroughly the new scholarship permeated European society. Full of references to Greek and Roman gods, his plots were sometimes drawn from Roman plays and even, as with Julius Caesar and Antony and Cleopatra, from Roman history. Even some of Shakespeare's plays set in his own time take place in Italian cities that gave rise to the Renaissance.

Packing something to read onboard a ship

Europe's growing literacy, which was rooted in a return to ancient classics and powered by the invention of printing, influenced matters much more down to earth than poems and plays. The ancients also wrote serious books about geography and navigation, and they drew maps that preserved what Greek and Phoenician navigators had learned about seas and land masses. After all, Greek and Phoenician navigators were the greatest travelers of their times. (Turn to Chapter 5 for more about Phoenicians.) Europeans of the Renaissance read those books too.

Advances in navigation and cartography (mapmaking) during the 15th and 16th centuries, like other intellectual advances of the time, had their roots in the relevant Greek and Roman texts. Explorers such as Christopher Columbus and Vasco da Gama (see Chapter 7 and Chapter 21) started with an atlas designed by the Egyptian–Greek astronomer Ptolemy (90–170 AD) and then radically redrew it. Their discoveries about the shape and size of the world went hand in hand with the theories of Copernicus and his heirs, Galileo and Johannes Kepler (discussed in Chapter 15).

Undermining Renaissance Gains with Conflict

All the cross-pollination of the Renaissance — with scholars and their ideas traveling from city to city and country to country — suggests a climate of political harmony throughout Europe. But the continent wasn't that harmonious. The Renaissance was a time of many borders and lots of political powers vying for dominance.

Battling for control of Italian city-states

Italy, the heart of the Renaissance, was nothing like the modern nation it is now. It was a hodgepodge of city-states, kind of like ancient Greece had been. (See Chapter 4 for more on ancient Greece.)

WHO KILLED LATIN?

Latin is a dead language, but it lived long after the fall of the Roman Empire. Only when Renaissance scholars tried to *save* Latin did the language begin to ossify into the sterile tongue it has been ever since.

Latin — the language of Rome, from everyday people to government, business, and scholarship — helped hold the Roman Empire together. And after the Rome-based Western Empire declined, Latin hung on in Western Europe. (The Eastern [Byzantine] Empire spoke Greek.) Educated people all over Western Europe continued to communicate in Latin. All the courses and debates at medieval universities were conducted in the language. The universality of Latin was really cool if you were a professor, because whether you were from Ireland or Italy, you could be just as much at home in a German classroom as a colleague from Cologne. Also, students didn't have to understand French to study in Paris.

As living languages do, Latin kept growing and changing. Grammatical uses shifted. Sentence structure became a little simpler here and a bit rougher there. Then, during the Renaissance, scholars began reading Latin from texts that were 1,500 years old and realized how different their Latin was from the language of the great Roman rhetorician Cicero.

With their newfound appreciation of pre-Christian classics, these scholars saw Cicero's Latin as exemplifying the original, uncorrupted language: the right stuff. So, they worked hard on turning the clock back on their own scholarly language, making strict rules of grammar and usage, and enforcing those rules as an important part of a *classical education*. Schoolboys all over Christendom conjugated Latin verbs, which may have been a good tool for building disciplined young minds but was the beginning of the end for Latin. By losing its flexibility, Latin no longer lived the way that ever-changing English, for example, lives today. It took centuries, but Latin eventually fell out of use, even in most areas of scholarship.

Some of these city-states, such as intellectually rich Florence, were wealthy trade centers. Their rulers — people such as the Medicis, a family that got financially rich from banking — hired the sculptors, painters, architects, and writers who made their renaissance the Renaissance.

Italian rulers also competed for influence and territory. Just as the bankers and traders who marked this age kept financial agents in other cities to look after their interests, the rulers (some of them also bankers and traders) placed political agents to watch out for them in competing capitals. From this strategy, both modern diplomacy and modern espionage were born.

The Italian states also hired mercenary soldiers, or condottieri. Moving as a unit, a military leader and his men provided armed support to anybody who paid for it. Some of their clients were foreigners. Englishman John Hawkwood and his men, the White Company, were among the fiercest. Some mercenaries were also lords of Italian cities. The Montefeltro family, rulers of Urbino, financed their municipal budget by hiring out as condottieri.

In *The Prince*, Machiavelli argues that a successful ruler needs to use cleverness and trickery. In heady times, Italian princes valued brainpower over brute strength, but sometimes, they outsmarted themselves. In 1494, Duke Ludovico Sforza of Milan invited the French to help him defeat Naples. Because the French king, Charles VIII, had a claim on the throne of Naples (these families intermarried and seldom agreed whose turn it was to rule), the French accepted.

The French army easily routed Naples's smaller force. But then Sforza and his Italian co-conspirators, including some from the island of Sicily, turned on their northern allies and forced the French to hightail it over the Alps. Boy, were those French angry! Sforza's trick humiliated them, and the French wanted revenge. Besides, they'd just enjoyed a taste of Italian wealth, and they wanted more. After Charles VIII died in 1498 at the age of 27, Louis XII succeeded him. Charles had been called "the Affable." Nobody called Louis affable. Also believing that he had a claim on Milan's throne, the new French king mounted another invasion force. This time, the target was Ludovico Sforza. Milan wasn't ready, so the French overwhelmed the city, captured Sforza, and threw him in prison, where he died. He wasn't so clever after all.

Things got worse for Italy — a lot worse. Remember those Sicilians who helped Sforza drive the French away in 1494? Their king was Ferdinand, who also ruled Aragon, one of the largest kingdoms in Spain, which was coming together as a united land. (His wife and joint ruler, Isabella, was queen of Castille. See Chapter 19 for more on them.) Ferdinand had a claim to Naples as well. And like the French, he had noticed how rich, and how politically divided, Italy was.

The Holy Roman Emperor, Maximilian, wanted in on the action in Italy too. The Holy Roman Empire, as I note in other chapters, wasn't really Roman. It started out French, under Charlemagne, but for a long time it was mostly German and Austrian. Yet Maximilian had hereditary "Roman" claims on northern Italy. Because he and Ferdinand were in-laws (two of Max's kids were married to two of Ferdie's), the emperor sided with Spain. This meant war — actually, a series of wars. Spaniards and Imperialists fought to get the French out of Italy. Various Italian city-states fought first on one side and then the other.

Spilling outside Italy's borders

The Italian Wars melded into more wars that spilled out into other parts of Europe. Charles I of the mighty Habsburg Dynasty became co-ruler of Spain in 1517 (along with his mother) and won election as Emperor Charles V of the Holy Roman Empire two years later. This political victory made the French nervous; it meant that they were in the middle of a Habsburg sandwich.

TECHNICAL STUFF

The election of Charles wasn't democratic, by the way. Just as the Holy Roman Empire wasn't Roman, it wasn't really an empire. The Holy Roman Empire was a conglomeration of states, some of which were practically kingdoms. The electors were the powerful princes of seven of those states who enjoyed the hereditary right to choose each new emperor. They elected Charles.

Being picked Holy Roman Emperor by the electors wasn't always a vote of confidence. Sometimes, the electors chose rulers whom they thought they could manipulate. Charles, however, had considerable success taking charge. He wrested Milan away from his French rival, Francis I (successor to Louis VII), and his Spanish troops even took Francis prisoner. Charles also got Naples, and the other Italian states knew not to mess with him.

Yet that didn't settle things. The Italian Wars melded into a long Habsburg-versus-France fight that lasted until the middle of the 18th century.

REMEMBER

Before he retired to a Spanish monastery in 1556, the embattled Charles found it necessary to split his empire back into two parts — Spanish and Austrian — to make it less unwieldy and easier to defend. If this reminds you of something that the Roman emperors did more than 1,000 years before Charles's time, good for you. If not, you can read about that event in Chapter 5.

By the time Charles called it quits, other things in Europe had changed profoundly, partly as a result of the financial strains of prolonged wars. To start, taxes rose. Princes were forced to borrow money, enriching new generations of bankers — and sometimes bankrupting the bankers when the princes defaulted on loans. Then came this big thing called the Protestant Reformation (Chapter 14).

An irony of the Renaissance is that the place where it began, Italy, ended this era in such disarray and decline. While Spain, Portugal, England, Holland, and other powers were starting worldwide empires and becoming richer and more powerful, the once-mighty Italian city-states remained divided and dominated. Foreigners ruled several of them.

Renaissance buildings and sculptures, once symbols of a thriving movement ahead of its time, became tourist attractions, which they remain today. The symbols of a vital present and a promising future turned into artifacts of yet another glorious past.

Tracking the Centuries

1396: Coluccio Salutati, chancellor of Florence, invites Manuel Chrysoloras, a scholar from Constantinople, to teach Greek to Italian students who were eager to probe ancient writings.

1400: English author Geoffrey Chaucer dies.

About 1420: The artist Filippo Brunelleschi invents the one-point system for giving perspective to paintings and drawings.

1453: Constantinople falls to the Ottoman Turks. Many scholars of the Byzantine Empire flee west to Italy.

About 1455: Johann Fust and his son-in-law, Peter Schöffer, publish the Gutenberg Bible, the first mass-produced book. Gutenberg surrendered his revolutionary press to Fust after being unable to repay a loan to the backer.

About 1473: William Caxton returns to London from Cologne, where he learned printing, and goes into the publishing business with a book about the Trojan War and a volume of sayings of the ancient philosophers.

About 1476: Caxton publishes the first printed edition of *The Canterbury Tales*.

1519: Charles I of Spain wins election as Emperor Charles V of the Holy Roman Empire. The French, who are geographically between Spain and the Holy Roman Empire, aren't reassured by this development.

1528: In his book *The Courtier*, Count Baldassare Castiglione spells out rules for gentlemanly behavior. He says you should be good at everything, but you shouldn't look like you're trying too hard.

1543: Andreas Vesalius, anatomy professor at the University of Padua, publishes *Seven Books on the Structure of the Human Body*.

1556: The Emperor Charles V of the Holy Roman Empire retires to a monastery in Spain.

1605: The first part of *The Adventures of Don Quixote* by Miguel de Cervantes is published; the second part will follow in 1615.

1835: The Roman Catholic Church lifts its 219-year ban on Copernicus's book *On the Revolution of the Heavenly Spheres*.

authority

» **Insisting on faith: Luther's protest**

» **Spurring revolution in the name of religion**

» **Declaring divine right: Henry VIII's break from Rome**

» **Preaching predestination: Calvin's Puritanism**

Chapter **14**

Breaking Away: The Reformation

S tarting with a disagreement over faith and turning political almost immediately, the Protestant Reformation provoked war and even revolution. It rearranged Europe's power structure. In its wake, the Holy Roman Empire was nearly ruined, and Spain, that most unshakeable of Catholic imperial powers (see Chapter 10), fell into decline.

In this chapter, I guide you through causes and effects of this religious revolution, which spread beyond Europe and eventually around the world.

Cracks in the Catholic Monopoly

To understand how the Reformation began, it helps to consider how ready some people were to rebel against the Catholic Church, which had been essentially the only Christian church in Europe. They rebelled for reasons that often had little or nothing to do with the question of how to get into heaven. As in so many conflicts, there were many reasons, including the following:

>> Money: Many nobles (and commoners too) thought that the Church had too much of it and demanded too much of theirs.

>> Land and other property: Regional and national rulers thought the Church possessed and controlled too much of it.

>> Power and autonomy: Local rulers, especially in Germany, wanted to wrest power, especially economic control, from the pope and the Holy Roman Emperor.

Losing authority

How vulnerable to a shake-up was the Catholic Church in the early 16th century? Pretty vulnerable, given that Renaissance trends undercut the Church's authority.

For one, the pre-Christian authors (those ancient Greek and Greek-style philosophers that I keep harping about) became part of Christendom during the Renaissance. These Classical authors now were seen as being manifestations of God's glory, but their voices and views were diverse and contradictory. Where once there was one supreme source of wisdom — the Church — now wisdom came in a variety of flavors.

The Church even lost its monopoly on interpreting scripture. The first mass-produced book was the Bible, and printers quickly saw how newly literate Europeans wanted to read in their own languages instead of in Latin or Greek. Scholars started translating the Bible into vernacular (common) languages. Desiderius Erasmus, the most famous scholar of the time, was a prolific translator of scripture. For more on the effects of the Renaissance on the Church establishment, turn to Chapter 13.

Satirizing the Church

Erasmus, who was from the Netherlands and lived in England, also wrote original works saying things that many people agreed with but that few stated as eloquently as he did. In 1509, he ridiculed silly, lazy, and incompetent churchmen in a popular satire called *The Praise of Folly*. Erasmus wasn't anti-Church, but he thought the Church could be run better.

REMEMBER

The Catholic Church was a huge, international bureaucracy with layers upon layers of officials. (Remember that virtually every Christian in Western Europe at this time — almost everybody — belonged to one church, the one based in Rome. That's why it was called the Church with a capital *C*. The word Catholic, which means *universal*, was part of its name, but there was no reason to say so because there were no Protestants — yet.) Like bureaucrats anywhere, some Church officials were inefficient, lazy, and dishonest. Imagine how much worse your state's Department of Motor Vehicles would be if rude, slow clerks claimed divine authority.

For centuries, there was a widespread feeling that churchmen had it too easy. Folks thought too many priests were hypocrites for telling the rest of society what to do while living in sin themselves. Erasmus knew about such resentment firsthand, because he started life in Rotterdam as the illegitimate son of a priest.

Some bishops, who were at a higher level of the priesthood and sworn to celibacy, kept mistresses and then used Church influence to get advantages for their out-of-wedlock offspring. Even popes had children. Pope Alexander VI, who served from 1492–1503, had many mistresses and many kids, and Pope Clement VII, who precipitated a separate branch of the Reformation in England by refusing to annul the marriage of King Henry VIII, reportedly fathered a son. (More on Henry VIII later.)

Alexander, Clement, and Pope Leo X (who was pope when the Reformation began in 1517) were privileged men from wealthy families who received cushy Church positions by virtue of their connections. Leo, for example, began life as Giovanni de Medici, part of the powerful Medici family that controlled the city-state of Florence. Elected pope on March 9, 1513, he wasn't ordained as a priest until more than a week later, the same day he was consecrated as a bishop. Two days after the ordainment and consecration he was crowned as supreme pontiff. That's how things could work for the rich and influential in the 16th century Church (although Leo was the last pope to be elected without first being a priest). In office, Leo nearly wiped out the Vatican treasury with his extravagant spending.

Pope Leo X pampered himself with the Church's money, but he also spent it on Renaissance glories. He accelerated construction of St. Peter's Basilica in Rome, a landmark of the period's architecture, and he enlarged the Vatican library. Many Christians, especially in Northern Europe, weren't impressed with these developments; they were tired of seeing their hard-earned coins carted off to Rome to pay for sculptures and painted ceilings. "What good do those things do us?" asked the Germans and the Swiss.

REMEMBER Don't get the impression that all priests (or monks, bishops, cardinals, and popes) were hypocritical or corrupt. Many, and probably most, led devout lives of worship, service to others, and self-sacrifice. Those honest churchmen, such as Germany's Martin Luther, resented the bad reputation that followed their corrupt brothers and rubbed off on the Church at large. Church officials promised reforms, and some really tried to clean things up, but abuses persisted.

Erasmus wasn't the first to mock or criticize churchmen. John Wycliffe, an English priest and theologian, had anticipated the Reformation by more than a century when, in the 1370s, he began attacking the worldliness of the Church. Wycliffe argued for limited papal authority over government matters and insisted that churchmen who fell into mortal sin forfeit their authority. But Erasmus's international prominence (he was widely read) and the timing of *The Praise of Folly* directly paved the way for widespread public criticism of Church abuses — one that followed his book by less than a decade. It has been said that Erasmus laid the egg and Martin Luther hatched it.

Luther Challenges the System

Many of history's great changes can be traced to a visionary, someone who did what it took to make a dream come true. Martin Luther wasn't one of those visionaries: He didn't set out to trigger religious revolt, let alone unleash international tensions, but that's what he did.

Luther — a monk, priest, and theology professor at Wittenberg University — pondered the individual's relationship to God. His thoughts on that topic interacted with other forces building in Europe in the early 16th century, starting a movement that profoundly changed the world even beyond Europe and North America (a continent most Europeans hadn't heard of when the Reformation began). Yet it all began with a rather small gesture: a one-man protest.

Luther possessed deep moral conviction, powerful faith, and stubborn resolve. But if he had known that he was going to split the Church six ways to Sunday, he might not have tacked his protest literature on the door of a Wittenberg church on October 31, 1517. The *95 Theses* (95 arguments) was a list of Luther's objections to the way that Church leaders in his neck of Europe sold indulgences.

Selling salvation

An indulgence was a grant of forgiveness, issued either to a living person or to someone who had died and whose soul was believed to be in purgatory (a sort of anteroom in which sinners must be cleansed before entering heaven).

TIP

You can think of an indulgence like this: Suppose that you do a good deed. Your reward is that God doesn't make you suffer so much for your bad deeds, so you get into heaven a little more easily. Now suppose that you need a good deed to earn this consideration. Giving money to the Church counts as a good deed.

But what if your brother died before he could build up his spiritual credits? Not a problem. You, his surviving relative, can give money to the Church by purchasing an indulgence and then transfer your credit to your bro, getting him off the hook in the afterlife.

Okay, that's a simplistic explanation of the concept, which also involved a sort of bank account of godly merit, built up through the good works of Jesus and the saints. The important thing to remember is that the practice of selling indulgences led to an impression among common people that they could buy an express, one-way ticket to heaven.

Peddling to pay the pope

When he crafted and posted his 95 Theses, Martin Luther was ticked off in particular at a friar called Tetzel, from the Dominican Order, who traveled around peddling indulgences. The friar came into a village or city and gathered a crowd, much as a snake-oil salesman would do in a frontier American town three centuries later. Imagine Tetzel hawking indulgences as though they were the latest things in patent medicines for your soul.

Why did he do it? Well, Tetzel wasn't an entrepreneur, as it may seem, but a deputy sent out by the newly appointed Archbishop of Mainz.

Another Church practice bred widespread skepticism: Anyone appointed to a high ecclesiastical office, such as archbishop, had to pay fees to the pope as a sort of recompense for the appointment. If that arrangement sounds like a kickback, you've got the idea. In 1514, when the Archbishop of Mainz got his job, Pope Leo X was spending a lot of money in Rome — especially on the building of St. Peter's Basilica — so Leo set a high fee.

The new archbishop lacked ready cash, so he borrowed from an Augsburg family called Fugger. (No remarks, please.) Powerful banking families, another Renaissance phenomenon that started in Italy, had risen in northern Europe by this time. (The Welser family, also of Augsburg, was the other big banking force in Germany.)

The archbishop needed to repay the Fuggers. To help, the pope gave him an easy way to raise funds: He made the archbishop regional distributor for holy indulgences. Tetzel was the archbishop's sales rep.

Insisting on faith

If you wanted to rub Martin Luther the wrong way, you couldn't come up with a better method than mass-marketing indulgences. As a theology teacher, Luther had thought hard about the correct path to heaven. What did God expect of a Christian?

He decided that God was merciful. As Luther saw it, you must honestly believe. Belief, rather than good works, was the key. In some ways, Luther reflected the Renaissance philosophy of humanism (Chapter 13), in that he saw a direct relationship between the individual mortal and God. But in other ways, Luther returned to St. Augustine's idea that good works on Earth won't earn you entrance to heaven (Chapter 12). Instead, you had to rely on God's grace.

Luther thought that a good Christian would do good works — go to church, pray, and be kind to others — as a result of belief, not as a way to escape punishment or win reward. How much one paid to an itinerant salesman–monk didn't count at all toward eternal bliss.

In his theses, Luther condemned the indulgence campaign as exploitation, and he slammed the corrupt clerical bureaucracy. But he didn't mean to raise a call for mass rebellion. As a scholar, he observed a tradition that had grown up in the medieval universities: Professors argued points of religion. Luther thought that Tetzel was wrong, so he challenged anyone who supported Tetzel to a debate. He did this on October 31, or All Hallows Eve (the night before November 1, All Souls Day), but this was no trick-or-treat prank. By pinning his theses to the door of the church, Luther issued a public challenge.

A Precarious Holy Roman Empire

REMEMBER

Besides the writings of Erasmus and a general unhappiness with the Church, there were other reasons why Europe, and especially Germany, were ready to erupt early in the 16th century. (Keep in mind that Germany wasn't Germany yet; that wouldn't happen for centuries. It was still the Holy Roman Empire, a conglomeration of semi-independent states where Germany and Austria are today.)

It had been a long time since the Holy Roman Empire embodied the vision held by the pope when he crowned Charlemagne Emperor of the West in 800 AD. The emperor was supposed to serve as the pope's partner and chief protector of the Church (see Chapter 6), but popes and emperors quarreled often and bitterly.

Searching for sources of cash

When Luther posted his theses, the emperor was Maximilian I, who ruled from 1493–1519. In Chapter 13, I discuss how Max hooked up with Spain to attack the French in Italy. A big reason for that excursion was that the emperor, like everybody else in this story, needed money.

Max enjoyed spending his dough on art. He also liked hunting, flashy clothes, and armor — the perks of being the emperor. Beyond that, he had expensive plans to strengthen the empire. Even money couldn't help him there, however, as long as the individual German princes, whose land made up the empire, held power in their own hands. They were getting stronger and turning their states into little nations.

Max was so strapped for cash sometimes that he couldn't pay his soldiers, or *landsknechts,* which made it hard for him to keep an army. Some landsknechts hired themselves out as mercenary units, even to the emperor's enemies, or even resorted to robbery and extortion.

Fighting crime and inflation

Times were hard for other Germans too. With no strong national government to keep order, and with the line between knight and robber blurred, merchants had to pay protection money or hire their own muscle just to transport goods safely. The high cost of shipping contributed to inflation. Prices rose, not just in Germany, but all over Europe.

The situation was more complex than this (isn't everything?), but the inflation also was tied to an increase in population. A decrease in the number of people in Europe caused by the bubonic plague helped bring about the Renaissance, because plague survivors and their children had more material wealth to go around. (For more on the bubonic plague, see Chapter 7.)

Good times bred more people, however, and by the 16th century, the population burgeoned. People needed work, food, clothing, and shelter, but there weren't enough of those things for everybody. Goods cost more despite the fact that no one had more money to pay. The price of a loaf of bread, for example, just about quadrupled between 1500 and 1600. Cash-strapped landlords put the squeeze on peasants to get more work for less. People were poor, overworked, overtaxed, hungry, and nervous.

Setting the stage for dissent

Crises of finances, violence, and hunger all help explain why Luther's protest became more than a theological discussion. People took the *95 Theses* as a rallying cry against the Church and its high-handedness. Some who agreed with the priest copied Luther's arguments, took them to printing shops, and sent copies all over Germany and beyond. Suddenly, Luther was famous.

Luther's action still wouldn't have had the impact it did, however, if rulers hadn't also been ready to challenge the Church. Some German princes were as edgy as their subjects were. They sought to limit the emperor's meddling in their kingdoms, and they were even more resistant to the pope for sticking his nose where they thought it didn't belong.

Seven German princes called the electors got to choose the emperor. One of them — Frederick, Prince Elector of Saxony — backed Luther in the religious dispute that broke out after 1517. Frederick didn't necessarily agree with Luther, but because Frederick had founded the University of Wittenberg not many years before, he had a stake in protecting his faculty member, the overnight celebrity.

Here Luther Stands (Up to the Emperor)

When Martin Luther really needed a friend, Frederick, Prince Elector of Saxony — known as Frederick the Wise — came through for him. It happened shortly after Emperor Charles V, who succeeded his grandfather Maximilian I in 1519, tried to make Luther change what he had said about indulgences and the Church.

Charles made his challenge in 1521 at the Diet of Worms, which wasn't nearly as disgusting as it sounds. In the Holy Roman Empire, the word diet had nothing to do with keto or intermittent fasting. A diet (from the medieval Latin dieta, meaning *a day's work*) was an all-day meeting — a day in court, in this case the Imperial Assembly. Worms referred to a city on the Rhine River near Mannheim, Germany. At the Diet of Worms, Emperor Charles V met with the empire's princes and with churchmen, including Luther. Although no one asked him to ingest squirmy, legless invertebrates, Luther gagged anyway — at the suggestion that he give ground.

Oh, he thought about it. When the emperor tells you to change your tune, you have to at least think about it. Luther turned the issue over and over in his mind before he came back the next morning with his answer.

Luther faced up to the emperor, the princes, and the bishops and said, "Here I stand. I can do no other. God help me. Amen." At least, that's how the story goes. There's some doubt about whether he ever really said that, but the quote is too good to throw away. (So here I quote it. I can do no other.) Whether those were his exact words or not (and come to think of it, he didn't even speak English), they sum up what Luther meant.

In the 2003 movie *Luther*, Joseph Fiennes doesn't speak any English, either, but the DVD includes English subtitles. This German biopic takes some liberties with the facts (as all movies do), but it vividly portrays the tensions and excitement of the time.

Luther Gains a Following

After the Diet of Worms, Martin Luther was an outlaw, and he headed home to Wittenberg to prepare for his arrest and a probable death sentence. But on the way, he disappeared. It turned out that Prince Frederick's men kidnapped him. The prince–elector locked Luther up for his own protection.

In the castle of Wartburg, Prince Freddy gave Luther a study in which to work, and work he did. Instead of taking back his theses, Luther noisily attacked other beliefs of the Church. Realizing the power of the printing press, he published his ideas — among them, his claim that priests weren't the big deal they thought they were. You could get into heaven without one, Luther said. It was cut-out-the-middleman spirituality. Luther said that Christians should read the Bible for themselves, and he translated his own user-friendly German version. He also wrote the (German) words and the music for hymns such as "A Mighty Fortress Is Our God" — the theme song of the Reformation.

A pamphlet he published in 1520, *To the Christian Nobility of the German Nations*, was especially popular. Some nobles, scholars, and other people who agreed with Luther's writings began to think of themselves as his followers. Just a few years after the *95 Theses*, some Christians began to call themselves Lutherans.

The German princes, especially the less devout among them, tended to like Luther's argument that they should rein in the out-of-control Church. In those times of inflation, a reasoned excuse for confiscating the Church's wealth appealed to free-spending aristocrats. If a powerful noble or merchant became a Lutheran, it often meant that his followers, who depended on him for their livings, became Lutheran too — by persuasion or coercion.

Losing control of the Lutheran movement

Anti-Church sentiment, once unleashed, spread. A bunch of knights attacked the Archbishop of Trier in 1522 in an attempt to oust him in the name of Luther. (Luther had nothing to do with it.) Other malcontents, among them former priests and self-appointed preachers, used Luther's rebellion as a jumping-off point to spread radical ideas far beyond Luther's. They said nobles and the rich should embrace the poor and share the wealth. Luther was much too conservative to have taught such a thing, but there was so much pent-up discontent that the extreme ideas took hold and spread.

Unrest turned to violence in 1524 as the Peasants' War ripped through central and southwestern Germany and into Austria. "Hey," said Luther, "this wasn't supposed to happen." (My own loose translation.) He thought people who twisted his teachings were even more wicked than churchmen who sold indulgences. On this topic, he wrote a scathing pamphlet titled *Against the Murdering, Thieving Hordes of the Peasants*.

Luther urged the German princes to crush the rebels. The princes complied (as they would have done without Luther's encouragement), calling in soldier-for-hire landsknechts. Thousands of peasants died in battle, and more were captured and put to death.

Choosing sides

After the Peasants' War was settled, the German princes tried to sort out what to do about Lutheranism. Several sided with Luther; after all, he had sided with them. More to the point, Lutheranism offered them freedom to rule with less interference from Emperor Charles and none from the pope. Some Lutheran partisans formally broke religious ties with Rome and set up their own Lutheran churches. Other princes stuck with Rome and tried to force the Lutheran princes to change their minds.

The Lutheran rulers came to be known as Protestants, because they protested their peers' attempts to force them back into the old Church. In 1531, they formed a mutual protection alliance, the Schmalkald League. Their relations with Paul III (who became pope in 1534) and Emperor Charles deteriorated further.

The Empire Strikes Back

REMEMBER

Charles V was Holy Roman Emperor from 1519–58. As the Protestant movement grew, his resources were strained for reasons I discuss in Chapter 13. He was fighting in Italy and taking care of his lands in Spain. He also had a major rivalry with the French. He didn't want to fight the Protestant princes. He wanted to settle the issue with diplomacy.

Finally despairing of that option, the emperor marched an army into Germany in 1546, the same year Luther died. Thus began the first of the Religious Wars of the 16th century.

Savoring a bitter victory

In 1547, at the Battle of Mühlberg, Emperor Charles led the loyal Catholic princes of the Holy Roman Empire against the rebel Protestant princes of the Schmalkald League. Although Charles's forces defeated them handily, the Protestants wouldn't submit. In the Treaty of Passeau, which ended the war in 1552, Charles offered to make changes in the Catholic Church if they would support him. (Pope Paul III was actually working on the reforms of the Counter-Reformation.) The Protestants stood fast.

Even more frustrating for the emperor, some of the Catholic princes who had been loyal to him during the war started to worry that with the Protestants defeated, the emperor was getting too powerful. As a result, they turned on him and drove him out of Germany.

Achieving compromise

Charles finally had little choice but to recognize Protestantism. The Religious Peace of Augsburg said that each prince in the empire could choose the official church in his own kingdom or duchy. The princes and the emperor signed this agreement in 1555. The Augsburg agreement wasn't a move toward a stronger or more united empire; it was really quite the opposite, but it kept the confederation from falling apart.

Religious war in the Holy Roman Empire wasn't over, however. It would erupt again in the next century with the Thirty Years' War (see the later section "Along Comes Calvin").

Reform Spreads to England

During the Reformation, Church reform wasn't limited to the Holy Roman Empire. Kings outside Germany reformed their churches too. Lutheranism spread into the Scandinavian countries, for example, and variants took hold throughout Northern Europe. Ultimately, the Reformation didn't create one new church; it created many (see Chapter 10).

As in Germany, some rulers in other parts of Europe agreed with Luther's religious convictions; others saw the growing Reformation as a great excuse to confiscate Church wealth. King Henry VIII of England was one who certainly didn't agree with Luther, yet he was strong-willed and took opportunities as he found them.

Creating the Church of England

In the 16th century, England was primed for religious reform, although perhaps not in the same way that Germany had been. Papal taxes stirred widespread resentment. The dissident priest John Wycliffe had set the stage, even winning the support of England's royal family, with his arguments about Church abuses in the 14th century. Wycliffe also organized the first English translation of the Bible. Also, Desiderius Erasmus, author of the satire on Church abuses, *The Praise of Folly*, lived in England in the early 16th century. (Refer to "Satirizing the Church" earlier in this chapter for more on these guys.)

But after the Reformation began, especially when it turned violent, Erasmus rejected it. He wanted orderly reform, not revolution. Erasmus's friend Sir Thomas More represented King Henry VIII in Parliamentary arguments against Lutheranism in 1523.

Divorcing and annulling in Tudor court

England's king built a reputation as vociferously anti-Luther. Henry VIII issued writings condemning the German rebel priest, and a grateful Pope Leo X rewarded Henry with the title Defender of the Faith.

Relations between Rome and London soured, however, when Henry decided that he needed to dump his wife, Catherine of Aragon, shown in Figure 14-1. Note that she was "of Aragon" and a daughter of Ferdinand and Isabella, the Catholic monarchs whose marriage united a large chunk of Spain (see Chapter 19).

FIGURE 14-1:
To be rid of wife
Catherine of
Aragon, Henry VIII
cut England's ties
with the pope.

ND/Getty Images

Catherine was also the aunt of Charles V, who was both Holy Roman Emperor and king of Spain (as Charles I). All these circumstances gave her pull with the pope.

Henry had gotten engaged to Catherine when he was only 11 and she was the widow of his elder brother, Arthur. She bore Henry five children, but only one — a daughter, Mary — survived. Henry wanted a son to be his heir.

Until Arthur died, Henry wasn't the crown prince. He'd actually been educated to become a churchman, maybe an archbishop. So he knew a bit about religious law and thought he knew a lot. He decided that his lack of a son was God's punishment for having married his brother's widow. Henry presented that argument as reason enough for the pope to rule that his marriage to Catherine had never been proper to begin with. Under Church rules, annulment was the only path to legal divorce.

Leo's successor, Pope Clement VII, didn't buy Henry's argument for annulment. Maybe the Emperor Charles, Catherine's nephew, carried more weight in Rome than Henry did. Or maybe Leo knew Henry's other reason for wanting a divorce: Anne Boleyn, the king's mistress.

Finding a way to get his way

Henry's chancellor (chief adviser) was a churchman, Cardinal Thomas Wolsey. Wolsey's ambition was to become pope, so he supposedly knew his way around Church politics.

Henry gave Wolsey the specific job of getting Pope Clement to give in on the divorce question so that Henry could ditch Catherine and make Anne his queen. When Wolsey failed, the king impeached the cardinal and seized his property.

Henry exiled Wolsey and decided to execute him, but Wolsey died in 1530, before the king could get him from York to the chopping block in London.

Next, Henry tried to hit the pope in the pocketbook. He arranged for Parliament to pass laws cutting English fees and offerings paid to Rome. Actually, one of his advisers, a fellow called Thomas Cromwell, came up with this clever idea. If Parliament cut the payments, Cromwell told the king, Henry could pin the blame on the members.

Clement still didn't budge, so in 1533, Henry married Anne Boleyn anyway. He had an old buddy, Thomas Cranmer, Archbishop of Canterbury, perform the ceremony. (What was Cranmer going to do? Say no to the king? You could lose your head for that.)

Catherine, having never seen *The Good Wife*, lived out her days quietly in a convent and died in 1536. Clement hadn't given permission to the king to marry again, and when the deal was done, he didn't offer forgiveness. Paul III, who became pope in 1534, held the line and excommunicated the king of England.

Breaking ties with Rome

Henry made a big move in 1534, telling Parliament to declare the king Supreme Head of the Church in England. With that, England broke away from Rome, like the duchies of those Protestant German princes Henry had so eloquently disagreed with. But Henry still said he wasn't siding with the Lutherans. If a Lutheran was found in England, the king dutifully ordered the heretic to be burned at the stake. Henry claimed that he wasn't changing religions — just correcting the pope's boo-boo.

In practice and theology, Henry's new English Church was little changed from the old Roman Church. He did allow a few small reforms, however. For one, he had English translations of the Bible installed in the churches. It was an English church, after all.

Paying the penalty for disloyalty

The converted Henry had no more mercy for Catholics than he had for Lutherans. Never mind that he'd been a Catholic until recently.

Those who remained loyal to Rome were now considered disloyal to Henry VIII and thus labeled traitors. That could draw a death sentence. Sir Thomas More, who had helped the king attack Protestantism, became chancellor in Wolsey's place and refused to swear obedience to the king's church. Henry ordered More to be decapitated.

Only one English bishop, John Fisher of Rochester, publicly opposed the new church. Henry ordered Fisher to be executed too. Is there any wonder more people didn't speak up?

The king stirred more opposition with his next step. On the advice of More's replacement, the crafty Thomas Cromwell, the king confiscated the monasteries and convents.

Cromwell pointed out to Henry that he could present the confiscation of Church property as a reform measure. He could accuse those monks, friars, and nuns of not doing their jobs, and thus that they were undeserving of the properties they controlled. What Henry really wanted were the monastery lands and their treasures — centuries' worth of offerings that pilgrims had given the monks.

Henry sold most of the monasteries, convents, and lands because he suddenly needed a lot of money. Remember that Emperor Charles V and Francis I of France were always fighting. When the two of them made peace and started acting threateningly toward England, Henry decided to boost defense spending.

Many of the former abbeys and priories were abandoned and left to decay, although the valuable land around them, if not sold, was sometimes awarded to favored noble families for their country estates. That practice continued under Henry's successors. Highclere Castle, where the TV series *Downton Abbey* was filmed, had been the site of a bishop's palace until Edward VI, Henry's son, confiscated it in 1551 and granted it to Sir William Fitzwilliam.

Making the Pilgrimage of Grace

Up in northern England, especially Yorkshire, some people came to the defense of the monks. They thought Henry VIII was taking too much power for himself, so in 1536, they marched south. This march, called the Pilgrimage of Grace, must have looked more like an invasion force.

Astoundingly, Henry was able to talk these armed marchers into going home. He blamed all the problems on Cromwell. Then he ordered his guards to overtake the homeward-bound Yorkshire rebels and kill as many of them as they could in the ugliest, most conspicuous ways possible. He ordered pieces of their hacked-apart bodies set out in all the towns where the rebels had lived to serve as warnings to anyone else who might think about marching on the king.

Realizing Henry's legacy

The former Catholic Defender of the Faith had severed the English Church from its allegiance to Rome, making his realm something like a Protestant nation, although the meaning of "Protestant" wasn't firmly settled yet, especially not in England. To some, it simply meant anti-Rome. Henry had little to no interest in the kinds of reforms advocated by Luther or another prominent rebel priest, John Calvin (coming up in this chapter). The king's church still followed the doctrines and practices of Catholicism, just without the reverence for the pope and without the money flowing to Rome.

Yet he had opened up his country's official state religion to a lot of change and turmoil, to trouble that would continue well into the following century.

More immediately, Henry's son, Edward VI (ruled 1547-1553), was a teenaged reformer who tried to ban Catholic practices from the Church of England. Henry's elder daughter, Mary I (ruled 1553 to 1558) reinstated Roman Catholicism, briefly. Then, even after Henry's other daughter Elizabeth I (ruled 1558-1603) reestablished the Anglican (English) Church, the Catholic-Protestant conflict continued to rumble through the land (see the English Civil War in Chapter 8 and Guy Fawkes in Chapter 22). So, for such an unsettled legacy, what did the king get for his break from Rome?

Well, he *did* get to marry Anne Boleyn, but she never gave him the son he wanted (only another daughter, who turned out to be Elizabeth I). Henry had Anne beheaded and went on to wed four more wives, only one of whom, Jane Seymour, gave him a son: the sickly, short-lived, and anti-Catholic Edward VI.

Along Comes Calvin

Martin Luther wasn't the last word in Church reformers. Also in the 16th century, a young fellow from France moved to Switzerland and shared Protestant teachings that resulted in widespread changes. This was John Calvin.

Reforming the Swiss church

The Reformation in Switzerland started about the same time it did in Germany and in much the same way. In 1518, a priest named Huldreich Zwingli opposed the selling of indulgences.

As in Germany, fighting broke out over the reform movement. Zwingli, unlike Luther, was in the thick of the violence; he died in battle near Kappel, Switzerland, in 1531. Like the Holy Roman Empire, Switzerland was a confederation of smaller states (which the Swiss called cantons). Protestantism eventually won official recognition, meaning that the rulers of the cantons were allowed to decide which brand of Christianity to follow.

Establishing Puritanism

Calvin was a Classics scholar when the Reformation began. He was steeped in Greek and Roman philosophy as well as Christian theology. (Those Greeks keep popping up, don't they?) His thinking reached back to St. Augustine's Christian version of Platonic thought, which is built on the idea that humanity is a false and corrupt shadow of God's perfect Idea. Like Augustine, Calvin came to think that people are bad and have been so ever since Adam and Eve sinned. But Calvin agreed with Luther that God is merciful. Instead of condemning everybody to Hell, God chooses to save some.

This type of thinking put Calvin, an author, lawyer, and later a churchman, at odds with Catholic scholars. He moved from Paris to Strasbourg and then to Geneva, where he was invited to teach reform theology. His ideas became the basis of what's called Calvinism or Puritanism. Calvin set them down in an influential 1536 book called *Institutes of the Christian Religion*.

Calvin went much further than Luther in embracing predestination. Although he supported Luther's idea that good works alone can't win salvation, he dissented regarding the importance of faith in securing a place in heaven. Calvin thought that God decided each person's salvation or damnation at the beginning of creation. Nothing you do or believe influences whether you'll be saved or damned.

But predestination didn't mean that you could do anything you wanted, according to Calvin. He taught that to live a godly life, you must be vigilant and strict — not to win God's favor or reap a reward, because Calvin's God doesn't bargain. But if you believe, you have the opportunity and obligation to act on that belief.

Calvin's followers had to watch for every sort of sin and be ready to cast the unworthy out of their church. Those who crossed the Reformed church could be exiled or tortured to death. Geneva, once a party town, became a place where you could be punished for singing a dirty song or even wearing clothes that were too colorful. The Puritans disapproved of feasts. They banned dancing and thought the theater was sinful. They believed in hard work, thrift, and honesty. By working hard and practicing thrift, many Calvinists prospered, and some even became wealthy, which contributed to the prosperity and security of Switzerland itself. Well-heeled Puritans also shared their wealth with the Calvinist church, adding to its growth and influence.

Calvin's ideas were so strict that more-liberal Genevans initially resisted and even threw him out of town. But Calvin returned, and by the time he died in 1564, Geneva was considered to be Calvin's town — a Puritan town. His critics called him "the Pope of Geneva." Puritanism soon became influential in other parts of the world as well.

Causing turmoil in France

Because John Calvin came from France, it seems right that his teachings returned there. Ministers from Geneva spread the word, but as had happened with the Reformation in the Holy Roman Empire and in Switzerland, some French nobles broke with Catholicism for reasons that were more political than religious. They clashed with Catholic rivals. The conflict erupted into armed violence in 1562, with intermittent fighting taking the form of nine separate French Wars of Religion over the next 36 years.

The French royal family saw the French Calvinists, or Huguenots, as a threat. The Huguenots suffered severe persecution. King Henry II, who came to power in 1547, wanted to kill every Protestant in France and the Netherlands. His sons Charles IV and Henry III continued this policy. Before he became king, Henry III was among the soldiers who slaughtered 50,000 Huguenots at the Massacre of St. Bartholomew in 1572.

It wasn't until Henry IV gained France's throne in 1598 that the country settled down. Henry IV had been a Calvinist, but he had to become Catholic to rule. That year, he enacted the Edict of Nantes, a law that legalized Protestantism and, in effect, ended the Wars of Religion.

Sparking rebellion in Holland

Calvinism caught on in the northern Netherlands, called Holland. This development didn't sit well with the king of Spain, Phillip II, who also ruled that country (inherited from his dad, Holy Roman Emperor Charles V).

While the southern Netherlands remained Catholic and Spanish, the Calvinist north broke free in 1608 and became the United Provinces.

The Calvinist teachings of hard work and thrift helped push the Dutch to successes in navigation and trade. They excelled as merchants and colonists through the 17th century.

Weakening the Holy Roman Empire

By 1618, both Protestantism and Catholicism had changed. Militant Calvinism infused the Lutheran movement. Catholicism, through a reform movement called the Counter-Reformation, had managed to reinvigorate itself.

Protestants and Catholics clashed again in the last big religious war of the Reformation, the Thirty Years' War (1618–48). It broke out after Protestants in

Bohemia tried to appoint a Protestant king in place of the Catholic emperor of the Holy Roman Empire.

Emperor Mathias sent forces to oppose the Protestants. German Catholic states waded in behind the empire. Protestant states backed the Bohemians. Spain, still ruled by Habsburg cousins of the emperor, sent soldiers to help him, and the Catholics got the upper hand.

Bohemians in Bohemia (today part of the Czech Republic) weren't free-spirited artists and vagabonds. Well, maybe some were, but the word Bohemian wasn't used to describe anti-establishment types until a few centuries later, among the French. The label was based on the mistaken notion that wandering Roma people (often referred to as Gypsies, although they reject that term), who are also often considered free-spirited outsiders, had come to France by way of Bohemia. They hadn't, but the term stuck, and spread.

After the Catholic gains in the Holy Roman Empire, the Swedes entered the war on the Protestant side, commanded by King Gustavus Adolphus. The Protestants regained the advantage until Gustavus died in battle. Then the Catholics were poised for victory — except that one more country was about to enter the war. That country was Catholic France.

Did this mean the end for the Protestants? Well, not exactly. France under Louis XIII and his top government minister Cardinal Richelieu (that's right, a high official of the Roman Catholic Church) got into this conflict on the Protestant side. Richelieu's interest was France's security. He mobilized against the Habsburg family — rulers of the Holy Roman Empire and Spain — to keep them from getting too powerful. You may have noticed that conflicts labeled as "religious" are often just as much about political and strategic issues.

French troops helped secure the Peace of Westphalia, ending the war in 1648. After decades of fighting, Germany was an economic wreck. Spain was bankrupt; fighting the Reformation sent it into a long decline. In retrospect, it would have been better to let the Bohemians have their Protestant king.

Pushing for Puritanism in England and Scotland

As Calvinist teachings caught on in England, some people there wanted to make Puritanism part of the Church of England. This movement eventually led to the English Civil War in 1642, the execution of King Charles I, and the establishment of the Commonwealth and the Protectorate (see Chapter 8).

Scotsman John Knox (1523–72) was a Catholic priest who became a Lutheran and came under Calvin's influence during the time he spent in Geneva. Knox founded the Church of Scotland in 1560. The Scottish Calvinists, called Presbyterians, organized their worship and religious authority after the Swiss model, but they faced a powerful critic in King James VI, who hated Puritanism and installed bishops in the Scottish Church. James VI became King James I of England in 1603 and, thus, the head of the Church of England (see Chapter 19).

Emigrating to America

The so-called Pilgrims who came from England to North America on board the Mayflower, landing at Cape Cod Bay, Massachusetts, in 1620, were in their own time called Separatists. They broke away from the Church of England so that they could freely observe their Calvinist beliefs. They were soon followed by somewhat less-radical Puritans, who would have preferred to stay within the English church but make it more Calvinist. In New England, the two groups became virtually indistinguishable.

Considered to be founders of American society, these people adhered to a highly moralistic brand of Christianity — not unlike the rigorous Calvinism practiced in Geneva — and shaped social attitudes and civil policy for centuries.

New England Puritans earned notoriety for labeling certain women as witches and persecuting or killing them. This practice wasn't exclusive to America, Puritans, or even Protestants. Catholics burned accused "witches" throughout medieval times. The judgmental strictures of Calvinism, however, tended to encourage this kind of thing. Scottish Presbyterians were also especially strident in their witch hunts.

Tracking the Centuries

1509: Desiderius Erasmus publishes his satire on Church corruption, *The Praise of Folly*.

October 31, 1517: Martin Luther nails his *95 Theses*, a protest against Church abuses, to a church door in Wittenberg, Saxony.

1524: The Peasants' War, a rebellion of the poor against nobles, rips through central and southwestern Germany and into Austria.

1534: On the orders of Henry VIII, the English Parliament declares the king Supreme Head of the Church in England, superseding the authority of the pope.

1536: French–Swiss religious leader John Calvin publishes his influential book *Institutes of the Christian Religion*, setting down the tenets of Calvinism.

1555: The Religious Peace of Augsburg grants each prince in the Holy Roman Empire the right to decide the official church affiliation of his own kingdom or duchy.

1572: The future King Henry III of France is among the soldiers who slaughter 50,000 Huguenots (French Protestants) at the Massacre of St. Bartholomew.

1608: The Protestant northern region of the Netherlands (Holland) breaks free of Catholic Spanish rule and becomes the United Provinces.

1620: English Separatists arrive in Massachusetts seeking religious freedom.

1648: The Peace of Westphalia ends the Thirty Years' War.

» Inciting the Enlightenment with the Scientific Revolution

» Driving the Industrial Revolution through technological advances

» Spurring new economic philosophies

Chapter **15**

Opening Up to Science and Enlightenment

S cience and engineering shape everything in today's society — not just smartphones, smart speakers, drones, and the Global Positioning System. I mean everything. For centuries, human beings have used scientific inquiry, method, and invention to remake the world.

Every scientific advance traces back to an idea. Yet because so much of science's incredible yield is right here where you can touch it, use it, and curse at it (especially when your laptop crashes), the fact that all this hardware and software owes its distant origins to philosophers is easy to overlook.

In this chapter, as in every chapter in this part of the book, you can follow the ways that ideas — expressed through philosophies that traced their traditions back to ancient Greece — shaped the way people lived and shaped the way the world got to be as it is now. You can appreciate how, for centuries, the word "philosopher" described all kinds of thinkers, writers, observers, tinkerers, and theorists—people that today we call astronomers, mathematicians, physicists, political scientists, geneticists, and economists. You'll see how philosophy gave birth not just to modern science but to new nations and experiments in government and industry.

Mingling Science and Philosophy

The liquid-crystal display that forms images on your phone screen is an example of how science touches you. So is the phone itself, obviously. So is your shirt, which may be made of a synthetic fiber — a product of chemistry. Even if your shirt is made of a natural fiber such as cotton, consider that the fiber comes from a plant that was almost certainly grown by scientific methods and harvested with machines powered by internal combustion engines — more science and engineering. Then the fabric was woven mechanically on electric-powered looms and probably colored with chemical dye — yet more science.

What you eat, how you travel, what you do for a living, and the way you spend your leisure time are all marked in some way by scientific discoveries and inventions, new and old.

REMEMBER

Where did all this inventiveness come from — besides the marvelous human mind? The scientific and engineering versatility that defines today's world stems from a tradition tracing back to the ancient Greek philosophers, a tradition of asking questions about the world and how it works. (See Chapter 11 for more about the Greek philosophers and the beginnings of science.)

Things really got cooking when the Renaissance (Chapter 13), an economic and intellectual movement that reached back to Greek and Roman scholarship, brought forth a Scientific Revolution in the 17th century. And that event led to the Industrial Revolution in the 18th century. Discoveries and inventions — and the habits of thought they inspire — have been revolving madly ever since. Science shaped technology, which shaped industry, which shaped economies, which shaped society at large.

The Scientific Revolution was born of philosophy and brought forth new ways of thinking. Rationalism and empiricism, both influential ways of thinking about the world, came out of scientific perspectives. The Enlightenment of the 18th century, also called the Age of Reason, had its roots in science. Philosophy fed science. In the 18th century, scientists were still called natural philosophers. (The word scientist wasn't coined until 1833, by an English philosopher, William Whewell.) Philosophy inspired new notions about government, justice, wealth, labor, and even mechanical inventions. Ideas birthed during this age fueled the American and French revolutions (see Chapter 9). And philosophers who followed in the 19th century inspired later revolutions, including those in Russia and China.

The scientific and engineering applications that created the Industrial Revolution changed the way people made their livings, bringing fantastic rewards to a canny (or lucky) few, improving lives, but also causing hardship for many in the working class. Social changes including child labor, slums, and new industrial wealth influenced philosophy and inspired the new field of economics.

Starting a Scientific Revolution

Humans have a drive to come up with useful tools, from a sharpened stick to a campfire to those flaked stone blades that early humans taught themselves to make to silicon microcircuits to quantum computers. So even without the Greek philosophers and their followers, people might still have devised some of the modern wonders you take for granted every day.

But as it happened, Renaissance scholars — European guys steeped in old Greek ideas — were the ones who kick-started scientific inquiry and headed humanity toward this modern, scientific world.

Gazing at the heavens: Astronomy

Among the most influential scientists were astronomers. The Renaissance spirit (see Chapter 13), as embodied in the Polish-born Copernicus, brought about new theories concerning Earth's place in relation to the sun and planets. Copernicus's theories challenged the medieval beliefs (founded on the work of Aristotle and the Greek–Egyptian astronomer Ptolemy) that Earth was the center of the universe and that the stars were eternal and fixed in place.

Brahe sees a comet

Other philosophers of the 16th century carefully scanned the night sky. A Dane named Tycho Brahe (1546–1601) pioneered modern astronomy, even though he had no telescope, by making painstaking measurements and multiple observations.

Brahe was from a noble family in what was then Danish Sweden. As a teenager in 1560, he witnessed a partial eclipse of the sun and was inspired to study the stars and planets. Frederick II (1534–1588), king of Denmark and Norway, helped by giving Brahe an island (Hven) and money to build his observatory there. The young man had the wealth, the instruments (such as navigator's sextants for measuring the positions of stars), and assistants to help him explore the skies as nobody before him had ever done.

Among his discoveries, Brahe realized in 1572 that a *nova,* or exploding star, was farther away than the planets. As something new in the sky, a nova (the word means *new)* wasn't supposed to be among the stars, because the stars were considered to be eternal. In 1577, he realized that a comet was farther away than the moon. This finding also upset conventional assumptions about how the sky was arranged. The comet's distance and movement especially clashed with a long-held idea about transparent spheres that supposedly carried the planets around Earth.

Brahe was daring enough to conclude that if the comet could move through them, perhaps the spheres didn't exist. Perhaps the planets moved independently. This theory began astronomy's shift from geometry (tracing the curves and relationships of the spheres) to physics (trying to understand the motion of independent heavenly bodies).

Brahe couldn't embrace one daring idea of Copernicus's: that the Earth moves. Besides overturning Aristotle's cosmology, a moving Earth challenged the Lutheran Brahe's religious sensibility.

IN THEIR
WORDS

He fell back on an old proof for a fixed, immobile Earth: If you shoot an arrow straight up on a windless day, it falls straight down, landing at the spot where you fired it. "If the earth rotates toward the east," he wrote, "a body thrown from it would travel toward the west; birds which fly from their nest would be carried miles away before they alighted." Remember that this was more than a century before Isaac Newton wrote about gravity and posited laws of motion.

Furthermore, Brahe couldn't detect the parallax (a movement in the positions of the stars), which would have shown him that the ground from which he observed them was a moving platform. The idea that the stars were so far away that his instruments couldn't detect this movement made no sense to him. The entire universe, he thought, was only about 14,000 times as large as Earth.

These theories and disagreements illustrate how difficult it was for science to slough off old prejudices. Even Brahe, a star watcher from the time he was a teenager and the guy with the best information yet gathered, couldn't get past some of his essentially nonscientific ideas about how the universe must work.

Kepler charts planets

After Brahe died, his assistant and scientific heir, the German Johannes Kepler (1571–1630), took Brahe's copious data and applied it to support Copernicus's theories.

Kepler, who couldn't see well and had limited use of his hands (both afflictions the result of having a severe case of smallpox when he was a toddler), nonetheless came up with laws of planetary motion that have been the basis for study of the solar system ever since. The first of these laws is something you probably ran across in elementary school: Each planet travels in an elliptical orbit around the sun.

Galileo gazes through a telescope

While Kepler worked with Brahe's data, a multitalented Italian, Galileo Galilei (1564–1642), came up with a fresh, exciting way to check out the stars by using cutting-edge technology. Only recently developed as a tool for gathering military intelligence, the telescope turned out to work even better for expanding scientific intelligence.

Galileo (best known by his first name) saw heavenly visions no one had seen before, such as mountains on the moon and Jupiter's own moons. In 1610, he reported his findings in a pamphlet called *Sidereus Nuncius* or *Sidereal Message*. (Sidereal means pertaining to constellations or stars, and Nuncius, often translated as messenger, can also mean message.)

Galileo also saw just how right Copernicus was: Many heavenly bodies clearly didn't orbit Earth. He published these findings in 1632, a move that got him in trouble with Church authorities. Rome's branch of the Inquisition, which wasn't as notorious as the Spanish Inquisition (covered in Chapter 10) but still fiercely conservative, forced him to recant and sentenced the then-69-year-old Galileo to prison, although he was allowed to live the rest of his life under house arrest.

In true Renaissance fashion (find more on the Renaissance in Chapter 13), Galileo was much more than an astronomer. He was also an artist, musician, engineer, and mathematician.

His work in physics paved the way for England's brilliant Isaac Newton, born the year Galileo died. Perhaps the best-known physical principle that Galileo established is that weight doesn't determine the rate at which an object falls. In other words, if you discount or equalize wind resistance or any other friction, a bowling ball and a soccer ball fall at the same speed. Legend says that Galileo established this principle by dropping balls off the Leaning Tower of Pisa, but that's not so. His experiment involved timing balls of equal size but unequal weights rolling down an incline.

Galileo approached his work with careful observation, experimentation, and mathematics. In his wake, science came to depend increasingly on unbiased inquiry, coming at a question without prejudice so as to base any conclusion on hard evidence or a solid mathematical model.

Advancing the scientific method

All kinds of discoveries came from people who followed Galileo's example in physics, mathematics, anatomy, astronomy, and many more fields.

English nobleman, statesman, and philosopher Francis Bacon (1561–1626) did a good job of putting his ideas into words. He argued in favor of induction, working from observed or demonstrated specifics to a general principle. Bacon's certainty that nature could be understood and even controlled became the orthodoxy of natural philosophy.

Another Englishman, the genius physicist and mathematician Isaac Newton, came along a bit later (1642–1727). Newton is also cited as establishing the scientific method, although he's more famous for establishing things such as the law of gravity (his niece began the legend that an apple falling from a tree inspired him), among other useful physical laws. He also invented calculus.

REMEMBER

Newton applied his work with gravity to Kepler's laws of planetary motion. All the fellows mentioned in this chapter built on one another's work. Although the Internet didn't exist, the printing press (see Chapter 13) made keeping up with others much easier for scholars.

Here's a sampling of other advances from this time:

>> William Harvey (1678–1757), who studied at Padua, Italy, discovered the circulation of the blood.

>> Carl Linne (1707–78), who was known by his Latin name, Linnaeus, classified the species of the plant and animal kingdoms for the first time.

>> Robert Bakewell (1725–95) explored scientific methods for breeding bigger, stronger farm animals.

Waking Up to the Enlightenment

IN THEIR WORDS

In "Rules of Reasoning in Philosophy," an essay included in his 1687 book *Principia*, Isaac Newton writes, "We are to admit no more causes of natural things than such as are both true and sufficient to explain their appearances."

This approach toward exploring the world — objectively, without prejudice — was also a foundation for a branch of philosophy called empiricism, the idea that knowledge is based on experience and derived from the senses.

Along with rationalism (a contrasting way of seeking truth based in inherent reason rather than experience), empiricism signaled more than a growing openness to new ideas. These and related philosophies, together called the Enlightenment, rearranged conventional thinking, and then politics and government, in earth-shaking ways.

Experiencing empiricism

John Locke (1632–1704), an English medical doctor and philosopher, introduced empiricism in his 1689 *Essay Concerning Human Understanding*. He and his empiricist heirs — among them the Scotsman David Hume (1711–76) — took the natural sciences as their model for all knowledge.

REMEMBER

Locke's work was tremendously important to philosophy, but he had just as big an influence on political thought, especially with his idea that authority derives solely from the consent of the governed.

If you contrast that idea with older notions about the divine right of kings (see Chapter 10), you can see how Locke's idea led to political upheaval. His work influenced the men who set the American Revolution in motion. Some French guys whom you can read about later in this chapter were on a similar wavelength.

Living a "nasty, brutish, and short" life

Not every 17th- and 18th-century philosophy rooted in scientific thinking seemed to point toward popular revolt. Thomas Hobbes (1588–1679) was an Englishman who took an intellectual route from mathematics to political theory, a path that led him to advocate absolute monarchy.

The Oxford-educated, well-traveled Hobbes became interested rather late in life in why people allowed themselves to be ruled and in what the best government would be. In 1651, he wrote his famous work *Leviathan*. (Although the word *leviathan* means *sea monster* and sometimes refers to a whale, Hobbes applied it to the powerful state, or commonwealth.)

In *Leviathan*, Hobbes argued that each person is self-interested and, thus, the people can't be trusted to govern society. He's probably best remembered for that book's passage describing what he thought humanity would be like without government, a condition which he called "the state of nature," bereft of industry, navigation, arts, letters, and any other hallmark of civilized society. It concludes with his declaration that "the life of man," so unregulated, would be "solitary, poor, nasty, brutish, and short."

For all his distrust of human nature, Hobbes was interested in justice and advocated that people band together so that the monarch would hear their concerns. He even coined the phrase "voice of the people."

Reasoning to rationalism

Rationalism, another 17th-century philosophy, chose reason rather than observation (the senses) as the basis for knowledge.

That way of thinking traces back to René Descartes (1596–1650), the French mathematician who invented analytical, or Cartesian (for *Descartes*), geometry. (Cartesian geometry uses algebra to solve geometric problems, in case you were wondering who to blame for that.)

Descartes believed that reason could be based on knowledge that just exists, independent of sense-experience. (Think of the way that mathematical principles seem to exist on a plane separate from everyday reality.)

**IN THEIR
WORDS**

He decided that the only thing beyond doubt was his own thinking, a decision that resulted in one of the most memorable quotes in all philosophy: "I think, therefore I am."

Rationalism grew into a political movement too. Based in Paris, it was embodied in a group of writers that included the poet Voltaire (1694–1778) and the Swiss-born essayist Jean-Jacques Rousseau (1712–78).

Expanding to the Encyclopedists

In the 1770s, Voltaire and other leading thinkers, led by the critic Denis Diderot (1713–84), published *Encyclopèdie,* a collection of social and political writing that uses reason to attack France's old order, the ancien régime.

REMEMBER

The Encyclopedists were intensely interested in the American Revolution, which broke out in the same decade as their collaboration. The interest was mutual. Many of America's rebels were Enlightenment thinkers — especially Thomas Jefferson, who wrote the Declaration of Independence. Signed in 1776, the Declaration contains phrases such as "We hold these truths to be self-evident" (rationalism) and "certain unalienable Rights" that seem to be inspired by Locke and Rousseau.

Jean-Jacques Rousseau's works — especially his 1755 *Discourse on the Origin and Foundations of Inequality Amongst Men,* which emphasized the natural goodness of human beings, and 1762's *The Social Contract* — had a big influence on political thinking of the time. *The Social Contract* introduced the slogan "Liberty, Equality, Fraternity," the battle cry of the French Revolution in 1789 (see Chapter 8).

Engineering the Industrial Revolution

Some thinkers were more interested in solving practical problems in the material world. If physical reality wasn't just knowable, but also controllable (as Francis Bacon thought), it fell to engineers to devise ways to control it.

One of these engineers, England's Jethro Tull (1674–1741), invented the seed drill (which hardly seems a good reason for a 1970s folk-rock band to steal his name). The seed drill (unlike the flute, the featured instrument in the Jethro Tull band) allowed crops to be planted more quickly, in neat rows that you could weed between. Crop production rose as a result.

England's Thomas Savery (1650–1715) thought along practical lines too. In 1698, he patented a device that used steam pressure to pump water out of tin and coal mines. With the help of blacksmith Thomas Newcomen, Savery improved his device until he had a commercially feasible steam engine, used primarily for pumping water. But using the steam engine to turn grinding wheels, as in a flour mill, occurred to other, equally practical folks.

In the second half of the 18th century, Thomas Hargreaves (1774–1847), an illiterate carpenter in Nottingham, England, built a machine that put several spindles on a frame to spin several threads at the same time, making possible a textile production volume far beyond that of the spinning wheel. He patented his spinning jenny (named after his wife) in 1768. The next year, Richard Arkwright came out with a similar device that was powered by a water wheel, as grindstones in mills often were.

For centuries, women had spun thread and yarn by hand and woven textiles on hand looms. These enterprises were called cottage industries because they were carried out in people's homes. But Arkwright's machine and others were too big, too expensive, and too complex for people to use at home. So, businessmen put up large buildings where several of Arkwright's water frames could be set up in one huge room, with hired laborers to operate them. This process got bigger, faster, and more powerful in 1779, when Samuel Crompton (1753–1827) came up with the spinning mule (named after his brother-in-law — no, just kidding). The water-powered mule could spin up to 1,000 threads at a time and could also be rigged to a newfangled steam engine.

Large-scale industrialization was off and running. Scotland's James Watt perfected the steam engine in 1790, and more and richer investors got behind this new factory system. Mass production of goods created a need for better ways to transport them and the raw materials that manufacturing required. Industrialization led to widespread networks of canals for barge traffic. Then some bright inventors figured out how to make the steam engine mobile, which meant railroads and steamships and, as you well know, innovations ever since. (See more about inventions that speeded up transportation and communication in Chapter 9.)

Dealing with the social fallout

The Industrial Revolution was just as profound a change as any political upheaval. It killed cottage industries and separated home from workplace, forcing people to move to the cities for jobs. England, and then other countries, became urban as never before. It wasn't just established cities like London that were growing like weeds; brand-new towns sprang up around mills, mines, and factories.

Although they created wealth for factory owners and employment for thousands of people, these social changes also caused serious problems. Country folk who relocated for factory jobs found themselves in small, crowded dwellings with inadequate ventilation and sanitation. Working-class neighborhoods rapidly deteriorated into miserable industrial slums.

REMEMBER

Factory owners had absolute control. Remember that Europe's population had grown rapidly through the Renaissance, so labor was plentiful and cheap. Workers had no leverage and worked under conditions you wouldn't put up with: A work-day was a hard 12 hours or more; factories ran six days a week, and so did workers.

Many of the new machines didn't require a man's strength. Power looms and spinning machines could be run by women and children, many of whom had little choice but to work those long hours — for less pay than men got. Figure 15-1 shows one such worker.

FIGURE 15-1:
Children often tended the machines of the Industrial Revolution.

Niday Picture Library/Alamy Stock Photo

The Industrial Revolution created a new, urgent need for coal and iron. Coal fired the steam engines that powered the machinery, after all. In the 1850s, an engineer called Henry Bessemer (1813–98) came up with the first inexpensive process for mass-producing steel from molten pig iron. Steel mills rose and mining boomed.

In the mines, even little kids did grueling physical labor, such as pulling heavy coal wagons along tracks deep underground, through tunnels too small for even a donkey to work easily. For all the work there was to do, poverty was cruel. You took the job on the factory owner's terms, or your family starved.

Such conditions inspired new lines of social philosophy, the most influential developed by the German Karl Marx, whom I discuss in the later section "Developing capitalism and Marxism."

Raging against the machines: Luddite uprising

Legend says that in 1782 (or, by some accounts, 1779), a laborer in Leicestershire, England, Ned Ludd, destroyed some machinery used to make stockings. Ludd blamed the machines for putting local hand-knitters out of work.

Ludd's name came up in 1812 when workers in Nottingham rioted, attacking and destroying power looms. The rioters blamed the new machinery for causing their misery. These people were called the Ludds, or Luddites, after the man who supposedly inspired them. The authorities rounded them up and tried them together in London. Many were hanged; others were deported to Australia.

Ever since, people who blame or fear technology have been called *Luddites.* The word saw resurgence in the late 20th century with the dawn of the Digital Age, when many people resisted using computers.

Marketing Economics

Just as philosophy gave rise to individual scientific disciplines, it split off into other branches of philosophical thought. In the 18th century, economics became its own separate discipline.

Playing the money game with Adam Smith

Scotsman Adam Smith (1723–90) used his professorships in logic and moral philosophy at Glasgow University to study the operation of markets and new manufacturing methods, such as division of labor.

Smith traveled to Paris and met with philosophers who were transforming French political thought (and who are mentioned in the earlier section "Expanding to the Encyclopedists"). He found himself particularly in tune with Francois Quesnay, who opposed tariffs and other government intervention in international trade. Smith's ideas fit the French Encyclopedists' notion of an inherent and just social order.

TECHNICAL
STUFF

Smith believed that if government left the marketplace alone, people pursuing selfish economic ends would be led, as if by an invisible hand, to benefit society as a whole. Things haven't always worked out that way, of course, especially not when you take into account the squalor and poverty that accompanied the Industrial Revolution. The worldwide economic crisis of 2008–09 can be seen as another example of Smith's invisible hand failing to do its job.

Over the long term, Smith's ideas about economic freedom, which he presented in his 1776 book *An Inquiry into the Nature and Causes of the Wealth of Nations*, were enormously influential in the development of modern economic theory and continue to be cited today.

Developing capitalism and Marxism

Adam Smith's theories support free-market capitalism, although he never used that term. Another philosopher now viewed as a classical economist (the field of scholarship Smith founded) invented the word capitalism and saw capitalists — those who own the means of production — as oppressors.

Karl Marx was born in Trier, Germany, in 1818 and grew up seeing the effects of industrialization. He was attracted by the ideas of Georg Friederich Wilhelm Hegel (1770–1831). Hegel, an idealist, developed his own brand of dialectic, a philosophical technique for inquiry. Dialectic traces back to fifth-century BC Athens and the philosopher Socrates, who pretended that he didn't know the answers to questions he asked as a way of using those questions to coax truths out of the people who answered him. Hegel's dialectic involves putting forth something as true (thesis), denying it (antithesis), and then combining the two (synthesis) to arrive at a greater truth.

Unlike Hegel, Marx came to believe that everything is composed exclusively of physical bits within time and space. In other words, he was a materialist. Forms of materialist philosophy go back to another Greek, Epicurus. Marx nonetheless applied Hegel's dialectic as he worked toward his own theories about economics and class struggle. (You can find out about Socrates and Epicurus in Chapter 11.)

REMEMBER

Marx saw capitalism — his word for the Industrial Revolution's economic system, dominated by factory and mine owners — as a primitive societal stage just above feudalism. Capitalism was a plateau on the path toward socialism and ultimately to what he thought was the ideal arrangement: communism.

In his major 1867 work, *Das Kapital*, Marx described the state as an instrument of class rule, supporting private capital and suppressing the masses. In contrast to Smith's theories about economic freedom benefiting society as a whole, Marx looked at the realities of the Industrial Revolution and argued that the need to earn a profit forces wages down to a subsistence minimum.

Marx wrote that capitalist societies are unstable, defined by contradictions. Because the need for profit keeps wages down, workers can't achieve purchasing power to acquire the goods that the economy produces. (He failed to anticipate the letter that starts "Good news, Karl: You have been preapproved for a Citi credit card account.")

Capitalism's inherent tendency toward booms and slumps, Marx said, will worsen until it incites a working-class revolution. He argued that the working class, or proletariat, would grab the reins of the state and establish a people's dictatorship. He also argued that because an industrial economy is capable of producing enough for everybody, there's no need for social strata: Communal ownership would lead to the abolition of social class, and a classless society would lead to the withering away of the state, resulting in communism.

Marx and his collaborator, Friederich Engels (1820–95), envisioned this change taking place in Germany and then spreading through the rest of industrialized Europe. The last place they figured their economic theories would click was rural, economically backward Russia. Yet with a little reworking by Vladimir Lenin (more on him in Chapter 9), Russia became the starting place for an experiment in Marxism.

The Union of Soviet Socialist Republics (USSR) didn't work out quite as Marx and Engels predicted. The state never achieved anything close to the economists' ideal of communism. And eventually the state — a totalitarian socialist state — fell away, all right, in 1991, but it happened largely because the USSR was bankrupt and had lost its political credibility. The USSR was replaced by another state: today's Russian Federation.

REMEMBER

Still, Marxism took hold in various forms adapted to China, Cuba, Vietnam, North Korea, and a few other outposts, and it was a major influence on the 20th century — although Marx may not have recognized many of the interpretations of his ideas. Many nations in the 20th century, including those of Western Europe, developed forms of democratic socialism that were influenced by Marx but not chained to his ideas.

In general, the 20th century showed that allowing people to pursue wealth creates more robust and resilient economies driven by incentive. Putting everything under government ownership tends to breed economic stagnation. Even China, the largest Marxist nation, reintroduced capitalist elements to its economy at the end of the 20th century.

By contrast, however, many governments were forced to intervene in the worldwide banking industry — committing public money to shore up struggling private firms, for example — during the economic crisis of 2008. Financial firms that had presented themselves as flagships of free-market economics found themselves forced to seek rescue from the state. Marx may have relished the irony.

Tracking the Centuries

1560: Tycho Brahe, a teenager in Denmark, sees a partial solar eclipse and decides to devote himself to astronomy.

1564: Galileo Galilei is born in Pisa, Italy.

1610: After aiming a new invention, the telescope, at the night sky, Galileo reports his findings in his book *Sidereal Message.* He observed that Copernicus was right that planets don't orbit Earth.

1687: Isaac Newton's greatest book, *Principia*, establishes the basic laws of physics, including his famous Third Law of Motion: "For every action, there is an equal and opposite reaction."

1768: Thomas Hargreaves invents a machine that can spin several threads at the same time: the spinning jenny.

1770s: In Paris, Denis Diderot collects the works of his fellow thinkers and writers, including Voltaire, into *Encyclopèdie,* an anthology attacking France's old order.

1776: In *An Inquiry into the Nature and Causes of the Wealth of Nations*, Adam Smith argues that if government left the marketplace alone, people pursuing selfish economic ends would be led, as if by an invisible hand, to benefit society as a whole.

1812: Rioting workers in Nottingham, England, destroy power looms. They call themselves Luddites, after Ned Ludd, an earlier rebel against factory machines.

1867: In the book *Das Kapital*, Karl Marx describes the state as an instrument of class rule, supporting private capital and suppressing the masses.

1991: The Union of Soviet Socialist Republics, founded on Marxist principles, collapses.

2008: The U.S. Congress approves a plan to prevent the collapse of the American economy by rescuing foundering private financial-services companies with public funds.

4

Fighting, Fighting, Fighting

Appreciate the tragic reality that groups of humans seem to have always fought other groups of humans, and look at some of the ways that ancient warriors — such as Greeks, Persians, and Romans — organized their battle plans.

Find out about innovations in military equipment and weaponry, from the stirrup (which kept cavalrymen in the saddle) to gunpower and artillery.

Encounter the philosophy of Total War and the terrible new weapons that made armed conflicts in the 19th century — and ever since — deadlier than ever before.

» **Organizing armies within civilizations**

» **Battling deadly Assyrian and Persian versatility**

» **Gathering the Roman legions**

» **Standing together as Greeks: The phalanx**

Chapter **16**

Wielding Sticks and Stones: Old-Fashioned War

Without warfare, the human story would be unrecognizable. War stories are among the earliest and most influential folklore and literature. A prime example is *The Iliad*, which I discuss in Chapter 4. For millennia, everybody knew who fought the Trojan War and that the Greeks had won, thanks to the epic poem.

In this chapter, you'll find out about how war seems to be universal among our species. You'll meet cultures that worshipped war gods and defined themselves by military conquest. You can think about the weapons that ancient armies used, how their forces were organized, and what strategies they employed. By looking at how long-ago wars were fought, you can get a better idea of what set this violent species on the path toward smart missiles, stealth aircraft, and experimental laser cannons.

Fighting as an Ancient Way of Life

When outsiders first stumbled across the interior valleys of New Guinea in the 1930s, they found village after village of Stone Age farmers who looked on the people of the other villages around them as being either enemies or potential enemies. Revenge wars whose root causes were lost in time were the overwhelming rule.

In the late 1970s, anthropologist Carol Ember reported that 64 percent of remaining hunter–gatherer societies in the world at the time fought a war at least every two years. War was rare or absent in only 10 percent of groups studied. In the 1980s, another anthropologist, K.E. Otterbein, turned up even more dismaying results: Studying both hunter–gatherer and primitive farming peoples, he found that 92 percent waged war.

Archaeologists note how often ancient human skulls appear to have received violent, bone-breaking blows from objects such as clubs and axes. The evidence suggests that ancient times were violent times and that people have always fought wars or at least engaged in armed skirmishes.

WE'RE NOT THE ONLY ONES MAKING WAR

Scientists say humankind isn't the only war-making species. What other animal indulges in such mass violence? For one, humanity's closest genetic cousin, the chimpanzee. Researchers have seen bands of male chimps from one group raid another band. If they can, they kill all the other group's males and gain mating privileges with the females.

Jane Goodall, the most famous researcher to study chimps, said, "If they had firearms and had been taught to use them, I suspect they would have used them to kill." This study and other evidence caused biologists such as author and biologist Michael P. Ghiglieri to believe that human beings didn't invent war at all — that rather, war is part of prehuman behavior.

Raising Armies

Cave people made war, but war got organized on a large scale when civilization did. Armies arose among early cultures in the Middle East (see Chapter 4), as did formations, such as the column and the line, and classic military strategy, such as the *flanking maneuver* (going around the side of the enemy line).

Sometime after 10,000 BC, the sling and the bow both joined the arsenal. Like the earlier spear and ax, these items surely doubled as hunting tools, but they changed the way wars were fought. A wooden bow, with its string of animal gut, could propel a stone-tipped arrow farther than a football field is long.

TECHNICAL STUFF

Made of a leather pad with two thin straps attached, the sling had even more range. The slinger put a rock or a solid baked-clay projectile into the pad; swung it around his head by the straps; and then let go of one of the straps, sending the missile flying. The Bible says that hero David felled the Philistine giant Goliath with a sling. Stone carvings from the 10th century BC show Mesopotamian soldiers (from what is now Iraq) using the weapon.

Keeping out attackers

Ancient cities had defensive walls, perhaps to keep out predatory animals, but most prehistorians who study defensive walls think they were built to protect against attackers. Jericho (see Chapter 4), perhaps the oldest town that left substantial ruins, was distinguished by a defensive ditch around the community, a stone wall, and a tower with an inside stairway. Towers let you see the attacking force while it's still far away, and from the top, you can rain projectiles on unwelcome visitors.

Another ancient ruin, the town of Çatalhöyük in southern Turkey, is made up of mostly windowless, doorless houses — again, probably designed for security against attackers. Under siege, residents of the houses could (theoretically) pull up their ladders, drop the ladders and themselves through their rooftop hatches, close the hatches, and sit out the attack.

Defenses evolved wherever people clashed, which was just about everywhere people lived. European villagers as long as 4,000 years ago built hill forts ringed by earthen ramparts. By 220 BC, the Chinese had put up the first parts of the Great Wall to protect against northern nomads. Eventually, the Great Wall stretched 2,550 miles. When European explorers arrived in New Zealand in the 18th century, they found Maori warriors in timber forts atop steep coastal cliffs.

Escalating weapons technology: Using metal

As defenses evolved, so did weapons. A big leap came with metal blades and points. A mummified man from about 3230 BC, found in the Italian Alps, carried a copper ax. Copper is a soft metal, which may have limited its usefulness as a weapon, although the man (Chapter 2) had been hit on the head with something hard enough to do serious damage. By 3000 BC, Middle Eastern metalsmiths were mixing copper with tin to form the harder metal bronze.

Bronze made tougher cutting blades and piercing points. People could also pound bronze into helmets, shields, and armor. Bronze battle-axes and swords became standard. Iron, which was even harder, followed. The Iron Age, which is a label that much later archaeologists invented for a time when large-scale iron production superseded that of bronze, began around 1200 BC in Turkey. Technology spread much more slowly than it does now, so the Iron Age began hundreds of years later in other parts of Asia, Europe, and Africa.

Riding into battle: Hooves and wheels

Around 300 BC, Mesopotamian armies used wheeled wagons to transport their fighters. The people of Sumer, perhaps the first great urban civilization, fashioned heavy, clumsy vehicles with four solid wooden wheels that were pulled by donkeys or plodding oxen.

After about 1800 BC, armies preferred horsepower, hitching horses to two-wheeled chariots, which were faster and lighter than the wagons but still big. Unlike the racing chariots in the classic 1959 movie *Ben*-Hur (set in early first-century AD Rome), these earlier chariots carried several men: warriors, javelin throwers, and a driver. The Assyrians, whose civilization arose from the city-state of Assur on the upper Tigris River, made especially good use of chariots in battle.

Avoiding Assyrian Arsenals

Around the Middle East, the Sumerians, Egyptians, Babylonians, and Hittites were military powers in an ebb and flow of early martial power. But other, lesser-known peoples — Hurrians, Mitanni, Kassites, Elamites, and Amorites — fielded armed forces too.

The Assyrians, about whom I tell you more in Chapter 4, grew particularly warlike. Perhaps Assyrian aggression began with defense. In the 11th century BC, waves of nomadic northern invaders beat the Assyrian kingdom down to an area of only 50 by 100 miles along the Tigris River in northern Mesopotamia. But at the end of the next century, Assyrian warriors began to overrun other societies until they ruled an empire 1,000 miles from border to border, stretching from Egypt to the Caucasus (between the Black and Caspian seas).

Assembling the units

At their height, the Assyrians could field an army of 100,000 men. They also relied on specialized units: quick-moving, lightly armored infantry and slower but heavily armored infantry; warriors with spears, bows, slings, pikes, and swords; and war chariots.

Perhaps most impressive, the Assyrians had engineering units. Advance corps blazed trails and laid roads for supply wagons. When the army needed to cross a river, engineers built a pontoon bridge (and army engineers did the same for thousands of years afterward). For pontoons, they used inflated animal skins and log or reed boats lashed together to float a roadway.

Assyrians also pioneered ways to get past a city's defenses. They built *siege engines*, which were towers on wheels or sometimes on pontoons that could be moved right up next to a city's walls. Siege engines were made of timber frames covered with layers of tough cowhide that could fend off arrows. Attackers could stay inside until the engine was in place and then climb up the inside, emerge on top, and go over the wall. Another method involved building a ramp of dirt and rubble to scale the wall.

Sometimes, Assyrian engineers went down instead of up, digging under a city's wall and shoring up their tunnel with wooden beams, like a mine shaft. When they were under the wall, the engineers would set the tunnel supports on fire and then turn around and run for daylight. The supports burned up, the tunnel collapsed, and the wall above — literally undermined — crumbled. Then soldiers advanced through the gap.

Wreaking havoc

Atrocities such as the wholesale slaughter of a city's residents and the mass deportation of entire populations are among the worst aspects of modern war, but slaughter and deportation are anything but modern. The Assyrians did both. In one instance, they deported 27,000 Jews — the Lost Tribes who supposedly disappeared from history — to eastern Syria. The Assyrians used captives as forced laborers.

TRIBES CALLED 'LOST' HAVE NEVER BEEN FORGOTTEN

In the 10th century BC, the Kingdom of Israel split itself in two. Its northern part became a new Israel, home to 10 of the 12 tribes who traced their ancestry to Jacob, son of Abraham. The southern part was the Kingdom of Judah, home to the other two tribes, Judah and Benjamin.

The 27,000 people that the Assyrians are believed to have captured and transported away in about 721 BC belonged to the north, Israel. Their tribes were called Dan, Ephraim, Gad, Issachar, Manasseh, Naphtali, Reuben, Simeon, and Zebulon. These became known as the Lost Tribes of Israel. Most historians think they weren't lost at all. Scholars posit that the captives' descendants mixed and assimilated with the Syrian population and that some among the "lost" found their way back to Israel or to other parts of the Middle East. But over the centuries since their capture, the tribes have become the subject of lore, rumor, and wild speculation.

Many ethnic, religious, and regional groups, meanwhile, have either claimed to be descended from the "Lost Tribes," or have had that heritage claimed on their behalf. The Pashtuns of Afghanistan, Assyrian Christians, indigenous Americans (sometimes called Indians), Ethiopian Jews, Jewish communities in India, and — maybe most surprisingly — the Japanese have all been put forward as descendants of the tribes.

The Assyrians finally fell from power at the end of the seventh century BC, when neighboring peoples united against them, but that didn't mean Assyrian military methods were lost. The Persians built their own vast empire with war tactics inherited from the Assyrians.

Farming and Fighting Together in Greece

Like the ancient Greeks' way of governing (which you can read about in Chapter 4) and the Greek way of thinking (see Chapter 11), a Greek style of warfare grew out of the geography of mainland Greece and its agricultural economy.

Greek soldiers of the sixth and fifth centuries BC were largely small landholders, family farmers who made their livings from fields scraped out of rocky hillsides. Their landholder status made them members of a privileged middle class: the citizenry. Because these farmers were determined to maintain control of their property and their communities, they volunteered as *hoplites*, or heavily armored foot soldiers. Military service for no pay was the mark of full membership in the community.

Every Greek citizen who could afford the equipment — a bronze breastplate; a helmet with a fashionable horsehair crest; a short iron sword; leg protectors called *greaves*; and the most essential item, a 9-foot-long spear — joined up. The hoplites took their name from one other piece of equipment: the heavy wooden shield, which they carried by its double handle. They slid one loop over the left forearm to the elbow and grasped the other loop at the rim of the shield in the left hand.

Soldiering shoulder to shoulder

The heavy hoplite weaponry fit the way Greeks fought: in a tight, porcupine-like formation called the *phalanx*. This formation grew out of conflicts between competing city-states.

In formal disputes, usually over farmland, the two sides decided the issue through an afternoon's worth of armored columns facing each other on cleared fields. Each side tried to bulldoze the other to a resolution.

TECHNICAL STUFF

When you hear somebody describe any group of aggressive people (say, reporters covering a big story) as a phalanx, remember that the original phalanxes were much deadlier. In battle formation, one guy's spear stuck out beyond the guy in the rank in front of him.

Hoplites fought shoulder to shoulder. They couldn't see well because of their helmets, and they couldn't move quickly because of the heavy gear. What the hoplites could do was advance behind their shields, which protected the bearer's shield side and his neighbor's weapon side.

IN THEIR WORDS

The Greek historian Xenophon put this interdependence in its agricultural context: "Farming teaches a person to help others. In fighting enemies, just as in working the earth, each person needs the help of others."

When two Greek phalanxes clashed, one would break through the other. The disrupted phalanx became ineffective because its helmet-blinded, armor-encumbered members were likely to become confused and fight one another. That happened at the Battle of Delium in 424 BC, when the Spartans broke through the Athenian line; the separated Athenians grabbed their swords and commenced hacking at anything that moved, including their comrades.

Standing up to the Persians

In time, the phalanx proved to be effective against other cultures' military formations, including quicker-moving light infantry (foot soldiers without such heavy gear) and even attackers on horseback.

Hoplites passed their biggest test in 490 BC, when King Darius I of Persia invaded mainland Greece. Athenian and allied hoplites, outnumbered two to one, confronted the Persians at Marathon.

Persians organized their armies along lines developed by the Assyrians (see the earlier section "Assembling the units"), with horses, archers, swordsmen, engineers — the whole, coordinated, multitiered shebang. To Darius's forces, this bunch of spear-carrying soldiers who looked like shields with stubby bronze legs promised easy pickings. But the Greeks wouldn't fall back. When a hoplite stumbled, the hoplite in the rank behind him stepped over him and shored up the advance. The Greeks pushed forward until their *flanks* — the far ends of their line — overwhelmed the most vulnerable part of the Persian forces and then folded the Persians in toward the middle. At that point, Darius's army wisely turned around and hightailed it for their boats.

The outnumbered Greeks beat the Persians again 11 years later at Platea. The Greek phalanx made heavy infantry the essential force of its time. For centuries, commanders thought cavalrymen and archers were best used in support of well-armored foot soldiers.

Facing Macedonian ferocity

When the Greeks finally fell to a foreign force, it wasn't to mighty Persia, but to a strongman king from the north of Greece, Philip of Macedon, who applied his own version of the phalanx.

Imagine Danny Trejo in the role of Philip, a hard guy. Phil put cavalry behind his infantry, and each rider was armed with a *xyston,* a 12-foot-long lance with a foot-long iron point at both ends. The cavalry's job was twofold:

>> To support the foot soldiers

>> To kill any comrade who turned and ran

Macedon arranged its infantry in a phalanx but made crucial improvements. Philip's soldiers strapped a small, round shield that wasn't as heavy (or as protective) as the bigger hoplite shield to their left shoulders, leaving both hands free to wield a long pike called a *sarissa*. The sarissa was like the cavalry xyston but even longer, at 13–21 feet, with a metal spike on its butt end. A soldier could plant the spike in the ground and then impale a charging horseman with the swordlike business end. The sarissa was so long that the tips of weapons carried by the soldiers in the fourth rank of a phalanx extended beyond the first rank (see Figure 16-1). The operation sounds incredibly awkward, and it must have taken a lot of practice to handle this weapon.

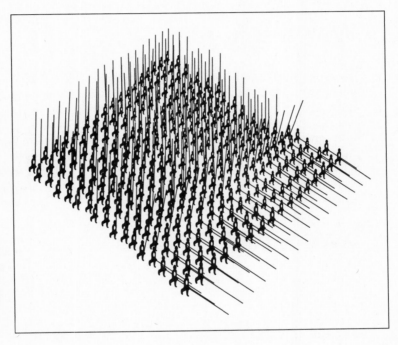

FIGURE 16-1:
Macedon's phalanx was a marching hedgehog of muscular men, wood, and metal.

Macedon's army also used the best Assyrian–Persian weaponry and tactics. Philip of Macedon deployed archers, javelin throwers, and slingers (experts at whipping about a leather sling to propel small but deadly stones). As the Assyrians had, he absorbed conquered armies into his force and told them to use their own weapons and formations. Philip also employed Assyrian-style combat engineers. His inventors improved the siege engine, adding a drawbridge and many platforms for archers to stand on. This new siege engine didn't have to be right up next to the target city's wall; if it came fairly close to the wall, attackers could let down the drawbridge and cross it onto the battlements.

Even more inventive than the improved siege engine was the catapult. Macedon's engineers built one that unleashed the tension of wound animal hair or sinew to hurl a large rock 1,000 feet.

Philip's approach to warfare spurred the successes of his son, Alexander the Great (chapters 4 and 20). Alex took the conquered Greeks with him as he turned the tables on the Persians, thoroughly defeated them, and marched through Mesopotamia and beyond to grab part of India. His troops weren't even fazed by the Indians' ultimate weapon: armored battle elephants.

Making War the Roman Way

The *Latins,* shepherds who built a city on the Tiber River in what is now Italy, were among many Mediterranean people who admired and imitated the way the Greeks fought.

At the end of the sixth century BC, Latins organized themselves into a Greek-style phalanx and challenged their northern overlords, the Etruscans. The Latins won, and their city, Rome, became the center of a new culture built on military prowess. (This is among those many places where I oversimplify wildly, a necessity with a book like this one.)

Marching in three ranks

The Latin shepherds became the Romans, who soon found that the phalanx was nifty for fighting the Etruscans (another Greek-influenced people), but it wasn't perfect for fighting less-advanced neighboring tribes.

REMEMBER

Greeks developed the phalanx on farmland — battlefields. The Romans' tribal neighbors weren't interested in marching formation to formation on a cleared hillside. Faster-moving than the shield-carrying Romans, a gaggle of tribesmen could come around the flank or hide behind trees and dart out in a raid.

Even the Greeks eventually found the traditional phalanx to be less and less effective, especially as their armed forces evolved, in the later decades of Classical Greece, from neighborly bands of farmer–citizen–soldiers to a mix of citizens and resident aliens, some of whom were paid mercenaries. A shoulder-to-shoulder, soldier-to-soldier style didn't work so well when you weren't quite sure about the guy next to you.

Needing their own, more flexible military style, the Romans came up with the *legion* in the fourth century BC. The legion consisted of three lines of foot soldiers. Only the third line carried traditional spears. The first two lines carried a variation called a *javelin* (or *pilum*), which was designed for throwing and boasted a cool technological advance: The head was designed to bend and break off, making the javelin useless to the enemy after it struck its mark. The bent spearhead also tended to stick in an opponent's shield, armor, or flesh.

The Roman legion worked like this:

>> Hastati: The first line, made up of young guys, threw their javelins, and then drew their swords and charged. If they had to fall back, they scrambled for a position behind the second rank.

>> Principes: The more-experienced second rank also threw their javelins and then charged. If they too found that they had to fall back, they got behind the third rank.

>> Triarii: The third rank of steady old hands stood fast in a solid defensive line to let the other guys retreat in safety. But Rome's battles rarely came to that.

IN THEIR WORDS

The legion usually won, but even when Rome didn't win, the other side suffered. In 279 BC, Pyrrhus, king of Epirus, defeated troops led by the Roman Consul Laevinus. (Consul was the top administrative post in the Roman Republic.) Both sides suffered horrible losses. After the dust cleared, 15,000 lay dead. Pyrrhus said, "If we win another battle against the Romans, we shall be completely ruined." That's where the phrase *pyrrhic victory* comes from.

Like the Greek phalanx, the legion began as a citizen corps. Most soldiers came from the small landholder class, and just about every man served. Each citizen (as in Greece, women weren't citizens) between age 17 and 45 had to devote 10 years to military service. A leader had to prove himself in battle before he could win political office. Failure in soldiering was failure, period.

Recruiting a standing force

Despite successes — and because of them — Roman commanders realized by 100 BC that they needed to change the empire's military. Battling foes from Germany to Africa to the Black Sea, the Roman Empire grew so fast that its legions of citizen–soldiers couldn't keep up. Troops posted far away on those frontiers couldn't come home and tend their property after a few months' campaign.

Besides that, the prosperity that came of Rome's expansions and the resulting boost in trade made the wealthy patrician class in Rome even wealthier. Rich guys were amassing big estates cultivated by slaves instead of by citizen–farmer–soldiers, the small landholders who traditionally manned the legions. And slaves were exempt from military service.

Recruiters began conveniently overlooking the property-ownership requirement for service. Commanders turned to the urban poor to fill out their rosters, but things just weren't the same. These new guys didn't have the same stake in the republic. They were harder to discipline. Gaius Marius, a lowborn soldier who rose to the political office of consul, figured that the time had arrived for Rome to ditch the old civil militia idea and officially make the army a full-time professional gig.

The military became an attractive career choice and a means of upward mobility. There was a downside, however: Instead, being loyal to Rome, as the citizen–soldiers were, the new pros were loyal to their commanders. The republic became vulnerable to civil wars. A military leader whose troops were more loyal to him than to the government may have fancied himself a dictator or emperor. Rome officially (that is, in the books of later historians) became an empire (that is, ruled by an autocratic emperor) with the coronation of Augustus Caesar in 31 BC (see chapters 5 and 19).

Diversifying the legion

The rise of Augustus wasn't the end of the citizen–soldier. Roman strategy in the later centuries of the Western Roman Empire (the Eastern Roman Empire became the Byzantine Empire) involved much defensive work. Resident defenders were important in the work of holding fortified outposts and cities against barbarian attack.

How warlike were the tribes that hammered away at Rome's borders? The Langobard people were named after their weapon: Langobard means *long axe*. Saxons took their name not from a sexy-sounding musical instrument (not invented until the 19th century) but from a machete-like knife, a *sax*. Imagine a modern nation called the Stealth Bombers.

In Chapter 5, I talk about the waves of people who came down through Europe, each clashing with the previous residents and some settling and becoming defenders against later waves. The Roman Empire's task of standing up to these assaults took plenty of personnel. Residents in places such as Gaul (now France) pitched in to defend their towns. The old idea that warriors fought better in defense of their own land came back.

When Attila the Hun invaded Gaul in 451, he and his fearsome allies spent months trying to break down the defenses of walled cities. They ran out of food and had no forage left for their horses. While Attila hammered away at the city of Orleans, the army of Roman General Aetius, consisting of Germanic soldiers raised mostly in Gaul, attacked and pursued the Huns to Châlons. The Huns turned and fought, but they were too depleted to prevail. (Note, however, that it took Roman cavalry to beat Attila.) You can find more on Attila the Hun in Chapter 20.

Returning to riders

Military strategists considered cavalry to be secondary to infantry for centuries. But after the murderous Huns swept into Europe on horseback, terrorizing everyone with their swift fury, war strategists woke up again to the importance of speed.

By the sixth century AD, Rome no longer ruled Western Europe, but the eastern branch of its empire, based in Constantinople, endured. There, swift-riding horse units patrolled the vast borders of the Byzantine Empire (more about the Byzantine Empire in Chapter 6), backed up by lightly armored archers who could move faster than the heavy infantry that were the backbone of traditional Roman and Greek forces. The old-style shield-carriers now operated mostly as garrison defense.

Tracking the Centuries

About 10,000 BC: The bow and the sling are added to the warrior's arsenal.

10th century BC: Assyrian warriors overrun neighboring peoples, building an empire that stretched from Egypt to the mountains between the Caspian and Black seas.

490 BC: Although badly outnumbered, Athenians and their allies defeat King Darius I's invading Persian forces at Marathon.

424 BC: Spartans break through the Athenian line at the Battle of Delium. The disoriented troops from Athens drop their spears, grab their swords, and begin hacking indiscriminately, wounding many of their own.

451 AD: In Gaul (today's France), Aetius, a Roman general commanding Germanic troops, drives Attila the Hun away from his siege on Orleans. Then Aetius pursues the Huns and defeats them at Châlons.

1980s: Anthropologist K.E. Otterbein discovers that 92 percent of the hunter-gatherer societies and primitive farming people that he studied waged war.

Chapter **17**

Upgrading the War Machine

t's hard to imagine anybody coming up with a horrific substance such as *Greek fire*, a highly combustible liquid that long predated 20th-century napalm, if not to use it as a weapon. And metalworking seems to have fed on the needs of weapons-makers and armorers. But inventions spur warfare too.

More than a millennium ago, two dandy little innovations from Asia enabled and demanded many adjustments in how wars were fought and even how war was perceived. These innovations were

» **Gunpowder:** The Chinese mixed up the first batch in the ninth century AD, although they didn't try to blow anybody up with it until a while later.

» **The stirrup:** Probably first devised by horse-savvy nomads of Central Asia, this piece of equestrian gear is far less flashy than gunpowder but exceedingly practical. The low-tech stirrup — that thing that you put your foot into to climb onto and ride a horse — became part of a Chinese horse soldier's gear in the fourth century AD.

In this chapter, you can find out about the way warfare has always stimulated technology and how technology, in turn, has escalated warfare. You can follow the ways that Assyrian military engineers, Macedonian inventors, and Roman fortification engineers were the weapons techies of their respective times. And you'll see how pyrotechnics — the art and science of setting certain chemical mixtures on fire — grew into a central part of inflicting violence on one's enemy.

Reinventing the Cavalry

Both gunpowder and the stirrup eventually filtered west through Asia to Europe, but the simpler stirrup came first. It coincided with a reemphasis on speed and mobility, which I talk about in Chapter 16. Horseback warfare gained greater importance in medieval times, and it took diverse forms, ranging from the lightly armed Arab conqueror on his small, fast-turning steed to the steel-plated European knight on his ponderous, metal-clad charger.

Standing tall and staying astride with stirrups

Stirrups make it vastly easier for a rider to stay balanced while swinging a sword, aiming an arrow, and especially while wheeling around in a strategic maneuver. That stability in turn allows the violence-prone equestrian to wield bigger weapons with better control. Europe's armor-clad age of chivalry would have been unthinkable without stirrups. Figure 17-1 shows some 13th- and 14th-century styles.

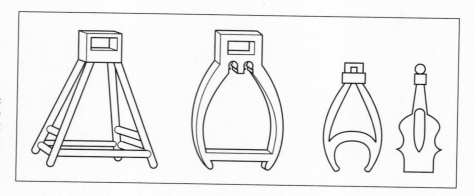

FIGURE 17-1: Front and side views of different stirrups, a technological innovation that changed warfare.

Imagine a rider encased in a pounded-steel suit, bracing a long, heavy lance with one arm while trying to use his metal-shielded thighs and buttocks to grip the undulating flanks and back of a galloping steed. It wouldn't work. But give that same knight two hanging platforms, one for each foot, so he can lift and center his weight, and the heavy armor and lance become more formidable than cumbersome.

Raiding as a way of life on horseback

Chinese soldiers started using the stirrup around the fourth century AD, but the hard-riding Asian nomads called *Avars* probably had the invention as early as the first century BC. Their riders' feet were tucked into stirrups when the Avars stormed into Eastern Europe in 568 AD, taking Danube Valley lands away from the Byzantine Empire.

Avars and other barbarian peoples used the stirrup while attacking towns and cities to get what they wanted: valuable trade goods, food, money, and sometimes even control of a region or an empire. (You can find out more about barbarian raiders and conquerors in chapters 6 and 7.) Raiding became a way of life for some nomadic tribes from interior Asia's steppes. Because these herders and hunters had little to offer in trade to settled farmers and townsfolk, such as the Chinese, they resorted to getting things they wanted by force.

REMEMBER

Raiding is best performed quickly. You make the hit and then put plenty of ground between yourself and your target. Horsemanship gave raiders an edge, and the stirrup sharpened it.

Guarding Byzantine borders

The rich Byzantine Empire (see Chapter 6) was a prime target of raiders, so fast horse patrols were a must to guard its borders. Stirrups, probably copied from the Avars, gave the Byzantine patrols an advantage over Western Europeans, who didn't have the technology yet. This superiority coupled with the use of a *commissariat* (a support organization that made sure cavalrymen and foot soldiers had enough to eat, even during long sieges) made the Byzantine Empire extremely difficult for outsiders to penetrate. Constantinople, the Byzantine capital, needed every advantage in the seventh and eighth centuries as its troops faced a new and persistent foe: Muslim Arabs of successive dynasties, who fought several wars against the Byzantine Empire between the middle of the 7th century AD and about 1050.

These Arab fighters used stirrups too, on relatively small, quick horses. More than just great riders, the Muslim Arabs focused their zeal to spread their religion, which arose in the 7th century. They gained control of much of the the Middle East and lands eastward into India and westward across North Africa and Spain (see Chapter 6).

Yet Constantinople withstood the Arabs. The Byzantine capital (today, it's Istanbul, Turkey) enjoyed a terrific strategic position, sitting on a point of high land jutting into the Sea of Marmara, between the Black and Aegean seas. Unable to take the capital on horseback, in the eighth century the Arabs tried ships, mounting a naval blockade that might have succeeded if not for Greek fire. A military secret, *Greek fire* may have been mostly naphtha, refined from coal oil that seeped to the surface from underground deposits. Whatever Greek fire was, it ignited on impact and floated.

The Byzantines catapulted clay pots full of Greek fire onto the decks of enemy ships, setting them aflame. Even if a pot missed, its contents burned atop the water. Sometimes, the Byzantines squirted Greek fire out of hand-powered pumps. After losing too many ships, the Arabs called off the blockade.

Battling mounted Moors

Arabs may not have brought down Constantinople, but their light-cavalry strategy worked just about everywhere else. (*Light cavalry* refers to lightly armored horse units with an emphasis on speed.) In 711 AD, Muslim Arabs conquered most of Spain, which remained in Muslim control long after the great Arab Empire broke up into regional Islamic kingdoms.

The Muslims in Spain, who advanced from North Africa, quickly came to be called *Moors.* (Find more about the Moors in Chapter 6.) Christians living a little north of them, especially the Franks, didn't like them as neighbors.

Ruling what was Gaul (now it's France and part of Germany), the *Franks* were old-style barbarian ground fighters who were also disciplined and willing to adapt. When quick-riding Moors raided his borders, the Frankish king knew that he needed more speed. His solution was to build up his cavalry.

Ironically, to defeat the invading Moors at Poitiers in 732 AD, that king, Charles Martel, ordered his horsemen down on their feet. Facing the attacking riders with shields and spears, the Franks stood fast and successfully repelled the Moors.

Despite that return to infantry tactics, this battle marked the beginning of the age of chivalry, a time when armored knights dominated European warfare.

Charging into chivalry

The words *chivalry* and *chivalric* are related to the French *chevaux*, meaning *horse*, and to other horse-based words, such as *cavalier* and the Spanish *caballero*. These words show that people of the Middle Ages associated nobility, gentility, and courage, not to mention wealth, with mounted warriors. As in ancient Rome, the mounted soldier enjoyed a status denied to the foot soldier.

The era of chivalry, like so many before it and since, glorified violence. People thought of fighting skills as being a mark of civilization.

IN THEIR WORDS

Jean Froissart, a 14th-century French chronicler, wrote, "Gentle Knights were born to fight, and war ennobles everyone who engages in it without fear or cowardice."

Ennobling or not, war costs money, and it became extremely expensive to outfit an armored, mounted knight. The Frankish king Charles Martel helped his riders pay for their gear by taking land from the medieval Church and giving it to the warrior–nobles. Under the system of feudalism (refer to Chapter 6), a landlord profited from his tenant farmers' harvests.

Charlemagne, a slightly later Frankish king and the first to unite a big piece of Europe after the Romans fell, accomplished that unification with his cavalry.

Donning the Steel Suit

A culture of chivalry lasted for hundreds of years in Europe. In movies, this armor-clad culture is associated with the legendary King Arthur, who may not have existed at all (see Chapter 19). If he did exist, Arthur probably led Celtic Britons against invading Saxons in the sixth century AD, but he certainly didn't do it in plate-metal armor. Plate armor didn't come into fashion until 800 years later, in the 14th century.

Wearing metal rings: Chain mail

Before plate armor, knights wore chain mail; before chain mail, they wore scale armor, which had been a defense against arrows since Assyrian times. (See Chapter 16 for more on the Assyrians.) *Scale armor*, like a lizard's scales, consisted of small metal plates sewn into overlapping rows on a leather vest. *Chain mail* was a bit more ingenious than scale armor; it consisted of interlocking metal rings made into a doublet (a close-fitting jacket).

The Crusaders wore mail as they rode east in their zeal to pry the Holy Land away from Muslim control (see Chapter 7). Chain mail became obsolete only when archers got better bows — bows that could shoot an arrow or a deadlier metal bolt — with enough force to pierce the material.

Putting more power into the archer's bow

The crossbow was yet another Chinese invention, and an ancient one at that, dating back to the fourth century BC. European archers rediscovered the crossbow's deadly power in the tenth century AD.

TECHNICAL STUFF

A short, extremely stiff bow was mounted on a stock with a mechanism for cranking back the bowstring and holding it there at a higher tension than an archer (usually, a man) could achieve by pulling the string back manually. The missile was loosed with a finger-lever trigger.

The crossbow usually shot short bolts rather than arrows. These bolts were often made of metal, and they penetrated materials that an arrow from a conventional bow could not. The Normans who conquered England in 1066 used the crossbow.

Pope Urban II condemned the crossbow in 1096, calling it "hateful to God." In 1139, the Church banned the crossbow for use against Christians. (Curiously, he deemed it okay to use the weapon against pagans such as the *Saracens*, a name for Turks and other Muslims.)

Charging behind the lance

Although Crusaders used the crossbow, something about it seemed to be less than honorable about it. Chivalric values centered on personal combat. When there wasn't a war to fight, knights rode against each other in fierce and often deadly jousts.

The *lance*, a long-pointed weapon that a jousting knight tucked under his arm, delivered incredible force. Increasingly metal-clad riders balanced on their stirrups and braced against high-backed saddles as they used this variation on the ancient spear to try to knock each other off their horses. Heavier armor kept them from being pierced through.

Mock battles let knights win status and stay sharp for the real thing, but the mock battles were still real. At a 1241 tournament in Neuss, Germany, about 80 competitors (men and boys) died.

Marrying precision to power with the longbow

The English *longbow*, a refinement of ancient Welsh technology, became the latest thing in weaponry during the 14th century. Both precise and powerful in the hands of a skilled archer, the longbow gave knights another reason to wear solid metal armor.

The crossbow was powerful, but its accuracy and range were limited, and it took too long to load. An English longbow could do damage at 750 feet and be reloaded rapidly. Only a skilled archer could use a longbow well, however, so England required yeomen to practice marksmanship. (*Yeomen* were small landowners who served as soldiers when needed, as small farmers had in ancient Greece and Rome; see Chapter 16.)

In 1346, at the Battle of Crécy (in the Hundred Years' War between France and England), English archers with longbows brought down wave after wave of French opponents. France lost more than 1,500 knights that day and 10,000 foot soldiers. England lost only two knights and fewer than 200 soldiers overall.

In the short term, Crécy led the French and other European knights to strap themselves inside heavier suits of armor. No one knew then that armored knights were on the way out and guns were on the way in. A century later, firearms outshot and outpierced any bow yet invented.

DID THE HUNDRED YEARS' WAR REALLY LAST 100 YEARS?

The name of the Hundred Years' War suggests ten solid decades of constant battle. Actually, it wasn't one war but a series of back-and-forth conflicts from the 1330s to the 1450s.

In 1337, Philip IV of France snatched Aquitaine (today, a region of southwestern France) from Edward III of England, and Edward invaded France. The next century featured many battles and raids. But there were also truces, including a 28-year peace after Richard II of England married the daughter of Charles VI of France in 1396.

France eventually won, largely because England — weakened by an internal struggle, the Wars of the Roses — gave up trying to conquer its neighbor across the English Channel.

Adding Firepower with Gunpowder

Between the 12th and 18th centuries, guns spread from China to western Asia, to Europe, and then around the world, advancing from primitive experiments to precision technology. Warriors were forced to revise their strategies, sometimes adapting ancient battle formations to the new weaponry, and defenders had to find new ways to fortify outposts and cities.

Lighting the fire of discovery

Light a fire on a patch of dirt that has sulfur in it, and you get a sizzling, popping reaction. Somebody whose name is lost to history noticed this effect a long time ago in China, and the observation led other Chinese to experiment with putting concentrated sulfur together with charcoal. By the ninth century AD, another genius added potassium nitrate crystals (saltpeter). Burn that mixture, and you get sparkly effects that made a nice backdrop to formal ceremonies. Taoist monks played with these chemicals until they resulted in fireworks.

Over time, *pyrotechnicians* (makers of fireworks) realized that their flammable mixture could make stuff fly — dangerous stuff. Soldiers noticed too. By the 12th century, the armies of the Sung Dynasty had added metal grenades to their arsenal. China pioneered fragmentation bombs, whose casings shattered into deadly shrapnel. Within another 100 years, Chinese factories made hundreds of military rockets and bombs, some filled with poisons (such as arsenic) that released on impact; others were packed with tar and oil and were designed to start fires. The Chinese also built early guns in the form of metal barrels packed with this mixture (later called gunpowder) that shot out rocks or metal balls.

Spreading explosive news

News of Chinese explosives spread west along the ancient trade route, the Silk Road (see Chapter 6). The Arabs got primitive firearms by the late 13th century. In 1267, the recipe for gunpowder turned up in Europe in the hands of English scientist and friar Roger Bacon, a Christian empiricist (see Chapter 15).

Less than a century later, European armies began using crude cannons. Archers with longbows — not their innovative comrades who were trying out noisy, stinky little firepots — won the Battle of Crécy, mentioned earlier in this chapter, but the primitive cannon was a sign of things to come. The early European cannon was called a *firepot* because it was pot-shaped. It propelled an arrow (yes, an arrow) with impressive force but little reliability and no accuracy. The earliest European gunmakers were craftsmen who, until then, had made church bells. Often, they melted down bells to make cannons. Soon, the gunmakers found out that a tubular barrel worked better and that it should propel a metal shot, because you could knock down a castle gate or level a house that way.

Bringing in the big guns

By the early 16th century, the Italian writer Niccolo Machiavelli observed, "No wall exists, however thick, that artillery cannot destroy in a few days."

Guns were already big, although some of the biggest didn't work so well. In the early 15th century, some early cannon, sometimes called *bombards,* weighed 1,500 pounds and discharged balls 30 inches in diameter. How did anybody back then make a cast-metal barrel that big? At first, the barrel wasn't cast, but pieced together out of forged iron staves, like the curved boards used to form a pickle barrel. Iron hoops held the staves together — temporarily, anyway.

For an example of how crude and dangerous early canon were, consider that in 1460, one of King James II of Scotland's big guns exploded, killing the king and many members of the royal party.

Battering down Constantinople's walls

Sometimes, a big gun was just the thing. In the 7th and 8th centuries, Arab warriors had tried to take Constantinople — first using their fancy new stirrups and then boats — but failed. (For more on those attempts, see "Guarding Byzantine borders" earlier in this chapter.) In the 15th century, deciding to break out the big guns to breach the city, Ottoman Turkish Sultan Mehmet II hired a Hungarian gunmaker, who built him a cannon that sent a ball flying a full mile.

In 1453, the sultan fired that gun, nicknamed *Mahometta,* at the Byzantine capital's ramparts and kept firing. Like so many of these giants, the cannon cracked after the second day and became unusable after a week. But Mehmet had other big guns. After 54 days of pounding, the 1,000-year-old Byzantine Empire finally fell, a victim of technological advance.

Refining the new weaponry

Although massive bombards worked, military leaders knew that there had to be less-cumbersome ways to win battles with big guns. Weapons-makers went to work devising field artillery weapons that were more useful and more versatile — and that fit specific niches in the Renaissance arsenal.

Making guns lighter and more maneuverable

Eventually, artillery experts figured out that they could cast some guns in light-yet-strong bronze rather than iron. These lighter, less-cumbersome guns could be moved into place faster, fired more often (some of the bigger ones could deliver a shot only once in two hours), and weren't so likely to explode, so they could do even more damage than the giants could.

Improving gunpowder with brandy

Guns got better, but gunpowder needed improvement because sulfur, carbon, and saltpeter had three different weights. The saltpeter crystals settled to the bottom, and the carbon came to the top. The only way to ensure that the gunpowder worked was to mix the ingredients right before loading the weapon, which was difficult and time-consuming. Then somebody came up with a way to make the ingredients stick together: mixing the gunpowder with brandy and letting the resulting paste dry into corns (grains) containing all three ingredients.

But what a waste of brandy! Soldiers tried substitutes such as vinegar, which worked okay, but human urine worked even better — especially the urine of soldiers who had put that brandy to more pleasurable use. (It didn't improve the smell of gunpowder, however.)

Putting guns in soldiers' hands

Guns were first seen as replacements for the catapult and the battering ram — destructive, but not precise. As gunnery improved, however, guns gained accuracy and usefulness.

Soon, gunmakers came up with models for use on the battlefield — both as light artillery (usually, a horse-drawn cannon on wagon wheels) and as weapons that soldiers could carry. *Handcannon,* as the smallest guns were called, scared the enemy's horses (and your own, for that matter) and perhaps intimidated a knight or two. But for quite a while, handcannon didn't seem to be a practical replacement for bows and swords. How did you hold a gun, aim it, and also effectively set fire to the gunpowder charge?

TECHNICAL STUFF

In the middle of the 15th century, the solution was a wick soaked in alcohol and coated with saltpeter, attached to a trigger. Pulling the trigger lowered this so-called *slow match* into the gun's touchhole to light the powder charge.

The *matchlock,* shown in Figure 17-2, freed a marksman's hands to aim a weapon, including one called a *hackbut* or *harquebus* — variations on the German *Hakenbuchse,* which meant *hook-gun.* Some matchlocks had a hook that you could brace on the edge of a wall when firing over it. The hook caught some of the shock from the gun's powerful recoil.

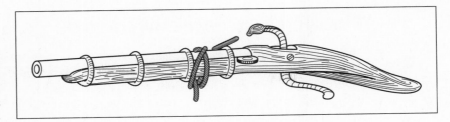

The term *musket* comes from *mosquito*, because the weapon was supposed to irritate the enemy (like its namesake). But muskets were anything but mosquito-like in size. Many a musket had to be propped on a forked rest, like a crutch, to be aimed and fired. So in addition to the heavy gun, a musketeer had to lug around this cumbersome prop.

Striking sparks

Because a slow match could send off a spark that lit the charge too soon, the musket was dangerous for the musketeer. Gunsmiths came up with other ways to fire a powder charge, such as the *wheel lock*, a piece of flint held against a spring-loaded steel wheel. If you've examined the moving parts of a cigarette lighter, you have a pretty good idea of how the wheel lock struck sparks. Eventually, the simpler *flintlock*, consisting of a spring-loaded hammer that struck a flint, became the dominant technology from about 1650 into the 19th century.

Adapting old strategies for new weapons

Until the introduction of the *breechloader* (a gun loaded from the back), a musketeer put everything — gunpowder and shot — down the barrel. He had to stand up to stuff all this material into the tube. Prince Maurice of Nassau, commander of the Netherlands troops in their religious war of independence against Spain (see Chapter 14), revived the *countermarch*, a Roman archery strategy. He put his musketeers in precise rows and had the ones in front fire at the same time; then they moved to the rear to reload while the next rank fired.

REMEMBER

Under Maurice and leaders like him — Sweden's King Gustav Adolph II (1594–1632) and French Inspector General Jean Martinet (died in 1672) — armies emphasized rigid discipline more than ever. (Martinet's name became a synonym for an unbending authority figure.) Military commanders of the 17th and 18th centuries wanted soldiers to be more than fierce; they wanted them to be willing and able to charge into concentrated gunfire. This trait — suicidal as it often proved to be — became a weird new definition of manly bravery.

Floating fortresses on the sea

Through the 16th century, warships were often oar-powered galleys, and the most effective naval maneuver was to ram an enemy ship and then board it with fighters armed with swords and pikes. But as gunpowder redefined battlefield weaponry, cannon and firearms redefined the naval arsenal and the tactics of a sea battle. At the Battle of Lepanto in 1517, the galleys of the Turkish navy on one side and the allied Christian nations of Europe on the other were fitted with two to four cannons on their bows, but the Europeans won the battle via hand-to-hand combat aboard Turkish ships.

By the middle of the 17th century, galleys had fallen out of favor as warships, partly because guns had become the key weapon in naval battles, and vessels needed to bristle with gunports, not oars and oarsmen, along both sides. Sea captains still sought to board enemy ships but generally did so only after disabling them with cannon broadsides.

Adapting fortifications to the artillery era

Ever since the earliest walled towns were built, a good defensive barrier was as tall as possible. But cannon fire could topple such a wall, so architects came up with a new way to build a fort in the mid-15th century. In Genoa, Leon Battista Alberti (see Chapter 13) drew designs for star-shaped fortresses with relatively low but extremely thick walls. Figure 17-3 is a simplified depiction of Castillo San Marcos, built by 16th-century Spaniards in St. Augustine, Florida, where it still stands.

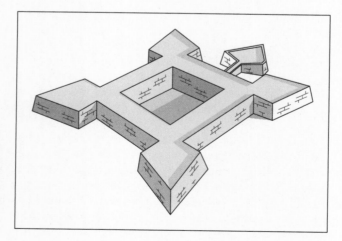

FIGURE 17-3: With thick walls and a star-shaped design, the Renaissance fort was built for cannon battles.

Jutting angles let a fort's defenders aim their cannons diagonally across the enemy lines so that a cannonball could skip down the line, wiping out more men, guns, horses, and equipment.

Tracking the Centuries

Fourth century AD: Chinese cavalry begin using stirrups.

568 AD: Avar horsemen, using stirrups, win battles to take Danube Valley lands from the Byzantine Empire.

732 AD: At Poitiers in Gaul, Charles Martel, king of the Franks, and his troops turn back invading Moorish horsemen from Spain.

Tenth century AD: European archers adopt the powerful crossbow.

1096: Pope Urban II condemns the crossbow, calling it "hateful to God."

1267: England's Roger Bacon has the recipe for gunpowder.

1396: Richard II of England marries the daughter of Charles VI of France, creating a 28-year peace in the Hundred Years' War.

1460: A Scottish military cannon explodes, killing King James II and many members of his retinue.

modern war

» Enlarging the scale of armed conflict with world wars

» Turning to guerilla tactics and terrorism in the nuclear age

Chapter **18**

Modernizing Mayhem

Many history books say that modern war started with the U.S. Civil War in the 1860s or the Crimean War in the 1850s. But maybe modern war traces back several decades earlier, to when a Prussian scholar–soldier began to teach the concept *total war.*

Those authors who call the Crimean War the first of the modern era's wars cite the way it proved the value of new technologies, such as rifled muskets and telegraph lines to the front. Those who credit the U.S. Civil War as the first of its kind note that it used those technologies and more, and that it was a bigger, more devastating conflict. Furthermore, the Civil War seemed to personify the teachings of Karl von Clausewitz, who had taught his young Prussian officers in the early 19th century that they must do more than defeat opposing forces: They must cripple entire regions. The Civil War's breadth and ferocity provided a glimpse of the future and previewed the global wars of the 20th century.

In this chapter, you'll find out how viewpoints regarding war — about, for example, the morality of destroying essential crops or sacrificing civilian lives to defeat a military foe — changed the nature of armed conflict. You'll meet weapons technologies and consider how inventions have fed every escalation in modern fighting styles. You'll also glimpse how backlash against the giant war-making capabilities of the post-World War II period revived age-old tactics such as guerilla raids and terrorist sabotage.

Following Three Paths to Modern War

What's so modern about wars fought before armored tanks, airplanes, and the threat of nuclear explosions? For our purposes, we'll say *modern war* started with these three military milestones:

» Prussian generals in the early 19th century embraced the concept of *total war* (a campaign of devastation) and *blitzkrieg* (a quick-strike campaign).

» In 1853, just at the time when the armies of Western Europe were rearming with faster-firing, easier-to-load weapons and employing such innovations as the steamship and telegraph to support fighting, England and France took on Russia in the Crimean War.

» Devastation wrought upon an entire region (the American South) and its economy, accompanied by a massive death toll, far surpassed the expectations of dismayed military commanders and civilians on both sides in the U.S. Civil War.

But don't get hung up on the label. "Modern war" is another of those frustratingly imprecise terms that I talk about in Chapter 3. That is, "modern" doesn't mean the same thing to historians as it does to, say, architects or software designers. And even historians don't necessarily agree on the meaning of "modern," so it's easy to get confused. War evolved and changed with every conflict.

Promoting devastation in Prussia

Officers in the militaristic German state of Prussia, around the time of the Napoleonic Wars (1803-1815), saw total war as the model for how warfare ought to be conducted. The most influential of these soldiers was Carl von Clausewitz (1780–1831), director of the Prussian army school. He wrote a book called *On War*, published posthumously in 1832, a manual for fighting an all-out campaign marked by the *scorched-earth* advance.

TECHNICAL STUFF

The scorched-earth advance is a way of crippling an enemy by targeting any resources that could help it. The strategy includes destroying or stealing weapons, roads, bridges, and factories, but it extends to anything that might support or sustain the opposing army. It can mean burning crops and slaughtering farm animals, fouling water sources, and even attacking the civilian population, although that last carries the strategy to an awful extreme.

Helmuth Graf von Moltke, commander of Prussia's army, took Clausewitz's ideas and harnessed them to new technology: needle guns, new long-range artillery, and railroads. Moltke reorganized and vastly enlarged his military. Then he used

Prussia's forces to win wars against Denmark in 1864, Austria in 1866, and France in 1870. (You'll find more on 19th-century weapons advances during the Crimean War in the next section.)

Overwhelming in number and devastatingly efficient, the Prussians in the Franco-Prussian War advanced on Paris in a troop movement so quick it was called a *blitzkrieg* (lightning war). The Prussians surrounded the French Army; killed 17,000 French soldiers in a rain of artillery; and took more than 100,000 prisoners, among them Emperor Napoleon III. The lightning-war strategy would emerge again, especially during World War II.

Prussia's military preeminence allowed its prime minister, Otto von Bismarck, to unite Germany in 1871. Bismarck became the first chancellor of a new German Empire, which was a formidable military power through the age when total war became world war.

Putting technology to deadly uses: The Crimean War

Why did France and the United Kingdom declare war on Russia to start the Crimean War? Well, for one thing, Russia was nibbling away at the crumbling Ottoman Empire, which was scary, because other countries didn't want any of their neighbors to be too big or powerful. This brings up that favorite phrase of history teachers, "balance of power," that I talked about in Chapter 9. It just means that having a very powerful nation next door tends to make a government seek to get militarily stronger so as not to be a pushover. One way to do this is to spend more money on troops and weapons. Another, often smarter way is to team up with other countries in an alliance tough enough to stand up to the powerful neighbor. The downside of balance of power alliances is that if your strategic friends get into an international scrap, you're obligated to back them up.

The Ottoman Empire, dating back to the Ottoman Turks' conquest of Constantinople in 1453 (see Chapter 17), was a wreck by the mid-19th century. As diplomatic friends of the Ottomans, France and Britain bristled when Russia marched troops across the Danube River into Turkish territory in Romania. These powers didn't want Russia to control the Black Sea area and the overland trade routes to India, much less establish a seaport on the Mediterranean.

Yet neither the French nor the British wanted open hostilities, either. Armed conflict with Russia, they knew, would be costly. At an 1853 conference in Vienna, they tried to get the Ottomans to compromise with the Russians, but the Turks declared war instead and their allies, pledged to mutual defense, were drawn in. Ironically, the war proceeded even after Russia gave in to Austrian demands (and the threat of the Austrian army) and withdrew from the disputed parts of Romania (Wallachia and Moldavia).

After Russia replied to the Turks' declaration of war by destroying the Ottoman fleet at Sinope, a port on the south coast of the Black Sea, the United Kingdom and France, as allies of the Ottomans, saw no alternative but to weigh in and teach the czar a lesson.

The British, French, and Sardinia (an island nation that also ruled parts of the Italian mainland) sent forces to confront the Russians on the Crimean Peninsula in southern Ukraine, between the Black Sea and the Sea of Azov.

Adding accuracy and speed with new rifles

By the time of the Crimean War, the flintlock musket was old technology (refer to Chapter 17). A new device, the *percussion lock*, replaced the flintlock's friction-spark system (see the nearby sidebar "The clergyman's new gun"). In the percussion-lock weapon, the powder charge ignited within a reliable, easy-to-load cartridge.

REMEMBER

What else was new about firearms? The rifled barrel was a big change. To *rifle* is to etch spiral grooves into the inside of a gun barrel. These grooves cause the shot to spin as it travels up the barrel, and that spin helps it fly straighter through the air. Think of the way a football thrown with a spin, or *spiral*, flies true, whereas one that doesn't spin develops a wobble.

For the rifled barrel to be most effective, it needed ammunition that fit the barrel tightly enough to engage the groove and take its spin. That kind of shot was difficult to load through the mouth, or *muzzle*, of the barrel. If the metal slug was tight enough to engage the grooves, the slug was also tight enough to catch on the way in, blocking the barrel and making the gun useless.

The *minié* ball — named not for its size but for its inventor, Captain Claude-Étienne Minié of France — offered an early solution. Minié hollowed the bottom of a lead bullet, turning its back edge into a semiflexible flange. When the explosive charge went off under it, the hollow expanded, pushing out the flange to fit more tightly against the sides of the barrel. The flange caught the rifling, and the bullet spun and flew true.

Then came an even better solution for getting the bullet into the barrel. With the percussion lock and its self-contained powder charge, it became practical to load the weapon from the back, or *breech end*, instead of through its muzzle. A snug fit on the way in was no longer an issue. Even better, breech-loading weapons eliminated the soldier's reliance on gravity to get the ammunition down the barrel. A rifleman no longer had to stand up to reload; he could stay flat against the ground, presenting a minimal target.

THE CLERGYMAN'S NEW GUN

The Reverend Alexander John Forsyth of Belhelvie, Scotland, wanted to shoot birds, not soldiers, when he came up with the idea for the percussion lock — a major advance in firearms technology.

Forsyth enjoyed hunting grouse and ducks. He didn't enjoy missing a shot. Shooters missed a lot in Forsyth's time (the early 19th century) even if they were handy with a musket, because the flash of a flintlock frightened the birds. Frustrated, the reverend devised a self-contained gunpowder capsule that ignited without flashing when the musket's hammer drove a firing pin into the capsule. This capsule was the prototype for what became a self-contained shell, in which the powder charge and slug (bullet) were one package.

The Prussian *needle gun* (named for its long firing pin) came first among these breech-loaders, followed by the French chassepot and the British Snyder-Enfield. With better weapons, range more than doubled — in some cases to more than 4,000 yards. Accuracy improved tremendously, and increased rate of fire allowed a skilled rifleman with a Snyder-Enfield to get off six shots in a minute.

How much difference did new firearms make? At the Battle of Inkerman in 1854, an early landmark in the Crimean War, the allies had breech-loading rifles, and the Russians did not. The score: 12,000 Russians dead to only 3,000 allies.

Transporting troops via steamship

Steam power allowed shippers to deliver freight on time, keeping to a schedule instead of depending on the whim of the wind. The steamship did the same for military leaders.

Men, horses, and artillery transported to a battle site by sea have a better chance of arriving fresh rather than ground down from a long march. But a wind-powered ship sometimes stalled in becalmed waters for days or even weeks. If supplies ran out while troops were onboard, the soldiers arrived weak from hunger. With the steamship, ready troops could be shipped from England and France to Turkey and the Crimea faster and more reliably. Strategists could make plans with reasonable certainty that the soldiers would arrive on or near the date promised. (There's more about steam power, including its industrial uses, in Chapter 9.)

Laying down railroad tracks to the front lines

No rail line was handy for British and French troops when they got to the port of Balaklava in the Crimea, so they built one to serve the inland battle headquarters — the first railroad built expressly for a war effort. The train did on land what the steamship did on water, providing a reliable way to get fresh troops and supplies to a battle site.

Stringing telegraph wires to the battlefield

The most modern device employed in the Crimea, the electric telegraph, allowed commanders to communicate with their troops almost instantaneously. Support troops strung wires to wherever fighters were deployed.

Previously, armies had communicated by messenger or sometimes by systems of signals, such as smoke puffs or flag code relayed by line of sight from station to station. With the electric telegraph, information and orders pulsed along at the speed of electric current.

Not only were commanders and field lieutenants in touch, thanks to the telegraph, but also, the governments in Paris and London communicated with their armies by wire (for much of the distance, anyway). Getting a message back home no longer took weeks.

Civilians, notably members of the press, also could send messages quickly and easily, presenting a new public-relations problem for British officers in the Crimea. W.H. Russell, an Irish reporter working for an English paper, became the first war correspondent to file a *wire report,* as newspapers called them. His stories in *The Times* of London told the English about the disastrous "Charge of the Light Brigade," a brave but mistaken British cavalry attack on Russian artillery positions during the Battle of Balaklava. Russell wrote about the way that poorly equipped allied troops suffered through the long winter siege of Russia's fort at Sebastopol in 1854 and 1855, noting that some of their commanders spent that winter onboard private yachts offshore. Outraged readers demanded reforms.

INTO THE VALLEY OF DEATH

The English of the mid-19th century learned about the Light Brigade's mistaken charge through newspaper accounts, but they remembered it through verse. Lord Alfred Tennyson (1809–92) landed the post of England's poet laureate in 1850 and wrote a heroic verse that begins, "Half a league, half a league, / Half a league onward, / All in the valley of Death / Rode the six hundred." The poem caught the popular imagination as few poems ever have. Readers could almost feel the galloping horses in the galloping cadences of the lines "Cannon to the right of them, / Cannon to the left of them, / Cannon behind them / Volleyed and thundered."

Redefining armed conflict: The U.S. Civil War

If the Crimean War changed the tools of warfare, the U.S. Civil War changed war itself by showing how big, deadly, and devastatingly costly a modern war could be. Four million men mobilized over the course of the war, and more than 600,000 of them died in widespread battles.

REMEMBER

Although estimates differ, as many as 751,000 died in the U.S. Civil War. That's not as many as the reported number killed by the COVID-19 pandemic (754,000 as of November 2021). It is, however, more than the deaths from World War I, World War II, the Korean War, the Vietnam War, the 1990-91 Gulf War, and the wars in Afghanistan and Iraq combined. And if you think of how much smaller the U.S. population was then — fewer than 31.5 million by the 1860 census compared with almost 331.5 million in 2020 — you can begin to imagine the impact.

Waging total war on Sherman's March to the Sea

For the South, the Civil War meant the wreck of its economy. This war was the one in which General Ulysses S. Grant, commander of the Union armies, used the word *attrition* to describe his strategy. He announced his intention to pound the enemy until they could do nothing but surrender. And so Grant did.

Although German theoretician Clausewitz (covered earlier in this chapter) pioneered the concept of total war, the U.S. Civil War was the first large-scale demonstration of his idea. Before war's end, the Union wreaked brutal and absolute devastation — military, economic, and societal. Union General William Tecumseh Sherman wiped out virtually everything in his army's path on an 1864 march from Chattanooga, Tennessee, through Atlanta to the coastal town of Savannah, Georgia. On this campaign, known to history as Sherman's *March to the Sea,* Union troops destroyed farms; trashed machinery; spoiled any foodstuffs they didn't steal; slaughtered cattle and chickens; loosed mules; encouraged enslaved people to run away; sacked and burned not just Atlanta, but also dozens of towns along their way; and in Sherman's words "generally raised hell."

IN THEIR WORDS

Sherman gets credit for the phrase "War is hell." If he didn't actually say it, he acted it out.

Sorting through the Civil War's causes

Also called the War of the Rebellion and the War Between the States, the U.S. conflict started in 1860, although a violent prelude foreshadowed it. The abolitionist John Brown (see Chapter 22), fresh from committing antislavery violence in the western territory of Kansas, went east with his men in 1859 to capture the U.S.

armory at Harper's Ferry, in what would soon be the new state of West Virginia. U.S. troops commanded by Robert E. Lee captured Brown. Convicted of treason and hanged, Brown became a martyr for the abolitionist cause.

Abolitionists wanted to outlaw slavery (see Chapter 8), the labor base of the American South. This issue more than anything else led to the South's rebellion at the end of 1860. Southerners saw enslaved people as property and abolition as a threat to take that property from its owners. The rebellion erupted after Abraham Lincoln of Illinois, the Kentucky-born candidate of the new antislavery Republican Party, won the presidency in 1860.

In December, South Carolina resigned from the Union, citing in particular Northern states' willful failure to apprehend people who had escaped from slavery and return them to Southerners who claimed ownership. Ten other states said "Us, too." The following April, troops of the newly formed Confederate States of America attacked Fort Sumter, a U.S. military post in Charleston, South Carolina. Neither side was prepared for what would follow. Who could have been? Most Americans of the mid-19th century had never seen war.

Exceeding expectations with grim determination

In the summer of 1861, when Union troops marched south from Washington, D.C., intent on thrashing the Confederate forces camped in nearby Virginia, the capital city's public treated the impending conflict as a lark. Sightseers toting picnic baskets tagged along behind the troops. Civilians and soldiers alike expected a neat victory and a quick peace.

What they got instead was a decisive defeat and a shock. Before the day was over, many of the 18,000 Union soldiers who met the enemy at Bull Run near Manassas, Virginia, turned and ran for their lives. The Confederate victory showed that the war wasn't going to be easy or predictable.

That early encounter is usually called the first Battle of Bull Run, after a nearby stream. Northern chroniclers of the war generally named battles after nearby waterways. Southerners called the same fight, and the one that occurred there the next year, the First and Second Battles of Manassas. Casual readers of Civil War history are sometimes confused by a single battle being known by two different names.

Believing fervently in their cause, Southerners thought that a decisive victory or two, like the first at Bull Run, would convince the Union to turn them loose. But the Union had overwhelming economic advantages — factories, railroads, and a much larger population base — that the rebels lacked, and it had a deep-seated resolve of its own. The canny, articulate Lincoln convinced the public that the Union must be saved.

SPEWING BULLETS FROM THE MACHINE GUN

Ever since the cannon and musket became basic tools of warfare, inventors had struggled to find ways to load and fire guns faster. Early attempts to meet this challenge included weapons with multiple barrels or multiple charges to be fired in succession. The first practical design was the *Gatling gun,* named after American inventor Richard Gatling. An opportunist inspired by the U.S. Civil War, he used percussion lock technology and devised a hand-crank mechanism to feed charges into his gun's chambers, fire them, and then extract the spent cartridges. Gatling claimed that this gun would fire 200 rounds a minute.

Although he was a Southerner, Gatling offered his invention to both sides in the war. Neither side bought it. Only after the war did it become part of the U.S. arsenal. Britain, Japan, Russia, Turkey, and Spain all placed orders too.

In the 1880s, another American inventor, Hiram Maxim, came up with an improved machine gun that required no cranking. A gunner could hold down the trigger, and the gun would just keep firing, making this gun the first automatic weapon. It used the power of each charge's recoil to eject the cartridge and move the next one into the chamber. The gun could spit more than 600 bullets a minute. By World War I, the Maxim and its imitators were major parts of just about every battle.

The Civil War evoked the kind of popular involvement among Americans that Europe had seen in the French Revolution (see Chapter 8) and hooked the nation up to the new industrial technology. In some ways, the Civil War was a throwback to earlier ages, when sacking and burning were commonplace. But as the Civil War employed the same new technologies as in the Crimean War — on a larger scale and over a longer time — it pointed toward a horrible future. Military leaders figured out, for example, that the improved range and accuracy of a rifled gun barrel added enormous risk to the infantry charge. Units learned to dig in; the spade, or *trenching tool,* came into tactical use. All this and more previewed the grinding, static, morale-killing style of ground fighting that would characterize World War I.

Tying Tactics to Technology in the 20th Century

Twentieth-century wars spread European-based conflicts around the world, rearranging borders and bringing down economic and political empires. World War I reset the global stage for a new era in international relations by inspiring the world's first attempt at an organization to prevent war: the League of Nations. It did that, at least in part, by demonstrating how war had been changed by the killing trends of the 19th century. (For more on these conflicts, refer to Chapter 9.)

World War II added new weapon after new weapon to the increasingly technically sophisticated arsenal. Each perilous escalation in weaponry made industrialized nations better able to rain down death with an ease beyond any imagined by ancestors of even a century earlier. This so-called progress brought civilization all the way to the perilous, fiery brink of the nuclear age.

Trapping valor in a trench: World War I

With the Maxim machine gun (see the nearby sidebar "Spewing bullets from the machine gun") and its improved descendants so widely used in WWI, the tactic of charging enemy positions, more dangerous with every advance in weaponry, became suicidal.

This lesson sank in at the first Battle of the Marne, fought in France in September 1914. After that battle, the front lines of the war's Western Front turned into thousands of miles of parallel trenches across Europe; the trenches were wet, rat-infested ditches in which cold, dirty, terrified men hid for days, weeks, months, and years, scratching at lice and warily watching the other side's trenches. On occasion, the horrible order would come, and the men would obediently climb out and fling themselves into a barrage of bullets and exploding mortar shells. Trying to break the stalemate, both sides developed new weapons, including hand grenades for lobbing into the enemy trenches; mortar shells that could be fired up and over the opposite embankment; and exploding canisters of poison mustard gas, an oily chemical that left victims blistered outside and inside — especially in their lungs — and often permanently disabled.

In 1915, a British officer came up with the idea of putting an armored casing around the kind of tractor that ran on metal chain treads. The officer thought that he could mount guns on this fortified crawler and drive it toward enemy machine-gun positions. The armored tank was born, and by war's end, British units were using it to cross German trenches.

Also in that war, a German engineer figured out how to time a machine gun to fire through a spinning propeller without hitting the blades. Fighter aircraft resulted. Airplanes began to drop bombs too, although on nothing like the scale that was to come in WWII. The submarine, in the form of the German U-boat, showed its value in WWI as its crews enjoyed the advantage of underwater surprise.

Retooling the World War II arsenal

In WWII, technology in the service of mass destruction accelerated at a pace that would have astonished even General Moltke. Bazookas, aircraft carriers, anti-aircraft guns, antisubmarine depth charges, long-range fighter planes, missiles, radar, sonar, and atomic weapons all came out of that war.

What are all these things? Many of the names are self-explanatory — although *bazooka* is a weird name for anything, including a brand of bubble gum. (The so-named weapon is a small, portable antitank rocket launcher that an infantryman can carry and fire.) Most of the inventions — even some of the most chilling among them — are now taken for granted as part of the modern world. Some of them serve peaceful purposes, however, including these two examples:

>> **Radar** (originally RADAR, an acronym for RAdio Detecting And Ranging) began as an idea based on the echo. Radar bounces radio waves off objects and then detects the pattern of the returning waves to *see* objects (especially airplanes) beyond the range of visual detection. Radar allowed Britain's outnumbered Royal Air Force to detect German bomber squads, spoiling Nazi plans to invade the British Isles. After the war, it was an invaluable tool for commercial aviation and law enforcement, because radar can tell how fast an object (such as an automobile) is moving.

>> **Sonar** (an acronym for SOund Navigation And Ranging) did much the same with sound waves underwater as radar did with radio waves in the air. With sonar, a ship could detect enemy submarines. Numerous postwar uses range from salvaging sunken ships to finding good fishing spots.

The United States dropped two atomic bombs on Japan in 1945 to end WWII. Historians, military strategists, and peace activists still argue, and probably always will, about whether those attacks were justifiable. In any case, it's certain that those *A-bombs* and the even deadlier nuclear weapons developed after the war changed the way that war is perceived and fought.

Warring On Despite the Nuclear Threat

At the end of WWII, some people thought that nuclear weapons would make any further warfare unthinkable. Things haven't turned out that way.

A growing number of countries built and tested nuclear weapons in the postwar years. (For more about nuclear proliferation, see Chapter 9.) But in much of the world, the nuclear option remained irrelevant, especially in South America, Southeast Asia, and Africa, where revolutions and civil wars raged on.

Despite the massive ability of the post-WWII superpowers (the Soviet Union, until its 1991 breakup, and the United States) to wreak large-scale mayhem, small-scale warriors — especially those who believed in their causes of revolution or retribution for perceived political wrongs — found ways to undermine the security of major nations. Often, they reached back to pretechnological strategies such as the guerilla raid and the difficult-to-prevent terrorist strike.

Drawing strength from stealth: Guerilla tactics

Paradoxically, the nuclear age of the late 20th century was also the era of foot soldiers treading softly in the night. *Guerilla war* is often fought by outnumbered, ill-financed bands of revolutionaries moving stealthily against better-armed powers. Guerilla units venture out under cover of darkness to conduct small-scale raids and set booby traps.

REMEMBER

Guerilla (Spanish for *little war*) first referred to the Spanish peasants who harassed Napoleon's conquering forces early in the 19th century. Then, as now, guerilla tactics followed precedents as old as war itself — the same tactics that the sneaky Italian tribes who frustrated early Rome's Greek-style phalanx (Chapter 16) probably used. Similarly, the improvisational soldiering of American revolutionaries sometimes caught Britain's infantry off guard in the 1770s. Americans sometimes fired from cover, putting a marching formation of Brits at a disadvantage.

The British faced guerilla tactics again more than a century later in South Africa. The First Boer War began in 1899, when Boers, descendants of 17th century Dutch (and some German and French) colonists, stood up to the ruling British government. The United Kingdom had taken control of South Africa almost a century before, in the Napoleonic Wars. The Boers, whose descendants are now called Afrikaners, were independent farmers who resented British rule and established their own, separate governments (and, yes this is another place where I oversimplify wildly) in the region of South Africa called the Transvaal. For decades, the British left them mostly to themselves until the Boers began to profit from gold and diamond mining in the territory they claimed. Naturally, the British wanted control of the wealth, and asserted ownership of that land. As happens in these situations, greed bred war.

Expecting to beat down this rebellion in a few months, the British failed to consider Boer determination, toughness, familiarity with the terrain, and mastery of guerilla tactics. Against Britain's superior weaponry, the determined Boers resorted to hiding, raiding, and bombing. Realizing that this foe would hold on indefinitely, the British resorted to the kinds of extreme measures that generals Grant and Sherman had in the United States during the Civil War. They fought a war of attrition. British troops burned farms and herded Dutch civilians into concentration camps.

REMEMBER

Twentieth-century opposition forces ranging from the French Resistance in WWII to the Communist Viet Cong in 1960s Vietnam (see Figure 18-1) to the anti-Communist Contras in 1980s Nicaragua made effective use of backwoods evasiveness, quickness, mobility, and well-timed, small-scale raids against stronger foes.

FIGURE 18-1:
Guerilla fighters such as Vietnam's Viet Cong, South Vietnamese insurgents who supported the North Vietnamese cause, stage raids against stronger foes.

Three Lions/Hulton Archive/Getty Images

Wielding the weapon of fear: Terrorism

Whereas the targets of guerilla forces are generally military or at least within an area at war, terrorist violence frequently seems to be indiscriminate and arbitrary, as in the bombing of a shopping mall, a city bus, or a commercial airliner full of passengers.

REMEMBER

The perpetrators of terrorism are usually members of minority groups who feel that violence is the only way to advance their cause, which is often the overthrow of the established order. By definition, terrorists use terror, or fear of the next unpredictable strike, as a weapon.

The Provisional Irish Republican Army (IRA), a nationalist group that wanted to unite British-controlled Northern Ireland with the self-ruled Irish Republic, was frequently labeled *terrorist* from the 1970s to the 1990s. Although IRA bombs were often directed at military targets, they also went off among passersby in English cities.

Although they're often labeled criminals, terrorists usually consider themselves to be warriors engaged in honorable acts of battle. Such is the case with the members of *al-Qaeda*, the terrorist group responsible for the notorious September 11, 2001, attacks on the United States. Formed in the 1980s to support Muslim resistance to a Soviet incursion into Afghanistan, al-Qaeda became an international network with an increasingly antagonistic attitude toward the United States. Its devastating 2001 attacks on the World Trade Center in New York and the Pentagon just outside Washington, D.C., as well as a hijacked plane that went down in Pennsylvania, killed almost 3,000 people.

Terrorism is extremely difficult to defend against because its perpetrators often deliberately take their own lives so that they can kill others around them with explosives. From the late 20th century and into recent decades, Islamic terrorists in the Middle East frequently resorted to this tactic, known as *suicide bombing*. In 1983, two suicide bombers driving trucks killed 300 people — 241 of them U.S. servicepeople, mostly Marines — by driving trucks filled with explosives into two troop barracks in Beirut, Lebanon. In the years since, suicide bombers have many times struck civilian targets in Israel. Palestinian militant groups such as Hamas, which seek an end to Israeli governance, are generally credited with inciting and financing such attacks. Islamic insurgent groups have also used the tactic in Iraq, Afghanistan, Pakistan, Sri Lanka, Yemen, and several other countries.

Terrorist attacks are also difficult to retaliate against because the terrorists officially represent no sovereign nation. After the 2001 attacks on the World Trade Center buildings in New York City, the United States attacked first Afghanistan, where al-Qaeda had its headquarters, and later Iraq. American forces defeated the ruling regimes in both countries, although the subsequent wars dragged on for many years. The U.S. invasion led to no lasting or significant peace for Iraq. And U.S. withdrawal from Afghanistan in 2021 allowed the Taliban, the very group that Americans had ousted twenty years before, to regain governing power in that country.

As for the difficulty of retaliation against terrorist attacks. Note that it was almost a decade after the attacks on the World Trade center that United States forces were able to find the supposed mastermind behind that deadly plan. In 2011, a team of U.S. Navy SEALs tracked down al-Qaeda leader Osama bin Laden not in Afghanistan but in neighboring Pakistan.

Tracking the Centuries

1832: Carl von Clausewitz's book *On War*, published after his death, teaches deliberate devastation.

1854: French and British infantrymen with new breech-loading rifles outgun Russians armed with muskets in the Crimean War.

1861: A determined Confederate force routs Union troops at the first Battle of Bull Run in Virginia.

1899: British troops fight Boer rebels in the Transvaal, South Africa.

1914–18: Parallel trenches define the Western Front of WWI, stretching from the North Sea to Switzerland.

1945: Atomic bombs devastate the cities of Hiroshima and Nagasaki, forcing Japan's government to surrender and ending WWII.

1973: The Vietnam War nears an end as U.S. forces withdraw and North Vietnamese troops take possession of the south.

October–December 2001: The United States bombs and then invades Afghanistan with ground troops, overthrowing the ruling Taliban government.

2011: A team of U.S. Navy SEALs attacks a residential compound in Abbottabad, Pakistan, where they find and kill al-Qaeda founder and leader Osama bin Laden.

2021: U.S. forces withdraw from Afghanistan after 20 years. The former rulers, the Taliban, regain control.

5
Meeting the Movers and Shakers

Find out about people who have become legendary — and in some cases mythic — for founding cities, societies, civilizations, and cultures.

Meet warriors, raiders, and tacticians whose lasting fame rests on the battles they fought — for conquest, defense, or a cause — and the foes they challenged.

Trek alongside explorers in search of new frontiers, or treasure, or a way to get somewhere before any other human being.

Get the scoop on rebels and revolutionaries who fought for freedom and self-determination to cut the reins of authority held by royalty and foreign overlords.

Chapter **19**

Starting Something Legendary

Societies, nations, and cultures don't just happen. Well, maybe they do, but somebody always takes credit. Or a few hundred years after the fact, somebody looks back and assigns credit for the founding of the city-state, the empire, the nation, or the culture.

REMEMBER

In Chapter 3, I talk about the way historians label eras, movements, and trends, choosing what to include and what to leave out. Trying to make sense of the hodgepodge of human experience, historians have to make choices.

In this chapter, I cover only a fraction of history's founders; they're my choices based on their impact in their own times and their political and cultural legacies. (Okay, one or two made the cut just because I felt like putting them in.) You'll find out how some of those legacies rest more on reputations and stories than on demonstrable accomplishments. But you can also glimpse some of the ways that exceptionally able people laid the foundations for great nations and their laws.

Spinning Legends

Many historical figures, even in relatively recent times, take on mythic stature. Those from long ago can be shrouded in such heavy layers of lore that the truth about them and what they did may never be known. Did a demigod really ever found a city-state? Did a wizard's spell ever grace an enchanted age? My guess is that no, those things didn't happen. All the following legends may have been inspired by real leaders, or they could be make-believe, but they affected history all the same:

>> **Agamemnon** (legendary, but probably based on a real king of the 12th century BC): In *The Iliad,* a Greek epic poem credited to Homer, King Agamemnon commands the alliance of fellow Greeks (or the pre-Greeks called *Achaeans*) who besiege Troy. Agamemnon, the wealthy ruler of Mycenae, was the brother of Menelaus, king of Sparta. The Greeks had a bone to pick with Troy because the Trojan prince Paris stole Menelaus's beautiful wife, Helen. Because *The Iliad* is laced with supernatural acts by the gods, nobody can say how much of it is literally true, but many centuries of Greeks found cultural identity in the tale. (For more about *The Iliad* and the Trojan War, see Chapter 2.)

>> **Romulus** (mythical, although his legend could be based on a king of the eighth or seventh century BC): In a story about Rome's founding, Romulus is one of the twin sons of Mars (the god, not the planet or the candy bar) conceived when Mars dallied with a Vestal Virgin (a priestess of Vesta, another goddess; see the nearby sidebar "Vesta's girls"). There are many variations of the story, including some in which Hercules was the twins' dad. In most, the mythical King Amulius of Alba Longa throws the illegitimate infants in the Tiber River, where a river god protects them, and wash up on the riverbank at the future site of Rome. A she-wolf finds them and suckles the babies. As young men, they clash with King Amulius and Romulus kills him, then the twins set out to build their own city, Rome. (It took more than a day.) They argue about the city site, Romulus gets mad and kills Remus, and later, a thunderstorm blows Romulus away. How much of this wild tale is true? Probably none of it, but Romulus still gets credited as being the first Roman king. (Romulus's brother is not the same as Uncle Remus, an American fictional character who told fables about talking rabbits, bears, and foxes.)

>> **King Arthur** (perhaps sixth century AD): Maybe, just maybe, Arthur was a real person. Scholars and enthusiasts have suggested many historical figures as the real-life inspiration for the legend. Yet the history of Wales around the time when a real Arthur may have fought and ruled is exceedingly murky. Among the more intriguing possibilities is a Welsh king, Owain Ddantgwyn, who could have united his fellow Celts against invading Germanic tribes. If so, Ddantgwyn may have given himself the battle name Arth-Ursus, combining the Welsh and Latin words for bear. Welsh chronicles say that Arthur died fighting in 537, a date fairly consistent with what little is known about Ddantgwyn. Other candidates for the role of King Arthur include Scots and Romans, but the most famous Arthurian tales are the fanciful inventions of Sir Thomas Malory, written 900 years after any real Arthur would have lived. Based on legends, not history, the tales are fiction.

Uniting for Strength

Many a founder is the one person strong enough for other leaders to rally around. The leaders in this section made a difference through a combination of physical force and force of personality:

>> **Saul** (11th century BC): Saul became the first king of the Israelites after Samuel, a holy man, poured oil on Saul's head. (As the greasy pompadour hairstyle was not yet in vogue, this oil was not a grooming aid.) By anointing Saul, Samuel signaled that (according to their faith) Saul was God's choice to unite a tribal confederation of Jews. Saul defeated the Philistines and ruled the Israelites from his capital at Hebron. As king, Saul took over religious

ceremonial duties, angering the high priest, that same Samuel. So, Samuel began to favor David, a brave young war hero. David was best pals with Saul's son and married Saul's daughter, making him a member of the family but also making Saul jealous of all the attention paid to David. Samuel secretly anointed David as the next king. After Saul and his son Jonathan died in another battle against the Philistines, David became leader of the tribe of Judah, later reuniting the Israelites as their second king.

» **Qin Shi Huang** (259–210 BC): This king, whose name is sometimes written Shi Huangdi, became known as an innovative warrior who adopted iron weapons and told his cavalry to ditch the chariots and sit right on top of those horses, making them faster and more adaptable. With his father held hostage by a hostile neighboring state, the 13-year-old prince, then called Zhao Zheng, became king of the state of Qin, which was about 600 miles southeast of modern Beijing. Until he came of age in 238 BC, a regent ruled in his place. When he took personal control of the throne, he began exiling and executing rivals for power. Qin was by that time already a powerful kingdom, but Zhao Zheng set out to conquer the rulers of neighboring lands. He used not just clever warfare, but also espionage and bribery, until he could name himself Qin Shi Huang, or First Emperor of a united China. Then the emperor standardized writing and units of measure, including weights, across the lands he had conquered. This conformity helped successive dynasties rule China as a unified land. He feuded with Confucian scholars (see Chapter 10 to find out about Confucianism), burned Confucian books, and surrounded himself with alchemists and magicians. His tomb, full of terra-cotta warriors to protect him in the afterlife, is an archaeological and historical gold mine. Shi Huangdi's own Qin Dynasty survived him by only four years, until 206 BC, when the long-lasting Han Dynasty came to power. Yet the name Qin (also spelled Chi'in) is the root of the name *China*. (See Chapter 4 for more about early civilization in China.)

» **Clovis** (about 465–511 AD): Roman officials trying to hang onto Gaul (or France) after the Western Roman Empire crumbled had to give up when Clovis, the king of the Franks, took over. After he succeeded his father, Childeric, Clovis extended his rule over everything between the Somme and Loire rivers by 496 AD. That year, Clovis was the first Frankish king to convert to Christianity. Credit his wife, a princess from Burgundy, for that conversion. If Clovis ever said, "My wife is a saint," he was more right than he knew; the Catholic Church later canonized her as St. Clotilde. When Clovis converted, so did several thousand of his warriors. As Frankish leaders did in those days, Clovis had to battle Visigoths and Ostrogoths (Germanic barbarian tribes) to stay in power.

- **Alfred the Great of England** (849–99 AD): The Danes were moving in on the Saxons when Alfred came to power as king of Wessex (the Western Saxons). Danes had their own kingdom in the north of England, and they were expanding into such Anglo-Saxon parts of Briton as Northumbria and East Anglia. Alfred (see Chapter 6) put a stop to that at the Battle of Edington in 878 AD. Then he pushed back, regaining London in 886 AD. He assembled a standing army, navy, and network of forts that gave him the military advantage over his northern neighbors. Alfred got the Saxons together with other English peoples, descendants of fellow Germanic tribes such as the Angles and Jutes, so they could work together against the Danes. He emphasized Christianity (as opposed to Norse paganism) and literacy, and he codified laws. No other English king or queen is called "the Great." Alfred paved the way for his grandson, Æthelstan, to unite the territory ever since defined as England under a single king.

- **Brian Boru** (about 926–1014 AD): Also called Brian Boroimhe (meaning Brian of the Tribute), this Irish warrior was a chief of the Dal Cais clan and fought his way to the Crown of Leinster. (See Chapter 6). The fact that the Irish were tired of absorbing Viking blows helped Brian rally support. He fought regional rivals until he united Ireland, which was the beginning of a nation (although many hard centuries lay ahead). Brian's forces beat the Vikings at Clontarf, but Brian, by then too old to join the fray himself, was murdered by fleeing Viking warriors.

Playing for Power

When the going gets tough, the toughest found dynasties. The guys in this list didn't need assertiveness training; they stepped forward to shove rivals out of the way as they made themselves, and their governments, the ultimate authority. Stand aside for military strongmen and emperors:

- **Augustus Caesar** (63 BC–14 AD): Rome's first official emperor was Gaius Julius Caesar Octavianus, or Octavian, the son of a senator and a great nephew of *the* Julius Caesar. (See Chapter 20 for more about Julius Caesar and Chapter 5 for more on the Roman Empire.) When conspirators killed Julius Caesar, who was dictator, Octavian was a student, but he closed his books; raised an army, dealt with the assassins; and defeated his rival for power, Mark Antony. Then he forced the Senate to make him consul — the top administrative job in the Roman government. Later that year, 43 BC, Octavian made a deal with Antony and another Roman big shot, Lepidus, to form a triumvirate (or "ruling three"). Octavian's part of the bargain was Africa, Sardinia, and Sicily. Later, he got the entire western half of the Roman world, and after defeating Antony and the Egyptian queen Cleopatra at Actium in 31 BC, Octavian became sole ruler. The Senate gave him the name *Augustus,* or "exalted." Under his rule, Rome saw peace, reform, and rebuilding. The Roman Senate declared him *Pater Patriae* (father of his country) in 2 BC. When he died, the Senate declared him a god.

» **Charlemagne** (742–814 AD): The Franks, like the Romans before them, had problems with intruders. Barbarians from up north kept horning in on Gaul (today's France), and there were rumblings from the Muslims in Spain when Charlemagne (Charles the Great) came to power — first as king of the eastern Franks (his brother Carloman got the western bunch) and then as Great King of the Franks in 771 AD. The title *Great King* meant that he ruled over lesser kings and princes, which was the feudal style of leadership. Charlemagne brought Europe together under one rule as nobody had since the Romans, fighting Saxons, Avars, and Lombards to do it. On Christmas Day 800 AD, Pope Leo III crowned Charlemagne Emperor of the West or Holy Roman Emperor, starting the Holy Roman Empire (which had almost nothing to do with the original Roman Empire). Charlemagne built palaces and churches, and promoted Christianity, education, agriculture, and the arts. Commerce thrived under his administration, which came to be known as the Carolingian Renaissance — a *little* awakening hundreds of years before the big Awakening. The empire fell apart after he died, though, because Charlie's sons lacked his vision and authority. (For more about Charlemagne and his family, see Chapter 6.)

» **William the Conqueror** (about 1028–87): When St. Edward the Confessor died, he left a mess. As king of England, he apparently designated one noble — William, Duke of Normandy — and then another — Harold Godwinson — to succeed him. Harold took the Crown as Harold II, but William thought that Harold had promised to uphold *his* claim to the throne. William and his Norman army invaded, killed Harold at the Battle of Hastings, was crowned king on Christmas Day 1066, and forever after has been *the Conqueror.* He stayed in power by replacing all the leaders of the old Anglo-Saxon nobility with a new ruling class of French-speaking Normans, Bretons, and Flemings. Their descendants are English nobility.

» **Genghis Khan** (around 1167–1227): Before he was Genghis Khan, he was Temujin, who at age 13 became chief of a desperately poor clan of nomadic Mongols. Temujin was hungry, so he went to work defeating other clans, including the Naimans and the Tangut (names that nobody much remembers anymore, but they were tough in their time). In 1206, after the Turkish Uigurs bowed down to him, Temujin changed his name to Genghis Khan, which means "very great ruler" or "universal king." In several campaigns, he overran the empire of North China and other East Asian territories. Between 1206 and his death in 1227, he extended the Mongol Empire from the Pacific Ocean west into Eastern Europe.

» **Babur** (1483–1530): He was called Zahir-ud-din Muhammad before taking the name Babur, which means "tiger" in Arabic. The first Mogul emperor of India, Babur was born in Ferghana, Kyrgyzstan. A genius at war, he invaded India and defeated leaders of its separate kingdoms to unite an empire and found a dynasty marked by its mixed Mongol and Turkish origins and by its attitude of conciliation toward the Hindu majority. Babur was interested in architecture, music, and literature. He passed these interests down through a line of successors whose empire remained strong until the early 18th century but eventually fell under the domination of the British East India Company in the 19th century. (See Chapter 8 for more on European influence in 18th- and 19th-century Asia.)

Building Bridges

The way to build something big — from a house to an empire — is to put together smaller components. As in carpentry, so in the hammering together of nations, regions, and cultures. The people in this section used means as diverse as battles and alliances to link geographic, religious, and ethnic components into new combinations. Some of them built so well that their constructions still stand:

» **Kublai Khan** (1214–94): Genghis Khan's grandson established his capital where Beijing is now. As Mongol emperor of China and founder of the Yuan Dynasty, starting in 1279, he was vigorous and forceful in the way he used power, launching military campaigns against Java, Burma, Japan, and other Asian nations, although with limited success (none against Japan, for example). Kublai Khan, like many of history's most interesting people, was a study in contradictions. He was adaptable, making the Chinese style of civilization his own, yet he kept his Mongol ruling class separate from the Chinese natives and appointed many foreigners, especially Muslims, to high government offices while making Buddhism the state religion. Some accounts describe him as a cruel ruler, others as reasonable and merciful. His court is legendary for luxury and splendor.

» **Ferdinand** (1452–1516) and **Isabella** (1451–1504): When Ferdinand, king of Aragon (part of today's northern Spain), married Isabella, queen of Castille (also part of today's northern Spain), in 1469, their kingdoms got hitched too, coming together as the forerunner of modern Spain. Co-ruled by this happening couple, Spain finally ousted the last of its Moorish rulers in 1492, when Ferdinand and Isabella took over the Sultanate of Granada. That same year, Isabella sponsored Christopher Columbus on his voyage to find a westward sea route to Asia (see Chapter 8). That led to Spain's supremacy in the Americas. In 1478, Ferdinand and Isabella, with backing from Pope Sixtus IV, began the Spanish Inquisition, a Catholic reform movement aimed at rooting out non-Christian (especially Islamic and Jewish) ideas that had dominated the Iberian Peninsula (Spain and Portugal) over centuries of rule by Moorish caliphates. (The Moors had been tolerant of Judaism.) The Inquisition also helped keep the Protestant Reformation out of Spain (see Chapter 14 for more about the Reformation). In 1512, after Isabella died, Phillip completed Spain's unification when he took over the kingdom of Navarre.

» **Nobunaga Oda** (1534–82), **Toyotomi Hideyoshi** (1536–98), and **Tokugawa Ieyasu** (1543–1616): The three great unifiers of Japan finally broke the cycle of warring feudal lords dominating the country. Noble-born Nobunaga Oda subjugated Owari Province, threw out the sitting *shogun* (a feudal big boss), occupied the capital at Kyoto in 1568, and defeated the priests at Osaka, destroying the power of the Buddhists. Just to make sure that Buddhism didn't bounce back, he briefly encouraged Christianity. When he died, he controlled half of Japan, paving the way for his general, the lowborn Hideyoshi Toyotomi and Hideyoshi's erstwhile ally, Tokugawa Ieyasu, to unite the country at last. Toyotomi banned swords for anybody but the *samurai*, or warrior class. Tokugawa eventually turned on Toyotomi and his family, and established the long-lived but repressive and isolationist Tokugawa Shogunate, which lasted until the mid-19th century.

» **James I of England/James VI of Scotland** (1566–1625): Scotland's King James didn't conquer neighboring England; he simply ascended its throne as the legitimate successor (through his English great-great-grandmother) to the childless Elizabeth I in 1603. His position unified the Crowns of the two realms — the first step toward the unification of the two kingdoms, which happened in 1707, when the Act of Union created the United Kingdom. After James I became their king, the English no longer tried to annex Scotland, because there was no point to it. James was a scholarly type who wrote pamphlets, sponsored Shakespeare's acting troupe, and commissioned an enduring and beautiful English translation of the Christian scripture known as the *King James Bible.* He imprisoned and executed Sir Walter Raleigh — not because he hated Raleigh's newfangled habit of smoking tobacco (which he did), but for other offenses against the Crown. James also hated the extreme form of Calvinist–Protestant belief called Puritanism that gained momentum in England at the beginning of the 17th century. (Find out more about the Puritans in Chapter 14.) James drew criticism for his habit of playing favorites and resisted Puritan pressure to purge Catholic practices from the English Church. Ironically, Catholic conspirators such as Guy Fawkes, not Puritans, tried to blow up the new king and Parliament in the Gunpowder Plot of 1605 — and almost succeeded. (For more about Fawkes and the Gunpowder Plot, see chapters 3 and 22).

» **Frederick the Great** (1712–86): As a young prince, Frederick II of Prussia studied military skills, music (he even composed some), and French literature. As king, he fought the neighboring Austrians and other Germanic states, adding Silesia (along the Oder River in east-central Europe) and parts of western Germany to his kingdom. In the First Partition of Poland (1772), he acquired part of Poland. (Poland had ruled part of Prussia until his father's time.) Prussia doubled in size under Fred's rule and became a leading power, both militarily and economically, and the forerunner of modern Germany.

» **George Washington** (1732–99): The first president of the United States of America used enslaved people as servants and laborers. In the 21st century, it's impossible to forgive that practice. Yet there was a lot more to Washington, who set a remarkable precedent in 1796 by declining to run for a third term of office. Many a new nation has stumbled over the issue of peaceful transfer of power, as the first administration balks at handing over authority to successors. Washington achieved this crucial transition gracefully. (He had turned down Congress's earlier offer to make him king.) With natural authority rather than rhetoric, Washington brought disagreeing Americans together at two critical times. In the 1770s, the self-possessed Virginia planter and British military veteran was the clear choice to lead a revolutionary army. In the 1780s, his willingness to revise the Articles of Confederation (the loose agreement by which the newborn country tried to operate) led to the drafting of the U.S. Constitution. It's hard to imagine the American Revolution succeeding without him. It's even more difficult to imagine the nation succeeding without his example. For more on George Washington, check out *U.S. History For Dummies,* 4th Edition, by Steve Wiegand (John Wiley & Sons, Inc.).

» **Nelson Mandela** (1918–2013): Like George Washington, Nelson Rolihlahla Mandela could be listed along with other revolutionaries in Chapter 22, but his greatest legacy lies in his commitment to reconciliation as the first post-apartheid president of South Africa. Raised to become a Thembu tribal chief, Mandela was a college student when he started working to overturn *apartheid,* the legal separation of races. As a young Johannesburg lawyer in the 1950s, he organized a black underground movement. He was arrested and convicted of conspiracy to overthrow the government and sentenced to life in prison.

During 27 years in jail, Mandela became a worldwide symbol for justice. After his release in 1990, he helped negotiate the end of apartheid; shared the Nobel Peace Prize with F.W. de Klerk; and at age 75 succeeded de Klerk as president, becoming his country's first leader chosen in an all-race election. Never seeking revenge, Mandela consulted his former captors as he rebuilt South African society. When he left office in 1999, crime and poverty still plagued South Africa, and racial tensions persisted well into the 21st century, but Mandela had seen the country through an extraordinary transition.

Writing Laws

Often, a society's identity flows from the way it defines morality and administers justice. Consider the fact that most modern jurisprudence is based on precedent. The way an issue was decided before becomes part of the current definition of what is legal or illegal, right or wrong. This precedence business doesn't date back just a few decades or even a few centuries; it's rooted in decisions about justice and punishment that go all the way to the foundations of human society. No wonder so many lawgivers — good and bad — are remembered in history. A tiny sampling follows:

>> **Ur-Nammu** and **Shulgi** (22nd and 21st centuries BC): A ruler of the ancient Mesopotamian kingdom of Ur, in today's Iraq, instituted the earliest code of laws that survives in written form. Which ruler? Researchers aren't sure, but it was either Ur-Nammu, who is credited in the preface to the code, or his son and successor Shulgi, who may have been the one who codified the list of rules. Modern archaeologists unearthed two fragments of clay tablets in 1952 at the ruins of Nippur, a Sumerian city in what is now Iraq. They could read only five laws from the artifact. More copies were later unearthed at Ur, allowing for the translation of 30 laws that show that even 4,200 years ago, civilized people had a legal system requiring testimony under oath, as well as special judges who could order a guilty party to pay damages to a victim. The code also allowed for the dismissal of corrupt officials, protection for the poor, and punishment proportionate to the crime.

TIP

If you ever have a chance to visit the Istanbul Archaeological Museums, near the Topkapi Palace in Istanbul, Turkey, you can see Ur-Nammu's code, or at least the two fragments uncovered in 1952.

» **Moses** (14th or 13th century BC): The Bible's book of Exodus says that God gave mankind the Ten Commandments through his servant Moses, a Hebrew reared as an Egyptian prince. It says that Moses led the Israelites out of slavery in Egypt and on a meandering, 40-year route through the desert to Canaan. With his brother Aaron, he set up the religious community of Israel and founded its traditions through practice and writings. Moses is considered to be the author of the first several books of the Bible, the only source of information about these events. (For more about Judaism and Moses, see Chapter 10.)

Moses's story has inspired some bad films. The worst may be 1975's ill-conceived epic *Moses,* with Burt Lancaster in the title role and cheesy special effects undercutting his performance. Director Cecil B. DeMille did it better in 1956 when he made *The Ten Commandments.* In that one, Charlton Heston plays Moses, heading an all-star cast speaking nonsensically shallow, pseudo-Biblical lines amidst marvelous photography. The animated musical cartoon *Prince of Egypt* from 1998 may be the best version of the Moses story on film.

» **Draco** (seventh century BC): Athens picked this official to write its laws, the first such written code in Greece, in about 620 BC. Draco's severe laws made the state exclusive prosecutor of those accused of crime, outlawing vigilante justice. But many offenses merited the death penalty, and the word *draconian* still refers to harsh punishment. Yet Athenians loved Draco. As Draco entered an auditorium to attend a reception in his honor, Athenians gave him the customary celebratory greeting, showering him with their hats and cloaks. He fell down and was strangely still, so they pulled all the clothing off him and found him dead — suffocated.

» **Solon** (about 630 BC–about 560 BC): Solon was an Athenian statesman and reformer, not to mention a wizard at reciting verse. This Greek's breakthrough as a public figure came when he spurred Athenians to military action against the Megarians with a rousing poem. His eloquence made Solon the choice to rewrite Draco's harsh code of laws. Solon had other talents too: He reorganized public institutions, including the senate and the popular assembly; minted coins; reformed weights and measures; and strengthened Athenian trade. The result is that his name came to be a synonym for *legislator,* especially in 20th-century newspapers in which the word *"congressman"* wouldn't fit in a headline.

» **Justinian** (482 AD–565 AD): "The things which are common to all are the air, running water, the sea, and the seashores" is a bit of Roman law, interpreted and set down by the Byzantine Emperor Justinian in a series of books that have been an important source for legal codes ever since. The word *justice* comes from Justinian's name.

TECHNICAL STUFF

If you're wondering why a Byzantine emperor was writing Roman law, remember that the name *Byzantine* is a label that historians have given to the Eastern Roman Empire, which survived until 1453 — almost a thousand years after the Western Roman Empire finally collapsed in 476. (For more about the Romans and the Byzantine Empire, turn to chapters 5 and 6.)

>> **Muhammad** (about 570 AD–about 632 AD): The son of a poor Arab merchant, Muhammad was orphaned at age 6 and grew up tending sheep. As a young man, he led caravans owned by a rich widow. Later, he married her and became a merchant. But for a businessman, Muhammad (sometimes spelled Mohammed or Mohamet) was a bit of a loner who liked to go off and think. He was 40 when he said the Angel Gabriel commanded him in the name of God to preach the *true religion*. After a few years, Muhammad began urging people to live a pious, moral life. He taught his followers to believe in an all-powerful, all-just God, or *Allah,* whose mercy could be obtained through prayer, fasting, and the giving of alms. Authorities in Mecca, alarmed by his growing popularity, threw him out in 622 AD, so he went to Medina, where he became high judge and ruler. Mohammed led a war against enemies of Islam, taking Mecca in 630. After his last pilgrimage in 632, he fell ill and died. His moral rules, set down in the Quran, remain a basis of law throughout the Islamic world. (You can find out more about Muhammad, Islam, and the Arabs in chapters 6 and 10.)

>> **James Madison** (1751–1836): The fourth president of the United States kept enslaved people and used their labor. From a 21st century perspective, that casts a disfiguring shadow over his accomplishments. Yet his knowledge of history and keen ability to forge compromises served Madison well at a 1787 convention in Philadelphia. A graduate of Princeton (then called the College of New Jersey), Madison represented his native Virginia at the convention. The delegates were supposed to beef up the Articles of Confederation, governing relations among the newly independent American states. Instead, the convention threw out the articles and replaced them with the U.S. Constitution. Influenced by Enlightenment political philosophers such as Charles Montesquieu, (more about the Enlightenment in Chapter 14), Madison read widely and thought deeply about how best to govern a society. He studied the democracy of ancient Athens, the Roman Republic, and European federations such as the Holy Roman Empire, and he knew that the United States needed a strong central government, so he deftly managed agreements allowing the convention to hammer out a working document. Many of Madison's ideas became foundations of U.S. law, which is why he's called the Father of the Constitution. Madison's notes also contributed to the historical record, providing the most complete account of the Constitutional convention. For more on Madison and the Constitution, see *U.S. History For Dummies,* by Steve Wiegand (John Wiley & Sons, Inc.).

Tracking the Centuries

About 2200 BC: The king of Ur, a Mesopotamian kingdom (today's Iraq), institutes a legal system that requires testimony under oath and authorizes judges to order a guilty party to pay damages to a victim.

About 230 BC: Shi Huangdi, self-proclaimed First Emperor of China, standardizes writing and units of measure across the lands he has conquered.

630 AD: Muhammad leads his army of Islam to capture Mecca.

886 AD: Alfred the Great, formerly king of the West Saxon, becomes king of the Anglo-Saxons and wrests control of London from Danish forces.

1066: At the Battle of Hastings, invader William of Normandy defeats the forces of Harold II, conquering England.

1206-1227: Genghis Khan rules a Mongol Empire that, at its height, stretched from the Pacific Ocean west beyond the Black Sea and into Eastern Europe.

1469: Queen Isabella of Castille and King Ferdinand of Aragon get married, forging their lands into a forerunner of modern Spain.

1772: Frederick the Great of Prussia adds West Prussia to his kingdom in the First Partition of Poland.

1787: At the Constitutional Convention in Philadelphia, James Madison's knowledge and bright ability to apply history's lessons earn him the title Father of the Constitution.

1990: Nelson Mandela walks out of jail after 27 years in the custody of the South African government.

» Casting long shadows with Alexander, Caesar, Napoleon, and Hitler

» Crossing the Alps by elephant with Carthage's Hannibal

» Fending off the English with Scotland's Robert the Bruce

» Commanding tanks across North Africa's desert with Germany's Rommel

Chapter **20**

Battling Toward Immortality

"War is the father of all and the king of all," said Heraclitus, a Greek–Ephesian philosopher of the fifth century BC. "It proves some people gods, and some people men; it makes some people slaves, and some people free." War also makes people famous. Those in this chapter are among many more who owe their reputations to battles won or lost.

WARNING

Neither complete nor absolute, my headings in this section — like any historical labels — are arbitrary. That means I made them up. History authors have some latitude, after all.

In this chapter, you can find my selected examples of some of history's feistiest fighters. You'll probably notice, too, that many of these fierce characters had other distinctions, too. You may have already discovered Genghis Khan and other battle-scarred founders of empires in Chapter 19. Here, you can check out some more of history's famous military leaders. You'll meet other generals remembered for their ability to amass lands, some who are considered especially ferocious, clever tacticians, and steadfast defenders.

Towering Over Their Times

Some historical figures are so huge that . . . well, they're just *major*. That's why I give them a category to themselves. Alexander the Great, Julius Caesar, Napoleon, and Hitler changed the world profoundly and achieved monstrous fame (or notoriety) for ambitious, world-wrenching military conquests:

» **Alexander the Great** (356–323 BC): By the time Alexander the Great died in Babylon, everybody knew about Macedon's brilliant young prince–soldier–general–king–emperor. The kingdom of Macedon lay mostly in what is now the northern Greek province of Macedonia. (The modern nation of North Macedonia is part of a larger region that the Romans later labeled Macedonia just to confuse us, apparently.) The son of Philip II, Alex thought he was descended from gods and loved the epic poems of Homer. Enjoying the best upbringing available, he studied under the philosopher Aristotle, his tutor. (Aristotle appears in Chapter 11.) As a teenager, Alexander commanded his dad's Macedonian–Greek forces, showing sharp military skills and remarkable maturity. After his dad's assassination, he took the throne as Alexander III and took the world by storm. He was handsome, charismatic, and so popular that many of the peoples he conquered welcomed his rule, but he also had a temper and lashed out at those closest to him. Alexander's brief empire stretched beyond the limits of what people of the time considered to be the known world (see Chapter 4).

» **Julius Caesar** (about 100–44 BC): Gaius Julius Caesar didn't become emperor (at least, he didn't wear that title), but his ambition helped bring down the ailing Roman Republic, and his death led to the new Roman Empire. A talented general, Caesar pushed Rome's frontier all the way to Europe's Atlantic coast in the Gallic Wars. In Egypt, he put Cleopatra VII back on the throne after her brother kicked her out. Why did Caesar help Cleopatra? The fact that she bore him a son (or at least said it was his) may be a clue. In trouble-wracked Rome, he formed a three-man ruling body, or *triumvirate,* with Pompey and Crassus, but the arrangement dissolved into a power struggle. In 49 BC, Caesar led his troops south across the Rubicon River toward Rome. This move violated a Roman law intended to protect the city against a military coup, but Caesar had come too far to turn back. His action started civil war, and the phrase *crossing the Rubicon* has meant "point of no return" ever since. He emerged with sole control, taking the title Dictator for Life. A group fed up with Caesar's airs assassinated him in 44 BC.

>> **Napoleon Bonaparte** (1769–1821): The Mediterranean Island of Corsica became part of France the year Napoleon was born there. He attended French military school and joined the nation's service at age 16. The French Revolution of 1789 proved to be an opportune moment for a smart, ambitious young officer, because just about every monarch in Europe declared war on the revolutionary government in Paris. Napoleon scored important victories, became a general, and in 1799 joined co-conspirators in a *coup d'état,* or takeover of government. Napoleon emerged as sole ruler of France and conqueror of neighboring countries; by 1807, he ruled Europe's largest empire since the Romans. His reforms improved education, banking, and the legal system. (Many countries still base their laws on his Napoleonic Code.) Because his wife, Josephine, had not borne him an heir, Napoleon dumped her for Marie Louise, an Austrian princess. When their son was born, Napoleon made the baby king of Rome, a title traditionally bestowed upon the heir apparent to the French throne. (The title had nothing to do with Rome, but everything to do with the lasting cultural/political influence of the ancient Roman Empire.)

Napoleon's biggest mistake was his 1812 invasion of Russia, in which thousands of his troops froze to death or starved (see Chapter 9). The next year, Russia joined Austria, Prussia, and Sweden to crush Napoleon at Leipzig, Germany. His enemies exiled Napoleon to the Mediterranean island of Elba, where in 1814 he raised a small army and headed toward Paris. Napoleon ruled again for a period famously called the *Hundred Days,* which ended in 1815 at the Battle of Waterloo in Belgium, as English and Prussian forces delivered a defeat from which Napoleon couldn't rebound. This time, he was sent to St. Helena, an island in the south Atlantic. He died of stomach cancer six years later, although there were rumors that he'd been poisoned.

>> **Adolf Hitler** (1889–1945): Hitler, shown in Figure 20-1, wanted to be an artist, but the Vienna Academy turned him down twice. Directionless for a time, the young Austrian eventually enlisted in a Bavarian army regiment and served honorably as an infantryman in World War I. After the war, he turned to right-wing politics to vent his rage at the terms of peace, which were punitive toward Germany. As leader of the extremist National Socialist German Workers' Party, he tried to overthrow the Bavarian government in 1923 and was jailed. Over the next several years, he built support for his Nazi party, blaming so-called outsiders, especially Jews, for weakening Germany. In 1932, Hitler won the office of chancellor and then suspended Germany's constitution. When President Paul von Hindenburg died in 1934, Hitler became president and supreme commander — *Der Führer* (the leader). He ordered Jews, Arabs, Roma, homosexuals, and people with disabilities (especially those with cognitive differences), to be rounded up and sent to concentration camps, where hundreds at a time were gassed. Nazis killed at least six million Jews under Hitler's leadership.

After forcefully uniting Germany with Austria, Hitler invaded Poland in 1939, starting World War II. As Germany's war strategy deteriorated under Hitler's personal direction, Colonel Claus von Stauffenberg of the German command staff led a conspiracy to assassinate Hitler. The attempt failed.

Having escaped death, *Der Führer* purged the army of anyone he suspected of disloyalty, which weakened Germany further. As Soviet troops advanced on Berlin, Hitler hid in an air-raid shelter with his longtime mistress, Eva Braun. He and Braun married in that bunker and then, determined to avoid capture by the Allies, the newlyweds killed themselves. Germany had lost the war.

FIGURE 20-1: Adolph Hitler started World War II in 1939 when he sent German troops into Poland.

Shawshots / Alamy Stock Photo

Building Empires

A conqueror's motivation isn't just to show toughness. Virtually every one of history's most fearsome characters was fighting for material gain. Motives for conquest included land, of course. Conquerors sought more territory and more people to rule because of the prestige that such gains brought — and because additional territory and population brought greater trade advantages and military power. Other incentives included booty (in this context, not an anatomical term, but a word for goods stolen in warfare) and tribute (money paid to a conqueror by the conquered). The following historical figures were determined to acquire the spoils that go to the victor:

» **Nebuchadnezzar II** (about 630–562 BC): Before succeeding to the throne of Babylon, Nebuchadnezzar led his father's army to victory over Egypt. Crowned in 605 BC, Nebuchadnezzar launched campaigns against western neighbors.

Babylonian forces captured Jerusalem and took thousands of Jews, including the newly crowned King Jehoiachin, back to Babylon as slaves. Jehoiachin remained in captivity for 37 years. Nebuchadnezzar appointed Zedekiah as his vassal king in Jerusalem. (The job of a *vassal king* was to govern as the deputy of an overlord, or great king.) After Zedekiah rebelled, Nebuchadnezzar came back and destroyed Jerusalem in 586 BC. Legend says that Jewish slaves built or helped build the fabulous Hanging Gardens of Babylon, a wonder of the ancient world. Historians know little about the gardens, which were destroyed long ago, but according to tradition, Nebuchadnezzar II or his predecessor, Queen Samu-ramat, ordered their construction. So little is known about Samu-ramat, however, that historians have often referred to her as semilegendary.

» **Wu Ti** (156–87 BC): Wu the Martial's original name was Lui Ch'e. An empire-building ruler of China's Han Dynasty, he annexed parts of Southern China, upper Vietnam, northern and central Korea, and the northern and western frontiers where the Hsuiung-nu nomads (a warlike people known elsewhere as Huns) roamed.

» **Attila the Hun** (about 406–453 AD): Known as the *Scourge of God,* Attila co-ruled the aggressive, nomadic Huns with his big brother Bleda, controlling a region from the Rhine to the edge of China. In 445 AD, Attila murdered Bleda and assembled a vast horde of Huns based in Hungary. In 451, when Attila invaded Gaul (France), Roman commander Aëtius (you can find him in the later section "Mounting a Defense") and king of the Visigoths Theodoric I resisted him. Attila pulled an end run into Italy, where Pope Leo I pleaded with Attila to spare Rome. Leo must have been remarkably persuasive because Attila was convinced. The Hun Empire fell apart after Attila died.

» **Canute the Great** (995–1035 AD): Canute was a tall, strong, warrior son of Sweyn Forkbeard, king of Denmark. Sweyn invaded and seized control of Anglo-Saxon England in 1013, making him king of both countries, but he died the following year. After Sweyn's death, the former Anglo-Saxon ruler, known as Æthelred the Unready (it meant "ill-advised" rather than "unprepared"), regained control, briefly. Canute responded with a devastatingly large invasion force made up largely of well-armed and provisioned Vikings from the noble houses of Scandinavia. Canute, already king of Denmark through inheritance from his father, became king of England in 1016. His warrior force of men and ships continued their aggressive campaigns until Scotland submitted to him in 1017 and he added Norway to his empire in 1028. Remarkably, he achieved peace throughout this far-flung realm. It's sometimes said that Canute thought he was such a big shot, he tried to make the waves on the sea obey him. This story is a bad rap, however. If anything like this ever happened, it was more likely that Canute was demonstrating that he was *not* some kind of god and could *not* tell nature what to do.

>> **Shaka** (about 1787–1828): The founder of the Zulu Empire conquered most of southern Africa with a military system that could deploy 40,000 well-trained, highly disciplined warriors. The downside was that they were equipped only with shields and short spears. A ruthless dictator, Shaka repressed his tribal rivals but died at the hands of his power-hungry half-brothers. Still, his tactics and empire survived for another half-century until the British used modern weapons to break the back of Zulu power in 1879.

Actor Henry Cele played the part of Shaka in two successful TV miniseries, *Shaka Zulu* in 1986, and *Shaka Zulu: The Citadel* in 2001. As always with dramatic presentations of history, neither adheres strictly to the actual history.

Launching Attacks

All the following men made their names as audacious attackers, employing speed and audacious daring, not to mention well-conceived planning, to gain the advantage over their enemies. Yet not all of them emerged as victorious in the end. Some of them lost crucial battles and ended up on the losing side:

>> **Xerxes I** (485–465 BC): Xerxes suppressed revolts all over the Persian Empire, including Babylon and Egypt. Because his dad, Darius the Great (548–486 BC), died trying to teach the Greeks a lesson, Xerxes thought he would finish the job. He burned Athens before going home to Persia, but the Greeks weren't down for long. They whipped the army that Xerxes left behind and burned the Persian fleet on the same day in 479 BC. Artabanus, his own *vizier* (captain of the guards), murdered Xerxes.

>> **Genseric** (unknown–477 AD): Genseric was one of the barbarians who threatened the Western Roman Empire during its waning decades. King of the Vandals, he took over much of Spain and from there attacked North Africa. He captured Carthage from the Romans and made it his capital. He also sacked Rome but stopped short of destroying the city in 455.

>> **Harald III Sigurdsson** (1015–66): It must have been tough to be the brother of an actual saint, but Harald seemed to cope with it. His half-brother became St. Olaf (he's listed in the section "Instigating Inspiration"), but both brothers were Norwegian Viking mercenaries. Olaf, who was king first, died in 1030 while fighting against Norwegian rebels allied with Denmark. Having to flee, Harald hired himself out as a warrior for the prince of Kiev Rus (an early edition of Russia, where Ukraine is now) before returning to Norway. There, Harald became king in 1045, earning his nickname "The Ruthless" in wars against

Denmark. He invaded England in 1066 to claim the throne after St. Edward the Confessor died, but a fellow with a similar name, Harold II of England, killed Harald. That would have been the end of the story, but William of Normandy (see Chapter 19) succeeded where Harald failed. Had it turned out differently, maybe Harald III of Norway would be Harald the Conqueror, and perhaps this book would be in Norwegian.

>> **Richard Lionheart** (1157–99): Also remembered as the Lionhearted, Richard I was king of England for a decade, starting in 1189, but he spent only five months of that time in the country. No wonder his brother John tried to steal his throne. Actually called *Coeur de Lion,* because English rulers spoke French in those days (they *were* French), he was the third son of Henry II and an outstanding soldier. Richard was on his way back from Jerusalem and the Third Crusade when he landed in a Vienna jail. (Chapter 7 has more about the Crusades.) His mom, Eleanor of Aquitaine, paid the ransom to get him released. Richard went on to fight, and die, for England's claim to lands in what is now France.

>> **Erwin Rommel** (1891–1944): Rommel, a German field marshal in World War II, made his name leading a mechanized division that charged through France to the English Channel in 1940. Rommel led more attacks on allied forces in North Africa, where his inventive tank warfare strategies earned him the name "Desert Fox." Nazi officials suspected Rommel of conspiracy in a plot to kill Hitler, and he was recalled from his post and forced to commit suicide by poison.

Mounting a Defense

Some fighters were at their best (or worst) when invaders came calling. Several of the people in the list that follows were just as aggressive and ambitious as any empire-builders known to history. It just so happened, however, that each of these fighters became known for an important defensive stand, whether it succeeded or not:

>> **Flavius Aëtius** (about 350–454 AD): For 20 years, this Roman general was in charge of keeping the barbarians at bay, which was often a losing battle. Coming from the *patrician* (or aristocratic) class, he became the empire's general-in-chief and also a consul, the top government administrator. (There's more about Roman social classes in Chapter 5.) Aëtius scored a big success at Châlons in 451 AD, when he commanded the allied forces that beat the invader Attila the Hun. After that, Aëtius was flying high, the most popular guy in the empire, which ticked off Emperor Valentinian III. The jealous emperor stabbed Aëtius to death.

>> **Charles Martel** (about 699–741 AD): The Carolingian kings of Charlemagne's family (see Chapter 19) started with Charles Martel, who ruled much of Gaul (today's France) but never got to call himself king. He was called "The Hammer," however, for his military campaigns against Saxons, Frisons, and assorted other rivals through the region. He fought the invading Muslims and kept them from penetrating Western Europe (beyond Spain, that is) at the Battle of Poitiers in 732 AD.

>> **Harold II** (about 1022–66): The last Anglo-Saxon king of England had a short, violent, disputed reign. He fought off Harald III Sigurdsson of Norway and then turned around to take on the Duke of Normandy at the Battle of Hastings. But all poor Harold got for his efforts was an arrow through the eye.

>> **Shagrat al-Durr** (unknown–1259): Also known as Shajarat, she was a onetime slave girl who married two of Egypt's sultans, ran the government from behind the scenes for years, and for two months bore the title of sultan. In 1249, her first husband, Salih Ayyub, was out of town when Crusaders under Louis IX of France landed at the mouth of the Nile. Acting for the absent sultan, Shagrat organized Egypt's defense. Her hubby returned but soon died. Shagrat pretended that Salih was still alive and kept acting in his name until her stepson Turan showed up and claimed his inheritance. Turan, with Shagrat's guidance, beat the Crusaders and took Louis prisoner. Egyptian army officers preferred Shagrat, a Turk like them, to Turan, so they killed Turan and installed Shagrat as sultan. But the Caliph (chief Muslim religious and civil leader) in Baghdad said nope, a woman wasn't allowed to be sultan. Shagrat resigned, and then wooed and married her replacement, Aibak. She remained the power behind the throne until he decided to add a new wife to his harem (a group of wives and concubines kept by a rich Muslim man), angering her. She killed Aibak in his bath, riots broke out, and harem slaves beat Shagrat with their shoes and threw her into the palace moat. Egyptians later enshrined her bones in a mosque named for her.

>> **Robert the Bruce** (1274–1329): In 1296, the Scottish Earl of Carrick, better known as Robert the Bruce, swore loyalty to the king of England, Edward I, who was trying to establish English sovereignty over Scotland. Then Bruce changed his mind and backed William Wallace, a Scottish patriot fighting the English. (You may recognize Wallace's name from Mel Gibson's 1995 film epic *Braveheart*, but don't let that throw you off. Gibson dons a kilt in the movie, but kilts weren't in fashion until the 17th century.)

After Edward tortured and beheaded Wallace in 1306, Robert the Bruce advanced his own claim on Scotland's Crown by killing political rival John Comyn with a dagger. Bruce was crowned Scotland's king, and after a brief exile in Ireland (some people didn't consider this stabbing business to be fair), he came back in 1307 and thrashed the English at Loudoun Hill. Bruce and his lads trounced the English again at Bannockburn in 1314. Finally, the English signed the Treaty of Northampton (1328), agreeing that Bruce was the rightful king.

Devising Tactics

A battle's outcome often hinges on strength, as in superior numbers or better weapons. But strategy and tactics just as often make the difference between winner and loser. When two forces are evenly matched, strategic advantage comes in second only to luck in determining the result. The following fighters used wits and innovation, although not all of them achieved success:

» **Sun Tzu** (About 544-496 BC): He may have been a minister to the Chinese King Helü of Wu, but there's little historical evidence of his life. Tradition says he was a philosopher, military strategist, and commander of troops, but his reputation rests upon a long-lasting and influential, 13-chapter book, *The Art of War*, credited to him. As its title indicates, it's a treatise on military strategy but the approach includes finding alternatives to battle and even alternatives to war itself. Sun Tzu's stratagems include delay, espionage, employing misinformation, and building alliances. They extend to the strategy of submitting to a superior enemy, temporarily, to gain an advantage. The book's great influence on military thinking, and on other strategic pursuits such as business, has led to it being studied continuously in Asia and around the world.

» **Hannibal** (247–182 BC): In his mid-20s, Hannibal of Carthage subdued most of southern Spain. He blindsided the Romans in the Second Punic War (refer to Chapter 5) by invading Italy from the north, over the Alps mountain range, with battle-trained elephants. (The Romans assumed that Hannibal would come at them by sea from North Africa.) Scoring multiple victories against Roman defenders, Carthage controlled much of the Italian peninsula for a decade. The occupation crumbled, finally, when Carthage called Hannibal home to defend against a Roman invasion force led by Scipio Africanus (below).

Scipio Africanus (About 236-183 BC): In full, he was Publius Cornelius Scipio Africanus, a Roman general best known for defeating Hannibal in the Second Punic War. Before attacking Carthaginian forces in Spain in 209 BC, he trained his army in novel tactics that involved splitting his main force to push the enemy from its flanks. It was something he learned from Carthage's Hannibal. Then, after being elected Roman consul in 205 BC, Scipio attacked the Carthaginian forces in North Africa, considered an audacious move and one unexpected by the enemy. At the battle of Zama that year, Scipio's forces faced a force commanded by Hannibal and prevailed.

» **William Tecumseh Sherman** (1820–91): Born in Ohio and educated at West Point, Sherman resigned his U.S. Army commission in 1853 to become a California banker. The bank failed, and he became superintendent of the Louisiana Military Academy (which eventually became Louisiana State

University), the post he held when that state seceded from the Union. Sherman resigned, went north, and rejoined the Union Army, commanding a brigade at the first Battle of Bull Run in 1861 (the North lost) and then heading up defensive forces in the border state of Kentucky. (Border states were slaveholding states that didn't secede from the Union.) After recovering from a nervous breakdown, he served under the command of his friend Ulysses S. Grant, leading units effectively at several decisive battles. His drive to capture Atlanta, destroying and burning towns and farmsteads along the way, stands as a definitive landmark of modern war. See Chapter 18 for more about modern war.

» **George Patton** (1885–1945): The California-born Patton, educated at West Point, had first seen action as a young U.S. Army officer against Mexican revolutionary leader Pancho Villa in 1915. (Villa was blamed for raids across the U.S. border into New Mexico). Two years later, Patton was assigned to the brand-new American Expeditionary Force tank corps, serving in France in World War I. He is best remembered for his aggressive command tactics in World War II, first during the successful Allied invasion of Sicily and then, in 1944 and 1945, as commander of the 3rd U.S. Army in its relentless, victorious sweep across France into enemy Germany. He died in late 1945 of injuries suffered in a traffic accident in Manheim, Germany.

Instigating Inspiration

A few of history's warriors inspired others with their bravery or dedication to a cause. Some soldiers inspired those who followed them into battle; others left legends that inspired later generations of warriors. Here are a few:

» **St. Olaf** (about 995–1030 AD): As a 15-year-old mercenary in 1010, Olaf joined his Viking buddies in ripping down London Bridge. (The British rebuilt it several times, most recently in the 1970s.) Three years later in Normandy, Olaf found religion. He went home to Norway, seized the throne (he probably wasn't yet 20), and worked to establish Christianity in place of the old Norse gods, earning posthumous sainthood. Olaf was Catholic, but he lived long before Martin Luther (see Chapter 14) started the Protestant Reformation. Many Lutheran churches in Scandinavia and America are now named St. Olaf's. Danish-backed rebels killed King Olaf.

» **Peter the Hermit** (about 1050–about 1115): Imagine joining an army led by a monk, Peter the Hermit, and an impoverished knight, Walter the Penniless. Thousands of Christians said, "I'm in!" in 1095, forming the People's Crusade, which was part of the First Crusade (see Chapter 7). Also called Peter of Amiens, Peter the Hermit was an ex-soldier who got his followers fired up about liberating the Holy Land from the Muslims. Most of Peter's followers — including co-leader Walter — died the first time they faced the Turks. Peter survived to join the better-armed branch of the First Crusade, which conquered Jerusalem in 1099. He later founded a Belgian monastery.

» **Robin Hood** (likely legendary; if he lived, it was sometime between the 12th and 14th centuries): English ballads dating from about the 14th century credit the legendary Robin with protecting the poor and attacking corrupt officials. The stories may be rooted in discontent that led to the Peasants' Revolt of 1381 (see the story of Wat Tyler in Chapter 22). Some accounts place Robin in the 12th century, during the rule of the unpopular King John. Robin Hood is the hero of many movies, as well as books, plays, and TV series.

» **Joan of Arc** (about 1412–31): This 13-year-old girl (shown in Figure 20-2) claimed that she heard the voices of saints telling her to rescue France from English domination during the Hundred Years' War — a tall order for a kid, but something about her was convincing. Charles VII, at that time the *dauphin* (crown prince) of France, let her lead the army against the English at Orleans. In white armor, she inspired her troops to victory and then escorted Charles to Reims for his coronation. In her next campaign, she was captured, handed over to the English, tried for sorcery and other grievous crimes against Christian sensibilities (notably wearing men's clothes), and sentenced to burn at the stake in 1431. The Catholic Church canonized her in 1920, making her St. Joan. Joan hasn't been the subject of as many movies as Robin Hood, but the Maid of Orleans (as she is also called) has inspired several films. Many critics rank a black-and-white antique from 1928, *The Passion of Joan of Arc,* as the best cinematic version of the story. More recently, New Yorker film critic Richard Brody included a French *Joan of Arc*, starring adolescent Lise Leplat Prudhomme in the title role, as one of the best movies of 2020.

FIGURE 20-2: Joan of Arc led French troops to victory over the English in the Hundred Years' War.

Hulton Archive/Getty Images

A TALE OF TWO — OR MORE — BRIDGES

St. Olaf's teen vandalism probably didn't inspire the children's song "London Bridge is Falling Down (My Fair Lady)." The wooden bridge that the Vikings demolished in 1010 was one of a series of early structures across the River Thames linking London with Southwark (now part of London).

Perhaps the most memorable London Bridge (and the likely inspiration for the song) was a 19-arch stone bridge built in the 12th century, which included not just traffic lanes, but also shops and houses along each side. Dangerously overloaded, that bridge, like its wooden predecessors, began crumbling long before it was replaced in 1831 by another stone bridge. The 1831 model was a handsome, no-nonsense, five-arch structure that stood until 1968. Then it was dismantled block by block and shipped to Lake Havasu City, Arizona, where you can see it today. Its replacement over the Thames, today's London Bridge, is rather plain.

Because the name "London Bridge" is famous, people confuse the plain replacement with Tower Bridge, modern London's best-recognized landmark. Tower Bridge, which opened in 1894, stands downriver from London Bridge and next to the Tower of London, a castle that dates to the time of William the Conqueror. Tower Bridge has tall, handsome towers, whereas London Bridge has none. Tower Bridge can be raised to let large ships pass beneath it; London Bridge can't.

Tracking the Centuries

586 BC: Babylonian troops led by Nebuchadnezzar destroy Jerusalem and take King Zedekiah prisoner.

479 BC: Troops from Greek city-states allied against Persia defeat King Xerxes' army and burn his fleet in a single day.

49 BC: Julius Caesar leads his troops across the Rubicon, the stream that marks the boundary of his province, beginning a Roman civil war.

445 AD: Attila the Hun murders his big brother and co-ruler, Bleda, and begins forcibly assembling a vast horde of Hun warriors in Hungary.

1028: Canute, king of England and Denmark, adds Norway to his empire.

1431: Joan of Arc is convicted of sorcery and burns to death at the stake.

1828: His power-hungry half-brothers kill Shaka, emperor of the Zulu.

1853: William Tecumseh Sherman resigns his commission in the U.S. Army to become a banker in California.

1944: Germany's Nazi Gestapo, suspecting war hero Field Marshal Erwin Rommel of conspiracy in Colonel Claus von Stauffenberg's plot to kill Hitler, recalls Rommel from his command post in northern France and forces him to commit suicide by swallowing poison.

Chapter **21**

Exploring and "Discovering"

Many people made history by traveling to new places. Sometimes, they went for the sake of going, but more often, they headed out for the sake of getting something they couldn't get at home, such as new territory, the glory of being first, and (of course) wealth.

In this chapter, you can find out about some of the world's greatest voyagers, travelers, wanderers, and explorers. You'll be able to glimpse, in these at-a-glance biographies what motivated the kind of people remembered for wanting to see just what, and who, was over that mountain or beyond that ocean. You'll notice that many of them are from the 15th to 17th centuries because restless Europeans in particular were "discovering" the rest of the world during that time. And you can reflect on the reality that people in the rest of the world didn't ask to be discovered, but that was how it went.

Famous Pioneers: Arriving Before Their Time

Some pioneers arrived at places that were new to them before the world was quite ready for them to get there. Getting from point A to point B is always an accomplishment, but what if no cultural influence or trade links result? Some explorers, including the following, didn't even know what they'd found:

>> **Pytheas** (fourth century BC): Ancient Greeks traveled and settled just about everywhere around the Mediterranean. Pytheas, born in Massilia, Gaul, went further — much further. Around 330 BC, he sailed from Massilia (today's Marseilles, France) past Spain, out through the Strait of Gibraltar, and up the Atlantic coast of Europe. His personal account of his travels, titled *Peri tou Okeanou* (*On the Ocean*) is lost, so it's only through the works of later geographers and historians that his story has come down to us. But it seems that Pytheas visited Cornwall, where he encountered tin miners, and continued up the west coast of the island of Great Britain. Then he proceeded north, reaching a place he called Thule. Scholars disagree about whether Thule was Iceland or Norway or somewhere else. Pytheas went even farther than Thule, however, describing what must have been the frozen Arctic Ocean.

>> **Leif Eriksson** (late 10th–early 11th centuries AD): Icelandic sagas say that around the year 1000, this tall, strong, smart, and fair-dealing son of the murderous Erik the Red (see the later section "Famous Mavericks: Taking Advantage of Opportunity") set out from Greenland with a crew of 35 to explore land sighted in the west. He found Baffin Island, just north of the Hudson Strait; then he spied the coast of Labrador (calling it Markland) and camped on Newfoundland's northeastern tip. Eriksson called that place Vinland, for the wild grapes or perhaps berries that grew there. (It's now known as L'Anse aux Meadows.) The party stayed all winter before returning to Greenland. They would have gone to Vinland again if Leif's dad, Erik, hadn't died, making Leif head of the family back in Greenland. More Viking boats did travel from Greenland to Canada carrying other members of the clan, and some tried to settle there, but they fought with the native people (whom they called Skraelings) and among themselves. A Norse settlement never took hold. Leif also brought Christianity to Greenland.

>> **Zheng He** (unknown–about 1433): A Muslim court eunuch (ouch!) in China's royal household, Zheng He was also an admiral, sea explorer, and ambassador. From 1405–07, Zheng commanded a 62-ship flotilla that went all the way to India. Then he led six more expeditions into the Persian Gulf and eventually to East Africa. He brought back giraffes, ostriches, and zebras, but the Chinese never seemed to have much use for the relationships that Zheng He established with the rulers of the countries he visited. China didn't do very much to

pursue trade advantages or cultivate political influence abroad. Legends claim that Zheng crossed the Pacific Ocean and visited the Americas, but no evidence of that journey exists. (Zheng He's name is also often written as Cheng Ho. The spelling has to do with the different ways that Chinese names have been transcribed in Western alphabets.) Figure 21-1 shows many of Zheng He's voyages.

» **Christopher Columbus** (1451–1506): Some people still celebrate Columbus, while many others vilify him for his so-called discovery of America. But the tall, red-haired, eccentric sailor died never realizing what he accomplished. Born in Genoa (then an independent Italian city-state), Columbus was a crack navigator who sailed along the Atlantic coast of Africa and probably north to Iceland. He explored the Caribbean for Spain, becoming the first European navigator to land at the Bahamas, Cuba (he thought it was Japan), Puerto Rico, Hispaniola (the Dominican Republic and Haiti), Jamaica, and Trinidad before he stumbled on the South American mainland (Venezuela). Yet Columbus insisted that China, his real goal, was close by (see Chapter 7). As a Spanish governor of the West Indies, he became notorious for his cruelty toward natives, many of whom he enslaved. A rival sea captain brought charges and arranged for Columbus to be hauled back to Spain in chains. After some time in jail, Columbus was able to appeal to his sponsors, co-rulers Ferdinand and Isabella (see Chapter 19), who set him free and gave him another expedition. On his fourth trip, Columbus fell ill with the maladies that eventually killed him. He never found Asia, and even by the time he died in 1506, Europeans had not yet grasped what a world-changing event his "discovery" would prove to be.

By act of Congress, Columbus Day is an official federal holiday in the United States. It is also observed in many other Western Hemisphere countries. But since the 1980s, many Americans (North, South, and Central) have learned about the dark side of Columbus's legacy and decided he is not worthy of celebration. Governors and/or legislatures of many U.S. states and mayors and governing councils of hundreds of U.S. cities, more every year since the 1990s, declared the second Monday in October (the federal Columbus holiday) be observed as Indigenous Peoples Day. In 2021, Joe Biden became the first U.S. president to proclaim Indigenous Peoples Day. Many expected Congress to follow with a law changing the name of the holiday.

» **Neil Armstrong** (1930–2012): When he set foot on the moon in 1969, Armstrong was supposed to say, "That's one small step for *a* man, one giant leap for mankind." It came out "one small step for man," which garbled the meaning a bit ("man" without the article "a" in those pre-feminism days often meant the whole human species), but his wording didn't diminish the fact that somebody had finally walked on the moon. Ohio-born Armstrong was fighter pilot and test pilot before training as an astronaut. After commanding the Gemini 8 orbiter in 1966, he was picked for Apollo 11, the first moon-landing expedition.

On July 20, 1969, Armstrong climbed out of the landing module as spellbound Earthlings watched on TV. Co-pilot Buzz Aldrin (1930–present) was the second guy to step on moondust. The first moon landing proved to be a great turning point in history, but that fact wasn't immediately apparent. Other manned U.S. moon landings followed, but only through 1972. For the next few decades, the 1969 moonwalk seemed to be an achievement ahead of its time. Nobody, not even the inventive people at the National Aeronautics and Space Administration (NASA), were certain what to do on the moon. Subsequent robotic craft were sent to orbit and probe, but no more people made the journey. After decades, China sent unmanned landers to the lunar surface in 2013 and again in 2019; India also sent a lander in 2019. By then, NASA had again turned its attention to the moon and was planning to put people on the surface once more in 2025, including women this time. Meanwhile, private space-exploration companies such as Blue Origin and SpaceX, which hadn't existed in 1969, were also contemplating moon missions.

Courageous Couriers: Carrying Messages

Some historical figures traveled to spread news. Most spread the word about where they were after they returned. Either way, travelers have always been important sources of information about the world beyond the horizon and even inspiration about what could be found by anybody willing to follow such intrepid voyagers, including the following:

>> **St. Paul** (about 10–67 AD): First, he was Saul, a Jew who came to Roman Judaea from his native Turkey. He became a rabbi of the strict Pharisee sect and believed in persecuting Christians, whom he saw as *heretics* (holders of religious beliefs that contradict official doctrine). Then, on a journey to Damascus to advise that Christians be rounded up, he said that Jesus came to him in a vision. Saul went blind for a while, and upon recovery, he was Paul, a traveling Christian apostle who wrote 13 New Testament letters. He roamed widely as a missionary and participated in debates about whether *gentiles* (non-Jews) could be admitted to the Church (he was in favor) and, if so, how. Other religious and civil leaders, both Jewish and Roman, still held Paul's earlier opinion that Christian ideas threatened the established order. Roman policy held that those who spread Christianity should be jailed — or worse — so Paul spent his final years as a prisoner.

>> **Marco Polo** (1254–1324): Born into a Venetian merchant family, Marco Polo tagged along with his dad and uncle on a trip to China in 1271. (Figure 21-1 maps out his journey.) By Polo's account, the Emperor Kublai Khan appointed him as an envoy and then governor of Yangzhou before the Italian went home

in 1292. A soldier for Venice in a war against the Genoese, Marco Polo was captured and thrown in jail, writing *The Travels of Marco Polo* while imprisoned. The book was widely read and broke through the provincial consciousness of many literate Europeans. Many of Polo's contemporaries thought the book contained lies, and many latter-day scholars also doubt Polo's truthfulness, thinking that he may have padded his Chinese résumé. But the book's descriptions of the East still stand as a remarkably accurate, cross-cultural milestone. (See Chapter 24 for more on Marco Polo.)

>> **Ibn Battuta** (1304–68): Some people call this writer the Arab Marco Polo, but that nickname fails to do Ibn Battuta justice, because he wrote about so many places. Born in Tangiers, Morocco, he spent almost three decades (from 1325–54) covering more than 75,000 miles. Like Polo, he visited China and was well received. He also visited all the Muslim countries, writing about Mecca (in present-day Saudi Arabia), Persia (now called Iran), Mesopotamia (now Iraq), Asia Minor, Bokhara (in present-day Uzbekistan), southern Spain, and the North African city of Timbuktu, as well as India and Sumatra. He finally settled in Fez, Morocco, in 1354 and dictated the story of his journeys. The resulting book, *Rihlah,* is a memoir of cultural, social, and political observations.

>> **Amerigo Vespucci** (1454–1512): Vespucci, a sailor from Florence, wrote about his 1499 voyage to Venezuela and points south. But Martin Waldseemüller (around 1470–1518), a clergyman in northeastern France, is the one who tacked the navigator's name onto the New World. In a little publication called *Cosmographiae Introductio* (you might call it *Cosmo* for short), Waldseemüller spread the idea of a fourth part of the world beyond Europe, Asia, and Africa. He called this new mainland *America,* a Latinized tribute to Vespucci. The name stuck. Other mapmakers made it South America, using Vespucci's name for North America too.

Vespucci later became a victim of historical libel, as the charge spread that he stole credit for discovering America from Columbus or that he was the mapmaker who egotistically applied his own name to the New World. These false accusations are perhaps rooted in the irrational dislike that an American philosopher, Ralph Waldo Emerson (1803–82), held toward Vespucci. Emerson wrote that the Italian was a "pickle vendor" and "boatswain's mate in an expedition that never sailed." It's not clear where Emerson got the impression that Vespucci never traveled to the Western Hemisphere or that Vespucci was anything but a well-born and literate mariner. He became pilot-major of Spain, the government's top navigator, in 1505.

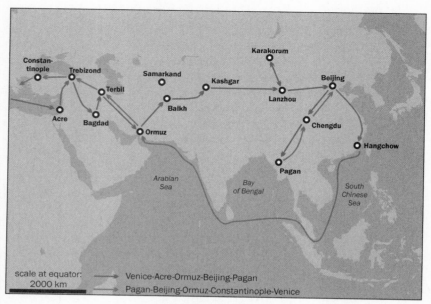

FIGURE 21-1:
Marco Polo's travels took him to places that include today's Israel, Turkey, Iran, Afghanistan, Mongolia, and much of China.

scale at equator: 2000 km
→ Venice-Acre-Ormuz-Beijing-Pagan
→ Pagan-Beijing-Ormuz-Constantinople-Venice

Wikimedia Commons, https://en.wikipedia.org/wiki/File: Travels_of_Marco_Polo.png. CC BY-SA 3.0

Trailblazing Explorers: Seeking New Routes

Many travelers left home in search of something specific, and many of them, especially in the 16th to 19th centuries AD, were looking for something that promised to be highly lucrative for the shipping trade. They wanted sea routes between Europe and Asia, where spices and silks could be purchased. Even in later centuries, the promise of another water route between the Atlantic and Pacific — one shorter and less harrowing than sailing south around Cape Horn (the southern tip of South America) or the Cape of Good Hope (Africa) seemed worth tremendous risks. Some of the risktakers were:

» **Henry the Navigator** (1394–1460): Prince Henry had a singular dream of finding a sea route to India and China. To realize that vision, this member of Portugal's royal family founded a school of scientific navigation and sponsored expeditions along the west coast of Africa. In the same interest, he built Portugal's first observatory to advance the science that taught sailors how to steer by the stars. Although he died before his students sailed around Africa, the prince paved the way for his country's greatest nautical and commercial successes.

>> **Juan Ponce de León** (1460–1521): Running a Spanish plantation on the island of Hispaniola (today's Dominican Republic and Haiti), this veteran officer (he may have been onboard Columbus's second mission to the Caribbean) developed a reputation for efficiency, which among early Spanish authority figures in the Caribbean, was often the same as ruthlessness. De León crushed a rebellion by the local Taino people. He then won a royal appointment to the office of governor of Puerto Rico, a post he later lost in a dispute with Diego Columbus, son of Christopher. Perhaps inspired by a native story about island where a spring made anyone who drank from it feel young and healthy, he sailed toward what turned out to be the North American mainland. He never found that island or its fabled Fountain of Youth, but he did land in Florida (and name it) early in 1513. He died of an arrow wound suffered on his second expedition to Florida.

>> **Meriwether Lewis** (1774–1809) and **William Clark** (1770–1838): Better known as Lewis and Clark, these buddies crossed North America looking for the thing that so many seafarers failed to find: a northern water route between oceans. Backed by the U.S. government, Lewis and Clark wanted to find a route defined by rivers with a short, manageable overland stretch at the Continental Divide. Like all other residents of the newly independent United States of America, they thought of mountains in terms of the Appalachian range, never imagining how high, steep, wide-ranging, and . . . well, *rocky* the Rockies are. The Lewis and Clark expedition was supposed to reach the headwaters of the Missouri River and then *portage* (carry their canoes and supplies) to the nearby headwaters of a westward-flowing river, which would carry them to the Pacific. Such a route would have been a commercial boon to U.S. traders, who wanted to establish a Pacific trading post on the West Coast (despite the fact that the United States had no territorial claims on the West Coast at the time).

President Thomas Jefferson chose Lewis, his private secretary, to lead the expedition in 1804. Lewis took Clark along as co-commander of a party that journeyed by canoe, horse, and foot up the Missouri River and into the Rockies. They found the mountain crossing to the Columbia River to be too long and rugged for commercial use, but they traveled down the Columbia to the Pacific and wintered in Oregon before returning east. Their observations of lands, people, plants, and wildlife were invaluable, although Lewis failed to publish their journals.

Lewis became governor of the Louisiana Territory in 1807. A troubled man, he killed himself while traveling through Tennessee on a trip east to Washington, D.C. Clark went on to hold numerous government posts and negotiated several treaties with native tribes.

>> **Sir John Franklin** (1786–1847): British naval officer Franklin fought in the Napoleonic Wars (see Chapter 9) and served as governor of Tasmania. Like so many sailors before him, he set out to find the Northwest Passage — a northern sea route around North America. Franklin's expedition can't exactly be termed a success, given that he and all his crew members died in their icebound ship. Yet they got so close — within a few miles — of finding the channel that Franklin gets credit for discovering the passage. Nobody successfully sailed the treacherous route until the Norwegian explorer Roald Amundsen (see "Famous Firsts" later in this chapter) did it in the early 20th century. An ice-breaking oil tanker was the first commercial vessel to use the passage, in 1969. In the 21st century, as Arctic ice recedes due to global climate change, the Northwest Passage appears at long last to be a viable route for general navigation between the Atlantic and Pacific oceans.

Notorious Conquerors: Bad Company

Not all explorers had positive motives for seeking new worlds. And most Europeans of the Age of Discovery were far less interested in making friends than they were in taking charge. Even when their motives were strictly businesslike, many saw violence and fear as the most effective tools for getting what they wanted when they wanted it. The following few fellows were among those many, the ones that just barged in and took over:

>> **Vasco da Gama** (about 1469–1525): Born in Sines, Portugal, he was one in a series of Portuguese explorers who were trained and dispatched for the purpose of exploring the African coast, rounding the continent's southern tip, and establishing a trade route with the East. The first to succeed in reaching India, da Gama returned to Portugal with a load of spices in 1499. His success was followed by a voyage by fellow Portuguese explorer Pedro Alvarez Cabral (about 1467–about 1520), who accidentally touched the coast of Brazil on his way south, thus establishing Portugal's claims in South America. After resentful Arab merchants killed a party of Portuguese traders that Cabral had left in Kozhikode, on India's southwest coast, da Gama returned in 1502 as an enforcer, establishing a pattern for brutal European colonialism in Asia. When Portuguese authority in India slipped during the 1520s, the government called da Gama out of retirement and sent him as a get-tough viceroy. He fell ill on that trip and died. Check out Chapter 8 for more about da Gama's voyages from Portugal to Kozhikode.

>> **Francisco Pizarro** (about 1478–1541): Pizarro, a soldier from Trujillo, Spain, was crafty and brutal. He used both qualities to defeat the mighty Inca Empire of South America in the 1530s, capturing King Atahualpa by trickery and killing

him. (For more about the Spanish conquest of the Inca, see Chapter 8.) Pizarro also fought with his fellow conquistador, Diego de Almagro (about 1475–1538). (*Conquistador* is the Spanish name for the conquering commanders who took lands away from indigenous Americans.) When Almagro, the conqueror of Chile, challenged Pizarro's authority in Peru, the ailing Pizarro sent his brothers to capture and kill Almagro.

» **Hernan Cortés** (1485–1547): Cortés helped his commander, Diego Velázquez de Cuéllar (1465–1524), conquer Cuba. After quarreling with Velázquez, Cortés, a proud nobleman from Medellin, Spain, accelerated his planned departure from Cuba to the mainland of Mexico, founding the port city of Vera Cruz before heading inland. Making allies of natives opposed to Aztec rule, he then marched on the Aztec capital. The Aztec king, Moctezuma, welcomed Cortés as a god at first, but when the Aztecs became suspicious of the Spaniard's motives, Cortés took Moctezuma captive. Velázquez sent an expedition to bring Cortés back to Cuba, but Cortés persuaded the party's leader to join him and even burned their ships so that he couldn't be taken back to Cuba. After other natives rebelled against the Aztecs, Moctezuma's death at the hands of the rebels, and a brief Spanish retreat, Cortés conquered Mexico in 1521. He also tried but failed to conquer Honduras. (You can find more about Cortés in Chapter 8.)

Famous Firsts

As Jean-Luc Picard (not a historical figure but a science-fiction character) once said, the explorer aims "to go where no one has gone before." (Yes, *Star Trek* fans; James T. Kirk said it first, but his gender-specific version — "where no *man* has gone" — has become unacceptably sexist.) Anyway, what's true in the make-believe future was certainly true in the real-world past, as explorers competed to be the first ever to conquer a geographic barrier or to slip the bonds of geography. The following people fit that description, and those who survived won the bragging rights that go with the title "first."

REMEMBER

If you've noticed that other explorers in this chapter were first to go where no one had gone before, congratulations; you're paying attention. A chapter about explorers is bound to be full of *firsts*. But as I explain in Chapter 3, the study of history is divided into arbitrary categories — valid largely as memory devices. The section titles in this chapter are just such labels.

» **Ferdinand Magellan** (about 1480–1521): What Columbus dreamed of doing — reaching the East by sailing west — Magellan accomplished. The Portuguese captain sailing under Spain's colors traveled from Seville, Spain, around South America, and across the Pacific to the Philippines, where he died in a clash with locals. His expedition continued, commanded by Juan Sebastian del Cano, and a small, scurvy-weakened, surviving crew completed the first trip all the way around the world. When Magellan first entered the new ocean west of South America, the weather stayed nice and the water calm for weeks on end, so he named the ocean the Pacific, or "peaceful." The Pacific proved to be at least as violent as the Atlantic when a storm hit, but the name stuck. (For more about Magellan's voyage, see Chapter 8.)

» **Robert E. Peary** (1856–1920) and **Matthew A. Henson** (1866–1955): Peary and Henson, credited as first to get to the North Pole, may not have touched the exact geographic pole in 1909. It was tough to tell, because there's no actual pole to mark the North Pole and no land either — just ice floating so swiftly that a campsite drifts miles overnight. Still, Peary's observations show that he and Henson came within 20 miles of the pole and probably closer.

A U.S. Navy officer from Pennsylvania, Peary commanded several Arctic expeditions, at least four of which aimed to reach the North Pole. Henson, whom Perry hired as a valet (personal servant) in 1897, was his navigator, trailbreaker, and translator. They almost lost their claim of being first to the North Pole to a former member of Peary's expedition, Frederick A. Cook (1865–1940), who claimed to have reached the pole a year earlier. But Cook, who also said that he climbed Alaska's Mount McKinley (later renamed Denali), had a habit of exaggerating. Peary's other projects included a surveying expedition in Nicaragua. Henson wrote the 1912 book *A Black Explorer at the North Pole*.

» **Roald Amundsen** (1872–1928): Norway's Amundsen never finished the race to the North Pole, although he was first to locate the magnetic North Pole (not the same as the geographic North Pole, a discrepancy that caused hassles for northern navigators who used compasses, which point to the magnetic pole). When he found out that Robert Peary had beaten him in the northern competition, Amundsen headed for the South Pole, reaching it in December 1911. Amundsen's other accomplishments included sailing the Northwest Passage (see John Franklin in the section "Trailblazing Explorers: Seeking New Routes" earlier in this chapter) and flying across the North Pole in a blimp.

» **Yuri Gagarin** (1934–68): Gagarin, the first *cosmonaut* (Russian astronaut) died young, before the age of manned space exploration reached beyond its beginnings. Gagarin was a member of the Soviet air force and became the first human being to travel outside the Earth's atmosphere when he made one trip around the planet in the Vostok spaceship in 1961. He was alive to see American John Glenn achieve sustained orbit by circling the earth three times in 1963, but Gagarin died in a plane accident the year before men first walked on the moon. (See the entry for Neil Armstrong in the earlier section "Famous Pioneers: Arriving Before Their Time.")

NAME THAT EXPLORER

To make remembering history easier, keep in mind that explorers often got things — cities, rivers, and lakes, for example — named after them. Here are a few notable examples:

- **Sir Francis Drake** (about 1540–96): Drake was an Englishman who fought the Spanish Armada and sailed around the world. His ports of call ranged from Virginia to the Caribbean to California, where a bay north of San Francisco bears his name.

- **Samuel de Champlain** (1567–1635): He was France's man in Canada — explorer, diplomat, and governor. He established French alliances with several native tribes and founded Quebec. The British captured Quebec in 1629 and made Champlain their prisoner until 1632. When Quebec was restored to French rule, Champlain served as its governor from 1633 until his death. Lake Champlain, which lies mostly between the states of New York and Vermont but also extends into Canada, is named for him.

- **Henry Hudson** (unknown–around 1611): Nothing is known about this navigator's early life, but he sailed for the Dutch and the English, making claims for both countries along the northeast coast of North America. Like other European navigators, Hudson was looking for the Northwest Passage. He explored a river (in New York), a strait (in Canada), and a bay (also in Canada), all of which now bear his name. Late in 1610, he found himself in Hudson Bay and decided to winter there. When the ship ran short of food, the crew rebelled, setting their captain and eight other men adrift to die.

Renowned Guides

Some people just know how to get places. Out ahead of many travelers was a knowledgeable explorer who had learned how to get places and was willing to show the way. These two were great guides:

» **Ahmad Ibn Majid** (early 1430s–around 1500): When Portugal's Vasco da Gama (discussed earlier in this chapter and in Chapter 8) rounded the southern tip of Africa, sailing through the perilous waters between that continent's east coast and the island of Madagascar, he knew he'd need help to travel all the way to India. He hoped to find an Arab ship pilot to guide him. Perhaps overqualified, the man da Gama found in Malindi was Ahmed Ibn Majid, also known as "the Lion-of-the-Sea-in-Fury." (Nobody has great nicknames like that anymore.) This greatest of Arab navigators wrote more than three dozen books about seafaring, oceanography, and geography. He specialized in the Arabian Sea, the Red Sea, and the Indian Ocean, and his knowledge was precisely what da Gama needed to open that part of the world to European sea trade. Many Arabs and other Muslims — not to mention Indians, Indonesians, Chinese, and more — later regretted that Ibn Majid shared what he knew.

>> **Sakagawea** (unknown–1812): A rival tribe captured the young Shoshone woman from her native village (in today's Idaho) and sold her to Toussaint Charbonneau, a Canadian fur trapper. Charbonneau claimed to have married her in a native tribal ceremony and he took her along when Lewis and Clark hired him as their expedition guide. (Refer to the earlier section "Trailblazing Explorers: Seeking New Routes" for more on Lewis and Clark.) Sakagawea proved to be a better guide than Charbonneau, and she also served as interpreter, trader, ambassador, and quick-thinking aide, once rescuing Lewis's priceless journal from floating down a river. Pregnant when they set out, she gave birth along the way and then carried the baby boy on her back. Her name, which means "Bird Woman," has various English spellings, including Sakajawea.

Famous Mavericks: Taking Advantage of Opportunity

Traveling well often means grabbing your chance when it presents itself — turning banishment into a chance to found a settlement, for example, or taking over the colony when you see an opening. The following voyagers are among many in history who broke a few rules on the way to discovery:

>> **Erik the Red** (tenth century AD): Erik was a violent person who apparently came from a violent family. He grew up in Iceland after his father, Thorvald, was banned from Norway for killing a man. It followed that Erik, called the Red for the color of his hair and beard (and perhaps his temper), would later be banned from his hometown in Iceland for the same offense. After his involvement in repeated disputes that ended with somebody getting killed and Erik being banished, he realized that it was time to get out of Iceland entirely. He knew there was land to the west, because a sailor named Gunnbjorn had reported it after being blown off course 50 years before. So, Erik sailed and found Greenland, rich with game and grassy enough to make

good pasture. After his latest banishment was up, Erik and his crew returned to Iceland and rounded up 25 ships full of Icelanders eager for life in another new land. Erik would have been aboard for his son Leif Eriksson's expedition to North America (see "Famous Pioneers: Arriving Before Their Time" earlier in this chapter) if he hadn't been thrown from a horse just before leaving and decided that it was an omen against his travel plan. He told Leif to go without him.

» **Vasco Núñez de Balboa** (1475–1519): Balboa came to Darién (now part of Panama) as a stowaway on a Spanish ship. He seized power during an insurrection and extended Spanish influence into nearby areas. Extending influence required traveling through low jungle and wetlands, but he found some high ground too, and from atop a hill, Balboa sighted what he called the Southern Ocean and claimed it for Spain. Later, the navigator Magellan called this ocean the Pacific. Despite Balboa's industry, Spain appointed Pedro Arias Dávila (about 1440–1531) governor of Darién. Balboa made the best of this arrangement by leading several expeditions for Dávila. But in 1519, Dávila and Balboa clashed, and the governor had Balboa beheaded.

Tracking the Centuries

Around 330 BC: Pytheas of Massilia (today's Marseilles) sails out through the Strait of Gibraltar, up the west coast of Great Britain, and then on to what may have been Iceland or Norway.

First century AD: St. Paul, a former rabbi of the Pharisee sect, travels widely through southern Europe and the Middle East, spreading the new Christian faith.

1354: The scholar Ibn Battuta settles in Fez, Morocco, to dictate his book *Rihlah*, a memoir of 30 years of travels from Spain to Uzbekistan, China, and Timbuktu.

1502: Vasco da Gama returns to Kozhikode, India, to settle the score after rival traders killed a group of Portuguese merchants.

1733: Samuel de Champlain becomes governor of French Quebec.

1804: Sakagawea helps American explorers Meriwether Lewis and William Clark find their way up the Missouri River toward the Great Divide.

1909: Robert E. Peary and Matthew A. Henson reach the North Pole, or close enough to it to be credited as the first explorers to achieve that goal.

1911: Roald Amundsen, a Norwegian explorer, arrives at the South Pole, becoming the first person to reach this frigid goal.

1961: Yuri Gagarin, aboard the Soviet spaceship Vostok, becomes the first human in space.

1969: Neil Armstrong, an American, steps out of his lunar landing module to become the first human being to set foot on the moon.

Chapter **22**

Turning Tables: Rebels and Revolutionaries

I n the United States of America, a democratic republic, the Constitution dictates a process whereby elections determine who leads. The transition from one administration to the next is supposed to be peaceful and usually has been. The candidate who receives fewer votes customarily concedes and congratulates the winner. Only rarely have resentments erupted into violence. Peaceful transition of power is the most important feature of a functioning democratic system. Throughout history, however, the quest for change in many societies has often involved brute force.

In this chapter, you'll get a sampling of those who sought and/or achieved change — reformers, revolutionaries, and a few usurpers. You'll be able to find out more about how people who held power clung to it. You'll glimpse ways that those who craved power pursued it and often seized it. And you'll gain perspective on how revolutionaries fought, plotted, and labored to usher in new eras.

Rising from Revolutionaries to Rulers

The goal of any political revolution is to kick out the people currently in power and replace them with new people. Usually, the leaders of the revolution become the leaders of the new political order. But forming a government and restoring order is a different job altogether from tearing down the old order.

The people in this section struggled to oust oppressors but then came up against a different set of challenges as leaders of their countries. The way in which each was changed by the transition illustrates what a tricky business it is to wield power wisely and with grace:

>> **Lucius Junius Brutus** (late sixth century BC): History knows this Roman hero by an unlikely nickname that became part of his formal name and was proudly handed down to his family. (See his much-later descendant, Marcus Junius Brutus, in "Dying for a Cause" later in this chapter). In the earliest days of Rome, then a city-state ruled by a king, *brutus* meant "stupid." Lucius Junius earned this title by pretending to be an idiot so that King Lucius Tarquinius Superbus wouldn't kill him. When Brutus's rich dad died, the king confiscated his property and killed Brutus's brother. He didn't bother to kill the "stupid" one.

After the king's son, Tarquinius Sextus, raped a nobleman's wife and she committed suicide, public sentiment turned against the king. Brutus led the Romans in a revolt, and they declared a republic in 509 BC. His fellow citizens elected "Stupid" to their top office: consul. But Brutus had two sons of his own who turned against him, conspiring to restore the Tarquin family (Tarquinius Superbus's clan) to the throne. With the fate of the new republic at stake, Brutus ordered his boys to be arrested and put to death. The Roman Republic survived, but Brutus didn't: He died in one-on-one combat with Tarquinius Aruns, another son of Tarquinius Superbus.

>> **Chu Yuan-chang** (1328–98): When he was 17, after his entire farm-laborer family died in an epidemic, Chu entered a Buddhist monastery. Eight years later, he left the monastery to lead the province of Anhwei against China's Mongol rulers. After years of struggle, Chu's forces occupied Beijing, the Mongol capital. At age 40, Chu Yuan-chang proclaimed himself the first emperor of the Ming Dynasty.

>> **Oliver Cromwell** (1599–1658): Cromwell was a staunch Puritan (see Chapter 14) and a persuasive member of England's Parliament during the reign of Charles I. He became an accomplished military officer during the English Civil War of 1642–51, a war between Royalists, who, like Charles, believed in absolute monarchy, and the Parliamentarians, who insisted that the king derived his authority from the governed. As leader of the victorious

Parliamentarians, Cromwell put Charles on trial and signed his death warrant in 1649.

After the execution, Cromwell stood looking at the king's lifeless body and muttered "Cruel necessity."

Cromwell replaced the monarchy with a *commonwealth* ruled by a single-house parliament over which he presided as chairman. When this form of government proved to be ineffective, he took the title lord protector, a kind of Puritan dictator with kinglike powers. He quashed opponents, reorganized the English church along Puritan lines, and ruthlessly put down an Irish rebellion. After Cromwell's death, his son Richard briefly succeeded him as lord protector, but the younger Cromwell was unable to withstand challenges from rivals, who removed him from office in 1659. Parliament restored the monarchy the following year. (For more on the English Civil War, see Chapter 8.)

» **Vladimir Ilyitch Lenin** (1870–1924): Lenin put the economic philosophy Marxism (see Chapter 15) to work in Russia. As a law student in St. Petersburg, he participated in leftist activities that got him sent to Siberia. He came back as leader of the far-left faction of the Russian Social Democratic Labor Party. Lenin spent much of World War I in exile. After Russia's government collapsed in 1917, Germany, enemy of the Czarist government, helped Lenin return to his native land. Lenin rallied Russians with the slogans "Peace and bread" and "All power to the soviets." (A *soviet* is a council of workers or peasants.) In October 1917, he led the Bolshevik Revolution and became head of the first Soviet government.

Counterrevolutionary forces tried reversing what Lenin had done, which led to the Russian Civil War of 1918–21. Lenin's Communists won the war after nationalizing major industries and banks and seizing control of farms. The measures helped Lenin defeat the counterrevolutionaries, but they sent the Union of Soviet Socialist Republics hurtling toward economic collapse and famine. Lenin reacted by instituting a *New Economic Policy,* permitting private production. This retreat from all-out socialism disappointed Lenin's harder-line Communist colleagues. The new policy came too late, though, because the farm economy recovered slowly, and thousands of Russians died in the famine of 1922–23.

» **Ho Chi Minh** (1892–1968): As Nguyen Tat Thanh, he was a well-educated young man from French Indochina (French-ruled Vietnam) who traveled widely and lived in England, the United States, France, and China. In Paris, he became active in France's Communist Party and then went to the newly established Soviet Union, where the government recruited him as a foreign agent and sent him to Guangzhou, in southern China. There, Ho Chi Minh (the name means "He Who Enlightens") organized Vietnamese exiles into an Indochinese Communist Party.

After his party's first efforts against the French government of Indochina failed in 1940, Ho (shown in Figure 22-1) took refuge in China, only to be thrown in jail by the anticommunist Nationalist government there. Japanese forces occupied Indochina during World War II, and in 1943, Ho returned home to organize Vietminh guerilla forces to fight back. The Vietminh succeeded, and Ho proclaimed the Democratic Republic of Vietnam in 1945, only to see French colonial forces return. Ho once again fought the French. By 1954, the Vietminh ousted the French, but Ho's struggle was lost; rival Vietnamese leaders seized control of the southern part of the country.

The Geneva Conference of 1954, which officially ended the French-Indochinese War, partitioned Vietnam along the 17th parallel, with Ho in charge of North Vietnam. Ho remained committed to a reunited Vietnam. After a 1963 military coup left South Vietnam vulnerable to North Vietnamese takeover, the United States sent military assistance to South Vietnam. The resulting war — marked by U.S. escalation through the 1960s and into the 1970s — was raging when Ho died, but his side eventually won, as U.S. forces withdrew from South Vietnam in the 1970s. The former South Vietnamese capital, Saigon, was renamed Ho Chi Minh City.

» **Fidel Castro** (1926–2016): Born into a prosperous Cuban family, Castro was a law student in Havana and a gifted baseball pitcher — some fans say he might have made the pros — but he became convinced that the corrupt government of dictator Fulgencio Batista (1901–73) had to be overturned. Castro joined a revolutionary uprising in 1953, but it failed, and he was imprisoned. Granted amnesty, he fled to the United States and then to Mexico, where he gathered support for another assault on Batista, starting in 1956. Castro and his supporters finally forced Batista to leave the island in 1959. Castro ordered many remaining Batista supporters to be executed, raising alarm in Cuba and abroad. Failing to negotiate diplomatic relations or a trade agreement with the United States, Castro turned to the Soviet Union for support. In 1961, he declared a Marxist–Leninist government. His far-reaching reforms depended for decades on Soviet financing, especially because the anticommunist United States imposed an embargo on trade with Cuba. Yet Castro's regime survived the 1991 collapse of the Soviet Union. In 2006, his brother and longtime number two, Raúl, filled in as provisional head of state for the ailing Fidel. Although Fidel recovered, he declined another term as president, and Raúl Castro officially succeeded him in February 2008. In his final few years, Fidel Castro served as his brother's adviser and as first secretary of the Cuban Communist Party.

FIGURE 22-1:
North Vietnamese leader Ho Chi Minh discovered communism as a young man in France.

Central Press/Getty Images

» **Robert Mugabe** (1924–2019): As a young teacher, Mugabe helped form democratic political organizations in Rhodesia, a British colony in southern Africa with limited, White-controlled self-rule. With Ndabaningi Sithole (1920–2000), Mugabe co-founded the Zimbabwe African National Union (ZANU), which sought Black liberation. Convicted of "subversive speech," Mugabe spent a decade in prison; while jailed, he earned a law degree and directed a coup that ousted Sithole from ZANU leadership.

In the late 1970s, Mugabe's ZANU joined forces with rival Joshua Nkomo's (1917–99) Zimbabwe African People's Union (ZAPU) in guerilla war against the White government. A 1979 democratic election, the nation's first, transformed Rhodesia into Black-ruled Zimbabwe. Mugabe was elected prime minister in a landslide election the following year, but then he undermined democracy by establishing one-party rule in 1987. His dictatorial reign turned increasingly repressive as his popularity waned throughout the 1990s and into the 2000s.

A contentious 2008 election, marred by violence by Mugabe supporters, resulted in what appeared to be a win for challenger Simba Makoni (1950–present). Weeks passed before an official but widely disputed vote count showed neither candidate with a majority. Then Mugabe "won" a run-off election. Faced with public anger over the rigged elections, civil chaos, widespread hunger, and an outrageous inflation rate, Mugabe agreed to a power-sharing agreement with Makoni's party but failed to abide by it. He remained in power for almost another decade, as opposition grew, and announced plans to run again for reelection in 2018. But in late 2017, the Zimbabwe National Army placed him under house arrest on charges of harboring criminals within his administration. With the national legislature poised to impeach him, he resigned, agreeing to a deal with legislators — one that guaranteed him a mansion, a staff, and millions of American dollars. Mugabe died less than two years later at age 95.

TOUCHY, TOUCHY

Although Chu Yuan-chang had been a Buddhist monk and brought other monks into his court, he also promoted Confucian rituals and scholarship. Among the Chinese of this time, few people felt that it was important to accept only one religious tradition while rejecting all others.

The emperor wasn't as tolerant about other things as he was about religion. He forbade any reference to his years in the monastery, for example — not because of religion, but because he was sensitive about his humble origins. (You didn't dare mention that he'd grown up a peasant either.) Once, two Confucian scholars sent Chu Yuan-chang a letter of congratulations in which they used the word *sheng,* which means "birth." The term was a little too close to the word *seng,* which means "monk." The emperor took it as a pun and had them killed.

Later, Chu got so touchy that he made it a capital crime to question his policies. When he thought the people of Nanjing didn't display proper respect to him, he slaughtered 15,000 of them.

Gaining Support As Charismatic Rebels

Rebellion carries a certain romantic cachet. As the 1962 pop hit "He's a Rebel," declares, the individual who goes against the grain boasts a defiant magnetism, whether it's the appeal of a wild-eyed idealist or gritty guerilla toughness. Many movements have charismatic leaders who attract interest and galvanize support. The following may fit that description:

>> **Toussaint Louverture** (1746–1803): François-Dominique Toussaint (nick-named "Louverture") was born to enslaved parents from Africa and rose up to free Black people on the Caribbean island of Hispaniola. As a member and then leader of Haiti's French Republicans, Toussaint faced armed opposition from the Napoleonic French overlords; the British, whom he drove off the island; the Spanish, who ran the other half of the island (today's Dominican Republic); and people of mixed Black–White heritage, who were opposed to losing their place in Haiti's racial hierarchy. Napoleon's agents captured the defiant Toussaint and shipped him to Paris, where he died in jail.

>> **Simón Bolívar** (1783–1830): Caracas-born Bolívar is a national hero in at least five countries: Venezuela, Colombia, Ecuador, Peru, and Bolivia (which is named for him). Known as "The Liberator" and "The George Washington of South America," he was instrumental in wars of independence that booted Spain from much of South America. The passionate Bolívar traveled the

continent, leading campaigns of independence. Yet he clashed with other freedom fighters and, as the first president of the Republic of Colombia (today's Colombia, Venezuela, and Ecuador), struggled with dissent and even civil war. Disheartened, Bolívar was headed to exile when he died. For more about Bolívar and the fight for independence in South America, see Chapter 9.

» **Sun Yixian** (1866–1925): Chinese Communists on the mainland and Chinese Nationalists on the island nation of Taiwan may not agree on much, but they both honor Sun Yixian as the founder of modern China. Also known as Sun Yat-sen, he founded China's *Tongmenghui,* or United League, in Tokyo in 1905. Sun lived away from China during the first decade of the 20th century because he was exiled after a failed 1895 attempt to bring down the aging Qing Dynasty. The decaying imperial government saw Sun as such a threat that its agents kidnapped him while he was visiting London during his exile. (The English negotiated his release.) The Qing were right to fear Sun, because his Tongmenghui evolved into the *Kuomintang,* or Chinese Nationalist Party, which was instrumental in bringing down the Qing in 1911 and setting up a short-lived Nationalist government. Sun was president briefly in 1912 before stepping aside in favor of another revolutionary leader, who repaid Sun by banning the Kuomintang. Sun set up a separate government in Canton in 1913 and oversaw an uneasy alliance with the newly formed Chinese Communist Party in the 1920s. He was trying to negotiate a unified government when he died. (For more about the Nationalists in China, see Mao Ze-dong and Jiang Jieshi, both discussed in "Making Ideals Reality" later in this chapter.)

» **Che Guevara** (1928–67): In the late 1960s, a popular poster on college dorm-room walls showed the shadowy, bearded face of Ernesto Guevara de la Serna, a one-time medical student from Argentina. After helping overthrow Cuba's government in the revolution of 1956–59, Che (as he was popularly known) served in various posts in Fidel Castro's regime (see the earlier section "Rising from Revolutionaries to Rulers"). He left Cuba in 1965 to lead guerillas in Bolivia. Che's shaggy good looks, jaunty beret, and especially the timing of his 1967 arrest and execution made him a martyr of the 1960s political left. His image still shows up on T-shirts today as a retro-radical fashion statement.

Making Ideas Reality

Ideas start revolutions, but thinkers don't always make the best revolutionaries. The men in this section weren't just writers who synthesized the ideas that rallied supporters to their cause; they were also doers who made momentous decisions involving others' lives and destinies. Transforming an idea into a practical result isn't easy, however, especially when politics are involved. The following people worked to put theories into practice:

» **Thomas Jefferson** (1743–1826): In 1774, Jefferson wrote *A Summary View of the Rights of British America*, expressing the unhappiness that led him to become a delegate to the Continental Congress in Philadelphia. Jefferson also wrote the Declaration of Independence, which was approved by that revolutionary body in 1776. His public service included serving as U.S. president (two terms), vice president (under John Adams), secretary of state (under George Washington), governor of Virginia, and ambassador to France. During his presidency, his nervy Louisiana Purchase more than doubled the size of the United States. He also commissioned the Lewis and Clark expedition (see Chapter 21 for more on the explorers), setting the precedent for U.S. expansion to the Pacific.

Jefferson was happiest in aesthetic pursuits, especially architecture. The University of Virginia and the Virginia statehouse are among his designs. His wife's death after ten years of marriage marred his private life, and four of the six children he had with her died young. In the late 1990s, DNA evidence supported the long-repeated rumor that Jefferson also fathered children with an enslaved woman in his household, Sally Hemings.

» **Mao Ze-dong** (1893–1976): This longtime chairman of the People's Republic of China (whose name is also spelled Mao Tse-tung) led his party through a hard-fought struggle for power and guided his country through a tumultuous stretch of the 20th century. Mao came from rural Hunan Province and was just out of college when he landed a job in the library of Beijing University. Marxist professors there changed his thinking.

Mao became involved in the Chinese Nationalist *May Fourth Movement*, which began in 1919 with a student demonstration against a Chinese trade agreement with Japan. He attended meetings of the May Fourth group that led to the formation of the Chinese Communist Party. As a newly converted Communist, he moved to Shanghai in 1923 as a political organizer for the Kuomintang, or Nationalist People's Party, which was fighting to establish a new Chinese Nationalist government in place of the Revolutionary Alliance that had ruled since 1911. When the Kuomintang decided in 1927 that it didn't want Communists among its fighters, the ousted Mao formed the Jiangxi Soviet, an outlaw guerilla force that watched the Nationalists take over but finally emerged victorious from a post-WWII civil war against forces led by Nationalist President Jiang Jieshi.

On October 1, 1949, Mao proclaimed the formation of the People's Republic of China. As chairman of the new government, Mao delegated administration to others, but he occasionally emerged with dramatic and disastrous reform proposals such as the *Great Leap Forward*, which lasted from 1958–1960. A drive for industrial and agricultural expansion, it resulted in crop failures and the starvation of as many as 13 million peasants. Mao tried again in 1966 with the *Cultural Revolution.* A drive to root out Western influences from every corner of Chinese society, the Cultural Revolution brought widespread chaos and violence. A prolific poet and essayist, Mao was a much-quoted source of leftist thought in the turbulent 1960s. The plump chairman's jovial, Buddha-like portrait became especially popular.

Standing Against Authority

Some people live by conscience, consequences be damned. The men in this section showed rare courage in standing up to the powerful and speaking out against injustice:

>> **Martin Luther** (1483–1546): Chapter 14 tells the story of how Luther, a German university professor and priest, started the Protestant Reformation. He spent three years in a monastery before earning his degree. Initially, his big issue was the Church's practice of selling indulgences, which many people understood as a way to buy entry into heaven. When he started taking on the papal system, Luther moved on to other issues, including priestly celibacy. He married Katharina von Bora, a former nun, in 1525.

>> **Mohandas Karamchand Gandhi** (1869–1948): His fellow Indians called him *Mahatma,* or "great soul." After studying law in England, Gandhi fought to end discrimination against Indian immigrants in South Africa. After two decades there, he returned to his native India in 1914. He led the Indian National Congress, a group seeking independence from British rule. Inspired by the American writer Henry David Thoreau, Gandhi preached and practiced nonviolent noncooperation, or *civil disobedience.* The colonial government jailed him for conspiracy from 1922–24.

Gandhi helped shape independent India's first constitution. Achieving his goal of self-rule for India in 1947, Gandhi's next challenge was to stop Hindu–Muslim violence, for which a Hindu fanatic killed him. Latter-day critics, citing passages in his writings, say that he harbored racist attitudes toward Black people in Africa.

>> **Martin Luther King, Jr.** (1929–68): Named for his father, who borrowed the "Martin Luther" part of his name from the German priest who started the Protestant Reformation, King guided the U.S. civil-rights movement during its most crucial years, from 1955–1968. As a young Baptist pastor in Montgomery, Alabama, he took up the cause that Rosa Parks had started and

led the 1955 boycott of that city's bus line to protest racial discrimination. Two years later, the newly formed Southern Christian Leadership Conference chose King as its leader.

King looked to India's Gandhi (see the preceding entry) for inspiration as he preached and practiced nonviolent opposition to racism. Arrested, jailed, stoned by mobs, his family threatened, his home bombed, and his privacy ravaged by a hostile FBI, King continued to lead protests. He made his famous "I Have a Dream" speech at the Lincoln Memorial in Washington, D.C., in 1963, and in 1964, he was awarded the Nobel Peace Prize. In 1968, an assassin killed King in Memphis, Tennessee, where he was supporting striking garbage collectors.

Changing Rules

Sometimes change, even radical change, comes from the top. The rulers in this section weren't content with the status quo and set about shaping their domains to fit their visions:

>> **Akhenaton** (14th century BC): As Amenhotep IV, he became Egypt's king in 1379 BC, but after six years, he changed everything — his own name, his capital city, and the state religion. Akhenaton was devoted to a cult that discarded Egypt's traditional array of gods (more on religions in Chapter 10) in favor of just one: the sun-disc god, Aton. He put the new center of government at Amarna, which he called Akhetaton, 300 miles from the established capital at Thebes. Art thrived under Akhenaton and his queen, the beautiful Nefertiti. (Many surviving sculptures depict her beauty.) But Akhenaton failed to take care of worldly business, and Egypt's commercial and military fortunes declined.

>> **Asoka** (third century BC): This king of India (whose name is also spelled Ashoka) was the last ruler of the Mauryan Dynasty. Early in his reign, Asoka led armies, but he didn't like bloodshed. He swore off fighting, converted to Buddhism, and spread the religion throughout India and beyond. His policy of *dharma* (principles of right life) called for tolerance, honesty, and kindness. His reign was beautiful while it lasted, but after Asoka died, the empire went downhill.

>> **Henry VIII** (1491–1547): Nineteenth-century novelist Charles Dickens looked back on big Henry as "a blot of blood and grease upon the history of England." You may remember this king as the fat guy who chopped off the heads of two of his six wives, but he was also England's first Renaissance prince — educated, handsome (before he packed on the pounds), witty, popular (until

he closed down the monasteries), and ruthless. Henry was thought to meet the very high expectations that educated people had for a ruler during the Renaissance. I talk about the ideas of the Renaissance, including the role of a king, in Chapter 13. Chapter 14 gives you the scoop on how Henry broke England away from Catholicism and founded the Church of England.

>> **Peter the Great** (1672–1725): As a kid, Peter I of Russia was a sort of co-czar with his half-brother, who had a mental disability. But this arrangement had their big sister Sophia calling the shots. In 1696, Peter sent Sophia to live in a convent, became sole ruler of Russia, and started changing things. He reformed the military, the economy, the bureaucracy, the schools, the Russian Orthodox Church, and even the way Russian people dressed and groomed themselves. He wanted Russia to mirror its Western European neighbors. How did he get Russians to do what he wanted? With brutality and repression, of course. Peter's many wars, especially a big victory over Sweden, made Russia a major power with a Baltic seaport where the czar built a new capital city, St. Petersburg. His second wife succeeded him as Catherine I, not to be confused with the later Catherine the Great.

Living and Dying by the Sword

Often, the person who gets power by force has it pried away by force. The following leaders are examples of the countless historical figures who resorted to violence in their climb to the top of the heap, only to be knocked down by another contender just as willing to fight for the summit:

>> **Atahualpa** (unknown–1532): Atahualpa, last Incan ruler of Peru, was one of history's many sons who wanted a bigger piece of his dad's estate. Rather than being grateful for inheriting the northern half of the Inca Empire, Atahualpa overthrew the king of the southern half, who happened to be his brother. Just a few months later, Spain's Francisco Pizarro (see Chapter 21) captured Atahualpa and killed him.

>> **Maximilien-François Marie-Isidore de Robespierre** (1758–94): He was called "The Incorruptible" and later "The Headless." Okay, I just made up that second name, but Robespierre, who energetically employed the guillotine on anybody he thought threatened the French Revolution (see Chapter 8), also died under the falling blade. He was a lawyer and a member of the Estates-General, an official gathering of the three estates of the French realm (the Church, the nobility, and the commons). The Estates-General had begun centuries earlier as an occasional advisory body to the king, but it had fallen into disuse a century and a half before King Louis XVI called it into session in

May 1789, with the unexpected (to the king) result of precipitating the French Revolution. Led by its radical fringes, the Estates-General transformed itself into the revolutionary National Assembly. Robespierre emerged as a leader of the revolution, becoming public accuser and, two years later, a member of the notorious Committee of Public Safety, directing a steady flow of executions over the three months known as the Reign of Terror. At this point, his ruthlessness scared even his former allies. The Revolutionary Tribunal, an institution he had helped create, sent him to get a bad haircut — fatally bad.

» **Jean-Jacques Dessalines** (about 1758–1806): He was born in West Africa, taken as a slave, and shipped to Haiti, where he proclaimed himself emperor. In Haiti's slave insurrection of 1791, Dessalines served as a lieutenant to rebel leader Toussaint Louverture (see the earlier section "Gaining Support As Charismatic Rebels"). With British help, Dessalines chased the French out of Haiti in 1803 and assumed the post of governor general. In 1804, he had himself crowned Jacques I. As monarch, he slaughtered Whites and took their land. His former political allies, Henri Christophe (1767–1820) and Alexandre Pétion (1770–1818), couldn't tolerate his self-importance, cruelty, and immorality; they arranged for Dessalines's assassination.

» **Bernardo O'Higgins** (1778–1842): Though born in Ireland, Ambrosio O'Higgins (about 1720–1801) fought for the Spanish and became Spain's captain-general of Chile and viceroy of Peru. His son Bernardo, however, was on the side of those Chileans who wanted to break away from Spain. (For more about the revolutions in the Spanish colonies of South America, turn to Chapter 9.) O'Higgins planned and helped carry out the revolt that unfolded between 1810 and 1817; then he became president of independent Chile. Yet another revolution threw him out of office, and he was forced to flee to Peru.

» **Jiang Jieshi** (1887–1975): Also known as Chiang Kai-shek, Jiang was the revolutionary leader who took over the Kuomintang, or Chinese Nationalist Party, in 1926 after founder Sun Yixian died (see "Gaining Support As Charismatic Rebels" earlier in this chapter). The Kuomintang was largely responsible for the overthrow of China's decrepit imperial government in 1911. Struggling against rival revolutionary forces, Jiang ousted Chinese Communists from the Kuomintang and in 1928 established his Nationalist government at Nanjing. (Westerners used to call it Nanking.) The Kuomintang had unified most of China by 1937, but World War II provided an opportunity for the Communists, who had regrouped under Mao Ze-dong (see "Making Ideas Reality" earlier in this chapter) to regain momentum. The Communists won the ensuing Chinese Civil War, forcing Jiang and his supporters into exile. In 1949, Jiang set up a government in exile on the island of Taiwan and surprised the world with that nation's dramatic economic growth.

Dying for a Cause

Many rebels die for a cause, and their failed revolutionary efforts can have lasting impact. The people in this section never rose to be presidents or prime ministers, but they left a legacy in the causes they championed and the sacrifices they made:

» **Spartacus** (unknown–71 BC): Born in Thrace, a region of northeastern Greece, Spartacus was a slave and gladiator who led the most serious slave uprising that Rome ever faced. Starting in 73 BC, Spartacus assembled a huge army of slaves and dispossessed people that more than challenged the mighty Roman army; his army actually scored numerous victories. Finally, a general called Crassus (about 115–53 BC) beat the rebels and killed Spartacus. Crassus had all the rebels crucified and left hundreds of their bodies hanging along the Appian Way, the main Roman road.

» **Marcus Junius Brutus** (about 85–42 BC): This Roman politician's name means "stupid," but he wore it with honor. The name was handed down from a legendary ancestor (see Lucius Junius Brutus in Rising from Revolutionaries to Rulers earlier in this chapter). When Pompey and Julius Caesar fought a civil war, Brutus sided with Pompey. Then he bowed to the winner, Caesar, who appointed him governor in a region of Gaul (present-day France). Because the first famous Brutus had helped drive the last Roman king out of town, Marcus Brutus fancied the idea of being a king-breaker himself. That made it easier for a fellow politician, Cassius, to enlist Brutus in a plot against Caesar in 44 BC.

After they assassinated the dictator, the conspirators fought Caesar's avengers, Antony and Octavian. Antony and Octavian defeated Brutus at Philippi. Brutus killed himself, and Octavian became Emperor Augustus Caesar, which wasn't the outcome Brutus had in mind.

» **Wat Tyler** (unknown–1381): In 1381, English peasants rebelled against working conditions in Kent and chose Tyler to lead them. He led a march to London to see King Richard II. The meeting ended in violence, and William Walworth, lord mayor of London, wounded Tyler. His supporters took him to St. Bartholomew's Hospital, but Walworth had Tyler dragged out of the hospital and beheaded.

Tyler's uprising, called the Peasants' Revolt, proved to be centuries ahead of its time. Workers' rebellions rarely again amounted to much in England until 1812, when a group calling itself the Luddites protested the injustices of the Industrial Revolution. The Luddite revolt also failed, but a call for workers' rights figured in widespread revolts in several European countries in 1848. The short-lived National Labor Union, formed in the United States in 1866, began an era of spreading workers'-rights movements in North America and Europe.

» **Guy Fawkes** (1570–1606): Though born in York to Protestant parents, Fawkes converted to Catholicism and served in the Spanish army, fighting Dutch Protestants. Back in England, where Catholics were an oppressed minority, he conspired with fellow activists to blow up King James I and Parliament in 1606. Fawkes was caught red-handed in a cellar full of gunpowder. He was convicted and hanged. Each November 5, on the anniversary of his death, the English joyfully burn him in effigy.

» **Emelian Ivanovich Pugachev** (1726–75): A Cossack soldier, Pugachev pretended to be an assassinated monarch and fueled a rebellion. The opportunity arose after political opponents killed Russia's weak Czar Peter III in 1762 and installed his widow, Catherine, in his place. Catherine the Great rose to the challenge, but not without turmoil. *Cossacks,* semi-independent tribes of roving warriors in southern Russia, resented her authority.

In the 1770s, a rebellion among rank-and-file Cossacks grew into a wider revolt, joined by peasants who flocked to support Pugachev when he proclaimed himself to be Peter III, the empress's murdered husband. With that claim, he led a fierce mass insurrection against Catherine, promising to strike down government repression. Catherine's officers captured Pugachev in 1774 and took him to Moscow, where they tortured and killed him. Long after his death, his name stood for the spirit of Russian peasant revolution.

» **John Brown** (1800–59): Brown's opposition to slavery dated back to his days as a youth in Ohio, but the tradesman and occasional farmer was in his 50s (and the father of 20 children!) when he decided that emancipation must be won by force. With six of his sons and a son-in-law by his side, he went to Kansas to fight slavery in that state. In retaliation for a raid on an antislavery town, Brown and his followers attacked the slavery stronghold of Pottawatomie Creek and killed five men. Then they headed east for the U.S. arsenal at Harpers Ferry, Virginia (later West Virginia). He took the arsenal in 1859, but U.S. Army Colonel Robert E. Lee (future commander of Confederate forces) captured Brown. Hanged for treason, Brown became a martyr for the abolitionist cause.

Tracking the Centuries

509 BC: Lucius Junius Brutus wins the top administrative post in Rome's new republican government.

71 BC: Roman General Crassus puts down a slave revolt led by the gladiator Spartacus. He executes Spartacus and hundreds of his followers by hanging them on crosses along the Appian Way.

44 BC: Marcus Junius Brutus, descendant of Lucius Junius Brutus, joins fellow conspirators in assassinating Roman dictator Julius Caesar.

1381: London Lord Mayor William Walworth orders the injured peasant leader Wat Tyler dragged out of a hospital and beheaded, ending England's Peasants' Revolt.

1532: Atahualpa, ruler of the northern half of the Inca Empire, overthrows his brother, king of the southern half, to reunite Inca lands. Within months, Spanish conquerors capture and kill Atahualpa.

1606: The Gunpowder Plot, a plan by Catholic rebel Guy Fawkes and co-conspirators to blow up King James I of England and the Parliament, fails.

1775: Officers under Russian Empress Catherine the Great torture and kill the leader of a widespread Cossack uprising, Emelian Ivanovich Pugachev.

1893: Mao Ze-dong, future founder and chairman of the People's Republic of China, is born in rural Hunan Province.

1922: The British colonial government of India imprisons nationalist leader Mohandas Karamchand Gandhi, known as Mahatma Gandhi, for conspiracy.

1949: Jiang Jieshi establishes a Chinese government in exile on the island of Taiwan.

2017: President Robert Mugabe of Zimbabwe, who came to power as a revolutionary leader in 1980, is arrested and charged with corruption. Faced with impeachment, he agrees to retire.

6

The Part of Tens

Take a look at an unforgettable ten dates (of the many thousands). Even if you hate memorizing them, dates can help you remember how long ago a big change happened and why it mattered.

See how certain writings — those regarding language, ideas, notions of how people should behave, and blueprints for how governments should work — have steered the course of human events for thousands of years.

IN THIS CHAPTER

» Breaking new ground with democracy in Athens

» Watching the Roman Empire crumble

» Kicking off the Crusades

» Starting an age of revolutions in Philadelphia

» Taking a turn against human bondage

» Opening the polling booths to women

Chapter **23**

Ten Unforgettable Dates in History

I f a teacher required you to memorize dates without bothering to get you interested in *why* whatever happened that day, month, or year matters, you know why I almost hate to mention them.

Still, dates give events context and help you remember the order in which things occurred. Many dates serve as shorthand, standing for a broad change that hinged on a particular day or year. So even if you hate memorizing dates (as I do), the ten that are spotlighted in this chapter are worth remembering.

But as I've reminded you throughout this book, much of the study of history is based on informed, but not infallible, judgments made by historians and other scholars. They don't know everything. I certainly don't. And as I've also stressed, this book is not complete. It couldn't possibly be a complete record of the entire course of human events on this planet. So, what I hope for with offering this tiny list of significant dates, is that it will help you think about the many, many more years (and days, decades, centuries, eras, ages, and epochs) that have brought us, our species, to the present.

460 BC: Athens Goes Democratic

The aristocratic leader Pericles achieved his goal of turning Athens into a democracy between 462 and 460 BC. It wasn't the first-ever participatory government, but Athens became powerful during this time, and it remains the early democracy that most inspired later ones. In fact, the founding fathers of the United States looked back to Athenian democracy as a model.

Athens's popular assembly, the principal lawmaking body, was open to any male citizen (but not to women or to enslaved people; were ineligible for citizenship). In addition to the popular assembly, there was a senate made up of citizens over age 30; it operated as an executive council that drew up the government's agenda and administered law enforcement. These two bodies set a precedent for two-house legislatures in later democracies. Think of Britain's House of Commons and House of Lords and the U.S. House of Representatives and Senate.

Although Athens's democracy was ruled by citizens, Athenian society hung onto some aspects of its former *oligarchy* (rule by a few), as aristocrats retained privileges won by birth or connection. The glaring example was Pericles himself, who functioned almost as a king. (I talk more about Pericles' Athens in Chapter 11.)

323 BC: Alexander the Great Dies

Born in 356 BC, Alexander the Great succeeded his dad as king of Macedon (north of Greece) in 336 BC. Those dates were big. So were the years of his victories, such as when he beat Persia's King Darius III in 334 BC. But the year of the conqueror's early death — 323 BC — is most worth remembering.

Alex's conquests probably wouldn't have ended while he lived. He was too ambitious for that. Instead, his victories stopped when a fever (probably malaria) killed him. This event was a beginning as well as an end, in that it began a remarkable period when Alex's generals became kings and founded dynasties in places ranging from Macedon to Persia to Egypt. Take Egypt, for example: Alexander's general Ptolemy founded a dynasty that continued until Rome's Augustus captured Queen Cleopatra in 30 BC.

476: The Western Roman Empire Falls

Rome didn't collapse in a day. Civil wars between competing military and political leaders rocked the Roman Republic from 88 to 28 BC, leading to the end of the republican form of rule and the beginning of government by one strong emperor. (Check out Augustus, the first emperor, in Chapter 19.)

Yet imperial rule eventually faltered too, as the combination of third-century AD attacks on many fronts along the Roman Empire's far-flung borders and internal revolts forced the emperor Diocletian to take an extreme measure in 286 AD: splitting the empire in two, installing himself as emperor of the East (Egypt and Asia) and his colleague Maximian as emperor of the West (Europe and northwest Africa). Although Diocletian still held authority over both halves, this system eventually led to the East becoming a separate empire, the one we call the Byzantine Empire, with its capital at the very eastern edge of Europe, at Constantinople, while the West, with its capital at Rome, went into a slow decline.

Huns, Vandals, Visigoths, and Ostragoths — all enemies of the Romans — kept pouring across the Rhine in the fifth century, eroding Rome's ability to defend its lands. By 476 AD, the empire had little authority left in most of Europe. Odoacer, the leader of barbarian mercenary troops that were supposedly allied with the Empire, attacked the weak and disorganized forces of Western Emperor Orestes, who died in battle. Orestes's young son Romulus Augustus (also known as Augustulus, or "little Augie") briefly succeeded his father, but Odoacer deposed him. He mercifully allowed the youngster to live, sending him into exile. That was the effective end of the Western Empire and the beginning of a feudal, fractured society from which the nations of Europe would eventually grow. (Find more about that ascendancy in chapters 7 and 8.)

1066: Normans Conquer England

A band of guys called Norman came to southern England in 1066, looking for a guy named Harold. The Normans got into a fight at a seaside town called Hastings and . . . oh, wait. These Normans were called that because they were from the duchy of Normandy, part of what became France, and they were coming to attack Harold II, the king of England.

I don't know how Britain would have turned out if William, duke of Normandy, hadn't won the Battle of Hastings on October 14, 1066. I do know that the effects of the Norman Conquest were felt for a long time. Harold II, the last Saxon king, died in that battle. William, crowned king of England on December 25, 1066, and his descendants ruled for almost a century, replacing English Saxon nobles with Normans, Bretons (also from France), and Flemings (from northern France and Belgium). From 1066 to 1144, England and Normandy had the same government, and Normandy remained in English hands until France's Philip II wrested it away in the 13th century.

Royal family ties and conflicting claims kept the English and French linked — and often at war — for centuries. You can trace the Hundred Years' War of the 14th and 15th centuries back to the Norman invasion. (For more about that war, see Chapter 17.)

1095: The First Crusade Commences

The Crusades, a prelude to worldwide European empires and colonialism, sent Western Europeans surging into another part of the world: the Middle East, where they threw their weight around and acted self-righteous.

The Crusades started after Seljuk Turks took over a large part of the Middle East from Arabs and from the Byzantine Empire, which resisted. The Turks had become Muslim, like the Arabs. But unlike Arabs of the 7th to 11th centuries, the Turks weren't tolerant toward Christians. The Byzantine emperor asked Pope Urban II, a fellow Christian, to help him resist this new Turkish threat. Urban also worried about reports of Christian pilgrims being harassed on their way to Palestine, the Holy Land (which was under Seljuk rule at the time).

On November 26, 1095, the pope called for Christian warriors to take on the Seljuk Turks. Two kinds of warriors answered:

>> Untrained, ill-armed peasants and townspeople, who headed east, getting into trouble on the way and then getting themselves killed.

>> Well-armed nobles and their troops, who defeated the Seljuk army defending Jerusalem in 1099 and massacred almost everybody in the city.

Later Crusades, which went on for centuries, were just as bloody and wandered even farther from the goal of restoring holiness to the Holy Land. (To find out how the Crusades foreshadowed the European imperialism of the 16th to 20th centuries, see Chapter 7.)

1492: Columbus Sails the Ocean Blue

Even if you've never memorized another date, you know 1492. The year marked the beginning of Europe's involvement with lands and cultures that would forever after bear the mark of Spain (the country Columbus represented), Portugal (his home base for years), and other European nations.

Columbus's discovery rearranged the world — or at least the way everybody thought of the world — by feeding a growing European hunger for conquest and helping bring about an age of imperialism that lasted into the 20th century. Columbus's voyages (he kept going back to the New World, trying to establish that it was really part of Asia) also devastated the people who already lived there. European diseases decimated their numbers, and European immigration pushed them from their lands.

For all the changes it brought, however, Columbus's feat was disappointing to his fellow Europeans at the time — especially compared with what Portugal's Vasco da Gama did in 1598 by rounding Africa and reaching India, a coveted trade destination. (For more about Columbus, da Gama, and other European explorers, see Chapter 7.)

1776: Americans Break Away

The spirit of July 4, 1776, when the Continental Congress adopted the revolutionary Declaration of Independence, brought forth what would eventually become the most powerful nation in the world. But there's another reason why this date is unforgettable.

The American Revolution, which was inspired by the Enlightenment thinking of the 18th century (see Chapter 15), began an age of revolutions. It set the stage for the culturally shattering French Revolution of 1789 and for many successive revolts both in European colonies and in Europe.

Rebellion swept South America early in the 19th century, and the middle of the century (especially 1848 and 1849) saw many more revolts in places such as Bohemia and Hungary. In the 20th century, revolutionary fervor finally ended the colonial age. Revolutions also took on Marxist rhetoric and continued to overturn the old order in places as diverse as Russia and China.

1807: Britain Bans the Slave Trade

In the 18th century, more and more free people in Britain and elsewhere realized how wrong slavery is. They focused on the worst abuses, especially the cruelty of the transatlantic slave trade. Denmark was first to outlaw the trade in 1803. But because of Britain's stature in trade and naval power, the British ban a few years later marked a huge international shift. Parliament took the crucial step with the Abolition Act in 1807. In 1815, after the Napoleonic Wars, Britain leaned on France, the Netherlands, Spain, and Portugal to also stop trading in enslaved people.

The change grew out of Enlightenment ideas (see Chapter 15), specifically notions about natural law and human rights that also fed the revolutions in America and France. Religious and political sentiment turned. England's Quakers formed a Christian abolition society in 1787. Britain's top judge, Lord Mansfield, ruled as early as 1772 that fugitives who had been enslaved became free upon entering British soil. In the 1830s, Britain ordered all enslaved people freed.

Although idealism drove antislavery sentiment, the movement got a boost from economic pragmatism. By 1807, Britain's Industrial Revolution was taking off. The English saw more profit in Africa's natural resources and overseas markets than in slave labor.

1893: Women Start Getting the Vote Around the World

The democratic revolution is still happening. Women first won the right to vote in New Zealand (then a British colony) in 1893, but many other nations followed. Among them were Australia in 1894, Norway in 1907, and Russia in 1917. British women over age 30 gained *suffrage* (voting rights) in 1918, and the voting age for women there was lowered to 21 in 1929.

Women in the United States won this right when the 19th Amendment to the Constitution was ratified in 1920, although some states had passed women's suffrage earlier. France was a relative latecomer to this party, granting women the vote in 1944. In Switzerland, women didn't gain suffrage until 1971.

The 20th and 21st centuries also saw a rapid, generation-by-generation expansion of women's roles and status in many societies worldwide. In Western industrial nations especially, women took on professions formerly reserved for men and excelled in science, medicine, law, and journalism, among many other pursuits. Women ran for and won elective offices. Major democracies — notably Britain, India, Pakistan, and Israel — had female prime ministers in the second half of the 20th century. In 1997, Madeleine Albright (1937–present) became the first woman to serve as U.S. secretary of state, the top post in the president's cabinet. Following this precedent, Condoleezza Rice (1954–present) and Senator Hillary Clinton (1947–present) also filled this important job in the early 21st century. In January 2021, Senator Kamala Harris (1964-present) took the oath of office as the first woman to have been elected U.S. vice president. Meanwhile, women in other countries — especially some parts of the Muslim world — were just beginning to seek greater freedoms, often meeting fierce resistance from Islamic traditionalist men.

1945: The United States Drops the A-Bomb

On August 6, 1945, at least 70,000 people died in the brilliant flash and impact that demolished 75 percent of Hiroshima, Japan, after an American plane dropped the first nuclear bomb ever used in war. The explosion and the fire that followed wounded another 60,000 people, many of whom later died of radiation sickness and cancer. Three days later, Americans dropped another atomic bomb on Japan, this one on Nagasaki. Another 40,000 people died instantly.

The two atomic bombs caused indescribable, indiscriminate death and destruction. World War II finally ended, and the world entered the nuclear age.

These two bombings remain the only times that nuclear weapons have been used against people. I hope that they remain the only times. But the very existence of atomic bombs and the far-more-powerful thermonuclear weapons that succeeded them make 1945 a huge, fearsome turning point.

» Collecting scriptural riches in one
volume

» Forcing a contract with the king

» Breaking free: America's template

» Reshaping empires with an economic
treatise

» Shocking the world with an
evolutionary idea

Chapter **24**

Ten Essential Historical Documents

D ocuments give humankind its history, in that they preserve history. If no
one had ever invented writing or started making formal records of battles,
beliefs, laws, treaties, and so on, you'd have to sift history out of oral
accounts.

Did you ever play the telephone game, in which you whisper something into your
neighbor's ear, and they whisper what they heard to the next person, continuing
around the room? If you have, you know how oral history changes from person to
person, even in a span of a few minutes. Over centuries of relying on oral history,
people would be left with little idea of what really went down. As for contractual
agreements, everybody knows that the important stuff should be put in writing.

Documents are important, and some documents prove to be extra-important, not
just in preserving the past, but also in shaping it. Documents set down basic tenets
of understanding, societal identity, and principles of right and wrong. Rule of law
is a concept that's crucial to modern democracies; it means that no king,

president, mayor, police officer, or anybody else can make up the rules on the spot. To legally take any action — whether it be to negotiate a treaty between nuclear powers, appoint a town dogcatcher, or make an arrest — public officials are supposed to go by the book. And the book is a document.

In this chapter, you'll encounter ten of the most important documents ever. You can find out about how a document opened doors to understanding lost history. You'll encounter books that tell the stories and set down the principles of belief systems. You can also read about how certain documents changed expectations and standards regarding how people should be governed.

The Rosetta Stone

As much artifact as document, the Rosetta Stone is a slab of black basalt that bears an inscribed text in ancient Greek and in two forms of old Egyptian writing: formal hieroglyphics (as seen on royal tomb walls) and the more common demotic script. In 1799, during Napoleon's occupation of Egypt, some of his soldiers found this rock on the Rosetta fork of the Nile River at Raschid, near Alexandria. The stone had been carved about 2,000 years earlier, in 196 BC.

When the French soldiers recovered the stone, nobody knew how to read hieroglyphics. (For more on hieroglyphics, see Chapter 4.) Ancient Egyptian history seemed to be lost forever.

Scholars Thomas Young and Jean François Champollion worked long and hard to decipher the Rosetta Stone, establishing that the three texts all said the same thing in different languages. Using his knowledge of ancient Greek, Champollion was able to announce in 1822 that he could read hieroglyphics. The Rosetta Stone provided an entryway into the remote Egyptian past.

TIP

You can see the Rosetta Stone in London's British Museum.

Confucian Analects

In much of the world, people attribute the Golden Rule to Jesus. But 500 years before Jesus, a humble Chinese teacher told his students, "Do to others what you would have them do to you."

Remembered in the Western world as Confucius, he lived from around 551 to 479 BC. He became a government official as a teenager, was put in charge of grain stores and pastures at fifteen, and worked his way up to high office. Confucius's ideas for reform made him popular with the public but also angered some privileged people.

After enemies forced him to leave his native province, he traveled and spread his ideas about respect for others, reverence for ancestors, obedience, shared values, loyalty, and self-improvement. He stressed the concepts of *li* (proper behavior) and *jen* (sympathetic attitude). His students gave him the respectful title *Futzu*, meaning "venerated master." Appended to his Chinese name, which was pronounced something like "Kung," it is often Romanized (written in Western letters) as "Kung Futzu," which forms the basis for "Confucius."

Late in Confucius's life and after he died, followers gathered his sayings into the *Analects*, a tremendously influential source of Chinese thought. Confucianism shaped Chinese character, blending with other philosophical and religious schools such as Taoism, Buddhism, and Legalism. Until the 20th century, every student training to be an official in the Chinese government had to study the *Analects*. Confucianism also influenced other Asian cultures and was especially important in Japan during the Tokugawa, or *Edo*, period, which lasted from 1603 to 1867. Over most of those years, Confucian values endorsed and enforced by a military dictatorship called the Shogunate helped maintain a remarkable level of social stability in Japan.

The Bible

This book is a package deal — a treasure chest of documents all wrapped up into one volume. Which version of the Bible you're talking about depends on which tradition you follow, but regardless of how you know the Bible, it's an indispensable document for understanding the course of many world events.

In its Christian form, the Bible includes writings that are at the heart of two major religions: Judaism and Christianity. (Chapter 10 talks about world religions.) The Bible contains the *Pentateuch*, or Jewish Priestly Law (the written Torah) and both the Ten Commandments (Old Testament) and the Christian Golden Rule.

Bible stories stand as important sources of history, even as historians challenge their literal truth. The Bible's teachings have shaped the courses of great nations, including the Roman and Byzantine empires, as I discuss in chapters 5 and 6. The Bible also figures in a huge technological change, courtesy of Johannes Gutenberg, who chose it as the first book to come off his revolutionary printing press.

The Bible played a role in important linguistic changes too. Both the German and English languages were shaped by early major translations of the Bible into those languages. For German, it was Martin Luther's 1530 translation. For English, it was the King James Version of 1611. It may sound funny, but the way you talk right now owes a lot to a 400-year-old book full of "thee" and "thou."

The Quran

A holy book like the Bible, the Quran (also spelled Qur'an or Koran) is the foundation of not just religious practice, but also daily life, formal law, and government policy in most of the Islamic world — a huge, wealthy, and powerful part of humanity more than a millennium ago and today too.

The Quran defines Islam's place in history. Its verses spurred the Arab conquests of the seventh and eighth centuries, and they continue to shape the Muslim worldview today.

Muslims believe that the Quran is Allah's (God's) direct, infallible word and that the angel Gabriel revealed it, as written in heaven, to the Prophet Muhammad, founder of Islam, in the seventh century AD (see Chapter 10). Muslims consider the text to be sacred. In addition to revering the text, many consider the physical book to be a symbol of Islam and even a talisman to ward off illness or misfortune. When it is read aloud, listeners are expected to show respect by staying silent. Muslim leaders strictly forbid as sacrilege any mockery or parody of the book's verse style.

REMEMBER

Like other religious scriptures, the Quran has been subject to conflicting interpretations. Some extremist Islamic teachers cite the book as a source of justification for acts of violence carried out by anti-Israeli, anti-American, anti-Indian, and other terrorist organizations. The vast majority of Muslims worldwide, however, see nothing in the Quran that justifies modern terrorism.

In addition to its impact on world events, the Quran is the book from which Muslims traditionally learn to read Arabic, which makes the Quran one of the most widely read books ever.

The Magna Carta

The idea of the divine right of kings (covered in Chapter 12) was based on the understanding that the monarch, as God's deputy, had to care for creation's lesser children. A subject, whether commoner or noble, had a duty to respect and obey the king. But the king's godly duty in return was to defend and protect his subjects. A certain mutual respect was implied.

Often, though, things didn't work like that. John, the most unpopular of England's kings, upset his barons, and they rebelled. In 1215, the barons got the upper hand, forcing King John to sign a contract, the Great Charter, or *Magna Carta* in Latin (official language of 13th-century Europe).

By signing, King John agreed to specific rules on respecting his subjects. The Magna Carta contained 63 clauses, most relating to King John's misuse of his financial and judicial powers. Clauses 39 and 40, the two most famous, say that

> *No freeman shall be taken or imprisoned except by the lawful judgment of his equals or by the law of the land.* (A freeman was an adult male subject of the crown who wasn't a serf or enslaved.)
>
> *To no one will we sell, to no one will we deny or delay right or justice.*

This first formal attempt at separating kingship from tyranny didn't solve all the problems between King John and the barons, but the charter set a precedent for laws regarding rights, justice, and the exercise of authority in England, the British Empire, former colonies, and beyond. Clause 40, for example, was the inspiration for the 14th Amendment to the U.S. Constitution and the whole "equal protection under the law" thing.

The Travels of Marco Polo

When 13th- and 14th-century Venetians called Marco Polo *Il Milione*, they were repeating one title of his well-read book about his travels and his life in China. (Polo's book appeared under other titles in various translations and editions.) *Il Milione* referred to the vast wealth (millions) possessed by China's emperor, Kublai Khan.

But some of Polo's fellow Europeans also used the term *Il Milione* to mean that Marco Polo told a million lies. Many of them couldn't believe his tales of Kublai Khan's magnificent empire. China seemed to be almost as remote as another planet; only a few other Western travelers of the 13th century had seen Beijing, including Polo's father and uncle, who took the lad along on their second journey east in 1271.

Marco Polo's knowledge of the East and its riches gained believers because he put his experiences in writing. More and more people became fascinated by his reports, and his book, known in English as *The Travels of Marco Polo*, became a 14th-century must-read. It fed hunger for silk, ceramics, and other exotic goods, and drove the quest to find a sea route to transport those goods. As historian Daniel J. Boorstin puts it in his book *The Discoverers*, "Without Marco Polo . . . would there have been a Christopher Columbus?" You could go so far as to trace the age of European conquest and colonialism to Polo's account of travels through the Far East. For more about his adventures and the impact of his book, turn to Chapter 7.

The Declaration of Independence

When in the Course of human events, it becomes necessary for one people to dissolve the political bands which have connected them with another . . . they should declare the causes which impel them to the separation.

Say what? It's my pared-down version of the opening sentence from a great document written largely by Thomas Jefferson and approved by the Continental Congress on July 4, 1776. (See Chapter 23 for more on that monumental date.)

The Revolutionary War was already on, so the Declaration of Independence wasn't about war. The Congress had unanimously approved a resolution calling for independence two days earlier, on July 2, so it wasn't the first expression of that decision. Rather, the Declaration served as an *explanation* of why America's colonial leaders felt they had to do what they were doing. The document is full of specific grievances against King George III, for example. But Jefferson — with assists from Benjamin Franklin and John Adams — also did a brilliant job of summing up some of the most compelling political and social philosophy to come out of the 18th-century philosophical movement called the Enlightenment. Here's a perfect example:

> *We hold these truths to be self-evident, that all men are created equal, that they are endowed by their Creator with certain unalienable Rights, that among these are Life, Liberty and the pursuit of Happiness.*

REMEMBER

The Declaration doesn't mention women and didn't apply to all men; it tacitly excluded enslaved people, for example. Still, Jefferson's were powerful words. The document says that people have not just a right but also a *responsibility* to stand up to government when the exercise of authority is unjust. Those words echoed through the rest of the 18th century and the two centuries that followed it, and into this one. (Chapter 15 has more information about revolutionary philosophies.)

The Bill of Rights

Drawn up in 1789 and added to the U.S. Constitution on December 15, 1791, the first ten Constitutional amendments were powerful afterthoughts intended to limit the power of government and to guarantee certain rights — civil liberties — to everybody.

Freedom of speech, freedom of the press, and freedom of religion come from the First Amendment, which specifically guarantees those freedoms. The Second Amendment, the one that begins with "A well-regulated Militia, being necessary to the security of a free State . . .," is the one that gun-control advocates and gun-rights advocates continue to argue about more than 230 years after the amendment was drafted.

People argue all the time about the Bill of Rights. Everyday citizens, members of Congress, talk-show hosts, and judges continually interpret and reinterpret this essential American document. Supreme Court justices spend much of their time deciding what the framers of the Constitution meant when they wrote these amendments.

REMEMBER

Debatable but indelible, the Bill of Rights provides a permanent curb on what government can get away with. Like the Declaration of Independence, these amendments have been copied and elaborated on by many other democracies around the world.

Das Kapital

The 1848 *Communist Manifesto*, by Karl Marx and Friedrich Engels, and Marx's exhaustive opus Das Kapital, first published in 1867, seemed to be thoroughly discredited for some time. The governments founded on Das Kapital's arguments either collapsed (the Soviet Union in 1991) or made concessions to private property and individual incentive (the People's Republic of China).

Still, the worldwide impact of this economic–political book has been incredible. The work has incited numerous revolutions and dramatically reshaped societies.

The *Communist Manifesto* attacks government, religion, and traditional culture as tools of a repressive *capitalist class*, defined as people who own factories and mines and use other people to get profit from these properties. Marx and Engels present communism — collective ownership of industry and farms and equal distribution of resources among everybody — as the only economic system that's fair to everybody. In theory, their arguments struck a powerful chord among working people worldwide in the 19th century. In practice, no so-called communist society ever achieved anything close to its ideal of a classless society in which all are equal and none enjoys special privilege. Communist Party leaders in the Soviet Union, for example, became a new aristocracy, enjoying the confiscated summer homes that once belonged to Russian nobles.

Despite such failures, socialist ideas linked to Marx's theories are still powerful influences on workers' rights and government responsibility in virtually every developed country. Western European nations, with their national health services, generous unemployment benefits, and numerous government-run social programs, are widely understood to be socialist democracies with capitalist economies. Even in the United States, where many people, especially those who identify themselves as conservative, consider "socialism" a dirty word, labor-protection laws and programs such as Medicare and Social Security are still rooted in the socialist concept of a society's responsibility to its citizens.

On the Origin of Species

Charles Darwin's theory of evolution by natural selection, set forth in his 1859 book *On the Origin of Species*, underlies the way that scientists have approached the study of living things since then. Modern biology, anthropology, and paleontology are all based on the idea of evolution.

In the 19th century, most naturalists thought that plant and animal varieties were unchanged since God created the world. Others acknowledged change but thought that a trait acquired in life could be passed on to offspring, as in a mare with a bad hoof giving birth to a limping colt. In his 20s, Darwin (1809–92) traveled around the world as a naturalist onboard a British naval survey ship. His observations made him doubt both theories.

The idea of species evolving by natural selection is called *Darwinism* even though Darwin recognized at least 20 other scientists who had proposed similar ideas. Prominent among them was his fellow British naturalist Alfred Russell Wallace (1823–1913). What Darwin did that the others didn't, though, was support his theory with boatloads of hard data from all over the world and publish his findings first.

Darwin also wrote in plain-enough language that anybody could read *On the Origin of Species.* This accessibility brought him fame but also attracted opposition. Many religious people decried any theory of life that didn't rely on direct divine creation and intervention. Some religious conservatives were especially shocked by the Darwinist notion that humankind evolved like other animals. Others hijacked Darwin's ideas, fixing on the concept of "survival of the fittest," and applied it incorrectly to human society in ways that supposedly justified the exploitation of native peoples and the impoverished. That exploitation, which characterized imperialism and colonialism, was long established by the time Darwin published his book, but the loose set of misbegotten theories labeled "social Darwinism" provided a supposed justification for injustice.

Even respected scholars and government leaders in the United States bought into the false idea that members of certain ethnic groups and social classes are more highly evolved than other people. This belief led to state laws that allowed doctors and judges to order involuntary sterilization of citizens judged to be "unfit" to reproduce. These victims included the mentally and physically ill, as well as habitual criminals, alcoholics, and even the unemployed. Social Darwinism was a tool for the racist lawmakers who drafted Jim Crow laws that discriminated against Americans who were the descendants of slaves. Germany's anti-Semitic National Socialist Party used such American laws as a template when fashioning the policies that eventually led to wholesale slaughter of Jews and others deemed undesirable by dictator Adolf Hitler.

Meanwhile, scientists made legitimate use of Darwin's ideas by developing such fields of study as genetics and molecular genetics. In the late 20th and early 21st centuries, the study of DNA led to an ever more detailed and complex understanding of how living things pass on genes to their offspring and how evolution actually works.

Index

Numerics

460 BC, Athens goes democratic, 375

323 BC, death of Alexander the Great, 375

476, fall of Western Roman Empire, 376

1066, Normans conquer England, 277–378

1095, First Crusade commences, 378

1492, Columbus's discovery, 29, 114, 123, 379

1776, American Declaration of Independence, 379

1807, Britain bans slave trade, 380

1893, women start getting the vote, 380–381

1945, US drops A-bomb, 381

A

Abbasid Caliphate, 94

Abbasid Dynasty, 89

Abdur Rahman Khan, 142

Abraham (Abram or Ibrahim), 165, 169, 183

Abu Bakr, 88, 96

Achaeans, 316

Achaemenid Persian Empire, 54, 70, 71

Act of Union, 322

AD (Anno Domini), 33

Adams, John, 388

Adelaide (queen), 87

Adi-Granth, 182

The Adventures of Don Quixote (Cervantes), 223, 228

Aeschylus, 193

Æthelred the Unready, 332

Æthelstan, 106

Aetius, 281

Aëtius, Flavius, 335

Afghanistan
    Soviets' failure to quash Muslim rebels in, 157
    as theocratic state, 164
    US invasion of, 16, 157–158, 311
    US troops pull out of, 18, 160, 310, 311

Africa, 46–47, 59, 139–142, 145, 158. *See also specific African peoples*

Afrikaners, 308

Agamemnon, 21, 316

agriculture, 10, 17, 46–47. *See also* farming

aircraft carriers, 307

airplanes, 150, 151, 306, 307

Ajita of the Hair Blanket, 189, 199

Akbar (emperor), 72

Akhenaton (Amenhotep IV) (king), 166, 366

Aksum, 75, 88

Alans, 80

al-Bakr, Ahmed Hassan, 14

Alberti, Leon Battista, 221, 294

Albertus, Graf von Bollstädt (later St. Albertus Magnus or St. Albert the Great), 208

Al-Biruni, 95

Albright, Madeleine, 381

Aldrin, Buzz, 346

Alexander I of Russia, 138

Alexander III (pope), 174

Alexander the Great
    Aristotle as teacher, 196
    conquests of, 14–15, 54, 58, 278, 330
    death of, 16, 17, 33, 49, 60, 70
    declaring himself a god, 163
    life of, 57–58

Alexander VI (pope), 231

Alexandria (city), 58, 198, 199, 204

Alfred the Great (king), 82, 84, 91, 106, 319, 327

Algeria, 156

The Algarves, 144

Ali ibn Abi Talib, 96

Alighieri, Dante, 223

Almagro, Diego de, 351

alphabetic writing, 53

al-Qaeda, 16, 97, 157, 160, 164, 181, 182, 183, 310, 311

Amboyna (city), 123

American Revolution, 17, 39, 130–133, 379

Americas, 74–75, 110, 112, 116–117

Amerindians, 116

Amorites, 15, 272

Amundsen, Roald, 352

Analects (Confucius), 384–385

Anaxagoras, 193

Anaximander, 189, 192

Anaximenes, 187, 189, 191

ancient, use of term, 34

Angkorian Dynasty, 90

Angles, 82, 84

Anglican (English) Church, 245

Anglo-Saxons, 82, 85

animism, 167–168

Anselm (saint), 208

anti-aircraft guns, 307

antiglobalism/antiglobalists, 159

antipopes, 174

anti-semitism, 169

Antisthenes, 197

anti-U.S. sentiments, 16

apartheid, 323–324

Apollo (god), 204

apostles, 173

Aquinas, Thomas, 207–209, 210

Arabian Peninsula, 96

Arabian Sea, 95

Arabic numerals, 94

Arabs

    Arab Empire, 86, 88, 94–97, 127, 180

    attack of Constantinople by, 79, 285–286, 291

    conquering of Egypt by, 88

    cultural transmission by, 93

    hatred between Israelis and Arabs, 170

    religions of, 88, 285

    slave trade, 127

    weapons of, 290

Arawak people, 110

Archbishop of Mainz, 177

archeology, 10, 15, 20–21, 74, 80

Ardashir (soldier), 71

Argentina, 143

Aristippus, 197

Aristophanes, 193, 199

Aristotle, 185, 188, 191, 195–196, 198, 199, 202, 207, 208, 210

Arkwright, Richard, 259

armor, 287–289

armored tank, 306

Armstrong, Neil, 345–346

Arsaces, 71

art, 40, 216–218

The Art of War (Sun Tzu), 337

Arthur (king), legend of, 317

Aryan, use of term, 50

Asante people, 141

Asoka (king), 71, 72, 76, 172, 183, 366

Assyrians, 48, 88, 272–274, 281

astrolabe, 95

astronomy, 52, 56, 74, 90, 189, 219, 253–255

Atahualpa (king), 120, 350, 367, 371

Athena (goddess), 204

Athens/Athenians, 35, 55, 57, 60, 63, 275, 281

Atlantis, 21–22, 27

atomic bombs/weapons, 151, 155, 156, 307–308, 381

atoms, 189

Aton (god), 166

Attila the Hun, 80, 85, 280, 281, 332, 340

Atum (Re) (god), 166, 168

Augustine (saint) (formerly Aurelius Augustinius), 205–207, 208, 210, 214, 234, 245

Augustus (emperor), 16, 18

Augustus Caesar (emperor), 66, 280, 319–320, 369

Australia, 137, 155, 159

Australian Aborigines, 137

Austria, 146

Austro-Hungarian Empire, 152

automobiles, 150

Avars, 96, 285, 295

Averroës, 208

Aztecs (Mexica), 74, 117–119, 133

B

Babur (formerly Zahir-ud-din Muhammad) (emperor), 122, 321

Babylon/Babylonians, 14, 15, 17, 46, 48, 49, 272

Bacon, Francis, 255

Bacon, Roger, 290, 295

Baghdad (city), 14, 18, 89, 104

Bakewell, Robert, 256

balance of power, 138, 299

Balboa, Vasco Núñez de, 355

Balfour, Arthur, 170

Balfour Declaration, 170

Balkans, 152, 181

Bandinelli, Orlando (Roland), 174

Bantu people, 79, 81

Baptists, 129, 178

barbarian peoples, 79, 80, 104, 285

Bastille, 132, 133

Batavia (city), 123, 133

Batavii, 123

Batista, Fulgencio, 360

battering ram, 292

Battle of Balaklava, 302

Battle of Bull Run, 304, 311

Battle of Crécy, 289, 290

Battle of Delium, 275, 281

Battle of Hastings, 320, 327

Battle of Inkerman, 301

Battle of Kadesh, 48

Battle of Lepanto, 102, 294

Battle of Mühlberg, 239

Battle of the Marne, 306

Battle of Thermopylae, 57

Battle of Waterloo, 144, 331

Battles of Manassas, 304

bazookas, 307

BC (Before Christ), 33

BCE (Before the Common Era), 33

Becket, Thomas, 174

Bell, Alexander Graham, 150

Bell, Patrick, 149

Benz, Karl, 150

Berbers, 96

Berners-Lee, Tim, 150

Bessemer, Henry, 261

Bible
    as essential historical document, 385–386
    Gutenberg Bible, 215, 228
    King James Bible, 322, 386
    New Testament (Christian Bible), 173, 203, 204
    Old Testament (Hebrew Bible or Jewish Bible), 169, 173, 203, 385

Biden, Joe, 18, 37

Bill of Rights (US), 389

bin Laden, Osama, 310, 311

Birhadratha (king), 71

Bismarck, Otto von, 140, 299

Bjarni Herjolffson, 83

Black Death. *See* bubonic plague (Black Death or Black Plague)

Black Hole of Calcutta, 125

blitzkrieg (lightning war), 299

blood circulation, 220

Blue Mosque, 95

Boccaccio, Giovanni, 213

Boers, 308, 311

Boleyn, Anne, 241, 242, 245

Bolívar, Simón, 143, 362–363

Bolivia, 143

Bolsheviks, 148, 149

bombards, 291

bombs, 151, 155, 156, 290, 306, 307–308, 381

Bonaparte, Joseph, 143, 159

Bonaparte, Napoleon. *See* Napoleon Bonaparte

Boniface VIII (pope), 219

Boorstin, Daniel J., 388

Bosnia/Bosnians, 15, 102, 152, 158, 160

Boston Tea Party, 131

Brahe, Tycho, 253–254, 264

Brahma (god), 170

Brahmanism, 182

Brazil, 115, 143–144

breech end, 300

breechloader, 293

breech-loading rifles, 301, 311

Brexit, 18, 160

Brian Boru (Brian Boroimhe), 84, 91, 319

Britain. *See* England; Great Britain

British East India Company, 123–124, 126

Britons, 82

Brown, John, 303–304, 370

Bruce, James, 139

Brunelleschi, Filippo, 217, 221, 228

Brutus (senator), 65

bubonic plague (Black Death or Black Plague), 13, 83, 107–109, 112, 213

Buddhism, 71, 88, 90, 91, 124, 165, 171, 172, 182, 183, 321, 322, 366, 385

Bush, George W., 14, 17, 157

Byzantine Empire, 22, 67, 78–79, 91, 96, 101, 121, 285

Byzantium (city), 78, 91, 176

C

Cabral, Pedro, 115

Cajamarca (city), 120

Calcutta (city), 123

calendar, 33, 74, 90

Calistus III (antipope), 174

Calvin, John, 207, 245–248, 249

Calvinism, 176, 245, 246, 249

Canaanites, 169

cannons, 270, 290–291, 292, 294–295, 305

Cano, Juan Sebastian del (de Elcano), 121, 352

The Canterbury Tales (Chaucer), 223, 228

Canton (city), 126

Canute the Great (Cnut) (king), 82, 332, 341

capitalism, 262–264, 389–390

Carib people, 110, 112

Caribbean, 111

Carolingians, 85, 86

Carolman (king), 86

Carolus Augustus (Charlemagne), 86. *See also* Charlemagne (Charles the Great) (king)

Carter, Howard, 26, 27

Carthage (city), 63–64, 67

cartography, 224

Cassius (senator), 65, 369

castes, 171

Castiglione, Count Baldassare, 222, 228

Castillo San Marcos, 294

Castro, Fidel, 360

Castro, Raúl, 360

Çatalhöyük (town), 271

catapult, 292

Catherine of Aragon, 240, 242

Catherine the Great, 370, 371

catholic, use of term, 69, 173

Catholicism, 129, 175, 176, 244, 246, 367, 370. *See also* Roman Catholic Church

cavalry, 276, 280–281, 284–287, 295, 302, 318

Caxton, William, 215, 223, 228

Celts, 24, 75–76, 82

Central Powers, in World War I, 152

centuries, naming and numbering of, 33–34

Cervantes, Miguel de, 212, 223, 228

chain mail, 287–288

Chaldeans, 49

Chamberlain, Neville, 154

Champlain, Samuel de, 353, 355

Champollion, Jean François, 384

Chandragupta I, 72

Chandragupta II, 72, 89

Chandragupta Maurya (Candra Gupta Maurya), 71

Charbonneau, Toussaint, 354

"Charge of the Light Brigade" (Tennyson), 302

Charlemagne (Charles the Great) (king), 15, 69, 85, 86, 87, 91, 174, 226, 287, 320

Charles I (king), 129, 130, 133, 226, 228, 247, 358, 359

Charles IV (king), 246

Charles Martel (king), 86, 286, 287, 295, 336

Charles V (emperor), 178, 227, 228, 236, 238, 239, 243

Charles VI (king), 289, 295

Charles VIII (king), 226

chassepot, 301

Chaucer, Geoffrey, 223, 228

Chavin people (Peru), 52

Cheat Sheet, 3

Chechnya, 158

Childeric (king), 318

Children's Crusade, 105

Chile, 143

China. *See also specific dynasties*

  as believing themselves center of the world, 98

  civil war in, 156, 368

  cultural influences from, 51, 79

  dynasties for, 51

  food production in, 126, 51

  Great Wall of, 72, 73, 99, 271

  innovation in, 97–98, 112, 283, 288, 290

  invasion of, 99–100

  Japan as gaining territory from, 146

  People's Republic of China, 156, 364

  philosophical traditions of, 190–191

  uniting of, 72–74

  war against Britain, 145

  war with Japan, 156

  in World War I, 152

  in World War II, 155

Chinese Communist Party, 363, 364

Chinese Manchuria, 146

chivalry/chivalric, 287

Chola, 89

Christian Bible (New Testament), 173, 203, 204

Christian Church, use of term, 69

Christianity. *See also* Crusades; Jesus of Nazareth; Protestant Reformation

  Augustine's influence on, 205

  belief that king was God's representative, 163, 174

  Constantine's conversion to, 68

  early centers of state-sanctioned Christianity, 68

  feelings of Muslims toward Christians, 16

  fundamentalist-style, 178

  interpretation of, 203–204

  as monotheistic religion, 165

  as official religion of Roman Empire, 68

  origins of, 172

  shrines of, 104

  as unifying focus in Europe and beyond, 88

  as winning converts in Arab culture, 88

Christophe, Henri, 368

Chrysoloras, Manuel, 213, 215, 228

Chu Yuan-chang (emperor), 172, 358, 362

Church, use of term, 69, 173

Church of Christ, 178

Church of England, 129, 178, 240–243, 367

Cicero, 225

Cinco de Mayo, 144

cities, 43, 45–51, 78. *See also specific cities*

citizenship, 55, 62–63

city-state, 55, 56, 57

civil authority, decentralization of, 78

civil disobedience, 365

civil rights movement, 39, 365

civil wars

  American Civil War, 151, 297, 298, 303–305

  among Arabs, 96

  Chinese Civil War, 156, 368

  English Civil War, 130–131, 247, 358

  in Japan, 90, 124, 145

  Roman civil war, 64, 65, 76, 330, 340, 369, 377

  Russian Civil War, 359

  in South America, Southeast Asia, and Africa, 308

civilizations, 21, 45, 47–48, 81, 107, 116, 163

Clark, William, 349

classical, use of term, 35

Classical Greece, 35, 40, 55–59, 165, 166, 274–278

Clausewitz, Carl von, 297, 298, 303, 311

Clement VII (pope), 231, 241

Cleopatra VII (queen), 58, 65, 330

climate change, 13, 47, 80, 83

Clinton, Hillary, 381

The Clouds (Aristophanes), 193, 199

Clovis (king), 85, 318

Cold War, 149, 157

Colet, John, 214

Colombia, 143

Colombo, Matteo Realdo, 220

colonization, 110, 142, 145

Columbus, Christopher, 29, 103, 109–112, 112, 113, 114, 116, 123, 345

commerce, 106

commissariat, 285

Commonwealth, 130, 247

communism, 148, 156, 263, 361, 390

Communist Manifesto (Marx and Engels), 389, 390

communities, origins of, 43–44

Condorcanqui, Jose Gabriel, 142, 143

Confederate States of America, 304, 311

Confucianism, 167, 385

Confucius, 167, 190, 384–385

A Connecticut Yankee in King Arthur's Court (Twain), 8

consolidated power, 87

Constantine (later Constantine the Great), 66, 68, 76, 78, 91, 174, 176, 183, 204

Constantinople (formerly Byzantium, later Istanbul), 66, 76, 78, 79, 91, 96, 176, 177, 228, 285–286, 291

Constantius, 66

contradictory characters (in history), 38–39

Contras, 309

Cook, Frederick A., 352

Copan, 74

Copernicus, 219, 224, 228, 253, 254, 255, 264

Cortés, Hernan, 114, 116, 118, 119, 351

Cosmographiae Introductio (Waldseemüller), 347

countermarch, 293

coup d'état, 144

The Courtier (Castiglione), 222, 223, 228

COVID-19 pandemic, 7, 14, 18, 107, 303

Cranmer, Thomas, 242

Crassus (general), 369, 370

creation stories/myths, 166, 189, 206

Crete, 55

Crimean War, 151, 297, 298, 299–302, 311

Crompton, Samuel, 259

Cromwell, Oliver, 358–359
Cromwell, Richard, 359
Cromwell, Thomas, 242, 243
crossbow, 288, 289, 295
Crusades
  Children's Crusade, 105
  defined, 100, 103
  First Crusade, 16, 37, 105, 378
  Fourth Crusade, 105
  impacts of, 105–106
  launching of, 102–105, 112, 174
  main players in, 103–104
  People's Crusade, 105, 338
  Second Crusade, 105
  Third Crusade, 105
cultural diffusion, 58
cultural dominance, 107
cuneiform, 53, 189
Cuzco (city), 119, 120, 142
cynicism, 197
Cyprus, 102, 112
Cyrenaics, 197
Cyrus (king), 54, 60
czar (tsar), 69

D

da Gama, Vasco, 95, 113, 114–116, 120, 136, 224, 350,
    353–354, 355, 379
da Vinci, Leonardo, 218, 219, 221
Daesh, 16
Daladier, Édouard, 154
Damascus (city), 96
Darius I (king), 54, 57, 72, 192, 276, 281
Darius III (king), 58, 375
Dark Ages, 207
Darwin, Charles, 137, 390–391
Darwinism, 391
Das Kapital (Marx), 263, 265, 389–390
David (king), 318
David (Michelangelo), 216–217
Declaration of Independence (US), 258, 379, 388–389
Declaration of the Rights of Man (1792), 132
Delian League, 192, 199
democracy, 35, 40, 58, 62, 146, 376
Denmark, 146

Denovisans, 32
Descartes, René, 258
Dessaline, Jean-Jacques, 133, 368
dharma, 172, 183
dialectic, 262, 263
Dickens, Charles, 366
Diderot, Denis, 258, 264
Diet of Worms, 236
Diocletian (emperor), 66, 377
Diogenes of Sinope, 197
Dionysus (god), 204
Diponegoro (prince), 145
disasters, 13
Discourse on the Origin and Foundations of Inequality
    Amongst Men (Rousseau), 258
The Discoverers (Boorstin), 388
disposable income, 108
dissections, 29, 220
Divine Comedy (Alighieri), 223
divine right of kings, 129, 203, 257, 387
documents, ten essential historical documents, 383–391
Dom Pedro (prince), 144
Donatello (Donato di Betto Bardi), 217, 218
Draco, 325
Drake, Francis, 353
Dresden (city), 155
dress, modes of, 165
Dublin, 33
Duma, 148
Durkheim, Emile, 168
Dutch East India Company, 123
dynasties. See specific dynasties

E

Earth, formation of, 30, 40
East Germany, 155
East India Company, 122–125, 137
East Indies, 123
Eastern Han, 74
Eastern Orthodox Church, 176–177
Eastern trade, 100–103
economic crisis (2008), 264, 265
economics, 131, 261–264
Edict of Milan, 174, 183, 204
Edict of Nantes, 246

Edward III (king), 289

Edward the Confessor, 82

Edward VI (king), 243, 245

Egypt/Egyptians

  burying of dead in, 27

  creation story of, 166

  development of practical scientific and engineering methods in, 52

  hieroglyphics of, 53

  invention of writing, 44

  military power of, 272

  mummies found in, 26

  Muslim Arabs' conquering of, 88

  villages springing up in Nile Valley of, 47

Elamites, 272

Eleanor of Aquitaine, 335

Elizabeth I (queen), 35, 122, 245

Elizabethan era, 35, 36

Ember, Carol, 270

Emerson, Ralph Waldo, 347

Empedocles, 188, 189, 199

empires. *See also specific empires*

  managing unprecedented ones, 136

  rise and fall of, 61–76

empiricism, 252, 256–257

Encyclopèdie, 258, 264

Encyclopedists, 258

Engels, Friederich, 263, 389

England

  in Crimean War, 298–301

  English Civil War, 130–131, 247, 358

  English Revolution, 129

  in Hundred Years' War, 289

  meaning of name, 85

  as part of United Kingdom, 86

  slave trade, 128, 380

The Enlightenment (Age of Reason), 17, 130, 131, 252, 256

Epic of Gilgamesh, 46

epic poems, 19–20, 57, 166, 269, 316, 330

epicureanism, 197

Epicurus, 197

Episcopalian denomination, 178

epistemology, 187

equestrians (riders), 64

eras, naming of, 34–37

Erasmus, Desiderius, 214, 230, 231, 232, 240, 248

Eratosthenes, 199

Erik the Red, 83, 354–355

"Essay Concerning Human Understanding" (Locke), 256

ethics, 187

Ethiopia, 141–142

"ethnic cleansing," 158

Etruscans, 278

eunuch, 99

Euphrates River, 45, 59

Euripides, 193

Eurocentrism, 107

Europe

  challenging the dominance of, 142–146

  as dividing Africa, 139–142

  early cultures of, 59

  growing literacy of, 224

  Industrial Revolution of, 140

  movement away from imperialism, 135

  mummies found in, 24

  planting seeds of nations of, 84–88

  rebuilding of after World War I, 153

  redrawing of map of, 15

  revolutionary movements in, 159

  ricocheting unrest as coming home to, 146

  World War II as redrawing map of, 155

European Union, 18, 159, 160

Evangelical Lutheran Church in America (ELCA), 178

evangelical movement, 178

Evans, Arthur, 21

evolution, 31

explorations/explorers, 103, 109–112, 113–133, 140, 209, 348–350. *See also specific explorers*

explosives, 290

F

Faisal I, 14

farming, 10, 43, 46–47, 51, 52. *See also* agriculture

Farnsworth, Philo T., 150

Fawkes, Guy, 38, 323, 370, 371

Ferdinand (king), 111, 175, 226, 240, 322, 327

Ferdinand VII (king), 143

Fertile Crescent, 10, 11, 15, 17

feudalism, 287

Ficino, Marsilio, 213

fighter planes, 307

firearms, 289, 290, 294, 300, 301

firepot, 290

First Boer War, 308

First Crusade, 16, 37, 105, 378

First Nations, 116

First Triumvirate, 64–65

Fisher, John, 243

Fitzwilliam, William, 243

Five Pillars, 179

flanking maneuver, 271

flanks, 276

flintlock, 293, 300, 301

flooding, 46

Florence (city), 213, 225

Ford, Henry, 150

foreign luxuries, market for, 107, 109

Forkbeard, Sweyn (king), 332

Forsyth, Alexander John, 301

fortresses, 294–295

Four Noble Truths, 172

Fourth Crusade, 105

Fracastoro, Girolamo, 220

fragmentation bombs, 290

France. *See also* Gaul

  Calvin as causing turmoil in, 246, 247

  in Crimean War, 298–301

  French Resistance, 309

  French Revolution, 129, 130–133, 138, 139, 143, 144, 252, 258, 305, 331, 367, 368, 379

  Habsburg-versus-France fight, 227

  in Hundred Years' War, 289

  invasion of Mexico, 144

  letting go of Algeria, 156

  post-revolution, 138–139

  preventing insurrections in, 131

  during Protestant Reformation, 175

  serfdom in, 147

  women's suffrage in, 380

  in World War I, 152, 306

  in World War II, 155

Francis I (king), 227, 243

frankincense, 88

Frankish Empire, 15

Franklin, Benjamin, 388

Franklin, John, 350

Franks, 84, 85, 86, 286, 295, 318

Frederick (Frederick the Wise) (elector of Saxony), 178, 236, 237

Frederick I (Barbarossa) (emperor), 105, 174

Frederick the Great (Frederick II) (king), 253, 323, 327

freedom fever, 114

French and Indian War, 131, 151

Froissart, Jean, 287

Fugger family, 233

Fulton, Robert, 149

Funan (city), 90

Fust, Johann, 215, 228

G

Gagarin, Yuri, 352

Gaius Julius Caesar Octavianus (Octavian), 319, 320

Gaius Marius, 65

Galerius, 66

Galileo Galilei, 219, 224, 254–255, 264

Gallic Wars, 65

Gandhi, Indira, 182

Gandhi, Mohandas Karamchand (Mahatma), 39, 40, 171, 365, 366, 371

Gatling, Richard, 305

Gatling gun, 305

Gaul, 76, 80, 84, 85, 280, 281, 286, 320, 333, 336, 369

Geb (god), 166

Genghis Khan (formerly Temujin), 15, 99, 100, 106, 122, 320–321, 327

Genoa (city-state), 101, 102, 103

genocide, 158

Genseric (king), 334

geometry, 198

Germany

  competition with Britain for naval superiority, 152, 159

  German Empire, 15, 140, 154, 299

  revolutionary movements in, 146

  Third Reich, 154

  in World War I, 152

  in World War II, 154

Ghiglieri, Michael P., 270

Giovanni, Conte Pico della Mirandola, 210, 213, 214

Glenn, John, 352

globalization, 149

Gnaeus Pompeius Magnus, 65

Goa Velha (old Goa) (city), 122

Göbekli Tepe, 43

god(s), belief in, 165

Godwinson, Harold (Harold II, king), 320

Golden Rule, 384, 385

Goodall, Jane, 270

Gospels, 173

Grant, Ulysses S., 303

Great Britain

  Angles, Saxons, and Jutes in, 82

  British-French rivalry, 138

  competition with Germany for naval superiority, 152, 159

  empire, size of, 138

  setback of from America, 137

  use of name, 85

  war against China, 145

  withdrawal of from India, 156

  in World War I, 152

Great Chain of Being, 202–203

Great Dying. *See* bubonic plague (Black Death or Black Plague)

Great Pyramid at Giza, 52

Great Wall, 72, 73, 99, 271

Great Zimbabwe, 81

greaves, 275

Greece, Classical, 35, 40, 55–59, 165, 166, 274–278

Greek fire, 283, 286

Greek language, 67

Gregorian calendar, 33

Gregory XIII (pope), 33

guerilla tactics, 308, 309, 360, 361, 362, 363, 364

Guevara, Che (Ernesto Guevara de la Serna), 363

Gulf War, 303

gunmakers, 290–293

Gunnbjorn, 354

gunpowder, 98, 112, 117, 283, 284, 290–295, 301

Gunpower Plot, 40, 371

Gupta Dynasty, 71, 72, 89

Gustav Adolph II (king), 293

Gustavus Adolphus (king), 247

Gutenberg, Johann, 215, 385

Gutenberg Bible, 215, 228

Gutenberg press, 223, 228, 385

Guthrum, 82, 91

H

Habsburg Dynasty, 144, 175, 226–227, 227

hackbut (harquebus), 292

Hagia Sophia, 177, 183

Haiti, 132–133, 133

hajj (pilgrimage), 179

Hakenbuchse (hook-gun), 292

Halakh, 169

Hamburg (town), 106, 112

Hammurabi (king), 48, 53

Han Dynasty, 73–74, 97–98, 99, 318

handcannon, 292

Hannibal, 337

hansa, 106, 112

Hanseatic League, 106, 112

Hanukkah, 170

Harald III Sugrdsson (king), 334–335

Harappa, 49, 51

Hardicanute (king), 82

Hargreaves, Thomas, 259, 264

Harold II (king), 82, 320, 327, 335, 336, 377

Harris, Kamala, 381

Harsha, 89

Harvey, William, 220, 256

hastati, 279

Hattusilis III (king), 48

Hawkwood, John, 226

Hebrew Bible (Jewish Bible or Old Testament), 169, 173, 203, 385

Hebrews, 88. *See also* Judaism

hedonism, 197

Hegel, Georg Friederich Wilhelm, 262, 263

Hellenistic Age/culture/philosophies, 58, 196–198, 204

Hellenization, 71

Hemings, Sally, 364

Henry II (king), 174

Henry III (king), 246, 249

Henry IV (king), 246

Henry the Navigator, 111, 348–349

Henry VIII (king), 38, 178, 231, 240–244, 249, 366–367

Henson, Matthew A., 352

Heraclitus, 192, 329

Herbert, George (Earl of Carnarvon), 26

Herero people, 145

Hero, 199

Herodotus, 32, 52

Herzegovina, 158

Hessians, 137

Hidalgo y Costilla, Miguel, 144

hieroglyphics, 53

Hindenburg, Paul von, 331

Hindi language, 50

Hinduism, 170, 171, 182

Hiroshima (city), 151, 155, 381

Hissarlik, 20

history

  biases in writing about, 36

  as constantly being reevaluated, 35

  different perspectives in viewing of, 38–39

  as full of periods divided by arbitrary lines, 34

  putting it in perspective, 29–40

  as six degrees of separation, 16–17

  as slanted, 36

  as tapestry, 13–16

  ten essential historical documents, 383–391

  ten unforgettable dates in, 375–381

  terminology of, 30

  as told in chronological order, 13

  view of, that sees only progress, 12

  war as good material for books on, 12–13

Hitler, Adolf, 15, 154, 331–332

Hittite Empire/Hittites, 48, 107, 272

Ho Chi Minh (Nguyen Tat Thanh), 359–360, 361

Hobbes, Thomas, 257

Holy League, 102

Holy Roman Empire, 15, 18, 69, 86, 91, 226

Holy Trinity, 173

Homer, 20, 27, 166, 167, 189, 204, 316

hominids, 40

Homo erectus, 31, 40

Homo Neanderthalensis, 32

Hong Kong, 126, 133

hook-gun (Hakenbuchse), 292

hoplites, 274, 276

horses

  equestrians (riders), 64

  introduction of to Americas, 117

  terra-cotta horses, 73

  in war, 98, 272, 276, 277, 281, 284–286, 288, 295, 301

Horus (god), 168

Houthi rebels, 97

how-to genre, 32

Hrolfr (or Rollo), 82, 91

Hsia Dynasty, 51

Hudson, Henry, 353

Huguenots, 246, 249

Huitzilopochtli, 118

human anatomy, 219–220

human perfection, pursuit of, 220–222

human species, modern, 30

humanism, 209–210, 213–214, 220, 234

Hume, David, 257

humors, 219

Hundred Years' War, 289, 295

Hungary, 146

Huns, 72, 80, 89, 96, 280, 281

hunter-gatherers, 9, 10, 17

Hurrians, 272

Hussein, Saddam, 14, 17, 160

Hutus, 158

Hypertext Markup Language (HTML), 150

I

Ibn Battuta, 347, 355

Ibn Majid, Ahmad ("the Lion-of-the-Sea-in-Fury"), 95, 353–354

Ibn Rushd, 208, 210

ice ages, 17, 32, 83

icons, explained, 3

Ideas (Forms), theory of, 195

Il Milione, 387

The Iliad (Homer), 19, 21, 57, 269, 316

Imamis, 181

immunities, 117, 127–128, 137

imperialism, 135

Incas, 119–120, 163, 350–351

India

  British withdrawal from, 156

  castes, 171

  cultural influences from, 79

  East India companies, 122–124

  empires in, 71

Indian Empire, 89
  number system from, 94
  rebounding guptas in, 89
  religious disagreement and conflict in, 171
Indians, origin of term, 110, 116
indigenous peoples, 137
Indus River, 49–51, 60
Industrial Revolution, 140, 149, 252, 258–261, 262, 263, 369, 380
Innocent III (pope, antipope), 129, 174
An Inquiry into the Nature and Causes of the Wealth of Nations (Smith), 262, 265
Inquisition (Rome branch of), 255
Ionian Greeks, 54
Ionians (Milesians), 189
Iran, 164
Iranian Revolution, 181
Iraq, 14–15, 18, 44, 157–158, 160, 310
Iraq War, 14, 16, 18
Ireland, 33, 84, 91, 146, 175
iron, 117
irrigation canals, 45, 59, 74
IS, another name for ISIS, 16
Isabella I (queen), 111, 175, 226, 240, 322, 327
ISIL (Islamic State of Iraq and the Levant), 16
ISIS (Islamic State of Iraq and Syria), 16, 17, 97, 164, 181, 182
Islam. *See also* Muhammad (Mohammed or Mohamet)
  defining of, 179
  dynasties of, 89
  emerging fervor of, 88–89, 181
  factions/sects of, 96, 180
  feelings of Muslims toward Christians, 16
  founding of, 91, 178, 183
  meaning of name, 179
  as monotheistic religion, 165
  spread of, 94
Israel
  belief that God promised it to Abraham, 170
  establishment of state of, 16, 157, 170, 183
  hate between Israelis and Arabs, 170
  as Jewish and democratic state, 164
  kingdom of, 169, 183, 274
  Lost Tribes of, 274
Istanbul (city), 66, 95. *See also* Constantinople (formerly Byzantium, later Istanbul)
Italian Wars, 226–227

Italy, 146, 152, 154, 224–225
Iturbide, Augustin de, 144
Itzcóatl, 118

J

Jakarta (city), 123, 133
James (apostle), 173
James I (king), 38, 40, 248, 322–323, 371
James II (king), 291, 295
James VI (king), 248, 322–323
Janjaweed, 158
Japan
  civil war in, 90, 124, 145
  cultures in, 59
  influence of China in, 90
  during Iron Age, 76
  isolation of, 123
  unleashing pent-up power in, 145–146
  war with China, 156
  warrior class in, 123
  in World War I, 152
  in World War II, 154
Java, 145
javelin (pilum), 278
Jefferson, Thomas, 258, 349, 364, 388–389
Jerez, Rodrigo de, 111
Jericho, 43–45, 59, 271
Jerusalem, 104, 112
Jesus of Nazareth, 104, 172–173, 180, 183, 204–205
Jewish Bible (Hebrew Bible or Old Testament), 169, 173, 203, 385
Jiang Jieshi (Chiang Kai-shek), 368, 371
jihad (holy struggle), 179–180
Joan of Arc, 339, 341
João VI (king), 143–144
John (king), 129, 387
John XII (pope), 87
Jomon era (Japan), 59
Juan-Juan, 104
Judah (Judaea), 169, 274
Judaism, 88, 165, 169, 213–214
Julius Caesar, 33, 64, 65, 76, 319, 330, 340, 369
Julius Caesar (Shakespeare), 65
junta, 143
Justinian, 79, 91, 325–326
Jutes, 82, 84

K

Kabbalah, 213–214
Kacchayana, Pakudha, 189
Kadesh, Battle of, 48
kaiser, 69
Kanauj, 89
Kangxi (emperor), 125–126
karma, 170, 172
Kassites, 272
Kepler, Johannes, 224, 254, 256
khanates, 100
Khanbaligh (later Beijing), 100
Khmer, 90
King, Martin Luther, Jr., 39, 40, 365–366
King James Bible, 322, 386
Klerk, F.W. de, 324
Knox, John, 248
Korea, 146
Korean War, 303
Kozhikode (Calicut) (city), 95, 115, 116
Kublai Khan, 15, 99, 100, 101, 122, 321, 346
Kuomintang (Chinese Nationalist Party), 363, 364, 368
Kush (Upper Nubia), 47, 60
Kuwait, 157

L

La Paz (city), 142
labor pool, 108, 109
Laevinus (consul), 279
Lamaism, 172
lance, 276, 285, 288
landsknechts, 235
Langobard people, 280
language, 32, 223. *See also specific languages*
Lao-tzu, 190
Latin, 62, 69, 85, 225
Latin America, 142–144, 176
Latins, 278–281
Lavoisier, Antoine, 130
laws, 53, 324–326
League of Nations, 14, 15, 153, 158, 159, 306
Lee, Robert E., 304, 370
legalism, 190
legends, 316–317
legion, 278, 279
Leif Eriksson, 83, 90, 91, 344, 355
Lenin, Vladimir Ilyitch, 148, 263, 359
Leo III (pope) (later St. Leo), 15, 69, 86, 91, 174, 320
Leo X (pope), 231, 233, 240
Leucippus, 189
Leviathan (Hobbes), 257
Lewis, Meriwether, 349
liberation movements, 135
Licinius (co-emperor), 174, 183, 204
Lima (city), 143
Lincoln, Abraham, 304
Linne, Carl, 256
Livingstone, Davie, 140
Locke, John, 130, 256–257
Lombards, 86, 87
London Bridge, 340
longbow, 289, 290
"lost" civilizations, 21
Lost Tribes of Israel, 274
Louis Napoleon, 146
Louis Phillipe (king), 146
Louis VII (king), 227
Louis XII (king), 226
Louis XIII (king), 131, 247
Louis XIV (the Sun King) (king), 131
Louis XVI (king), 130, 131–132, 139
Louis XVIII (king), 139
Louverture, Toussaint (François-Dominique Toussaint), 132, 133, 362
Lubeck (town), 106, 112
Lucius Junius Brutus, 358, 370
Ludd, Ned, 261, 265
Luddite uprising, 261, 265, 369
Luther, Martin, 175, 176, 177, 183, 232–234, 234, 236, 237–239, 239, 248, 365
Lutheranism, 176, 178, 238, 246

M

Macedon, 57
Machiavelli, Niccolo, 222, 223, 226, 291
machine guns, 305, 306
Madison, James, 326, 327
Madras, 123
Madrasapattinam (Madras Town), 123

Magadha, 71

Magellan, Ferdinand (Fernao de Magalhae), 113–114, 120–121, 133, 136, 351–352

Magna Carta (Great Charter), 129, 387

Mahayana, 172

Mainz, Archbishop of, 177

maize (corn), 90

Manchukuo, 146

Mandela, Nelson Rolihlahla, 323, 327

The Mandrake (Machiavelli), 223

Manicheism, 206

Manuel I (Manuel the Fortunate) (king), 114, 115

Manuzio, Aldo (Aldus Manutius), 215

Mao Zedong (Mao Tse-tung), 156, 364–365, 371

Maori culture, 90

March to the Sea, 303

Marconi, Gugliemo, 150

Marcus Antonius (Mark Antony), 65

Marcus Junius Brutus, 369, 371

Marcus Licinius Crassus, 65

Marie Antoinette, 139

Marius, Gaius, 280

Martinet, Jean, 293

Marx, Karl, 148, 261, 262–263, 264, 265, 389

Marxism, 262–264

Mary (saint), 173

Masaccio, 217

Masada, 170

mass production, 259

Massacre of St. Bartholomew, 246, 249

matchlock, 292, 293

mathematics, 52, 56, 90, 189, 255, 257

Mathias (emperor), 247

Maurice (prince), 293

Mauryan Dynasty, 71, 89

Maxim machine gun, 306

Maximian (general), 66, 377

Maximilian (Ferdinand Maximilian Joseph) (archduke), 144, 226

Maximilian I, 235

May Fourth Movement, 364

Maya, 52, 74, 90, 116

Mecca (city), 179

Medes, 54, 60

Media (Medea), 54

medical breakthroughs, 220

Medici, Cosimo de,' 213

Medici, Giovanni de. *See* Leo X (pope)

Medici family, 225

Medina (city), 96, 179

Mehmet II (sultan), 291

Meiji (emperor), 145

Meiji Restoration, 146

Memphis, Egypt, 47, 60

Menes (Normer) (king), 47, 60

Merovingians, 85

Mesopotamia, 45, 46, 48, 52, 53, 58

Messiah (anointed one), 169, 173, 204

Mestopotamians, 88

metaphysics, 187, 196

Methodists, 178

Mexican-American War, 144

Mexican-Guatemalan Empire, 144

Mexico, 118, 144

Michelangelo (Tommaso di Giovannie de Simone Guidi), 216–217, 218, 221

microcosm, 210

microscopic contagion, 220

Middle Ages, 77–91

middle class, 109

migration, 80

Milesians (Ionians), 189

Minamoto Yoritomo, 90

Ming Dynasty, 35, 125

Minié, Claude-Étienne, 300

minié ball, 300

Minoans, 21, 22, 54–55

missiles, 157, 270, 307

Mitanni, 272

Mithradates I, 71, 72, 76

mobile phones, 150

Moche culture, 75

Moctezuma I (Montezuma), 118, 351

Moctezuma II, 118, 119

modern, use of term, 34

modern war, 298–305

Mogul Dynasty, 122

Mohammad Reza Pahlavi, 181

Mohenjo-Daro, 49, 50, 51

Moltke, Helmuth Graf von, 298–299, 307

Mongols/Mongol Empire, 80, 101, 104, 106, 121, 122

Montefeltro family, 226

Montesquieu, Charles, 326

moon landing, 345–346

Moors, 86, 100, 175, 286, 295

morals, 187

More, Thomas, 240, 242

Morelos y Pavon, Jose Maria, 144

Morse, Samuel, 159

Moscow (city), 148

Moses, 165, 180, 325

movable-type printing, 98

Mugabe, Robert, 361, 371

Mughal Empire, 72

Muhammad (Mohammed or Mohamet), 88, 91, 94, 165, 178–179, 180, 183, 326, 327

Mumbai (city), 123

mummies, 22–26

muskets, 293, 297, 300, 301, 305, 311

Mussato, Albertino, 223

Mussolini, Benito, 142, 154

mustard gas, 152, 306

muzzle, 300

Mwenumatapa civilization, 81

Mycenaeans, 55

myrrh, 88

Mysore Wars, 137

N

Nagasaki (city), 151, 155, 381

Nama people, 145

Namibia, 145

Nanak, 182, 183

Nanjing (later Nanking), 137

napalm, 283

Napoleon I (Napoleon Bonaparte), 132–133, 136, 138–139, 146, 159, 331

Napoleon II, 146

Napoleon III (emperor), 144, 146, 299

Napoleonic Wars, 143–144, 298

National Socialists (Nazis), 154, 169, 331

nationalism/nationalists, 159, 169

Native Americans, 116

navigation, 95, 98, 111, 114, 120–121, 123, 209, 224, 246, 348, 350

nawab, 123

Nazca culture, 75

Neanderthals, 31–32

Nebuchadnezzar II, 49, 331–332, 340

needle gun, 298, 301

Neoplatonism, 188, 209

New Rome (later Constantinople), 66

New Testament, 173, 203, 204

New World, 114, 121, 129

Newcomen, Thomas, 259

Newgrange, Ireland, 59

Newton, Isaac, 130, 219, 255, 256, 264

Nicaea (Nicea) (city), 204

Nichiren, 172

Nicholas II (czar), 147–148

Nile Valley, 47, 52

95 Theses, 177, 183, 232, 233, 235, 248

Nobunaga Oda, 322

Nok people, 59

Normandy, 82

Norsemen, 83, 165

North Atlantic Treaty Organization (NATO), 158

Northern Ireland, 86, 175

novas, 253

nuclear bombs/weapons, 151, 155, 156, 307–308, 381

Nuclear Test Ban Treaty, 157

Nun, 166

Nut (Geb), 166

O

Octavian, 65, 66, 76

Odin (Wodin), 165

The Odyssey (Homer), 19, 57

O'Higgins, Bernardo (Ambrosio O'Higgins), 143, 368

Olaf (saint), 334, 338, 340

Old Persian Empire, 70

Old Testament (Hebrew Bible or Jewish Bible), 169, 173, 203, 385

oligarchy, 375

Olmec, 52

Olympias, 57

Olympics, 57

Omayyad Dynasty, 89

On the Origin of Species (Darwin), 390–391

On the Revolution of Heavenly Spheres (Copernicus), 219, 228

On War (Clausewitz), 298, 311

opium, 126, 145

Opium War, 126

Orestes (emperor), 377

orient, use of term, 101

original sin, 206

Orkney, 59

Otterbein, K.E., 270, 281

Otto I (Otto the Great) (king), 18, 69, 87

ottoman, origin of term, 121

Ottomans/Ottoman Empire, 14, 18, 37, 101, 102, 121–122, 142

Ötzi, 23, 27

Outline of History (Wells), 34

P

Pachacuti, 119

Padua (city), 101

Pakistan, 71, 171

Palenque, 74

Palestine, 16, 18, 104, 157, 183

Palestinian Liberation Army (PLO), 170

Palestinian West Bank, 44

pandemic, COVID-19, 7–8

pantheon, 166, 187, 204

paper, 74, 97

Paracas, 74–75

Paracas Necropolis, 75

Paré, Ambroise, 220

Park, Mungo, 139

Parks, Rosa, 365–366

Parthians, 70–71

Paschal III (antipope), 174

patricians, 64, 279, 335

Patton, George, 338

Paul (apostle), 173

Paul (saint), 203, 346, 355

Paul III (pope), 238, 239

Peace of Westphalia, 247, 249

Peary, Robert E., 352

Peasants' Revolt, 369, 371

Peasants' War, 238, 248

Peloponnesian War, 56, 60, 193, 194

Pentateuch, 385

People's Crusade, 105, 338

percussion lock, 300, 301, 305

Peri tou Okeanou (*On the Ocean*) (Pytheas), 344

Pericles, 56, 193

Persian Wars, 57, 192

Persians/Persian Empire, 54, 276

persuasion, art of, 192–193

Peru, 74, 142, 143

Peter (apostle), 173

Peter I (Peter the Great), 147, 367

Peter III (czar), 370

Peter the Hermit (Peter of Amiens), 105, 338–339

Pétion, Alexandre, 368

Petrarcha, Francesco (Petrarch), 213

Petrograd (later St. Petersburg), 148

phalanx, 275, 276, 277, 278

pharaohs, 48

Philip II (king of France), 105

Philip IV (king), 289

Philip of Macedon (king), 57, 276–278

Phillip II (king of Spain), 246

philosophy, 58, 59, 167, 185–200, 202, 252

Phoenicians, 63

pictograph symbols/pictographic writing, 51, 53, 90

Pilgrimage of Grace, 243

pioneers, 344–346

Pizarro, Francisco, 114, 119, 120, 350–351, 367

plastic surgery, 220

Plato, 21–22, 27, 185, 188, 191, 194, 195, 196, 199, 202, 205

Platonic Academy, 213, 214

plebeians, 63, 64

Pleistocene Epoch, 17

Plotinus, 188

polis, 55

Polo, Marco, 100, 101, 112, 346–347, 348, 387–388

Polynesians, 90

Ponce de Léon, Juan, 349

popes, 173, 174, 234. *See also specific popes*

porcelain, 74, 98

Portuguese/Portugal, 123, 127, 133, 139, 142, 152

Porus (king), 58

The Praise of Folly (Erasmus), 230, 240, 248

pre-Columbian, 35

predestination, 206–207, 245

prehistory, as becoming history, 11, 44

Presbyterians, 178, 248

pre-Socratic philosophers, 191–192

Priam, 20

The Prince (Machiavelli), 222, 223, 226

principes, 279

Principia (Newton), 264

printing press, 215, 223

progress, 13

Protectorate, 247

Protestant Reformation, 129, 173, 174, 175, 177–178, 211–212, 227, 229–248

Protestantism, 175, 177–178, 178, 238, 239, 245, 246

Provisional Irish Republican Army (IRA), 175, 310

Prussians, 298–299

Ptolemaic Dynasty, 58, 70

Ptolemy (astronomer), 110, 224, 253

Ptolemy (general), 58, 70, 375

publications, early ones, 215

Pugachev, Emelian Ivanovich, 370, 371

Punic Wars, 64

Puritans/Puritanism, 129, 133, 245, 247–248

pyramids, 52–53

pyrotechnics/pyrotechnicians, 284, 290

pyrrhic victory, 279

Pyrrho, 198

Pyrrhus (king), 279

Pythagoras, 188, 189, 191

Pythagorean theorem, 189

Pytheas, 344, 355

Pythias of Marseilles, 80

Q

Qaysar, 70

Qin Dynasty, 318

Qin Shihuangdi (Qin Shi Huang or Shi Huangdi) (king), 72, 73, 76, 318, 327

Qing (Ch'ing) Dynasty, 125–126, 363

Quakers, 129

questioning, 58

Quetzalcóatl, 118

Quran (Qur'an or Koran), 94, 180, 386

R

Rabelais, François, 223

radar, 307

radio, 150

railroads, 149, 259, 298, 301–302, 304

Raleigh, Walter, 322

Ramses II (pharaoh), 48

rationalism, 252, 256, 257–258

record keeping, 52

Reformed Church, 178

Reign of Terror, 132, 368

Reinhard, Johan (archaeologist), 24–25

religion. *See also specific religions*

  as adapting Aristotelian and Platonic ideas, 202

  animism, 167–168

  clashing cultures among, 180

  creation stories/myths, 166

  defining of, 164–167

  divergent ideas in, 203

  enmity among believers of different religions, 179, 180, 181

  impact of on history, 163

  as intermingled with philosophy, 187–188, 202

  monotheistic religions, 165–166

  most societies as having been organized around, 164

  official religions, 164

  polytheistic religions, 165, 166–167

  role of in New World, 129

  theistic religions, 165

  volatility of, 88

Religious Peace of Augsburg, 239, 249

Renaissance

  art, 216–218

  contributors to, 209

  cross-pollination of, 224

  drama, 223–224

  as leading to the Enlightenment, 17

  origins of, 108

  pursuit of human perfection during, 220–222

  redefining human role during, 213–216

  returning to science during, 219–220

  scope of, 212–213

  sparking of, 207

  undermining of gains of with conflict, 224–227

  as uniting flesh and soul, 216–218

  writing for the masses during, 223–224

renaissance, defined, 214

Republic of Georgia, 158

The Republic (Plato), 195, 196

Revolution of 1917, 177

revolutions. *See specific revolutions*

Rice, Condoleezza, 381

rice growing, 59

Richard I (Lionheart) (king), 105, 335

Richard II (king), 295

Richelieu (cardinal), 131, 247

rifled barrel, 300

righteous killing, condoning of, 205

Rihlah (Ibn Battuta), 347

"Ring around the Rosie," 109

rivers, cities as growing along, 45–51

Robert the Bruce, 336

Robespierre, Maximilien-François Marie-Isidore de, 367–368

Robin Hood (likely legendary), 339

Roma (formerly Gypsies), 169, 247

Roman Catholic Church

  conflicts with Protestants, 175

  cracks in monopoly of, 229–232

  initiating of, 173

  in Latin America, 176

  power of, 78

  Rome and, 68–70, 173

  Spanish Inquisition, 175–176, 255, 322

  as unifying force in Europe, 174

Roman Empire

  attempts to split it in two, 66

  civil wars in, 64, 65, 76, 330, 340, 369, 377

  crossing the Rubicon, 64–65

  as distinct from Holy Roman Empire, 15, 69

  eastern branch as persisting, 67

  end of, 78

  expansion of, 63–64, 66

  fall of western empire, 67–68, 377

  as first a city-state, 70

  at its height, 67

  legacy of, 61

Roman Senate, 62

Romanovs, 69–70

Rome

  ascent and demise of, 61–70

  as borrowing freely from other cultures, 62

  fall of, 34

  First Triumvirate, 64–65

  founding of, 62, 76

  power shift away from, 67

  rivals to, 63–64, 78

  and the Roman Catholic Church. *See* Roman Catholic Church

  Roman Republic in, 62, 65, 76

  sack of, 67

  stratified society in, 62–63

Rommel, Erwin ("Desert Fox"), 335, 341

Romulus (king), 62

Romulus (mythical), 62, 316

Romulus Augustus (Augustulus) (emperor), 68, 76, 377

Rosetta Stone, 53, 384

Rousseau, Jean-Jacques, 130, 258

The Royal Hunt of the Sun (film), 120

"Rules of Reasoning in Philosophy" (Newton), 256

Russell, W.H., 302

Russia. *See also* Union of Soviet Socialist Republics (USSR) (Soviet Union)

  civil war in, 359

  in Crimean War, 298–301

  as fighting against Islamic independence movement in Chechnya, 158

  Napoleon's invasion of, 138, 331

  revolting in, 146–148

  Russian Democratic Socialist Party, 148

  Russian Federation, 149, 263

  as special case among European nations, 147

  unfair land settlement in, 147

  war with Republic of Georgia, 158

  in World War I, 152

Russian Orthodox Church, 177

Russo-Japanese War, 146, 147

Rwanda, 158

S

saints, 173–174. *See also specific saints*

Sakagawea, 354

Saladin, 105

salat (formal prayer), 179

Salutai, Coluccio, 213, 228

salvation, 206–207, 232–233, 245

Samoothiri (Zamorin), 115

Samudragupta, 72

samurai, 90

San Martín, José de, 143

Santorini (Theta), 22, 27

Sapa Inca (Son of the Sun), 163

Saracens, 288

Sarajevo (city), 160

sarissa, 276

SARS-CoV-2, 7. *See also* COVID-19 pandemic

Sassanid Dynasty, 71, 96

Saul (king), 33, 169, 183, 317

saum (fasting), 179

Savery, Thomas, 259

sax, 280

Saxons, 82, 84, 86

scale armor, 287

Schliemann, Heinrich, 20–21, 27

Schmalkald League, 238, 239

Schöffer, Peter, 215, 228

scholarship, 207, 213, 224

scholasticism, 208, 209

School of Names, 190

science, 219–220, 252

scientific approach/method/thought, 59, 130, 255–256

Scientific Revolution, 252, 253–256

Scipio Africanus (Publius Cornelius Scipio Africanus), 337

scorched-earth advance, 298

Scotland, 86

"Scramble for Africa," 140

Scriptures, 169. *See also* Bible

sea routes, 95, 101, 109, 113, 114, 120, 121, 122, 136, 213, 322, 348, 350, 388

secular humanism, 209

seed drill, 259

Seleucid Dynasty, 70, 169

Seleucus (general), 70, 71

self-rule, 135

Seljuk Dynasty, 16, 101, 103–104

Seljuk Turks, 121, 378

Seneca, 214, 223

Separatists, 248, 249

Sepoy Rebellion (or Mutiny), 125

September 11, 2001, al-Qaeda attack on US, 16, 18, 157, 160, 181, 183, 310

Serbians/Serbs, 102, 152, 158

serfs/serfdom, 147

Servetus, Michael, 220, 221

Seven Years' War, 151

Seymour, Jane, 245

Sforza, Ludovico of Milan (duke), 226

Shagrat al-Durr (Shajarat), 336

shahada (profession of faith), 179

Shaka, 334, 341

Shakespeare, William, 61, 65, 212, 223, 224

Shang Dynasty (Yin Dynasty), 51

Sherman, William Tecumseh, 303, 337–338, 341

Shiite (Shia), 96, 97, 181

Shiva (god), 170

shogun, 90, 123, 145, 322

Shu (god), 166

Shulgi, 324

Siddhartha Gautama, 172

Sidereus Nuncius (*Sidereal Message*) (Galileo), 219, 255, 264

Sikhism, 182–183, 183

Silk Road, 79, 83–84, 98–99, 101

silks, 100

Siraj-ud-Daulah, 123–124, 125

Sixtus V (pope), 322

Skanda (god), 170, 171

skepticism, 198

slave trade/slaves/slavery, 63, 64, 126–128, 147, 304, 380

Slavs, 106, 152

slow match, 292, 293

smallpox, 128

Smith, Adam, 262, 263, 265

Snyder-Enfield, 301

The Social Contract, 258

socialism, 263, 264, 359, 390

Socrates, 185, 191–195, 199

Socratic method, 194

Soka Gakkai, 172

Solon, 21, 325

sonar, 307

Song (Sung) Dynasty, 100

sophists, 193

Sophocles, 193

South America, 52

Southern Baptist Conference, 178

Southern Christian Leadership Conference, 366

soviet, 359

Soviet Union. *See* Union of Soviet Socialist Republics (USSR) (Soviet Union)

Spain, 111, 128, 142

Spanish Inquisition, 175–176, 255, 322

Spartacus, 369, 370

Sparta/Spartans, 56–57, 60, 275, 281

spices, 100, 115, 123

St. Peter's Basilica, 231, 233

St. Petersburg (city), 146

St. Petersburg Soviet of Workers' Deputies, 147

Stalin, Josef, 149, 154, 156

Stanley, Henry Morton, 140

Stauffenberg, Claus von, 341

steamships, 149, 259, 298, 301–302

stirrup, 98, 104, 283, 284–285, 288, 291, 295

Stoics/Stoicism, 188, 198, 213

Stonehenge, 59

submarine, 151, 152, 306, 307

suffrage (voting rights), 380

Sui Dynasty, 74

suicide bombing, 310

Sumerians, 53, 272

Summa Theologica (Aquinas), 208, 210

A Summary View of the Rights of British America (Jefferson), 364

Sumuabum (king), 48

Sun Tzu, 337

Sun Yixian (Sun Yat-sen), 363

Sung Dynasty, 290

Sunga Dynasty, 71

Sunni, 96, 97, 180

Surat (city), 123

survival of the fittest, 391

Sweyn Forkbeard, 82

Switzerland, 146

T

Tagliacozzi, Gaspare, 220

Taliban, 157, 158, 160, 164, 181, 310, 311

Talmudic laws, 169

Tang Dynasty, 74, 98, 112

Tanzania, 145

Taoists, 190

Tarquinius Superbus (king), 62, 65, 76

Tasmania, 137

Taylor, Edward, 168

technology, 94, 149–150, 284, 305–307

Tefnut (god), 166

telegraph, 150, 298, 302

telephone, 150

television, 150

Ten Commandments, 165, 169, 385

Tendai, 172

Tennyson, Lord Alfred, 302

Tenochtitlán (city), 116–117, 119, 133

terrorism, 309–310

Tetzel (friar), 233, 234

Thales, 186, 190, 191

Thebes/Thebans, 56–57

theistic religions, 165

theocratic governments, 164

Theodosius I, 67, 68

theologians, 204

theological determinism, 207

Theravada, 172

Thermopylae, Battle of, 57

Third Reich, 154

Thirty Years' War, 174–175, 239, 246–247, 249

Thoreau, Henry David, 365

Through the Dark Continent (Stanley), 140

Tiersch, H., 199

Tigris River, 45, 59

Tikal, 74

The Time Machine (Wells), 8, 34

time travel, 8–9

Timur (Tamerlane or Timur the Lame), 15, 122

To the Christian Nobility of the German Nations (Luther), 237

tobacco, 29, 90, 103, 111, 128

Tokugawa Dynasty, 133

Tokugawa family, 123

Tokugawa Hidetada, 123

Tokugawa Iemitsu, 123, 133

Tokugawa Ieyasu, 123, 322

Tokugawa Yoshinobu, 145

Toltecs, 74, 91

Tongmenghui (United League), 363

the Torah, 169

Torres, Luis de, 111

total war, 303

totemism, 168

Toussaint, François-Dominic (Toussaint Bréda) (later Toussaint Louverture), 132, 133, 362

Tower Bridge, 340

Toyotomi Hideyoshi, 322

trade, 10, 102–103, 106–107, 110

Trajan (emperor), 67

transcultural diffusion, 58

The Travels of Marco Polo (Polo), 100, 101–102, 347, 387–388

Treaty of Nanjing, 126

Treaty of Passeau, 239

Treaty of Tordesillas, 142

Treaty of Versailles, 15, 18, 153

trenches, 151, 305, 306, 311

Trevithick, Richard, 149

triarii, 279

Trojan War, 20, 27, 269

Troy (city), 20–21, 27

Tuchman, Barbara (historian), 12

Tula (city), 91

Tull, Jethro, 259

Tulsa Race Massacre, 37

Tupac Amaru II, 143

Ture, Samory (Samir) (emperor), 141

Turkestan, 24

Turks, 102, 104, 121, 180. *See also* Seljuk Turks

Tutankhamen (king), 26, 27

Tutsis, 158

Twain, Mark (novelist), 8

Tyler, Wat, 108, 112, 369, 371

U

U-boats, 151, 306

Umayyad Dynasty, 89, 91

Union of Soviet Socialist Republics (USSR) (Soviet Union)

agricultural reforms in, 149

collapse of, 160, 263, 265

establishment of, 15

as increasingly exclusionary and closed off, 156

taking power in, 148–149

World War I as helping to create, 153

in World War II, 155

United Kingdom, 9, 18, 38, 86, 155, 160. *See also specific countries of*

United Kingdom of Portugal, Brazil, and the Algarves, 144

United Nations, 16, 18, 158–159, 159

United Provinces, 246, 249

United States. *See also* American Revolution

in Afghanistan, 16, 157–158, 160

Bill of Rights, 389

Civil Rights Act of 1964, 39

civil war in, 151, 297, 298, 303–305

creation of, 130

Declaration of Independence, 258, 379, 388–389

emergence of as leader of West, 156

September 11, 2001, al-Qaeda attack on US, 16, 18, 157, 160, 181, 183, 310

in Vietnam War, 12, 18, 157, 303, 311

War on Terror(ism), 16

in World War I, 152

in World War II, 155

universities, 207

Upper Nubia (Kush), 47, 60

Ur (city), 46, 165

Urban II (pope), 16, 104, 174, 288, 295, 378

Ur-Nammu, 324, 327

V

Vandals, 80

Vandalusia (later Andalusia), 80

vassal king, 332

Veda, 170

Velázquez de Cuéllar, Diego, 351

Venetians, 102

Venezuela, 143

Venice (city-state), 101–102, 103, 112

Verona (city), 101

Vesalius, Andreas, 220, 228

Vespucci, Amerigo, 347

Vestal Virgins, 316, 317

Vicenza (city), 101

viceroy, 70

Victor IV (antipope), 174

Victorian era, 36

Viet Cong, 309

Vietnam War, 12, 18, 157, 303, 311

Vikings, 81–83, 91, 106, 127

Vishnu (god), 170

Visigoths, 67, 86

Vitruvian Man (drawing), 218

Vladimir (grand prince), 177

Voltaire, François, 130, 258

W

Waldemar IV (king), 106
Waldseemüller, Martin, 347
Wales, 86
Wallace, Alfred Russell, 391
Wallace, William, 336
Walworth, William, 371
War of 1812, 137
War of the Roses, 289
War of the Worlds (Wells), 34
warfare. *See also specific wars*
  among chimpanzees, 270
  of ancient Greeks, 274–278
  of ancient Rome, 278–281
  of Assyrians, 272–274, 281
  cavalry, 276, 280–281, 284–287, 295, 302, 318
  civil wars. *See* civil wars
  Cold War, 149, 157
  deaths from, 303
  as good material for history books, 12–13
  guerilla tactics. *See* guerilla tactics
  human advances as influenced by, 12–13
  nuclear threat in, 307–308
  opposition forces, 309
  as part of prehuman behavior, 270
  paths to modern war, 298–305
  regional wars, 157
  as stimulating technology, 284
  strategies of, 271–272
  total war, 297, 298
  transportation used in. *See* aircraft carriers; airplanes; horses; railroads; steamships; submarine; U-boats; warships
  tying tactics to technology in 20th century, 305–307
  universality of, 269, 281
  weapons of, 271, 272, 277, 278–279, 280, 281, 283, 287–289, 290–295, 300–301, 305. *See also specific weapons*
  world wars, 151–156
Wars of Religion, 246
warships, 147, 294
Washington, George, 39, 40, 323
Watt, James, 259
weapons technology. *See* warfare, weapons of
Wells, H.G., 8, 34, 35
Welser family, 233
West Germany, 155
West Indies, 110, 111, 123
wheel lock, 293
Whewell, William, 252
White Company, 226
White Lion (ship), 128
Whitehead, Alfred North, 195
Wilhelm II (kaiser), 152, 159
William the Conqueror, 33, 82, 320, 327, 377–378
Wilson, Woodrow, 153, 158
wire report, 302
Wolsey, Thomas, 241, 242
workers'-rights movements, 369
World War I
  charging of enemy positions in, 306
  combatants in, 152–153
  deaths from, 303
  as depleting resources and resolve of colonial powers, 136
  as ending with 1919 Treaty of Versailles, 15, 18
  impacts of, 305–306
  mechanization in, 151–152
  precipitating events and attitudes, 152
  reacting to the carnage, 153
  as redefining war, 151–153
  as sowing seeds for World War II, 153
  triggering of, 160
  weapons of. *See* warfare, weapons of
World War II
  assessing damage of, 155
  beginning of, 160
  combatants in, 154–155
  deaths from, 303
  as depleting resources and resolve of colonial powers, 136
  Germany as breaking the Treaty of Versailles, 154
  as redrawing map of Europe, 155
  retooling arsenal in, 307
  as return to conflict, 153–156
  weapons of. *See* warfare, weapons of
World Wide Web, 150
worshipping, 163–183. *See also specific religions*
Wright, Orville, 150
Wright, Wilbur, 150
writing, 44, 51, 53, 90
Wu Ti, 332
Wycliffe, John, 232, 240

X

Xenophanes, 188, 189
Xenophon, 275
Xerxes I (king), 57, 334, 340
Xiongnu people, 99

Y

Yellow River, 49, 51
yeomen, 289
Yorvig (later York), 81
Young, Thomas, 384
Yuan Dynasty, 99, 321
Yugoslavia, 158
Yung Lo (emperor), 99

Z

zakat (purification), 179
Zen Buddhism, 172
Zeno of Citium (Cyprus), 198, 199
Zeno of Elea, 190
Zeus (god), 165, 166, 204
Zheng He (Chung Ho or Cheng Ho), 99, 100, 344–345
Zhou Dynasty, 51
Zimbabwe, 145
Zimbabwe African National Union (ZANU), 361
Zimbabwe African People's Union (ZAPU), 361
Zionist movement, 170
Zulu people, 141, 334, 341
Zwingli, Huldreich, 245
Zworykin, Vladimir K., 150

About the Author

Peter Haugen is an editor, journalist, and author whose books include *Was Napoleon Poisoned?: And Other Unsolved Mysteries of Royal History* (John Wiley & Sons, Inc.). A graduate of the University of California–Berkeley, he has contributed to *History* magazine and is among the co-writers of *The Armchair Reader: The Amazing Book of History* (West Side Publishing), *Mental Floss Presents Condensed Knowledge* (HarperResource), and *Mental Floss Presents Forbidden Knowledge* (Collins). He also wrote *Biology: Decade by Decade* (Twentieth-Century Science series, Facts on File). He was a staff member on several newspapers, including *The Sacramento Bee* and *The Tampa Bay Times*, and an editor of the online publication *Best Thinking*. Haugen has been an adjunct instructor at the University of Wisconsin–Madison and California State University–Fresno and is a U.S. Army veteran. He lives in Boston.

Dedication

Author's Acknowledgments

Thanks, to my family — sons Marcus Haugen and Lucas Haugen, and my wife, Deborah Blum — for their love and support. Thanks too to the team at Wiley — Michelle Hacker, Elizabeth Stilwell, Victoria Anllo, and Christina Guthrie — who helped make the process of writing this third edition painless. I'd also like to thank historian David McDonald yet again for his invaluable help with the first edition of this book, along with all the wonderful history writers whose works I have combed through, pored through, and compared while once again skimming the surface of the wonderful body of scholarship that is world history.

Publisher's Acknowledgments

Acquisitions Editor: Elizabeth Stilwell

Project Manager and Development Editor: Victoria Anllo

Managing Editor: Michelle Hacker

Copy Editor: Keir Simpson

Technical Editor: Randall Fuchs

Production Editor: Mohammed Zafar Ali

Cover Image: © Tryfonov/Adobe Stock Photos